Family Communication *in the* Age *of* Digital *and* Social Media

LIFESPAN COMMUNICATION

Children, Families, and Aging

Thomas J. Socha
GENERAL EDITOR

Vol. 9

The Lifespan Communication series
is part of the Peter Lang Media and Communication list.
Every volume is peer reviewed and meets
the highest quality standards for content and production.

PETER LANG
New York • Bern • Frankfurt • Berlin
Brussels • Vienna • Oxford • Warsaw

Family Communication *in the* Age *of* Digital *and* Social Media

Edited by Carol J. Bruess

PETER LANG
New York • Bern • Frankfurt • Berlin
Brussels • Vienna • Oxford • Warsaw

Library of Congress Cataloging-in-Publication Data

Family communication in the age of digital and social media /
edited by Carol J. Bruess.
pages cm. — (Lifespan communication: children, families, and aging; vol. 9)
Includes bibliographical references and index.
1. Communication in families. 2. Internet and families. 3. Interpersonal communication.
4. Social media. 5. Internet—Social aspects. I. Bruess, Carol J.
HQ519.F295 302.23'1—dc23 2015019989
ISBN 978-1-4331-2746-5 (hardcover)
ISBN 978-1-4331-2745-8 (paperback)
ISBN 978-1-4539-1668-1 (e-book)
ISSN 2166-6466 (print)
ISSN 2166-6474 (online)

Bibliographic information published by **Die Deutsche Nationalbibliothek**.
Die Deutsche Nationalbibliothek lists this publication in the "Deutsche Nationalbibliografie"; detailed bibliographic data are available on the Internet at http://dnb.d-nb.de/.

Cover image by Tammy Brice Photography

The paper in this book meets the guidelines for permanence and durability of the Committee on Production Guidelines for Book Longevity of the Council of Library Resources.

29 Broadway, 18th floor, New York, NY 10006
www.peterlang.com

Printed in the United States of America

This volume is dedicated to everyone who kindly puts up
with my over-use of emoji in text messages, email, and on Facebook, thereby
embracing my crazy-expressive self! 😘💘🙏😎👍😍

Contents

Foreword

LYNN TURNER
Marquette University

I am delighted to write the foreword for this important volume. This book, which explores challenges and opportunities experienced by families communicating in the era of digital and social media, is both fresh and timely. The topic is a critical one, as all the authors in this volume acknowledge when they cite the ubiquity of social media, as well as the enormous impact social media exert on family communication practices. This idea was vividly brought home to me because during the time I was preparing this foreword, the Supreme Court decision on same-sex marriage was announced. The way the decision was communicated highlights how social media intertwines with issues of family. Partners texted one another, #SCOTUSmarriage became a trending hashtag on Instagram, Facebook profile pictures were overlaid with rainbow filters, and families appeared on social media expressing their feelings about this landmark decision that clarified the definition of marriage. Certainly, now the time is ripe for scholars to examine relationships among family and technologically assisted communication.

This book, expertly edited by Carol J. Bruess, brings together an interdisciplinary group of authors to do just that. *Family Communication in the Age of Digital and Social Media* contributes several things to our knowledge of family communication: 1) it is no longer sufficient to ask whether social media helps or harms the family; 2) multiple, current theories are useful in our studies of social media and family; and 3) it is critical to think about practical applications for our research on technology and family life.

First, I applaud the authors in this collection for avoiding a "good or bad" dichotomy when probing the impact of social media on family life. Instead of fixating on WHETHER technology brings families together or drives them apart, the authors here opt to interrogate HOW digital and social media penetrate and affect the communication practices of families. In so doing, it becomes clear that media have both positive and negative impacts on family (as Webb clearly articulates in Chapter 1), and researchers should move to more nuanced investigations, such as those provided within this volume. For example, in Chapter 2, Child and Petronio unpack how families address privacy concerns given that social media make a great deal of information public that we might have previously thought belonged within the realm of privacy. In Chapter 8, Hall and Feister argue persuasively that communication technologies impact the transition from childhood to adulthood. Piercy and his colleagues address a unique topic in Chapter 10, and cogently discuss how social and digital media might be used during couples therapy. Vaterlaus and Tulane, in Chapter 20, explore the different uses of interactive technology employed by adolescents, who are digital natives, and their parents, who are, for the most part, digital immigrants. In all the chapters, the authors focus on multiple impacts of social media and technology, and thus their findings are informative and reveal subtleties. As an example, in Chapter 15 Daws points to the complex way that "wedsites" (wedding websites) use new technology to reinforce the old norms of heteronormativity.

Second, this collection makes clear both that research of this type should and can be theoretically sound, and that many of our existing theories are still useful in examining issues of technology and family. For instance, theories including, but not limited to Uncertainty Reduction Theory (Chapter 18), Uses and Gratifications (Chapter 20), Ecological Theory on Parenting (Chapter 16), Privacy Management (Chapter 2), Narrative Performative Theory (Chapter 15), and Systems Theory (Chapter 6), illustrate both the theoretical grounding of this collection, as well as the utility of "old" theories to frame and explain "new" communication contexts and channels. In Chapter 18, Sharabi, Roache, and Pusateri, for example, find that a theory from 1975 (URT) can help us understand how parents use Facebook to seek information, and reduce uncertainty, about their children who are away from home in college.

Finally each chapter includes an application section, revealing how theory and practice easily coexist within the topic of family life and social and digital communication. For example, Blumer and Hertlein in Chapter 22 illustrate how the traditional genogram can be modified to a technological genogram. With these technologically focused genograms, it is possible to answer research questions such as how families communicate across generations using social media. But, it also likely that these genograms can be applied in a variety of employment settings as well as medical contexts for assessing things such as cancer risk, for instance.

This collection excites me, and I invite you to enjoy its range and depth. It will be an absorbing read, inspiring you to think about family, communication, and life in our contemporary world in many different ways. This book makes it clear that family communication is altered by the presence of digital and social media, but still remains vibrant and can be investigated using theories and methods available to researchers today. I invite you to learn from each of the chapters, and to be motivated to study this ever-evolving, relevant topic yourself.

—Lynn H. Turner, Professor, Communication Studies and
Director of the Interdisciplinary Family Studies Minor, Marquette University

Series Editor's Preface

Thomas J. Socha
Old Dominion University

Family Communication in the Age of Digital and Social Media, expertly edited by Professor Carol Bruess, represents a bold and significant step forward in the research literatures of lifespan communication, family communication, and digital media. Globally, digital communication technologies have been fast- woven into the everyday communication fabric of family life, and as this volume highlights, have spotlighted new paths as well as challenges for families. Included among these challenges are cultural concerns such as the commodification of intimacy (Karraker, this volume), misconceptions about technology (Webb, this volume), "technoference" (McDaniel, this volume), privacy issues (Child & Petronio, this volume), the role of digital media and optimal child development (e.g., Fletcher & Blair, this volume), and parenting in the digital age (e.g., Tikkanen, Afifi, & Merill, this volume). Yet, with mindful use, we also find digital media opening new paths toward deeper understanding and appreciation of family history (Blumer & Hertlein, this volume), potentially higher levels of personal and relational satisfaction, feelings of closeness, and inventiveness at home (Piercy et al., this volume), and new, creative family-presentation rituals via Facebook (Bruess, Li, & Polingo, this volume). This groundbreaking volume is a must-read work that will, like all of the other volumes in Peter Lang's *Lifespan Communication: Children, Families, and Aging* series, spark research, conversation, and contribute important insights into life's dynamic and ever-evolving communication processes from first words to final conversations.

Acknowledgments

To my husband, Brian, and my beautiful teenagers, Tony and Gracie: You are the model of support, love, and joy—even when I'm stressin'. Thank you!! To Tom Socha: You are an inspiring managing editor and scholar, even when I'm asking too many novice questions. Thank you! To Tammi Polingo: Your cheerleading and micro-attention to every detail has been priceless, even when I'm sending you 126 emails a day. How can I ever thank you?! To Mike Stoffel: Your eagle eyes are a gift. Thanks for sharing them with this project. To Kate Woodman Middlecamp and Tammy Brice, your combined artistic brilliance made the cover come to life. Wow—thank you! And to all of the authors in this volume: Your passion for studying and discerning families in the digital age is beyond impressive. Without all you, this book wouldn't be a thing! Thank you for trusting me with your beautiful, smart work.

Section One

Plugged-In Families: Characteristics, Frameworks, and New Realities in a Digital Age

1

Research on Technology and the Family

From Misconceptions to More Accurate Understandings

LYNNE M. WEBB
Florida International University

Introduction

For more than a decade, the popular press in the United States has featured news stories on the negative impact of new media on children. As a result, parents are repeatedly urged to monitor their children's Internet use. Media panic concerning children's safety was particularly fueled at three points:

- In 2003, and for the 10 years following, various national and international jurisdictions began arresting users for illegally downloading copyrighted material, primarily music and films but also videos of sports events and videogames. The arrested and prosecuted users included minors as young as 12 years old. Parents were urged to more closely monitor their children's online behavior and discourage illegal downloads.
- From 2004 to 2007, NBC broadcast the "reality" television program *To Catch a Predator* in 11 two-part episodes, in which pedophiles were lured to pretend children for sexual encounters; the show's host and website warned parents to talk to their children about predators trolling the Internet for victims.
- In 2005, MySpace was purchased by News Corporation for $580 million dollars. Under the intense media monitoring that followed, MySpace began experiencing a series of safety issues, including hacked accounts. At that

> time, MySpace users were primarily adolescents and marketers targeting adolescents; parents were advised to warn their children about placing personal and financial information such as credit card numbers on social media websites, as this information could be easily stolen during a security breach.

Currently, the traditional news media cover a wide variety of stories about families and their online behavior. In 2014 alone, stories appeared on the effects of smartphones at the dinner table, parental-control options on smartphones, and video-monitoring children's bedrooms to proctor Internet use. One headline read, "OMG, the Internet Can Be a Scary Place with Kids!" (Byers, 2014).

Like many phenomena featured in contemporary news stories, negative reports garner the most attention—even though such negative outcomes are rare and the stories often contradict research findings concerning the phenomenon. Nonetheless, as these stories settle into our collective consciousness, we begin to believe (and perpetuate by sharing with others in our social networks) multiple cultural misconceptions about how families use personal communication technologies (PCTs) such as cell phones, tablets, and laptop computers. We might fear for the future of the prototypical American family as more and more of us acquire laptop computers for individual use, as children begin using cell phones at younger and younger ages, and as entire families "play" on their tablets while they eat dinner together at the neighborhood eatery, speaking only to the wait staff and rarely to each other.

In contrast, the original research reviewed in this chapter paints a picture quite different from the news depictions described above and from the cultural misconceptions and misunderstandings surrounding such representations. For example, family conflicts about children's use of PCTs tend to occur when parents attempt to regulate children's access to the Internet via conversation rather than simply employing parental control settings on cell phones. The conflicts rarely originate with strangers or with children's actions on the devices, per se. Instead, it is typically the very attempt to keep children safe that leads to ongoing parent–teen, parent–child, and/or parent–adolescent conflicts that can significantly disrupt family life.

This chapter identifies eight widespread misconceptions about families and their PCT use. The misconceptions include notions such as ever-present Internet "stranger danger," children's overuse of technology as the etiology of parent–child conflicts, and the availability of the Internet prompting users to focus on relationships with users outside the family versus face-to-face interaction with family members. Each of the eight misconceptions is either completely false or an oversimplification of the facts according to the latest research. This chapter clarifies the eight misconceptions via a review of the published research concerning families and their technology use. Because the misconceptions are so far-reaching, the chapter also provides a broad overview of existing research about families in an age of digital and social media.

Eight Misconceptions about Families and Personal Communication Technologies

Misconception One: Children's Use of PCTs Prompts Family Conflicts

The existence of family conflicts surrounding PCT use is well documented. However, what is not as widely known or acknowledged is the source of these conflicts. Contrary to popular belief, typically children's PCT use does not prompt family conflicts; most technology-related family disagreements are the direct result of parents' communication when attempting to monitor or limit their children's Internet access. Furthermore, a growing body of research indicates that intense monitoring is largely unnecessary and that the parents' fears that are driving such behaviors are largely unfounded.

Conflicts are parent-provoked. Parents' attempts to regulate their children's Internet use often provoke family conflicts (Mesch, 2006b; Mesch & Frenkel, 2011) and lead to verbal arguments. From the child's viewpoint, parents should trust them to make well-reasoned, sound judgments concerning Internet use. From the parent's viewpoint, keeping their children out of harm's way constitutes a primary parental responsibility—and the Internet offers many forms of harm including seductive online advertising (Cornish, 2014), cyberbullying (Schrock & boyd, 2011), gaming addiction (Lemmens, Valkenburg, & Peter, 2009), online harassment (Lindsay & Krysik, 2012), online pornography (McCartan & McAlister, 2012), and sex texting (Lunceford, 2011). Parents might view adolescent children as especially susceptible to such "harms," given their inexperience with such matters, their desire for positive adult attention, as well as their naïve attraction to gaming and sexual matters. See Fletcher and Blair (this volume) for a recent assessment of the dangers of visual online media to adolescents. A recent 25-country multinational study (Mertens & d'Haenens, 2014) documents that parents' primary reason for mediating their children's Internet use is concern for their children's well-being. According to Mertens and d'Haenens, the only cultural dimension related to parents' level of concern was uncertainty avoidance: The more parents desired to avoid uncertainty and increase certainty, the more they expressed concern and attempted to mediate their children's Internet access.

Mertens and d'Haenens's finding raises the question of whether parents attempt such mediation purely out of concern for their children or rather, at least in part, to increase their own sense of security and certainty. For instance, Tikkanen, Afifi, and Merrill (this volume) found that parents who experience longer-than-expected delays in their child's cell-phone response time experience more uncertainty about their child's activities than those who do not experience such a delay. Furthermore, Sharabi, Roache, and Pusateri (this volume) found that uncertainty reduction can drive parents' viewing of their young adult child's Facebook posts.

Related research indicates that motivations for parental mediation of cell phones in particular can differ by sex (Mascheroni, 2013). Mothers tend to serve as the enforcers of family rules governing children's PCT use. Mothers also tend to see cell phones as tools for safety, connection, and monitoring—and are more likely to view cell phones as providing opportunities to call their children at any time to discover where they are and what they are doing. Fathers tend to view cell phones as providing children with educational opportunities, given the Internet access availability on smartphones.

Clark (2013) identified four primary types of parents, based on their mediation beliefs and behaviors concerning their children's cell phone use:

- *Engaged parents* favor active mediation and will use parental controls built into the cell phones to limit their children's Internet access;
- *Helicopter parents* favor restrictive mediation but are ambivalent about using parental controls built into the telephones; they might restrict their children's cell phone use, for example, to two hours after homework is complete;
- *Permissive parents* appreciate the arguments in favor of mediation but do not engage in much regulation of their children's media use; and,
- *Digital immigrants* believe that mediation of their children's media use is simply futile.

Interestingly, Dworkin, Walker, Rudi, and Doty (this volume) examine the multiple ways parents use new media technologies to fulfill and understand their parenting responsibilities, including seeking support and ideas from other parents in online communities about how to manage PCT use of their child(ren).

Parents' regulation may be so limited or so subtle that children fail to perceive it (Sorbring & Lundin, 2012). In one study (Wang, Bianchi, & Raley, 2005), 61% of parents reported regulating their adolescent children's Internet access, whereas only 38% of their adolescent children reported such oversight. Adolescents might fail to perceive parental regulation as actual regulation because they can easily circumvent it (Byrne & Lee, 2011) using various technological affordances such as screening parents' calls, deleting browser histories, and posting on social media websites under assumed identities. Such circumvention might explain why many parents do not attempt to regulate their children's Internet use even when they perceive the Internet as dangerous (Staksrud & Livingstone, 2009). Many parents report attempting to balance concerns about online risks with the educational benefits of Internet access (Tripp, 2011). In sum, parents are more likely to take either a hands-off approach to their children's PCT use or attempt to monitor and limit their children's Internet access (which both practice and research suggests might be virtually impossible).

Parental fears disproportionate to reality. Much evidence suggests parents' fears of Internet dangers are not well founded. For example, recent advances in Internet monitoring have led to successful automatic monitoring of cyberbullying (Van Royen, Poels, Daelemans, & Vandebosch, 2015) and email screening software typically prevents pornographic messages from reaching users. Furthermore, research suggests adult predators stalking children on the Internet are rare; more often, middle school and high school students engage in cyberstalking and harassment of peers (Schrock & boyd, 2011). On the rare occasions teenagers attend offline meetings with strangers they have met on the Internet, the teens cite "the discrepancy between expectations and reality as the core reason" for their negative feelings about the meetings; they do not report molestation, rape, or robbery (Dedkova, Cerna, Janasova, & Daneback, 2014, p. 327).

Recent research suggests that children might need less guidance on Internet use than parents imagine. In one survey of more than 600 college-student users of Facebook, the more popular users (those reporting larger numbers of "friends") were more likely than unpopular users (those with fewer contacts on Facebook) to say nothing on their Facebook page that would surprise their offline family members (Zywica & Danowski, 2008). The more popular the young adult users, the more likely that their "friends" included multiple offline contacts such as family members, and thus the more likely to present an honest and accurate portrayal of his or her offline life on Facebook. Such findings suggest that the more embedded the young adult child is on Facebook, the less parents needs to worry about him or her engaging in inappropriate or embarrassing online behavior.

Similarly, Mostmans, Bauwens, and Pierson's (2014) study documents that, at least among their sample, even younger children articulate rather sophisticated ideas about digital age choices. The pre-adolescents in their study could easily imagine "the moral consequences of disclosing personal information [online]. Their moral reflections were embedded in a more general concern for children's vulnerability to other, more powerful information circulators in their social networks, such as older children, siblings, but also parents or the Internet crowd" (p. 347). Given that one of parents' primary concerns is their children's willingness to disclose personal information—allowing online adult predators to find them offline—the results of this study provide powerful evidence that parents' concerns may be misplaced, and that the need for training in Internet use might be exaggerated.

Nonetheless, many parents attempt to regulate their children's access to the Internet and such attempts can (and often do) lead to conflict (Mesch, 2006b; Mesch & Frenkel, 2011). Regulatory strategies vary with parenting style and not with adolescents' amount of time spent online (Eastin, Greenburg, & Hofschire, 2006). More frequent and intense conflicts occur when parents employ authoritative and permissive parenting styles (Byrne & Lee, 2011) rather than consultative and deliberative decision-making. Additionally, as Mesch (2006a) explains, "intergenerational conflicts over the Internet were higher in families in which parents expressed concern over the potentially negative consequences of Internet use" (p. 473). Such conflicts can lead adolescents to perceive their parents as difficult to talk to about the very matters of concern: online dangers.

Because most children and adolescents use their PCTs for direct and private access to peers (Ling & Bertel, 2013; Ling & Ytrri, 2002), they often perceive attempted parental regulation as privacy invasion (Mascheroni, 2014). Children typically defend against such privacy invasions using the same medium that the parents attempt to regulate (Ledbetter et al., 2010). For example, adolescents often maintain a Facebook page that parents can access and a second Facebook page for peer interaction that their parents cannot access. Such tactics avoid conflict and maintain privacy. If children maintain only one account on a given social medium, they often manipulate their privacy settings to prevent parental monitoring of peer interactions (Mascheroni, 2014). For a detailed discussion of online privacy in family communication, see the Child and Petronio chapter in this volume. For examples of recent research on marital communication and privacy/boundary issues, see two other chapters in this volume: Cravens and Whiting, as well as Hertlein and Blumer.

Given ubiquitous access to smartphones and wireless Internet access around the globe, children typically experience unlimited online access. Middle school aged children report taking advantage of free Wi-Fi and hacking into their school's Wi-Fi (Mascheroni, 2014). If parents deny their children cell phones and access to the Internet via the family computer, parents often fail to account for their children's friends who are happy to share their unlimited access to such technology with their phoneless peers.

Limiting children's Internet access might inflict social harm. An argument can be made that parents who deny their children PCTs are inflicting social harm. Given that by 2008, 57% of children ages 7 to 17 owned their own cell phone (Kennedy, Smith, Wells, & Wellman, 2008)—and it is likely the percent has since increased—the phoneless child can become an object of pity or ridicule among peers. Additionally, many offline peer conversations discuss games and information garnered online (Lee, 2009). Denying a child access to those bits of information is tantamount to denying him or her much of the social currency of face-to-face interchange among age-appropriate peers.

Children without ready access to the Internet may become vulnerable to undue influence from others who will provide such access. The access provided by a peer or an adult outside the family might involve activities the parents would deem as not age appropriate, such as viewing pornography. Nonetheless, the child may feel compelled to engage in the activity because his or her parents limit any opportunities for Internet access. Conversely, if the parents provide the child with his or her own cell phone, the parents could activate control settings that significantly reduce the odds of the child viewing material that is not age appropriate.

In sum, parents often prompt family conflicts by attempting to monitor or limit through oral argument their children's access to the Internet—a virtual impossibility; in contrast, cell phone control settings provide an easy, no-conflict method of limiting children's Internet access. The fears driving parents' desire to protect their children from Internet harm are not well founded given that negative elements appear to be rapidly disappearing and/or nearly nonexistent. Parents who fail to provide children with cell phones or Internet access might be doing more harm than good by limiting or reducing their children's social currency with peers.

Misconception Two: Technology Is Primarily Being Used in Family Member–to–Family Member Interactions to Stay in Touch with Out-of-Town Relatives

From grandparents texting their grandchildren to free Skype chats across continents, PCTs offer families multiple means to stay in touch, especially for family members living in far-flung locations. Inexpensive technologies and widespread Internet access allows every U.S. citizen to interact (should they desire to) with every known, living family member every day. A recent Pew survey revealed that more than half (60%) of surveyed users thought the Internet and cell phones made them better informed about their family than they were 5 years ago (Purcell & Rainie, 2014). To what extent do users avail themselves of these opportunities? Two lines of communication research address this question:

- A number of researchers are documenting the ways geographically distant families employ technologies, often in fairly challenging circumstances such as during military deployment or catastrophic illness.
- Other researchers are examining simple, often mundane relationship maintenance behaviors in face-to-face family relationships and the ways technology assists and challenges such maintenance.

Relationship maintenance in face-to-face family relationships. Social media such as Facebook allow users to "keep up with" face-to-face friends, colleagues, and family members (Bruess, Li, & Polingo, this volume; Young & Quan-Haase, 2013). Research documents that most social media contacts are people that users know in their offline lives (Lampe, Ellison, & Steinfield, 2006), including family members. Multiple studies document users' tendency to employ technology to interact with immediate family members (Bruess, Li, & Polingo, this volume; Dorrance-Hall & Kenny, this volume; Kennedy et al., 2008; Smith, this volume), often people the user sees every day. Such interactions can address both social goals (e.g., e-birthday cards) and task goals (e.g., planning birthday parties; Boase, Horrigan, Wellman, & Rainie, 2006). Pew data indicate that couples with children in the home often use their cell phones to "coordinate their lives" (Kennedy et al., 2008, p. ii). For example, cell phones can facilitate fluid task achievement, such as deciding who will pick up the children from daycare or who will stop at the grocery store after work. Families often employ such so-called micro-coordination (Ling & Yttri, 2002) to manage family obligations simultaneously with other activities such as volunteering and work demands (Webb, Ledbetter, & Norwood, 2014). Indeed, users report that technology has "blurred the traditional lines between work and family" (Kennedy et al., 2008, p. iii).

Multiple researchers examine parent–child Facebook interactions (Young & Quan-Haase, 2013) and document the benefits of such interactions, particularly in contentious relationships (Binder, Howes, & Smart, 2012; Child & Westermann, 2013; Kanter, Afifi, & Robbins, 2012). Bruess et al. (in this volume) found that Facebook served as a ritual of connection between family members and served multiple positive functions for families, including reminiscing, increasing knowledge of each other, and reestablishing ties with extended family. Vitak, Ellison, and Steinfield (2011) reported that "friending" family members was associated with increased perceptions of social support.

Interestingly, most "Facebook fights" involve a primary users' contacts disagreeing in the comments sections of one of the primary user's recent posts. Such disagreements typically occur at sites of social diversity such as where family, friends, and work associates converge (Binder et al., 2012). Often these socially diverse groupings include one or more family members who have never met the user's other "friends" face to face. Indeed, Binder et al. reported a connection between the number of Facebook disagreements and the number of family members who were Facebook friends with the user. In other words, the battling commenters are arguing with complete strangers online but know offline associates of the primary user, whose account has become the site of the "Facebook fight." The primary user might then hear comments at the next face-to-face family gathering about, for example, his or her "weirdo Facebook friends." One way to reduce online arguments of this type is to create groups of contacts and then post to specific groups. Another is to hide all posts from certain individuals, including contentious family members.

In addition to "keeping up" with the day-to-day events in family members' lives, social media afford families the option to stay in daily touch when crisis strikes. For example, some blog hosting websites such as caringbridge.com provide a venue for caregivers to keep family members informed about serious health-related events such as surgeries and cancer treatments. When a natural disaster such as a hurricane strikes, family members might be scattered across locations; social media (such as Facebook) provide venues for family members to reconnect and share information (Knight, 2013)—and to do so quickly to reduce the anxiety caused by ambiguity about the health status and location of loved ones.

Communicating with geographically distant family members. Modern communication technologies provide workable venues for interaction among geographically distant family members (see Karraker, this volume). Indeed, more than half (52%) of the survey respondents in a Pew survey viewed PCTs as particularly useful for staying in touch with family members who live at a distance (Kennedy et al., 2008). Furthermore, the communication technologies employed by transnational families has significantly changed across the past three decades (Webb et al., 2014): Families moved from biweekly postal mail contact before the 1990s, to phone contact facilitated by decreasing long-distance rates in the mid-1990s, and then to email and other online contact by the end of the decade (Wilding, 2006). Today, family blogs allow multiple family members, regardless of geographical distance, to maintain regular contact as they have time and interest (Nardi, Schiano, & Gumbrecht, 2004). Choice of online venue for family communication can vary with family size and patterns of communication (Cramer & Edward, this volume).

In addition to regular interaction, new media allow far-flung family members to "be there" during important moments. For example, instant-messenger services allow male American military personnel to maintain a sense of being present at their children's births while they serve overseas (Schachman, 2010). Via Skype or

FaceTime, family members at multiple locations can sing "Happy Birthday" to a child as he or she blows out the candles on the cake; a doting aunt never need miss the look on a young adult's face as he or she opens a special graduation present.

Linking distant family members can be enjoyable and beneficial—but not in all cases. Sometimes family members "migrated precisely because they found their home country socially or culturally stifling or their kin dominating and difficult. An increased capacity to connect with home [may enable] feelings of suffocation and restriction to extend across time and space" (Wilding, 2006, pp. 135–136). Thus, although modern communication technologies offer geographically distant family members the means to stay in touch as if they lived in the same neighborhood, some family members elect to not exercise that option.

Beyond transcending geography, research in the communication-accommodation theory tradition recognizes that age differences can hinder communication between family members (Soliz & Harwood, 2006). However, telephone and written media (including email) can effectively transcend generational barriers, with increased contact positively associated with relational quality and relational satisfaction in grandparent–grandchild relationships; indeed, grandparents and grandchildren tend to initiate email contact with equal frequency (Harwood, 2000).

In summary, the notion that families use new media to stay in touch with geographically distant relatives is borne out by research. But, the misconception that families use PCTs *exclusively* or even *primarily* to stay in touch with out-of-town relatives provides too limited an understanding of the "reach" of the stay-in-touch function of social media. Families also use new media to maintain relationships with family members they see daily and to achieve important coordination and task goals. Modern communication technologies provide multiple venues for family members to communicate, whether they live in close proximity or in distant geographic locations. Pew reports that 64% of surveyed users reported staying in touch with family was their major reason for using social media (Smith, 2011). Using PCTs to maintain family relationships, both near and far, has become so common that family genograms of technical connections can be mapped (Blumer & Hertlein, this volume). Additionally, PCTs allow a sense of social presence at special moments across locations and generations.

Misconception Three: Internet Use Threatens Healthy Family Functioning

Communication technologies are not inherently bad for family relationships. In fact, many users think that PCT use can increase family closeness. Pew researchers report "25% of our survey respondents feel that their family is now closer than when they were growing up thanks to the Internet and cell phones, while just 11% say their family today is not as close as families in the past" (Kennedy et al., 2008, p. iii). The balance of their respondents (approximately 60%) reported that PCTs had neither increased nor decreased their family's closeness.

PCT use can impact family functioning in *both* positive and negative ways. In many circumstances, family functioning is supported and/or restored via social support provided by specialized online communities (e.g., bulletin boards for parents of children with cancer). Facebook interaction can renew and enhance family relationships across space, time, and generations, serving as a highly desirable digital-age family ritual (Bruess et al., this volume). Family members can offer social support to college students during their first year away at college (Smith, this volume). Romantic and married couples also create digital love letters and keep digital mementos of relationship experiences and feelings (Janning and Christopherson, this volume).

When they are not interacting with family members, users might spend time online engaging in family-related activities such as buying birthday gifts online for family members and answering e-invitations to family gatherings. Additionally, when users interact online with non–family members, they often discuss family issues and engage their family identities (Webb et al., 2014), as exemplified in the following research reports:

- Foster parents write, read, and discuss their adoption stories with other foster parents on narrative blogs (Suter, Baxter, Seurer, & Thomas, 2014).
- Grandparents may spend time on grandparenting websites discussing their grandparenting role (Harwood, 2000).
- Mommy bloggers reinforce their identity as mothers by sharing contemporary solutions to parenting problems (Lee & Webb, 2012; Webb & Lee, 2011).
- Engaged couples construct wedding websites that present a relationship narrative and couple identity consistent with what they believe their families expect (Daws, this volume).

In other circumstances, of course, family functioning can be negatively affected. The marital relationship is especially vulnerable to damage via online interactions with non–family members (e.g., cyber-affairs).

The potentially negative impact of cyber-cheating and -sex on marriage. Online interactions with users outside the family can harm existing family relationships, especially the marital relationship. Research indicates that many married men and married women participate in cyber-cheating (Millner, 2008). Multiple websites will match partners who desire extramarital cyber-affairs (e.g., nostringsattached.com and marriedsecrets.com). Other websites match married users who desire "discreet" affairs with other married users who do not want to "get caught" (e.g., AshleyMadison.com). Explanations for cyber-cheating include the recreational hypothesis (cyber-cheaters are sexually permissive sensation seekers) and the compensation hypothesis (cyber-cheaters look for others to compensate for their own inadequacies) (Peter & Valkenburg, 2007). Cyber-cheaters can experience online sexual harassment and cyber-stalking (Kelly, Pomerantz, & Currie, 2006; Philips & Morrissey, 2004) that disrupts family life.

Internet pornography poses a unique threat to marriages. Men often view Internet pornography as visual stimulation for masturbation with no emotional attachment (Limacher & Wright, 2006), but their heterosexual spouses often hold an alternative viewpoint. "Getting caught" by the partner can transform a safe and loving relationship into one of mistrust and distance (Hans, Lee, Tinker, & Webb, 2011). In heterosexual relationships, wives who discover their husbands viewing Internet pornography typically decode the situation as the wife being no longer attractive to the husband; the wives typically experience emotional pain from the husbands' "involvement" with other women (Hans et al., 2011). The higher the frequency of the heterosexual husband's pornography use, the greater the marital issue in the wife's view (Hans et al., 2011). Research on wives' cyber-affairs and the impact of such affairs on their spouses is virtually nonexistent; however, it is easy to imagine any spouse's negative reaction to the realization that his or her marital partner is "seeing other people" online.

A more common PCT problem among marital dyads is partners' use of devices, especially mobile telephones, to communicate with non–family members during family or couple time together. Spouses who work outside the home are especially susceptible to the desire to, for instance, finish one more work-related email before turning back to a conversation with partners and/or children. McDaniel (this volume) examined the nature of "technoference"—the tendency for technology to interfere with couple relationships and couples' parent–child time. Piercy, Riger, Voskanova, Chang, Haugen, and Sturdivant (this volume) also uncovered, through their national surveys of marriage and family therapists, ways couples face difficulty when technology creates conflict and difficulties for couples. Furthermore, Iaccheri and Tyma (this volume) found, through a Critical Discourse Analysis of couples' discussions about technology in their relationship, that sometimes unhealthy power dynamics are created and maintained in couple relationships around the technology.

The positive influence of social-support communities. Many online interactions facilitate healthy family functioning in communities of social support (for instance, see Dworkin, Walker, Rudi, and Doty, this volume, for an examination of parents' use of new media to support their parenting practices and choices). Especially in times of crisis or when offline family support is unavailable, online social support communities can stabilize the family system. For example, if a young married couple is living far from family and experiences the birth of their first child—a child with Down Syndrome—they can find information and advice via online social-support groups of parents who have children with Downs. Online social support communities are available for parents on almost any relevant topic.

Benefits of social support to individual family members include positive changes to perceptions of self, strategies for coping with stress, and an enhanced sense of self-worth and stability (Cohen & Wills, 1985). Social-support communities have broad appeal to parents. Dworkin et al. (this volume) examined demographic differences in parents' use of digital media and the ways parents develop complex communities to support parenting; among many differences across gender, income, ethnicity, geography, education level, and age, they report rural parents participated in online classes more frequently than suburban parents, potentially a reflection of convenience and access. As Walker (this volume) reveals, social media is not a platform that has singular effects on parent development, knowledge, attitudes, or behavior, but influences both the structure and processes of parents' relationships.

PCTs often provide access to support resources that are unavailable, inconvenient, or perceived as intimidating in offline settings. Family members coping with stress, illness, or loss can easily locate online venues for social-support provision. Illness blogs provide online social support, often substituting for support unavailable offline (e.g., Donovan, LeFebvre, Tardif, Brown, & Love, 2014; Rains & Keating, 2011). The death of a family member can prompt users to seek online social support; approximately 10% of Internet support groups are for bereaved parents (Carlson, Lammert, & O'Leary, 2012). Such groups are more likely to draw bereaved fathers, who historically are less likely to attend offline bereavement groups (Carlson et al., 2012).

Finally, family members facing stigma can seek social support in online communities. Websites for families with gay, lesbian, bisexual, or transgender members provide educational material, discussion boards, and information about support groups. Online support is available to families who depart from cultural ideals (Baxter et al., 2009) such as large families with four or more children (Arnold, 2005) and transnational/transracial families (Meyers, 2014), as well as family members who depart from cultural ideals such as birthmothers who relinquish parental rights (Baxter, Norwood, Asbury, Jannusch, & Scharp, 2012) and stepmothers (Christian, 2005). Members of almost any type of family system can seek and find social support online.

In sum, interaction with non–family members via PCTs can challenge healthy family functioning when users violate implicit relational contracts (e.g., cyber-cheating). Conversely, and primarily, online interactions with non–family members can enhance and improve family functioning, especially in challenging situations, when family members avail themselves of the opportunity to receive social support from online communities. Access to others via the Internet is a neutral phenomenon; how family members use this potential resource determines its impact on family functioning.

Misconception Four: Using Technology Leads to Fewer Face-to-Face Family Interactions

Although a few early researchers reported that technology reduced the amount of time family members spend in face-to-face interaction, very few contemporary scientists believe that PCT use displaces face-to-face interaction. In fact, a major Pew Research survey contradicted the early research; their participants reported that their increased time online did not reduce the amount of face-to-face time they spent with family members but rather reduced the amount of time they spend watching television (Kennedy et al., 2008). Today, scholars believe that communication via PCTs largely augments and enhances offline relationships, including family relationships.

Early research. Some early research linked Internet use to negative outcomes, such as increased depression and loneliness, reduced face-to-face interactions with family and friends, and neglect of close offline relationships (Brenner, 1997; Kraut et al., 1998; Mesch, 2006b). Negative outcomes widely reported about children's use of a personal computer in bedrooms (rather than use of a family computer in a common room in the home) increased parental fears of social isolation (Roberts, Foehr, Rideout, & Brodie, 1999). Other researchers linked increased Internet interactions with strangers (such as fellow interactants on fan blogs) to shrinking family and community interaction in everyday life (Turner, 2004). Such tales of doom and gloom are largely irrational; most recent studies cannot replicate these early findings.

To assume that PCT use will displace face-to-face interaction in the family engages a zero-sum view of time use (Lee, 2009) and is grounded in the assumption that multitasking is not a possibility. Research suggests users often multitask by communicating via multiple communication channels simultaneously, often in the presence of a face-to-face relational partner (Turner & Reinsch, 2011). For example, an entire family can watch a movie being live-steamed onto a computer and talk about the movie while they watch it. Face-to-face family visits can occur among geographically distant family members via Skype or FaceTime. In other words, engaging on PCTs can increase face-to-face family interaction.

Recent research. Recent research documents that many users employ social media precisely to stay in touch with offline family and friends (Haythornthwaite, 2005; Wasike & Cook, 2010; Zhao, Grasmuck, & Martin, 2008). Indeed, the closer the relationship, the more likely users are to employ multiple media to maintain contact and communicate regularly (Haythornthwaite, 2005), including face-to-face interactions, Facebook, Twitter, email, and texting. Some users view PCTs as absolutely necessary to maintain close relationships with their family members; for example, nonresidential parents extensively employ technology for daily communication with their children (Kartch & Timmerman, this volume). Mobile phones function as a favored device to maintain close relationships (Kim, Kim, Park, & Rice, 2007).

Use of PCTs can reduce conflict between family members (Child & Westermann, 2013; Kanter, Afifi, & Robbins, 2012). For example, rather than two adult siblings quarreling about factual matters (e.g., Who won the 1987 World series?), they might discover factual information with a quick Google search. Similarly, when children ask parents challenging questions (e.g., How does photosynthesis work?), parents could quickly research the answer on a smartphone and share it with their children. Internet-streaming educational programs (e.g., *Sesame Street, National Geographic* documentaries) can enrich children's lives; parents may be grateful that such media exposes their children to the world beyond their neighborhood in a positive way and thus broadens their children's horizons.

In sum, rather than assuming every moment spent online is a moment not spent in face-to-face interaction, PCTs can be more accurately viewed as a tool to augment face-to-face interactions, decrease conflict, and expand family members' horizons. PCTs offer means to supplement rather than displace offline interaction.

Misconception Five: Families Abuse Technologies, Using "Screens" as Babysitters and to Avoid Face-to-Face Family Interaction

Children sometimes use their parents' tablets to play games and watch cartoons (Rideout & Hamel, 2006). However, the characterization of such technology use as "babysitting" is too narrow and negative to accurately describe how most parents and children together engage in PCT use for mutual benefit.

PCT use to facilitate family functioning. There can be no denying that some parents use mass media programming and interactive online activities (e.g., the popular digital game *Angry Birds*) as means of keeping children occupied while parents engage in alternative activities such as completing household chores, scheduling appointments, and running errands. Parents quickly learn that children's emersion in PCT use can ease transitions, keep children quietly engaged rather than quarreling with siblings, and become a part of helpful bedtime routines (Rideout & Hamel, 2006). However, no research to date documents (1) that parents are not present with children while the children use PCTs; (2) that parents are using PCTs as "babysitters" and thus ignoring their children during the PCT use; or (3) that children using PCTs for short periods has any adverse effect on family functioning. In fact, the published research paints the opposite picture: Parents employ PCTs to facilitate family functioning, as described above, and engage in cooperative activities as described below.

Family use of PCTs for cooperative activities. Families with children often employ PCTs to engage in cooperative activities, such as playing games together (Aarsand & Aronsson, 2009) and co-viewing films or television shows (Clark, 2011). Joint game playing allows family members of diverse ages to interact as peers and learn from one another (e.g., *Words with Friends*). Many parents find that co-playing video games is an effective mechanism for mediation of sexual and violent content. As Nikken & Jansz (2006) noted, "parents more often co-play video games with their children when they expected positive social-emotional effects from gaming" (p. 181).

Additionally, families have been watching television together since the advent of the medium, and often consider such joint viewing as quality time spent together. Streaming televisions shows, films, and cartoons via laptop computers and tablets operates in precisely the same way, allowing joint viewing and accompanying discussions. Joint watching enables family members to share their favorite genres of televisions shows (e.g., mysteries) and sporting teams (e.g., "I married into a Green Bay Packer family"). Joint viewing can provide the catalyst for challenging but timely discussions between parents and adolescents on such topics as safer sex practices, as well as drug and alcohol use (see Kam & Lee, 2013, for a thorough review of the research documenting this phenomenon).

Finally, Pew researchers note that family members often go online together for joint activities (Kennedy et al., 2008). Additionally, family members individually may view something interesting on the Internet, but then bring their PCT device to other family members to share in the experience: a "Hey, look at this!" experience (Kennedy et al., 2008, p. iii).

In sum, parents strategically use PCTs to assist family functioning (e.g., easing the transition from school to home by allowing the child to watch a cartoon in the car), but there is no scientific evidence that parents use PCTs to babysit their children. Additionally, parents and children together use PCTs for collaborative engagement such as playing online games together, co-viewing streamed films, and sharing interesting content. Such collaborative engagement facilitates more family together time and conversation.

Misconception Six: The Family Elder as a Source of Wisdom and Reliable Information Is Being Replaced by "Googling the Internet"

We can reasonably question the credibility of many Internet sources. Only the most naïve user would think that all statements on the Internet are true. Conversely, many highly credible sources employ the Internet for information distribution, including, for example, the U.S. government, the Mayo Clinic, and scholarly journals. Therefore, users often turn to the Internet to seek information. "Googling" a question is a common activity among PCT owners. They turn to the Internet to learn when a game will be broadcast, when the sun will set today, what food is on sale this week at their local grocery store, and how to reduce a fever. Typically users seek information from the Internet under two conditions:

- The information they seek is not immediately available from a trusted face-to-face source.
- The user believes that the most accurate information on the subject is available on the Internet.

These conditions also apply to information related to families and family functioning. A user might text his or her mother to ask for the date of an uncle's birthday or email a family member to ask for grandmother's apple pie recipe, but users are less likely to contact a relative to ask when the sun will set today or when the game starts tonight.

Gathering information related to family concerns. It should come as no surprise that many family members search the Internet to address a wide variety of information needs related to both individual and family concerns. The Internet offers information on how to cook the family's Thanksgiving Day turkey, how to "come out" to the family, how to have DNA tested for inherited diseases, for ideas about birthday gifts for older family members in nursing homes, as well as countless other family-related topics. New mothers and fathers visit parenting websites to learn about pregnancy and childbirth (e.g., Johansson, Rubertsson, Radestad, & Hildingsson, 2010), parenting skills (Radey & Randolph, 2009), as well as children's health and nutrition (Atkinson et al., 2009; Knapp et al., 2011). Some new parents perceive online information from fellow parents as more current and relevant than information from other sources, including relatives and healthcare providers (O'Connor & Madge, 2004). Plantin and Daneback (2009) observed: "Today's parents are no longer satisfied with simple descriptions of parenthood, but instead require knowledge that conveys the experiences of others in similar situations as themselves" ("Parents go online—needs and motives," para. 2). Given that knowledge about child development, medicine, and nutrition is constantly increasing, perhaps current information from fellow contemporary parents on the front lines of childrearing might be perceived as more accurate and credible than grandparent's recollections of child-rearing practices from the past. Furthermore, online information about child rearing comes without unwanted advice and hurtful comments from in-laws (An, 2014).

Gathering information about the family itself. If an Internet-user wants to learn the outcome of a cousin's surgery, a family member is likely the best source of such information. However, there may exist more accurate or credible sources of information about a family than family members themselves. Sometimes family members lack the knowledge or the willingness to share needed or desired family-centric information. Indeed, older adults often carry family secrets to the grave. In such cases, PCTs provide access to Internet-based records that might provide desired and useful information.

Many users search the Internet to discover information about their biological family, especially in cases where detailed information cannot be gathered in face-to-face conversations with family members. For example, an Internet search is adult adoptees' primary means of seeking information about their biological relatives (Powell & Afifi, 2005). Similarly, online genealogical research is an increasingly popular pastime fueled by the proliferation of genealogical websites and easy-to-use online search tools for mapping biological family trees (Bishop, 2008). Offline conversations with family members might precede an Internet search to guide users' efforts. Such conversations might further encourage explorers to dig for information on the Internet, information revealed only in bits and pieces in family stories. Conversely, many fruitful offline family conversations can surround the Internet findings.

In sum, the family elder may be consulted, but there are two cases in which users tend to turn to the Internet for information to augment offline conversations with family members: when the user perceives that more accurate information is available online (e.g., new parents seeking medical advice), and when live conversations fail to reveal the information sought (e.g., genealogical research revealing information long forgotten by or never passed along from living elders in the family). Family members seek information on the Internet related to family concerns (e.g., relevant medical information) as well as searching information about the family per se (e.g., using genealogical websites).

Misconception Seven: Children Are Technology Experts in Families Because They Possess Greater Knowledge Than Parents

Some children indeed possess greater technical knowledge than their parents about PCTs, affording them technological authority in the family (Belch, Krentler, & Willis-Flurry, 2005). Such a position comes with drawbacks, as detailed later in this section. However, recent evidence calls into question the assumption that technology is a young person's game (Eynon & Helsper, 2015). Eynon and Helsper argue the future of technological expertise might lie with parents; it is often the parents who use a wider variety of hardware and software for a wider variety of purposes; many parents use PCTs extensively for work and many work 40 or more hours per week. Similarly, Vaterlaus and Tulane (this volume) call into question the very nature of a digital "generation gap."

Disadvantages of children's tech savvy. Researchers find that children who believe their parents perceive them as technological experts can experience difficulty talking with parents about online dangers. For example, Mesch (2006b) reported "adolescent–parent conflicts over Internet use proved strongly related to the perception that the adolescent was a computer expert" (p. 473). One possible explanation for these negative outcomes is that the adolescent as family expert represents a reversal of traditional family roles; usually the parents provide adolescents with guidance and expertise (Mesch & Frenkel, 2011). Such a reversal of roles might present an interpersonal communication challenge for family members who need to quickly "reverse back" when the adolescent seeks advice from parents about how to address cyber-threats. However, future generations of parents will be increasingly tech-savvy, closing the intergenerational knowledge gap (Webb et al., 2014) and potentially providing parents with a distinct advantage that can be used for the mutual benefit of multiple family members.

Mixed research findings. If we assume tech-savvy children are helping their parents with online access, then we might assume parents' Internet use should be related to their children's technological savvy. However, a recent multinational study failed to document such a relationship; children's Internet savvy did not predict parents' use of the Internet (Eynon & Helsper, 2015). The best predictors of parents' Internet use included parents' age, educational level, and social capital (Eynon & Helsper, 2015). Social capital is the primary reason users of all ages engage in social networking—to gain relational contacts and to use those relational contacts, including relationships with family members, for personal gain, most often to acquire needed information to achieve personal goals (Vitak & Ellison, 2012).

Scales tipping in the parents' favor. Today, many parents know much more about communication technologies than do their children, given that parents increasingly work online, employing a wide variety of technologies (Mesch & Frenkel, 2011). Their children (and most adolescents), on the other hand, typically use only applications that are popular among their peer groups (Back channel, 2015). Given that social media and tablet-based applications are extremely user-friendly, little technical knowledge is required for parents to become sophisticated users of such formats. The readers of this chapter might be among the last generation to witness a youth advantage in technological expertise.

In summary, children who serve as family technology experts might encounter difficulties, including reluctance to talk with parents about online dangers. Recent research fails to document a relationship between children's and their parents' Internet use, perhaps indicating a decline in the number of children serving as family technology experts. Given PCTs' increasing ease of use and the increased demands for technological know-how in the workplace, parents might be rapidly becoming more technologically knowledgeable than their children.

Misconception Eight: Families Are Formed and Then *Use Technology*

U.S. families, of course, preexist the Internet. Indeed, the concept of family appears eternal and has existed since pre-civilization. Tomb drawings and statuary depict families in ancient Egypt; medieval depictions of Madonna with the infant male child were quite common. From this viewpoint, the Internet is a relatively new invention and its use by families a recent innovation. Generalizing from this historical perspective to the misconception that *all* families predate the Internet is simply inaccurate for many U.S. families in the first quarter of the twenty-first century. Many families now form on the Internet, and they do so in three ways: via online dating, via adoption websites, and via surrogacy websites.

Online dating. Many online daters are looking for fun and casual relationships. Others, however, desire what so many dating websites advertise: the opportunity to meet their permanent life partner, to marry, and to begin a family (Heino, Ellison, & Gibbs, 2010). Online dating websites employ a marketplace orientation to finding a life partner (Webb et al., 2014) by providing opportunities to peruse multiple profiles, begin conversations with those that appear attractive (while ignoring those less attractive), abruptly end budding relationships at the first sign of incompatibility, and "test drive" as many potential partners as desired before committing to one.

Adoption websites. The market metaphor also aptly describes online facilitation of adoption (Webb et al., 2014). Hopeful adoptive parents market themselves as ideal families via parent profiles and "Dear Birth Mother letters" on adoption websites

(Norwood & Baxter, 2011). Birth mothers become online consumers who select parents for their unborn child. Moreover, such websites encourage hopeful adoptive parents to construct particular notions of adoption and family, including depictions of adoption as the primary and preferred means to parenthood, as a process of gain rather than loss, and as the birth mother being a good parent who can elect continued contact with the adoptive family (Wahl, McBride, & Schrodt, 2005). Such positive frameworks counter the stigma surrounding adoption but ignore the negative aspects of the online adoption experience, such as hopeful parents who remain unchosen by birth mothers. Wahl et al. summarized the situation as follows: "On one hand, the technology makes it seem easy to start your own family, but through commodification, family members can now be bought and sold" (p. 291).

Surrogacy websites. Finally, the market metaphor also can be applied to online facilitation of assisted reproductive technology (Webb et al., 2014). Infertile couples often access the Internet to locate surrogates (May & Tensek, 2011), obtain donor egg and sperm (Terman, 2008), and negotiate reproductive-related international travel (Speier, 2011). Such services are available offline, of course, but the Internet affords access to more options (Terman, 2008) and offers anonymity that protects users from the potential embarrassment often associated with infertility (Ishikawa & Keaveney, 2001). Many users believe that the online fertility market creates mutually beneficial situations. However, critics contend that the online fertility marketplace potentially exploits all parties involved (Tober, 2001).

In sum, access to the Internet assists in creating new families; nonetheless, the online reproductive marketplace comes with potential complications and negative consequences. As noted above, U.S. families engage new media in a wide variety of ways, most notably and simply to stay in touch with one another, but also to enact family identities, to seek social support for family roles, and to manage the work/family interface. At least equally important is the recognition that individual users employ PCTs literally to form new families that endure long into the future.

Conclusions

What can we conclude from this discussion of misconceptions concerning technology and the family? Certainly, the situation concerning families and their use of digital communication technologies is far more complicated than previously thought. Thoughtful and considerate use of technology holds the potential to improve family relationships by providing family members with additional means and opportunities for communication and, when used skillfully, technology-mediated communication holds the potential to build lasting, positive family bonds.

Perhaps most importantly, the Internet and twenty-first-century communication technologies are, in so many ways, simply tools and channels of interaction. They are neutral—neither inherently good or bad for individual users, for their families, or for our society. Tools and channels are simply the means to a variety of ends. A knife can be used to kill, but also to perform lifesaving surgery, and more commonly to simply prepare food for family dinners. Similarly, the Internet and PCTs function as commonplace communication tools and social utilities among family members and in households (Kennedy et al., 2008). Users can employ PCTs to benefit and/or to harm their family members. The notion of neutrality is consistent with Walker's (this volume) view that social media provide frameworks and platforms but not outcomes. Family members remain in control of their discourse and thus can shape the outcomes of their online interactions.

As with any tool, PCTs can be used to facilitate change or to maintain the status quo, to improve the quality of life for the individual family members and the family unit. For example, Ye, Sarrica, and Fortunati (2014) make a compelling argument that online bulletin boards are changing the traditional concepts of marriage and family in contemporary China by offering younger family members more compelling options and opportunities to engage in more individualistic rather than collectivist conversations regarding family matters. Conversely, other studies suggest that multiple social-support groups offer opportunities for family members to strengthen family ties in times of crisis (Carlson, Lammert, & O'Leary, 2012; Donovan et al., 2014; Rains & Keating, 2011).

Family conflicts surrounding PCT use seems to fall into two categories that might be usefully avoided: conversations concerning attempts to control another family member's Internet use (e.g., parents attempting to regulate children's usage) and violating family norms and rules for behavior using the PCTs (e.g., cyber-affairs) and privacy. Indeed, the ability of PCTs to link family members in new and multiple ways raises important privacy issues (Holladay & Seipke, 2007).

PCTs offer the opportunity to regularize family communication among far-flung as well as nearby family members via easily accessed and inexpensive venues such as Skype and FaceTime—but only if family members are open to mediated conversation. Although most online, text-based venues offer a limited number of nonverbal cues and can involve time lags between the visual and audio signals, nonetheless PCTs provide the means to regularly enact communicative closeness among family members, should users choose to do so. The question becomes: Will families avail themselves of these new, unprecedented, and unlimited opportunities? Or, conversely, will they allow the largely unfounded cultural misconceptions and the negative hype to prevail?

Application

For Family Members

PCTs offer the tools to achieve diverse, positive outcomes, including staying in touch on a day-to-day basis with family members near and far, as well as staying in touch in times of crisis and disaster. They offer tools to maintain relationships, to revitalize relationships, and to discover new family relationships (e.g., adoptions and searching family histories). Given the many potential positive outcomes, family members might benefit from learning the basic technological skills to take advantage of these affordances.

For Family Communication Theorists

PCTs offer many new and exciting channels of communication. Like television, which presented a new communication channel that necessitated new and innovative thinking to explain the communication phenomena surrounding it, PCTs offer similar challenges. The sooner we stop comparing online communication to offline communication, the sooner we create opportunities for new and helpful insights into the communication surrounding PCTs. Our most frequently cited family communication theory, the theory of family communication patterns/environments, was initially developed to theorize about how families watched and together decoded television news. What amazing new theory will evolve next to explain how families use PCTs?

To Family Communication Researchers

Large quantities of online data exist for the harvesting (Webb & Wang, 2013). Family communication scholars have only begun to harvest and analyze the vast trove of existing dialog that awaits analysis (e.g., Suter et al., 2014). Insights into family communication, both on- and offline, are there for the taking. Never before has so much data been so available to so many with so little effort. Communication researchers could greatly benefit from embracing these opportunities.

To Students and Professors of Family Communication

Through service-learning projects, so much of the knowledge in this book could be conveyed to appropriate community groups. Through class projects, including workshops, websites, and dedicated Twitter accounts, information could be conveyed to first-year students and their families that could smooth the transition to college and improve retention; inform parents about the many communities of support available via mediated forums; remind couples of power dynamics in how technology is perceived, positioned, and used, as well as help families of all shapes, sizes, and life stages make informed choices about technologies—choices that ultimately move them toward strengthening their family systems and subsystems.

References

Aarsand, P., & Aronsson, K. (2009). Response cries and other gaming moves: Building intersubjectivity in gaming. *Journal of Pragmatics, 41*, 1557–1575. doi:10.1016/j.pragma.2007.05.014

An, Z. (2014). The dilemma of receiving support from in-laws: A study of the discourse of online pregnancy and childbirth support groups. *China Media Research, 10,* 3–42.

Arnold, L. B. (2005). Don't you know what causes that? Advice, celebration, and justification in a large families bulletin board. *Communication Studies, 56,* 331–351.

Atkinson, N. L., Saperstein, S. L., Desmond, S. M., Gold, R. S., Billing, A. S., & Tian, J. (2009). Rural e-health nutrition education for limited-income families: An iterative and user-centered design approach. *Journal of Medical Internet Research, 11*(2), e21.

Back channel. (2015). A teenager's view on social media. Retrieved from https://medium.com/backchannel/a-teenagers-view-on-social-media-1df945c09ac6

Baxter, L. A., Henauw, C., Huisman, D. M., Livesay, C. B, Norwood, K., Su, H.,... Young, L. B. (2009). Lay conceptions of "family": A replication and extension. *Journal of Family Communication*, *9,* 170–189.

Baxter, L., Norwood, K., Asbury, B., Jannusch, A., and Scharp, K. M. (2012). Narrative coherence in online stories told by members of the adoption triad. *Journal of Family Communication, 12,* 265–283.

Belch, M. A., Krentler, K. A., & Willis-Flurry, L. A. (2005). Teen Internet mavens: Influence in family decision making. *Journal of Business Research, 58*, 569–575.

Binder, J. F., Howes, A., & Smart, D. (2012). Harmony and tension on social network sites: Side-effects of increasing online interconnectivity. *Information, Communication, & Society, 15,* 1279–1297.

Bishop, R. (2008). In the grand scheme of things: An exploration of the meaning of genealogical research. *Journal of Popular Culture, 41*, 393–412.

Boase, J., Horrigan, J. B., Wellman, B., & Rainie, L. (2006, January 25). *The strength of Internet ties.* Pew Internet & American Life Project. Retrieved from http://www.pewinternet.org/Reports/2006/The-Strength-of-Internet-Ties.aspx

Brenner, V. (1997). Psychology of computer use: XLVII. Parameters of Internet use, abuse, and addiction: The first 90 days of the Internet Usage Survey. *Psychological Reports, 80*, 879–882.

Byers, C. (2014, December 23). OMG, the Internet can be a scary place with kids. Retrieved from http://www.news-gazette.com/living/2014–12–23/omg-internet-can-be-scary-place-kids.html

Byrne, S., & Lee, T. (2011). Toward predicting youth resistance to Internet risk prevention strategies. *Journal of Broadcasting & Electronic Media, 55*, 90–113.

Carlson, R., Lammert, C., & O'Leary, J. M. (2012). The evolution of group and online support for families who have experienced perinatal or neonatal loss. *Illness, Crisis, & Loss, 20*, 275–293.

Child, J. T., & Westermann, D. A. (2013). Let's be Facebook friends: Exploring parental Facebook friend requests from a communication privacy management (CPM) perspective. *Journal of Family Communication, 13,* 46–59.

Christian, A. (2005). Contesting the misconception of the "wicked stepmother": Narrative analysis of an online stepfamily support group. *Western Journal of Communication, 69,* 27–47.

Clark, L. S. (2011). Parental mediation theory for the digital age. *Communication Theory, 21,* 323–343.

Clark, L. S. (2013). *The parent app.* Oxford, UK: Oxford University Press.

Cohen, S., & Wills, T. A. (1985). Stress, social support, and the buffering hypothesis. *Psychological Bulletin, 98,* 310–357.

Cornish, L. S. (2014). "Mum, can I play on the Internet?" Parents' understanding, perception, and responses to online advertising designed for children. *International Journal of Advertising, 33,* 437–473.

Dedkova, L., Cerna, A., Janasova, K., & Daneback, K. (2014). Meeting online strangers offline: The nature of upsetting experiences of adolescent girls. *Communications, 39,* 327–346.

Donovan, E. E., LeFebvre, L., Tardif, S., Brown, L. E., & Love, B. (2014). Patterns of social support communicated in response to expressions of uncertainty in an online community of young adults with cancer. *Journal of Applied Communication Research, 42,* 432–455.

Eastin, M. S., Greenberg, B. S., & Hofschire, L. (2006). Parenting the Internet. *Journal of Communication, 56,* 486–504.

Eynon, R., & Helsper, E. (2015). Family dynamics and Internet use in Britain: What role do children play in adults' engagement with the Internet? *Information, Communication, & Society, 18,* 156–171.

Hans, M. L., Lee, B. D., Tinker, K. A., & Webb, L. M. (2011). Online performances of gender: Blogs, gender-bending, and cybersex as relational exemplars. In K. B. Wright & L. M. Webb (Eds.), *Computer-mediated communication in personal relationships* (pp. 302–323). New York: Peter Lang Publishers.

Harwood, J. (2000). Communication media use in the grandparent–grandchild relationship. *Journal of Communication, 50,* 56–78.

Haythornthwaite, C. (2005). Social networks and Internet connectivity effects. *Information, Communication & Society, 8,* 125–147.

Heino, R. D., Ellison, N. B., & Gibbs, J. L. (2010). Relationshopping: Investigating the market metaphor in online dating. *Journal of Social and Personal Relationships, 27,* 427–447.

Holladay, S. J., & Seipke, H. L. (2007). Communication between grandparents and grandchildren in geographically separated relationships. *Communication Studies, 58,* 281–297.

Ishikawa, M. & Keaveney, M. M. (2001). A modern meeting of the egg and the sperm: A neoclassical analysis of egg donation/surrogacy web sites. *Electronic Journal of Communication, 11,* Retrieved from http://www.cios.org/EJCPUBLIC/011/3/01139.HTML

Johansson, M., Rubertsson, C., Radestad, I., & Hildingsson, I. (2010). The Internet: One important source for pregnancy and childbirth information among prospective fathers. *Journal of Men's Health, 7,* 249–258.

Kam, J. A., & Lee, C. I. (2013). Examining the effects of mass media campaign exposure and interpersonal discussions on youth's drug use: The mediating role of visiting pro-drug websites. *Health Communication, 28,* 473–485. doi:10.1080/10410236.2012.699873

Kanter, M., Afifi, T., & Robbins, S. (2012). The impact of parents "friending" their young adult child on Facebook on perceptions of parental privacy invasions and parent–child relationship quality. *Journal of Communication, 62*, 900–917.

Kelly, D. M., Pomerantz, S., & Currie, D. H. (2006). "No boundaries?" Girls' interactive, online learning about femininities. *Youth and Society, 38*, 3–28.

Kennedy, T. L. M., Smith, A., Wells, A. T., & Wellman, B. (2008). Networked families: Parents and spouses are using the Internet and cell phones to create a "new connectedness" that builds on remote connections and shared Internet experiences. *Report of the Pew Internet & American Life Project.* Retrieved from http://www.pewinternet.org/files/old-media//Files/Reports/2008/PIP_Networked_Family.pdf.pdf

Kim, H., Kim, G. J., Park, H. W., & Rice, R. E. (2007). Configurations of relationships in different media: Ftf, email, instant messenger, mobile phone, and SMS. *Journal of Computer-Mediated Communication, 12*, article 3. Retrieved from http://jcmc.indiana.edu/vol12/issue4/kim.html

Knapp, C., Madden, V., Marcu, M., Wang, H., Curtis, C., Sloyer, P., & Shenkman, E. (2011). Information seeking behaviors of parents whose children have life-threatening illnesses. *Pediatric Blood & Cancer, 56*, 805–811.

Knight, M. (2013). Communicating in a crisis. *Business Communication Quarterly, 76*, 3–4.

Kraut, R., Patterson, M., Lundmark, V., Kiesler, S., Mukhopadhyay, T., & Scherlis, W. (1998). Internet paradox: A social technology that reduces social involvement and psychological well-being? *American Psychologist, 53*, 1017–1031.

Lampe, C., Ellison, N., & Steinfield, C. (2006, November). A Face (book) in the crowd: Social searching vs. social browsing. In *Proceedings of the 2006 20th anniversary conference on computer supported cooperative work* (pp. 167–170) New York: ACM. doi: 10.1145/1180875.1180901

Ledbetter, A. M., Heiss, S., Sibal, K., Lev, E., Battle-Fisher, M., & Shubert, N. (2010). Parental invasive and children's defensive behaviors at home and away at college: Mediated communication and privacy boundary management. *Communication Studies, 61*, 184–204.

Lee, B. D., & Webb, L. M. (2012). The ICC (identity, content, community) theory of blog participation. In R. A. Lind (Ed.), *Producing theory: The intersection of audiences and production in a digital world* (pp. 177–193). New York: Peter Lang Publishers.

Lee, S. J. (2009). Online communication and adolescent social ties: Who benefits more from Internet use? *Journal of Computer-Mediated Communication, 14*, 509–531.

Lemmens, J. S., Valkenburg, P. M., & Peter, J. (2009). Development and validation of a game addiction scale for adolescents. *Media Psychology, 12*, 77–95.

Limacher, L., & Wright, L. (2006). Exploring the therapeutic family intervention of commendations. *Journal of Family Nursing, 12*, 307–331.

Lindsay, M., & Krysik, J. (2012). Online harassment among college students. *Information, Communication, and Society, 15*, 703–719.

Ling, R., & Bertel, T. (2013). Mobile communication culture among children and adolescents. In D. Lemish (Ed.), *The Routledge international handbook of children, adolescents, and media* (pp. 127–133). London: Routledge.

Ling, R., & Yttri, B. (2002). Hyper-coordination via mobile phones in Norway. In J. Katz & M. Aakhus (Eds.), *Perpetual contact* (pp. 139–169). Cambridge, UK: Cambridge University Press.

Lunceford, B. (2011). The new pornographers: Legal and ethical considerations of sexting. In B. E. Drushel & K. German (Eds.), *The ethics of emerging media: Information, social norms, and new media technology* (pp. 99–118). London: Continuum Books.

Mascheroni, G. (2014). Parenting the mobile Internet in Italian households: Parents' and children's discourses. *Journal of Children & Media, 8,* 440–456.

May, A. & Tenzek, K. E. (2011). Seeking Mrs. Right: Uncertainty reduction in online surrogacy ads. *Qualitative Research Reports in Communication, 12,* 27–33.

McCartan, K. F., & McAlister, R. (2012). Mobile phone technology and sexual abuse. *Information & Communication Technology Law, 21,* 257–268.

Mertens, S., & d'Haenens, L. (2014). Parental mediation of Internet use and cultural values across Europe: Investigating the predictive power of the Hofstedian paradigm. *Communications, 39,* 389–414.

Mesch, G. S. (2006a). Family characteristics and intergenerational conflict over the Internet. *Information, Communication, & Society, 9,* 473–495.

Mesch, G. S. (2006b). Family relations and the Internet: Exploring a family boundaries approach. *Journal of Family Communication, 6,* 119–138.

Mesch, G. S., & Frenkel, M. (2011). Family imbalance and adjustment to information and communication technologies. In K. B. Wright & L. M. Webb (Eds.), *Computer-mediated communication in personal relationships* (pp. 285–301). New York: Peter Lang.

Millner, V. (2008). Internet infidelity: A case of intimacy with detachment. *The Family Journal: Counseling and Therapy for Couples and Families, 16,* 78–82.

Mostmans, L., Bauwens, J., & Pierson, J. (2014). "I would never post that": Children, moral sensitivity, and online disclosure. *Communications, 39,* 347–367.

Myers, K. W. (2014). "Real" families. *Critical Discourse Studies, 11,* 175–193.

Nardi, B. A., Schiano, D. J., & Gumbrecht, M. (2004). Blogging as social activity, or would you let 900 million people read your diary? Proceedings from *2004 ACM Conference on Computer Supported Cooperative Work.* New York: ACM. doi:10.1145/1031607.1031643

Nikken, P., & Jansz, J. (2006). Parental mediation of children's videogame playing: A comparison of the reports by parents and children. *Learning, Media, & Technology, 31,* 181–202.

Norwood, K., & Baxter, L. A. (2011). "Dear birth mother": Addressivity and meaning-making in online adoption-seeking parental letters. *Journal of Family Communication, 11,* 198–217.

O'Connor, H., & Madge, C. (2004). "My mum's thirty years out of date": The role of the Internet in the transition to motherhood. *Community, Work, & Family, 7,* 351–369.

Peter, J., & Valkenburg, P. M. (2007). Who looks for casual dates on the Internet? A test of the compensation and the recreation hypotheses. *New Media & Society, 9,* 455–474.

Philips, F., & Morrissey, G. (2004). Cyberstalking and cyberpredators: A threat to safe sexuality on the Internet. *Convergence: Journal of Research into New Media Technologies, 10,* 66–79.

Plantin, L., & Daneback, K. (2009). Parenthood, information, and support on the Internet: A literature review of research on parents and professionals online. *BMC Family Practice, 10.* Retrieved from http://www.biomedcentral.com/1471–2296/10/34

Powell, K. A., & Afifi, T. A. (2005). Uncertainty management and adoptees' ambiguous loss of their birth parents. *Journal of Social and Personal Relationships, 22,* 129–151.

Purcell, K., & Rainie, L. (2014). Americans feel better informed thanks to the Internet. *Report of the Pew Internet & American Life Project.* Retrieved from http://www.pewinternet.org/files/2014/12/PI_InformedWeb_120814_02.pdf

Radey, M. A., & Randolph, K. A. (2009). Parenting sources: How do parents differ in their efforts to learn about parenting? *Family Relations, 58*, 536–548.

Rains, S. A., & Keating, D. M. (2011). The social dimension of blogging about health: Health blogging, social support, and well-being. *Communication Monographs, 78*, 511–534.

Rideout, V., & Hamel, E. (2006). The media family: Electronic media in the lives of infants, toddlers, preschoolers, and their parents. Menlo Park, CA: Kaiser Family Foundation.

Roberts, D. F., Foehr, U. G., Rideout, V. J. & Brodie, M. (1999). *Kids & Media @ the New Millennium.* Washington, DC: Henry J. Kaiser Family Foundation.

Schachman, K. A. (2010). Online fathering: The experience of first-time fatherhood in combat-deployed troops. *Nursing Research, 59*, 11–17. doi:10.1097/NNR.0b013e3181c3ba1d

Schrock, A. R., & boyd, d. (2011). Problematic youth interactions online: Solicitation, harassment, and cyberbullying. In K. B. Wright & L. M. Webb (Eds.), *Computer-mediated communication in personal relationships* (pp. 368–396). New York: Peter Lang.

Smith, A. (2011). Why Americans use social media. *Report of the Pew Internet & American Life Project.* Retrieved from http://www.pewinternet.org/Reports/2011/Why-Americans-Use-Social-Media.aspx

Soliz, J., & Harwood, J. (2006). Shared family identity, age salience, and intergroup contact: Investigation of the grandparent–grandchild relationship. *Communication Monographs, 73*, 87–107.

Sorbring, E., & Lundin, L. (2012). Mothers' and fathers' insights into teenagers' use of the Internet. *New Media & Society, 14*, 1181–1197.

Speier, A. R. (2011). Brokers, consumers, and the Internet: How North American consumers navigate their infertility journeys. *Reproductive BioMedicine Online, 23*, 592–599.

Staksrud, E., & Livingstone, S. (2009). Children and online risk. *Information, Communication, & Society, 12*, 364–387.

Suter, E. A., Baxter, L. A., Seurer, L. M., & Thomas, L. J. (2014). Discursive constructions of the meaning of "family" in online narratives of foster adoptive parents. *Communication Monographs, 81*, 59–78. doi:10.1080/03637751.2014.880791

Terman, S. (2008). Marketing motherhood: Rights and responsibilities of egg donors in assisted reproductive technology agreements. *Northwestern Journal of Law & Social Policy, 3*, 167–184.

To Catch a Predator website. (2004–2007). Retrieved from http://www.nbcnews.com/id/10912603/ns/dateline_nbc-to_catch_a_predator/

Tober, D. M. (2001). Semen as gift, semen as goods: Reproductive workers and the market in altruism. *Body & Society, 7*, 137–160.

Tripp, L. M. (2011). "The computer is not for you to be looking around, it is for schoolwork": Challenges for digital inclusion as Latino immigrant families negotiate children's access to the Internet. *New Media & Society, 13*, 552–567.

Turner, G. (2004). *Understanding celebrity.* London: Sage.

Turner, J. W., & Reinsch, N. L. (2011). Multicommunicating and episodic presence: Developing new constructs for studying new phenomena. In K. B. Wright & L. M. Webb (Eds.),

Computer-mediated communication in personal relationships (pp. 302–323). New York: Peter Lang Publishers.

Van Royen, K., Poels, K., Daelemans, W., & Vandebosch, H. (2015). Automatic monitoring of cyberbullying on social networking sites: From technological feasibility to desirability. *Telematics & Informatics, 32,* 89–97.

Vitak, J., & Ellison, N. B. (2012). "There's a network out there you might as well tap": Exploring the benefits of and barriers to exchanging informational and support-based resources on Facebook. *New Media & Society, 15,* 243–259.

Vitak, J., Ellison, N., & Steinfield, C. (2011). The ties that bond: Re-examining the relationship between Facebook use and bonding social capital. In *Proceedings of the 44th Annual Hawaii International Conference on System Sciences.* New York: Computer Society Press. Retrieved from http://www-personal.umich.edu/~enicole/VitakEllisonSteinfield2011.pdf

Wahl, S. T., McBride, M. C., & Schrodt, P. (2005). Becoming "point and click" parents: A case study of communication and online adoption. *Journal of Family Communication, 5,* 279–294.

Wang, R., Bianchi, S. M., & Raley, S. B. (2005). Teenagers' Internet use and family rules: A research note. *Journal of Marriage and Family, 67,* 1249–1258.

Wasike, B., & Cook, J. A. (2010). Hispanic students and social networking. *Web Journal of Mass Communication Research, 25.* Retrieved from http://wjmcr.org/vol25

Webb, L. M., Ledbetter, A., & Norwood, K. M. (2014). Families and technologically assisted communication. In L. H. Turner & R. West (Eds.), *Sage handbook of family communication* (pp. 354–369). Thousand Oaks, CA: Sage.

Webb, L. M., & Lee, B. S. (2011). Mommy blogs: The centrality of community in the performance of online maternity. In M. Moravec (Ed.), *Motherhood online: How online communities shape modern motherhood* (p. 244–257). Newcastle upon Tyne, UK: Cambridge Scholars Publishing.

Webb, L. M., & Wang, Y. X. (2013). Techniques for sampling on-line data sets. In W. C. Hu & N. Kaabouch (Eds.), *Big data management, technologies, and applications* (pp. 95–114). Hershey, PA: IGI Global Publishers.

Wilding, R. (2006). "Virtual" intimacies? Families communicating across transnational contexts. *Global Networks, 6,* 125–142.

Ye, W. M., Sarrica, M., & Fortunati, L. (2014). A study of Chinese bulletin board system forums: How Internet users contribute to set up the contemporary notions of family and marriage. *Information, Communication, & Society, 17,* 889–905.

Young, A. L., & Quan-Haase, A. (2013). Privacy protection strategies on Facebook. *Information, Communication, & Society, 16,* 479–500. doi:10.1080/1369118X.2013.777757

Zhao, S. Y., Grasmuck, S., & Martin, J. (2008). Identity construction on Facebook: Digital empowerment in anchored relationships. *Computers in Human Behavior, 24,* 1816–1836. doi:10.1016/j.chb.2008.02.012

Zywica, J., & Danowski, J. (2008). The faces of Facebookers: Investigating social enhancement and social compensation hypotheses; predicting Facebook and offline popularity from sociability and self-esteem, and mapping the meanings of popularity with semantics networks. *Journal of Computer-Mediated Communication, 14,* 1–34.

2

Privacy Management Matters in Digital Family Communication

JEFFREY T. CHILD
Kent State University

SANDRA PETRONIO
Indiana University-Purdue University

Introduction

Over the last decade, social media and interactive communication technologies have had a dramatic impact on the way family members interact with one another, creating a number of challenges (Padilla-Walker, Coyne, & Fraser, 2012). Privacy management, in particular, is a main concern for parents and children (Petronio, 2010). The way family members manage their privacy online amid so many possible ways to use interactive communication technology is often confusing and can lead to privacy turbulence and ultimately privacy breakdowns (Child, Haridakis, & Petronio, 2012; Petronio, 2010). Given the newness of these communication options, families have had to develop unique sets of privacy rules for the way members regulate the flow of personal and family information online (Child & Westermann, 2013).

Families manage privacy among family members in many ways, but the ones that prove most difficult are the ways parents regulate children's choices about managing private information online—information both about themselves and other family members. For example, a mom writes about purchasing a smartphone for her young teenage son (Italie, 2013): It is the first time he has had a smartphone, and his mom is concerned about the disclosure choices he might make online. She is not sure what her son might think is acceptable to tell others about himself and his family. She also worries that her son might not be as open with her as now he has a vast audience of friends and others online to which he instead might confide his emotions, activities, and thoughts. Mom feels that if she sets some clear rules to guide her son in his decision making about privacy management using a smartphone, he will be better equipped to make good choices (see Fletcher & Blair's chapter in this volume; Italie, 2013; Petronio, 2013). This and other stories—such as those about negotiating Facebook disclosures and parents' access to their children's passwords (Hone-McMahan, 2013), as well as unexpected issues like problems relatives might have accessing a deceased family member's Facebook account (Gambino, 2013)—are examples of how families are confronted with learning how to navigate privacy control and ownership of information related to social media use.

No doubt you have experienced challenges not only establishing new privacy rules for yourself but also negotiating such rules among your family members. Have you thought about whether you want any of your family members to have access to all of your social media content? Think about a time when you were surprised that your sister or brother did not understand which of your posts on Facebook they should not have told your parents. How do you feel if your privacy expectations could be violated by Facebook independently releasing your password to a family member after you passed away? As a parent, how might you deal with privacy issues and concerns related to social media use by your children? Finally, if you were a child or teen negotiating with your parents about getting your first smartphone, what privacy rules would be important to you? These questions help family members of all ages consider the intersections between social media use, privacy management, and family communication. In this chapter we present the theoretical framework of Communication Privacy Management (Petronio, 2002, 2013) as one way to consider these and other related issues about communication through social media, as well as interactive communication technologies used by and among family members.

Contextualizing Social Media Use and the Family

The list of unique social media sites continues to rapidly grow as individuals create new ways to expand networking and social interactions on the Internet. Broadly speaking, *social media* refers to a series of online, Web-based platforms and applications that allow members to interact and share information (and user-generated content) with one another in a networked group (Child et al., 2012). A social media platform is simply the website or location where the computer-mediated communication (CMC) occurs, like Facebook.com, Myspace.com, or Twitter.com (Child & Petronio, 2011). The content that people share varies from platform to platform and includes text, images, website links, and videos. Some of the most popular types of social media include personal journal or diary blogs (e.g., Myspace.com, LiveJournal.com, and Blogger.com), social networking websites (e.g., Facebook.com and Linkedin.com), micro-blogs (e.g., Twitter.com), and video and/or picture-based social media (e.g., YouTube.com, Pinterest.com, and Vimeo.com). Amid this range of social media options, Facebook.com is still the most visited social media site in the United States, accessed by more than 70% of U.S.-based Internet users (Edison Research, 2012; Nielsen, 2011). Approximately 58 million Americans incorporate social media use into their daily routines (Edison Research, 2012), which means social media present a convenient and popular way for many people to keep in touch with family and friends.

Facebook allowed anyone to create a webpage for the first time in 2006. This move essentially opened up the Facebook social media platform to greater use for family communication. Since the loosening of membership restrictions, the makeup of Facebook has drastically changed from the primarily 18–22-year-old audience (Lenhart, 2009; Pempek, Yermolayeva, & Calvert, 2009) to a middle-aged and older audience of users. Current users across age groups increasingly use Facebook to interact with their closest confidants, including family members (Bruess, Li, & Polingo, in this volume; Child & Westermann, 2013; Hampton Goulet, Rainie, & Purcell, 2011). In fact, parents and older adult users of Facebook reflect one of the fastest growing demographics adopting and using the social networking site (Edison Research, 2012; Facebook, 2014; Hampton et al., 2011; Lenhart, 2009; Nielsen, 2011; Qualman, 2009). Across a two-year time span (2008–2010) the number of people using social networking sites doubled, and the average age of users shifted from 33 to 38 years old (Hampton et al., 2011). The longer an individual maintains a Facebook account, the more frequent their usage patterns are for all of the interactive functions offered through the site, including status updates, commenting on content, tagging and liking behaviors, and sending private messages (Hampton, Goulet, Marlow, & Rainie, 2012). Collectively, evidence suggests Facebook users are currently older, more interactive across time, and comfortable integrating Facebook interaction into daily routines. This chapter presents research from a range of social media platforms and considers how family members communicate through social media and enact privacy management strategies. We highlight more information about Facebook above simply because of its prominence and use today by multiple generations of the family, which is not the case with other forms of social media.

Communication Privacy Management (CPM) Theory

When considering family communication, social media, and privacy, social media use within the family can produce both positive and negative effects (Child, 2007; Child, Pearson, & Petronio, 2009). For example, parental surveillance of their children's social media interactions can be seen as a threat when perceived as attempts to invade the child's privacy or as an encroachment on autonomy (Hawk, Keijsers, Hale, & Meeus, 2009; Ledbetter, Heiss, Sibal, Lev, Battle-Fisher, & Shubert, 2010; Petronio, 1994). However, social media use within the family can also give family members a convenient way to maintain ties across multiple generations and over great distances. As a consequence, families are more readily able to maintain strong bonds and familial connections (Fife, LaCava, & Nelson, 2013; Kanter, Afifi, & Robbins, 2012). Communication Privacy Management (CPM) theory (Petronio, 1991, 2002, 2013) explains how users may come to evaluate their own privacy needs and develop unique rules for social media use with family members (Child & Petronio, 2011; Metzger, 2007).

Private information is defined in CPM theory as information that makes people feel some level of vulnerability, thereby resulting in the desire to control the further dissemination of that information (Petronio, 2002, 2010). For example, individuals with a stigmatized disease such as HIV/AIDS tend to protect their status and are highly selective about who can co-own and disseminate this private information (Greene, Derlega, Yep, & Petronio, 2003). On the other hand, research shows that individuals with strongly held religious beliefs, for instance, tend not to be concerned about disclosing their religious identification with others through social media (Bobkowski & Pearce, 2011).

CPM theory proposes that effective management of private information includes considerations of three main principles: privacy ownership, privacy control, and privacy turbulence. These three interrelated principles are related to the axiomatic predictions of the theory for the way people regulate access and protection of their private information (Petronio, 1991, 2010, 2013; Petronio & Reierson, 2009). CPM asserts that individuals have both access and privacy needs, forming a dialectical tension that drives choices for privacy management. Therefore, people need to both disclose private information to others and, at the same time, protect other information in order to manage relationships effectively. CPM is an evidence-based theory about how people manage private information, both theirs and others' to which they have been granted access (Petronio, 2002).

First, CPM contends that people believe they own their private information, as well as have the right to protect their information and control access to it.

When individuals share private information with others they grant co-ownership rights to selected others for the future management and regulation of that private information. They select others to be co-owners based on several decision criteria that can include privacy orientations they learn in their families, motivations they wish to fulfill, and assessments of risk and benefits of disclosing or protecting information (Petronio, 2002, 2010, 2013; Morr Serewicz & Canary, 2008). The theory illustrates this principle of ownership rights through different types of metaphorical privacy boundaries (Petronio, 2002). Privacy boundaries that are thick indicate higher levels of privacy while thinner, permeable boundaries suggest more openness for the individual or collective. Information identified as private and protected resides within an individual privacy boundary. Once private information is disclosed to others, it transitions from an individual privacy boundary to a shared boundary that is managed among the original owner and authorized co-owners (Petronio & Caughlin, 2006; Petronio & Gaff, 2010).

In the case of social media, personal information that individuals protect, and therefore do not share with others on social media, remains in their individual privacy boundaries. However, when a person posts status updates, photos, and allows comments on the person's posts, any of these actions converts some of the information in that person's individual privacy boundary into a co-owned, collective boundary (Child & Petronio, 2011). Sharing or disclosing private content with a social media network is seen as a decision to invite some level of co-ownership for that information within the online community of those who have access to the information (Bateman, Pike, & Butler, 2011; Child, Petronio, Agyeman-Budu, & Westermann, 2011). In other words, the willingness to share suggests people believe that the online community represents an environment of people within their collective privacy boundary. Although it is often a fallacy, posters tend to assume that others will respect their privacy rules when those others post information online and remain consistent with the original posters' preferences to have their personal privacy boundary regulated (Child et al., 2011, 2012; Child & Westermann, 2013).

Second, CPM predicts that individuals control their privacy and make decisions about disclosing or concealing private information through the use of privacy rules (Petronio, 2002). Privacy rules function as a way to regulate the management of both individual privacy boundaries and collective privacy boundaries (Petronio & Reierson, 2009). At the individual level, people not only develop privacy rules for selecting co-owners of private information, based on decision criteria mentioned above (such as cultural expectations, gender, motivational goals, contextual issues, and risk–benefit assessments), they also have privacy rules to establish and regulate how much is known, and when, where, and how it is conveyed (Petronio, 2002).

Once information is shared, creating collective privacy boundaries with others considered authorized co-owners, these boundaries are managed through the use of three types of privacy rules, which are jointly negotiated among co-owners: privacy boundary linkages, privacy boundary permeability, and privacy boundary ownership (Petronio, 2002, 2013). Privacy boundary linkage rules determine who else may know the collectively held information (i.e., "Do not tell my parents what I have said about my family on Facebook"). Privacy boundary permeability rules specify how much and what types of information can be shared outside the social media privacy boundary (i.e., "Mom, you can comment on what I post but never share any embarrassing baby photos of mine through social media"). Privacy boundary ownership rules stipulate what rights authorized co-owners have to make independent decisions about disclosure of the collectively held information to third parties (i.e., "Please ask me before you disclose anything I have said through social media to someone else; I want to decide who else knows") (Child & Agyeman-Budu, 2010; Child et al., 2009, 2011).

Although negotiating privacy rules allows for the optimal agreed-upon level of privacy management, people often assume that others in their online community will use the same types of privacy rules that they would use to manage their private information, without necessarily discussing or negotiating these rules (Child & Petronio, 2011; Petronio, 2002). Not openly setting privacy rules and establishing acceptable parameters for third-party dissemination increases the probability of breakdowns in regulating the access to information in acceptable ways for the collective—the final tenant of CPM theory.

The third tenet of CPM addresses situations of privacy turbulence and privacy breakdowns. Accordingly, people can experience minor disturbances to full breakdowns in the management of their private information online, as well as in face-to-face settings (Petronio, 2013). There is a gradation of disruption that can occur in the privacy management system. Because not all privacy management is synchronized between the original owner and authorized co-owner(s), there is a potential for trouble. Therefore, CPM argues that it is necessary to theoretically accommodate the possibility that privacy rules might not be followed or mistakes might be made in privacy management (Petronio, 2013). Although often disruptive, the recognition that there is a privacy management problem, followed by consideration of what adjustments in privacy rule changes are necessary, has the potential to make the privacy management system stronger and more effective. Often the process of repairing the privacy management system includes updating, correcting, and recalibrating the adequate functioning of privacy rules (Child et al., 2011; Petronio, 2002). Nevertheless, full breakdowns, such as intentionally snooping or invading someone's privacy by taking information without permission, make correcting the privacy problems more difficult to unpack and require more consideration.

When social media users experience privacy turbulences or disturbances in their expected privacy regulation routines, it is possible to avert a full breakdown in the management of their private information by adapting or recalibrating their privacy rules in light of evolving concerns (Child et al., 2011). One way to do this is to retrieve private information through deleting previously posted information, essentially asserting greater protection of privacy by reclaiming individual privacy rights (Child et al., 2011, 2012). When cognizant of disruptions, many social media users engage in such strategies rather than leaving the information posted on their social media sites (Child et al., 2011).

There are several examples of ways family members might respond to turbulence on a social media site when a member shares "too much" information belonging to the whole family. For example, a user could delete the family-based posts and interact with the overstepping family member further in order to establish a new permeability rule for their social media collective boundary (i.e., "Mom, I would appreciate it if in the future you would please show me any photographs that have me in them before you upload them to Facebook"). Or, if the problem is a person habitually posting inappropriate context, righting the disruption might mean making boundary linkage rules more restrictive. The social media user in these circumstances might also decide to unfriend the person and remove him or her from the user's social media collective boundary altogether, tightening ownership rules so that another breakdown does not occur (i.e., "I have decided to remove my brother from my social media site because he cannot abide by my privacy rules. If you know my brother, please do not share my posts with him").

Family Communication, Privacy Management, and Social Media

Individual Privacy Boundaries and Family Influence over the Life Span

Privacy boundaries change over the course of an individual's life (Petronio, 2002, 2010). Children begin with inclusive privacy boundaries where parents make many decisions related to what and how much is shared about them and under what circumstances others are allowed to access the children's private information (Petronio, 2002). This overarching rule extends to the parents' decisions about what to post about their children on social media. As they age and enter adolescence, children assert more ownership and control over managing their own privacy boundaries. This is often seen when youth engage in privacy protection behaviors such as posting "keep out" signs on bedroom doors, keeping a diary, or asking their parents to allow more latitude over what they share with others. Consistent with the need to deindividuate during adolescence, there is often a tug between the child claiming rights and the parents wanting to preserve control. As a consequence, parents of adolescents are more likely to take an increasingly active role in reviewing social media activity and posts while simultaneously allowing the child to interact and learn (Madden, Cortesi, Gasser, Lenhart, & Duggan, 2012; Weeden, Cooke, & McVey, 2013). As young adults continue to age, they are more likely to assert greater independence and want more control over the management of their own private information (Petronio, 2002). In the case of parental review of what a young adult posts, the child might eventually change his or her password and not allow a parent to co-own that private information any longer. Young adult users of social media also disclose more private information and use fewer privacy setting than do older adults overall (Christofides, Muise, & Desmarais, 2012a). Adolescents tend to more freely share certain kinds of private information than do adults because they are more likely than adult users to use social media platforms as a way to explore and develop their identities (Livingstone, 2008; McCullagh, 2008; Shapiro & Margolin, 2014).

In general, throughout adulthood, individual privacy boundaries continue to thicken, and in older age privacy boundaries usually become more permeable again, often when aging adults exchange control over private information for meeting healthcare needs (Petronio & Kovach, 1997; Petronio, 2002). Extended family members such as grandparents may want to use social media to maintain connections and closeness with their grandchildren (Harwood, 2000; Siibak & Tamme, 2013). When grandparents and relatives live far apart, use of social media helps maintain the integrity of intergenerational bonds. However, to participate in social media use overall, these older adults have to learn about the new communication technologies that their younger relatives use and may need to seek the aid of their adult children, younger adults, and grandchildren, who are likely to be more adept at using social media and interactive communication technologies to manage privacy and meet diverse interaction goals with others (Child & Petronio, 2011; Siibak & Tamme, 2013).

Family Privacy Orientations and Family Social Media Linkages

Communication Privacy Management theory and research demonstrates that families play a significant role in socializing children about privacy rules to use throughout life. The first place an individual learns privacy rules is within the family (Morr Serewicz & Canary, 2008; Petronio, 2002). Further, families also attempt to socialize new members, such as spouses of children, teaching them the family privacy orientations held by the members as a whole (Morr, 2002; Morr Serewicz & Canary, 2008; Morr Serewicz, Dickson, Morrison, & Poole, 2007; Petronio, 2002). Family privacy orientation refers to rules that have been developed and endorsed over time by a family of origin (Petronio, 2002; Petronio, 2010). The privacy orientation reflects a value structure of the family and is a whole family perspective concerning how members define privacy. Family privacy orientations can range from very open to completely closed (Petronio, 2010). Within these orientations, families manage two types of privacy boundaries: internal and external privacy cells. Internal cells are where private information is held and controlled by only certain members. These cells shift and change, depending on the disclosure and privacy needs of the particular members within the privacy chamber. Families also have an external privacy boundary where the whole family ascribes to a rule about what can and cannot be disclosed to outsiders as well as the general level of access to information outsiders are given.

With more people joining and using social media, young adults are faced with considering the role of their parents in their social media spaces as well, as if they would consider parental involvement as privacy violations and invasions of individual privacy expectations (Child & Westermann, 2013; Kanter et al., 2012). It is also important to understand if the privacy management practices guiding disclosure behavior within the home help explain the types of choices family members make about interacting with one another through social media.

Research supports that young adults overall are more likely to accept than deny social media requests from their parents (Ball, Wazner, & Servoss, 2013; Child & Westermann, 2013). Young adult children are also less likely to adjust their privacy settings when considering giving access to a parent on their Facebook site (Ball et al., 2013; Child & Westermann, 2013). Interestingly, daughters are more likely to be Facebook friends with their parents than sons (Ball et al., 2013). However, when their relationships are not as trusting and satisfying with their mothers, young adults are less willing to provide mothers the same type of open access to them through social media than they would had there been stronger relational bonds (Child & Westermann, 2013).

The value of openness (or not) cultivated by families helps explain some of the ways young adults interact with their parents through social media (Child & Westermann, 2013). Curiously, families who are more open with one another are more likely to have children who link in their moms, being more willing to disclose private information with her on their own social media sites and being more willing to disclose private information to her. This is in comparison to families who are more closed and private (where there is less willingness to allow moms to be within the social media privacy boundary). Finally, the results of an experimental study show that when parent–child dyads are paired to interact over a period of time through Facebook, those parent–child social media interactions decrease the frequency of conflict within the parent–child relationship and increase relational closeness (Kanter et al., 2012). Social media use has expanded beyond sites that mostly facilitate peer-to-peer communication (Pempek et al., 2009) to now also facilitating parent-to-child communication (Child & Westermann, 2013; Kanter et al., 2012).

Individual Motivations, Online Privacy Management, and Family Communication

Applying the theoretical frame of CPM to social media interactions opens many avenues of inquiry not considered previously. The research reviewed in this section increases understanding about how individual family members may interact through social media. CPM predicts that decision criteria grounded in understanding individual motivations drive the kinds of privacy rules that people apply to communicative situations related to interaction through social media (Child et al., 2009; Durham, 2008; Petronio, 2002). From existing research, it is clear there are a number of decision criteria leading to the development and implementation of privacy rules that function in the background for a person (Petronio, 2002). For example, self-consciousness, self-monitoring, and social media disclosure orientations all impact the choices for privacy regulations and, by implication, the privacy rules influenced by the criteria that are used as a result by family members (Child et al., 2009).

Family members who have higher levels of self-consciousness spend more time processing and thinking through the possible implications and ramifications of their disclosures in light of others (Buss, 1980; Fenigstein, Scheier, & Buss, 1975). Greater depth in this personality disposition of processing more information in light of others also translates into more sharing of private information through social media for an individual family member. Therefore, family members who have a higher level of self-consciousness use the social media platform as a venue for also working out and seeking feedback about their own perspectives (Child et al., 2009). Self-monitoring is another personality disposition related to how a family member might manage privacy online.

Someone who has high self-monitoring needs is more likely than a low self-monitoring person to guard what they say to someone else and perhaps refrain from sharing opinions because they do not want to offend (Shaffer & Pegalis,

1998; Tardy & Hosman, 1982). This personality disposition is more common in someone who carefully manages impressions with others (Bello, 2005; Flynn, Reagans, Amanatullah, & Ames, 2006; Shaffer & Pegalis, 1998; Tardy & Hosman, 1982). Child and Agyeman-Budu (2010) found that high self-monitors are also more likely to guard themselves online and maintain a higher level of privacy management than low self-monitors. These findings support that some of the interaction-based personality dispositions family members experience impact the privacy management choices they are individually motivated to seek out and use when managing their privacy online (Child & Agyeman-Budu, 2010; Child et al., 2009; Guadagno, Okdie, & Eno, 2008; Miura & Yamashita, 2007).

Six different disclosure goals serve as an orientation for how family members set up privacy rules and consider what to say when interacting with others online (Child et al., 2012). Three of these disclosure orientation profiles (the utilitarian user, the planner, and the sharer profiles) were related to the overall levels of privacy management that a family member practiced (Child et al., 2012). Self-centric users set up privacy rules in ways that relied more on their own perspectives and often neglected to consider expectations from others in their online community. By contrast, utilitarian social media users worried more about consequences that might result from their online disclosures to others. Family members who connected more with the utilitarian disclosure profile also engaged in more privacy management online. Planners tended to have rational purposes for, and engage in clear and thought out, social media disclosures. Family members who more strongly identified with this disclosure orientation engaged in less privacy management online, perhaps because messages they shared were all vetted and intentional. Finally, the sharer disclosure profile reflected the type of person who discloses information in order to make a connection with people. Unsurprisingly, family members who were stronger in this disclosure orientation were also more likely to freely share private information with others through social media. These findings demonstrate that certain goals are important to different family members and that these goals can drive the types of privacy rules used to enact privacy management behaviors with diverse social media audiences (Child et al., 2012).

From this body of research, an initial set of conditions emerge to advance our understanding of how family members might be motivated to utilize privacy rules for sharing or protecting private information when interacting with others through social media. Thus, family members' decisions about privacy rules are predicated on the degree to which people are private or public in their orientation to self-consciousness, whether they engage in high or low self-monitoring, and which disclosure orientation profiles they may endorse.

Understanding Privacy Breakdowns and Repair Work on Social Media

An area of growing importance is the increasing incidence of breakdowns in privacy management in social media environments. Of critical concern is how family members might navigate privacy repair strategies to adopt more functional privacy rules in their online interaction after a breakdown occurs. Some family members do not give much thought to the privacy rules they use, assuming their rules are acceptable without considering how their choices could create problems for other members (Child et al., 2012). However, other family members might actively think about the degree to which their privacy is being protected on social media sites and what they can do to prevent breakdowns from occurring (Child et al., 2012; Livingstone, 2008; Young & Quan-Haase, 2013). Although we talked about the function of family privacy orientations earlier, it should be noted here that not only are some families more opened or closed, they also vary in the degree to which each member complied with the basic orientation. As a consequence, family members being more or less concerned about which privacy rules are used and when can result in privacy breakdowns. Likewise, because privacy regulation behaviors in certain families can sometimes be taken for granted, especially among those who articulate expectations poorly, the functionality of some privacy rules may be unclear and thus more easily violated (Petronio, 2002; Petronio, Jones, & Morr, 2003). However, once a violation occurs, though often problematic, the members have a more clear sense of what they and others expect (Petronio, 2010).

Examining the effectiveness of family members' current privacy management rules for social media is critical in preventing embarrassment, loss of employment, or other negative outcomes resulting from ineffective disclosure and privacy management practices that can occur in an era of increased organizational surveillance (Acquisti & Gross, 2006; Athavaley, 2007; Berkshire, 2005; Child et al., 2011; Jamieson, 2011; Needleman, 2010; Smith & Kidder, 2010). A primary way that family members prevent negative fallout from their social media disclosure is by reviewing their posts and deleting content that either creates or has the potential to end in turbulence (Child et al., 2011, 2012).

Common deletions that family members make in readjusting their social media privacy include: information that stirs up conflict, details that make someone's identity too transparent to unwanted others, information that puts personal safety in jeopardy (such as when stalking occurs), information that could lead to retribution (such as a child getting grounded), information that could cause the loss of a job if dispersed too widely, information that might leave others with a negative impression if gleaned only from the limited information available on social media, disclosures that were more emotionally motivated than rationally thought out, and expressions of anger or other negative emotions from going through a break up or even any online evidence of the relationship (Child et al., 2012).

Considering gender differences in using deletion practices, research finds that women are more likely than men to delete social media content in order to remove evidence of a past relationship. Also interesting: When family members initially engaged in less overall protection of privacy on their social media sites, they were more likely to use one or more deletion strategies to recalibrate effective privacy management. Such results demonstrate that family members are likely to vigilantly monitor their social media posts and respond to evolving privacy concerns in the hope that minor breakdowns in privacy regulation do not become major incidents (Child et al., 2012).

Research about privacy breakdowns among adolescents demonstrates that people who have not yet had negative experiences with the privacy rules used on social media tend to disclose more, with an increased potential for privacy problems in the future (Christofides, Muise, & Desmarais, 2012b). Adolescents and young teenagers are also not as concerned as older audiences about using privacy settings to prevent third parties from accessing their private information (Madden et al., 2013). These results suggest that having a parent instruct younger children and monitor their social media interaction could help prevent unnecessary breakdowns (Madden et al., 2012). The most common online causes of turbulence for adolescents include: being the victim of online bullying, encountering unwanted messages by unknown people on their social media sites, and having a peer or family member post information than the adolescent preferred not to have shared with their social media network (Christofides et al., 2012b). Other evidence suggests that when a family member experiences an actual privacy breakdown on social media, they tend to be more cautious and mindful of the vulnerabilities stemming from their current privacy rules (Child et al., 2012).

We must further examine privacy breakdowns and turbulence (Petronio, 2013). Less evidence exists about the factors that cause people to dramatically change the trajectory of an online relationship with someone, such as a family member privy to social media disclosures who then ends up getting unfriended (Bevan, Ang, & Fearns, 2014). Preliminary research demonstrates that being unfriended through social media carries both emotional and cognitive consequences. People experience hurt feelings and become more contemplative in reconstructing what might have gone wrong in the social media relationship (Bevan, Pfyl, & Barclay, 2012). Some social media users who have been unfriended might rationalize that being unfriended was a glitch in the technology and not a message about relationship status with that person (Bevan et al., 2012). This emerging body of research demonstrates that family members invest deeply in the decisions made by others about the ability to interact, socialize, and share private information through social media as a type of relational status symbol.

CPM Theory, Social Media, Family Communication, and Future Research

The study of family communication, social media, and privacy is still in its infancy. Communication Privacy Management theory (Petronio, 2002) provides a rich theoretical base for grounding significant future research about the many social media platforms and interactive communication technologies and applications, especially those that both shape and help us understand family communication. For example, the relatively new smartphone application Snapchat is growing in use among the younger generation, yet there is little research about how parents and children consider privacy issues when making decisions about whether to use the application (see the Fletcher & Blair chapter in this volume).

Snapchat allows a user to take a picture or video, or create a text message, and send it to another user under the premise that the message will self-destruct in a matter of seconds and will not be stored on the company's servers after a short interval established by the original owner (from 1 to 10 seconds) after the viewer opens it (Gillette, 2013). Individual users nevertheless can make a digital copy of Snapchat messages by taking a screen capture. When this occurs, the original owner is notified about the screen capture (Fogel, 2014).

The application has been popular among teenagers and young adults, and is growing in popularity among adults and parents as well. The company notes that more than 50 million Snapchat messages are sent each day and that it is one of the most downloaded new applications (Gillette, 2013). The appeal of the app is in providing a user a way to shoot a quick video or snap a picture without the user having to worry about its permanency. Because messages still can be captured and made permanent, users might be functioning under different privacy expectations. Research should explore how often users respond when someone screen captures a Snapchat message not intended to be preserved. When does such an event result in severing use of the application with someone because of privacy expectation violations?

Since the application allows young adults to send messages to others that their parents might not approve of, without any trace of the message it is sent, it is virtually impossible for a parent to monitor use of the application, unless that parent is receiving the Snapchats sent by the child. As such, research might also examine how parents develop and reinforce expected privacy norms for these types of applications. What discussions, if any, do parents have with their children about online privacy? (For some early research, see the Fletcher & Blair chapter in this volume.) How do individuals respond when they receive Snapchat messages they do not wish to co-own, such as sext-messages? More research is needed on evolving communication technologies to show how families can or do influence privacy protection and access behaviors employed by their members. This work could further develop the family privacy orientations related to additional types of social media (Child & Westermann, 2013; Morr Serewicz & Canary, 2008; Petronio, 2002).

In addition to the difficultly of keeping pace with new communication technologies, future research might also more fully examine the unique experiences of family members across multiple generations simultaneously using social media. Research should examine a range of privacy concerns from a family communication perspective. For example, the generation that grew up with Facebook as a college-only application has been using this social media platform for a much longer time than members of other generations in the same family (Child & Petronio, 2011). Therefore, they may have more expertise about how to use social media and protect information effectively. Future research might examine the privacy-rule socialization processes that occur with multiple generations of the same family using social media to achieve similar or different goals.

Another question worthy of exploration concerns parental and family member decisions regarding what to share about their infant or young children with their own online community. What are generally agreed-upon rules for couples about what is appropriate to share within a social media collective privacy boundary? What might other general social media users identify as too much information? Some parents now provide a chronology of their children's lives in video, text, and picture—all linked to their own social media sites; how, when they become young adults, do these children navigate conversations with parents about hiding these virtual baby books when they desire more independence from inclusive privacy boundaries created by their parents' disclosure practices? The comfort with which individuals today use social media to interact with friends and family begs for more scientific research about these types of potential privacy breakdowns and sharing practices that occur through social media.

One final area of future research we wish to highlight is how persons may respond to privacy turbulence among family members in the forms of unfriending, untagging content, and interacting differently with family members because they are a part of that person's own social media privacy boundary. Research has identified how being unfriended can be hard for someone to process and accept (Bevan et al., 2012). Being unfriended removes someone from access to another person's digital online community. Other less final forms of turbulence might include disassociating tagged information from a family member's own social media page. When do family members use these ways of responding to social media turbulence for content posted by other family members? Information is also needed to better understand what happens when one family member divorces or otherwise breaks up with a partner and yet has other family members who are still friends through social media with the divorced partner. When would such family members prefer to erect a thicker collective family privacy boundary and ask others in the family to unfriend the individual? Would the person maintain such social media ties and privacy boundaries in different ways going forward and how?

An additional way to adapt to a diverse social media network is to adopt greater use of what has been deemed "vague-booking" or using coded language to disclose private information online. Using unclear, nonspecific, and veiled language on a social media site that only certain audiences might understand, allows communication to occur to the intended parties while excluding all others. Such practices raise many questions: In what situations do family members prefer to use these privacy protection practices rather than limiting the audience who can view the message? Or, when do family members prefer to send a message through an alternative channel, such as face-to-face interactions, rather than through a social media channel?

Application

Research about social media, family communication, and privacy management practices can guide parents, children, and family educators in considering a range of applications, each grounded in scholarly evidence. Doing so means that developing training sessions, teaching parents and children about social media use, and creating resources to help families make the difficult but necessary decisions about social media can be translated into meaningful practice. There is also greater likelihood the suggestions will be effective because they have been scientifically tested. The bulk of this chapter frames the research according to Communication Privacy Management (CPM) theory (Petronio, 2002, 2010, 2013). CPM theory is inherently an evidence- and practice-based theory (Petronio, 2002). As such, the theoretical framework allows consideration of many applications related to social media, disclosure, and privacy management practices.

Parents can consider the information found in this chapter as a guide for how they might interact with their children about and through social media channels.

For example, while there has been much discussion about whether privacy is "dead," the research in this chapter shows that, whether we are talking about face-to-face interactions or considering social media–based interactions, people of all ages rely on the same privacy management practices. Privacy remains important to people and is evident in how and why they make choices about what they allow others to know through social media. Coordinating social media privacy management is a challenge for families. We provide some clues about what to consider when deciding how to achieve the best outcomes for yourself and your family members.

Parents can take comfort knowing that their children engage in a range of privacy management behaviors with family members and others in their online networks (Child et al., 2011, 2012). Young adults regulate what they say through social media based on how appropriate it is to share information to those allowed to read and co-own the disclosed content (Child & Petronio, 2011; Child et al., 2009, 2011, 2012). Understanding the criteria that young adults use to regulate their social media privacy boundary can help parents better judge when to raise privacy issues or question their children about what they may think is acceptable to share online. More discussion about appropriateness on social media can help younger family members with less social media experience, and the same is true for parents, grandparents, and other family members (Madden et al., 2012, 2013). When family members have less social media experience, more discussion about online privacy norms and acceptable disclosure practices can help prevent privacy breakdowns. Engaging in more collective decision making about effective online privacy management with less knowledgeable family members (as a way to increase familiarity and competence with social media interactions) can also create a stronger sense of trust between family members and strengthen relational bonds.

The literature also suggests that family members may interact face to face and through social media in ways that are congruent with own their general personality dispositions (Child & Agyeman-Budu, 2010; Child et al., 2009). In their daily routine, children who are less likely to attend to who their audience is and what their audience might be thinking, or to how diverse people might react to and interpret messages, are likely to embody these same communication dispositions when interacting through social media (Child & Agyeman-Budu, 2010; Child et al., 2009). Depending on children's age and level of cognitive development, they are more or less able to anticipate consequences and recognize how differently their messages might be interpreted online. Keeping those variables in mind, parents can then help kids consider their choices and their potential consequences by together discussing reasons for online disclosures that children have made.

Parents should keep in mind that the way they reinforce privacy values within the home and interact with their children can create a comfort level for children to figure out effective ways to interact on social media (Child & Westerman, 2013; Morr Serewicz et al., 2007). Parents who share more with their children and have more openness between family members in general will also feel more secure with, willing to engage in, and interactive on social media with other family members. Thus, one way a parent might increase family involvement through social media (if it is a desired goal) is to work more generally on the family privacy culture through sharing more, asking more questions, and being more open within the family unit, if doing so is not a normative family disclosure and privacy management practice. Further, multiple studies suggest young adult children are comfortable interacting with family through social media (Ball et al., 2013; Child & Westermann, 2013; Kanter, 2012). As such, parents should not feel nervous extending social media friend requests to their children out of concern that such actions might be interpreted as an invasion of privacy.

Family educators and researchers can apply the current scholarship on digital age privacy management to their work in several ways. In social media and family communication it is important to recognize that family members experience diverse motivations for disclosure and privacy management practices (Child et al., 2011; 2012; Petronio, 2002). While one family member might set up privacy rules to encourage and enable deeper sharing through social media, another might be more concerned with making sure his or her own individual perspectives and opinions are heard by others. Privacy motivations change from time to time and are also related to how people make decisions about reclaiming individual privacy through deleting content (Child et al., 2001; 2012; Petronio, 2002). Studying social media, privacy management, and family communication requires more attention to what motivations are relevant to individuals as they express identity through social media and protect privacy online with diverse audiences.

Final Thoughts

Social media has changed how families interact. Communication Privacy Management theory provides family communication scholars the apparatus for exploring some of the complex questions about the role of family communication in helping members consider privacy issues in the overall use of social media (Petronio, 2002, 2010, 2013). We have just scratched the surface of how social media interaction impacts expectations and norms for the sharing of private information among family members (Child et al., 2012). This chapter offers a functional beacon to begin the process of understanding how privacy management functions in social media within family communicative systems. Exploring privacy regulation at the intersection of family and media use pushes many of the assumptions we have made theoretically. The yield of understanding is very promising, yet challenges basic hypotheses and beliefs about how family members communicate with each other.

References

Acquisti, A., & Gross, R. (2006). Imagined communities: Awareness, information sharing, and privacy on Facebook. *Lecture Notes in Computer Science, 4258,* 36–58. doi: 10.1007/11957454_3

Athavaley, A. (2007, June 20). A job interview you don't have to show up for. Retrieved from http://online.wsj.com/public/article_print/SB118229876637841321.html

Ball, H., Wazner, M. B., & Servoss, T. J. (2013). Parent–child communication on Facebook: Family communication patterns and young adults' decisions to "friend" parents. *Communication Quarterly, 61,* 615–629. doi: 10.1080/01463373.2013.822406

Bateman, P. J., Pike, J. C., & Butler, B. S. (2011). To disclose or not: Publicness in social networking sites. *Information Technology & People, 24,* 78–100.

Bello, R. (2005). Situational formality, personality, and avoidance–avoidance conflict as causes of interpersonal equivocation. *Southern Communication Journal, 70,* 285–300.

Berkshire, J. C. (2005, April 1). 'Social network' recruiting. *HR Magazine.* Retrieved from http://www.shrm.org/Publications/hrmagazine/EditorialContent/Pages/0405berkshire.aspx

Bevan, J. L., Ang, P., & Fearns, J. B. (2014). Being unfriended on Facebook: An application of expectancy violation theory. *Computers in Human Behavior, 33,* 171–178. doi: 10.1016/j.chb.2014.01.029

Bevan, J. L., Pfyl, J., & Barclay, B. (2012). Negative emotional and cognitive responses to being unfriended on Facebook: An exploratory study. *Computers in Human Behavior, 28,* 1458–1464.

Bobkowski, P. S., & Pearce, L. D. (2011). Baring their souls in online profiles or not? Religious self-disclosure in social media. *Journal for the Scientific Study of Religion, 50,* 744–762. doi: 10.1111/j.1468–5906.2011.01597.x

Buss, A. H. (1980). *Self-consciousness and social anxiety.* San Francisco: Freeman.

Child, J. T. (2007). *The development and test of a measure of young adult blogging behaviors, communication, and privacy management.* Unpublished doctoral dissertation, North Dakota State University.

Child, J. T., & Agyeman-Budu, E. (2010). Blogging privacy rule development: The impact of self-monitoring skills, concern for appropriateness, and blogging frequency. *Computers in Human Behavior, 26,* 957–963. doi: 10.1016/j.chb.2010.02.009

Child, J. T., Haridakis, P. M., & Petronio, S. (2012). Blogging privacy rule orientations, privacy management, and content deletion practices: The variability of online privacy management activity at different stages of social media use. *Computers in Human Behavior, 28,* 1859–1872. doi: 10.1016/j.chb.2012.05.004

Child, J. T., Pearson, J. C., & Petronio, S. (2009). Blogging, communication, and privacy management: Development of the blogging privacy management measure. *Journal of the American Society for Information Science and Technology, 60,* 2079–2094. doi: 10.1002/asi.21122

Child, J. T., & Petronio, S. (2011). Unpacking the paradoxes of privacy in CMC relationships: The challenges of blogging and relational communication on the Internet. In K. B. Wright & L. M. Webb (Eds.), *Computer-mediated communication in personal relationships* (pp. 21–40). New York: Peter Lang.

Child, J. T., Petronio, S., Agyeman-Budu, E. A., & Westermann, D. A. (2011). Blog scrubbing: Exploring triggers that change privacy rules. *Computers in Human Behavior, 27*, 2017–2027. doi: 10.1016/j.chb.2011.05.009.

Child, J. T., & Westermann, D. A. (2013). Let's be Facebook friends: Exploring parental Facebook friend requests from a communication privacy management (CPM) perspective. *Journal of Family Communication, 13,* 46–59.

Christofides, E., Muise, A., & Desmarais, S. (2012a). Hey mom, what's on your Facebook? Comparing Facebook disclosure and privacy in adolescents and adults. *Social Psychological and Personality Science, 3,* 48–54.

Christofides, E., Muise, A., & Desmarais, S. (2012b). Risky disclosures on Facebook: The effect of having a bad experience on online behavior. *Journal of Adolescent Research, 27,* 714–731. doi:10.1177/0743558411432635

Durham, W. T. (2008). The rules-based process of revealing/concealing the family planning decisions of voluntarily child-free couples: A communication privacy management perspective. *Communication Studies, 59,* 132–147.

Edison Research. (2012, June). *The social habit.* Retrieved from http://socialhabit.com/research/

Facebook (2014). Press room. Palo Alto, CA: Facebook. Retrieved from http://www.facebook.com/press/info.php?statistics

Fenigstein, A., Scheier, M. F., & Buss, A. H. (1975). Public and private self-consciousness: Assessment and theory. *Journal of Consulting and Clinical Psychology, 43,* 522–527.

Fife, E. M., LaCava, L., & Nelson, C. L. (2013). Family communication, privacy, and Facebook. *The Journal of Social Media in Society, 2,* 107–125.

Flynn, F. J., Reagans, R. E., Amanatullah, E. T., & Ames, D. R. (2006). Helping one's way to the top: Self-monitors achieve status by helping others and knowing who helps whom. *Journal of Personality and Social Psychology, 91,* 1123–1137.

Fogel, K. (2014, January 29). Privacy apps like Snapchat make a promise they can't keep. *Slate.* Retrieved from http://www.slate.com

Gambino, L. (2013, March 1). 'Digital assets' of deceased often out of families' reach. *Akron Beacon Journal,* p. A2.

Gillette, F. (2013, February 13). Snapchat and the erasable future of social media. *Business Week.* Retrieved from http://www.businessweek.com

Greene, K., Derlega, V. J., Yep, G. A., & Petronio, S. (2003). *Privacy and disclosure of HIV in interpersonal relationships: A sourcebook for researchers and practitioners.* Mahwah, NJ: Erlbaum.

Guadagno, R. E., Okdie, B. M., & Eno, C. A. (2008). Who blogs? Personality predictors of blogging. *Computers in Human Behavior, 24,* 1993–2004.

Hampton, K. N., Goulet, L. S., Marlow, C., & Rainie, L. (2012). Why most Facebook users get more than they give. *Pew Internet & American Life Project.* Retrieved from http://www.pewinternet.org/Reports/2012/Facebook-users.aspx

Hampton, K. N., Goulet, L. S., Rainie, L., & Purcell, K. (2011). Social networking sites and our lives. *Pew Internet & American Life Project.* Retrieved from http://www.pewinternet.org/Reports/2011/Technology-and-social-networks.aspx

Harwood, J. (2000). Communication media use in the grandparent–grandchild relationship. *Journal of Communication, 50,* 56–78. doi: 10.1111/j.1460–2466.2000.tb02863.x

Hawk, S. T., Keijsers, L., Hale, W. W., & Meeus, W. (2009). Mind your own business! Longitudinal relations between perceived privacy invasion and adolescent–parent conflict. *Journal of Family Psychology, 23,* 511–520. doi: 10.1037/a0015426

Hone-McMahan, K. (2013, March 17). Tracking kids' activity on Facebook is fair game. *Akron Beacon Journal,* pp. E1, E6.

Italie, L. (2013, January 1). Mother goes viral with smartphone code. *Akron Beacon Journal,* p. A1.

Jamieson, D. (2011, August 9). Facebook firings: Employers need to mind labor law, report finds. *Huffington Post.* Retrieved from http://www.huffingtonpost.com/2011/08/09/facebook-firings-labor-law_n_922389.html

Kanter, M., Afifi, T., & Robbins, S. (2012). The impact of parents "friending" their young adult child on Facebook on perceptions of parental privacy invasions and parent–child relationship quality. *Journal of Communication, 62,* 900–917. doi: 10.1111/j.1460–2466.2012.01669.x

Ledbetter, A. M., Heiss, S., Sinbal, K., Lev, E., Battle-Fisher, M., & Shubert, N. (2010). Parental invasive and children's defensive behaviors at home and away at college: Mediated communication and privacy boundary management. *Communication Studies, 61,* 184–204. doi: 10.1080/10510971003603960

Lenhart, A. (2009). Adults and social network websites. *Pew Internet & American Life Project.* Retrieved from http://www.pewinternet.org/Reports/2009/Adults-and-Social-Network-Websites.aspx

Livingstone, S. (2008). Taking risky opportunities in youthful content creation: Teenagers' use of social networking sites for intimacy, privacy, and self-expression. *New Media & Society, 10,* 393–411. doi: 10.1177/1461444808089415

Madden, M., Cortesi, S., Gasser, U., Lenhart, A., & Duggan, M. (2012). Parents, teens, and online privacy. *Pew Internet & American Life Project.* Retrieved from http://www.pewinternet.org

Madden, M., Lenhart, A., Cortesi, S., Gasser, U., Duggan, M., Smith, A., & … Beaton, M. (2013). Teens, social media, and privacy. *Pew Internet & American Life Project.* Retrieved from http://www.pewinternet.org

McCullagh, K. (2008). Blogging: Self-presentation and privacy. *Information & Communication Technology Law, 17,* 3–23.

Metzger, M. J. (2007). Communication privacy management in electronic commerce. *Journal of Computer-Mediated Communication, 12,* 335–361.

Miura, A., & Yamashita, K. (2007). Psychological and social influences on blog writing: An online survey of blog authors in Japan. *Journal of Computer-Mediated Communication, 12,* 1452–1471.

Morr, M. C. (2002). *Private disclosure in a family membership transition: In-laws' disclosures to newlyweds.* Unpublished doctoral dissertation, Arizona State University.

Morr Serewicz, M. C., & Canary, D. J. (2008). Assessments of disclosure from the in-laws: Links among disclosure topics, family privacy orientations, and relational quality. *Journal of Social and Personal Relationships, 25,* 333–357.

Morr Serewicz, M. C., Dickson, F. C., Morrison, J. H., & Poole, L. L. (2007). Family privacy orientation, relational maintenance, and family satisfaction in young adults' family relationships. *Journal of Family Communication, 7,* 123–142.

Needleman, S. E. (2010, March 10). Facebook, Twitter updates spell trouble in small workplace. *The Wall Street Journal.* Retrieved from http://online.wsj.com/article/SB10001424052748703701004575113792648753382.html

Nielsen. (2011). *State of the media: Social media report q3.* New York: Nielsen.

Padilla-Walker, L. M., Coyne, S. M., & Fraser, A. M. (2012). Getting a high-speed family connection: Associations between family media use and family connection. *Family Relations, 61,* 426–440. doi: 10.1111/j.1741–3729.2012.00710.x

Pempek, T. A., Yermolayeva, Y. A., & Calvert, S. L. (2009). College students' social networking experiences on Facebook. *Journal of Applied Developmental Psychology, 30,* 227–238. doi: 10.1016/j.appdev.2008.12.010

Petronio, S. (1991). Communication boundary management: A theoretical model of managing disclosure of private information between marital couples. *Communication Theory, 1,* 311–335. doi: 10.1111/j.1468–2885.1991.tb00023.x

Petronio, S. (1994). Privacy binds in family interactions: The case of parental privacy invasion. In W. R. Cupach & B. H. Spitzberg (Eds.), *The dark side of interpersonal communication* (pp. 241–257). Hillsdale, NJ: Erlbaum.

Petronio, S. (2002). *Boundaries of privacy: Dialectics of disclosure.* Albany: State University of New York Press.

Petronio, S. (2010). Communication privacy management theory: What do we know about family privacy regulation? *Journal of Family Theory and Review, 2,* 175–196.

Petronio, S. (2013). Brief status report on communication privacy management theory. *Journal of Family Communication, 13,* 6–14. doi: 10.1080/15267431.2013.743426

Petronio, S., & Caughlin, J. P. (2006). Communication privacy management theory: Understanding families. In D. O. Braithwaite & L. A. Baxter (Eds.), *Engaging theories in family communication* (pp. 35–49). Thousand Oaks, CA: Sage.

Petronio, S., & Gaff, C. (2010). Managing privacy ownership and disclosure. In C. Gaff & C. Bylund (Eds.). *Family communication about genetics: Theory and practices.* London: Oxford Press.

Petronio, S., Jones, S., & Morr, M. C. (2003). Family privacy dilemmas: Managing communication boundaries within family groups. In L. R. Frey (Ed.), *Group communication in context: Studies of bona fide groups* (pp. 23–55). Mahwah, NJ: Erlbaum.

Petronio, S., & Kovach, S. (1997). Managing privacy boundaries: Health providers' perceptions of resident care in Scottish nursing homes. *Journal of Applied Communication Research, 25,* 115–131.

Petronio, S., & Reierson, J. (2009). Regulating the privacy of confidentiality: Grasping the complexities through communication privacy management theory. In T. D. Afifi & W. A. Afifi (Eds.), *Uncertainty, information management, and disclosure decisions: Theories and applications* (pp. 365–383). New York: Routledge.

Qualman, E. (2009, August 11). Statistics show social media is bigger than you think. Retrieved from http://socialnomics.net/2009/08/11/statistics-show-social-media-is-bigger-than-you-think/

Shaffer, D. R., & Pegalis, L. J. (1998). Gender and situational context moderate the relationship between self-monitoring and induction of self-disclosure. *Journal of Personality, 66,* 215–234.

Shapiro, L. A., & Margolin, G. (2014). Growing up wired: Social networking sites and adolescent psychosocial development. *Clinical Child Family Psychological Review, 17,* 1–18. doi: 10.1007/s10567–013–0135–1

Siibak, A., & Tamme, V. (2013). "Who introduced granny to Facebook?" An exploration of everyday family interactions in Web-based communication environments. *Northern Lights, 11,* 71–89. doi: 10.1086/nl.11.71_1

Smith, W. P., & Kidder, D. L. (2010). You've been tagged (Then again, maybe not): Employers and Facebook. *Journal of Applied Developmental Psychology, 30*(3), 227–238. doi: 10.1016/j.bushor.2010.04.004

Tardy, C. H., & Hosman, L. A. (1982). Self-monitoring and self-disclosure flexibility: A research note. *Western Journal of Speech Communication, 46,* 92–97.

Weeden, S., Cooke, B., & McVey, M. (2013). Underage children and social networking. *Journal of Research on Technology in Education, 45,* 249–262.

Young, A. L., & Quan-Haase, A. (2013). Privacy projection strategies on Facebook: The Internet privacy paradox revisited. *Information Communication & Society, 16,* 479–500.

3

Global Families in a Digital Age

MEG WILKES KARRAKER
University of St. Thomas, Minnesota

AUTHOR NOTE: I thank Changhyuk Byun, Morten Ender, Lea Hagoel, Brandon Haugrud, Michael Murphy, Shady Shalik, and Alexander Tsadwa for sharing their personal experiences and professional insights on digital connections with their own global families. Thanks also to Mark Karraker, P. E., who researched the data from the United Nations International Telecommunications Union. Correspondence concerning this chapter should be addressed to Meg Wilkes Karraker, University of St. Thomas, 2115 Summit Avenue, Mail #4048, St. Paul, MN 55105–1095, U.S.A. Contact: mwkarraker@stthomas.edu

Introduction

If the global mass media are "a driving force behind transnational life plans" (Beck-Gernsheim, 2001, p. 62), then information communication technology (ICT) is a driving force on steroids! As editor Carol Bruess stated in her call for the chapters in this volume, mobile cellular telephones, Facebook and its spinoffs, the Internet, online chat rooms, text messaging, and other ICTs are increasingly "affecting family systems and interactions over the life span." Families increasingly use ICTs to negotiate the full range of family functions across life cycle stages and subsystems, while extending in revolutionary ways the very ecology of their families.

This chapter examines the ways transnational families use information communication technologies to communicate, thereby accomplishing family functions and stretching family subsystems across national borders. Throughout this chapter, members of transnational families offer their own accounts of how their families have moved beyond what today seems like painfully slow surface mail and prohibitively expensive transcontinental fixed-line telephone calls to organize family life across great—often transcontinental—divides in new, more efficient and often (but not always) more effective ways. Throughout this chapter I report the results of interviews (most conducted via email) with individuals who are themselves members of transnational families. Those individuals will be introduced throughout the chapter.

I begin with an important qualification. The newest technology does not render older technologies useless. Access to the newer, most effective, and most cost-efficient global communication systems are certainly shaped by technical development and household economics but also by personal preferences. In the case of migrant families, development, access, and preference issues play out in both the sending (home) and the receiving (host) countries, with the potential for disruption at any point in the interpersonal communication process. For example, a young man living in Minnesota reports that one of his aunts in Ethiopia has a Facebook™ profile and is "friends" with him, but the aunt rarely interacts with him via that medium. The man's mother, also living in Minnesota and with access to a broad range of ICTs, nevertheless buys phone cards to communicate with her sisters living in Ethiopia.

> [She] prefers phone cards because they are cheap, ranging from 2 to 5 dollars, depending on the number of minutes the card gives you, and there are no fees outside of the initial purchase of the card. Calls can be made through cellphone service providers but roaming charges vary and are generally high.

This chapter extends the conversation on family communication in a digital age to a more global milieu and does so by exploring answers to the following questions:

1. What is the current status of ICTs worldwide, and what is the frequency of their use based on global dispersion and user characteristics?
2. How do digital technologies shape the quantity and quality of global family communication, including among temporarily dispersed families, such as deployed military?
3. How are new communication technologies shaping caring capital, especially among migrant families and others living transnationally?
4. Along with the benefits, do ICTs create dysfunctions, including threats to families through the "commodification of intimacy"?

5. What practical applications does this chapter offer for those who serve global families, be they researchers, teachers, or students; for family life educators, therapists, or other family professionals; and for family members themselves?

The Growth of ICT Worldwide

The United Nations International Telecommunication Union (UNITU) collects data on not only the frequencies of fixed (landline) telephone subscriptions but also mobile-cellular telephone, active mobile-broadband, and fixed (wired) broadband subscriptions. From the same source, data exist on households with a computer, households with Internet access at home, and individuals using the Internet. These data confirm the dramatic acceleration of mobile, cellular telephone subscriptions, and Internet usage worldwide, notwithstanding the persistence of regional and demographic disparities. The UNITU (2013) estimates the number of fixed telephone subscriptions worldwide at 1.1 billion. However, at 6.8 billion, the number of mobile-cellular telephone subscriptions is already six times that number—and growing. At the same time, the number of active mobile-broadband subscriptions is more than 2 billion and the number of individuals using the Internet exceeds 2.7 billion.

Transnational communication systems, including ICTs, demand capital and capital-intensive infrastructures (e.g., electricity, communication towers, and telephone and Internet providers). While worldwide access is growing at breakneck speed, access to ICTs varies across regions of the globe, countries within the regions, and families and individuals within countries. For every type of ICT, the rates of access for developed countries are dramatically higher than the rates for developing countries. The number of households in the developed world with Internet access at home approaches three times the number of such households in the developing world; the developed world has both active mobile- and fixed-broadband subscriptions 3.8 and 4.5 times that in developing world (Sassen, 2000).

Likewise, ICT usage differs widely across continental regions. At 39.0, 28.4, and 25.7, respectively, Europe, the Americas (North, Central, and South), and the Commonwealth of Independent States (CIS, the loose, regional organization of states formed after the break-up of the Soviet Union) have the highest ICT usage rates per 100 inhabitants. For these three regions, the rate of mobile-cellular subscriptions is highest in the CIS, while fixed telephone and both types of broadband subscriptions are highest in Europe. Country estimates of the percentage of the population living in poverty are based on weighted, stratified samples, and definitions of poverty vary considerably, with rich nations applying more generous standards of poverty than poor nations (Central Intelligence Agency, 2014). Still, ICT usage varies considerably within continental regions, as between affluent nations in the Americas like the United States (where approximately 15 percent of the population lives in poverty) and Haiti, one of the poorest nations in the Americans and in the world (where approximately 80 percent of the population lives in poverty) (Central Intelligence Agency, 2014).

The UNITU estimates that one third of the world's seven billion inhabitants uses the Internet and that 45 percent of those users are under the age of 25 (UNITU, 2011). In developed countries 77 percent of those under age 25 are using the Internet, compared to 71 percent of those over age 25. In developing countries, 30 percent of those under 25 are using the Internet, compared to 23 percent of those over age 25. Such an age divide has implications across family relationships across the life cycle, such as transnational communication about pressing lifespan issues, including, for instance, adult children negotiating and managing the caregiving of aging parents.

Critically, access to ICTs is shaped by inequalities of social locations (and intersections among those inequalities) (Parreñas, 2008a, 2008b). As Parreñas reveals, "[t]echnology not only enforces inequalities between groups, it also exacerbates relations of economic inequality among nations" (Parreñas, 2010, p. 14). Digital divides exist between and within developed and developing regions, as well as across age, gender, and likely other social locations. Differential access to cost-effective technologies privileges some families and individuals and disadvantages others, essentially constructing some families and individuals as more effective in their transnational or global efforts to stay connected (Baldassar, Baldock, & Wilding, 2007).

Gender is among the most prominent of these digital divides. In November 2013 the Task Group on Gender (TGG) of the Partnership on Measuring ICT for Development (2013) met to address the need to improve the availability of sex-disaggregated data on ICT usage, especially in developing countries. Citing an "almost total absence of ICT statistics and indicators from international gender equality statistics and indicators," the TGG argues:

> Men and women the world over have different realities, roles, positions and constraints. Too often the situation of men is taken to be the norm for both men and women, ignoring the differences between them. The 2012 UNDP Gender Inequality Index2 shows that no country in the world has achieved gender equality. Most women tend to be poorer than men and in many countries they are less educated. The majority of the world's illiterates are women. Women in general tend to earn less, hold fewer positions of power and make fewer decisions in the family, in businesses and in political and public life. These inequalities

> impact women's ability to benefit equally from the opportunities offered by ICT and to contribute fully to shaping the developing global knowledge economy and society. (p. 5)

Consistent with United Nations Millennium Development Goals (MDGs) and the World Summit on the Information Society (WSIS), the TGG seeks "the achievement of a globally equitable information society" (p. 5). We can argue that reducing the digital divide will enhance the quality of life not only for women and girls but also for their families.

Global Communication in Wired (and Wireless) Families

Rapid advancements in technology are increasingly enabling families to maintain intimacy across broad spatial distances. *Family Communication in an Age of Digital and Social Media* moves us beyond considering the role of ICTs in the most obvious places—economics and employment—to include emerging adulthood, conjugal relations, parenting roles, and intergenerational communication in the family. As discussed in other chapters in this volume, ICTs and the values and norms in which they are contextualized can influence virtually every aspect of individual, family, and communal life, including maintaining the conjugal relationship, performing long-distance parenting, executing elder caregiving, and supporting other life cycle functions. We are also compelled to consider implications of ICTs on age and gender roles; childhood, youth, and adult socialization; sexualities and mate selection; and the role of ICTs in the very formation of family identity.

ICTs play a role in other types of family communication as well. In the aptly titled "Not the Romantic, All Happy, Coochy Coo Experience," Brady and Guerin (2010) found that online support groups may help fill the gap in decreasing face-to-face social networks in modern society. For example, their research indicates that parenting websites are seen as safe, supportive places "in which mothers could develop an enhanced frame of reference in which to better understand the role of parenting" (p. 14). This chapter focuses more on ICT usage within the global or transnational families, such as that described by Parreñas (2008a), a scholar who has studied migrants and globalization for almost 20 years. Regarding her own extended family, with members residing in the sending country of the Philippines and the receiving country of the United States, she writes:

> transnational communication usually occurred unidirectionally, from the United States to the Philippines. Aunt Letty called frequently to instruct my cousin Mimi, her designated head of household, on how to budget her remittances and how to accordingly allocate funds to each of her children.... In my household,

> transnational communication occurred in a variety of ways, including via telephone calls, e-mails, SMS mobile phone messages, air-mailed letters, balikbayan* packages, and bank remittances. (p. 65)

An international student who studied for a semester at a university in the United States describes how he uses IMessage, Viber, and WhatsApp on his mobile telephone to keep in touch with family and friends in Africa and Europe. He says, "I know that my parents and friends always have their mobile phones with them." And, for only 10 dollars a month, he could access 3G Internet on his mobile phone and make free Internet phone calls. But he also liked to use Skype to keep in touch with his mother in France and his father in Egypt. He told me:

> We used to call and see [via Skype] each other once or twice a week. … It was possible to start a video conference with my mother to see how she actually was … [which is important] for someone who lives abroad and who started to miss his parents and friends. … These new technologies make the distance shorter than it seems to be.

Likewise, a high school student living in Minnesota uses Apple™ technology, including his iPod™, to connect with friends and family back home in Korea. His preferred medium is Kakao Talk, a worldwide messenger application well known to Koreans (but less known to U.S. Americans). Kakao Talk is not only free, but its Voice Talk option "is great" and has a high audio quality of phone call. But he reports that he has had some (but not insurmountable) difficulty connecting with relatives in Korea with whom he does not have compatible devices or applications. He says, "I switched to Skype because Skype is available on every device, but Facetime from Apple is only for Apple devices. My relatives didn't have Apple devices except for my aunt."

Although the focus above has been on relatively privileged youth and their families, some research has examined the place of ICTs in mediating culture for refugee youth. Wilding (2012) found that ICTs can provide "virtual interaction" so that such youth, living for example in Australia, have expanded opportunities for sources of individual identity and cultural renewal that can enable family, peer, and other networks to transcend spatial limitations. ICTs certainly enable youth and the families to maintain personal contacts with kith and kin. However, the greater benefit may be the venue ICTs provide for development of authentic personal identities that integrate rather than alienate youth from their indigenous cultures.

Digital communication has many upsides but also has limitations. Communication is not just sight and sound; intimate family communication engages all the senses. For instance, human touch is a powerful form of family communication, illustrated well in the comments offered to me by a woman who lives in Israel but who maintains close connections with her daughter, son-in-law, and grandchildren living in Japan:

> My little granddaughters love our "group hugs," which are impossible on Skype, so even when we met on Skype for hours, we would still feel the kissing and touching was missing, and remained what we would be looking for the next time we meet.

Touch is not the only sense deprived when ICTs are used for family communication across the miles. The same woman, writing of her Skype™ calls from Israel to her granddaughters, who have now moved from Japan to Israel, explained to me:

> I was cooking the other day and my granddaughter came downstairs following the smell. We reminded ourselves of the days we used Skype to meet and for me to show her my cooking, and then it occurred to me that it's not only touch that Skype cannot mediate—it's smells, too.

As Wilding (2006) found in her large comparative study of ICT usage among transnational families in Australia, Iran, Ireland, Italy, the Netherlands, New Zealand, and Singapore, the decisions individuals and families make about the use of ICTs are grounded in "the social and cultural contexts of family life, which render some ICTs more desirable than others at specific points in time" (p. 125). In contrast to the perception of cyberculture—what some consider utopian but others consider a dystopian "Cyberia" (Escobar, 1994)—as a radical means for conducting the human endeavor, global families make decisions daily about how to incorporate various ICTs into everyday family life. The time required to facilitate an exchange, as well as the technology's reliability and its material cost, certainly affect such choices, but so do the objectives of the communication.

As a parent, when I want to determine something routine like our daughter's flight schedule, email will do and might even be preferred, for the reliability and relative permanence of a forwarded message from the airline. However, if I am interested in knowing how she is taking the news of a relationship ending, I would rather see her facial expressions and other nonverbal cues as we Skype via our webcams. Obscurement is still possible but perhaps less likely, especially if the digital communication occurs via visual technology. This leads some scholars to refer to Skype™ as the "quintessential social glue for virtual connectedness" (Pearce, Slaker, & Ahmad, 2013, p. 2147).

Families seem to favor the addition of visual cues in video-mediated communication over other ICTs (Furukawa & Driessnak, 2013; Madianou, 2012). This is not surprising, given that the majority of meaning is derived from facial expression and other nonverbal cues. In fact, the smallest portion (perhaps only 7 percent) of most interpersonal communication is verbal (Mehrabian, 2007). This may not be true in every case. Madianou (2012) found that Filipina mothers living apart from their children seem to prefer mobile telephones not only for their mobility but for their synchronicity and spontaneity. As is true of most communication technologies, their use is not without risks, as described by the Israeli woman: "On email, if you don't double check the addressee or wait to "cool down" before [you hit] reply, that's when errors you're really sorry for, easily occur."

ICT usage might also have latent dysfunctions for family relationships. In particular, intergenerational conflicts seem to accompany family use of the Internet (Kiesler et al., 2000; Turow, 2001). While most parents view the Internet as a positive thing in their children's lives, conflicts arise over time displacement, when both quantity and quality of family time may be compromised by heavy Internet use. Lenhart, Lewis, and Raine's (2001) study for the Pew Research Center's *Internet Project* found that a majority (55 percent) of parents with online teens report that the Internet is "a good thing" for their teens but that almost two thirds (64 percent) of online teens themselves say that use of the Internet reduces young people's time spent with their families. Some research indicates that frequency and type of Internet use by adolescents is associated with perceptions of lower family cohesion (Mesch, 2006), although we must question the causal versus correlational nature of such a relationship.

Other factors shape the quality of digital communication for global families attempting what Wilding (2006, p. 134) calls "imagined proximity." Loss of hearing or sight, the ability to manipulate a keyboard or pad, or the decline of cognitive skills can make some forms of communication less meaningful to the receiver, the sender, or both, thus further compromising global families' ability to maintain a connected presence with long-distance elders or other family members. Baldassar, Baldock, and Wilding (2007) articulate a variety of global barriers to family communication in transnational caregiving. These include lack of access to specialized knowledge and equipment (e.g., a computer and the ability to use it), as well as physiological and cognitive skills (e.g., mental and physical dexterity) and the absence of debilitating impairment (e.g., arthritis or dementia) in those areas.

A large body of research, including other chapters in this volume (i.e., Bruess, Li, and Polingo on Facebook family rituals; Hertlein and Blumer on couple and family systems; Piercy, Riger, Voskanova, Chang, Haugen, and Sturdivant on couples; Sharabi, Roache, and Pusateri on parenting; and Smith on college transitions, among others) confirms that effective family communication promotes the well-being of families and their members. A comprehensive, interdisciplinary review of the conceptual and empirical literature finds that connectedness reduces the risk for psychological distress, health risks, and other individual, family, and social problems (Townsend & McWhirter, 2005). Families separated by geography need to find ways other than face-to-face communication to impart information, resolve conflict, and (of utmost importance) create and share meanings (Panagakos & Horst, 2006; Segrin & Flora, 2005; Wilding, 2006). For example, social support, especially spousal support, during deployment in the form of "delayed" modalities (e.g., letters, care packages, email) appears to buffer against posttraumatic stress disorder (PTSD), albeit only among married soldiers who evidenced high on marital satisfaction. However, "interactive" communication modalities (phone calls, instant messaging, instant messaging with video) buffered against PTSD, exclusive of interaction with marital satisfaction (Carter, Loew, Allen, Stanley, Rhodes, & Markmanet, 2011).

Virtual copresence, communication facilitated by ICT, enhances family connectedness and family cohesiveness. For example, while 90 percent of fathers in the United States are present at the births of their children, such is not the case for fathers deployed in the military. In the case of combat-deployed new fathers, frequent communication via email, instant messaging, Facebook™, blogs, chatrooms, and other ICTs enables those men to maintain greater connectedness to their wives and infants (Schachman, 2010).

The various branches of the United States military have long recognized the value of ensuring effective family communications for their members. For example, combat troops receive gratis postage from their points of deployment back to their families in the United States. I remember my mother returning from our mailbox in Florence, South Carolina, with letters from her husband then serving in Vietnam, not even waiting to enter the house before she opened the envelopes. Several years ago, I came across a few of those letters and was touched by the deep expressions of love my parents (neither of whom was normally given to great displays of emotion) expressed for one another in writing. Likewise, I remember the letters my father wrote to me during that year, letters which were full of love and always a little silly humor, as well as expressions of pride and advice from a father to his daughter.

How far we have come! In a recent email, Morten Ender, professor of sociology at the United States Military Academy and a military sociologist specializing in families of troops in Iraq, recounted to me:

> Personal communication media is ubiquitous in the war zone. Cell phones, satellite radio, email, Skype, CNN, … are all available. … Indeed, a soldier in his 12 by 12 trailer room in Iraq probably had better comms [communication technologies] in Baghdad in 2008 than he had in his barracks back at Fort Hood,

> Texas, or Fort Carson, Colorado. However, commanders … could shut down power sources for personal communications such as phones and email in the event of a casualty and the need to notify next-of-kin. … Of course, a communications blackout sent families into a tizzy, as it became an indicator that something with their loved one's unit had occurred.

However, the availability of technology has not always been entirely universal. A former Marine told me that, in his experience while deployed in Iraq in 2006–2008 and in Afghanistan in 2008, the cost of bandwidth limited the availability of certain ICTs.

> Troops stationed in a headquarters element behind the wall of a secured base have limited access to Non-classified Internet Protocol Router Network (NIPRNet for short), which is a military Internet service [that service people] securely log in to to check email, Facebook, Amazon, etc. The service is so slow, however, and computers so limited, that most troops instead opt to visit the Morale, Welfare, and Recreation Center on base (MWR for short), which operates as a USO-type facility. There are also phone centers that contractors like Halliburton provide (for a price) that troops with an international phone card will use to call family.

He added that, because he was stationed with an intelligence-collection team, he and his fellow marines had access to a satellite phone, which enabled them to call family regularly.

In this digital age, we are beginning to see some research on the power of ICT usage on the well-being of military members separated from their families. Family APGAR is a Likert-type scale that measures individual satisfaction with five family functions: adaptation, partnership, growth, affection, and resolve (Smilkstein, 1978). In an exploratory study conducted online using 341 participants aged 18 to over 70, Furukawa and Driessnack (2013) found higher Family APGAR scores associated with more positive comments about the use of video-mediated ICT. At the same time, some participants in the study voiced negative experiences associated with video-mediated ICT, citing specifically the changes of the need to schedule communication sessions (68 percent) and technical difficulties (49 percent), including poor video images (27 percent).

Family Care in Global Families

Global parents (and grandparents) are using ICTs to keep in touch with often far-flung adult children and grandchildren and with their own parents, siblings, and spouses. In an age when children increasingly move away from the family of origin for education, employment, or to establish families of their own, Skype™

enables grandchildren to know their grandparents and their grandparents' world. For example, the grandmother living in Israel while her grandchildren were living in Japan shared:

> I was used to inviting them [my two grandchildren] to my kitchen when we met on Skype™.... I would show them what I was cooking, and they would ask, "Grandma, show us what's in your refrigerator today!" So I would open the door and slowly pass the laptop in front of the shelves.

In global families, grandparents may even "babysit" their grandchildren across continents.

> A few months ago I babysat from Haifa my two little (ages five and two-plus) granddaughters in Tokyo, while their mother was on an errand and their father had to go out for a short while. I was reading a Dr. Seuss story to them, showing them the drawings on each page. They accepted my presence from the other side of the globe as reassuring.

In some cases, families make use of cameras placed throughout the home or left engaged for long periods of time. In this way, distant parents can assist their children with homework and other tasks, while "generating a feeling of co-presence" (Madianou, 2012, p. 289).

Migrants, Gender, and Transnational Care

Immigration scholars in particular have taken the time to ask migrant workers, "how do you keep in touch with the family you left behind?" The increasing feminization of migration has led to a rise in transnational mothering (Hondagneu-Sotelo & Avila, 1997; Karraker, 2012; Parreñas, 2001), what Parreñas has termed "displaced mothering" or, more generally, "displaced caretaking" (Parreñas, 2000, p. 576). ICTs can have very positive effects on families, including providing parents, especially mothers who have migrated for employment, to have a more "empowered experience of distant mothering" (Madianou, 2012, p. 277) and "intensive mothering at a distance" (Madianou, 2012, p. 277), all in the interests of the expressive tasks of care on behalf of family members that Ducey (2010) refers to as "affective labor" (p. 18).

ICTs may also reduce inequalities as a wider range of kin can be encouraged to become involved in care for family members. While letter writing and telephone calling appear to remain in woman's domain, email (perhaps because of its more technological base) has at least the potential to introduce not only broader engagement in such family matters as caring for elders but also to a breakdown of traditional gender barriers to the involvement of male members (Wilding, 2006).

In particular, research on Filipina mothers who have migrated for employment and who have left behind children in the Philippines indicates that ICT-mediated interaction can relieve some of the ambivalence those mothers experience (Madianou, 2012). The migration of fathers generally maintains traditional gendered divisions of household labor. As Parreñas (2005, 2008b) has discovered, intimacy presents more of a challenge for away-fathers, and men do not adjust their role performance to accommodate being away. In contrast to transnational mothers, transnational fathers tend not to communicate with their children, but, when they do, they engage in "distant disciplining" (Parreñas, 2008b, p. 1068). In a study of Ecuadorian male migrants to Europe and New York, Kyle (2000) found that transnational husbands are also more likely to restrict the information they share with their wives.

Parreñas (2005a), whose own family story of ICT-mediated communication was recounted earlier, demonstrates the extent to which transnational families, including those of migrant mothers, maintain traditional gender roles. These children acknowledge the care their mothers provide. Their mothers "achieve intimacy in separation," many relying on mobile-cellular telephones, planning meals, asking about school and extracurricular activities, checking up on their children's health, and even sending text messages of bible verses to their children, to be read as they start the day. One of the daughters in Parreñas' (2005a) study reported about her mother that "[s]ometimes she calls three times a week. Especially if one of us is sick, then she will call one day, then she will call again a day later" (p. 104).

Parreñas further reports on how children become almost protective of their away-mothers, not willing to burden them with emotional needs. In the words of a 17-year-old daughter:

> My mother calls and asks me if I have any problems, if I have a boyfriend. (Laughs). But I do not share with her any serious problems. I try to take care of them on my own. … So, it's better if I carry my problems on my own than bother her all the way there. (Parreñas, 2005a, p. 99)

As a result of this intensive, if physically distant, communication, these children define their relationships with their mothers as "very close" (Parreñas, 2005a, p. 105).

ICTs aside, transnational mothering is not universally accepted. Transnational mothers encounter strong public opinion that they have abandoned their children. In fact, Parreñas (2010) found substantial resistance in Philippine society and adverse effects on intergenerational relations and reinforcement of asymmetrical gender divisions of labor. Her research reveals that the geographical distance posed by maternal migration encourages fathers to avoid housework, while burdening female daughters and extended kin. What remains to be seen is if ICTs could help lift such burdens or simply add to maternal migrants' already often crushing burdens in the receiving countries. Technologies such as the Internet can be time consuming and may be used at the expense of face-to-face relationships (Mesch, 2006) and community-based relationships (Mesch & Levanon, 2003) that might provide social and other capital for women facing a difficult life in a society not their own. In other words, just as labor-saving technology in the home increased the time required to accomplish housework by elevating standards, new technology creates new requirements for relationships across distances, too often meaning "more work for mother" (Parreñas, 2010, p. 14).

For all the richness of the predominantly qualitative data we have on how migrant mothers manage their caring capital, we have much more to learn about how the various pieces of the digital puzzle fit together for diverse families. First and foremost, we know that migrant families have widely variable access to ICT resources necessary for maintaining effective family communication and that the interruption of that communication increases children's sense of abandonment by their absent parents (Parreñas, 2005b). Other research suggests that the actual execution of transnational care for families via ICTs is quite diverse. In their study of Filipina domestic workers in Hong Kong, Peng and Wong (2013) found three patterns for the performance of maternal duties: intensive, collaborative, and passive. They argue that the diversity in ICT mothering is shaped by factors such as mothers' agency, children's response, and the role of substitute caregivers in child care. Another quantitative study of ICT use among transnational families left behind in Armenia indicates that some ICT usage (i.e., frequency of Internet use, Internet subscription, and Skype™ use, but not mobile-cellular telephone ownership, email, Facebook™, and other ICTs) is affected by migrant-family status (Pearce, Slaker, & Ahmad, 2013). How do all of these pieces fit together? And, as addressed in the following section, what are the dysfunctions of ICTs in global family life?

Dysfunctions of a Digital World: The "Commodification of Intimacy"

We know that ICTs shape family communication in powerful ways, from mate selection to elder care, from financial support to parent–child interaction. Research, especially the innovative research on American military families and the strong qualitative tradition on women who have immigrated from the global South to the global North for domestic work, reveals that the wider distribution of more affordable ICTs facilitates transnational families' maintenance of the conjugal relationship, performance of long-distance parenting, elder caregiving, and other family tasks.

However, we must also ask if the growth of ICTs in family ecology is an insidious part of not only cultural imperialism but also what some critics of postmodern society have called the "commodification of intimacy" in global capitalism. Members of real global families offer cautions about the use of ICTs in family communication, from the need to "cool down" before responding to an email, for example, through the challenges of confronting incompatible technologies, to the great anxiety of being unexpectedly cut off from their usual ICTs. But beyond those challenges, we must ask: Is there an underside to all this digitalization of family communication—what Bacigalupe and Lambe (2011) refer to in their research on transnational families in therapy as "virtualizing intimacy"?

As illustrated throughout this chapter, ICTs can aid global families in achieving more intimate unions (Cobble, 2010) as they use technologies to recreate intimacy under new circumstances (Boris & Parreñas, 2010) in order to meet their intimate obligations (Parreñas, 2010). Globalized media and ICTs play a substantial role in what the United Nations Educational, Scientific, and Cultural Organization (UNESCO, 2003) has termed the "transnationalization of culture" by "disrupting established boundaries … and … rearticulating the private and public spheres in new ways" (p. 64). In fact, the United Nations has even declared "the right of all individuals to seek, receive and impart information and ideas of all kinds through the Internet" (U.N. Human Rights Council, 2011).

Through their ability to close great geographical distances, ICTs play a major part in creating, maintaining, enhancing (Baldassar, Baldock, & Wilding, 2007), but can they not also disrupt family life and family relationships? Postmodern life is characterized by the rapid movement not of just people and goods but also messages and technologies (Appadurai, 1999), to the point that time and space can seem to collapse in upon us (Harvey, 1989). Ender et al. (2007) have written of the "intense and uncalculated impact on some Army wives" when live television coverage of Operation Iraqi Freedom increased their use of other types of communication media, ostensibly in their efforts to seek out additional sources of information on the situations in which their husbands were fighting. Some of the wives in the study engaged in television viewing that the researchers described as "compulsive" (watching six hours of more of television per day). As one wife reports, "I watched TV all day even though I knew it was not good for me … I felt anxious about things when not watching—then I'd go online and monitor" (Ender, Campbell, Davis, & Michaelis, 2007, p. 57).

This chapter has not addressed how the growth in ICT impacts family relations and communication through the transportation of human beings for exploitative labor and the trafficking of women and children for sex. For an analysis of the place of social networking sites and online classifieds on sex trafficking, see reports from the University of Southern California Annenberg Center on Communication Leadership & Policy's Technology and Human Trafficking Project (Latonero, 2011, 2012). Some social scientists, including feminist scholars, offer dire cautionary tales of latent dysfunctions of other aspects of globalization and the role of ICT in such disparate family functions as adoption (Briggs, 2010), the medicalization of egg and sperm donations (Almeling, 2010), and birth tourism from less developed countries to Canada and the United States, the only developed nations where citizenship is conferred by virtue of birth in-country (Yelaja, 2012).

Family scholars should be concerned with postmodern issues such as cultural imperialism, which may result in conflict within families as norms and values spread from the developed global North to the global South and from developed societies to developing societies. We should also be watchful for the challenges of individualism and materialism (Nederveen Pieterse, 2004; Ritzer, 2004). Appadurai (1996) has referred to this cultural shift as not so much the triumph of the West over the rest of the world but rather the continuing history of cultural convergence or even cultural hybridization. Has the subject of this chapter been, in essence, an apologia for that "most striking feature of contemporary global capitalism … the heightened commodification of intimacy that pervades social life … the colonization of the intimate" (Boris and Parreñas, 2010, p. 1)?

The growth of ICT, as discussed in this chapter and elsewhere in this book, can certainly be seen as one of the hazards faced by postmodern families, hazards that include fragmentation, instability, risk, and uncertainty (Costa, 2013), along with individualization and deinstitutionalization (Bauman, 2003; Beck-Gernsheim, 2002; Brannen & Nielsen, 2005; Giddens, 1993). In other words, while technology can enable families to reduce the strain spatial distance places on intimacy, technology may also be "the antithesis of intimacy" (Parreñas & Boris, 2010, p. 13). Most likely, as with every social change confronted by the family, technology will sometimes enhance long-distance intimacy for global families and will sometimes diminish it, while certainly changing the dynamics of global families in a digital age.

Applications

This chapter has examined the rapidly expanding prevalence of ICTs worldwide, while recognizing important digital divides by development, age, and gender. I have considered how digital technologies shape the quantity and quality of global family communications in different areas of family life. This chapter has been informed by accounts from global families, consideration of the place of ICTs in shaping families such as those of deployed military troops, as well as applications of ICTs to caring capital among migrant families and others living transnationally. The previous section includes what we might call "cautionary tales" offered by scholars who are concerned that increased reliance on digital communication may compromise the quality of family life.

What, then, are the practical applications of what we know about global families in a digital age for those of us who serve global families through scholarship and practice? First, we must carefully consider assumptions about the functions and dysfunctions of global families' use of digital communication. Meeting global families where they live regarding digital communication will force family scholars to continue to critically examine our very suppositions of what it means to be "family." Of the Ethiopian man who shared with me that he rarely communicates with his aunt even though they are Facebook™ "friends," and who furthermore may have little expectation of seeing her face to face in the near future, let alone of living on the same continent any time soon: Are they still "family"? Of an Irish American man who discovered and remains connected with his Irish and then Italian extended family via ICTs, when did they become "family"? Likewise, in the case of someone who loses ICT contact with a distant family member, when do they stop being "family"?

Second, as demonstrated by the Task Group on Gender of the Partnership on Measuring ICT for Development (UNITU, 2013), family scholars and policy makers must press organizations like the UNITU to deconstruct previous measurements of ICT usage. These women and girls whose ICT usage is going uncounted are the daughters, mothers, sisters, and wives who not only share with their sons, fathers, brothers, and husbands the responsibility for their families of origin but also for the next generation. For, "when aggregate data collection masks gender differences, women's realities go unrecorded and are ignored, not only in statistics but also in policy formulation" (p. 5).

Third, we have a burgeoning body of scholarship on the use of cell phones, the Internet, social media, and other ICTs on the lives of American families (see, for example, the Pew Research *Internet & American Life Project*, 2014). Although this chapter has documented research on the effects of ICTs on migrant families, the time has come for a more systematic examination of their effects on a broader range of families, families like those who contributed insights to this chapter. We might ask, for example, how does the quantity and quality of digital communication vary over the life course of "global grandmothers" and their grandchildren?

Fourth, when citizens are sent abroad on behalf of national interests, we have a pressing digital communication policy need. The Marine who had been deployed to Iraq and Afghanistan offered me this poignant comment on the need to prioritize family well-being as part of a national agenda:

> It goes without saying that wars are expensive, and when the top brass climb Capitol Hill to request the money for bullets and fuel needed to fight these wars, they give little thought to the technology that might sustain the morale or sanity of their troops.

Fifth, research indicates that families divided by national borders may experience more problems than other families. For example, using data from both the Early Childhood Longitudinal Study and the Mexican Family Life Survey, Landale, Oropesa, and Noah (2014) found that Mexican children under age six whose parents had immigrated experienced more family instability, including transitioning from two-parent to single-parent families and from extended family households to simple households. Could such "erosion of children's family support across generations" (p. 24) be ameliorated through the use of ICTs? And, if so, is it not time for a dialogue regarding the responsibilities of not just single-national but also transnational organizations?

Finally, for the families. One of the members of a global family with whom I spoke for this chapter suggested several strategies that help her and her family make the most of ICTs. For example, recognizing the critical importance of family rituals (Fiese, Tomcho, Douglas, Josephs, Poltrock, & Baker, 2002), she suggested that families make the most of significant family times. She spoke of how her own family turns on the technology so everyone, regardless of their global location, can "have Christmas in the same room." Other suggestions included:

- Schedule "quality family time" via ICTs
- Use ICTs to deal with issues as they arise
- Employ face time whenever possible
- Stage not just one-on-one communications but family group communications
- Celebrate the global and its potential to enrich family life

This sounds to me like an action agenda for family-life educators wishing to expand service to global families in a digital age!

Note

* Balikbayan boxes are collections of items sent back to the Philippines, e.g., clothing, electronics, household items, nonperishable food, toiletries, toys, designer clothing, or items hard to find in the Philippines.

References

Almeling, R. (2010). Selling genes, selling gender: Egg agencies, sperm banks, and the medical market in genetic material. In R. S. Parreñas & E. Boris (Eds.), *Intimate labors: Cultures, technologies, and the politics of care* (pp. 63–77). Stanford, CA: Stanford University Press.

Appadurai, A. (1996). *Modernity at large: Cultural dimensions of globalization.* Minneapolis: University of Minnesota Press.

Appadurai, A. (1999). Globalization and the research imagination. *International Social Science Journal, 51*(160), 229–238.

Bacigalupe, G., & Lambe, S. (2011). Virtualizing intimacy: Information communication technologies and transnational families in therapy. *Family Process, 50*(1), 12–26.

Baldassar, L., Baldock, C. V., & Wilding, R. (2007). *Families caring across borders: Migration, ageing and transnational caregiving.* New York: Palgrave Macmillan.

Bauman, Z. (2003). *Liquid love: On the frailty of human bonds.* Cambridge, UK: Polity.

Beck-Gernsheim, E. (2001). Household-migrant women and marriage-migrant women in a globalizing world. In E. Beck-Gernsheim, J. Butler, & L. Puigvert (Eds.), *Women and social transformation* (pp. 61–80). Oxford, UK: Berg.

Beck-Gernsheim, E. (2002). *Reinventing the family: In search of new lifestyles.* Cambridge, UK: Polity.

Boris, E. & Parreñas, R. S. (2010). Introduction. In R. S. Parreñas & E. Boris (Eds.), *Intimate labors: Cultures, technologies, and the politics of care* (pp. 1–12). Stanford, CA: Stanford University Press.

Brady, E., & Guerin, S. (2010). "Not the romantic, all happy, coochy coo experience": A qualitative analysis of interactions on an Irish parenting website. *Family Relations, 59*(1), 14–27.

Brannen, J., & Nielsen, A. (2005). Individualization, choice, and structures: A discussion of current trends in sociological analysis. *The Sociological Review, 53*(3), 412–428.

Briggs, L. (2010). Foreign and domestic: Adoption, immigration, and privatization. In R. S. Parreñas & E. Boris (Eds.), *Intimate labors: Cultures, technologies, and the politics of care* (pp. 49–62). Stanford, CA: Stanford University Press.

Carter, S., Loew, B., Allen, E., Stanley, S., Rhodes, G., & Markman, H. (2011). Relationships between soldiers' PTSAD symptoms and spousal communication during deployment. *Journal of Traumatic Stress, 24*(3), 352–355.

Central Intelligence Agency. (2014). *The world factbook: Population below the poverty line.* Retrieved from https://www.cia.gov/library/publications/the-world-factbook/fields/2046.html

Cobble, D. S. (2010). More intimate unions. In R. S. Parreñas & E. Boris (Eds.), *Intimate labors: Cultures, technologies, and the politics of care* (pp. 280–296). Stanford, CA: Stanford University Press.

Costa, R. P. (2013). Family rituals: Mapping the postmodern family through time, space, and emotion. *Journal of Comparative Family Studies, 44*(3), 269–289.

Ducey, Ariel. (2010). Technologies of caring labor: From objects to affect. In R. S. Parreñas & E. Boris (Eds.), *Cultures, technologies, and intimate labors* (pp. 18–32). Stanford, CA: Stanford University Press.

Ender, M. G., Campbell, K. M., Davis, T. J., & Michaelis, P. R. (2007). Greedy media: Army families, embedded reporting, and war in Iraq. *Sociological Focus, 40*(1), 48–71.

Escobar, A. (1994). Welcome to Cyberia: Notes on the anthropology of cyberspace. *Current Anthropology, 35*(3), 211–231.

Fiese, B. H., Tomcho, T., Douglas, M., Josephs, K., Poltrock, S., and Baker, T. A. (2002). Review of fifty years of research on naturally occurring family routines and rituals: Cause for celebration? *Journal of Family Psychology, 16*(4), 381–390.

Furukawa, R., & Dressnack, M. (2013). Video-mediated communication to support distant family connectedness. *Clinical Nursing Research, 22*(1), 82–94.

Giddens, A. (1993). *The transformation of intimacy: Sexuality, love, and eroticism in modern societies.* Cambridge, UK: Polity.

Harvey, D. (1989). *The postmodern condition.* Baltimore, MD: Johns Hopkins University Press.

Hondagneu-Sotelo, P., & Avila, E. (1997). "I'm here, but I'm there": The meanings of Latina transnational motherhood. *Gender & Society, 11*(5), 538–571.

Karraker, M. W. (2012). *Global families.* Thousand Oaks, CA: Sage.

Kiesler, S., Zdaniuk, B., Lundmark, V., & Kruat, R. (2000). Troubles with the Internet: The dynamics of help at home. *Human–Computer Interaction, 15*, 322–351.

Kyle, D. (2000). *Transnational peasants: Migrations, networks, and ethnicity in Andean Ecuador.* Baltimore, MD: Johns Hopkins University Press.

Landsdale, N. S., Oropesa, R. S., & Noah, A. J. (2014). Immigration and the family circumstances of Mexican-origin children: A binational longitudinal analysis. *Journal of Marriage and the Family, 76*(1), 24–36.

Latonero, M. (2011). *Human trafficking online: The role of social networking sites and online classifieds.* University of Southern California Annenberg Center on Communication Leadership and Policy, Technology and Human Trafficking Project. Retrieved from https://technologyandtrafficking.usc.edu/files/2011/09/HumanTrafficking_FINAL.pdf

Latonero, M. (2012). The rise of mobile and the diffusion of technology-facilitated trafficking. University of Southern California Annenberg Center on Communication Leadership and Policy, Technology and Human Trafficking Project. Retrieved from https://technologyandtrafficking.usc.edu/files/2012/11/HumanTrafficking2012_Nov12.pdf

Lenhart, A., Lewis, O., & Raine, L. (2001). *Teenage life online.* Retrieved from Pew Research Center website, http://www.pewInternet.org/2001/06/21/teenage-life-online/

Madianou, M. (2012). Migration and the accentuated ambivalence of motherhood: The role of ICT in Filipino transnational families. *Global Networks 12*(3), 277–295.

Mehrabian, A. (2007). *Nonverbal communication.* Piscataway, NJ: Aldine.

Mesch, G. S. (2006). Family relations and the Internet: Exploring a family boundaries approach. *The Journal of Family Communication, 6*(2), 119–138.

Mesch, G. S., & Levanon, Y. (2003). Community networking and locally-based social ties in two suburban localities. *City & Community, 2*(4), 336–351.

Nederveen Pieterse, J. (2004). *Globalization and culture: Global mélange.* Lanham, MA: Rowman & Littlefield.

Panagakos, A. N., & Horst, H. A. (2006). Return to Cyberia: Technology and the social worlds of international migrants. *Global Networks, 6*(2), 109–124.

Parreñas, R. S. (2000). Migrant Filipina domestic workers and the international division of reproductive labor. *Gender & Society, 14*(4), 560–581.

Parreñas, R. S. (2001). *Servants of globalization: Women, migration and domestic work.* Stanford, CA: Stanford University Press.

Parreñas, R. S. (2005a). *Children of global migration: Transnational families and gendered woes.* Stanford, CA: Stanford University Press.

Parreñas, R. S. (2005b). Long distance intimacy: Class, gender, and intergenerational relations between mothers and children in Filipino transnational families. *Global Networks, 5*(4), 317–336.

Parreñas, R. S. (2008a). *The force of domesticity: Filipina migrants and globalization.* New York: New York University Press.

Parreñas, R. S. (2008b). Transnational fathering: Gendered conflict, distant disciplining, and emotional gaps. *Journal of Ethnic and Migration Studies, 34*(7), 1057–1072.

Parreñas, R. S. (2010). Transnational mothering: A source of gender conflict in the family. *North Carolina Law Review, 88*, 1825–1856.

Parreñas, R. S., & Boris, E. (2010). Introduction to Part I. Remaking the intimate: Technology and globalization. In R. S. Parreñas & E. Boris (Eds.), *Intimate labors: Cultures, technologies, and the politics of care* (pp. 13–17). Stanford, CA: Stanford University Press.

Partnership on Measuring ICT for Development. (2013, December 4–6). Stocktaking and assessment on measuring ICT and gender. Eleventh World Telecommunication/ICT Indicators Symposium (WTIS-13), Mexico City, Mexico. Retrieved from Partnership on Measuring ICT for Development website, http://www.itu.int/en/ITU-D/Statistics/Documents/events/wtis2013/001_E_doc.pdf

Pearce, K. E., Slaker, J. S., & Ahmad, N. (2013). Transnational families in Armenia and information communication technology use. *International Journal of Communication, 7*, 2128–2156.

Peng, Y., & Wong, O. M. H. (2013). Diversified transnational mothering via telecommunication: Intensive, collaborative, and passive. *Gender & Society, 27*(4), 491–513.

Pew Research Center. (2014). *Internet & American life project.* Retrieved from http://www.pewInternet.org/about/

Ritzer, G. (2004). *The globalization of nothing.* Thousand Oaks, CA: Pine Forge.

Sassen, S. (2000). *Cities in a world economy.* (2nd ed.). Thousand Oaks, CA: Pine Forge.

Schachman, K. A. (2010). Online fathering: The experience of first-time fatherhood and ubiquitous computing. *Nursing Research, 159*(1), 11–17.

Segrin, C., & Flora, J. (2005). *Family communication.* Mahwah, NJ: Lawrence Erlbaum.

Smilkstein, G. (1978). The family APGAR: A proposal for a family function test and its use by physicians. *Journal of Family Practice, 6*(6), 1231–1239.

Townsend, K. C., & McWhirter, B. T. (2005). Connectedness: A review of the literature with implications for counseling, assessment, and research. *Journal of Counseling and Development, 83*(2), 191–201.

Turow, J. (2001). Family boundaries, commercialism, and the Internet: A framework for research. *Applied Developmental Psychology, 22*(1), 73–86.

United Nations Educational, Scientific, and Cultural Organization (UNESCO). (2003). World television day celebrated today. Retrieved from UNESCO website, http://portal.unesco.org/ci/en/ev.php-URL_ID=13630&URL_DO=DO_TOPICS7URL-SECTION=201.HTML

United Nations Human Rights Council. (2011). *Report of the special rapporteur on the promotion and protection of right to freedom of opinion and expression, Frank LaRue.* Retrieved from Office of the High Commissioner for Human Rights website http://www2.ohchr.org/english/bodies/hrcouncil/docs/17session/A.HRC.17.27_en.pdf

United Nations International Telecommunications Union (UNITU). (2011). *ICAT facts and figures.* Retrieved from UNITU website, http://www.itu.int/ITUD/ict/facts/2011/material/ICTFactsFigures2011.pdf

United Nations International Telecommunications Union (UNITU). (2013). *Measuring the information society.* Retrieved from UNITU website, http://www.itu.int/en/ITU-D/Statistics/Pages/stat/default.aspx

Wilding, R. (2006). "Virtual" intimacies? Families communicating across transnational contexts. *Global Networks, 6*(2), 125–142.

Wilding, R. (2012). Mediating culture in transnational spaces: An example of young people from refugee backgrounds. *Continuum: Journal of Media & Cultural Studies, 26*(3), 501–511.

Yelaja, P. (2012, March 5). "Birth tourism" may change citizenship rules. CBC News. Retrieved from CBC Radio-Canada website, http://www.cbc.ca/news/canada/birth-tourism-may-change-citizenship-rules-1.1164914

4

The Couple and Family Technology Framework

Katherine M. Hertlein
University of Nevada, Las Vegas

Markie L. C. Blumer
University of Wisconsin–Stout

Introduction

There is no longer a question that technology and new media have impacted the lives of individual children, adults, and their relationships. Mobile phones, laptops, and tablets are a primary way many of us work, spend leisure time, and connect with family and friends, a shift from previous leisure activities (Woodard & Gridina, 2000). They accelerate the speed of our communication (for good or for bad) and provide a chance to simultaneously dissociate and connect.

In this chapter, we present the theoretical underpinnings and therapeutic application of the Couple and Family Technology (CFT) Framework. We describe the ecological elements of the framework and the ways relationships are helped and hindered by these elements. We also attend to the areas in which the ecological elements affect couples and families in specific ways: through roles, rules, boundaries, relationship initiation, relationship maintenance, and relationship dissolution.

Psychological Effects Associated with Technology Usage

Individuals who use the Internet more frequently have higher levels of aggression and conflict in their online interactions than those who do not (Yum & Hara, 2006). Those individuals who scored as having more pain while text messaging also scored lower on a five-item mental health scale (Hupert et al., 2004). Researchers found a link between anxiety and Internet usage when controlling for depression, noting those with higher degrees of social anxiety will be more likely to have used the Internet in problematic ways than those without such symptomology (Lee & Stapinski, 2012). In a sample of college students aged 18–22, anger/irritability, lack of concentration, anxiety, and lack of sleep were also noted as common effects related to mobile phone usage. In some cases, the results were tied to friends not returning texts or messages (Acharya et al., 2013). Cyberbullying, defined as "any behavior performed through electronic or digital media by individuals or groups that repeatedly communicates hostile or aggressive messages intended to inflict harm or discomfort on others" (Tokunaga, 2010, p. 278), is also a prevalent concern.

Technology use also has implications for power differentials in a couple or family relationship. Individuals in a relationship likely have varying levels of technology competence (see Blumer & Hertlein, in this volume), and because technologies are developing so rapidly, it is often difficult to keep up. Additionally, partners may be more computer literate than another (this may be related to gender roles such as degree of masculinity or femininity) (Kang, 2012), thus contributing to another power imbalance (Hertlein & Blumer, 2013; Kang, 2012).

Published Information on Technology in Relationships

To date, published work on technology and relationships has had a overwhelming tendency to be individually focused, specifically investigating the sociodemographic characteristics of those using the Internet as well as seeking to understand motivation for usage (Hertlein & Desruisseaux, 2012). Attention in clinically focused journals is most often spent on problematic behavior, such as Internet infidelity, Internet addiction, and Internet pornography usage (Cravens, Hertlein, & Blumer, 2013; Hertlein & Cravens, 2014) and less often on the processes in relationships. Overall, the literature on technology and relationships is published in a diverse set of journals and disciplines, making it difficult for practitioners or scholars to collaborate easily (Hertlein & Blumer, 2013).

Generally speaking, information about couples and the technology in their lives has had a slow start. Blumer, Hertlein, Smith, and Allen (2013) completed a content analysis of technology in relationships in 17 top marriage and family therapy journals. Across 15 years, there were only a few journal articles that attended to technology at all (79 of more than 13,000), and only 18 attended specifically to couple relationships. Further, most of the articles related to couples focused specifically on online infidelity only (Blumer, Hertlein, Smith & Allen, 2013), and therapists are further limited in their access to journals (Lambert-Shute, Hertlein, & Piercy, 2009). Finally, many practitioners who work with couples are not well-versed in areas of technology to conduct a proper assessment, do not inquire about children and technology usage, and limit couples assessment to infidelity without consideration of other key areas that might affect couples and families, such as online gaming, online addiction, cyberstalking, and the relation between time spent on the computer and family cohesion (Blumer, Hertlein, Smith & Allen, 2013).

The New Field of Couple and Family Technology

Research on families, couples, and technology is growing, yet remains fragmented and spread across multiple fields and scholarly journals, including media studies, communication, information systems, sociology, psychology, family science, and education, among others. One way to provide integration is to organize the information related to technology, couples, and families under a broad umbrella: the field of Couple and Family Technology (CFT) studies (Hertlein & Blumer, 2013). An important outcome of a field of Couple and Family Technology—which has a primary focus on clinical and therapeutic applications of relevant research—is that mental health providers and therapists have a source for the best empirical information on technology and relational systems as it is translated into practice (Hertlein & Blumer, 2013). As more scholars translate empirical information into practice, family scholars are also then better able to develop further research for answering essential questions about technology and relational systems. Couple and Family Technology attends to multiple aspects of technology in couple and family life and advances understanding of benefits and drawbacks of technology on relational life (Hertlein & Blumer, 2013). Currently, limited literature exists for mental health practitioners and, as a result, many clinicians tend to discuss the negative aspects of technology on relationships without weighing its benefits (Hertlein & Webster, 2008). Scholars of the field are also interested in applying what is known about technology, individual motivations, and personality to relational contexts. For instance, much of the research related to motivations in Internet usage (Teo, Lim, & Lai, 1999) could be applied to couples but thus far has not been. Hertlein and Hawkins (2012), for example, conducted an analysis of the literature on personality characteristics and motivation related to online gamers and, through application of the concepts, proposed intervention strategies for couples based on the CFT model. Cho and Cheong (2005) found the process concepts of intimacy and family cohesion were related to shared browsing online with children and, in turn, results in parents being more knowledgeable about their children's Internet browsing behavior. Such integrative pieces are the hallmark of the Couple and Family Technology field: adaptation and application of the technology literature in a way that advances and provides a framework for understanding couple and family life.

Another element of the Couple and Family Technology field is to provide a place for the generation and development of CFT assessment tools (e.g., assessment tools for working with couples/families in clinical settings). Thus far, much of the assessment in CFT studies has again been dedicated to understanding and defining (or even diagnosing) problematic behavior. Yet because the field is based on the assumption that technology is neither exclusively positive nor negative for relationships but can be both, and even simultaneously positive and negative, assessment tools need to be broad enough to investigate and allow space for multiple potential outcomes. Further, the field of couple and family therapy supports the idea of establishing goals related to technology management and usage within the context of mental health and relationship treatment.

Key Components of the CFT Framework

Couple and Family Technology studies is a discipline intended to organize the information regarding technology and family systems through evaluating the impact of technology on couple and family life, the identification of electronic resources for couples and families, and the development of assessment tools regarding technology. One specialized part of the Couple and Family Technology field is the Couple and Family Technology Framework, designed to provide a conceptualization of how technology affects couple and family life (Hertlein, 2012). The CFT Framework is divided into three main sections: ecological influences, impact to structure of couple and family systems, and impact to processes in family and couple relationships. Ecological influences include seven factors that technology and new media bring to us, each unique to new media and each having a specific impact on families. Each element (independently and collectively) has implications for (1) the structure of couples and families, and (2) the processes of couples and families. Specifically, they affect the roles, rules, boundaries (structural) and relationship initiation, relationship maintenance, and dissolution (processes). Each element is described in greater detail below, with specific attention to the way they interact with the structural and process elements of relationships.

Ecological Elements

Accessibility. Accessibility was initially described by Spears and Lea (1994) and Cooper (2002) to refer to how accessible the Internet is in our daily lives. The existence of personal computers, laptops, and other devices that allow Internet accessibility surround us, thus having a pronounced impact on our lives. Accessibility has increased through the development of new technologies such as tablets in the later 2000s (Prey & Weaver, 2007) and more sophisticated smartphones. Accessibility can create challenges and/or positive changes in relationships. Dean and Mariana came to treatment to address Dean's relationships with other women. One particularly upsetting piece for Mariana was Dean's using his phone to message his other romantic interests while sitting on the couch with her. As far as advantages, accessibility can create additional contact with partners throughout the day when, without technology, relationship members might not have been able to do so. Hertlein and Blumer (2013) note technology allows one to be accessible to others, evidenced by potential contact via an online presence or contact through social media forums.

Implications for structure. Accessibility has a definite impact on the structure of couple and family relationships. The introduction of accessibility changes the boundaries around couples and families. Mesch (2006) stated boundaries are helpful for families in that we learn to interact with the world via boundaries, something the Internet challenges.

Mesch (2006) outlined his model on boundaries in the family as being influenced by several components: time spent online (considered a major factor), social uses, nonsocial uses, family conflict, family cohesion, and family time. Specifically, social use was the type of information providing the most family information to outside members of the family unit and is thus viewed by parents as the biggest threat to the family. This is due to how many places people can access the Internet—seemingly everywhere—so much so that being unable to access the Internet from a hotel, home, or place of business seems rare.

Because of the accessibility, boundaries between relationships and the outside world are permeated, and sometimes done so both out in the open yet secretly (Hertlein & Blumer, 2013).

With family relationships, the accessibility parents might experience with children may also improve or compromise relationships with their children. Daniel and Raja brought their oldest son, William, to therapy because they were concerned about his increased mood swings and argumentative nature. During the intake, William disclosed that when he was out with his friends for an evening, his mother would constantly call and text, making it impossible to enjoy himself. His response to her was to ignore her multiple attempts at contact, which then fueled her attempts to contact him, knowing that he was accessible and not responding.

Another example of the impact of technology on couple and family life with regard to boundaries and accessibility is work–family conflict (Chelsey, 2005). For most employees in the 21st century, work is something that can now be attended to at any hour of any day. There may be an expectation that boundaries around work and home become more diffuse; the result can be added pressure on couples and families, when a partner is expected to respond to requests outside of designated work hours (Harris, Marett, & Harris, 2011). The intrusion of technology into personal time outside of the traditional work week is a phenomenon especially familiar to academics, who find it particularly difficult to disengage from work because of flexibility in work schedules (Heijstra & Rafnsdottir, 2010).

Likewise, accessibility affects rules in relationships. In the case of Daniel, Raja, and William, Raja viewed her son William as breaking the rules of communication between parent and child by not responding to her when she made her attempts to contact him—with the notion that the accessibility offered to her by mobile phones further enforced the rules about immediate response to parental contact, no matter what the context (see Robbins, Afifi, & Merrill in this volume: an empirical examination of parents' anxiety in response to adolescent mobile phone delays). Rules for couples are also impacted; they must discuss with whom one provides social media contact information, as well as when and how technology is used in the household and in the presence of each other. For families with children, decisions have to be made in several additional areas. Parents have to negotiate the rules in the house related to cell phone use and their children—specifically at what age are children allowed to peruse the Web without a parent present; at what age are children allowed to have their own cell phone; at what age are children granted social networking accounts. Some concerns are related to questionable implications for health associated with cell phones and children (Rosenberg, 2013; Sudan, Khefiets, Arah, & Olsen, 2013) as well as potential impairment to cognitive functioning (Lin, 2010). Other concerns are related to balancing freedom with the potential risk gained from such freedom (Bond, 2011). Parents have to negotiate the issues that emerge. With a cell phone comes freedom and autonomy for some children; on the other hand, autonomy can be expressed by each person locking their phones with passwords or organizing/restricting the contact list of their child (Bond, 2010).

Another way accessibility influences rules in couple and family relationships is through presence and surveillance (Francisco, 2013). Because of increased accessibility, there is a perception of people always being present—and implications for relationships when people are not present. Isadora became upset when she did not receive a response from Manuel after sending multiple texts periodically throughout the day. Manuel's response the following day was that he was unusually tied up at work, which resulted in him not being able to respond to Isadora. He also became angry with her by the end of the day because her repeated texts and concerns began to feel more like surveillance, and a perception that she did not trust him. Isadora experienced a problem because Manuel was typically present and responsive, and thus the couple had to develop a rule in their relationship that Manuel must provide context if something about his level of presence changed.

Accessibility influences roles in relationships. For example, as adolescents are more adept at communicating via new media than their parents, they can acquire more power in the relationship, especially about technology (Marshall & Reday, 2007; Prensky, 2001). Such accessibility has resulted in teens being trusted with more responsibility in decision-making within family systems because of their expertise with the Internet (Belch, Krentler, & Willis-Flurry, 2005).

Implications for process. In terms of relationship processes, initiation is certainly one of the ways in which accessibility has impacted relationships. "Gating" features (usually physical characteristics that allow for individuals to select others such as hair color, body shape, and so on) often used in offline processes are not typically used in the development of online relationships (McKenna & Bargh, 2000; McKenna, Green, & Gleason, 2002). Thus, Internet users are exposed to a wider range of potential partners.

Relationships can also be maintained differently than they were before new media technologies were widely adopted. Largely, increased contact with one another creates more ways for connection. In this way, technology and new media can be a vehicle through which partners develop latent intimacy (characterized by warmth and connection), argued by some as the most important type of intimacy for sustaining a long-term relationship (Merolla, 2012; Sternberg, 1986). For example, couples who use cell phones to communicate with each other during the day as compared to couples who do not have calls of shorter duration and are more task-oriented (Kennedy, Smith, Wells, & Wellman, 2008; Wilding, 2006), thus demonstrating a need for couples to exert more effort to demonstrate warmth and connection.

On the other hand, relationship maintenance can be challenged with more frequent calls and calls of shorter duration. Doug expressed dissatisfaction that his girlfriend Elaine would not respond to his frequent calls throughout the day. Elaine noted that she did respond when she could but the frequency of the short calls, in addition to her perception that many were about household decisions—conversations she viewed as able to be addressed when she returned home from work—did not result in intimacy building. In terms of intimacy in the relationship, the calls where Elaine was not available impacted the couple's manifest intimacy: the type of intimacy shared when a couple experiences one another in the immediate present through specific actions (Sternberg, 1986).

In addition, accessibility of email has also been cited as an advantage in extending family networks, in family communication—especially when members are geographically distant from each other—and in the communication of romantic partners—both those living near and those living at a distance (Johnson, Haigh, Becker, Craig, & Wigley, 2008). For example, Johnson et al. (2008) found 38% of their sample had used email to communicate with a long-distance family member over a 1-week period and 32% exchanged emails with at least one long-distance friend over the week. Approximately the same percentage of the sample exchanged emails with their geographically close romantic partners, as did those who exchanged emails with their geographically distinct romantic partners (9% and 11%, respectively).

Relationship maintenance has also been influenced by the use of the global positioning systems (GPS) built into new media devices; in some circumstances, it can be used as a surveillance tool. Ana asked Roger to pick up their daughter and then bring her home for a nap. When Ana checked on Roger's whereabouts and whether he had gotten home, he indicated that he was not at home yet and told an elaborate story of how he was involved in an altercation with several men who had attempted to harm their daughter. When Ana checked his GPS location, however, it showed he was already at home and so was lying to her. Therefore, Ana had to make a decision about what she would and would not accept in their relationship due to the discovery of Roger's lies.

Finally, accessibility also impacts the lives of children. In many cases, children can connect with their peers who share the same technology, organize times to engage in social outings, and be included in conversation (Bond, 2011). Monitoring devices can be used to protect youth online (Mesch, 2006), but increased surveillance of online activities can also create arguments around autonomy. Further, mobile phones may have a different impact based on the subsystem. In a study on the role of mobile phone usage in Filipina migrant mothers and their separated children, mothers who used cell phones to mediate contact with their children felt empowered, while the children themselves were ambivalent about the consequences (Madianou & Miller, 2011).

Affordability. The general affordability of the Internet is what enables so many people to use it (Cooper, 2002). The more affordable the technologies, the more likely people have access to them. The use of such services is not restricted to those with more financial resources. Affordability influences the structure of relationships as well. With more affordable ways to connect with others, the roles in relationships may shift. For example, there may be equal opportunity for people to initiate communication in relationships if the initiation is equally affordable to both parties.

Implications for structure. Boundaries are also influenced by more affordability. Put simply, affordability for all affects accessibility in ways that promote relationship development, such as increasing opportunities for connection. On the other hand, affordability can also become a detriment to the primary relationship if it is used to fuel other relationships outside of the primary one. For example, topics of conversation formerly reserved for one's romantic partner are often expressed to groups of people (friends and acquaintances) via social media. This activity diffuses the boundary around the primary relationship because the same intimate behaviors can be shared with others. One partner in a couple found that the most distressing trigger that reminded her of her partner's infidelity was the receipts from her partner's dinner with someone else. Given that many Internet activities with another person can occur at little or no cost, the visual reminder (or evidence) of a receipt is less of a concern.

Boundaries are also diffused in positive ways to improve relational maintenance, such as in transnational families. These families use the Internet and new media to maintain the same familial relationships and connections in other ways (Bacigalupe & Lambe, 2011; Francisco, 2013; Kang, 2012; also see Wilkes Karraker's chapter in this volume). In many cases, transnational family connections are affected by pronounced economic conditions. For example, in migrant families, the affordability of technology and mobile phones allows the members who are more privileged financially to better understand the sacrifices and less affordable living situation of the other family members (Francisco, 2013).

Implications for process. Affordable new media technologies level the playing field with regard to relationship initiation. With the sheer number of individuals who use the Internet, meeting others outside of one's socioeconomic status is more probable. In addition, relationship maintenance can take a variety of forms. Websites provide information on how to enhance one's relationship through a series of short self-report quizzes, dating ideas, and so on. Technologies such as Web-based communication and video conferencing can promote intimacy development in relationships. This can be particularly useful in long-distance relationships where time, money, and other resources do not permit in-person interactions. In addition, new media allows relatives to watch their family member grow up, something not offered by phone communication only but critical to feeling present in many families, which offers a different sense of intimacy (Francisco, 2013).

Affordability also allows Internet and new-media users to end relationships in an emotionally affordable way. For some couples, it can be as easy as changing one's status on a social networking site from "in a relationship" to "single." There does not have to be a long conversation or emotional explanation to someone else when the relationship ends. It can be achieved through a quick email to a partner ending the relationship, or in some cases no notification of the relationship dissolution at all. One may even choose to block a partner from communicating via their phone, email, or social networking site.

Anonymity. The Internet and new media have the ability to render the user anonymous (Cooper, 2002). Anonymity within this context can mean several different things. At its most basic level, users of new media can make posts and comments under assumed names or nondescriptive avatars. Such anonymity can apply to one's relationship status: one can choose to reveal an accurate relationship status online via social media, or not and retain some level of anonymity. Likewise, one can choose to post photographs or not, and if the choice is made to post them, such photos can enhance or deemphasize physical characteristics (Hertlein & Blumer, 2013). Photos that deemphasize physical characteristics could be of pets, other family members, or can be out-of-date photos that do not accurately reflect present appearance.

Implications for structure. Anonymity has serious implications for structural issues in couples and families. Those who choose to remain anonymous to their partners have a boundary around themselves, not around the unit or partnership. This will invariably disrupt the cohesion within a family, as one person may not be bringing themselves fully to the table. On the other hand, boundaries and rules around when to disclose information can be exceedingly useful in pacing a relationship in a way that helps prevent those involved from investing emotionally too quickly and getting hurt. For example, children and adolescents may benefit from some degree of anonymity in their online interactions as it might prevent them from being victims of cyber-stalking or other potentially dangerous circumstances.

Implications for process. Technology also affects couple and family relationships through privacy (see Child & Petronio's chapter in this volume). While one partner in a relationship or family system might be hiding some of his or her or their activities, technology enables partners and parents to engage in spying practices to track their partner's behavior. The ability to immediately check phone records and install keylogging software can render the person looking anonymous to the other partner whose activities are being recorded. Such advances in technology can create problems in couples as the person who is being spied on feels anger at the violation of privacy; alternatively, they may be acting in ways that are in fact a violation of the relationship code. Such was the case for Tara and Jim. Tara expressed distress and offense that Jim was tracking her activities without telling her, thus invading her privacy; at the same time, Tara had stepped out of the relationship previously, so Jim's concerns seemed warranted.

Anonymity can also protect a person's emotional life and experiences. Through the screen, it can be difficult to detect whether persons on the other end are happy, mad, or sad, and so on, which means those persons have more control over the way in which they present themselves. One can choose to promote oneself as being distant or close, can be deceptive or sincere; and disclose as much or as little as one wants. In many ways, new media provides users with an invisibility cloak, which has significant implications for both relationship initiation and relationship maintenance. In terms of initiation, the development of relationships might be built on a self-presentation rather than an authentic representation of oneself. This can cause problems later if the couple moves toward a more serious relationship, thus also affecting relational maintenance. Jeremy and Melissa came to treatment because Melissa had developed a pattern of holding back her own feelings to spare her partner's, something that was easy to do, as most of their interactions were via text messaging because of conflicting work schedules.

Acceptability. Acceptability is the degree to which use of the Internet and new media are acceptable for communicating with partners, family, and friends. It is becoming commonplace to see phones and other new media emerge during dinners, meetings, and other social and work functions. It is also becoming more acceptable for children and teenagers to have their own phones (Aarsand, 2007). It is also very common that teens are online in some capacity (Hundley & Shyles, 2010) and even without phones, as an estimated 70–80% of teens digitally multitask (Pan, 2004). Using the Internet for sex is also becoming a more acceptable practice (Couch & Liamputtong, 2008; Daneback, Cooper, & Månsson, 2005), as is Internet infidelity (Mileham, 2007), and the practice of sexting, particularly among teens, college students, and young adults (Dake, Price, Maziarz, & Ward, 2012; Ferguson, 2011; Hertlein & Ancheta, 2014; Mitchell, Finkelhor, Jones, & Wolak, 2012; Peskin, Markman, Addy, Shegog, Thiel, & Tortolero, 2013; Strassberg, McKinnon, Sustaíta, & Rullo, 2013).

Implications for structure. The acceptability of these devices is apparent in their use in social situations. As already mentioned, it is acceptable for people to use a phone during shopping, and even during social events and gatherings. The responses to bringing out a phone during these activities can dictate the tone of the relationship. Recent data suggest that 95% of U.S. teens are online (Madden et al., 2013). Owning a cell phone is associated with a higher status among one's peers (Blair & Fletcher, 2011). Acceptability is also important when one considers cell phone usage in adolescents. In some ways, cell phones are a way for parents to retain control over their adolescent—particularly if the adolescent contacts the parent. They also provide ways for teens to connect and socialize with their friends (Blair & Fletcher, 2011). On the other hand, cell phone ownership represents increased autonomy for adolescents as they branch into new and different activities with the security of a cell phone on which to fall back if needed (Blair & Fletcher, 2011; Rizzo, 2008). The cell phone also provides an ability to monitor the adolescent easily and more frequently (Blair & Fletcher, 2011)—a reminder of the parent's role as supervisor in the adolescent's life.

Implications for process. Acceptability has implications for both couples and families. For example, using smartphone applications to meet people and date is quickly becoming an acceptable practice, particularly for persons seeking same-sex relationships (Rosenfeld & Thomas, 2012). In families, the role of the parent as a monitor and whether that is acceptable, might be confirmed by other parents engaged in the same practice. For example, Nora stated that she often checked in with her son's friend's parents to see if they were implementing the same monitoring procedures as she, in order to determine whether her monitoring behavior was acceptable among her peers.

Approximation. Developments in technology now make it easier to replicate real-life situations online, a concept known as approximation (Ross & Kauth, 2002). One way couples and family members experience this approximation is through the immediacy provided by phone calls and instant messaging. Users can create a rich, descriptive environment through text and email as a way to mimic real-life situations. They can stage a background for a Web camera session as a way also to create a sense of authenticity that may not really be there in the physical world.

Implications for structure. Approximation has particular relevance in sexual interactions. Ross (2005) claims that advances in technology have resulted in Internet users believing that the sexual fantasies they view online are things that can and do happen in real life. For example, Nathan entered treatment for a perceived sexual addiction. He indicated one of the factors contributing to his difficulty managing the addiction was that the scenes he watched online were becoming more explicit, and he began to need more stimulation in order to achieve satisfaction. Furthermore, Nathan's wife refused to participate in these activities, thus creating conflict between the two of them. For Nathan, the rules of the sexual relationship with his wife were changing without her knowledge or consent.

Implications for process. Approximation can also mimic a real-world relational maintenance experience. Characteristics of a relationship that have to be approximated over the Internet as a way to maintain the relationship include: positivity; openness; assurances; social networks; sharing tasks; joint activities; cards, letters, and calls; and humor (Canary & Stafford, 1994, as cited in Johnson et al., 2008). Of these, the order of importance in terms of maintaining family relationships appears to be openness, social networks, positivity, assurance, and joint activities; with romantic relationships, the order is assurances, openness, positivity, social networks, and reference to calls and letters (Johnson et al., 2008). Additionally, couples also use technology and new media to approximate physical affection as a way to enhance their connection when they cannot physically be together (Coyne et al., 2011).

Approximation also affects relationship maintenance through the sharing of everyday activities. People connect through Skype or another webcam technology and watch other family members do homework or cook dinner, as if the person on the other end of the computer was physically present in the same space for that experience (Francisco, 2013). Many people view online activities with someone else as constituting the same experience of betrayal as if the activities took place offline (see, for example, Whitty, 2005).

Ambiguity. With new media developing in our lives at such a rapid rate, couples and families have been hard pressed to stay ahead of its effect on relationships and the changing meaning of technology in their lives. As a result, ambiguity is a key component in how technology impacts couple and family life (Hertlein & Stevenson, 2010). Ambiguity can run the gamut in relationships—from what software can do to how technology will influence individuals and their relationships.

Implications for structure. Hertlein and Blumer (2013) posit there are two types of ambiguity—relational and technological—each having impact on family and couple roles, rules, and boundaries. Technological ambiguity was discussed earlier in the section on the extent to which individuals can successfully navigate new media. For example, men and women differ in knowledge of using the Internet to communicate with extended family and those who did not, thus exposing a barrier to family communication (Kang, 2012). Relational ambiguity, on the other hand, speaks more specifically to the roles, rules, and boundaries in relationships upon the introduction of new media into a person's interactions. Max and Will came to a first session of therapy to presumably address Will's alleged affair with a previous partner. Both Will and Max acknowledged that there was an extensive amount of pain between the two of them but disagreed as to the origin of the relational conflict. Max believed that Will's talking to another individual online late at night and keeping the relationship secret was a betrayal and breach of their relationship contract; Will flatly denied any wrongdoing on his part. Thus, new media necessitated a clarification of relationship rules, but the couple did not discuss them (for more on relationship rules about technologies, see Cravens and Whiting's chapter in this volume).

The same concept applies to families, specifically with regard to the rules related to technology use and children. For example, a family might have certain rules about a 10-year-old child's cell phone use (i.e., a restricted list of people with whom the child can speak or receive messages) but may not have rules about the amount of time the child can use the phone. Parents have a responsibility to adjust the usage rules based on the developmental level of the child, which is constantly changing. Rules governing children and technology have to be constantly revisited; this can be difficult for families to accomplish on a regular basis.

Implications for process. Ambiguity in couple and family rules has significant implications for how they manage their interactions. First, ambiguity within the couple as to the rules in their relationship can break down relationship maintenance, as each will be under the guidance of a different system of rules. Without clarity regarding roles and rules, couples and families may experience a disruption in cohesion.

The ambiguity around the technology itself can also result in relational maintenance problems. Emma had spent time via text with her sister, Linda, supporting her with a relationship problem. Emma inquired as to Linda's schedule and believed Linda had told her that she would be free during the day. The next day, Emma checked on Linda via text, but Linda did not respond. Emma grew increasingly concerned over the day and wondered whether she had written something to upset Linda. After Linda did not respond that night, Emma became angry that Linda had seemingly blown her off. The following day, when Linda returned her texts, Linda indicated that she meant that she was in fact going to be at work but acknowledged her brief message about it was not clear. Unfortunately, the ambiguous nature of Linda's message caused several hours of confusion and hurt for Emma. She felt that she had gone out of her way for Linda, only to feel that her care was not reciprocated.

Accommodation. People use new media technologies to accommodate behavior that they would not normally feel safe performing in real life (Hertlein & Stevenson, 2010). Similar to Higgins's (1987) concept of real versus ideal self, accommodation has been studied in the context of men's use of the Internet to fulfill sexual encounters with other men, even when they self-identify as heterosexual (Cooper, Galbreath, & Becker, 2004). Accommodation can function in both positive and negative ways in a relationship, depending on the context of each person involved (Hertlein & Blumer, 2013). For example, relationships may be more successful when both people are operating from a place of authenticity as compared to relationships in which partners are together operating from their idealized selves.

Implications for structure. Accommodation can impact relationship roles. Individuals can feel constrained in the roles assigned to them in day-to-day life and may use the Internet as an escape from those restrictions. In addition to avatars and living aspects of one's personality, individuals might also use the Internet to accommodate new and varied roles. For example, Barbara was someone who considered herself to have a feminine role in her relationship with Eric; however, online, she was able to portray a more masculine role in her relationship via her social media postings. Boundaries also play a role in the differences in the areas where people chose to express their "real self." For many, using the Internet to accommodate behavior they really want to express is best undertaken initially where there will be few, if any, people who might be able to compare the "real self" online with the idealized but constrained self offline.

Implications for process. Accommodation is a critical concept in relationship initiation. For example, as couples are beginning their relationship, the assumption is that this search for a partner will identify someone who is authentic and honest (i.e., a "real self"). Because it is more acceptable for couples to initiate their relationships in an online realm before moving it offline (see earlier discussion on acceptability), the concept of accommodation of one's real and ideal self emerges early in a couple's development. Interestingly, when writing an online personal ad in search of a long-term, face-to-face relationship, factors associated with success include the amount of self-disclosure, disclosure of personal information, and disclosing information by intention, with many disclosures being negative (Gibbs, Ellison, & Heino, 2006). This finding suggests that those making negative disclosures assume that such information will be discovered eventually if the online relationship transitions into a face-to-face relationship (Gibbs et al., 2006), supporting the idea that persons manage authentic versus ideal selves in computer-mediated communication. Alternatively, as much as the amount of disclosure predicted perception of success in online dating, greater degrees of honesty seemed to have a negative effect (Gibbs et al., 2006). Paired with the findings of the importance of intentional disclosures, this suggests those using the Internet for relationship initiation are indeed weighing presenting their real versus ideal self in various circumstances.

Relational maintenance is also impacted by one's level of accommodation. The characteristics people create in their online selves end up shifting into their offline lives (McKenna, Green, & Smith, 2001). This can have implications for relationship maintenance, as those who are integrating aspects of their online selves into their offline lives may meet with confusion in their partners, whose behavior may then change in response to the new persona.

Interaction of the Three CFT Framework Components

As mentioned throughout this chapter, the seven ecological elements independently and directly affect the structure and process of couple and family relationships. There is also an interaction between the structural elements (roles, rules, and boundaries) and the process elements (relationship initiation, maintenance, and termination) (see Figure 4.1). As one family renegotiated rules around their teen daughter's use of her cell phone, such a conversation enhanced relationship maintenance through intimacy building just by having the conversation. In this way, the accessibility of friends through cell phones changed the relationship rules in the family (structural), which had implications for the intimacy and connection between the family members (relationship maintenance). In other ways, the new rules around technology in the daughter's life might also have implications for the relationships that she initiates and maintains among her peer group. If there are rules (structure) around the types of sites or the times in which she can use the Internet or cell phone, there may be some impact to the types of disclosures that the daughter might make in these relationships (processes). In couples, as boundaries become blurred with the ambiguity of the Internet, each member of a couple might imply different things about their commitment (relational maintenance) to one another as one partner engages in particular behaviors the other partner finds problematic.

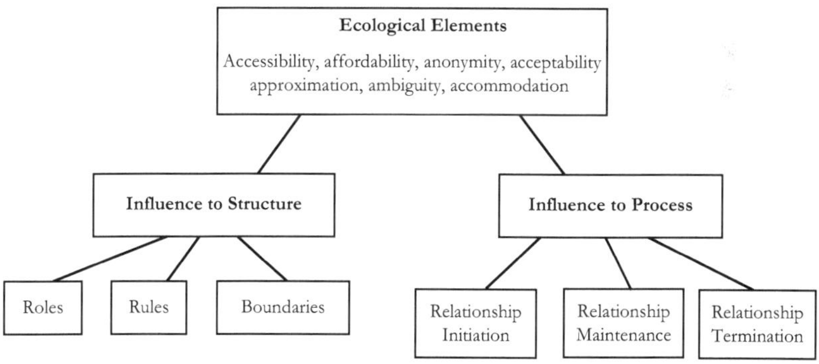

Figure 4.1. CFT Framework.

Application

For Therapists in Clinical Settings

Kara and Chris came to treatment to improve how Kara could come to express herself more honestly to Chris. Kara complained Chris was rarely able to hear any feedback about the relationship because Chris would initiate a problem (e.g. threats of self-harm, reports of health problems that would turn out to be medically undetectable, etc.) as a way of derailing Kara from discussing her concerns. Kara refused to acknowledge Chris' manipulation. The couple had been together for 1 year and both had experienced infidelity at different stages in their relationship. Kara noted she cheated on Chris recently, though this relationship had occurred primarily via text messaging and email exchanges. Chris did not admit cheating on Kara, something Kara did not believe, noting Chris hid some behaviors from Kara for "no reason": deleting text messages, keeping the phone nearby, and making the third party's messages be silent when they came in. Both partners acknowledged if their relationship were going to survive, they would both need to make changes in terms of safety with one another, specifically to their ability to be honest about the problems in their relationship.

In this case, understanding the couple's vulnerabilities begins with assessment of the ecological elements operating in the relationship. For both partners, their phones provided accessibility to other partners. Furthermore, when the couple would use their phones to discuss issues between the two of them, Kara hid behind anonymity—not directly communicating what her feelings were and instead texting her partner that things were fine, keeping her true emotions anonymous. Because each partner maintained separate phone accounts, their relationships with the other people were affordable and not easily discovered by the other. Once Kara admitted to her infidelity, she believed that it made Chris consider an electronically mediated affair as acceptable within their relationship. Approximation manifested in the sense that Kara's relationship with her partner involved sexting, which approximated a sexual relationship that she wanted desperately, but did not have, with Chris. The ambiguity in the couple's relationship revolved around whether Chris was having an affair as well. Chris was secretive regarding the activities shared with the third party but still denied that the activities would be considered infidelity. Kara, however, was not convinced what was happening was not infidelity, since she engaged in those same behaviors while trying to hide her own affair. Therefore, there was no acknowledgment of Kara's sense of betrayal as the couple could not agree on the activities that constituted infidelity. Finally, the only piece of the relationship with the third party that Chris would discuss was that Chris was able to be authentic in the relationship with the third party in ways Chris could not be in the relationship with Kara.

Each of these elements affected the structure and process of their relationship. The accessibility each had to the other's partners created the ambiguity in their rule system and opened their relational boundary around each other to include other people and, in some ways, limit the boundary around the couple themselves. The anonymity of using phones and emails to accommodate real feelings could be used to understand how the barriers to being oneself could be removed and applied instead to developing that type of intimacy in the relationship. Finally, the acceptability of involving other people into the relationship interfered with their ability to maintain the relationship in the way they always have.

Treatment would involve reducing these vulnerabilities and using the ecological elements to increase the overall couple intimacy. For example, accessibility used to develop relationships with other people could be used to increase the couple's connection with one another. This would involve prescribing the couple to initiate texts of self-disclosures until it became natural and self-reinforcing. It would also involve varying degrees of being more revealing and not being anonymous emotionally. This could begin with progressive disclosures—starting with small, safe disclosures building up to larger disclosures about the relationship. Ambiguity can be resolved through agreeing that each member of the couple feels betrayed, without necessarily getting both to agree on the activities until such a time that the cohesion in the relationship is built up enough to develop a new relational contract.

For Use in Multiple Contexts by Family Professionals, Educators, and Researchers

While the field of couple and family technology focuses in part on assessing what parts of technology and new media usage benefit and impair relationships, the CFT framework does not endorse one application over another or prescribe some activities as better than others for relationships. Instead, the framework only asserts that technology and new media influences couples and families in two ways: structure and process. The meaning the couple or family makes of such changes, on the other hand, is specific to each system. For example, there may be times where accessibility creates more positives than negatives. In a case where a couple participates in sexually nonmonogamous relationships, for example, the accessibility to others might support their relationship dynamic whereas in sexually monogamous couples, this may not be the case. Furthermore, there are differences in, for example, the acceptability of sexting between same-sex and heterosexual relationships (Shadid, Hertlein, & Steelman, 2014). Specifically, it is more acceptable to be sexting if one identifies as bisexual or same-sex oriented. Again, this does not mean that it is a problem, but that the couple and family therapist would need to consider that with higher levels of acceptability it might result in higher levels of accessibility, and potentially problematic behavior. In short, the CFT framework functions as a metaframework: It is broad enough to be adapted to couples and families from a wide variety of cultural backgrounds and allows therapists or other practitioners to work within their already identified framework as it serves primarily as a way to organize the potential varied impact in couples and families.

For Couples and Families

Couples and families need to identify the ways in which their personal relationships are organized around technology. One application for couples and families could be the technological genogram (see the Blumer & Hertlein chapter in this volume). This tool helps families clearly identify the roles technology holds within their family. Another application of this framework for couples and families is in identifying ways they can connect positively with one's family using the Internet and social media.

References

Aarsand, P. (2007). Computer and video games in family life: The digital divide as a resource in intergenerational interactions. *Childhood: A Global Journal of Child Research, 14*, 235–256. doi:10.1177/0907568207078330

Acharya, I. P., Acharya, I., & Waghrey, D. (2013). A study on some psychological health effects of cell phone usage. *International Journal of Medical Research and Health Sciences, 2*(3), 388–394.

Bacigalupe, G., & Lambe, S. (2011). Virtualizing intimacy: Information communication technologies and transnational families in therapy. *Family Process, 50*(1), 12–26. doi:10.1111/j.1545–5300.2010.01343.x

Belch, M. A., Krentler, K. A., & Willis-Flurry, L. A. (2005). Teen internet mavens: Influences in family decision making. *Journal of Business Research, 58*(5), 569–575.

Blair, B. L., & Fletcher, A. C. (2011). "The only 13-year-old on planet Earth without a cell phone": Meanings of cell phones in early adolescents' everyday lives. *Journal of Adolescent Research, 26*, 155–177.

Blumer, M. L. C., Hertlein, K. M., Smith, J. M., & Allen, H. (2013). How many bytes does it take? A content analysis of cyber issues in couple and family therapy journals. *Journal of Marital and Family Therapy, 40*, 34–48. doi:10.1111/j.1752–0606.2012.00332.x

Bond, E. (2010). Managing mobile relationships: Children's perceptions of the impact of mobile phones on relationships in their everyday lives. *Childhood, 17*, 514–529.

Bond, E. (2011). The mobile phone = bike shed? Children, sex and mobile phones. *New Media and Society, 13*(4), 587–604.

Chelsey, N. (2005). Blurring boundaries: Linking technology use, spillover, individual distress, and family satisfaction. *Journal of Marriage and the Family, 67*, 1237–1248.

Cho, C., & Cheong, H. J. (2005). Children's exposure to negative Internet content: Effects of family context. *Journal of Broadcasting & Electronic Media, 49*(4), 488–509.

Cooper, A. (2002). *Sex and the Internet: A guidebook for clinicians.* New York: Brunner-Routledge.

Cooper, A., Galbreath, N., & Becker, M. A. (2004). Sex on the Internet: Furthering our understanding of men with online sexual problems. *Psychology of Addictive Behaviors, 18*(3), 223–230. doi:10.1037/0893–164X.18.3.223

Couch, D. L., & Liamputtong, P. (2008). Online dating and mating: The use of the Internet to meet sexual partners. *Qualitative Health Research, 18,* 268–279. doi:10.1177/1049732307312832

Coyne, S. M., Stockdale, L., Busby, D., Iverson, B., & Grant, D. M. (2011). "I luv u:)!": A descriptive study of the media use of individuals in romantic relationships. *Family Relations, 60,* 150–162. doi: 10.1111/j.1741–3729.2010.00639.x

Cravens, J. D., Hertlein, K. M., & Blumer, M. L. C. (2013, March/April). Online mediums: Assessing and treating Internet issues in relationships. *Family Therapy Magazine*, 18–23. Retrieved from https://www.aamft.org/imis15/Documents/MAFTMSinglePages.pdf

Dake, J. A., Price, J. H., Maziarz, L., & Ward, B. (2012). Prevalence and correlates of sexting behavior in adolescents. *American Journal of Sexuality Education*, *7*(1), 1–15.

Daneback, K., Cooper, A., & Månsson, S. (2005). An Internet study of cybersex participants. *Archives of Sexual Behavior, 34*(3), 321–328. doi:10.1007/s10508–005–3120-z

Ferguson, C. J. (2011). Sexting behaviors among young Hispanic women: Incidence and association with other high-risk sexual behaviors. *Psychiatric Quarterly*, *82*(3), 239–243.

Francisco, V. (2013). "The Internet is magic": Technology, intimacy and transnational families. *Critical Sociology, 39*(3), 1–18.

Gibbs, J. L., Ellison, N. B., & Heino, R. D. (2006). Self-presentation in online personals: The role of anticipated future interaction, self-disclosure, and perceived success in online dating. *Communication Research, 33,* 152–177.

Haddon, L. (2013). Mobile media and children. *Mobile Media and Communication, 1*(1), 89–95.

Harris, K., Marett, K., & Harris, R. (2011). Technology-related pressure and work–family conflict: Main effects and an examination of moderating variables. *Journal of Applied Social Psychology, 41*, 2077–2103. doi:10.1111/j.1559–1816.2011.00805.x

Heijstra, T. M., & Rafnsdottir, G. L. (2010). The Internet and academics' workload and work–family balance. *The Internet and Higher Education, 13*(3), 158–163.

Hertlein, K. M. (2012). Digital dwelling: Technology in couple and family relationships. *Family Relations, 61*(3), 374–387.

Hertlein, K. M., & Ancheta, K. (2014). Advantages and disadvantages of technology in relationships: Findings from an open-ended survey. *The Qualitative Report, 19* (article 22), 1–11.

Hertlein, K. M., & Blumer, M. L. C. (2013). *The couple and family technology framework: Intimate relationships in a digital age.* New York: Routledge.

Hertlein, K. M., & Cravens, J. D. (2014). Assessment and treatment issues in Internet sexuality. *Current Sexual Health Reports, 6*(1), 56–63.

Hertlein, K. M., & Desruisseaux, J. (2012). Online intimacy problems. In Z. Yan (Ed.), *The encyclopedia of cyberbehavior* (pp. 885–899). Hershey, PA: IGI Global.

Hertlein, K. M., & Hawkins, B. P. (2012). Online gaming issues in offline couple relationships: A primer for MFTs. *The Qualitative Report, 17*(article 15), 1–48. Retrieved from http://www.nova.edu/ssss/QR/QR17/hertlein.pdf

Hertlein, K. M., & Stevenson, A. J. (2010). The seven "As" contributing to Internet-related intimacy problems: A literature review. *Cyberpsychology: Journal of Psychosocial Research on Cyberspace, 4*(1), article 1. Retrieved from http://www.cyberpsychology.eu/view.php?cisloclanku=2010050202

Hertlein, K. M., & Webster, M. (2008). A systemic research synthesis of the impact of technology on couples and families. *Journal of Marital and Family Therapy. 34*(4), 445–460.

Higgins, E. (1987). Self-discrepancy: A theory relating self and affect. *Psychological Review, 94*(3), 319–340. doi:10.1037/0033–295X.94.3.319

Hundley, H. L., & Shyles, L. (2010). US teenagers' perceptions and awareness of digital technology: A focus group approach. *New Media & Society, 12*(3), 417–433. doi:10.1177/1461444809342558

Hupert, N., Amick, B. C., Fossel, A. H., Coley, C. M., Robertson, M. M., & Katz, J. N. (2004). Upper extremity musculoskeletal symptoms and functional impairment associated with computer use among college students. *Work: Journal of Prevention Assessment & Rehabilitation, 23*(2), 85–93.

Johnson, A. J., Haigh, M. M., Becker, J. A. H., Craig, E. A., & Wigley, S. (2008). College students' use of relational management strategies in email in long-distance and geographically close relationships. *Journal of Computer-Mediated Communication, 13,* 381–404. doi: 10.1111/j.1083–6101.2008.00401.x

Kang, T. (2012). Gendered media, changing intimacy: Internet-mediated transnational communication in the family sphere. *Media, Culture & Society, 34,* 146–161. doi:10.1177/0163443711430755

Kennedy, T. L. M., Smith, A., Wells, A. T., & Wellman, B. (2008). *Networked families.* Retrieved from http://www.pewinternet.org/Reports/2008/Networked-Families.aspx

Lambert-Shute, J., Hertlein, K. M., & Piercy, F. P. (2009). The journal-reading habits of MFTs. *Journal of Family Psychotherapy, 20,* 28–45.

Lee, B. W., & Stapinski, L. A. (2012). Seeking safety on the Internet: Relationship between social anxiety and problematic Internet use. *Journal of Anxiety Disorders, 26,* 197–205.

Lin, J. C. (2010). Cognitive changes in children from frequent cell phone usage. *IEEE Antennas and propogation magazine, 52*(1), 232–234.

Madden, M. Lenhart, A., Cortesi, S., Gasser, U., Duggan, M., Smith, A., & Beaton, M. (2013). Teens, social media, and privacy. Pew Internet and American Life Project. Retrieved from http://www.pewinternet.org/2013/05/21/teens-social-media-and-privacy/

Madianou, M., & Miller, D. (2011). *Migration and new media: Transnational families and polymedia.* New York: Routledge.

Marshall, R., & Reday, P. A. (2007). Internet-enabled youth and power in family decisions. *Young Consumers: Insight and Ideas for Responsible Marketers, 8*(3), 177–183.

McKenna, K. Y. A., & Bargh, J. A. (2000). Plan 9 from cyberspace: The implications of the Internet for personality and social psychology. *Personality and Social Psychology Review, 4*(1), 57–75. doi:10.1207/S15327957PSPR0401_6

McKenna, K. Y., Green, A., & Gleason, M. (2002). Relationship formation on the Internet: What's the big attraction? *Journal of Social Issues, 58,* 9–31. doi:10.1234/12345678

McKenna, K. Y. A., Green, A. S., & Smith, P. K. (2001). Demarginalizing sexual self. *Journal of Sex Research, 38,* 302–311.

Merolla, A. (2012). Connecting here and there: A model of long-distance relationship maintenance. *Personal Relationships, 19*, 775–795.

Mesch, G. S. (2006). Family relations and the Internet: Exploring a family boundaries approach. *Journal of Family Communication, 6*(2), 119–138. doi: 10.1207/s15327698jfc0602_2

Mileham, B. L. (2007). Online infidelity in Internet chat rooms: An ethnographic exploration. *Computers in Human Behavior, 23*(1), 11–31. doi:10.4103/0019–5545.5829

Mitchell, K. J., Finkelhor, D., Jones, L. M., & Wolak, J. (2012). Prevalence and characteristics of youth sexting: A national study. *Pediatrics, 129*(1), 13–20. doi:10.1542/peds. 2011–1730

Pan, G. (2004, March 24) Seventy percent of media consumers use multiple forms of media at the same time, according to a study for the Media Center at API. Retrieved from Media Center at the American Press, www.werzit.com/intel/mirror/ZionismKills/www.americanpressinstitute.org/pages/apinews/api_news_releases/seventy_percent_of_media_consu/index.html

Peskin, M. F., Markham, C. M., Addy, R. C., Shegog, R., Thiel, M., & Tortolero, S. R. (2013). Prevalence and patterns of sexting among ethnic minority urban high school students. *Cyberpsychology, Behavior & Social Networking, 16*(6), 454–459. doi:10.1089/cyber.2012.0452

Prensky, M. (2001). *Digital natives, digital immigrants.* Retrieved from http://www.marcprensky.com/writing/Prensky%20-%20Digital%20Natives,%20Digital%20Immigrants%20-%20Part1.pdf

Prey, J. & Weaver, A. (2007). Tablet PC technology: The next generation. *Computer,* 40(9), 32–33.

Rizzo, S. (2008). The promise of cell phones from people power to technological nanny. *Convergence: The International Journal of Research into New Media Technologies, 14*(2), 135–143. doi:10.1177/1354856507087940

Rosenberg, S. (2013). Cell phones and children: Follow the precautionary road. *Pediatric Nursing, 39*(2), 65–70.

Rosenfeld, M. J., & Thomas, R. J. (2012). Searching for a mate: The role of the Internet as a social intermediary. *American Sociological Review, 77*(4), 523–547.

Ross, M. W. (2005). Typing, doing, and being: Sexuality and the Internet. *Journal of Sex Research, 42*, 342–352. doi:10.1080/00224490509552290

Ross, M. W., & Kauth, M. R. (2002). Men who have sex with men, and the Internet: Emerging clinical issues and their management. In A. Cooper (Ed.), *Sex and the Internet: A guidebook for clinicians* (pp. 47–69). New York: Brunner-Routledge.

Shadid, C., Hertlein, K. M., & Steelman, S. (2014, April). *Acceptability of sexting in same-sex relationships.* Poster, University of Nevada, Las Vegas, Greenspun College of Urban Affairs Annual Graduate Research Symposium. Las Vegas, NV.

Spears, R., & Lea, M. (1994). Panacea or panopticon? The hidden power in computer-mediated communication. *Communication Research, 21*(4), 427–459. doi:10.1177/009365094021004001

Starvinos, D., Byington, K. W., & Schwebel, D. C. (2011). Distracted walking: cell phones increase injury risk for college pedestrians. *Journal of Safety Research, 42*(2), 101–107.

Sternberg, R. J. (1986). A triangular theory of love. *Psychological Review, 93*(2), 119–135. doi: 10.1037/0033–295X.93.2.119

Strassberg, D., McKinnon, R., Sustaíta, M., & Rullo, J. (2013). Sexting by high school students: An exploratory and descriptive study. *Archives of Sexual Behavior, 42*(1), 15–21. doi:10.1007/s10508–012–9969–8

Sudan, M., Khefiets, L., Arah, O. A., & Olsen, J. (2013). Cell phone exposures and hearing loss in children in the Danish National Birth Cohort. *Paediatric and Perinatal Epidemiology, 27,* 247–257.

Teo, T. S., Lim, V. K., & Lai, R. Y. (1999). Intrinsic and extrinsic motivation in Internet usage, *Omega, 27*(1), 25–37.

Tokunaga, R. S. (2010). Following you home from school: A critical review and synthesis of research on cyberbullying victimization. *Computers in Human Behavior, 26,* 277–287.

Whitty, M. T. (2005). The realness of cybercheating: Men's and women's representations of unfaithful Internet relationships. *Social Science Computer Review, 23*(1), 57–67. doi:10.1177/0894439304271536

Wilding, R. (2006). "Virtual" intimacies? Families communicating across transnational contexts. *Global Networks, 6*(2), 125–142. doi:10.1111/j.1471–0374.2006.00137.x

Woodard, E. H., & Gridina, N. (2000). *Media in the home.* Philadelphia, PA: Annenberg Public Policy Center for the University of Pennsylvania.

Yum, Y. O., & Hara, K. (2006). Computer-mediated relationship development: A cross-cultural comparison. *Journal of Computer-Mediated Communication, 11*(1), 133–152.

5

Exploring the Interaction of Media Richness and Family Characteristics in Computer-Mediated Communication

EMILY M. CRAMER
North Central College

EDWARD A. MABRY
University of Wisconsin–Milwaukee

Introduction

In 2008, the Pew Internet and American Life Project published *Networked Families*, a comprehensive report on the use of technology within families in the United States (Kennedy, Smith, Wells, & Wellman, 2008). Using a sample of adults aged 18 and older (N = 2,252), the project concluded, "Technology now permeates American households and has become a central feature of families' day-to-day lives" (p. i). Of married couples with children, 95% of households have cell phones, 93% have computers, and 94% report at least one family member going online. Sixty-six percent of married-with-children households have a broadband connection, and 58% own two or more desktop/laptop computers. Moreover, 65% of households contain a husband, wife, and child who go online.

Families' ever-increasing use and reliance on computers, the Internet, and cell phones are remarkable, especially in light of concerns that technology would pull the family apart (Kennedy et al., 2008). On the contrary, adults surveyed by Pew felt computer-mediated communication (CMC) helped them stay closer to friends and family. These findings support extant research on the influence of information and communication technologies on social relationships (Boase, Horrigan, Wellman, & Rainie, 2006; Wajcman, Bittman, & Brown, 2008). Using data from a 2000 Pew study, Chesley and Fox (2012) found email use to be linked to perceptions of improved social ties and enhanced relationship quality among family members.

Chesley and Fox (2012) emphasize future research should focus on the role technology plays in supporting and sustaining different types of social relationships. Family communication scholars have come to similar conclusions about the need for closer examination of the impact of new technologies on everyday family life (Mesch, 2006; Wartella & Jennings, 2001). Indeed, Pew's *Networked Families* study offers some broad-brushstroke ideas about the growing use of technology in the modern family (Kennedy et al., 2008). But questions about the everyday use of technology within the family remain unanswered: What CMC technologies do family members prefer to use when they communicate with each other? What types of CMC technology may be more conducive for engaging other family members? How is CMC influenced by family characteristics such as size and patterns of communication?

The purpose of this empirical study is to examine how communication within families of different characteristics is constrained or enabled by CMC technologies. Of particular interest is how the messages families send to each other are impacted by the richness of the media channel used to communicate and how family characteristics such as size and communication patterns might affect richness and frequency of communication.

Media Richness and Message Type

Trevino, Daft, and Lengel (1990), in a study of managers' technology choices for communication, characterize communication media channels such as email, phone, and video conferencing as *rich* or *lean* based on "their capacity to facilitate shared meaning" (p. 75). A blend of four criteria predicts a medium's richness: (1) availability of feedback; (2) transmission of multiple cues such as facial expression, gestures, and vocal tone; (3) whether natural language can be used rather than numbers; and (4) the medium's personal focus. Shared meaning, "the basis for interaction among organization members" (Trevino et al., 1990, p. 74), may be amplified when the media offers instant feedback, can transmit many cues, facilitates the use of everyday language, and is focused on personal interaction.

Media richness theory (Trevino et al., 1990) not only describes differences between lean and rich media channels, the theory also purports the content of a message determines whether a rich or lean medium will be utilized. Proponents of the theory distinguish between messages that are *equivocal* (complex, with the potential for multiple interpretations) and *routine* (unambiguous, requiring little feedback). Managers were "more likely to process ambiguous, equivocal communications through rich media, such as face-to-face, while unambiguous communications were more likely to be sent via written or electronic media" (p. 77). When messages can be interpreted in many ways, individuals rely on cues, feedback, and language communicated explicitly through richer media.

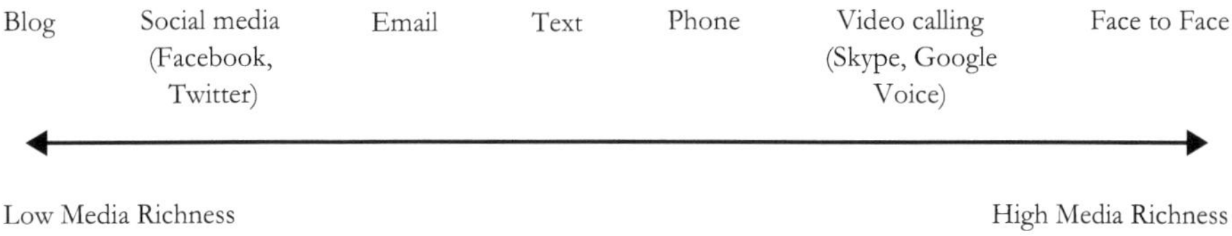

Figure 5.1. Adapted media-richnness hierarchy.

Families can be viewed as micro-organizations whose members also strive to create shared meaning through interaction. Just as organizations are constrained or enabled by determinants influencing the type of media used to communicate, so too are families impacted by factors such as distance (Taylor, Funk, Craighill, & Kennedy, 2006), which may require increased reliance on CMC technology to communicate. Figure 5.1 represents an adapted media-richness hierarchy including the media channels families might use to communicate both equivocal and routine messages. On the leaner end, according to the four criteria outlined by Trevino et al. (1990), blogs and social media are mediums providing: (1) fewer opportunities for immediate feedback; (2) limited transmission of multiple nonverbal cues such as gestures and vocal tone; (3) text-based communication only and; (4) a less-personal tone, in that posts are typically broadcasted en masse instead of sent directly to a unique receiver. On the other hand, face-to-face and video calling are regarded as richer channels, where the user can give and receive instant feedback, transmit multiple nonverbal cues, use natural language, and engage in a personal exchange with the receiver.

We hypothesize family members will use leaner channels (e.g., blogs, social media, email, text messaging) for routine communication such as making plans or recapping the day/week, typically messages that are unambiguous and require little feedback. At the same time, family members will use richer channels (e.g., face-to-face, phone calling, or video chatting) for equivocal messages, such as expressing worry or discussing a family member's health, which can be complex and/or contain the possibility for multiple interpretations.

H1: Message content is influenced by the richness of media families use to communicate: (a) leaner media channels will be used for routine messages while (b) richer media channels will be used for equivocal messages.

Family Size

Studies regarding the effects of family size tend to cluster around Blake's dilution model (1981), which claims a greater number of children in a family will result in increased division of parental resources and thereby impact the "quality" of each child within the family. Blake defines the term *quality* as "some objective measure of human capital such as educational or occupational attainment" (p. 422), rather than the child's intrinsic worth. When compared to only children and/or children from smaller families, children from large families historically attend fewer years of school, have less of a chance of getting through high school, possess decreased verbal ability, and have lower IQ scores (Blake, 1989). Blake's dilution model has been supported in recent studies by Downey (1995, 2001) examining educational performance and intellectual development. Other researchers, however, claim Blake's empirical methods in establishing a causal relationship between family size and intelligence are flawed (Guo & VanWey, 1999; Rodgers, Cleveland, van den Oord, & Rowe, 2000).

Despite some misgivings about its empirical validity, the dilution model may illuminate recent findings in the CMC realm, specifically regarding the size of online support groups. In a meta-analysis of computer-mediated support groups, Rains and Young (2009) hypothesized a larger network size would result in an individual's increased access to resources; as membership in a support group expanded, so too would sources of information and emotional/esteem support. But results indicated the reverse: The researchers were surprised to discover that group size and social support were negatively associated. The following rationale was offered:

> One explanation for this finding is that, as group size increases, so does the potential for individual members to feel isolated. In groups that are too large, individuals may feel a sense of alienation—as if they are lost in a crowd—and have difficulty making connections. (Rains & Young, 2009, p. 328)

Conceivably, the alienation that support-group members feel in large groups may be due to the same reason that members of large families may underperform academically: Resources are diluted. The number of individuals simultaneously seeking parental attention and social support impacts the distribution of these resources. Furthermore, the online support-group study offers a glimpse of how the size of a group (e.g., a family) might help or hinder communication in CMC contexts. Members of large families might experience difficulty making meaningful connections due to the number of individuals with whom they must connect. Some family members may feel "lost in a crowd" of siblings or stepsiblings.

Accordingly, we conjecture the temporal and communicative resources of larger families to be diluted; with more people to contact, family members from large families will spend less time communicating with individual family members.

> H2: Individuals from larger families will communicate less frequently with their parents and siblings across all mediums.

Individuals are becoming increasingly mobile, migrating to new countries and states during their lifetime (Jaffe & Aidman, 1998). Larger, geographically distant families may find it especially challenging to keep in touch with a greater number of family members. Regular phone conversations with parents and siblings, for example, might take up considerably more time than just-checking-in emails or text messages. Factoring in the effects of media richness theory, individuals from larger families, therefore, might be more likely to use leaner media to communicate with family members.

> H3: Family size influences the type of medium used to communicate with both parents and siblings: (a) larger families will use leaner media channels to communicate, while (b) smaller families will use richer media channels to communicate.

Family Communication Patterns

Family communication behavior is "largely the result of cognitive processes that are determined by family relationship schema developed over time and based on direct interaction experiences with family" (Koesten, 2004, p. 227). Ideas about family relationships, in combination with ongoing family interaction, shape how individuals communicate in the context of their family. The construct of family communication patterns emerged in the early 1970s with the work of Stone, Chafee, and colleagues (Stone & Chafee, 1970; Chafee, McLeod, & Wackman, 1970), who contended family communication to be influenced by the emphasis parents place on avoiding social conflict (socio-orientation) and considering all sides of an issue (concept-orientation). Ritchie and Fitzpatrick (1990) used the terms *conformity* and *conversation* instead of *socio* and *concept*, respectively, to distinguish between family orientations toward communication.

> Socio-orientation implies the use of parental power to enforce the child's overt *conformity* to the parent. Concept-orientation means parental encouragement of *conversation* and the open exchange of ideas and feelings. (Ritchie & Fitzpatrick, 1990, p. 523, emphasis added)

Family norms regarding the use of controlling (conformity) and supportive (conversation) messages have long been examined as part of family social science literature and have been found to have crucial impacts on the socialization of children (Ritchie & Fitzpatrick, 1990; Rollins & Thomas, 1979). However, limited research exists on the influence of family communication patterns, specifically conversation and conformity orientations, on the frequency and type of CMC technology used to interact with members.

Our predictions surround the interaction between family communication patterns and use of CMC technology. We surmise families with a high-conversation orientation will more likely to use richer media to communicate, because immediacy of feedback and use of multiple cues might be more valued among families who privilege open communication. Conversely, high-conformity families will communicate using leaner media enabling messages to be more controlled.

> H4: Families with a higher conversation orientation will communicate more frequently using richer media channels, such as face-to-face, video calling, and cell phone.
>
> H5: Families with a higher conformity orientation will communicate more frequently using leaner media channels, such as email, social media, and texting.

Methods

Participants

A 30-item survey was distributed via email to students enrolled in communication courses at an urban public university in the Midwest. Participants completing the survey were given extra credit in the course. A total of 214 ($N = 214$) participants completed the survey, and consent for participation was obtained through the survey instrument. Of the survey participants, 62% were female. The average age of participants was 21.2 ($M = 21.2$, $SD = 3.98$), with ages ranging from 18 to 56. The ethnicity of the sample was Caucasian/White (76%), African American (16%), Asian (7%), Hispanic (2%), American Indian/Alaska Native (1%), and "other" (6%).

Most participants in the sample (99%) reported having at least one surviving parent and a majority of participants had one or more siblings (91%). Family size was operationalized as the *number of children in the participants' family of origin*, since a common point of reference in research on family size is the number of offspring in a family (Blake, 1981, prefers the term *sibsize*). The sample reflected a balance of students from small-sized families (37%), comprised of one or two children; medium-sized families, consisting of three children (30%); and large families containing four or more children (33%). Families with three children represented the midpoint of the data (Md = 3.0); as a result, the categories of small, medium, and large were centered around the midpoint.

Not surprisingly, a majority of participants (99%) used a cell phone, with 94% using a cell phone daily and 99% reporting Internet access at home. Overwhelmingly, participants' parents used a cell phone (96%), but slightly less frequently than their children (87% used a cell phone daily; 8% used a cell phone 2–3 times a week). Siblings also had cell phones (94%) and used them daily (90%). Most parents (94%) had Internet access at home, along with a majority of siblings (97%).

Measures

Media richness. Media richness was measured using an adaptation of Trevino et al.'s richness scale (1990), incorporating newer technologies (e.g., video calling, social media, text messaging, and blogs) into the media richness hierarchy. Participants indicated on a five-item Likert scale how frequently they communicated with parents and siblings using: face-to-face, video calling (Skype or Google Voice), phone calling, text messaging, email, social media (e.g., Twitter and Facebook), and blogs. Descriptions of Likert-scale levels were included (e.g., "always" was defined as at least once a day; "frequently," at least once a week; "occasionally," at least once a month; "rarely," at least once every 6 months; "never," no communication using the particular technology). Participants then selected the medium preferred for communication with parents and siblings in *general*; when talking about *routine* topics, such as making plans or recapping the day or week; and when talking about *nonroutine* (i.e., equivocal) topics, such as expressing worry or discussing a family member's health.

Participants reported communicating *in general* with their parents face to face (41%) and over the telephone (40%), although participants also reported texting with their parents (14%). Besides talking with siblings face to face (35%), participants communicated *in general* with siblings using text messaging (34%), telephone (22%), and social media (7%). For *routine messages*, a majority of participants chose to talk with parents over the phone (52%) and siblings over text (34%). *Equivocal messages*, such as discussing worries or health concerns, primarily warranted face-to-face conversations with both parents (53%) and siblings (46%). Interestingly, 19% of respondents indicated they would discuss nonroutine messages with siblings over text, while only 2% of respondents would choose to text their parents with nonroutine messages.

Family communication patterns. The 26-item Revised Family Communication Scale (Ritchie and Fitzpatrick, 1990) measured family conversation orientation (e.g., "I really enjoy talking to my parents even when we disagree," "My family and I often have long, relaxed conversations about nothing in particular") and conformity orientation (e.g., "In our home, my parents usually have the last word," "When anything really important is involved, my parents expect me to obey without question"). The 15 items (α =.94) measuring conversation orientation and 11 items (α =.88) measuring conformity orientation were summed to create an average score for each orientation variable.

Results

Media Richness and Message Type

Hypothesis one conjectured message type to be influenced by the richness of media channels families use to communicate, in that (a) leaner media channels will be used for routine messages, while (b) richer media channels will be used for equivocal messages. Pearson correlations were conducted to examine the strength of the relationships between the type of message (general, routine, and equivocal) and the technology used to communicate. Significant positive correlations were found across all message types (see Table 5.1), indicating richer communication channels are more likely to be used regardless of whether messages were routine or equivocal. Therefore, H1 was not supported.

Table 5.1. Correlations between Message Type and Media Richness.

COMMUNICATION TO		PARENTS			SIBLINGS		
		General	Routine	Equivocal	General	Routine	Equivocal
General	Pearson Correlation	1	.534**	.474**	1	.650**	.542**
	N	210	208	210	195	195	195
Routine	Pearson Correlation	.534**	1	.494**	.650**	1	.675**
	N	208	208	208	195	196	196
Equivocal	Pearson Correlation	.474**	.494**	1	.542**	.675**	1
	N	210	208	210	195	196	196

** Correlation is significant at the 0.01 level (2-tailed).

Hypothesis two proposed individuals from larger families would communicate less frequently with parents and siblings across all mediums. To address H2, frequency scales for all mediums (face-to-face, Skype/Google Talk, phone calling, email, text messaging, social media, and blog) were combined into two variables representing (a) total communication frequency with parents and (b) total communication frequency with siblings. Weak but significant correlations were detected between the size of family and total communication with parents, $r(179) = -.182$, $p < .05$, and siblings, $r(176) = .162$, $p < .05$. The correlation was in a negative direction for total communication with parents, in that communication frequency decreased as the family size increased. Conversely, communication frequency increased among siblings as the family size increased.

To test for the interaction of family size on the specific type of technology used to communicate with parents and siblings, one-way ANOVAs were conducted to compare the frequency of each communication medium used to talk with parents and siblings (e.g., face-to-face, Skype/Google Talk, email, etc.) with three levels of family size (small, medium, large). Results were only significant for three mediums used in communicating with parents: over the phone, $F(2, 182) = 5.82$, $p < .01$; text, $F(2, 183) = 5.98$, $p < .01$; and email, $F(2, 183) = 3.26$, $p < .05$. Results were in the direction predicted: According to the results of post-hoc Scheffe comparisons, participants from larger families communicated less frequently with parents using these mediums (phone, text, and email). Significant relationships were not detected between family size and frequency of communication with siblings across communication mediums.

Table 5.2. Correlations between Family Size, Message Type, and Media Richness.

COMMUNICATON TO		PARENTS	SIBLINGS
General	Pearson Correlation	-0.023	.164*
	N	186	179
Routine	Pearson Correlation	0.016	0.09
	N	185	180
Equivocal	Pearson Correlation	-0.026	0.078
	N	186	180

* Correlation is significant at the 0.05 level (2-tailed).

Hypothesis three contended family size to impact the type of technology used to communicate with both parents and siblings, with (a) larger families using leaner media channels to communicate and (b) smaller families using richer media channels to communicate. To test H3, Pearson correlations were conducted to examine the strength of the relationship between family size and the types of technology used to communicate general, routine, and equivocal messages. A significant, positive correlation was detected only between family size and *general* communication with siblings, $r(177) = .164$, $p < .05$ (see Table 5.2). Interestingly, an evident but nonsignificant trend in the data suggested that as family size increased, individuals were more likely to use richer media to communicate with siblings overall.

Family Communication Patterns

Hypothesis four predicted families with a higher conversation orientation would communicate more frequently using richer media. For frequency of communication with parents, significant positive correlations were found between conversation orientation and every medium except blogging (see Table 5.3). In other words, families with a higher conversation orientation were more likely to communicate frequently across all mediums: face-to-face or using video calling, telephone, text, email, and social media. Similar significant positive relationships were observed between the frequency of communication with siblings and conversation orientation, as siblings from higher conversation orientation families communicated more frequently across all mediums except blogging. In all, a family's orientation toward conversation was related to the amount of communication occurring between family members regardless of medium (except blogging). Because the pattern of relationships between a conversational family communication style and media richness were similar for both parents and siblings, Hypothesis four could not be supported as stated because respondents did not appear to report clearly different media richness preferences (except for blogging) in their family communication.

Hypothesis five posited families with higher conformity orientations would communicate more frequently using leaner mediums, such as email and social media. H5 results were mixed: Respondents' frequency of communication with parents resulted in modest but significant negative correlations between conformity orientation and telephone, text messaging, and a nearly significant correlation for email; only a significant negative relationship was detected between siblings who communicated face to face. Participants from families with high levels of conformity communicated less frequently with parents over the telephone and Internet. Therefore, Hypothesis five was partially supported in that high-conformity families tended to communicate less frequently in face-to-face (i.e., richer) contexts.

Table 5.3. Correlations among Family Communication Patterns and Frequency of Technology Used to Communicate with Parents and Siblings.

		PARENTS		SIBLINGS	
		Conversation	Conformity	Conversation	Conformity
Face-to-face	Pearson Correlation	.211**	-.116	.230**	-.153*
	N	200	207	189	196
Video calling	Pearson Correlation	.192**	-.072	.214**	-.097
	N	202	209	189	196
Telephone	Pearson Correlation	.434**	-.269**	.144*	-.099
	N	202	208	189	195
Text messaging	Pearson Correlation	.318**	-.207**	.168*	-.091
	N	202	209	188	195
Email	Pearson Correlation	.330**	-.129	.148*	-.098
	N	202	209	189	196
Social media	Pearson Correlation	.216**	-.094	.167*	-.054
	N	202	208	189	196
Blog	Pearson Correlation	.017	.095	.017	.058
	N	201	208	188	195

**Correlation is significant at the 0.01 level (2-tailed). *Correlation is significant at the 0.05 level (2-tailed).

Discussion

This project represents a first step in understanding how family characteristics impact the frequency and richness of media families use to communicate. We found richer communication media were used among families regardless of whether messages were routine or equivocal. When sending both unambiguous *and* complex messages, families chose media channels allowing for more feedback, multiple cues, natural language, and personal focus (Trevino et al., 1990). This finding gives us some insight into how relational context (family, workplace, friendship, etc.) might impact the predictability of media richness theory. Perhaps family members select richer channels regardless of message type because the immediacy of a medium trumps its efficiency. Along these lines, drawing from interaction goals theory (Canary & Cody, 1993), Sheer and Chen (2004) contend media richness theory must be expanded to consider a broad range of goals beyond instrumental: Relational and self-presentation goals also play an important role in the media choices one makes. In other words, the day-to-day tasks of family life contain relational and self-presentational subnotes. For example, giving Mom a call to discuss dinner plans not only fulfills the caller's instrumental goal of putting a date on the calendar, the phone call also fulfills a relational goal of staying close by "hearing her voice" and a self-presentational goal of showing affection. Conversely, an email might also help the sender meet instrumental and self-presentational goals but, because the medium is less personal, might not fulfill the sender's relational goals of enhancing the relationship with Mom.

Results of the study also indicate family size to affect communication, although not always in predictable ways. For parental interaction, Blake's (1981) dilution model holds true: the greater number of children, the less frequent communication with parents overall. Parental communicative resources are further divided among large families, meaning parents have less time to talk with each child. Whereas a child with no siblings may get to communicate with Dad for an hour, a child with three siblings may only get 15 minutes. As the "group" size increases, therefore, the tendency for an individual member to be isolated from regular communication also increases (Rains & Young, 2009).

On the contrary, however, siblings from larger families communicate *more* frequently with each other across all mediums. The pattern might be explained using one of three rationales. First, more siblings simply means more individuals with whom to communicate. Second, because the communicative resources of parents in large families are diluted, siblings might rely on each other more to communicate. In a large family, a big brother or sister might take on some parental responsibilities for younger siblings, which leads to more frequent communication. Third, advanced CMC technologies enable more effective communication with a greater number of people, especially those of a younger age group. The mean age of the sample was 21, with a narrow standard deviation (SD = 4). The 18–24 demographic leads the way in use of mobile data applications (Smith, 2010), especially text messaging (Smith, 2011). Nine out of 10 young adults report owning a cell phone and young adults tend to use more mobile data applications, including non-voice applications (Smith, 2010). Adults in the 18–24 demographic send or receive about 40 text messages a day, while the average adult 18-plus sends or receives about 10 messages (Smith, 2011). The inclination of the younger demographic to use cell phone for voice calling, text messaging, checking email, and accessing social media sites therefore might transcend family size. Because young adults are communicating faster and more frequently using technology, the challenges associated with communicating within a large family decrease. Further study with a sample that represents an older age group is required to test the strength of family size impacting frequency of communication with different CMC technologies.

Results did not convey a significant relationship between family size and the type of messages—routine or equivocal—sent among members, which also may be due to complex interaction goals (Canary & Cody, 1993) family members may possess when sending messages to each other. Regardless of whether a family has one or 10 children, parents still prefer a phone call to a text message; accordingly, if a child wants to make Mom happy (relational goal) and show concern and care (self-presentational goal), the child will choose to make a phone call.

We also speculated families with a high conversation orientation would be more likely to use richer media to communicate, while high-conformity families would communicate using leaner media. Overall, results of the study support the following conclusions: (a) conversation orientation transcends media richness—members of families characterized by a conversational orientation are more likely to communicate with each other using various communication channels across the richness spectrum; (b) this pattern also appears to hold true for conformity-oriented families. Conformity-oriented families communicated with each other less frequently across the richness channel spectrum but were also characterized by a pattern of significant disaffinity for using individually targeted message channels like the telephone, text messaging, or face-to-face interaction.

Therefore, while neither communication-pattern hypothesis obtained clear confirmation, the cumulative implications of the results support the logical efficacy of the family communication patterns construct (Chafee, McLeod, & Wackman, 1970; Ritchie & Fitzpatrick, 1990; Stone & Chafee, 1970). Members of families characterized by greater interpersonal openness—conversational orientation—appear more likely to both communicate more often and use richer communication channels for their communication. Conversely, members of more interpersonally constrained, conformity-oriented families appeared to communicate less and were more likely to eschew more personal, and richer, communication channels.

Furthermore, we observed conversation orientation to be a stronger predictor of communication frequency than conformity orientation in CMC realms. Consistent, significant positive correlations were found between frequency of communication using all mediums and families valuing the open exchange of ideas. On the other hand, families that placed a premium on parental power demonstrated inconsistent communication behavior; whereas one would expect consistent, negative correlations across all mediums, significant inverse relationships were only found among phone, text, and email for communication with parents and face to face for communication with siblings. In all, conformity-oriented families do communicate less frequently, but not reliably so.

The imbalance between the strength of the conformity and conversation variable makes sense, however, given past empirical findings related to the underlying theory (Ritchie & Fitzpatrick, 1990). Studies have demonstrated the " perception of openness in the communication between parent and child…is more likely to predict harmony and lack of tension than is the perception of parental dominance" (Ritchie & Fitzpatrick, 1990, p. 525). In the same way, a family's conversation orientation predicts its level of communication, as interaction is inherent to being conversational. On the other hand, conformity orientation, or the desire to avoid conflict among members, does not necessarily imply that communication is reduced. It is easier to observe the impact of what a family tries to do (converse openly) than what it tries not to do (avoid conflict).

Limitations

We have identified several limitations of this exploratory study in order to guide more systematic research. First, although the adapted media-richness scale was a central construct to the study, the construct represents the researchers' own interpretation of how CMC technologies should be "scaled," so to speak, in terms of richness. Other scholars might have different interpretations of which media can or should be characterized as rich or lean. Texting, for example, was placed at the midpoint of the richness spectrum. Some might disagree that text messages represent a CMC technology that is both rich and lean. At the same time, evidence from this study shows texting to be used regularly by individuals to communicate with siblings and to send both routine *and* equivocal messages to siblings. Future research should examine whether, indeed, texting is a richer medium than we think, especially among younger generations.

Conversely, video calling may hold a tenuous position on the richness scale, largely due to lack of use. Of the survey respondents, 81% reported never or rarely using video calling to talk with parents and 75% never or rarely used video calling to connect with siblings. Moreover, video calling was hardly ever the preferred medium to communicate with parents (1%) and siblings (2%). At first glance, video calling seems to fulfill the four criteria for a rich medium: By using the technology's video and audio capabilities, feedback can be ascertained in (near) real time, multiple cues can be transmitted, natural conversation can occur, and it enables personal interaction (Trevino et al., 1990). However, despite its purported richness, video calling has yet to be integrated into family communication patterns. Perhaps some of its characteristics, such as requiring a webcam, sound speakers, and a downloaded application that may or may not be free, preclude family members from using video calling more regularly to communicate. Or, it may be that other technologies, such as phone and text messaging, are used on-the-go while video calling often requires an individual to be stationary at a computer (new applications, however, such as Apple's FaceTime do allow users to engage in video calling using a smartphone). Future study should further examine the usage of and barriers to video calling technology within families.

Finally, we must draw attention to the limitations of MRT in understanding media choices among families. Critics of MRT have observed the strength of the theory to wane in light of advances in CMC (Dennis & Kinney, 1998) and argued MRT does not account for "multidimensional relational messages" (Walther, 1992, p. 52). In particular, Walther (1992) points out that individuals motivated to engage in relationships will adapt communication to glean richer relational messages from media primarily offering only textual cues. Future research should continue to consider the value of MRT in exploring media choices. Perhaps theories of media synchronicity (Dennis, Valacich, Speer, & Morris, 1998), interaction goals (Sheer & Chen, 2004), or hyperpersonal interaction (Walther, 1996) can better help us understand why families choose certain technologies to communicate.

Application

In reviewing the results of the current investigation, two statements emerge summarizing the applications of our work for family communication, particularly families distanced by geography.

Size matters. Families with more members communicate less frequently with parents across all mediums. To stay in touch with Mom and Dad, large families might consider establishing a system of CMC interaction maximizing the number of participants. Depending on the richness of the medium family members' prefer, several new platforms can host conversations among many people. For example, Google Hangouts (Google+, n.d.) is a free service where multiple users can engage in a real-time, simultaneous video chat. Voxer (n.d.) is an app functioning as a walkie-talkie, where many users can broadcast and receive voicemail messages in a live format. GroupMe (2014) is group-texting app available on all iOS, Android, and Windows Phone devices.

Given the important communicative role of siblings in large families, perhaps a tech-savvy brother or sister might take the leadership role in putting such a system of communication in place. Parents might be likely to learn how to use a CMC platform to connect with their children especially because children often act as brokers connecting parents to new technologies (Katz, 2010). Recent research supports "bottom up" transmission of learning about information technologies from youth to parent (Correa, 2014). Simply put, knowing their children are "plugged in" and talking to each other encourages parents to "plug in" themselves.

Openness conquers all. Parents who encourage the open exchange of ideas and feelings among family members (Ritchie & Fitzpatrick, 1990) tend to communicate with children more frequently across all CMC mediums and also have children who talk more frequently with each other. Conversely, parents who try to control their children's behavior or to minimize conflict within the family end up establishing—either consciously or inadvertently—barriers to communication among family members. Because communication practices are heavily regulated, family members simply choose to talk less frequently.

Parents who desire frequent contact with children and those who want their children to connect with each other, then, should strive to establish a family environment where conversation is valued and judgment-free. An atmosphere of open and meaningful exchange helps family members perceive each other as important sources of trust, insight, and honesty. The wish to talk more to people whose ideas and advice one values seems like a natural outcome of conversation-oriented family communication patterns.

References

Blake, J. (1981). Family size and the quality of children. *Demography, 18*(4), 421–442. doi:10.2307/2060941

Blake, J. (1989). *Family size and achievement.* Berkeley: University of California Press.

Boase, J., Horrigan, J. B., Wellman, B., & Rainie, L. (2006). The strength of Internet ties. *Pew Internet & American Life Project.* Retrieved from http://www.pewinternet.org/

Canary, D. J., & Cody, M. J. (1993). *Interpersonal communication: A goals-based approach.* New York: St. Martin's.

Chafee, S. H., McLeod, J. M., & Wackman, D. B. (1970). Family communication patterns and adolescent political participation. In J. Dennis (Ed.), *Explorations of political socialization* (pp. 349–364). New York: John Wiley.

Chesley, N. & Fox, B. (2012). Email's use and its perceived effect on family relationship quality: Variations by gender and race/ethnicity. *Sociological Focus, 45*(1), 63–84. doi:10.1080/00380237.2012.630906

Correa, T. (2014). Bottom-up technology transmission within families: Exploring how youths influence their parents' digital media use with dyadic data. *Journal of Communication, 64*(1), 103–124. doi:10.1111/jcomm.12067

Dennis, A. R., & Kinney, S. T. (1998). Testing media richness theory in the new media: The effects of cues, feedback, and task equivocality. *Information Systems Research, 9*(3), 256–274. doi:10.1287/isre.9.3.256

Dennis, A. R., Valacich, J. S., Speer, C., & Morris, M. G. (1998). Beyond media richness: An empirical test of media synchronicity theory. *Annual Hawaii International Conference on System Sciences (HICSS) (1060–3425), 1*, 48–58. http://www.hicss.hawaii.edu/

Downey, D. B. (1995). When bigger is not better: Family size, parental resources, and children's educational attainment. *American Sociological Review, 60*(5), 746–761. doi:10.2307/2096320

Downey, D. B. (2001). Number of siblings and intellectual development: The resource dilution explanation. *American Psychologist, 56*(6–7), 497–504. doi:10.1037/0003–066X.56.6–7.497

Google+. (n.d.). Google+ features: Hangouts. Retrieved from http://www.google.com/+/learnmore/hangouts/.

GroupMe. (2014). Home page. Retrieved from https://groupme.com/.

Guo, G., & VanWey, L. K. (1999). Sibship size and intellectual development: Is the relationship causal? *American Sociological Review, 64*(2), 169–187. doi:10.2307/2657524

Jaffe, J. M., & Aidman, A. (1998). Families, geographical separation, and the Internet: A theoretical prospectus. In A. S. Robertson (Ed.), *Proceedings of the families, technology, and education conference October 30–November 1, 1997* (pp. 177–187). Champaign, IL: ERIC Clearinghouse System.

Katz, V. S. (2010). How children of immigrants use media to connect their families with the community. *Journal of Children and Media, 4*(3), 298–315. doi:10.1080/17482798.2010.486136

Kennedy, T. L. M., Smith, A., Wells, A. T., Wellman, B. (2008). *Networked families*. Washington, DC: Pew Internet and American Life Project. doi:10.1111/j.1460–2466.2000.tb02863.x

Koesten, J. (2004). Family communication patterns, sex of subject, and communication competence. *Communication Monographs, 71*(2), 224–244. doi:10.1080/0363775052000343417

Mesch, G. S. (2006). Family relations and the Internet: Exploring a family boundaries approach. *Journal of Family Communication, 6*(2), 119–138. doi:10.1207/s15327698jfc0602_2

Rains, S. A. & Young, V. (2009). A meta-analysis of research on formal computer-mediated support groups: Examining group characteristics and health outcomes. *Human Communication Research, 35*, 309–336. doi:10.1111/j.1468–2958.2009.01353.x

Ritchie, L. D. & Fitzpatrick, M. A. (1990). Family communication patterns: Measuring intrapersonal perceptions of interpersonal relationships. *Communication Research, 17*, 523–544. doi:10.1177/009365090017004007

Rodgers, J. L., Cleveland, H. H., van den Oord, E., Rowe, D. C. (2000). Resolving the debate over birth order, family size, and intelligence. *American Psychologist, 55*(6), 599–612. doi:10.1037/0003–066X.55.6.599

Rollins, B. C., & Thomas, D. L. (1979). Parental support, power, and control techniques in the socialization of children. In W. R. Burr, R. Hill, F. I. Nye, & I. L. Reiss (Eds.), *Contemporary theories about the family* (Vol. 1, pp. 317–364). New York: Free Press.

Sheer, V. C., & Chen, L. (2004). Improving media richness theory: A study of interaction goals, message valence, and task complexity in manager–subordinate communication. *Management Communication Quarterly, 18*(1), 76–93. doi:10.1177/0893318904265803

Smith, A. (2010). *Mobile access 2010.* Washington, DC: Pew Internet & American Life Project. Retrieved from http://www.pewinternet.org/

Smith, A. (2011). *Americans and text messaging.* Washington, DC: Pew Internet & American Life Project. Retrieved from http://www.pewinternet.org/.

Stone, V. A., & Chafee, S. H. (1970). Family communication patterns and source-message orientation. *Journalism Quarterly, 47*, 239–246. doi:10.1177/107769907004700203

Taylor, P., Funk, C., Craighill, P., Kennedy, C. (2006). As family forms change, bonds remain strong: Families drawn together by communication revolution. *Pew Research Center: Social Trends Report.* Retrieved from http://www.pewinternet.org/

Trevino, L. K., Daft, R. L., Lengel, R. H. (1990). Understanding managers' media choices: A symbolic interactionist perspective. In J. Fulk and C. W. Steinfield (Eds.) *Organizations and communication technology* (pp. 71–94). Thousand Oaks, CA: Sage Publications, Inc.

Voxer. (n.d.). Home page. Retrieved from https://voxer.com/.

Wajcman, J., Bittman, M., Brown, J. E. (2008). Families without borders: Mobile phones, connectedness, and work–home divisions. *Sociology, 42*, 635–652. doi:10.1177/003803850809162

Walther, J. B. (1992). Interpersonal effects in computer-mediated interaction: A relational perspective. *Communication Research, 19*(1), 52–90. doi:10.1177/009365092019001003

Walther, J. B. (1996). Computer-mediated communication: Impersonal, interpersonal, and hyperpersonal interaction. *Communication Research, 23*(1), 3–43. doi:10.1177/009365096023001001

Wartella, E., & Jennings, N. (2001). New members of the family: The digital revolution in the home. *Journal of Family Communication, 1*(1), 59–69. doi:10.1207/s15327698jfc0602_2

6 Facebook Family Rituals

An Investigation

CAROL J. BRUESS
University of St. Thomas, Minnesota

XIAOHUI (SOPHIE) LI
Northern Illinois University

TAMARA J. POLINGO
University of Chicago

Introduction

More than 50 years of research on family communication points to one conclusion: Type and quality of family communication is the best predictor of family satisfaction and family functioning. Research on family ritual—such as the family dinner, the daily "check in" email, and the large holiday tradition—suggests that large and small routines contribute to family strength, the creation and maintenance of family identity, and a number of other positive family outcomes. As both immediate and extended families begin using Facebook as a medium to regularly share information, engage in mundane or everyday talk, play games, touch base, keep up to date, and plan family gatherings, it is timely to understand the nature and function of Facebook as a common and potentially powerful twenty-first-century family ritual. The study reported in this chapter is an exploration of the way Facebook is functioning as an emerging forum for family communication. Specifically, we examine how Facebook interaction functions as a relationship ritual and what effect Facebook communication has on family relationships, with special attention to perceptions of family well-being and cohesiveness.

Family Communication and Facebook

Most families in the United States are "wired families" (Meszaros, 2004). The onslaught of new communication technologies has naturally resulted in them becoming part of the contemporary family landscape, and, as such, scholars are making urgent calls for family researchers to advance understanding of how technology is impacting, changing and/or altering family life and relationships (Lenhart, Madden, & Hitlin, 2005; Mesch, 2006; Meszaros, 2004; Papadakis, 2003). One of the most current and widespread new technologies used by family members of all ages is Facebook. As of 2014, Facebook ranks among the most used social networking sites in the world, with more than 1.3 billion monthly active users who spend an average number of 640 million minutes on the site each month (Facebook.com, 2014). While there is a dearth of academic investigations on how family communication and relationships are affected by Facebook, popular press reports suggest families using Facebook as their "No. 1 way to communicate" (Sutter, 2009, p. 1). Evidence of the way Facebook is spreading rapidly into families is the fact that its use has been growing most rapidly among women 55 years and older (Sutter, 2009), the primary kinkeepers in most families (Leach & Braithwaite, 1996; Lye, 1996; Monserud, 2008). Casper (2010) explicitly studied kinkeeping tasks via Facebook and found the majority of participants reported actually joining Facebook specifically to keep in touch with family members, and overall relationships were enriched as a result of the Facebook kinkeeping.

Facebook's attractiveness to families is not surprising given evidence of its value for social well-being generally (Bessiére, Kiesler, Kraut, & Boneva, 2008; Valkenburg & Peter, 2007). Urista, Dong, and Day (2009) found people use social networking sites like MySpace and Facebook for their ease and convenience for communicating with family and others in their close social network—and because the sites can fulfill users' social needs "constantly and instantaneously" (p. 217), they gratify multiple personal and interpersonal desires. Online technologies also create virtual connectedness for long-distance or not physically proximate families and members of social networks, substituting for a lack of co-presence (Laurier, 2001; Licoppe, 2004; Licoppe & Smoreda, 2005; Wilding, 2006) and even blurring, at times, the boundaries between absence and presence.

Debatin, Lovejoy, Horn, and Hughes (2009) adopt the theory of ritualized media use to examine the way Facebook is habitually used in individuals' life routines, taking the form of diversion and pastime, and is "subcutaneously built into users' daily life—a routinization" (p. 89). Facebook and other social networking sites "deeply penetrate their users' everyday life and, as pervasive technology, [and] tend to become invisible once they are widely adopted, ubiquitous, and taken for granted" (Debatin et al., 2009, p. 83). Facebooking, in these ways, is a ritual. Adopting Baxter and Braithwaite's (2006) conceptualization of family ritual, one situated in Goffman's (1967) work, provides a framework for exploring Facebook as ritual: "A voluntary, recurring, patterned communication event whose jointly enacted performance by family members pays homage to what they regard as sacred, thereby producing and reproducing a family's identity and its web of social relations" (Goffman, 1967, p. 263). While similar to routines, rituals are rich with symbolic meaning (Viere, 2001). When family members use Facebook for interaction with other family members, they pay homage to familial relationships and symbolize a family's historical connection. As such, and by design, recurring Facebook family interactions are ritual.

Wilding (2006) suggests that communication technologies via the Internet have not actually created a "brave new world" nor a radical new way of conducting family life; rather, new technologies are incorporated in ways that sustain and maintain the familiar, mundane patterns of social and family life. Similarly, we argue Facebook family interactions are best understood as potentially powerful rituals of digital age family interaction and, as such, are rightly investigated within the context of family ritual theory.

Family Ritual Theory

Although rituals have long been observed as central to the maintenance of cultures, societies, organizations, and religious practices (Bewley, 1995; Durkheim, 1965; Gluckman & Gluckman, 1977; Leach, 1966; Malinowski, 1954; Moore & Myerhoff, 1977), their profound place and function in personal relationships has also been well documented (Baxter, 1987; Bruess & Pearson, 1997; Bruess & Pearson, 2002; McCall, 1988). As the foundation of relationships, rituals reflect the core of a relationship; provide opportunities for members to share past, present, and future together (Bruess & Pearson, 1997); and are hallmarks of creating and sustaining relationship cultures (Baxter, 1987; Bossard & Boll, 1950; Bruess & Pearson, 1997; Bruess & Pearson, 2002). They promote the well-being of members and relationships with each other (Denham, 2003; Compañ, Moreno, Ruiz, & Pascual, 2002; Fiese et al., 2002; Markson & Fiese, 2000; Wolin & Bennett, 1984), and, according to a 50-year review of the research (Fiese et al., 2002), rituals are profound teachers of culture and essential in the positive development of individuals and families.

Rituals traditionally have played a central role in creating and recreating family identity (Baxter & Braithwaite, 2006). According to most family scholars, families create and recreate shared realities through rituals of daily interaction and connection (Baxter & Braithwaite, 2002; Bruess & Pearson, 1997, 2002; Jorgenson & Bochner, 2004; Imber-Black, Roberts, & Whiting, 1988; Wolin & Bennett, 1984). Rituals serve a variety of other functions, such as supporting individual and family development (Baxter & Braithwaite, 2006; Fiese et al., 2002); creating bonds between and among generations (Schvaneveldt & Lee, 1983); promoting closeness among family members (Meredith, 1985); teaching family values, shaping attitudes, and perpetuating a paradigm or shared belief systems (Bossard & Boll, 1950; Reiss, 1982); providing members with a sense of belonging (Wolin, Bennett, Noonan, & Teitelbaum, 1980) and a means for maintaining family contact (Meredith, 1985); creating a sense of cohesion (Wolin & Bennett, 1984) and commitment, especially in the early years of marriage (Weigel, 2003). Rituals are related to family strength (Meredith et al., 1989) and in general help maintain, create, and sustain healthy relationships (Bruess & Pearson, 1997, 2002; Fiese et al., 2002; Homer, Freeman, Zabriskie, & Eggett, 2007). Rituals can also protect alcoholic families from the generational recurrence of alcoholism (Wolin et al., 1980) and facilitate the health of members (Compañ, Moreno, Ruiz, & Pascual, 2002; Denham, 2003; Markson & Fiese, 2000). Absence of ritual actually can indicate relationship dissatisfaction (Aylor & Dainton, 2004).

Wolin and Bennett's (1984) family rituals theory suggests three primary forms of ritual: celebrations, traditions, and patterned family interactions. Each shares the properties of transformation, communication, and stabilization (Baxter & Braithwaite, 2006; Wolin and Bennett, 1984). To understand family ritual forms and functions is to advance our understanding of how families succeed and find meaning in their collective lives (Bruess & Pearson, 1997; 2002; Fiese et al., 2002). In fact, to study and understand ritual in family life is to "understand something of the local culture in terms of the specific symbol used, the relationships involved, the feelings and memories evoked" (Jorgenson & Bochner, 2004, p. 518).

New Technologies' Impact on Family Relationships

Researchers have indeed been examining how communication technologies affect everyday life, including studying the relationships between new communication technologies and social capital, community involvement, interpersonal relationships, relationship quality, family communication, and sociability (Hampton & Wellman, 2002; Harwood, 2000; Katz and Rice, 2002; Kavanaugh & Patterson, 2002; Mesch, 2006; Mesch & Levanon, 2003; Nie, Hillygus, & Erbing, 2002). Studying the impact of such technologies on family relationships is urgent. According to Forge and Blackman (2008), new information and communication technologies have the capability of significantly changing the family, specifically, and its daily existence by the year 2030. Already, they suggest, families are evolving and shifting their choices, functioning, definitions, and behaviors because of broad Internet use. For instance, families report the Internet's influence on most aspects of their family life including education, elder care, health care, consumption and acquisition of goods, banking, sharing information with extended family members, Internet telephone use (such as Skype), and career development and training (Forge and Blackman, 2008). Kennedy et al. (2008) report that owning multiple technological gadgets is a "standard feature of family life" (p. 1).

Most scholars agree we don't know much about how technology is affecting families in the twenty-first century; we lack data and coherent theories with a focus on families (Hughes & Hans, 2001; Lenhart, Madden, & Hitlin, 2005; Mesch, 2006; Meszaros, 2004; Papadakis, 2003; Perry & Doherty, 2003). What we do have is mostly about families' access to media, families' use of media, parental regulation, and sibling interactions around media (Jennings & Wartella, 2004; Lanigan, Bold, & Chenoweth, 2009). Jordan (2002), Mesch (2006), and Lanigan et al. (2009) offer some of the only contemporary theoretical work in this area; each study employed a systems theoretical approach to examine the role of technology in, or the impact of technology on, the family. But as Meszaros (2004) notes and others echo (Hughes & Hans, 2001; Lenhart, Madden, & Hitlin, 2005; Mesch, 2006; Perry and Doherty, 2003), we need to know much more about the "life worlds" of families: if, how, why, and when they are impacted as a result of widely used new communication technologies.

Much of the research on communication technologies and family addresses a key question: Are communication technologies "bringing together the family" or "distributing family members" (Christensen, 2009, p. 449)? Is it possible something altogether different is going on? As Ling (2007, 2008) and others suggest, new technologies seem to encourage mundane family interaction and rituals of connection, affirming and strengthening the social bond between members in an ongoing way. Mesch (2006) suggests technology is playing a significant role in "reshaping the meanings of family time" (p. 124).

Technology seems to fill a particular need for "distributed families" (Yarosh, Cuzzort, Mueller, & Abowd, 2009, p. 98), those separated by time and distance, giving parents and children synchronous opportunities for learning, contact, and play (Cao, Sellen, Brush, Kirk, Edge, and Ding, 2010). According to Christensen (2009, p. 433), "connected presence" practices in physically separated families reveal "the emergence of new ways of managing interpersonal relations within the family that would have been inconceivable 10 to 15 years ago" (p. 448). Most notable is the way mediated and ongoing rituals of interaction create the feeling of "presence-at-a-distance" (p. 449). Overall, online technologies appear to create virtual connectedness for long-distance/not physically proximate families and social networks, substituting for a lack of copresence (Laurier, 2001; Licoppe, 2004; Licoppe & Smoreda, 2005; Wilding, 2006), even blurring at times the boundaries between absence and presence.

Approximately 23% of adults say the Internet has greatly improved their relationships and connections with family members (Kennedy et al., 2008). Another 25% of adults believe Internet and cell phone technologies have helped theirs to be a stronger family than their own growing up. Families who reported the most technology use and ownership were more likely to say their family is closer because of the technology than those families with less technology use and ownership (Kennedy et al., 2008).

Family Satisfaction and Mundane/Everyday Talk

The link between communication and family/relationship satisfaction is long and strong (Caughlin & Huston, 2002; Caughlin, 2003; Emmers-Sommer, 2004; Koerner & Fitzpatrick, 2002a; Koerner & Fitzpatrick, 2002b; Schrodt, 2005; Schrodt, Soliz, & Braithwaite, 2008; Schrodt, Braithwaite, Soliz, Tye-Williams, Miller, Normand, & Harrigan, 2007; Sillars, Koerner & Fitzpatrick, 2005). As a perceptual variable, family satisfaction is difficult to assess, and is also challenging to discern because of the complexities of multiple family relationships (Burns & Pearson, 2011). Generally, measures of family satisfaction represent the quality of the relationships within a family (Olson, Larsen, & McCubbin, 1982).

Relationship satisfaction has been studied in relation to everyday talk (Schrodt, Witt, & Messersmith, 2008) and in a variety of family relationship subsystems such as in married couples and parent–child relationships (Caughlin & Huston, 2002; Sillars, Koerner, & Fitzpatrick, 2005) and in stepfamilies (Schrodt, Soliz, & Braithwaite, 2008; Schrodt et al., 2007). Family satisfaction is influenced by daily conversations among family members (Schrodt, Witt, & Messersmith, 2008). Specifically, family expressiveness positively affects satisfaction, while conflict avoidance and satisfaction are inversely related (Schrodt, 2009). Family cohesion is positively related to family time spent in recreational activities (Orthner & Mancini, 1991), which creates clearer boundaries and a stronger family identity (Hofferth & Sandberg, 2001).

Bryant and Bryant (2006) pointed to the heuristically rich area of study in mediated family communication as it is related to family happiness and strength, calling for theory and research on "mediated interactivity" (p. 302), a necessary next step beyond more traditional media–family interactions and family strength studied in the past when noninteractive technologies were prominent (e.g., Butner, 2003). Wilding (2006) and others (Licoppe & Smoreda, 2005) found that the *act* of communicating via the Internet with family and close social ties who are not copresent was as important as the content; email often consisted of mundane commentary, jokes, and/or brief comments about events or weather. As Wilding (2006) suggests, families continued doing "business as usual" (p. 132), simply using new forms of communication technologies to assist them. Some in Wilding's study even described the ability of the Internet and other communication technologies (e.g., cell phones) to connect their families over space and time as a "miracle" (p. 132).

Research Questions

Given that rituals of connection are central to strong relationships (Bruess & Pearson, 1997, 2002) and that relationships satisfaction is tied to rituals of everyday talk, it is worth investigating the connection between family members' mediated family communication using Facebook—a digital age venue for everyday talk—and satisfaction with their family relationships. Research suggesting families create and re-create shared realities through rituals of ongoing interaction would further suggest that by regularly using the Facebook interface with other family members, those members are engaging in ritual. As such, two primary questions guide the current study:

> RQ1: What types of rituals between family members are developed via Facebook?

Given the central role that new technology plays in contemporary families as well as the evidence, according to decades of research, that rituals play roles in multiple aspects of family functioning, the second question guiding this study is:

> RQ2: What functions do Facebook family rituals serve for families?

Finally, given evidence that rituals of connection are related to increases in family closeness and happiness, and communication technologies such as Facebook are creating new tools for relationship maintenance and kinkeeping, the following hypothesis is examined:

> H1: Facebook use with family members will be positively related to family satisfaction.

Method

Participants

After IRB approval, the research questions of this study were addressed by collecting data via an online questionnaire from 359 participants (227 female, 132 male; average age 30; ranging in age from 18 to 80) about Facebook use and general family satisfaction with family members. One hundred fifty three participants reported high school as the highest level of education; 41 reported two-year higher education degrees; 125 reported four-year degrees; 31 reported Masters/Professional Degree; and 4 reported MD/PSYD/PHD. In total, 67% (245) participants were not married; 31.4% (114) were married. Among the 114 married, the years they have been married ranged from 1 to 56. Those not married but in a committed relationship reported being in the relationship from 1 to 300 months. Among respondents, 33.6% participants reported that they were living with a romantic partner and 65.6% were not. Participants reported their ethnicity as White/Caucasian/American (80.4%, n = 292), Hispanic (2%, n = 7), Black (1.7%, n = 6), multiracial (1.1%, n = 4), African American (.9%, n = 3), Asian/Asian American (2%, n = 7), African (1.7%, n = 6), and Middle Eastern/Arab (2%, n = 7), with the remaining participants (n = 1 or n = 2, each) reporting as French Canadian, Mexican American, Hmong, Puerto Rican, Cameroonian American, Filipino American, Taiwanese, Indian/Indian American, Vietnamese/Vietnamese American, and Russian Slavic.

Participants provided detailed, narrative written responses to questions about Facebook use with a variety of family members, as well as responded to Likert-type questions assessing family cohesion and satisfaction. Participants were allowed to define who they would include as "family" as not to exclude or marginalize family forms not recognized by law. A snowball-sampling technique was employed beginning with undergraduate students at three mid- to large-size universities in the upper Midwest enrolled in 100- to 400-level communication courses. Each student was invited to complete the survey if he/she met the single criterion of participation for the targeted population (over 18 years of age) and signed the consent form. Students were then invited to distribute in person or via email at least five surveys to people in their social network of friends and family. All surveys were completed anonymously via a secure online survey tool.

Measures

The questionnaire included 16 open-ended questions addressing family members' use of Facebook with other family members in addition to Olson et al.'s (1982) measure of family satisfaction: Family Adaptability and Cohesion Evaluation Scale (FACES). FACES is commonly used for assessing family cohesion (the level of emotional bonding between members) and adaptability (the family's ability to adapt their structure, roles, and rules in response to situational or developmental needs). FACES has been used successfully to measure and quantify dimensions of family functioning, or family satisfaction, in a variety of clinical and research applications (e.g., Ide, Dingmann, Cuevas, & Meehan, 2010; Mirnics, Vargha, Toth, & Bagdy, 2010; Noller & Shum, 1990; Olson, Larsen, & McCubbin, 1982; Olson & Wilson, 1982; Place, Hulsmeier, Brownrigg, & Soulsby, 2005).

Data Analysis

To answer the research questions, triangulation of data analysis techniques was adopted. Descriptive statistical analyses were used to examine the effects of Facebook use on family relationships. All open-ended, narrative responses were analyzed in the tradition of qualitative/interpretive research (Strauss & Corbin, 1998). Specifically, analytic coding (Lindlof & Taylor, 2002) and grounded theory (Glaser, 1965; Glaser & Strauss, 1967; Strauss & Corbin, 1998) were used to identify Facebook ritual use and types, as well as the functions and effects of Facebook interactions between family members.

Analytic coding involves deriving themes through identifying meanings and categories emergent from participants' responses. Two teams of four coders began the process by independently engaging the conceptual development of ritual processes and outcomes when Facebook is used as a tool of family communication. Over 8 weeks, coders on each team were trained by the principle investigator in analytic coding (Lindlof & Taylor, 2002) and subsequently engaged in a two-stage process of thematic analysis. Teams one and two analyzed data toward answering RQs 1 and 2 respectively. Each team member became familiar with the literature on relationship ritual through work shared by the principle investigator with the goal of "stimulate(ing) theoretical sensitivity to clues of meaning in the data" (Lindlof & Taylor, 2002, p. 214). Stage one involved reading all raw data relevant to each RQ and developing "bins" (Spiggle, 1994) or high-inference categories toward beginning sense-making or development of "fuzzy categories" (Lindlof and Taylor, 2002, p. 214), stage one of the grounded theory approach (Glaser & Strauss, 1967) in which as many categories as possible are coded from the data. In this stage of open coding, each of the eight coders and the principle investigator went line-by-line through 133 pages of data; the process resulted in each coder identifying, naming, and defining a category or bin, for a total of 46 bins across both RQs 1 and 2. In stage two, coding teams with the PI used axial coding (Lindlof & Taylor, 2002) to identify any "new categories or a theme that spans many categories" (p. 220), under the principle of integration. Teams met in multiple sessions and engaged Spiggle's (1994) notion of "dimensionalization" (p. 494), attempting to "tease out the key variations (dimensions)" (Lindlof & Taylor, 2002, p. 222) of Facebook ritual types and effects. At this stage, team one identified 21 dimensionalized categories toward answering RQ1 and team two a total of 15.

A third and final stage of analysis was then conducted to ensure validity and reliability of themes emergent. One member of the original coding team and the principal investigator thoroughly read and examined teams' themes independently, and then in multiple face-to-face meetings used emergent categories and conceptualizations before going back and rereading the original data, looking for any necessary clarifications in logic and "integrating details" to ensure all categories were theoretically saturated (Glaser & Strauss, 1967, p. 110). Ultimately and as a result of stage three analysis, two of the authors of this study worked together to challenge and refine the analysis (Maxwell, 1996). As a result of stage three, 21 categories from team one's analyses were reduced to six types of Facebook family rituals; 15 categories from team two's analyses were reduced to one supra theme with four themes, one of which has two subthemes.

Results

Research Question One

RQ1: What types of family rituals are developed via Facebook? A total of six themes emerged to answer the question of Facebook family ritual types. Overall, the themes reveal that Facebook is indeed a space in which families construct rituals of connection, and that, because of the structure of the Facebook interface, the rituals are more numerous and different than rituals of connection that might occur using other channels of communication. Data reveal Facebook has become an overwhelmingly desirable tool for creating and sustaining communication and rituals of connection among and between many family subsystem groups. Rituals emerging via the Facebook interface take the form of: *Updates*, *Support, Thinking of You*, *Reminiscing, Play/Fun*, and *Monitoring.*

Updates rituals. The *Updates* ritual is defined as repetitive interactions during which family members use one or more Facebook functions with the primary purpose of sharing information and thereby increasing other family members' knowledge of about current lives, activities, thoughts, events, interests, and/or life experiences. Updates rituals pay homage to the relationship between those family members participating. Updates rituals were most commonly performed by sharing photos and videos, using the chat function, making wall posts, and sending private messages. Updates rituals often involve information about important or significant life events such as births, marriages, jobs, and trips/vacations, as well as sharing news items or discussing common interests. A participant's appreciation for pictures shared with geographically distant family members reflects how

Updates rituals increase knowledge of another's life: "My cousin just had a baby and she lives in Texas so I'm not sure when I'll be able to see her next, so it is really cool to be able to see what's going on via Facebook pictures." "Since my brother [25 years old] lives back home, we usually send each other private messages (at least once a week) about our daily activities, school, work…"

Support rituals. Rituals of *Support* include Facebook interactions between family members with the primary goal of supporting, comforting, or complimenting, often through an affirmation, expression, or exchange with the goal of care, concern, or congratulation. Support rituals pay homage to another family member or members' well-being, accomplishments, and/or challenges by providing a venue in which love and affection for a family member can be expressed. Participants reported repeatedly using Facebook for interactions in which one or more of the following is intended: emotional support, inspirational and uplifting advice and/or messages, encouragement, congratulations, or increasing another's sense of security.

Thinking of You rituals. *Thinking of You* rituals are expressions of brief, quick, and/or "random" acknowledgment of another family member. Participants reported Thinking of You rituals most often take the form of posting a message, quote, song lyric, or video on a family member's wall and are distinct from other rituals in their singular purpose: letting another know he/she was being "thought of."

Reminiscing rituals. *Reminiscing* as a Facebook ritual is characterized by exchanges emerging as the result of a connection members make to an event or experience in the past. Photos were commonly used in Reminiscing exchanges, as were stories shared through private conversations or comments, each with the intention of recalling something previously shared. Participants commonly engaged in Reminiscing rituals to share memories of tragedies—such as the death of a loved one—as well as to make light of, remember, and/or acknowledge childhood memories; recall and relive significant family events such as weddings or reunions; and/or to discuss or recollect stories, events, or moments of injury or mishap. The Reminiscing ritual often resulted in reestablishing relationships with family members who are geographically distant or with whom family member(s) have lost touch: "I recently found one of my favorite cousins, Pablo, that I hadn't seen or talked to in over 3 years. Facebook has helped us to connect. He commented on a photo of me and my sister that sparked a chain of comments where all three of us remembered funny things we did in our childhood."

Play/Fun rituals. Facebook rituals of *Play/Fun* include those that entertain or increase enjoyment through exchanges such as making jokes, playing games, sharing in-group humor, and/or using playful private language. Facebook Play/Fun rituals pay homage to good times past, present, and future shared or expected among family members. One participant revealed her family "post[s] funny stories we find over the Internet or YouTube on each others walls." Another reported "Playing scrabble. It gives us a chance to be competitive and brag when you win." In-group humor and inside jokes were common Play/Fun rituals, acts that pay homage to shared history or experiences: "My brother Ryan and I have developed a sort of ritual over time by making fun of each other and our dad over FB.... Neither of us will be friends with my dad even though he keeps trying. It started off as a serious request from my dad and eventually turned into a joke between all of us. To add to the hype, Ryan and I friended my dad's wife [Katie], right away. This made my dad even more exasperated and the situation even funnier."

Monitoring. *Monitoring* rituals are most often nonreciprocal acts by one family member used to observe, check up on, learning about, keep tabs on, and/or monitor another family member or members. The Monitoring ritual was most often accomplished through one or more of the following behaviors: checking status updates, reading wall posts, reading comments, or looking at photos, each with the explicit and articulated intention of finding information. Participants revealed Monitoring was most often motivated by the desire to protect, provide feedback, or intervene if something is perceived unhealthy or inappropriate: "My brother Luke, 16, and has had Facebook for about 2 years now. He doesn't like to share a lot of things with me in person, so I always like to creep on his Facebook wall to obtain some dirt on his life. For example, see what his new girlfriend looks like or what kinds of friends he is hanging out with."

Research Question Two

RQ2: What functions do Facebook family rituals serve for families? Four themes, one with two subthemes, emerged from the data analysis revealing the multiple ways Facebook use between family members functions in the family system. The four themes reveal a single supra theme, or overarching function: Family Facebook rituals *maintain* familial ties through ongoing, desirable, and meaningful communicative interactions.

Theme 1: Increase closeness/strengthen relationships. Facebook interactions with family members overwhelmingly increase feelings of closeness and perceptions of relationship strength. According to participants, Facebook serves as a relationship maintenance tool by bringing family members closer and providing contact and connection often over time, generations, and physical distance: "Facebook definitely 'strengthens' those strong ties, especially with my sister and me. I'd feel silly if I randomly texted her saying 'today I saw the most beautiful sunrise!' which is something that could be my status. But she can 'like' my status and that wouldn't be weird."

Theme 2: Share information/keep each other informed. Facebook rituals facilitate and support maintenance of family relationships by increasing information sharing. Participants report Facebook is a convenient, inexpensive venue for keeping informed of members' lives. Two subthemes of information sharing emerged: (a) information sharing as a *bonus* in the relationship, and (b) information sharing as *essential* for relational maintenance.

Subtheme 2a: Information sharing as a bonus in already strong family relationships. Many participants suggested information sharing via Facebook is a bonus—something that complements already strong familial ties: "It helps me keep up to date on things happening in the extended family. It is more of information providing than relationship building. We use face-to-face contact for that."

Subtheme 2b: Information sharing as essential for maintaining family relationships. In many cases, Facebook was essential for keeping family engaged in and informed of each others' lives over time and space. Respondents reported they might not have much if any interaction with some family members without Facebook as a communication tool: "It gives us more of a connection because other than Facebook we really have no communication with each other."

Theme 3: Have Fun/Play. Facebook ritual interactions were often reported as "fun" and used to facilitate laughter, joking, and playful family interactions. Members spoke of appreciating what Fun/Play rituals via Facebook add to already existing family tie(s): "I don't view Facebook as a relationship with my siblings; I have that without Facebook. We just use it to get a good laugh every once in a while." "[My husband and I]...we use FB more for fun."

Theme 4: Gain knowledge of other family members without obligation of reciprocity. The fourth theme is unique from theme two—share information/keep each other informed—in one distinct way: the lack of desire for *reciprocity* in information sharing. Theme 4 reflects participants' reports that Facebook functions as a means of "watching" or "keeping tabs" on family members from afar, often without their knowledge and without being intrusive: "I rarely see my cousins so it is nice to creep on their profiles once in a while just to see what they are up to."

Hypothesis One: Facebook Use with Family Members Will Be Positively Related to Family Satisfaction

Pearson correlations were conducted to examine Facebook use with individuals' family members and dimensions of their perceived level of family satisfaction, including (1) the relationship between Facebook use and degree of closeness between immediate family members; (2) the relationship between Facebook use and the quality of communication between family members; (3) the relationship between Facebook use and the amount of time spent together as a family; and (4) the relationship between Facebook use and overall family relationship satisfaction. Significant positive correlations (small effect sizes) were found between Facebook use and the quality of communication between family members (r =.113, p =.03), between Facebook use and the amount of time spent together as a family (r =.114, p =.03), and between Facebook using and overall family relationship satisfaction (r =.108, p =.05).

More than half of participants (59.8%, n = 217) reported they had a positive experience using Facebook with family. Very few (1.9%, n = 7) reported they had a negative experience. Only 3.3% (n = 12) participants reported ambivalent feelings (positive and negative) toward Facebook use with family. Did Facebook with a family member(s) change their relationship(s) and in which direction? Thirty nine percent of participants (n = 145) reported no change, 24.5% participants (n = 89) reported positive change and 1.1% (n = 4) reported negative change.

Chi-square analysis was used to examine whether gender, marital status, and being in a committed relationship was significantly different when measuring Facebook use with family members. Results show males were significantly different from females in Facebook use (p =.04). Inspection of the two groups indicates more females (n = 227) use Facebook to communicate with family members than males (n = 130). However, there was no significant connection between marital status and Facebook use, nor between being in a committed relationship and Facebook use with family members. There was no significant connection between Facebook use and education level or ethnicity.

Discussion

To understand family rituals in the digital age, we employed triangulation of methods to examine the nature and function of Facebook as mediated ritual of connection for family members. Our findings support pervious research revealing the opportunities of digital technologies to support family relationship building (Casper, 2010; Jennings & Wartella, 2004), particularly in physically separated families (Christensen, 2009), and generally giving families new communication tools for maintaining ongoing, mundane connection (Casper, 2010; Wilding, 2006). Further, Facebook ritual participants in this study appear to be "bringing together the family" more so than "distributing family members" (Christensen, 2009, p. 449) and doing so via many mundane ritual interactions—simple *Updates* and brief *Thinking of You* messages—and an overall affirmation of the social bonds between family members (Ling, 2007, 2008). As a ritual, Facebook family interactions appear to pay homage to the past, present, and anticipated future of family relationships (Goffman, 1967) by encouraging *Reminiscing*, enjoyment (*Play/Fun* rituals), frequent communication (*Updates* and *Thinking of You* rituals), and social support (*Support* rituals), as well as having access to information about others' lives (*Monitoring* rituals). Given the overwhelmingly positive perceptions and reports by participants of their rituals developed via Facebook, it is not surprising that such rituals—similar to family rituals in much of the extant research—are related to perceived relationship satisfaction and cohesion (Baxter & Braithwaite, 2006; Bruess & Pearson, 1997, 2002; Imber-Black, Roberts, & Whiting, 1988; Jorgenson & Bochner, 2004; Wolin & Bennett, 1984; Wolin et al., 1980).

Existing literature also alludes to families feeling closer *because* they use new communication technologies (Kennedy et al., 2008) and reporting better and stronger family relationships as a *result of* Internet use, particularly by enhancing cross-generational connections as well as renewing ties between extended family members (Pew Internet and American Life Project, 2002; Casper, 2010), each something our data also evidences. The strongest theme articulated by participants was how Facebook family rituals function to increase closeness and strengthen family relationships by providing opportunities for reestablishing relationships with family members with whom they have fallen out of touch, sharing information in a way that is essential for staying in touch and sustaining one or more family relationships, and simply providing a convenient and desirable venue for ongoing communication: the mundane, the playful, and the information-rich. Facebook rituals appear to be playing a kinkeeping role (Casper, 2010).

Our finding that Facebook rituals serve a maintenance function echoes Wilding (2006) and others (Licoppe & Smoreda, 2005) who believe the *act* of communicating via the Internet with family and close social ties who are not co-present was as important as the content, and that mundane commentary, jokes, and even brief comments are essential in relationship maintenance. Previous research (Christensen, 2009) revealed mediated rituals of interaction helping families create feelings of "presence-at-a-distance (p. 449), something our data also suggests; family members in our study reported feeling more connected to other members' lives even when they lived far apart and/or rarely interact face to face. In the words of one participant: Facebook is used to "shorten the distance between us as friends and cousins." Our data also illuminate previous research about families' use of the Internet for advice, social support, and guidance (Hughes and Hans, 2001) and to collaborate and communicate as a family (Kiesler et al., 2000; Orleans & Laney, 2000), something found both in the Support rituals reported by participants in our study, as well as articulated in the function of such rituals of strengthening relationships.

Applications

Family members of all ages—particularly those geographically or physically separated—are wise to consider the many ways Facebook can provide a highly accessible, low-cost, and efficient way to stay connected across time, space, and generations. Although it might seem obvious that maintaining family relationships is important, knowing how to actually do so in a healthy, ongoing way remains elusive for many families, especially as members become busier and as members move to other cities, states, and even countries. The results of this study suggest that ongoing rituals of connection, even those little behaviors that are consistent but meaningful such as sharing inside jokes and reminiscing about positive moments in the past, serve significantly positive functions for families—and they can be done just as effectively by using social networking tools like Facebook. No longer do Grandma and Grandpa have to wait for pictures of the grandkids in the mail; they can stay up to date with activities in almost real time by learning basic social networking. No longer must parents have lengthy phone calls and ask multiple questions of their son or daughter away at college; they can send messages via Facebook, something anyone can do on his or her own schedule. No longer do cousins or siblings living far apart need to wait until a major holiday or reunion to keep in touch; they can feel informed and connected about each others' life events, challenges, and accomplishments through posts and updates.

The results of this study suggest that families might even consider encouraging other family members to create a Facebook group exclusive to their own family, or simply encourage family members to "friend" each other and begin sharing parts of their daily lives. Then, as family members interact on Facebook, they would be wise to try various Facebook functions and tools for building new rituals of connection (playing Facebook games together such as Words with Friends) or sustaining older and prized rituals (such as sending each other jokes about a shared interest, now something they can do almost daily and with little effort on Facebook). Facebook tools also appear to help plan family gatherings, share photos and videos, and help family members who can't attend a family gathering or participate in a family event or tradition feel more connected and present. One caution about Facebook use that some participants offered and we echo: Avoid discussing difficult or emotional topics via Facebook. Complex, emotional, and sensitive topics are still best accomplished in a face-to-face context, or at minimum via phone when each person can hear the voice cues of the other. Further, to honor the privacy of families and individuals, members should explicitly discuss rules for sharing photos and information about family members (especially minor children), rules about what information should remain private (or who has the right to share different types of news first and with whom), and also be sensitive about those family members who do not enjoy or choose not to use social networking as way to stay connected as a family. In the latter case, family members are wise to consider the medium through which non-Facebook-using family members prefer to stay engaged and then make an effort to include and engage them in that medium—which might mean the good old-fashioned phone call, card, letter, or visit. While Facebook for many family members has become a new ritual for maintaining and enjoying relationships with each other, it shouldn't completely substitute (when possible) for being together and sharing a meal or a mundane conversation face to face.

References

Aylor, B., & Dainton, M. (2004). Biological sex and psychological gender as predictors of routine and strategic relational maintenance. *Sex Roles, 50*(9–10), 689–697.

Baxter, L. A. (1987). Symbols of relationship identity in relationship cultures. *Journal of Social and Personal Relationships, 4*(3), 261–280.

Baxter, L., & Braithwaite, D. (2002). Performing marriage: Marriage renewal rituals as cultural performance. *Southern Communication Journal, 67,* 94–109.

Baxter, L., & Braithwaite, D. (2006). Family Rituals. In L. Turner & R. West (Eds.) *The Family Communication Sourcebook* (pp. 259–280). Thousand Oaks, CA: Sage.

Bessiére, K., Kiesler, S., Kraut, R., & Boneva, B. S. (2008). Effects of Internet use and social resources on changes in depression. *Information, Communication, and Society, 11,* 47–70.

Bewley, A. R. (1995). Re-membering spirituality: Use of sacred ritual in psychotherapy. *Women & Therapy, 16*(2–3), 201–213.

Bossard, J. H., & Boll, E. S. (1950). *Ritual in family living.* Philadelphia: University of Pennsylvania Press.

Bruess, C. J., & Pearson J. C. (1997). Interpersonal rituals in marriage and adult friendship. *Communication Monographs, 64,* 25–46.

Bruess, C. J., & Pearson, J. C. (2002). The function of mundane ritualizing in adult friendship and marriage. *Communication Research Reports, 19,* 314–326.

Bryant, J., & Bryant, J. (2006). Implications of living in a wired family. In L. Turner & R. West (Eds.) *The family communication sourcebook* (pp. 297–314). Thousand Oaks, CA: Sage.

Burns, M., & Pearson, J. (2011). An exploration of family communication environment, everyday talk, and family satisfaction. *Communication Studies, 62,* 171–185.

Butner, R. (2003). *The relationship between family television use and family strength* (Unpublished doctoral dissertation). University of Alabama.

Cao, X., Sellen, A., Brush, A. B., Kirk, D., Edge, D., & Ding, X. (2010). Understanding family communication across time zones. In *Proceedings of the 2010 ACM conference on computer supported cooperative work* (pp. 155–158). New York: ACM Press.

Casper, G. M. (2010). *Kinkeeping and online social networks.* Retrieved via *ProQuest Dissertations and Theses* (Thesis No. 1482403, University of Wyoming) http://search.proquest.com/docview/759971770

Caughlin, J. P. (2003). Family communication standards: What counts as excellent family communication and how are such standards associated with family satisfaction? *Human Communication Research, 29,* 5–40.

Caughlin, J. P., & Huston, T. L. (2002). A contextual analysis of the association between demand/withdraw and marital satisfaction. *Personal Relationships, 9,* 95–119.

Christensen, T. H. (2009). "Connected presence" in distributed family life. *New Media & Society, 11,* 433–451.

Compañ, E., Moreno, J., Ruiz, M. T., & Pascual, E. (2002). Doing things together: Adolescent health and family rituals. *Journal of Epidemiology and Community Health, 56*(2), 89–94.

Debatin, B., Lovejoy, J. P., Horn, A. K., Hughes, B. N. (2009). Facebook and online privacy: Attitudes, behaviors, and unintended consequences. *Journal of Computer-Mediated Communication, 15,* 83–108.

Denham, S. A. (2003). Relationships between family rituals, family routines, and health. *Journal of Family Nursing, 9,* 305–330.

Durkheim, E. (1965). *The elementary forms of the religious life.* New York: Free Press.

Emmers-Sommer, T. M. (2004). The effect of communication quality and quantity indicators on intimacy and relational satisfaction. *Journal of Social and Personal Relationships, 21*(3), 399–411.

Facebook.com. (2014). Retrieved at Facebook.com. (2014). Retrieved at http://www.facebook.com/press/info.php?statistics

Fiese, B. H., Tomcho, T., Douglas, M., Josephs, K., Poltrock, S., & Baker, T. A. (2002). Review of fifty years of research on naturally occurring family routines and rituals: Cause for celebration? *Journal of Family Psychology, 16,* 381–390.

Forge, S., & Blackman, C. (2008). The role of information and communication technologies in shaping the family of the future. In *The Future of the Family to 2030: A Scoping Report.* Paris, France: Organization for Economic Cooperation and Development.

Glaser, B. G. (1965). The constant comparative method of qualitative analysis. *Social Problems, 12*(4), 436–445.

Glaser, B., & Strauss, A. (1967). *The discovery of grounded theory: Strategies for qualitative research.* Chicago: Aldine.

Gluckman, M., & Gluckman, M. (1977). On drama and games and athletic contests. In S. F. Moore & B. Myerhoff (Eds.), *Secular ritual* (pp. 227–243). Assen, Netherlands: Van Gorcum.

Goffman, E. (1967). *Interaction Ritual: Essays on face-to-face behavior.* New York: Pantheon.

Hampton, K. N., & Wellman, B. (2002). The not so global village of Netville. In B. Wellman & C. Haythornthwaite (Eds.), *The Internet in everyday life* (pp. 345–372). Oxford, UK: Blackwell.

Harwood, J. (2000). Communication media use in the grandparent–grandchild relationship. *Journal of Communication, 50*(4), 56–78.

Hofferth, S. L., & Sandberg, J. (2001). How American children spend their time. *Journal of Marriage and the Family, 63,* 295–308.

Homer, M. M., Freeman, P. A., Zabriskie, R. B., & Eggett, D. L. (2007). Rituals and relationships: Examining the relationship between family of origin rituals and young adult attachment. *Marriage & Family Review, 42*(1), 5–28.

Hughes, R., & Hans, J. (2001). Computers, the Internet, and families. *Journal of Family Issues, 22,* 776–790.

Ide, B., Dingmann, C., Cuevas, E., & Meehan, M. (2010). Psychometric testing of the FACES III with rural adolescents. *Journal of Family Social Work, 13*(5), 410–419.

Imber-Black, E., Roberts, J., & Whiting, R. (1988). *Rituals in families and family therapy.* New York: Norton.

Jennings, N., & Wartella, E. (2004). Technology and the family. In A. Vangelisti (Ed.) *Handbook of family communication* (pp. 593–608). Mahwah, NJ: Lawrence Erlbaum.

Jordan, A. D. (2002). A family systems approach to examining the role of the Internet in the home. In S. L. Calvert, A. B. Jordan, & R. R. Cocking (Eds.), *Children in the digital age: Influences of electronic media on development* (pp. 231–247). Westport, CT: Praeger.

Jorgenson, J., & Bochner, A. (2004) Imagining families through stories and rituals. In A. Vangelisti (Ed.), *Handbook of Family Communication* (pp. 513–538). Mahwah, NJ: Lawrence Erlbaum.

Katz, J. E., & Rice, R. E. (2002). *Social consequences of Internet use.* Cambridge, MA: MIT Press.

Kavanaugh, A., & Patterson, S. J. (2002). The impact of community computer networks on social capital and community involvement in Blacksburg. In B. Wellman & C. Haythornthwaite (Eds.), *The Internet in everyday life* (pp. 325–345). Oxford, UK: Blackwell.

Kennedy, T., Smith, A., Wells, A., & Wellman, B., (2008, October 19). Networked families. Pew Internet & American Life Project. Retrieved from http://www.pewinternet.org/files/old-media//Files/Reports/2008/PIP_Networked_Family.pdf.pdf

Kiesler, S., Zdaniuk, B., Lundmark, V., & Kraut, R. (2000). Troubles with the Internet: The dynamics of help at home. *Human–Computer Interaction, 15,* 322–351.

Koerner, A. F., & Fitzpatrick, M. A. (2002a). Toward a theory of family communication. *Communication Theory, 12*(1), 70–91.

Koerner, A. F., & Fitzpatrick, M. A. (2002b). Understanding family communication patterns and family functioning: The roles of conversation orientation and conformity orientation. In W. B. Gundykunst (Ed.), *Communication yearbook 26* (pp. 36–68). Mahwah, NJ: Lawrence Erlbaum Associates.

Lanigan, J. D., Bold, M., & Chenoweth, L. (2009). Computers in the family context: Perceived impact on family time and relationships. *Family Science Review, 14,* 16–32.

Laurier, E. (2001) Why people say where they are during mobile phone calls, *Environment and Planning D: Society and Space, 19,* 485–504.

Leach, E. R. (1966). Ritualization in man in relation to conceptual and social development. *Biological Sciences, 251*(772), 403–408.

Leach, M. S., & Braithwaite, D. O. (1996). A binding tie: Supportive communication of family kinkeepers. *Journal of Applied Communication Research, 24,* 200–216.

Lenhart, A., Madden, M., & Hitlin, P. (2005). *Teens and technology.* Washington, DC: Pew and American Life Project.

Licoppe, C. (2004) “Connected” presence: The emergence of a new repertoire for managing social relationships in a changing communication technoscape, *Environment and Planning D: Society and Space, 22,* 135–156.

Licoppe, C., & Smoreda, Z. (2005) Are social networks technologically embedded? How networks are changing today with changes in communication technology, *Social Networks, 27,* 317–335.

Lindlof, T. R., & Taylor, B. C. (2010). *Qualitative communication research methods.* London: Sage.

Ling, R. (2007). Mobile communication and mediated ritual. In K. Nyiri (Ed.), *Mobile studies: Paradigms and perspectives.* Vienna: Passagen Verlag. Retrieved from http://www.richardling.com/papers/2007_Mobile_communication_and_mediated_ritual.pdf

Ling, R. (2008). *New tech, new ties: How mobile communication is reshaping social cohesion.* Cambridge, MA: MIT Press.

Lye, D. N. (1996). Adult child–parent relationships. *Annual Review of Sociology, 22,* 79–102.

Malinowski, B. (1954). *Magic, science, and religion.* Garden City, NY: Doubleday.

Markson, S., & Fiese, B. H. (2000). Family rituals as a protective factor for children with asthma. *Journal of Pediatric Psychology, 25*(7), 471–480.

Maxwell, J. A. (1996). *Qualitative research design.* Newbury Park, CA: Sage.

McCall, G. (1988). The organizational life cycle of relationships. In S. Duck (Ed.), *Handbook of Personal Relationships: Theory, Research, and Interventions* (pp. 467–484). New York; Wiley.

Meredith, W. H. (1985). The importance of family traditions. *Wellness Perspectives, 2,* 17–19.

Meredith, W. H., Abbott, D., Lamanna, M., & Sanders, G. (1989). Rituals and family strengths. *Family Perspectives, 23,* 75–83.

Mesch, G. S. (2006). Family relations and the Internet: Exploring a family boundaries approach. *Journal of Family Communication, 6*(2), 119–138.

Mesch, G. S., & Levanon, Y. (2003). Community networking and locally based social ties in two suburban localities. *City and Community, 2,* 335–351.

Meszaros, P. S. (2004). The wired family. *American Behavioral Scientist, 48*(4), 377–390.

Mirnics, Z., Vargha, A., Tóth, M., & Bagdy, E. (2010). Cross-cultural applicability of FACES IV. *Journal of Family Psychotherapy, 21*(1) 17–33.

Moore, S. F., & Myerhoff, B. G. (1977). *Secular ritual.* Assen: Van Gorcum.

Monserud, M. A. (2008). Intergenerational relationships and affectual solidarity between grandparents and young adults. *Journal of Marriage and Family, 70,* 182–195.

Nie, N. H., Hillygus, D. S., & Erbing, L. (2002). Internet use, interpersonal relationships, and sociability: A time diary study. In B. Wellman & C. Haythornthwaite (Eds.), *The Internet in everyday life* (pp. 215–244). Oxford, UK: Blackwell.

Noller, P., & Shum, D. (1990). The couple version of FACES III: Validity and reliability. *Journal of Family Psychology,* 440–451. doi:10.1037/h0080548

Olson, D. H., Larsen, A. S., & McCubbin, H. I. (1982). Family strengths. In D. H. Olson, H. I. McCubbin, H. Barnes, A. Larsen, M. Muxen, & M. Wilson (Eds.), *Family inventories: Inventories used in a national survey of families across the family life cycle* (pp. 121–136). St. Paul: Family Social Science, University of Minnesota.

Olson, D. H., & Wilson, M. (1982). Family satisfaction. In D. H. Olson, H. I. McCubbin, H. Barnes, A. Larsen, M. Muxen, & M. Wilson (Eds.), *Family inventories: Inventories used in a national survey of families across the family life cycle* (pp. 25–32). St. Paul: Family Social Science, University of Minnesota.

Orleans, M., & Laney, M. C. (2000). Early adolescent social networks and computer use. *Social Science Computer Review, 18,* 56–72.

Orthner, D. K., & Mancini, J. A. (1991). Benefits of leisure experiences for family bonding. In B. L. Driver, P. J. Brown, & G. L. Peterson (Eds.), *Benefits of leisure* (pp. 215–247). State College, PA: Venture.

Papadakis, M. (2003). Data on family and the Internet: What do we know and how do we know it? In J. Turow & A. Kavanaugh (Eds.), *The wired homestead: An MIT Press sourcebook on the Internet and the family* (pp. 121–140). Cambridge, MA: MIT Press.

Perry, Y. V., & Doherty, W. J. (2003, November). *Developing theory about families and technology: The case of cell phones.* Paper presented at the Theory Construction and Research Methodology Workshop, National Council on Family Relations Annual Meeting, Vancouver, British Columbia, Canada.

Pew Internet and American Life Project. (2002, March 3). *Getting serious online.* Retrieved from http://www.pewinternet.org

Place, M., Hulsmeier, J., Brownrigg, A., Soulsby, A., (2005). The Family Adaptability and Cohesion Evaluation Scale (FACES): An instrument worthy of rehabilitation? *Psychiatric Bulletin, 29,* 215–218.

Reiss, D. (1982). The working family: A researcher's view of health in the household. *American Journal of Psychiatry, 139,* 1412–1428.

Schrodt, P. (2005). Family communication schemata and the circumplex model of family functioning. *Western Journal of Communication, 69,* 359–376.

Schrodt, P. (2009). Family strength and satisfaction as functions of family communication environments. *Communication Quarterly, 57,* 171–186.

Schrodt, P., Braithwaite, D. O., Soliz, J., Tye-Williams, S., Miller, A., Normand, E. L., & Harrigan, M. M. (2007). An examination of everyday talk in stepfamily systems. *Western Journal of Communication, 71,* 216–234.

Schrodt, P., Soliz, J., & Braithwaite, D. O. (2008). A social relations model of everyday talk and relational satisfaction in stepfamilies. *Communication Monographs, 75,* 190–217.

Schrodt, P., Witt, P. L., & Messersmith, A. S. (2008). A meta-analytic review of family communication patterns and their associations with information processing, behavioral, and psychological outcomes. *Communication Monographs, 75,* 248–269.

Schvaneveldt, J. D., & Lee, T. R. (1983). The emergence and practice of ritual in the American family. *Family Perspective, 17*(3), 137–143.

Sillars, A., Koerner, A., & Fitzpatrick, M. A. (2005). Communication and understanding in parent–adolescent relationships. *Human Communication Research, 31,* 102–128.

Spiggle, S. (1994). Analysis and interpretation of qualitative data in consumer research. *Journal of Consumer Research, 21*(3), 194–203.

Strauss, A., & Corbin, J. (1998). *Basics of qualitative research: Techniques and procedures for developing grounded theory* (2nd ed.). Thousand Oaks, CA: Sage.

Sutter, J. (2009). All in the Facebook family: Older generations join social networks. CNN.com. Retrieved from http://www.cnn.com/2009/TECH/04/13/social.network.older/index.html?iref=allsearch

Urista, M., Dong, Q., & Day, K. (2009). Explaining why young adults use MySpace and Facebook through uses and gratifications theory. *Human Communication, 12,* 215–229.

Valkenburg, P. M., & Peter, J. (2007). Preadolescents' and adolescents' online communication and their closeness to friends. *Developmental Psychology, 43,* 267–277.

Viere, G. M. (2001). Examining family rituals. *Family Journal, 9*(3), 285–288.

Weigel, D. J. (2003). A communication approach to the construction of commitment in the early years of marriage: A qualitative study. *The Journal of Family Communication, 3*(1), 1–19.

Wilding, R. (2006). "Virtual" intimacies? Families communication across transnational contexts. *Global Networks, 6*(2), 125–142.

Wolin, S. J., & Bennett, L. A. (1984). Family rituals. *Family Process, 23,* 401–420.

Wolin, S. J., Bennett, L. A., Noonan, D. L., & Teitelbaum, M. A. (1980). Disrupted family rituals; A factor in the intergenerational transmission of alcoholism. *Journal of Studies on Alcohol and Drugs, 41*(3), 199.

Yarosh, S., Cuzzort, S., Mueller, H., & Abowd, G. D. (2009). Developing a media space for remote synchronous parent–child interaction. In *Proceedings of the International Conference on Interaction Design and Children,* (pp. 97–105). New York: ACM Press.

Section Two

Adolescence and Emerging Adulthood in a Digital Age

7

Adolescent Use of Visual Media in Social Technologies

The Appeal, Risks, and Role of Parental Communication in Shaping Adolescent Behavior

Anne C. Fletcher
Bethany L. Blair
The University of North Carolina at Greensboro

Introduction

"Social technology"—technological devices and programs used for communicating with and maintaining connections to others—is a defining feature of the contemporary family experience, particularly among adolescents (Pfeil, Arjan, & Zaphiris, 2009). These technologies have introduced new relational and communication opportunities, as well as challenges, for parents of adolescents. As adolescents explore new ways of engaging with social technology, parents must try to understand these new ways of interacting, as well as their potential repercussions. One challenge for parents is children's use of "visual media" in communication: viewing, sharing, or interacting via digital photographs or video clips. Visual media is increasingly available in social technology, and young people have adopted it as a means for identity construction and self-presentation (Hum, Chamberlin, Hambright, Portwood, Schat, & Bevan, 2011; Zhao, Grasmuck, & Martin, 2008) and for establishing and maintaining intimacy with friends (Hsu, Wang, & Tai, 2011). Parents of adolescents in the digital age must navigate the complexities of social technology and develop strategies and rules for clear communication and healthy use. In this chapter we examine parental communication with their adolescent children regarding the use of visual media in social technology, as well as how such communication is linked with adolescent thoughts and behaviors regarding such use.

Prevalence and Content of Social Technology Use by Adolescents

Social technology can be Internet based, cell-phone based, or both, as the popularity of smartphones increases. In the United States, 83% of adolescents aged 14–17 report owning a cell phone (Madden, Lenhart, Duggan, Cortesi, & Gasser, 2013). Adolescents are particularly frequent and proficient users of the texting function on such phones, with adolescents ages 13–17 sending an average of 4,050 text messages a month (Nielsen Company, 2011). Adolescents are also more likely than adults to be active users of social networking sites (Lenhart, Madden, Smith, Purcell, Zickuhr, & Rainie, 2011) and to report positive feelings about the role of social technology in their lives (Macgill, 2007). Also, adolescents use social networking sites differently than do adult users, having more "friends," more same-aged "friends," and using a wider variety of media as a part of their online social networking activity (Pfeil et al., 2009).

Visual media plays a central role in much of current social technology. The specific social technology platforms that incorporate visual media components change over time. Current examples include the posting and viewing of visual media on social networking sites (e.g., Facebook) and the visual attachment component of text messaging on cell phones. Many popular social networking sites, such as Instagram and Snapchat, are built and have capitalized on the premise that users want to share photographs and videos with one another digitally and swiftly (Bilton, 2012; Instagram, 2014). Despite considerable research in recent years on adolescent use of social technologies (e.g., Brown & Bobkowski, 2011; Subrahmanyam & Greenfield, 2008; Underwood, Rosen, More, Ehrenreich, & Gentsch, 2012; Valkenburg & Peter, 2011), little of this work has focused specifically on adolescent experiences with visual media.

Research has indicated that adolescents use visual media in ways that reflect purposeful decision making and thought about how these media might influence others' perceptions of them. Furthermore, adolescents believe visual media are an important component of their social technology experiences (Mikkola, Oinas, & Kumpulainen, 2008) and are cognizant of the potential consequences of posting photos and videos, especially as they relate to how others may perceive them (Siibak, 2009). Many adolescents admit to making deliberate choices about how the photos they post will perpetuate a desirable image of self (Young, 2009). In fact, believing that they themselves look good in a photo is the most important consideration when adolescents choose profile pictures for social networking sites (Siibak, 2009). Young (2009) has emphasized the need for research that considers how the different components of social technology (including visual media) are selected to communicate with others. The current study helps fill that need.

Potential Risks Associated with Adolescent Visual Media Use in Social Technologies

The popular press often addresses the risks associated with use of visual media. Digital age parenting books—such as *A Survival Guide to Parenting Teens: Talking to Your Kids About Sexting, Drinking, Drugs, and Other Things That Freak You Out* (Geltman, 2014)—urge parents to consider scenarios such as "What if your daughter texts a naked picture to a 'boyfriend' ...which he then forwards to the entire class?" Adolescents' experiences of having degrading photographs or videos of themselves placed online is a frequent topic of television talk and news shows (e.g., Good Morning America, 2009). Newspapers and magazines report on the social, legal, psychological, and educational/occupational risks associated with posting compromising photographs on social networking sites (e.g., Howell & Stark, 2013). But are such concerns grounded in empirical evidence? Further, would parents' communication with their children about such risks be effective at reducing these risks?

There is currently little empirical research focused on risks associated with adolescent use of visual media in social technology, but what does exist indicates cause for concern. Sharing of naked photographs by adolescents has been linked with avoidant attachment styles (Weisskirch & Delevi, 2012) and risky sexual behavior (Benotsch, Snipes, Martin, & Bull, 2013). Posting photographs depicting alcohol use is one way adolescents construct identities as binge drinkers (Ridout, Campbell, & Ellis, 2012), and posting pictures that emphasize deviant behavior is longitudinally predictive of alcohol abuse (Szwedo, Mikami, & Allen, 2012). In addition, some argue that adolescent exposure to unsolicited visual images constitutes a form of cyber-bullying (Sansone & Sansone, 2013), although such suggestions have not been investigated empirically.

There are two plausible interpretations for the findings that link media use to adolescents' risky behaviors and negative psychological outcomes (Steinberg & Monahan, 2011). The first, referred to as differential selection, is that adolescents use visual media in a manner that reflects their current social and behavioral state. Such an interpretation suggests adolescents' traits and behaviors are the cause of their media use. In this case, visual media depicting troubling behaviors may serve as a warning sign of problems that adolescents are already experiencing. The second interpretation, referred to as media socialization, is that engaging in visual media practices that promote risky behaviors could place adolescents at greater psychological or behavioral risk than they might otherwise be. The latter interpretation may be cause for greater concern because it suggests visual media is the cause of adolescents' risky behaviors and psychological maladjustment. The differing interpretations reflect a current debate among scholars (Brown, 2011; Steinberg & Monahan, 2011). In either case, it is clear from previous empirical work (e.g., Benotsch et al., 2013; Szwedo et al., 2012) that adolescents' use of visual media is an area of concern for their current and future adjustment, and should be studied further.

Parental Perceptions of Adolescent Use of Social Technologies

Much of the research on adolescents' use of social technologies has focused on parents' perceptions about risks to adolescent users. For example, Weisskirch (2009) suggested that how adolescents use cell phones may differ based on particular characteristics of parent–adolescent relationships. In parent–adolescent relationships characterized by open, warm communication, cell phones may support and extend such relationships and serve as symbols of security and connection. In contrast, adolescents may perceive cell phones as tools of parental intrusion when parent–adolescent relationships are characterized by tension or hostility. Blair and Fletcher (2011) interviewed early adolescents and their mothers concerning adolescents' use of cell phones; both children and their mothers viewed cell phones as sources of connection to family and friends, facilitators of adolescent autonomy development, and indicators of social status. Research also suggests parents are more ambivalent about adolescent use of the Internet for interpersonal communication than they are about cell phones for such use. Although many parents believe the Internet is potentially a beneficial force in their children's lives (Macgill, 2007), parents also report concerns about perceived risks including their children giving out personal information, viewing sexually explicit images, or being exposed to content that might undermine parental values and belief systems (Turrow, 1999; Turrow & Nir, 2000). Parents also worry that strangers might contact their children online (Lenhart, Madden, & Hittlin, 2005; Mesch, 2006) or that adolescents will be exposed to content parents do not want them to see (Mesch, 2006). Although some of the concerns expressed by parents suggest parents view visual media as a potentially problematic aspect of social technology use, no research has specifically examined the topic. Furthermore, most of the current research examines parents' perceptions of their children as passive recipients of both contact requests initiated by and content received from strangers. In the current study, we examine adolescents as potentially active partners in the exchange of visual media with known others.

Parental Mediation of Adolescent Social Technology Use

As many as two thirds of parents of adolescents report talking with their children about social technology use (Livingstone & Helsper, 2008). However, little research has focused on understanding *how* parents communicate with adolescents about social technology use, or whether such communication has an impact on adolescent use of these technologies. Work in this area has focused almost exclusively on understanding parental mediation—parenting practices intended to shape children's use of social technologies or media (Nathanson, 2008). Dehue, Bolman, and Völlink (2008) found that, although parents reported setting rules for their children's use of the Internet, monitoring of Internet use (and presumably parent–child communication about Internet use) was sufficiently infrequent that parents were rarely aware when children experienced cyber-bullying. Wang, Bianchi, and Riley (2005) found that although 66% of parents of adolescents reported having family rules about adolescents' Internet use, only 38% of adolescents reported having such rules.

In a particularly informative investigation of parental efforts to exert authority over—to mediate—adolescents' Internet use, Eastin, Greenberg, and Hofschire (2006) conducted telephone surveys with mothers of adolescents to determine what types of mediation they used, as well as whether mediation efforts were associated with any parenting style. Mothers reported using both behavioral restriction and parental communication (e.g., discussing online content with adolescents) as strategies for promoting safe use of technologies by adolescents. Rates of virtually all types of mediation activities varied across parenting style groups, with authoritative parents the most likely to engage in mediation, followed by authoritarian parents.

To date, research investigating parental mediation of social technology has provided a broad picture of the ways parents manage and monitor their children's social technology use, as well as the predictors and outcomes of their strategies. However, little current research exists on *how* parents communicate with their adolescents about mediation strategies or about social technology use more generally. In addition, there has been no research explicitly focused on parent–adolescent communication regarding adolescent use of visual media. As such, our study sought to investigate multiple aspects of visual media use as a component of high school students' social technology activities, and does so with the following three research questions:

RQ1. What is the nature of adolescents' perceptions regarding visual media use?
RQ2. To what extent do parents engage in explicit communication with adolescents regarding both positive and negative aspects of visual media use?
RQ3. Is parent–adolescent communication regarding visual media use related to adolescents' perceptions regarding the potential dangers of such use?

Methods

Participants

Participants were 41 high school adolescents ranging in age from 14 years, 0 months, to 18 years, 6 months, with a mean of 16 years, 4 months. One female participant elected to provide no demographic data at all. The remaining 40 participants were ethnically diverse, describing themselves as European American (*n* = 16), African American (n = 14), multiethnic (*n* = 5), Hispanic American (*n* = 2), Asian American (*n* = 2), and Native American (*n* = 1). Participants were predominantly female (85%; *n* = 35), likely reflecting our use of a snowball sampling strategy in which girls were more likely to recruit female friends into the study than were boys to invite their male friends. Mothers' educational levels ranged from one mother who did not receive a high school diploma to ten who had received their graduate degrees, with a modal level of some college. Fathers' educational levels ranged from one father who had not completed high school to two who had received graduate degrees, with a modal level of some college education.

Procedure

Adolescents were recruited in 2010–2011 in two counties in the southeastern United States. Initial participants were recruited from church youth groups, a public high school, community agencies/organizations that worked with youth, and through distribution of project flyers in the community. We then used a snowball sampling strategy to recruit additional participants. Research assistants met with participants in a variety of settings that included participant homes, a private space at the agency/organization from which participants were recruited, and a public library. During meetings, participants completed a digitally recorded semi-structured qualitative interview and a packet of questionnaires (questionnaire data were not analyzed for this study). As an incentive for participation, participants were entered into a drawing for a fifty-dollar gift card to a local store of their choice.

Interview Protocol

Interview questions focused on use of cell phones for purposes of calling and texting, and use of social networking sites as accessed through computers or smartphones. Interview questions also focused on adolescent use of, and feelings about, the social technologies of cell phones and social networking sites. Specific areas of inquiry included: (a) experiences regarding technologies; (b) attitudes and perceptions regarding technologies; (c) feelings of proficiency regarding technology use; and (d) parents' and peers' attitudes and behaviors regarding technology use. We did not ask questions specifically about visual media use; instead, we allowed adolescents to raise aspects of social technology use that were important to them. We then probed further based on responses. We did ask adolescents to reflect on specific aspects of social technology use that seemed problematic to them. At the end of each interview, adolescents were provided the opportunity to tell interviewers anything important about social technology use they felt had not been covered in the interview.

Analytic Strategy

Interviews were transcribed verbatim and participants assigned pseudonyms. Data "chunks" (conceptually unified, related sections of transcripts) were identified throughout each transcript. First-cycle coding was applied to all data chunks. Although Miles, Huberman, & Saldana (2014) identify a number of categories of first-cycle coding that may be used, the current project used just two of these options. Descriptive codes were applied to summarize the basic content of data chunks. Process codes were applied to describe action within data chunks. These codes were broadly applied to describe content and action in all data chunks that made reference to visual media in any way. Second-cycle coding and charting were then used to identify and relate themes that emerged with respect to adolescents' discussion of visual media use and their perceptions of parents' values and rule setting. For example, themes emerged as they related to adolescent discussion of attractive versus concerning aspects of visual media use, content of parental communication regarding visual media use, and connections between presence of parental communication and the nature of adolescents' reflections regarding visual media use. We used a cross-case, variable-oriented strategy to understand the meanings and challenges adolescents experienced related specifically to visual media use. In other words, we considered points of consistency that emerged across adolescents (cases) with respect to the manner in which key concepts (variables) related to visual media use emerged and were connected.

Results

Nature of Adolescents' Perceptions Regarding Visual Media Use

Positive perceptions regarding visual media. Adolescents were highly consistent in their expressions of the salience and positive value ascribed to visual media in their use of social technologies. All but three participants mentioned use and enjoyment of photos and videos as a component of texting and social networking.

In some cases, visual media were described as the only component of social networking that was of interest to adolescents. One rather unenthusiastic Facebook user commented, "I'll go on there and I'll check and…I'll stay on there for a few minutes and that's about it. But if sometimes my friends post pictures and stuff then that's what I'll look at…I don't look at anything else" (Tiffany). The value of visual media as a component of social technology use was also illustrated by the sheer number of photos some adolescents maintained on their cell phones or on social networking sites: "I have over two thousand pictures…and before my phone got stolen I had five hundred on there" (Allison).

The participants also discussed why visual media were important to them and other adolescents. Two related themes emerged from interviews. First, adolescents used the posting and sharing of photographs to document and connect present and past. Participants posted pictures of important life events and time spent with friends, and discussed ways in which such posts were important to them as individuals—noting the value was represented in the social connections depicted in the photos: "We gossip and post pictures and stuff of like the night before if like we hang—like of us hanging out and stuff" (Natalie); "I had a whole bunch from when I was a little kiddy. I have, right now my profile picture is the very, very, very first day of school ever" (Brittany). The second theme suggested adolescents used visual media as a way to maintain positive connections to parents and friends. Comments focused on ways interactions with important others (primarily friends but sometimes parents or other relatives) were enriched by the content of photos—content that typically focused on positive aspects of relationships: "I have a really close friend…she always posts really funny things and just crazy stuff and like pictures and like, and I'm like, 'Why would you post that picture of me? I look like a fool,' or she posts crazy stuff. So I like to look on hers" (Jessica). "We just mainly post pictures on there about all of us and all the things we do, so I think it would make our relationship a little bit less closer [if we couldn't post pictures] 'cause you don't have those memories that you see" (Tiffany). Overall, adolescents expressed frequent use and enjoyment of visual media and considered it to be an essential component of their social technology activity.

Adolescent perceptions of risk in visual media use. At the same time they discussed the appeal of visual media in their social technology lives, adolescents also expressed serious concerns about the risks and potential for misuse of these media. Three interrelated themes emerged from interviews related to perceptions of risk/misuse: (1) visual media as encouraging an *overfocus on physical appearance*; (2) exposure to *sexually explicit content* through visual media; and (3) visual media as a tool of *social aggression*.

Overfocus on physical appearance. The content of visual media is frequently the adolescents themselves, i.e., "selfies," pictures taken by individuals of themselves. Some adolescents recognized that the posting of selfies promoted an overfocus on physical appearance, one that put them at risk of both developing appearance-based self-esteem difficulties and risking negative judgments from their peers. This risk was perceived as especially great for girls; participants reported that boys often publicly commented on the physical appearance of girls who shared selfies through texts or social networking:

> You know how people respond to, well, well like mostly guys, like how guys respond to girls' pictures? Like they pretty much base it off of looks and it's not like, ya know, from the inside, or whatever. They just focus on the looks or who looks better or something like that. (Keisha)
> This morning I was on Facebook and like this boy, he's putting up pictures of girls like that they have up there and like he was like writing stuff on the picture. Like he wrote on this one girl's it was like "Fishy, manly," like it was like, he was writing like all these negative things like on the picture, it was like a regular picture though but he was writing all these bad things on the picture and tagging everybody in it. (Mariah)
> There's these things on Facebook that I've noticed and they have websites out there too, just about, they'll put two girls' pictures up and they'll say, "rate this girl," "which one's prettier" and stuff like that. I cannot stand that. (Jenna)

Sexually explicit content. Adolescents we interviewed spoke frequently and in considerable detail about the manner in which the sharing of sexually explicit photos was a part of their own (occasionally) and their peers' (frequently) visual media use. Participants spoke of their own active involvement in such activities, the involvement of their peers, and their experiences as recipients of unsolicited and unwanted sexually focused photographs sent to their cell phones.

> *Participant involvement*:
> Okay so this girl and I were sexting, this was like a month ago and she had pics of body parts of mine. And apparently she didn't delete them and showed them to this other girl at my school. (Brad)
> *Peer involvement*:
> I was at her house. We were just hanging out, stuff like that. And she just got a cell phone like really, really nice one like and it had a camera on it. She was like "O my God! Look at this!" She was taking pics of her body…I didn't realize what she was doing until I turned around and saw it…first of all I said, "You know that's not cool," I explained to her, "Hey you know what you're getting yourself into?" She's like, "This is to my boyfriend. It's ok. It's fine. He loves me, I love him." (Lana)

> *Unsolicited receipt or viewing of photos*:
> I was in my room one day and then I received a picture of, you know, a guy's "whatever." Like, yeah, I didn't even ask for it or anything. (Kamia)
> I know a lot of girls that will send naked pictures. I had this one guy my freshman year, he was a senior and he had like forty girls in his phone and each girl had a naked photo… I mean, it disturbed me to the point of no end. He showed it to me and I literally just wanted to curl up in a ball with my blankie. It was horrible. (Jenna)

Virtually every story about sexual content recounted by adolescents was accompanied by details concerning negative outcomes from the experience. Outcomes were both public and widespread (photos circulating around schools) and private and internal (adolescents' feelings of discomfort or anger as a result of being exposed to unwanted sexual content).

Social aggression. Adolescents also made frequent reference to the ways their peers used visual media to perpetrate social aggression. In the majority of cases discussed by participants in this study, socially aggressive acts were related to the sharing of naked pictures. However, acts of social aggression also involved sharing nonsexual visual media with the intention of embarrassing or demeaning a specific peer. Participants discussed such incidents from the perspectives of both perpetrators (who felt this type of visual media use was justified) and disapproving spectators. For example, Jasmine described an incident: "Somebody made a hate page for one of my friends…the name on [the account] was her name, and there was the 'b' word…I just saw her picture, so I added it 'cause I knew it was her… And then when I actually went on and looked at it, it were talking mad junk about her and it was just making me angry." Allison told a story of an incident of social aggression that she herself perpetrated, in which the victim was a classmate who was interested in Allison's boyfriend and had mocked her in the past. "And she's never even kissed a boy, so I don't even know why she's going for him. But she was sitting in class, and you know, she was leaning over and her granny panties were hanging out so I had to take a picture of it and it's still on my phone. So if she decides to make fun of me I'll just have to [voice trails off]."

Parental Communication Regarding Visual Media Use

Parent–adolescent engagement related to visual media use. Adolescents reported engaging in positive interactions with parents related to visual media on their cell phones and social networking sites. Adolescents' discussion of such interactions suggested that visual media provided a means of maintaining personal connections with parents. Their references to interactions with parents were mostly lighthearted and funny, indicating parents clearly recognized the importance of visual media in their children's lives, as well as how much value adolescents placed on presenting the self to peers via photos. Visual media were often a point of mutual embarrassment and joking for parents and adolescents. "[My dad] posts pictures of prom and stuff and would tag me, and he would post these god-awful pictures of me without any make-up on. And it was a family thing and I'm gonna comment, 'Take this off!' and I'll comment, 'Hey, [Name], I made straight A's, go buy me breakfast.'" (Jenna). Allison noted that her father often teased her about the number of selfies she posted. "Every outfit, ya know, there's like ten pictures [posted]. Daddy [says he can't] decide whether I take more pictures of myself or I text" (Allison).

Parent–adolescent communication regarding visual media risks. Interview questions probed adolescents' perceptions of ways their parents had discussed potential risks of visual media use with them. Considerable within-sample variability was observed in terms of the extent to which participants reported communicating with their parents specifically about parental expectations regarding adolescent visual media use or the potential dangers of such use. Approximately 40% of participants (16 out of 41) discussed explicit communication with parents about potential dangers of visual media use and/or parental expectations regarding such use. According to the adolescents, such discussions were both proactive and reactive; parents both anticipated how adolescents might use visual media and responded to adolescents' experiences.

The general message adolescents received from their parents about visual media was to be cautious when posting pictures of themselves. "My mom just wants me to be careful. She told me, 'you're a pretty girl, you can't just be putting all these kind of pictures on there,' so…" (Brianna). According to the adolescents, most parents were fairly passive in their concerns about visual media, relying primarily on casual communication with their adolescent children to influence behavior: "They just say, like, be careful what you post on there, like, as far as status-wise or picture-wise, because colleges are already, ya know, looking at Facebook and Twitter and all that stuff now, so they just want me to have appropriate things" (Keisha). "My mom, we're so open with each other and she knows the type of person I am, the way I'm raised, she never really had to lay any rules. It was rules that I mostly set up for myself. But she would just always say 'Don't do anything that you wouldn't want somebody in the family or anybody else who knows me to see.' So from that, too, it was really no rules, I just really never did anything that I didn't want people to see" (Courtney).

According to the interviewees, some parents were quite active in monitoring whether their adolescent child was appropriately cautious with their photos.

Michele explained, "My mom asked me not to put too much information on there, and no pictures that anyone could use against me, but I mean, she doesn't set rules, because a lot, like I said, frequently she'll ask me to get on for her so she can see pictures of my family and then she'll ask to see my things, so she kinda keeps everything in check for herself." Briana's mother was also actively monitoring her daughter's account but did so as a "friend" on the site, with communication occurring via Facebook: "If she sees a picture she doesn't like, she'll put a message on it, like you need to get this off your wall right now."

Relationship between Parental Communication and Adolescent Beliefs and Behaviors

While the results are preliminary and qualitative in nature, strong themes emerged reflecting the way parental communication about visual media use affected the way adolescents talked about beliefs and behaviors surrounding visual media use and risks. Adolescents who reported receiving explicit communication from parents about the dangers and risks of visual media use expressed more thoughtful and wary attitudes about visual media use than did adolescents who reported not receiving explicit communication from parents. Adolescents who reported explicit discussions with parents on this topic were more elaborate during interview discussions about the reasons visual media use was risky than were their peers who reported little or no communication with parents. "She knows, like, if I post, like, a provocative message or something and then it'll, she knows what the damage can be, and I know what the damage can be" (Alisha). Participants were able to communicate not only why their parents had rules regarding use of visual media but also were able to reflect on how they themselves had internalized their parents' perspectives:

> I know I don't want to disappoint her.…I sent an inappropriate picture. I wasn't exposing anything but it was just very [slight pause], you know, like, [pause] sexy, let's put it that way. And I sent it to a person that I knew and we talked to each other in person and stuff. And I sent it to him but in the back of my mind I was, like, "My mom wouldn't want me to send this type of picture to anybody," and she never found out about it, but to this day she wouldn't have liked it.…It was tearing my conscience up. (Courtney)

In contrast, adolescents who did not discuss having engaged in explicit communication with parents regarding the risks of visual media use provided mostly unelaborated comments regarding such risks. Their answers overwhelmingly reflected a *lack of understanding about why* such risks were present, as well as a *lack of personal commitment to avoid* such risks. Further, adolescents who reported no explicit communication with parents about dangers and risks of visual media use tended to express a more *general* sense of emotional discomfort with inappropriate visual media use, one that was not grounded in a concrete explanation of why risks might result in discomfort. The comments were significantly and qualitatively different from those of the participants whose parents had discussed risks with them. For instance, Mariah did not report communicating with her parents about visual media, but did state, "I don't think sexting is safe at all." Similarly, Raven had a sense of what she was or was not comfortable with, but compared to the adolescents who explained how their parents' expectations had guided them, her reasons were more vague: "Kids in middle school that at the time they were going out and they sent each other pictures and it ended up getting through the whole school, their pictures…it was things I didn't want to see at all."

Discussion

Our interviews with high school students regarding their perceptions and experiences with visual media as a part of their social technology use highlighted its salience and value for these adolescents. This value was balanced with awareness, but not necessarily avoidance, of the myriad risks associated with visual media use. Visual media appears to represent a push-and-pull influence during this developmental period. Both psychological and social rewards associated with visual media pull adolescents toward its use, yet adolescents feel discomfort about the risks that accompany it. Interestingly, approximately 60% of adolescents in our sample did not report communicating explicitly with parents regarding any aspect of visual media use, positive or negative. Those adolescents who did report such communication discussed the risks of visual media use and their own involvement in such use in a more elaborate and internalized manner. While this finding is exploratory and emerged from a small sample of adolescents, it points to the potential significant benefit to youth when their parents discuss visual media use with them.

The appeal of visual media for adolescent users of social technologies is consistent with research indicating adolescents are more likely than adults to incorporate visual media into their social networking activity (Pfeil et al., 2009) and that they place a high value on it (Mikkola et al., 2008). Research focused on the posting of photos and videos by social networking users in general (not specific to adolescent users) suggests that part of the appeal of visual media might be due to it meeting psychosocial challenges such as identity construction and establishing and maintaining intimacy with friends (Hsu et al., 2011; Hum et al., 2011; Zhao et al., 2008). Although these tasks are present at all points in the lifespan, they are particularly salient during adolescence (Montgomery, 2005). Accordingly, visual media use is likely to be particularly attractive to adolescents. The recent growth and popularity of photo-centric applications like Instagram and Snapchat—both developed since the data for this study were collected—reveal that photos are likely the most attractive component of social networking, particularly for youth.

Yet despite the strong pull of visual media, adolescents in our sample were highly cognizant of the risks that accompanied its use. The frequency and matter-of-fact manner with which adolescents reported sharing or receiving sexual or socially aggressive visual content also suggests that such risky behavior is normative. Our findings are consistent with research from the Pew Institute indicating 30% of adolescents and 44% of young adults have received a sexually explicit image or message via text message (Lenhart, 2009; Lenhart & Duggan, 2014). Most adolescents in our sample reported experiences with sexting or social aggression in their own or friends' visual media use, and some (although certainly not all) reported being disturbed by unsolicited exposure to inappropriate visual media.

Given the serious nature of the risks associated with visual media use during adolescence (risks of which adolescents are clearly aware), why do adolescents engage heavily in posting and viewing photos and videos in their social networking activities? One potential answer is the high value adolescents place on visual media activity in general. The rewards of visual media are immediate and strong, and as such, adolescents are attracted to its use in such a way that they might ignore or minimize the risk. In this way, adolescent visual media behavior is similar to other adolescent risk-taking behaviors (Smith, Chein, & Steinberg, 2013). The most current research on adolescent risk taking (Chein, Albert, O'Brien, Uckert, & Steinberg, 2011) suggests the adolescent brain is highly sensitive to rewards (especially in the presence of peers—actual or virtual) and lacks critical control features that remain underdeveloped until the mid-twenties. In short, the adolescent brain might not be sufficiently mature to facilitate necessary caution in choices regarding visual media use.

If visual media is here to stay, what, then, is the role of parents to ensure healthy choices by their adolescent children? Our data suggest parents can play a critical role in shaping how adolescents think about visual media and make choices related to its use. Specifically, by engaging in clear and explicit communication with adolescents about expectations and values related to visual media use, adolescents in our study appeared more likely to develop thoughtful approaches to visual media use—approaches that appeared to directly reflect parents' ideas and expectations. Adolescents whose parents had engaged in conversations with them about media use were able to articulate the short- and long-term consequences associated with misuse of visual media. These adolescents were also able to articulate their parents' value systems about visual media use, and described those value systems as shaping their own moral standards and behaviors. Finally, adolescents who reported communication with their parents regarding visual media use also reported making behavioral choices based on explicit consideration of how their parents might perceive their behavior.

This study was not without its limitations. Primary among them are that we relied on adolescents to report not just on their own attitudes about visual media use but the nature of parental communication about such use. A broader and more complete perspective would have also included parents' perspectives regarding how they communicated with their adolescents about visual media use. Future research should have both adolescents and their parents provide information regarding communication about this topic. Although our sample was diverse with respect to both age and race/ethnicity, it was predominantly female. This might reflect greater interest in social technologies among girls (Barker, 2009). Future research should continue to involve diverse samples but make additional efforts to recruit adolescent boys, who may be less frequently represented in research on this topic. Finally, the constantly changing nature of technology means that research on technology becomes dated quickly. Accordingly, we recognize that the findings reported here represent a snapshot of a moment in time characterized by availability of and interest in a specific set of technologies as they relate to visual media use. Over time, these technologies may evolve in ways that limit the generalizability of the findings reported here. Accordingly, there is a need for continuing research that considers how parents communicate with their adolescent children regarding visual media use as it occurs within the context of new and evolving social technologies.

Although our sample was small and the study exploratory, our findings suggest that parental communication is influential in shaping adolescent behavior and choices in the digital age. In a number of contexts, parental communication has been shown to serve as a protective force against adolescent problem behavior. For example, when parents engage in open communication, adolescent girls are less likely to use alcohol (Ohannessian, 2012). Open parental communication about sex is linked with an increased likelihood that sexually active adolescents will use condoms (Malcolm et al., 2012). In Chinese families, parental communication about Internet use was linked with lower levels of pathological Internet use among adolescents (Liu, Fang, Deng, & Zhang, 2012). It's not surprising, then, that parental communication about visual media use would mediate adolescent choices about such use.

Application

Our findings suggest parents are wise to seize opportunities for clear, proactive, elaborated discussions with adolescents regarding their visual media use. Such communication needs to be informed by an understanding of how adolescents use visual media, the high value that visual media hold for adolescents, the range of risks that may accompany visual media use, and the parents' own values and expectations regarding visual media use. Parental communication regarding risks and expectations for responsible use of visual media are a potentially powerful force shaping how adolescents think about such use and structure their own behavior. With this in mind, we offer the following recommendations for parents regarding communication with adolescents about visual media use.

Make visual media use a positive part of the parent–adolescent relationship

We urge parents to focus on increasing positive interactions with their children about visual media. Parents can share photographs with their children as text attachments, "tag" youth on social networking sites, and set up their own accounts on photo-sharing applications—and then "friend" their children on these accounts. Although children might not appreciate having parents comment on their own postings in a public forum, they may well enjoy, for example, having a parent comment over dinner about how much fun they appeared to be having with their friends at the basketball game the previous night. Also, developing an ongoing pattern of joint viewing of visual media provides parents opportunities to discuss what constitutes appropriate and inappropriate use of this media. It also keeps youth aware that an interested parent is observing the photographs and videos they are posting. Discussions about appropriate and inappropriate visual media use might be more positively received by adolescents when they are grounded in an ongoing pattern of positive interactions related to such use.

Ask youth to be visual media use instructors

Parents should regularly ask adolescents how the multiple new visual media applications operate. Adolescents are often the best sources for information about which applications are current and popular, and such interactions can provide adolescents opportunities to be the expert, promoting feelings of self-worth and competence. Parents might also be pleasantly surprised how much enjoyment adolescents experience from showing their parents how such applications work—and possibly laughing at their parents' ineptitude in managing them. Such interactions can also provide parents opportunities to increase their own technological proficiency, skills they can then use to appropriately monitor their children's use of visual media.

Brainstorm about risks

Visual media use brings with it a unique set of risks that even parents might not fully understand. Discussions with adolescents concerning risks should be collaborative. Because parents may not always be as well informed as adolescents about how social media work and how visual components are incorporated into applications, the most comprehensive discussions of risk would be those to which both parents and adolescents contribute. Parents could share stories exemplifying consequences of poor choices (e.g., a coworker's son who was not admitted to the college of his choice due to photos of drinking posted his social networking site). In turn, adolescents might share experiences they have heard about or observed (e.g., a friend who wasn't sufficiently cautious about privacy settings and ended up sharing embarrassing photos with her youth minister). In such discussions about visual media and technology use, there are multiple opportunities to learn lessons about guidelines, best practices, ethical decision making, value judgments, and family rules and expectations. By actively engaging adolescents in such discussions, parents make visual media safety a collaborative process and acknowledge they are open to hearing their children's experiences and thoughts rather than simply presenting a set of parental rules to be resented.

Be clear about values and expectations

Within our study, parental communication with adolescents about visual media use was associated with adolescents being able to articulate their parents' values and expectations about such use, as well as internalizing these values. With this in mind, it is critical that parental communication about visual media use clearly articulate parents' beliefs about acceptable and unacceptable behavior, and why parents feel the way they do. Parents should clarify in their own minds, and then articulate to their children, exactly what makes a photo or video inappropriate and the risks associated with sharing it. They should then be extremely clear that their expectation is that adolescents' visual media use be consistent with parental values and expectations.

References

Barker, V. (2009). Older adolescents' motivations for social network site use: The influence of gender group identity, and collective self-esteem. *Cyber Psychology & Behavior,* 12, 209–213.

Benotsch, E. G., Snipes, D. J., Martin, A. M., & Bull, S. S. (2013). Sexting, substance use, and sexual risk behavior in young adults. *Journal of Adolescent Health, 52*, 307–313.

Bilton, N. (2012, May 6). Disruptions: Indiscreet photos, glimpsed then gone. *New York Times.* Retrieved on from http://bits.blogs.nytimes.com/2012/05/06/disruptions-indiscreet-photos-glimpsed-then-gone/?_php=true&_type=blogs&_r=0

Blair, B. L., & Fletcher, A. C. (2011). "The only 13-year-old on planet earth without a cell phone": Meanings of cell phones in early adolescents' everyday lives. *Journal of Adolescent Research, 26,* 155–177. doi: 10.1177/0743558410371127

Brown, J. D. (2011). The media do matter: Comment on Steinberg and Monahan (2011). *Developmental Psychology, 47*, 580–581. doi:10.1037/a0022553

Brown, J. D., & Bobkowski, P. S. (2011). Older and newer media: Patterns of use and effects on adolescents' health and well-being. *Journal of Research on Adolescence, 21*, 95–113. doi:10.1111/j.1532–7795.2010.00717.x

Chein, J., Albert, D., O'Brien, L., Uckert, K., & Steinberg, L. (2011). Peers increase adolescent risk taking by enhancing activity in the brain's reward circuitry. *Developmental Science, 14,* F1-F10. doi:10.1111/j.1467–7687.2010.01035.x

Dehue, F., Bolman, C., & Völlink, T. (2008). Cyberbullying: Youngsters' experiences and parental perception. *CyberPsychology & Behavior, 11*, 217–223.

Eastin, M., Greenberg, B., & Hofschire, L. (2006). Parenting the Internet. *Journal of Communication, 56*, 486–504.

Geltman, J. (2014) *A survival guide to parenting teens: Talking to your kids about sexting, drinking, drugs, and other things that freak you out.* New York: AMACOM.

Good Morning America. (2009). *The truth about teens sexting.* Retrieved from http://abcnews.go.com/GMA/Parenting/truth-teens-sexting/story?id=7337547

Howell, T., & Stark, E. (2013, June 12). Teens often ignore risks of sexting, experts say. *Calgary Herald.* Retrieved from http://www.calgaryherald.com/index.html

Hsu, C., Wang, C., & Tai, Y. (2011). The closer the relationship, the more the interaction on Facebook? Investigating the case of Taiwan users. *Cyberpsychology, Behavior, and Social Networking, 14*, 473–476. doi:10.1089/cyber.2010.0267

Hum, N. J., Chamberlin, P. E., Hambright, B. L., Portwood, A. C., Schat, A. C., & Bevan, J. L. (2011). A picture is worth a thousand words: A content analysis of Facebook profile photographs. *Computers in Human Behavior, 27*, 1828–1833. doi:10.1016/j.chb.2011.04.003

Instagram. (2014). Retrieved from: http://instagram.com/about/faq/

Lenhart, A. (2009). Teens and sexting. Pew Research Center's Internet and American Life Project. Retrieved from: http://www.pewinternet.org/2009/12/15/teens-and-sexting

Lenhart, A., & Duggan, M. (2014). Couples, the Internet, and social media. Pew Research Center's Internet and American Life Project. Retrieved from http://www.pewinternet.org/2014/02/11/couples-the-internet-and-social-media/

Lenhart A., Madden M., & Hitlin, P. (2005). Teens and technology. *Pew Internet & American Life Project.* Retrieved from: http://www.pewinternet.org/Reports/2005/Teens-and-Technology.aspx

Lenhart, A., Madden, M., Smith, A., Purcell, K., Zickuhr, K., & Rainie, L. (2011). Teens, kindness, and cruelty on social network sites. Pew Research Center's Internet and American Life Project. Retrieved from http://www.pewinternet.org/Reports/2011/Teens-and-social-media.aspx

Liu, Q.-X., Fang, X.-Y., Deng, L.-Y., & Zhang, J.-T. (2012). Parent–adolescent communication, parental Internet use and Internet-specific norms and pathological Internet use among Chinese adolescents. *Computers in Human Behavior, 28*, 1269–1275. doi:10.1016/j.chb.2012.02.010

Livingstone, S., & Helsper, E. J. (2008). Parental mediation of children's Internet use. *Journal of Broadcasting & Electronic Media, 52*, 581–599. doi:10.1080/08838150802437396

Macgill, A. R. (2007). Parent and teenager Internet use. Pew Research Center's Internet and American Life Project. Retrieved from http://www.pewinternet.org/Reports/2007/Parent-and-Teen-Internet-Use.aspx

Madden, M., Lenhart, A., Duggan, M., Cortesi, S., & Gasser, U. (2013). Teens and technology 2013. Pew Research Center's Internet and American Life Project. Retrieved from http://www.pewinternet.org/Reports/2013/Teens-and-Tech.aspx

Malcolm, S., Huang, S., Cordova, D., Freitas, D., Arzon, M., Jimenez, G. L., Pantin, H., & Prado, G. (2013). Predicting condom use attitudes, norms, and control beliefs in Hispanic problem behavior youth: The effects of family functioning and parent–adolescent communication about sex on condom use. *Health Education Behavior, 40*, 384–391. doi:10.1177/1090198112440010

Mesch, G. S. (2006). Family relations and the Internet: Exploring a family boundaries approach. *The Journal of Family Communication, 6*, 119–138. doi:10.1207/s15327698jfc0602_2

Mikkola, H., Oinas, M., & Kumpulainen, K. (2008). Net-based identity and body image among young IRC-gallery users. In K. McFerrin et al. (Eds.), *Proceedings of Society for Information Technology and Teacher Education International Conference 2008* (pp. 3080–3085). Chesapeake, VA: AACE.

Miles, M. B., Huberman, A., & Saldana, J. (2014). *Qualitative data analysis: A methods sourcebook* (3rd ed.). Thousand Oaks, CA: Sage.

Montgomery, M. J. (2005). Psychosocial intimacy and identity: From early adolescence to emerging adulthood. *Journal of Adolescent Research, 20*, 346–374. doi:10.1177/0743558404273118

Nathanson, A. I. (2008) Parental mediation strategies. In W. Donsbach (Ed.), *The International Encyclopedia of Communication*. Malden, MA: Blackwell Publishing. Available at www.communicationencyclopedia.com/public/book?id=g9781405131995_yr2010_9781405131995

Nielsen Company. (2011). *New mobile obsession: U.S. teens triple data usage*. Retrieved from http://blog.nielsen.com/nielsenwire/online_mobile/new-mobile-obsession-u-s-teens-triple-data-usage/

Ohannessian, C. M. (2012). Parental problem drinking and adolescent psychosocial adjustment: The mediating role of adolescent–parent communication. *Journal of Research on Adolescence, 22*, 498–511.

Pfeil, U., Arjan, R., & Zaphiris, P. (2009). Age differences in online social networking: A study of user profiles and the social capital divide among teenagers and older users in MySpace. *Computers in Human Behavior, 25*, 643–654.

Ridout, B., Campbell, A., & Ellis, L. (2012). "Off your Face(book)": Alcohol in online social identity construction and its relation to problem drinking in university students. *Drug and Alcohol Review, 31*, 20–26.

Sansone, R. A., & Sansone, L. A. (2013). Cell phones: The psychosocial risks. *Innovations in Clinical Neuroscience, 10*, 33–37.

Siibak, A. (2009). Constructing the self through the photo selection: Visual impression management on social networking websites. *Cyberpsychology: Journal of Psychosocial Research on Cyberspace, 3,* 1–9.

Smith, A., Chein, J., & Steinberg, L. (2013). Impact of socio-emotional context, brain development, and pubertal maturation on adolescent decision-making. *Hormones and Behavior, 64,* 323–332.

Steinberg, L., & Monahan, K. C. (2011). Adolescents' exposure to sexy media does not hasten the initiation of sexual intercourse. *Developmental Psychology, 47,* 562–576. doi:10.1037/a0020613

Subrahmanyam, K., & Greenfield, P. (2008). Online communication and adolescent relationships. *The Future of Children, 18,* 119–146. doi:10.1353/foc.0.0006

Szwedo, D. E., Mikami, A. Y., & Allen, J. P. (2012). Social networking site use predicts changes in young adults' psychological adjustment. *Journal of Research on Adolescence, 22,* 453–466.

Turrow, J. (1999). The family and the Internet: The view from the parents, the view from the press. A report from The Annenberg Public Policy Center at the University of Pennsylvania. Retrieved from http://www.appcpenn.org/Downloads/Information_And_Society/19991201_Internet_and_family/19991201_Internet_and_family.pdf

Turrow, J. & Nir, L. (2000). The Internet and the family, 2000: The view from the parents, the view from the kids. A report from The Annenberg Public Policy Center at the University of Pennsylvania. Retrieved from http://www.appcpenn.org/Downloads/Information_And_Society/20000516_Internet_and_family/20000516_Internet_and_family_report.pdf

Underwood, M. K., Rosen, L. H., More, D., Ehrenreich, S. E., & Gentsch, J. K. (2012). The BlackBerry project: Capturing the content of adolescents' text messaging. *Developmental Psychology, 48,* 295–302. doi:10.1037/a0025914

Valkenburg, P. M., & Peter, J. (2011). Online communication among adolescents: An integrated model of its attraction, opportunities, and risks. *Journal of Adolescent Health, 48,* 121–127. doi:10.1016/j.jadohealth.2010.08.020

Wang, R., Bianchi, S. M., & Riley, S. B. (2005). Teenagers' Internet use and family rules: A research note. *Journal of Marriage and Family, 67,* 1249–1258.

Weisskirch, R. S. (2009). Parenting by cell phone: Parental monitoring of adolescents and family relations. *Journal of Youth and Adolescence, 38,* 1123–1139. doi:10.1007/s10964–008–9374–8

Weisskirch, R. S., & Delevi, R. (2012). Its ovr b/n u n me: Technology use, attachment styles, and gender roles in relationship dissolution. *Cyberpsychology, Behavior, and Social Networking, 15,* 486–490.

Young, K. (2009). Online social networking: An Australian perspective. *International Journal of Emerging Technologies & Society, 7,* 39–57.

Zhao, S., Grasmuck, S., & Martin, J. (2008). Identity construction on Facebook: Digital empowerment in anchored relationships. *Computers in Human Behavior, 24,* 1816–1836. doi:10.1016/j.chb.2008.02.012

8

Navigating Emerging Adulthood with Communication Technology

Elizabeth Dorrance Hall
Megan K. Feister
Purdue University

Introduction

Digital communication technology is changing the landscape of the American family and can make a significant difference in the lives of emerging adults attempting to stay in close contact with their family of origin. Emerging adults experience a multitude of life events in rapid succession, making ages 18 to 25 a life stage for significant identity exploration and formation in the areas of love, career, and development of worldview (Arnett, 2000). The emerging adult life stage is marked by continuous change: moving away from home for college, job, or career; starting higher education and/or finishing formal education; seriously dating; cohabiting; and for some, getting married and having children. Family is an important source of support for emerging adults during this transitional period. Because most families are able to stay in contact with the emerging adults in their network via a variety of media—for example, as of 2010, 84% of families in the United States have Internet access—opportunities for offering support are numerous (Jennings & Wartella, 2013).

Jennings and Wartella (2013) suggest advancements in technology affect family roles, stages, and transitions. Technology is certainly affecting emerging adults. For example, social networking sites (SNSs) and other new communication technologies influence identity formation—an important aspect of emerging adulthood (Arnett, 2000)—and relationship maintenance (Steinfield, Ellison, &

Lampe, 2008). Despite the abundance of social science research using college students as participants, surprisingly little research has examined how college students and other emerging adults (e.g., those entering the workforce) communicate with their families using technology, how they use technology for connecting with family members, what they talk about with family members via mediated channels, and how technology affects their family relationships. This chapter will review what scholars currently know about technology use among emerging adults, including theoretical frameworks useful for making sense of the literature on emerging adults and their family relationships, particularly in the context of new communication technologies. Two research studies are then presented, each exploring key issues for digital age families: Study one examines how the frequency of communication with family members via technology is associated with family satisfaction, self-esteem, and loneliness. The second study explores how emerging adults use communication technology with family members and identifies barriers of such use. Finally, directions for future research and applications for scholars and family professionals are offered.

Emerging Adults' Use of Technology

Ever-expanding social networks are a defining feature of emerging adulthood. In the United States today, emerging adults "have a variety of communication technologies at their disposal to manage quickly and efficiently very large webs of social connections" (Manago, Taylor, & Greenfield, 2012, p. 369). Research on use of social networking sites (Cheung, Chiu, & Lee, 2011; Lenhart, Purcell, Smith, & Zickuhr, 2010; Pempek, Yermolayeva, & Calvert, 2009), cell phones (Chen & Katz, 2009; Gentzler, Oberhauser, Westerman, & Nadorff, 2011), instant messaging (IM; Junco, Merson, & Salter, 2010), and email (Harwood, 2000; Johnson, Haigh, Becker, Craig, & Wigley, 2008; Trice, 2002) suggests that emerging adults are using technology in robust ways, and that such technologies often impact family and other relationships.

Social Networking Sites

While blogging has declined in popularity among emerging adults, SNS use has become more common (Lenhart et al., 2010). According to Lenhart et al., one-third of adults between the ages of 18 and 29 use Twitter. Facebook continues to be the most popular SNS among college students (Cheung et al., 2011), with 34% of Facebook's 1.28 billion users in the 18–29-year-old age group (Smith, 2014). Despite those large numbers, only about 25% of college students report using Facebook to communicate with their parents (Gentzler et al., 2011). While Facebook could be a useful tool for communicating with family members, U.S. college students report multiple reasons they choose to use SNS, including: seeking friends, convenience (e.g., anywhere, anytime, easy), social support, information, entertainment, looking at and posting pictures, planning and finding out about events, messaging, posting and reading wall posts, and getting to know people (Kim, Sohn, & Choi, 2011; Pempek et al., 2009). Many students use SNS to observe others more than to post about themselves; 45% of college students admit to frequent "lurking" or to surveillance—such as looking at someone's profile page without posting a comment.

Research suggests Facebook is used to strengthen close relationships, including those among extended family (see Bruess, Li, & Polingo chapter in this volume; Manago et al., 2012). In Subrahmanyam et al.'s (2008) study, 48% of participants reported using SNS for social reasons such as keeping in touch with family members. Bruess et al. (this volume) found that Facebook provided rituals of connection for family members, ultimately providing relationship maintenance functions, especially when members lived or went to school in a different city, state, or country.

Despite varied reasons for use, SNSs represent a very real context for college students to interact and fulfill social needs. The literature suggests SNS use constitutes both a tool for relationship maintenance and a potential threat to emerging adult adjustment. Ellison, Steinfield, and Lampe (2007) suggest Facebook use is positively associated with all types of social capital—the ability to stay connected with people and build relationships. However, Gentzler et al. (2011) found college students who use SNS to communicate with their closest parent were lonelier, tended to have anxious attachment, and had more conflict with their parents. These same emerging adults report greater overall communication with parents, indicating they are not isolated. The authors suggest loneliness might stem from peer relationships, creating a greater dependence on parents. Other identified negative outcomes associated with SNS use include cyberbullying (i.e., aggression using communication technology; Erdur-Baker, 2010) and Facebook depression (i.e., depression caused by SNS use; O'Keeffe & Clarke-Pearson, 2011).

Cell Phones

According to Chen and Katz (2009), the cell phone has become an essential tool of college students living away from their families of origin. Junco et al. (2010) report 97% of college students own cell phones, a device simultaneously allowing students to both keep in touch with family members but also giving students freedom and independence; students can contact family almost anywhere and anytime, yet also have the power to answer or call parents when and if they choose (Gentzler et al., 2011). Chen and Katz (2009) report emerging adults use cell phones to contact family members, fulfill their roles within the family, share experiences, as well as receive and request emotional and tangible parental support.

Cell phone use has both positive and negative outcomes for the parent–child relationship. Chen and Katz (2009) report emerging adults use cell phones to ask for advice, complain, and share with their parents. Gentzler et al. (2011) found that college students who more frequently used cell phones to communicate with parents—as opposed to less immediate channels such as SNS, text messaging, and email—reported more satisfying, intimate, and supportive relationships with parents. However, Chen and Katz (2009) also observe the connection granted by cell phones can become a digital-age umbilical cord, tethering mothers and emerging adult children in unhealthy ways that inhibit independence.

Email and Instant Messaging

Little research has examined email and IM use among emerging adults, especially with family members. Trice (2002) examined emails sent by college freshman to parents and found students used email for relational maintenance and emailed their parents six times per week on average. Similarly, Johnson et al. (2008) found college students use maintenance strategies such as openness and positivity in emails with family members. Grandparents and emerging adult grandchildren also use email for communication, but past research yielded conflicting results on frequency of use compared to other media (see Harwood, 2000; Holladay & Seipke, 2007).

While less is known about use of IM with family, Junco et al. (2010) found no significant differences in access to and use of IM among college students based on gender, ethnicity, and income (unlike differences in cell phone access), perhaps due to widespread availability of computer labs on college campuses. Overall, research suggests emerging adults have a range of communication technology choices and most adopt a variety of options, with SNSs and cell phones being favored, especially for keeping in touch with close others.

Theoretical Frameworks

Several media and organizational communication theories, including social presence theory, media multiplexity theory, social identity theory, and communication privacy management theory, provide useful frameworks for understanding communication technology choices among emerging adults and their impact on family relationships.

Social Presence Theory

Social presence theory explains how two family members in separate locations can feel "together," as though they are able to *be* with each other (Biocca, Harms, & Burgoon, 2003), and why certain technologies are better than others at facilitating a sense of *being* together. For example, many SNSs were created specifically to enhance real-time interaction and provide access to others' thoughts and emotions. Biocca et al. (2003) found SNSs create "presence of real and virtual humans" (p. 458), further explaining why emerging adults prefer real-time technologies like the messaging function on Facebook for connecting with others (Cheung et al., 2011). According to Short, Williams, and Christie (1976), media with high *social presence* is "warm, personal, sensitive, and sociable" (p. 66). Burgoon and Hale (1987) posit that social presence is a product of behavioral indicators, emotion concerning the conversation, and involvement/interest in the interaction. Regardless of the definition, social presence has implications for technology-mediated family communication; family members seeking to maintain close relationships would be wise to use media that facilitate high levels of social presence. While there is little research on family communication using social presence theory, it would be prudent to explore whether using technology that facilitates higher social presence results in more satisfactory family relationships, especially with emerging adult children who tend to favor real-time technologies (Lenhart et al., 2010).

Media Multiplexity Theory

Media Multiplexity Theory (MMT) has been used to study how online communication impacts interpersonal relationships like those among family. MMT emerges from research on social networks and claims people use a variety of media to interact in any given relationship (Walther & Parks, 2002). MMT posits the more technologies a person uses to communicate with a relational partner, the more interdependent and higher quality the relationship.

Ledbetter and Mazer (2014) used MMT to understand the impact of relational interdependence on family communication, specifically the way relational interdependence—a component of MMT—relates to individuals' technology use. They explored how online communication attitudes about self-disclosure and social connection impact interpersonal relationships, claiming family communication orientations (i.e., conversation and conformity) are important influences on online attitudes about communication because family is a place where significant communication behavior is learned (Koerner & Fitzpatrick, 2002). Conversation orientation is the degree to which families encourage open communication on a variety of topics; conformity orientation is the degree to which families value homogeneity in members' attitudes, beliefs, and behaviors. According to the authors, "such orientations may influence the purposes, perceptions, expectations, and outcomes associated with communication behaviors, and particularly those enacted via online communication" (Ledbetter & Mazer, 2014, p. 5). For example, the results demonstrated that relational interdependence was positively associated with the interaction between online communication attitudes and frequency of technology use. Therefore, when Facebook use was high and online attitudes were positive, participants experienced greater relational interdependence. Family communication orientations and previous experiences with technology constitute online attitudes, which impact the frequency and relational outcomes of use of certain technologies with close others.

In a study comprising largely emerging adults, Ledbetter (2010) found that conformity orientation was significantly associated with online social connection. Online disclosure attitudes were predicted by conformity orientation directly and conversation orientation indirectly through communication competence. Ledbetter also found that those from high conversation- and moderate conformity-orientation families were most likely to have healthy online communication attitudes (e.g., not feeling nervous sharing personal information online for social connection). It is yet unknown how online attitudes impact unique aspects of the emerging adult life stage, such as negotiating independence from parents, or how a congruence (or discrepancy) of online attitudes and self-disclosure behavior with family members impacts family satisfaction.

Social Identity Theory

Emerging adults strive to manage multiple facets of their identities when interacting with family members using SNSs and other digital technologies. To help explain how individuals accomplish identity management, Social Identity Theory (SIT) (Tajfel, 1972) embraces a poststructuralist view of identity, that one's sense of self is socially created and discursively constituted through social interactions with others (Tracy & Trethewey, 2005). Identity is not fixed, rather is multifaceted and in certain contexts—such as in a work-versus-home settings—aspects of one's sense of self may be more or less salient or appropriate. Identities largely depend on receiving validation from significant others in relevant social groups, like from family members (Mead, 1934). Individuals create a "social identity" based on such affiliations (Alvesson & Robertson, 2006). Through validations and self-reinforcing associations with social groups, people negotiate and develop different senses of self (e.g., a family self and a friends self).

Negotiation of identity becomes especially interesting in the context of digital communication technology such as SNSs. Online profiles are a type of digital body, or as boyd (2006) suggests, "public displays of identity where people can explore impression management" (p. 4). Profiles contain vast amounts of personal information, and SNS users strategically manage the content and privacy of their online impressions (boyd, 2011). As such, online profiles are sites of identity production. Just as clothing can suggest a wearer's occupation, online profiles express identities (boyd, 2006). Because identity is multifaceted and individuals are motivated to share certain aspects based on appropriate social categorizations (Tracy & Trethewey, 2005), people are compelled to selectively present elements of the self and disclose information (and use SNSs) strategically as a result. Self-presentation affects how people manage profiles and engage in mediated forms of communication; individuals also strive to manage multiple facets of their identities on SNSs based on audience (boyd, 2011). Because emerging adults typically experience a significant transition, including a change in social groups and identity negotiation, strategic use of profiles and information sharing on SNSs is especially salient.

Indeed, past research suggests individuals are highly motivated to strategically manage impressions during online interactions (Walther, 1992; Walther, Van Der Heide, Kim, Westerman, & Tong, 2008). Impression management refers to the specific actions that people take in order to present favorable and appropriate images to others (Walther, 2007). Emerging adults accomplish impression management in a number of ways such as adjusting privacy settings, sending messages to just one or a number of individuals, and using different functions such as the "like" button on Facebook or leaving comments (boyd & Ellison, 2007; Child, Haridakis & Petronio, 2012). Information is managed differently with different groups of people, and information shared contributes to an online identity. Further, identities presented are expected by the self and others to be both "authentic" and "real" (boyd & Ellison, 2007), challenging individuals to balance impression management against a desire for authenticity (Ellison, Heino, & Gibbs, 2006).

Communication Privacy Management Theory

Privacy has become an essential topic of study and practical interest as individuals in nearly every age group increasingly use more and varied communication technologies. While Dwyer, Hiltz, and Passerini (2007) found many users of SNSs are very aware of the potential dangers of sharing personal information as well as options available for limiting access to information, few actually take measures to protect their information. Marwick and boyd (2011) urge SNS users to consider how to successfully navigate simultaneously sharing the same information with often disparate groups in their lives, from acquaintances to friends to coworkers to family. As emerging adults consider multiple audiences on their SNSs, research such as Communication Privacy Management theory (Petronio, 2002) suggests that they will experience potent tensions fueled by having to balance their own and others' privacy concerns with their desire for authentic identity production.

As emerging adults use SNSs to engage with a wide audience, it makes sense they might resist restricting access to their information. More often, they will use "boundary management," enabling them to tailor their communication and manage information among various social groups (Petronio, 2002). Privacy boundaries serve as information ownership lines, and can be either personal (i.e., restricted to self) or collective (i.e., restricted to a defined group, such as the family; Petronio, 2002). Emerging adults likely use these boundary lines strategically to explore their identities online while simultaneously maintaining a desired image with family members.

Because the primary purpose of SNSs is to share information with others, the social nature of SNSs means that collective privacy boundaries are often a salient issue. Tufekci (2008) suggests SNS users are not unconcerned with privacy; instead, they see privacy as "a process of optimization between disclosure and withdrawal" (p. 20). In other words, users want to maintain a basic level of privacy while also sharing certain information with certain groups of people. As a result of dynamic and developing identities and the emergence of new social groups (Schwartz, Côté, & Arnett, 2005), emerging adults are likely engaged in complex online boundary management. For emerging adults, strategies to manage boundaries include creating and selectively sharing aliases (Skeels & Grudin, 2009), creating layers of privacy allowing some contacts to see more information than others (Cohen, de Lussanet, Garon, & Wilkos, 2008), tailoring posts to a broad audience, and restricting visibility settings to "friends only" (Tufekci, 2008). For example, restricting certain posts to friends but not family allows emerging adults to construct a boundary in which they can test out new aspects of their evolving adult identity without changing their family's view of their authentic self.

Permeability, linkage, and ownership are three boundary characteristics with implications for the control of information (Petronio, 1991). Boundary permeability, or the possibility of information flow across boundaries, tends to increase as collectives get larger. Boundary linkage refers to the connections between individuals within the collective boundary. The strength of these connections changes the permeability of the boundaries, an issue salient in families because of typically strong bonds. As emerging adults move away from family, they renegotiate the strength of their boundary links with family (Ledbetter, Heiss, Sibal, Lev, Battle-Fisher, & Shubert, 2010). Finally, boundary ownership refers to the responsibility of each individual in the collective to manage shared information. As more people join the collective, privacy becomes contingent on the sharing behavior of more people making the boundary more permeable. For example, users can "share" other users' posts on Facebook with their own set of contacts, a behavior that can lead to unwanted flows of information across boundaries and between collectives (Petronio, 2002). Ledbetter et al. (2010) suggest new communication technologies are increasing boundary turbulence (i.e., asymmetry in the way two parties manage a privacy boundary) and parental intrusion, especially for emerging adults who live with their parents.

Two Studies

As evidenced by a review of the literature, relatively few studies have examined how communication technology impacts relationships between emerging adults and their families. Many of the studies that have included family members did so by collapsing categories of friends and family into a single group of "close relationships" or asking ambiguous questions about friends *and* family (e.g., Kim et al., 2011; Manago et al., 2012). Research is needed to understand just how emerging adults use communication technology to navigate emerging adulthood. The first of two empirical studies presented below examines how frequency of communication technology use with family is related to family satisfaction, and how emerging adults balance new college relationships while also maintaining family relationships during the transition to college. The second study examines how emerging adults make sense of communication technologies, weave them into everyday life, and how they impact family relationships. More specifically, the first study asks how well a structural equation model including direct and indirect pathways from frequency of communication technology use to self-esteem, loneliness, and family satisfaction represents the sample data (RQ1), and how emerging adults use communication technology to balance their family lives and new relationships while in college (RQ2). The second study asks how emerging adult students living away from home utilize communication technology with their families during college (RQ3).

Study One

Past research provides a starting place for constructing a predictive model of the relationship between self-esteem, loneliness, use of technology, and family satisfaction (e.g., the link between college students' loneliness and use of SNS to communicate with parents; Gentzler et al., 2011). A model including self-esteem, social loneliness, family satisfaction, and use of technology will be tested to answer the first research question. Despite what the research reviewed above has revealed, it is unknown how these variables operate within one model. To find out, a structural equation model (SEM) based on the associations identified in previous research is proposed (see Figure 8.1).

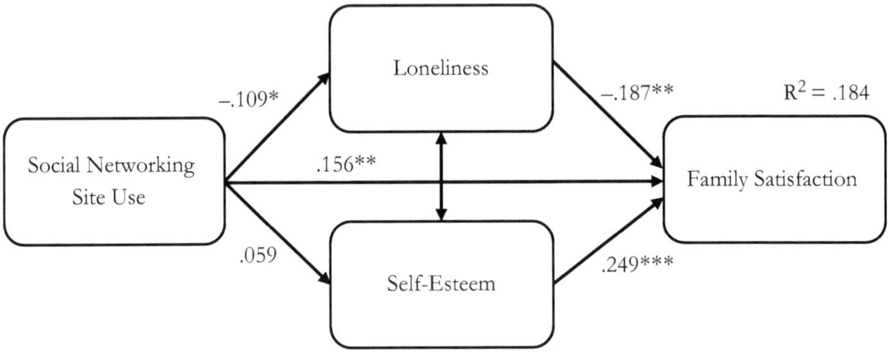

* $p < .05$. ** $p < .01$.*** $p < .001$.

Figure 8.1. The effect of emerging adults' use of communication technology with family members on self-esteem, loneliness, and family satisfaction: SNS use example.

To discover how family satisfaction and the transition to college are related to frequency of new technology use with family members, 453 college students were recruited from undergraduate communication courses at a large Midwestern university (260 males and 183 females, *M* age = 18.6, *SD* =.97) and were asked to report how frequently they use various communication technologies to communicate with family members in an online survey. Participants also completed scales for social loneliness (Oswald & Clark, 2003; α =.93), self-esteem (Rosenberg, 1965; α =.89), and family satisfaction (Campbell, Converse, & Rodgers, 1976; α =.92). Finally, students were given space to provide an answer as detailed as they wished to this question: "How do you balance your new life in college with your home life and relationships?" All open-ended data were examined using a qualitative grounded theory analysis method to search for "patterns of meaning" by identifying and refining themes and categories supported by these data (see Hatch, 2002, p. 161). Participants' responses to this question produced 36 pages of double-spaced data. The data were analyzed using the following steps: (1) read and become familiar with data; (2) create codes by making comparisons (i.e., comparing each incident of data with others to determine similarities and differences) and discover how data relate to each other; (3) dimensionalize the data by teasing out variations in properties of codes that run through all data further explain each code; and (4) determine theoretical saturation (Corbin & Strauss, 2008; Lindlof & Taylor, 2002).

Results. Emerging adults used texting most frequently (M = 4.90, SD = 1.73) to communicate with family while at college. Texting was followed in frequency of use by cell phones (M = 4.31, SD = 1.40), SNSs (M = 3.08, SD = 1.82), email (M = 2.70, SD = 1.64), and video chat (M = 2.39, SD = 1.52). The correlation matrix revealed that the use of landlines (M = 1.65, SD = 1.26) and blogging (M = 1.18, SD =.78) were the only forms of technology associated with lower self-esteem (landline r = -.173, p <.001; blogging r = -.107, p <.05) and greater loneliness (landline r =.181, p <.001; blogging r =.103, p <.05). Use of texting (r = -.176, p <.001) and SNSs (r = -.114, p <.05) was related to less loneliness while texting was also related to higher self-esteem (r =.114, p <.05). Frequent use of cell phones (r =.206, p <.001), texting (r =.232, p <.001), SNS (r =.184, p <.001), and video chat (r =.094, p <.05) were all positively and significantly associated with family satisfaction while blogging was negatively associated with family satisfaction (r = -.102, p <.05).

Table 8.1. Model Fit Indices and Standardized Betas.

Model	χ^2	DF	*p*-value	RMSEA	CFI	TLI	β (self-esteem to family satisfaction)	β (loneliness to family satisfaction)	β(technology use to family satisfaction)
Cell phone	256.93	60	.000	.085	.920	.878	.24***	-.20**	.21***
Texting	255.32	60	.000	.085	.921	.880	.26***	-.16*	.23***
SNS	244.85	60	.000	.083	.924	.885	.25***	-.19**	.16**
Email	249.50	60	.000	.084	.922	.881	.25***	-.20**	.04
Video Chat	271.07	60	.000	.088	.914	.869	.25***	-.21**	.10*
Blogging	255.86	60	.000	.085	.920	.878	.23***	-.204**	-.095 (trend)

* p <.05. ** p <.01. *** p <.001. trend: (p =.058)

SEM testing revealed several patterns in the data. All models exhibited adequate to good fit according to SEM standards for the model chi-square and degrees of freedom, comparative fit index, Tucker Lewis index, and the root mean square error of approximation (Bollen, 1989; see Table 8.1). Most models exhibited: (1) a significant positive pathway from the frequency of technology use to family satisfaction; (2) a significant positive pathway from self-esteem to family satisfaction; and (3) a negative significant pathway from loneliness to family satisfaction. This pattern was found for use of cell phones, texting, SNSs, and video chat and indicates those with higher self-esteem, lower loneliness, and more frequent use of technology (almost any kind) were also experiencing more satisfactory family relationships. The models explained 17–20% of the variance in family satisfaction. For example, the model testing cell phone use, self-esteem, and loneliness explained 20.2% of the variance in family satisfaction (R^2 =.20).

Inductive analysis of the open-ended data revealed that technology appeared to assist in the balancing act many emerging adults perform in order to maintain family relationships while being present in their new college environment. Emerging adults in this sample balance family and new friendships in two primary ways: (1) scheduled communication via technology and (2) small acts of connection via technology.

The data reveal that emerging adults are both cognizant of and intentional in their scheduled use of technology. For example, participants cited strategies such as: (a) setting certain days for communicating: "I have set days that I Skype with old friends. I try to communicate with each of my family members at least once a week"; (b) contacting family members every night: "I try to call my parents every night to keep in contact with them…I then spend the extra time studying and spending time with my friends here in college"; and (c) allotting portions of time to important relationships: "My mom and I have weekly Friday afternoon talks that I absolutely look forward to—I have that time slot blocked off just for her."

The second category, small acts of connection via technology, included excerpts from participants who perceived limited time for maintaining family relationships. These emerging adults felt technologies such as texting and email allowed them to engage in behaviors like spending just a few minutes connecting with family members. For example:

> If I am not doing an activity that requires a lot of attention I will be sure to send a text message to a friend, my mom, and occasionally my sister or dad. Also, during walks to and from campus I try to call my parents and see how they are doing and update them about what has been happening in college.

One participant expressed technology has helped close the physical distance gap in his relationships: "We Skype, talk over the phone, and text a ton in order to keep in touch and make it feel like we aren't that far apart." Data in this category revealed that several participants who felt pressure to be present at college and maintain home relationships sent text messages to family members between classes. The utility of texting was reflected in the response of this participant: "Sending an email or text or having a quick phone conversation can be done at any time."

Study one provides quantitative insights into how frequency of communication technology use impacts psychological and family relational outcomes and qualitative insights into the balancing act many emerging adults perform to maintain family relationships while building new friendships on campus.

Study Two

Study two extends the questions of study one by seeking to answer the third research question: "How do emerging adult students living away from home utilize communication technology with their families during college?" The researchers conducted eight separate focus groups ($N = 49$, 26 males and 23 females, M age = 20.26, $SD = 2.59$) consisting of between 3 and 11 college students in each group, all in the emerging adult life stage. Participants were recruited from introductory level communication classes and the focus groups were moderated by the authors. The semi-structured interview protocol was designed to elicit discussion about how participants use communication technologies with their family members, and how those communication technologies related to family relationships. Examples of guiding questions included: "In what ways do you feel communication technology brings your family together?" and "How do you use it to maintain your family relationships?"

Focus groups were recorded, transcribed verbatim and de-identified to protect the identities of the participants. Similar to study one, the researchers used a grounded theory approach (Glaser & Strauss, 1967) and open coding (Strauss & Corbin, 1997) to examine the themes that emerged from the participants' talk. A qualitative lens provided an opportunity for rich exploration into use of communication technologies (i.e., cell phone, video chat, IM, email, SNS, and text message use), their ability to facilitate or inhibit family communication, and the ways family members use technologies to maintain family relationships during the transition to college and throughout emerging adulthood.

Results. Two overarching categories emerged from the grounded theory analysis: (1) managing the transition to college through opportunities for communication and (2) challenges associated with communication technology. The first category demonstrated that emerging adults use technologies in structured ways to manage the transition and their busy schedules. Technology provides avenues for connecting with family members despite the interruption in communication caused by the transition to college. Communication technologies also assist college students by providing a means to navigate the constraints placed on their time by the rigorous schedule that comes with a full load of classes, social expectations, and often a part-time job. Busy students were able to fit in a quick text, phone call, or instant message to family members while walking to class or doing homework. Some emerging adults reported using text messaging to keep an open and ongoing connection with some family members. Others used texting to share trivial messages that were not important enough to warrant a phone call, thereby making a connection they might not have otherwise. One participant described this phenomenon:

> It's easier to keep in touch with parents and siblings over longer period of time texting just because it's such a slow process. Like 'hey' and they'll reply back 'hey' but dragging that conversation on through a longer time period you stay in touch with them longer than a five minute phone call then after that you're done. Instead, texting has kept me in better contact with my sister throughout a longer span of time than a phone call would.

The second category revealed that while communication technology was enhancing emerging adults' ability to stay connected to family members while away at college, it was also causing relational problems. First, participants cited two extremes in family members' use of technology: (a) overuse versus access and ability limitations and (b) communication technology discomfort. One participant expressed she felt she could not escape her mother because she had the ability to access the participant at any time through various forms of technology:

> Sometimes when she talks she never stops. So I could spend hours and hours talking to her from this medium to that medium because she has everything. She has Skype, she has smart phones, she has Facebook, she has Twitter. She has everything. She asks me on everything. So, and I can't just ignore her friend request because she would be yelling at me. So basically, she knows my life, my friends and everything like that. So the more she knows about it the more she wants to talk to me about it and that's where we're really spending a lot of time through technology.

On the contrary, participants noted some family members lacked access to some technologies they believed would enhance their communication. Grandparents and parents often did not have the skills necessary to use certain media and thus communication between those members and the student was hindered. One participant revealed: "My mom, she hates cell phones, she hates technology, she will never have her phone on her, and I hate that because I can't get a hold of her, ever. So I wish she would use it more." For others, the transition to college was a driving force for other family members to learn new technological skills.

Second, participants disclosed a sense of relational discomfort due to communication technology. Some felt unnatural when communicating with family members in person after only using communication technology for a period of time:

> You get so used to relying on technology to keep in touch with our family members that when we are actually all together it is kind of awkward. It's just like different, you know what I mean? Because everyone relies so heavily on texting and emailing and Facebook and stuff that when it's in person it becomes a different situation.

Another participant felt a similar strain in her relationship with her brother: "I think he overly relies on technology cause I'll get an email from him every once in awhile, and now when I see him in person, which is once every other year, we don't know how to talk to each other anymore. It's really awkward." Participants also expressed how relationships can feel strained or uncomfortable over technology because they are not face to face. For example, one participant stated, "I just, I feel weird talking to a computer screen. I know my dad's face is right there I just feel weird talking to a computer screen." Overall, results from study two revealed both benefits and challenges associated with technology for emerging adults communicating with family members.

Discussion

The results from study one provide quantitative insights into the frequency of technology use and the association of use with family satisfaction, self-esteem, and loneliness in emerging adults, while the qualitative results of both studies reveal *how* emerging adults are using technologies to maintain family relationships. Overall, results suggest communication technologies serve relational maintenance functions for emerging adults and their family members, and facilitate support; however, they are not without challenges (e.g., access and ability restrictions). Results from study two largely support what was found in study one (e.g., the intentional and systematic uses of technology by emerging adults for communicating with family), and specifically revealed barriers perceived by emerging adults using communication technologies with family members such as relational discomfort as a result of mediated face-to-face communication, along with lack of access or ability on the part of their family members.

Two interesting patterns were evident in the quantitative data from study one. First, frequency of technology use and self-esteem were positively related to family satisfaction while loneliness was inversely related. This pattern revealed that participants who reported the highest levels of family satisfaction also indicated higher self-esteem, less loneliness, and more frequent use of technology (of almost any kind). Those individuals likely receive more support from parents (Chen & Katz, 2009; Gentzler et al., 2011) and experience more adaptive transitions during emerging adulthood. A second pattern revealed that the pathway from frequency of technology use to self-esteem and to loneliness was almost never significant (except for SNS to loneliness and blogging), potentially meaning that technology use is not driving self-esteem or loneliness, but that a third variable (e.g., online attitudes; Gangadharbatla, 2008; or levels of social presence; Morahan-Martin & Schumacher, 2003) plays a mediating role in the relationship.

The model testing the frequency of blog use displayed a unique pattern. The blogging model was the only place in which both pathways from technology use to self-esteem and loneliness were significant. Unlike the pattern described above, an increase in frequency of blog use was associated with a *decrease* in family satisfaction (at the trend level, p =.58). Blogging is unique in that it is one of the least used communication technologies among emerging adults and has actually declined in use over the last decade (Lenhart et al., 2010). This finding might indicate that emerging adults who *are* frequently using blogs to communicate with family are doing so because they are experiencing unsatisfactory family relationships. Blogging can fulfill emerging adults' needs for social connection and relationships with close others as well as with a mass audience of acquaintances and strangers (Mazur & Kozarian, 2010). If emerging adult bloggers can experience social bonding and support online, they might rely less on family. Alternatively, those with unsupportive or unsatisfactory family relationships might turn to blogging to fill those voids.

The qualitative results in study one demonstrated that across participants a pattern of texting and using Facebook throughout the week, and scheduling nightly or weekly phone or video-chat calls with family members, was apparent. While not all emerging adults claimed to have achieved a desirable balance in their home and college lives, others found scheduling times for using various communication technologies allowed them to keep the two aspects of their lives separate yet maintained. These findings support MMT—that people use many different media to maintain their relationships and that the combined use of many technologies impacts the interdependence and strength of the relationship (Walther & Parks, 2002).

Study two also provided insight into the way emerging adults use technologies to communicate with their families during the transition to college. In using technology to manage busy schedules, emerging adults may be engaging in strategic boundary management (Petronio, 2002). For example, participants, use of text messaging to communicate with family while not taking much time away from a busy schedule, or using phone calls when one seeks to engage in a more in-depth conversation, represent ways emerging adults are distancing themselves and engaging in identity formation independent from family. The results from study two also indicate that when choosing a technology to convey a message, the access and ability of the message recipient makes a difference. Previous research has found that skill compatibility is a barrier to communication (Tee, Brush, & Inkpen, 2009). In this study, compatibility was not necessarily a barrier as much as it was an inconvenience; while they may have communicated less as a result, many emerging adults simply chose to communicate with a different technology. Because emerging adults have a variety of technologies in their communication arsenal, they tended to select the medium through which to connect with family that best fit the others'—as well as their own—needs, abilities, and preferences at a particular time and/or on a particular topic.

An unexpected theme that emerged from analyses was that participants reported feeling uncomfortable in face-to-face situations with their families after an extended time using only mediated communication. The phenomenon seemed to work both ways in that participants felt unnatural using mediated technology in the first place *and* they felt uncomfortable in face-to-face situations when they were reunited with family members. It is possible that the technologies they are using when apart are not facilitating adequate social presence; that is, they are not facilitating enough of a sense of being together to bridge the gap between face-to-face encounters (Biocca et al., 2003). In other words, the technologies may lack the ability to create a space where emerging adults and their family members feel a sense of being together. Alternatively, participants may have adopted specific communicative patterns used to manage privacy boundaries (Petronio, 2002). Their discomfort may manifest both in the struggle to set up and negotiate these boundaries when using mediated communication, as well as in the process of readapting when returning to face-to-face communication. The discomfort may be related to reframing or loss of strategies in the latter situation. Such questions are ripe for future research.

Much remains to be explored in the area of communication technology among emerging adults and the impact of its use on family relationships. While the two empirical studies reported here begin to the fill the knowledge gaps about how emerging adults use technology to communicate with family, there remain many important questions. We urge researchers to focus on how online attitudes influence relational outcomes, and examine how the model is different for individuals in the emerging adult life stage versus other life stages. For example, research and consumer trends indicate there should be differences in online behaviors across life stages (Jennings & Wartella, 2013). Emerging adults use many communication technologies more frequently than do other groups (Lenhart et al., 2010), but it is unknown just how such behavior is associated with online attitudes and perceptions of image and privacy, and especially how such attitudes and perceptions affect relationship communication and choices.

In addition, the research presented above suggests emerging adults are using technology to help maintain family relationships despite their hectic, often unsettled lives. However, little research explains how the process works, how the process is different from strategies emerging adults have employed in the past (e.g., writing letters and calling home from a community dormitory phone), what topics individuals feel comfortable talking about using which technologies, and how technology can be improved to further aid connections and closeness between family members.

Finally, as with any study, ours have limitations. First, the cross-sectional and situated design of both studies prevents claims of causality between variables or generalizations beyond the given samples. For example, study one was not able to assess whether use of technology actually predicts family satisfaction or vice versa. The cross-sectional design also prevented an analysis of how family relationships change over time, which is likely to happen during the transition to college due to role reconfigurations and increased independence (Paul & Brier, 2001; Terenzini et al., 1994). Levels of self-esteem and loneliness are also likely to change over time due to the transitional nature of the emerging adult life stage. It would be of interest to follow the same participants from the time they first move away from their families through their college careers to capture the distinct changes that occur in communication technology use. In addition, research that includes the college-aged participant along with the perceptions of their complete family group would allow researchers to assess whether communication technology choices are more or less successful at maintaining those relationships, as well as whether the technology choices mean the same thing to the message sender and recipient.

Application

The literature and studies presented in this chapter have both theoretical and practical implications for family communication and relationship scholars, as well as for students, professionals, and family members. The changes that occur during emerging adulthood affect the whole family, not just the individual experiencing such changes. A family member moving away, transitioning from school to work, and developing new interests can "shake up the whole family system" (Aquilino, 2006, p. 196). It's important to recognize that emerging adults' experiences can and do affect the whole family, and thus all members are wise to consider ways to support the emerging adults' transitions. For instance, parents and grandparents might consider adopting new technologies to facilitate and maintain connection with the emerging adult. Research suggests emerging adults who feel supported have more freedom to explore their identities and develop independence of career, relationships, and worldview. Access to and support from family members is essential for smooth and successful adaptation during this dynamic life stage. Family members who seek to communicate more with emerging adults might need to not only embrace new technologies but also consider which media is preferred and most often used by the emerging adult member. At the same time, family members—especially parents—must respect boundaries and grant the emerging adult child the space needed to explore new aspects of his or her identity and form ties with new social groups. Because frequent communication over a variety of technologies is associated with more satisfactory family relationships, emerging adults and their family members should consider attempting to connect over a variety of media when possible and accessible. Awareness of how emerging adults use SNSs can help parents and grandparents integrate their communication in a style and venue emerging adults already find useful (e.g., posting pictures, planning events, seeking support, making timeline updates—or simply post personal updates knowing that some emerging adults spend time "lurking" to gather information).

Family members can also be aware that certain types of media use (e.g., text messaging) are more desirable and beneficial for the emerging adult group because of the often erratic and dynamic schedules typical of college life. Emerging adults can be aware of and take advantage of the asynchronous nature of certain technologies, mindfully adapting their relationship maintenance skills to such technologies. Parents are wise to acknowledge that emerging adults can benefit from communicating quickly and at their convenience through text messages; emerging adults might be mindful of how even quick information transmission can make a significant difference in family members' sense of inclusion and connection, resulting in overall great family satisfaction for members. Both the emerging adults and their family members should be aware that while convenience is a strength of asynchronous technology, real-time technologies (e.g., Skype, Facetime, phone calls) are more effective at creating a sense of being together. While busy schedules of all family members might inhibit the frequent use of these technologies, family members should strive for a balance of synchronous and asynchronous communication technologies to keep in touch.

Although emerging adulthood will likely remain a life stage marked by an overall experience of being unsettled, research consistently suggests that how emerging adults and their families manage communication is key to successful adaptation to this life stage. It is essential that family members recognize the profound opportunities for identity development during emerging adulthood and the role communication technologies play in these efforts. Technologies provide profound opportunities for emerging adults to express distance from their family group (e.g., boundary setting on SNSs) while also maintaining connections to them (e.g., through ongoing text message conversations). Emerging adults and the many members of their family systems are wise to make careful, informed choices that consider how communication technologies can help ease the tensions and challenges, and also nurture the growth, of both the emerging adult *and* the larger family system during a time of great transition.

References

Alvesson, M., & Robertson, M. (2006). The best and the brightest: The construction, significance, and effects of elite identities in consulting firms. *Organization, 13*, 195–224.

Aquilino, W. S. (2006). Family relationships and support systems in emerging adulthood. In J. J. Arnett & J. L. Tanner (Eds.), *Emerging adults in America: Coming of age in the 21st century* (pp. 193–217). Washington, DC: American Psychological Association.

Arnett, J. J. (2000). Emerging adulthood: A theory of development from the late teens through the twenties. *American psychologist, 55*, 469–480.

Biocca, F., Harms, C., & Burgoon, J. K. (2003). Toward a more robust theory and measure of social presence: Review and suggested criteria. *Presence: Teleoperators and virtual environments, 12*, 456–480.

Bollen, K. (1989). *Structural equations with latent variables (SELV)*. New York: Wiley.

boyd, d. (2006, February). Identity production in a networked culture: Why youth heart MySpace. Talk given at American Association for the Advancement of Science, St. Louis, MO. Retrieved from: http://www.danah.org/papers/AAAS2006.html

boyd, d. (2011). Social network sites as networked publics: Affordances, dynamics, and implications. In Z. Papacharissi (Ed.), *A Networked Self* (pp. 39–58). New York: Routledge.

boyd, d., & Ellison, N. (2007). Social network sites: Definition, history, and scholarship. *Journal of Computer-Mediated Communication, 13*, 210–230.

Burgoon, J., & Hale, J. L. (1987). Validation and measurement of the fundamental themes of relational communication. *Communication Monographs, 54*, 19–41.

Campbell, A., Converse, P. E., & Rodgers, W. L. (1976). *The quality of American life: Perceptions, evaluations, and satisfaction*. New York: Russell Sage Foundation.

Chen, Y. F., & Katz, J. E. (2009). Extending family to school life: College students' use of the mobile phone. *International Journal of Human–Computer Studies, 67*, 179–191.

Cheung, C. M., Chiu, P. Y., & Lee, M. K. (2011). Online social networks: Why do students use Facebook? *Computers in Human Behavior, 27*, 1337–1343.

Child, J. T., Haridakis, P. M., & Petronio, S. (2012). Blogging privacy rule orientations, privacy management, and content deletion practices: The variability of online privacy management activity at different stages of social media use. *Computers in Human Behavior, 28*, 1859–1872

Cohen, S. M., de Lussanet, M., Garon, A., & Wilkos, D. (2008, September 9). Multiple identities allow teens to create boundaries in online social networks. Retrieved from http://www.forrester.com/Multiple+Identities+Allow+Teens+To+Create+Boundaries+In+Online+Social+-Networks/fulltext/-/E-RES47006

Corbin, J., & Strauss, A. (2008). *Basics of qualitative research* (3rd ed.) Thousand Oaks, CA: Sage.

Dwyer, C, Hiltz, S. R., & Passerini, K. (2007). *Trust and privacy concern within social networking sites: A comparison of Facebook and MySpace.* Proceedings of the Thirteenth Americas Conference on Information Systems, Keystone, CO.

Ellison, N., Heino, R., & Gibbs, J. (2006). Managing impressions online: Self-presentation processes in the online dating environment. *Journal of Computer-Mediated Communication, 11*, 415–441.

Ellison, N. B., Steinfield, C., & Lampe, C. (2007). The benefits of Facebook "friends": Social capital and college students' use of online social network sites. *Journal of Computer-Mediated Communication, 12*, 1143–1168.

Erdur-Baker, Ö. (2010). Cyberbullying and its correlation to traditional bullying, gender, and frequent and risky usage of Internet-mediated communication tools. *New Media & Society, 12*, 109–125.

Gangadharbatla, H. (2008). Facebook me: Collective self-esteem, need to belong, and Internet self-efficacy as predictors of the iGeneration's attitudes toward social networking sites. *Journal of interactive advertising, 8*, 5–15.

Gentzler, A. L., Oberhauser, A. M., Westerman, D., & Nadorff, D. K. (2011). College students' use of electronic communication with parents: Links to loneliness, attachment, and relationship quality. *Cyberpsychology, Behavior, and Social Networking, 14*, 71–74.

Glaser, B., & Strauss, A. (1967). The discovery of grounded theory. New York: Aldine.

Harwood, J. (2000). Communication media use in the grandparent–grandchild relationship. *Journal of Communication, 50*, 56–78.

Hatch, J. A. (2002). Analyzing qualitative data. In *Doing qualitative research in education settings* (pp. 147–210). Albany: State University of New York Press.

Holladay, S. J., & Seipke, H. L. (2007). Communication between grandparents and grandchildren in geographically separated relationships. *Communication Studies, 58*, 281–297.

Jennings, N. A., & Wartella, E. (2013). Digital technology and families. In A. Vangelisti (Ed.), *The Routledge Handbook of Family Communication* (2nd ed., pp. 448–462). London: Routledge.

Johnson, A. J., Haigh, M. M., Becker, J. A., Craig, E. A., & Wigley, S. (2008). College students' use of relational management strategies in email in long-distance and geographically close relationships. *Journal of Computer-Mediated Communication, 13*, 381–404.

Junco, R., Merson, D., & Salter, D. W. (2010). The effect of gender, ethnicity, and income on college students' use of communication technologies. *Cyberpsychology, Behavior, and Social Networking, 13*, 619–627.

Kim, Y., Sohn, D., & Choi, S. M. (2011). Cultural difference in motivations for using social network sites: A comparative study of American and Korean college students. *Computers in Human Behavior, 27*, 365–372.

Koerner, A. F., & Fitzpatrick, M. (2002). Toward a theory of family communication. *Communication Theory, 12*, 70–91.

Ledbetter, A. M. (2010). Family communication patterns and communication competence as predictors of online communication attitude: Evaluating a dual pathway model. *Journal of Family Communication, 10*, 99–115.

Ledbetter, A. M., Heiss, S., Sibal, K., Lev, E., Battle-Fisher, M., & Shubert, N. (2010). Parental invasive and children's defensive behaviors at home and away at college: Mediated communication and privacy boundary management. *Communication Studies, 61*, 184–204.

Ledbetter, A. M., & Mazer, J. P. (2014). Do online communication attitudes mitigate the association between Facebook use and relational interdependence? An extension of media multiplexity theory. *New Media & Society, 16*, 806–822.

Lenhart, A., Purcell, K., Smith, A., & Zickuhr, K. (2010). *Social media & mobile Internet use among teens and young adults* (pp. 155–179). Washington, DC: Pew Internet & American Life Project.

Lindlof, T. R., & Taylor, B. C. (2002). *Qualitative communication research methods*. Thousand Oaks, CA: Sage.

Manago, A. M., Taylor, T., & Greenfield, P. M. (2012). Me and my 400 friends: The anatomy of college students' Facebook networks, their communication patterns, and well-being. *Developmental psychology, 48*, 369–380.

Marwick, A. E., & boyd, d. (2011). I tweet honestly, I tweet passionately: Twitter users, context collapse, and the imagined audience. *New Media Society, 13*, 114–133.

Mazur, E., & Kozarian, L. (2010). Self-presentation and interaction in blogs of adolescents and young emerging adults. *Journal of Adolescent Research, 25*(1), 124–144.

Mead, G. H. (1934). *Mind, Self, and Society*. Chicago: University of Chicago Press.

Morahan-Martin, J., & Schumacher, P. (2003). Loneliness and social uses of the Internet. *Computers in Human Behavior, 19*, 659–671.

O'Keeffe, G. S., & Clarke-Pearson, K. (2011). The impact of social media on children, adolescents, and families. *Pediatrics, 127*, 800–804.

Oswald, D. L. & Clark, E. M. (2003). Best friends forever? High school best friendships and the transition to college. *Personal Relationships, 10*, 187–196.

Paul, E. L., & Brier, S. (2001). Friendsickness in the transition to college: Precollege predictors and college adjustment correlates. *Journal of Counseling & Development, 79*, 77–89.

Pempek, T. A., Yermolayeva, Y. A., & Calvert, S. L. (2009). College students' social networking experiences on Facebook. *Journal of Applied Developmental Psychology, 30*, 227–238.

Petronio, S. (1991). Communication boundary management: A theoretical model of managing disclosure of private information between marital couples. *Communication Theory, 1*, 311–335.

Petronio, S. (2002). *Boundaries of privacy: Dialectics of disclosure*. Albany: State University of New York Press.

Rosenberg, M. (1965). *Society and the adolescent self-image*. Princeton, NJ: Princeton University Press.

Schwartz, S. J., Côté, J. E., & Arnett, J. J. (2005). Identity and agency in emerging adulthood: Two developmental routes in the individualization process. *Youth & Society, 37*, 201–229.

Short, J., Williams, E., & Christie, B. (1976). *The social psychology of telecommunications.* London: John Wiley & Sons.

Skeels, M. M., & Grudin, J. (2009, May). When social networks cross boundaries: A case study of workplace use of Facebook and Linkedin. *Proceedings of the Association for Computing Machinery International Conference on Supporting Group Work* (pp. 95–104).

Smith, C. (2014, March 13). By the numbers: 123 amazing Facebook user statistics. Retrieved from http://expandedramblings.com/index.php/by-the-numbers-17-amazing-facebook-stats/#.U52eifldWSp

Steinfield, C., Ellison, N. B., & Lampe, C. (2008). Social capital, self-esteem, and use of online social network sites: A longitudinal analysis. *Journal of Applied Developmental Psychology, 29,* 434–445.

Strauss, A., & Corbin, J. M. (1997). *Grounded theory in practice.* Thousand Oaks, CA: Sage.

Subrahmanyam, K., Reich, S. M., Waechter, N., & Espinoza, G. (2008). Online and offline social networks: Use of social networking sites by emerging adults. *Journal of Applied Developmental Psychology, 29,* 420–433.

Tajfel, H. (1972). Social categorization. English manuscript of 'La catégorisation sociale.' In S. Moscovici (Ed.), *Introduction à la Psychologie Sociale* (Vol. 1, pp. 272–302). Paris: Larousse.

Tee, K., Brush, A., & Inkpen, K. (2009). Exploring communication and sharing between extended families. *International Journal of Human–Computer Studies, 67,* 128–138.

Terenzini, P. T., Rendon, L. I., Lee Upcraft, M., Millar, S. B., Allison, K. W., Gregg, P. L., & Jalomo, R. (1994). The transition to college: Diverse students, diverse stories. *Research in Higher Education, 35,* 57–73.

Tracy, S. J. & Trethewey, A. (2005). Fracturing the real-self⇔fake-self dichotomy: Moving toward "crystallized" organizational discourse and identities. *Communication Theory, 15,* 168–195.

Trice, A. D. (2002). First semester college students' email to parents: Frequency and content related to parenting style. *College Student Journal, 36,* 328–334.

Tufekci, Z. (2008). Can you see me now? Audience and disclosure regulation in online social network sites. *Bulletin of Science, Technology & Society, 28,* 20–36.

Walther, J. B. (1992). Interpersonal effects in computer-mediated interaction: A relational perspective. *Communication Research, 19,* 52–90.

Walther, J. B. (2007). Selective self-presentation in computer-mediated communication: Hyperpersonal dimensions of technology, language, and cognition. *Computers in Human Behavior, 23,* 2538–2557.

Walther, J. B., & Parks, M. R. (2002). Cues filtered out, cues filtered in: Computer-mediated communication and relationships. In M. L. Knapp & J. A. Daly (Eds.), *Handbook of interpersonal communication* (3rd ed., pp. 529–563). Thousand Oaks, CA: Sage.

Walther, J. B., Van Der Heide, B., Kim, S. Y., Westerman, D., & Tong, S. T. (2008). The role of friends' appearance and behavior on evaluations of individuals on Facebook: Are we known by the company we keep? *Human Communication Research, 34,* 28–49.

9

Staying Connected

Supportive Communication During the College Transition

MADELINE E. SMITH
Northwestern University

AUTHOR NOTE: This material is based upon work supported by the National Science Foundation Graduate Research Fellowship under Grant No. DGE-0824162. The author thanks Jeremy Birnholtz and Kathleen Galvin for supporting and advising this work, and the anonymous participants for sharing their stories.

Introduction

While it is typical for students in the United States to live with their families in high school, many move out of their family homes to attend college (Pryor et al., 2012). This chapter focuses on the transition to college, a major life change for students who move away from their family homes (Holmes & Rahe, 1967). When they arrive on campus, first-year students often experience a dramatically new environment, one in which they are expected to simultaneously perform academically, form new relationships, and become independent adults. This transition can be extremely stressful, plagued by homesickness, peer pressure, loneliness, and depression (Dyson & Renk, 2006). While many students are able to overcome these challenges and succeed, more than 40% of students who begin bachelors degree programs fail to graduate from those programs within 6 years (Kena et al., 2014), and depression is a significant predictor of dropping out (Eisenberg, Golberstein, & Hunt, 2009). Reducing stress during the transition to college might help reduce experiences of depression and, in doing so, support emerging adults successfully journey toward adulthood.

Social support (Cohen & McKay, 1984) can buffer the stressful effects of life changes, including the transition to college (Mattanah, Ayers, Brand, & Brooks, 2010). However, more than 60% of students move more than 50 miles from home to attend college (Pryor et al., 2012), physically separating them from family, the people most young adults rely on for significant social support (Licitra-Kleckler & Waas, 1993; Taylor, Doane, & Eisenberg, 2013). Today's college students use a variety of communication technologies (phone calls, texting, email, Facebook, Skype, and others) to communicate and maintain relationships with family members at home (Smith, Nguyen, Lai, Leshed, & Baumer, 2012). These technologies can communicate social support as effectively as face-to-face communication (Lewandowski, Rosenberg, Jordan Parks, & Siegel, 2011; Mikal, Rice, Abeyta, & DeVilbiss, 2013) and are associated with successful college adjustment and increased perceptions of social support (DeAndrea, Ellison, LaRose, Steinfield, & Fiore, 2012; Gray, Vitak, Easton, & Ellison, 2013).

During this transition, many students are dealing with changing family relationships (Lefkowitz, 2005). While supportive relationships with parents can smooth students' adjustment to college (Wintre & Yaffe, 2000) and distance from family can encourage the development of independence and autonomy (Arnett, 2000; Flanagan, Schulenberg, & Fuligni, 1993), overinvolved parents—often known as helicopter parents—can negatively impact students (LeMoyne & Buchanan, 2011). Finding the right balance is key, yet figuring out how to strike such a balance is not always easy. It is clear that students now use these affordable technologies to communicate with their families more frequently than ever before (Chen & Katz, 2009), yet it is unclear how this increased communication impacts students' development and adjustment to college (Eisenberg et al., 2009; Hofer, 2008). This chapter reviews literature on college transitions, emerging adulthood, and social support and uses interview data to explore the role of mediated family communication in supporting new students during their transitions to college.

Literature Review

Transition to College

Although beginning college can be an exciting opportunity for students, it also represents a major life transition. Such life changes can negatively impact individuals' health and well-being (Rahe, Meyer, Smith, Kjaer, & Holmes, 1964; Scully,

Tosi, & Banning, 2000). Because new college students typically experience multiple life changes, it is not surprising that the transition is viewed as one of the most difficult that emerging adults face and has been extensively studied (Fromme, Corbin, & Kruse, 2008; Gray et al., 2013; Kerr, Johnson, Gans, & Krumrine, 2004; Smith & Zhang, 2010; Taylor et al., 2013). Adjustment to college is multidimensional; students adjust academically, emotionally, socially, and to the institution they attend (Baker & Siryk, 1986). Students' adjustment is important for their success in college (Credé & Niehorster, 2011; Krotseng, 1992).

Reducing stress during this transition is important to increase the odds of successful adjustment to, and success in, college (Dyson & Renk, 2006; Eisenberg et al., 2009; Fisher & Hood, 1987). Research suggests millennial college students are often ill-equipped to handle such stress (Bland, Melton, Welle, & Bigham, 2012). The students who experience psychological issues during the transition to college are more likely to be students who find the transition difficult (Dyson & Renk, 2006; Fisher & Hood, 1987). Students who experience depression during college also have lower GPAs and are more likely to drop out of college than students who do not (Eisenberg et al., 2009).

Social Support

Providing social support to individuals navigating stressful life transitions is key to their well-being and success. According to Albrecht (1984) social support is "the way in which communication behaviors tie an individual to his or her social environment and function to enable the individual to positively relate to that environment" (p. 5), and can take the form of providing solutions and/or reducing the perceived importance of a stressful situation (Cohen & McKay, 1984). Social support helps people in four primary ways (Wills, 1985): (1) emotional support helps individuals feel valued; (2) informational support helps individuals understand and cope with problematic events; (3) social companionship helps individuals feel less isolated; and (4) instrumental support provides needed resources or services.

Research on social support demonstrates its usefulness for guiding people through various stressful situations and life changes (Cobb, 1976; Cohen & McKay, 1984). Recently, researchers have identified a number of ways social support benefits emerging adults during the transition to college. For example, Friedlander, Ried, Shupak, and Cribbie (2007) found that social support from friends improves students' adjustment to college. Similarly, Mattanah et al. (2010) developed an intervention that provided social support to new college students and effectively improved their adjustment to college. Further, Taylor, Doane, and Eisenberg (2013) found students with higher levels of perceived social support were less likely to internalize depression and anxiety symptoms. With the many benefits of social support on students' adjustment to college, how can we ensure that students access these crucial social support resources?

Most college students in the United States are residential students, and more than 60% move more than 50 miles from their family homes to attend college (Pryor et al., 2012). Research suggests students who live on campus—geographically separated from friends and family members who have provided social support in the past—perceive less social support and are more lonely and anxious than commuter students (Larose & Boivin, 1998). Fortunately, communication technologies now make it possible to receive social support from a distance (Lewandowski et al., 2011; Oh, Ozkaya, & LaRose, 2014). Further, some researchers argue that computer-mediated social support can be superior to face-to-face social support when managing the stress of life transitions because it enables people to keep in touch with their existing support networks while also finding and connecting with new supporters (Mikal et al., 2013).

Social media researchers have demonstrated that engaging with friends through Facebook and similar digital platforms can provide students with social support and positively impact their adjustment to college (Gray et al., 2013). Further, social media–based interventions, such as providing incoming students with access to a social media site designed to enhance their feelings of community on campus, have been shown to improve their expectations of support and overall adjustment to college (DeAndrea et al., 2012). Since most college students today are frequent users of computer-mediated communication and social media (Smith, Rainie, & Zickuhr, 2011), the role of such communication technologies in social support for college students deserves further research attention.

Changing Family Relationships

Developmentally, college students are emerging adults; they no longer see themselves as adolescents but don't consider themselves to be entirely adults yet either (Arnett, 2000). Their relationships with parents can play a significant role in their adjustment to college; specifically, benefitting when parents and students treat each other as equals and engage in open communication (Wintre & Yaffe, 2000). These relationships are shaped in the adolescent years (Aquilino, 2006) but also change during the transition to college (Parra, Oliva, & Reina, 2013). As students adjust to college, they are developing independence and must renegotiate roles and establish new dynamics with their parents, who often have different expectations about their own authority and their children's autonomy than do the students themselves (Kenyon & Koerner, 2009; Padilla-Walker, Nelson, & Knapp, 2014).

Students today use a wide range of digital communication tools to communicate with their parents while adjusting to college (Smith et al., 2012), and some research indicates that students who communicate more frequently with their parents are better able to adjust (Sarigiani, Trumbell, & Camarena, 2013). Although there are many benefits of student–parent communication during students' transition to college, other research suggests this increased communication can be problematic. For instance, students who communicate with parents most frequently are less autonomous and less satisfied both with their college experiences and relationships with parents (Hofer, 2008).

Many college students are supported financially by their parents, which can complicate expectations and renegotiation of parent–child roles (Aquilino, 2006). Additionally, parents today are often more involved in their children's college educations than were parents in previous generations (Cullaty, 2011). Many students find this additional involvement helpful and consult their parents when making important decisions during college (Pizzolato & Hicklen, 2011). In some cases, parents can become overinvolved, hindering students' development and well-being (Schiffrin et al., 2014). These parents are commonly referred to as "helicopter parents"—well-meaning parents who are more intrusive and hover more than is considered developmentally appropriate given the age of their children (Padilla-Walker & Nelson, 2012). Some evidence suggests college students with helicopter parents are more depressed and less satisfied with their lives than their peers (Schiffrin et al., 2014). Although family support can help students adjust to college, too frequent communication with parents might discourage independence and autonomy, a crucial developmental task of emerging adults.

Interview Study

As the literature reveals, adjusting to college is a major life change, and one that can be quite challenging. Communication technologies enable seeking and receiving social support from a distance and are frequently used by college students to communicate with family members. This in-depth interview study sought to bring together these areas and answer the following research question:

RQ: How do first-year college students use communication technologies to seek and receive support from family members?

Participants and Methods

Twenty-eight first-year undergraduate students from a selective midwestern United States university participated in this study. Students were recruited with flyers on campus and social media posts, and were compensated with $10 gift certificates to Amazon.com. All participants lived on campus at the time of the study and had grown up in the United States. Nineteen female students and nine male students participated; all were between the ages of 18 and 20 (M = 19.31). Students' hometowns ranged from 16 to 1730 miles from campus (M = 539.76). Five participants were undecided about their majors; the remaining 23 reported majors across a diverse range of fields including biology, cognitive science, engineering, journalism, and music. Participants' ethnicities reflected the racial breakdown of the overall freshmen class: Caucasian (n = 15), Asian (n = 6), Latino (n = 4) and African American (n = 3).

Each interview was semi-structured, followed an establish protocol, and was conducted by the author in a private room on campus between April and June 2013. Interviews began with general questions about the student, their family, and their overall adjustment to college. Participants were then asked to discuss specific situations that were stressful or challenging for them during their college transition. For each such situation, they were asked to describe what made it challenging, if/when they felt better about it, with whom they talked about it, what (if any) technology they used to communicate with those people, and how/if those people were helpful. At the end of the interview participants were asked about their general strategies for seeking social support and relieving stress.

After the interview, participants completed a short survey including demographic questions and questions about their communication technology practices. Specifically, students were asked how often (on an eight-item Likert scale from "never" to "multiple times a day") and with whom (romantic partners, close friends, other friends, acquaintances, parents, siblings, other family members, and other people) they used various communication technologies (phone calls, email, texting, instant messaging, video calling, social network sites (SNS), social games, and collaboration tools). Interviews lasted between 32 and 60 minutes (M = 48:02); all were audio recorded and fully transcribed for analysis, resulting in more than 23 hours of recorded audio and 411 pages of typed transcripts.

Interview transcripts were iteratively reviewed and coded to identify the themes presented next. The author first read through the transcripts and listened to the audio recordings using open-coding (Glaser & Strauss, 1967) to identify themes in the data related to the research question. Next, notes were compared across interviews to identify themes, and transcripts were reviewed again to identify interviewee comments related to each theme. This process was repeated as new themes emerged, and spreadsheets were used to track themes and comments. The transcripts were then reread to identify each stressful/difficult situation discussed. These situations were then coded to identify the type of situation, whom the interviewee sought support from, and which type(s) of communication technologies were used. Results presented in this chapter focus on themes emergent in the data, using specific examples from the interviews to illustrate these themes. All names have been changed to protect participant confidentiality.

Results

Key findings. There are several key findings from this study. First, students face diverse challenges while adjusting to college—some directly related to the college transition, and others unrelated but made more difficult by the stressful adjustment process. Second, students consider a number of factors when determining which communication technology to use, including the richness of the medium, the privacy available in their current physical environment, and the preferences of their communication partners. Third, communicating with family members regularly provides students with opportunities for seeking and receiving support. And finally, students use communication technologies to maintain connections with and seek support from a variety of contacts, including close family members and weak ties.

Challenges faced. Participants each described between two and five challenges ($M = 2.61$) faced, resulting in a collection of 73 detailed accounts of challenging situations students faced during the transition to college. As one might expect, the majority of challenges students faced were *college-related.* For purposes of this study, this theme includes situations related to both academics (e.g., taking exams, choosing a major, or registering for classes) and campus life (e.g., making new friends, living with roommates, getting involved in student organizations, and learning to do things independently that parents had done in the past). For example, David felt overwhelmed by midterm exams his first term:

> The first round of the midterms months [were stressful]. Just because I wasn't used to the amount of stuff I had to do to get ready for them. And so it was very stressful. And I spent a lot of time just reading through my notes and doing problem sets constantly. That was very, very difficult. I found it was much easier the second time around. But that first time was just [sigh].

David's experience illustrates a trend among participants: Stressful and challenging transitions were often considered stressful simply because they were unfamiliar. Once students had been on campus for a few months and were more accustomed to how things worked, the same situations were often perceived as less challenging.

Financial concerns emerged as another common theme among the challenging situations students described. Participants struggled with issues including finding a job on campus, learning to pay their own bills, and finding scholarships to help with tuition. Even students receiving financial support from their families expressed these concerns. For example, Kayla, a first-generation college student whose parents immigrated to the United States from Mexico, described a disagreement with her parents about her intended major (film) and the cost of college:

> My major was a big point of contention between my parents and I. And they were like "You are not going to make any money. You're going to like waste all this money that we're using to pay for your education on like this lame ass major." And I'm just like "Well, this is what I want to do. I don't want to do anything else." [...] So I guess I feel kind of guilty doing this to them.

Although many participants receiving financial support from parents were grateful, they also felt obliged to involve parents in their college decisions, limiting the freedom they expected when they moved away from home.

While the previous examples highlight challenges students faced that were directly related to starting college, students also described many challenges not directly related, including health issues, parents divorcing, death of a loved one, outing of one's sexual orientation, breakups, and technology failures. Although not caused by moving to campus, students often reported that being away from home exacerbated the difficulty of dealing with these already stressful situations. For example, Kelsey was diagnosed with an aggressive breast tumor on the day she moved to campus. One month later she returned to her hometown, over 700 miles from campus, to have the tumor surgically removed. She described the significant impact her diagnosis and subsequent surgery had on her college adjustment:

> It was hard to focus on school and just try and be positive. It definitely affected me in the beginning of school because it was just constantly on my mind. And then after surgery I couldn't do anything, like I couldn't drink or I couldn't exercise with any physical movement for two weeks, and I had a big bandage. And that definitely held me back a lot.

Because Kelsey had just arrived on campus, she felt uncomfortable sharing her diagnosis with new friends; instead, she relied on long-distance support from her mother and boyfriend at home.

Although dealing with such a serious health condition is an extreme example, Kelsey's case illustrates the complexity of dealing with additional challenges on top of adjusting to college. Many participants described struggling to develop close friendships when they first arrived on campus, and did not feel comfortable discussing deeply personal issues or seeking support from their new college friends.

Regardless of the specific issues they face, new college students can benefit from social support. The next theme reveals the ways students choose and use technology to communicate with family members and receive support during their transitions to college.

Technology choices. Students use a variety of technologies to communicate with others. Table 9.1 shows how often and with whom students reported using seven types of communication technologies.

Social network sites, texting, and email were most frequently used overall, with more than 90% of students reporting using them at least once a day. However, patterns of use were different between family and non-family contacts. All participants reported using phone calls to communicate with family members and a majority reported using texting, video calls, SNS, email, and instant messaging. Social games (e.g., Words with Friends) and collaboration tools (e.g., Google Drive) were commonly used with non-family contacts, but only a few participants indicated use with family members.

In interviews, participants expressed preferences for phone and video calls with family members because of the rich, personal conversations they afford. This was particularly true when seeking support during stressful situations, as Alexis discussed:

> [Facebook Messenger] is definitely not as personal; I think that might be part of the reason why it didn't feel like that deep of a conversation. And even with the phone it's kind of weird talking about a pretty serious life decision. It's kind of weird that I wasn't having that conversation with my parents just sitting down on the couch on the living room.

Like Alexis, many participants preferred to discuss these matters face to face, but resorted to using communication technologies when they were far from home.

Distance is not the only factor limiting students' abilities to have conversations with family members in the ways they desire; other external factors influenced their choices as well. First-year college students typically live on-campus with roommates, whose presence sometimes affected students' communication choices. Chelsea, who described an amicable relationship with her roommate, sought quiet places on campus for phone calls with her family that she did not want her roommate to overhear. Another student, Jenny, who was close with her roommate, also described being frequently unable to make phone calls from her room:

> My roommate she started doing crew, the rowing team. So she would go to sleep around 10 at night [before early morning practices]. And that was the time usually when I was done with schoolwork and I had gotten back from other activities. So at that point I couldn't really talk to them.

Table 9.1. Percentage of Participants Using Each Type of Communication Technology.

	Phone Calls	Email	Texting	Instant Messaging	Video Calls	SNS	Social Games	Collaboration Tools
Frequency of Use								
Multiple times a day	42.9%	85.7%	89.3%	50.0%	-	96.4%	10.7%	14.3%
Once a day	25.0%	10.7%	3.6%	10.7%	3.6%	-	7.1%	17.9%
Multiple times a week	25.0%	3.6%	7.1%	10.7%	3.6%	-	14.3%	28.6%
Once a week	-	-	-	14.3%	28.6%	-	7.1%	10.7%
Multiple times a month	7.1%	-	-	3.6%	28.6%	3.6%	7.1%	3.6%
Once a month	-	-	-	-	17.9%	-	10.7%	3.6%
Less frequently	-	-	-	-	17.9%	-	32.1%	17.9%
Never	-	-	-	10.7%	-	-	10.7%	3.6%
Use with Family Members	100.0%	64.3%	89.3%	53.6%	78.6%	71.4%	32.1%	7.1%
Parents	100.0%	57.1%	85.7%	17.9%	67.9%	39.3%	14.3%	3.6%
Siblings	57.1%	28.6%	75.0%	46.4%	35.7%	64.3%	17.9%	7.1%
Other Family	21.4%	21.4%	25.0%	3.6%	7.1%	25.0%	3.6%	-
Use With Non-Family	92.9%	96.4%	96.4%	89.3%	78.6%	100.0%	60.7%	71.4%
Romantic Partner	28.6%	7.1%	32.1%	14.3%	17.9%	25.0%	7.1%	3.6%
Close Friends	85.7%	17.9%	92.9%	85.7%	71.4%	100.0%	50.0%	25.0%
Other Friends	35.7%	21.4%	82.1%	75.0%	14.3%	92.9%	35.7%	21.4%
Acquaintances	35.7%	96.4%	60.7%	39.3%	-	57.1%	10.7%	60.7%
Other People	3.6%	7.1%	-	-	-	-	3.6%	-

Participants also reported considering the preferences and availability of the family members with whom they were communicating when choosing which technology to use. Although students often had free time between classes, they generally communicated with family members in the evenings, when parents were home from work. However, evening student organization meetings, time zone differences, and irregular work schedules added complexity. To avoid interrupting potentially busy family members, students often used asynchronous communication technologies, such as texting, as Ashley described:

> I usually text my grandma whenever I want to tell her anything, just because she works at night and I don't know when she works and I don't know when she's asleep. So I just send her a text and she'll respond to it whenever she can. [...] Most people in my family actually have weird work schedules and I never know when they are awake or asleep so I'll just send them a text.

Although Ashley revealed a preference for phone conversations, texting allowed her to communicate at her convenience without interrupting her working/sleeping family members. Students also consider family members' communication preferences. Although all participants used SNS such as Facebook, not all of their family members did. For example, Michelle reported using Facebook Messenger to communicate with friends and her brother, but not with her mom, "My mom really hates Facebook. She doesn't use it and she doesn't know that my brother and I use it either."

These findings reveal the complicated choices students make when choosing communication technologies to use with family members. Students must balance preferences for rich voice and audio calls with concerns for privacy in crowded campus residence halls, plus the needs and availability of family members. Such decisions are made even more difficult when students face challenging situations.

Routine connections. Before moving away to start college, participants lived at home and communicated with family members daily. In those settings, families routinely converse around the dinner table, keeping updated on each other's lives and providing support when needed. While continuing daily communication was impossible or prohibitively expensive for previous generations of college students, communication technologies now allow students to maintain regular contact. Participants described communicating with families regularly, not just when seeking support. For example, Anna's description of mundane calls to her parents was typical:

> I call them a couple times a week and we see how we're doing. I just tell them about the things that I'm getting involved in and the stories I've been writing, and we just catch up. It's honestly not that weird at all, like I don't feel homesick ever.

For Anna, regular phone calls helped her stay connected to her parents after she had moved away from home. When Anna was feeling sick, her mother noticed that her voice sounded different and encouraged her to seek medical care. Because she was in regular communication with her parents, Anna received support without having to seek it out.

Similarly, Rachel described communicating with family members everyday. Most evenings she called the family home and caught up with her parents and sister on speakerphone. When Rachel was having issues with one of the girls in her dorm, she was able to bring it up and get useful advice during one of those family phone calls. Both Rachel and Anna faced relatively minor challenges that they likely would not have sought support for, but because they were already in regular contact with their families, they received valuable support.

As these examples illustrate, regular family communication through communication technologies can create opportunities for students to seek and receive the support they need without additional effort. However, such communication was often quick and lacked the rich, personal conversations that many students reported preferring when seeking support. Many students described routine text messages to check in with parents, but switched to phone calls when difficult topics arose.

For example, Michael described getting support from his mother during a conflict with his long-distance girlfriend: "My mom asked me a couple of questions once she noticed something was up. [...] She asked via text message and then called me later about it." In this case, his mother picked up on cues that he was struggling in his text messages. The brief text exchange opened the door for a more in-depth, supportive phone conversation. Although he is not the type of person to seek support, he recognized the value of mother's input and, by following her advice, was able to resolve the conflict with his girlfriend.

Although many participants described situations when they contacted someone to seek support, routine family communication emerged as a convenient way for students to get support without specifically seeking it out or interrupting their family members. However, regular family communication did not guarantee students would seek and/or receive support from family members. Consider Tyler, for example, who chose not to mention concerns to his brother, although they communicated regularly via Facebook Messenger:

> My brother tries to ask sometimes and I'll talk to him about it a little bit and you know he has the experience and has gone through college and such. [...] But I still try to keep the romantic aspect and drugs and alcohol a little bit separate from my brother, even if he likes to talk about them more than I do.

Tyler chose to keep his concerns about his romantic relationship to himself, even though his brother specifically asked about the situation. Instead, Tyler sought support from a friend on campus with whom he felt more comfortable talking about it.

This last example highlights an important distinction emerging in the data: Although maintaining regular family communication can open the door to support, frequent communication does not necessitate support. Students can communicate frequently with their families without ever revealing the challenges they face. Further, although family members are important sources of support for students, it is not necessarily problematic when students do not receive support from family members, as revealed in the next theme.

Multiple sources of support. For many of my participants, family members were seen as the first line of defense and the people whom students immediately thought to contact when they needed support. Ashley, for example, defaulted to asking her mom for help: "If I don't know who else to call, I'll call my mom." Similarly, Rachel described counting on her family members to provide good advice no matter the situation:

> The immediate person would just be my mom. I'll just call her and be like "This is happening. What should I do?" And she'll give me whatever advice. And then [my younger sister] would probably weigh in. I might talk to [my older sister] about it. And my dad, if he's there, he'll tell me what to do. He's the greatest advice giver. He—I don't know—he should probably be a philosopher. He's awesome.

Given that students generally live with their parents until they move to college, it's not surprising that they continue to rely on family members for support during college.

Like Tyler, who preferred not to talk about his dating life with his brother, participants often considered particular topics to be off limits with family members and felt more comfortable seeking support from non-family contacts in those situations. Kelsey, for example, was comfortable talking to her mother about most issues in her life, but purposefully created conversational distance when it came to her romantic relationships:

> I wouldn't talk to her about boys, I guess. I mean, I had a boyfriend for two years and I would talk to her about more emotional problems with him. But I wouldn't tell her anything sexual. I'm sure that'd be awkward and unnecessary. She doesn't want to hear it.

Participants frequently avoided discussing sex, dating, drugs, and/or alcohol with parents. Some participants identified other family members—such as siblings, cousins, or aunts—they could turn to when seeking support related to topics they did not want to discuss with parents, or in situations when they did not think their parents would be able to provide appropriate support. For example, Chris sought support from an older cousin, rather than his parents, when he was trying to decide whether to look for a summer internship related to his major or return to his lifeguarding job:

> They [my parents] don't pretend like they know very much about, about the film industry or anything. I mean they might know that one day I might have to go to LA, and they know that I need money. [...] I have a cousin who also lived in DC for a while and she's like a 30-year-old professional. And at the same time I was looking for jobs, she was looking for a new job. So it was like a really great like parallel person to talk to, because she went through the same process and has way more experience than I have.

Like Chris, many students described using communication technologies to stay in touch with extended family members. These family members brought useful perspectives and expertise to students' social support networks. Further, students often preferred social support from people with contextual knowledge of the situation. For challenges that arose on campus, interviewees described peers who were already familiar with the situation as better able to provide immediate support than family members who lacked that background knowledge.

Just as communication technologies enable students to receive support from family members, interviewees revealed how they enable maintaining broad social networks including diverse contacts. SNS such as Facebook allow new college students to keep in touch with people they would not typically call when they are upset or need support, and provide students with opportunities to receive support in ways that were unexpected or surprising. Justin described "random" conversations with Facebook "friends":

> You know how on Facebook there are some people that are like available that you can chat? It's just that random high school friend that is available to chat, and then sometimes you just talk. [...] Sometimes you just go on Facebook and then people message you. It makes you really happy and you just get these random conversations.

A spontaneous conversation with one of these contacts provided Justin with some useful support and perspective when he was stressed about his final exams.

Providing connections to such "weak ties" is a significant benefit of Facebook and similar SNS (Ellison, Steinfield, & Lampe, 2011; Rozzell et al., 2014). Weak ties often differ from students' closest contacts, and such diversity can be particularly beneficial for new college students and other people seeking support (Granovetter, 1973; Wohn, Ellison, Khan, Fewins-Bliss, & Gray, 2013). Interview participants often described receiving support from multiple people about the same situation, including both strong and weak ties. These diverse perspectives helped them to understand the nuances of the situations and to better navigate the challenge.

Discussion

This study sought to shed light on first-year college students' use of communication technologies for seeking and receiving support from family members while adjusting to college. The transition to college is often the most significant life change emerging adults experience (Dyson & Renk, 2006; Fromme et al., 2008; Smith & Zhang, 2010); this study revealed the diversity of challenging situations students face during this transition, and how they use communication technologies for seeking and receiving support from family and other contacts. Many of the challenges students face are directly related to college adjustment, similar to aspects of college adjustment identified in prior research (Baker & Siryk, 1986; Taylor et al., 2013). The data also revealed the significance of other, non-college-related challenges that students face during this time; reminding us that problems normally perceived as insignificant can feel insurmountable to students in the midst of adjusting to college, a major life transition.

To help with these challenging situations, students often communicate with and receive social support from family members via communication technologies. Similar to Smith et al.'s (2012) study of student–parent communication, these data reveal a set of complex considerations students balance when choosing communication technology for these supportive conversations with family members. As suggested by Media Richness Theory (Daft & Lengel, 1986), students in the current study often preferred to use rich communication channels, such as video and phone calls, for these personal conversations. However, students frequently used less rich, text-based communication channels because they lacked privacy on campus or were unsure of family members' availability. Prior work suggests these mediated interactions can provide students with social support and minimize the potentially negative effects of the stressful college transition (Cohen & McKay, 1984; Lewandowski et al., 2011; Mattanah et al., 2010; Mikal et al., 2013).

Similar to past research suggesting students use technology to communicate with their family members frequently (Hofer, 2008; Smith et al., 2012) and not only when they are seeking support, the current study reveals that many first-year college students use technology to communicate with their family members in routine and rather mundane ways, such as daily text messages or weekly phone calls. The data reveal this regular communication creates opportunities for students to receive social support from family members without specifically seeking it. Research suggests that even in situations when the student does not specifically seek out social support, offered support can be beneficial (Cohen & McKay, 1984). Such opportunistic support encounters might be particularly advantageous for those students who are less inclined to seek out support (Taylor et al., 2004).

Communication technologies and SNS, in particular, enable new college students to maintain relationships with and receive support from a variety of people they knew before moving to college (Shklovski, Kraut, & Cummings, 2008). These connections form a support network students can rely on while they deal with the many challenges of adjusting to college. Maintaining connections to weak ties (Granovetter, 1973) diversifies students' support networks, providing them with a breadth of perspectives and knowledge to supplement their families' support. Those connections also provide support on taboo topics that young adults often avoid discussing with family members (Rozzell et al., 2014; Wohn et al., 2013).

Limitations and Future Work

When interpreting the findings presented in this chapter, it is important to consider the limitations of the study from which they emerged. All participants in this study were college students at a single institution. Future research would benefit from studying students at multiple and various types of institutions, such as small liberal arts schools, large public schools, community colleges, and technical schools. Further, only students who grew up in the United States were included in this study; future work should consider college adjustment for international students. Finally, this study relied only on self-report data, and future research would benefit from examining digital traces and communication logs to observe actual, day-to-day communication between students and family members.

Application

For Students

Adjusting to college is a major life change and it is likely that you will face some setbacks along the way. Do not be discouraged; it is "normal" to face challenges as you learn your way around a new place, are challenged academically, and take on more personal responsibility. Moving to college is like learning to ride a bike with training wheels: Your parents are no longer pushing you along so you must peddle on your own, but you still have training wheels to keep you on track. College is a time for you to explore your identity and learn more about what you want out of life, while you prepare to take the next big step. But you are not completely on your own yet; you have the support of your family and your campus to help you succeed.

Do not hesitate to seek support from your family members as you face unfamiliar challenges. That said, do not rely on them exclusively. Talk to your peers; they are often facing similar challenges, and you can lean on each other for support. Use SNS such as Facebook to maintain connections with weak ties, such as former classmates or teachers. Even though you don't talk to these people every day, they may be able to provide useful advice when you need it. You should also explore the many other resources available on your campus—from counseling centers and academic advisors to student organizations and residence assistants—there are many resources available on college campuses to help you succeed. Learn about the programs that your college offers and take advantage of them. Be mindful of the many serious and often hidden challenges that your peers may be facing and offer your support when you can.

For Families

Create regular communication routines to remind your children you are there for them, and create opportunities for them to seek support when they need it. Avoid pressuring your students to share every detail of their life with you; it is beneficial for them to get input and support from multiple and diverse perspectives as they make decisions on their own. Encourage your emerging adult children to talk to and learn from others in their campus communities. It can be hard to see your children grow up and move away, but it is important to give them the space and freedom they need to explore this new chapter of life. If your college student children come to you with questions, nudge them to find the solution on their own rather than handling it for them. Although they might make missteps along the way, and it might be painful to watch, know they are on the path to becoming independent adults.

For Researchers

The transition to college is a major life change, and students face a number of challenges during this time. Although some of these challenges are directly related to college adjustment, others are may appear unrelated but are more difficult when combined with a major life change. When studying college adjustment and other life transitions, researchers should consider not only challenges directly related to the transitions, but other aspects of peoples' lives that may be made more difficult as well. Researchers must take a broader perspective on families, beyond a narrow focus on parent–child relationships. Lastly, acknowledge that college students today use a variety of communication technologies and take a communication ecological approach rather than limiting your study to one specific communication channel.

References

Albrecht, T. (1984). Social support and life stress. *Human Communication Research, 11*, 3–32.

Aquilino, W. S. (2006). Family relationships and support systems in emerging adulthood. In *Emerging adults in America: Coming of age in the 21st century* (pp. 193–217). Washington, DC: American Psychological Association.

Arnett, J. J. (2000). Emerging adulthood: A theory of development from the late teens through the twenties. *American Psychologist, 55*(5), 469–480.

Baker, R. W., & Siryk, B. (1986). Exploratory intervention with a scale measuring adjustment to college. *Journal of Counseling Psychology, 33*(1), 31–38.

Bland, H. W., Melton, B. F., Welle, P., & Bigham, L. (2012). Stress tolerance: New challenges for millennial college students. *College Student Journal, 46*(2), 362–375.

Chen, Y., & Katz, J. (2009). Extending family to school life: College students' use of the mobile phone. *International Journal of Human–Computer Studies, 67*(2), 179–191.

Cobb, S. (1976). Social support as a moderator of life stress. *Psychosomatic Medicine, 38*, 300–314.

Cohen, S. E., & McKay, G. (1984). Social support, stress and the buffering hypothesis: A theoretical analysis. In A. Baum, S. E. Taylor, & J. E. Singer, *Handbook of psychology and health* (pp. 253–267). Hillsdale, NJ: Erlbaum.

Credé, M., & Niehorster, S. (2011). Adjustment to college as measured by the student adaptation to college questionnaire: A quantitative review of its structure and relationships with correlates and consequences, *Educational Psychology Review, 24*(1), 133–165.

Cullaty, B. (2011). The role of parental involvement in the autonomy development of traditional-age college students. *Journal of College Student Development, 52*(4), 425–439.

Daft, R. L., & Lengel, R. H. (1986). Organizational information requirements, media richness, and structural design. *Management Science, 32*(5), 554–571.

DeAndrea, D. C., Ellison, N. B., LaRose, R., Steinfield, C., & Fiore, A. (2012). Serious social media: On the use of social media for improving students' adjustment to college. *The Internet and Higher Education, 15*(1), 15–23.

Dyson, R., & Renk, K. (2006). Freshmen adaptation to university life: Depressive symptoms, stress, and coping. *Journal of Clinical Psychology, 62*(10), 1231–1244.

Eisenberg, D., Golberstein, E., & Hunt, J. B. (2009). Mental health and academic success in college. *The B.E. Journal of Economic Analysis & Policy, 9*(1).

Ellison, N. B., Steinfield, C., & Lampe, C. (2011). Connection strategies: Social capital implications of Facebook-enabled communication practices. *New Media & Society, 13*(6), 873–892.

Fisher, S., & Hood, B. (1987). The stress of the transition to university: A longitudinal study of psychological disturbance, absent-mindedness, and vulnerability to homesickness. *British Journal of Psychology, 78*, 425–441.

Flanagan, C., Schulenberg, J., & Fuligni, A. (1993). Residential setting and parent–adolescent relationships during the college years. *Journal of Youth and Adolescence, 22*(2), 171–189.

Friedlander, L. J., Reid, G. J., Shupak, N., & Cribbie, R. (2007). Social support, self-esteem, and stress as predictors of adjustment to university among first-year undergraduates. *Journal of College Student Development, 48*(3), 259–274.

Fromme, K., Corbin, W. R., & Kruse, M. I. (2008). Behavioral risks during the transition from high school to college. *Developmental Psychology, 44*(5), 1497–1504.

Glaser, B. G., & Strauss, A. L. (1967). *The discovery of grounded theory: Strategies for qualitative research.* Chicago, IL: Aldine Transaction.

Granovetter, M. S. (1973). The strength of weak ties. *American Journal of Sociology*, 78(6), 1360–1380.

Gray, R., Vitak, J., Easton, E. W., & Ellison, N. B. (2013). Examining social adjustment to college in the age of social media: Factors influencing successful transitions and persistence. *Computers & Education, 67*, 193–207.

Hofer, B. K. (2008). The electronic tether: Parental regulation, self-regulation, and the role of technology in college transitions. *Journal of the First-Year Experience & Students in Transition, 20*(2), 9–24.

Holmes, T. H., & Rahe, R. H. (1967). The social readjustment rating scale. *Journal of Psychosomatic Research, 11*, 213–218.

Kena, G., Aud, S., Johnson, F., Wang, X., Zhang, J., Rathbun, A.,... Kristapovich, P. (2014). *The Condition of Education 2014* (NCES 2014–083). U.S. Department of Education, National Center for Education Statistics. Washington, DC. Retrieved from http://nces.ed.gov/pubs2014/2014083.pdf

Kenyon, D. B., & Koerner, S. S. (2009). Examining emerging-adults' and parents' expectations about autonomy during the transition to college. *Journal of Adolescent Research, 24*(3), 293–320.

Kerr, S., Johnson, V. K., Gans, S. E., & Krumrine, J. (2004). Predicting adjustment during the transition to college: Alexithymia, perceived stress, and psychological symptoms. *Journal of College Student Development, 45*(6), 593–611.

Krotseng, M. V. (1992). Predicting persistence from the student adaptation to college questionnaire: Early warning or siren song? *Research in Higher Education, 33*(1), 99–111.

Larose, S., & Boivin, M. (1998). Attachment to parents, social support expectations, and socioemotional adjustment during the high school–college transition. *Journal of Research on Adolescence, 8*(1), 1–27.

Lefkowitz, E. S. (2005). "Things have gotten better": Developmental changes among emerging adults after the transition to university. *Journal of Adolescent Research, 20*(1), 40–63.

LeMoyne, T., & Buchanan, T. (2011). Does "hovering" matter? Helicopter parenting and its effect on well-being. *Sociological Spectrum, 31*(4), 399–418.

Lewandowski, J., Rosenberg, B. D., Jordan Parks, M., & Siegel, J. T. (2011). The effect of informal social support: Face-to-face versus computer-mediated communication. *Computers in Human Behavior, 27*(5), 1806–1814.

Licitra-Kleckler, D. M., & Waas, G. A. (1993). Perceived social support among high-stress adolescents: The role of peers and family. *Journal of Adolescent Research, 8*(4), 381–402.

Mattanah, J. F., Ayers, J. F., Brand, B. L., & Brooks, L. J. (2010). A social support intervention to ease the college transition: Exploring main effects and moderators. *Journal of College Student Development, 51*(1), 93–108.

Mikal, J. P., Rice, R. E., Abeyta, A., & DeVilbiss, J. (2013). Transition, stress, and computer-mediated social support. *Computers in Human Behavior, 29*(5), A40–A53.

Oh, H. J., Ozkaya, E., & LaRose, R. (2014). How does online social networking enhance life satisfaction? The relationships among online supportive interaction, affect, perceived social support, sense of community, and life satisfaction. *Computers in Human Behavior, 30*, 69–78.

Padilla-Walker, L. M., & Nelson, L. J. (2012). Black hawk down?: Establishing helicopter parenting as a distinct construct from other forms of parental control during emerging adulthood. *Journal of Adolescence, 35*(5), 1177–1190.

Padilla-Walker, L. M., Nelson, L. J., & Knapp, D. J. (2014). "Because I'm still the parent, that's why!" Parental legitimate authority during emerging adulthood. *Journal of Social and Personal Relationships*, 31(3), 293–313.

Parra, A., Oliva, A., & Reina, M. D. C. (2013). Family relationships from adolescence to emerging adulthood: A longitudinal study. *Journal of Family Issues.*

Pizzolato, J. E., & Hicklen, S. (2011). Parent involvement: Investigating the parent–child relationship in millennial college students. *Journal of College Student Development, 52*(6), 671–686.

Pryor, J. H., Eagan, K., Palucki Blake, L., Hurtado, S., Berdan, J., & Case, M. H. (2012). *The American freshman: National norms Fall 2012.* Los Angeles: Cooperative Institutional Research Program at the Higher Education Research Institute at UCLA. Retrieved from http://www.heri.ucla.edu/monographs/theamericanfreshman2012.pdf

Rahe, R. H., Meyer, M., Smith, M., Kjaer, G., & Holmes, T. H. (1964). Social stress and illness onset. *Journal of Psychosomatic Research, 8*(1), 35–44.

Rozzell, B., Piercy, C. W., Carr, C. T., King, S., Lane, B. L., Tornes, M.,... Wright, K. B. (2014). Notification pending: Online social support from close and nonclose relational ties via Facebook. *Computers in Human Behavior, 38*, 272–280.

Sarigiani, P. A., Trumbell, J. M., & Camarena, P. M. (2013). Electronic communications technologies and the transition to college. *Journal of the First-Year Experience & Students in Transition, 25*, 35–60.

Schiffrin, H. H., Liss, M., Miles-McLean, H., Geary, K. A., Erchull, M. J., & Tashner, T. (2014). Helping or hovering? The effects of helicopter parenting on college students' well-being. *Journal of Child and Family Studies*, 23(3), 548–557.

Scully, J. A., Tosi, H., & Banning, K. (2000). Life event checklists: Revisiting the social readjustment rating scale after 30 years. *Educational and Psychological Measurement, 60*(6), 864–876.

Shklovski, I. A., Kraut, R., & Cummings, J. (2008). Keeping in touch by technology: Maintaining friendships after a residential move. *Proceedings of the ACM SIGCHI Conference on Human Factors in Computing Systems*, 807–816.

Smith, A., Rainie, L., & Zickuhr, K. (2011). *College students and technology.* Pew Research Center's Internet & American Life Project. Retrieved from http://www.pewinternet.org/2011/07/19/college-students-and-technology/

Smith, M. E., Nguyen, D. T., Lai, C., Leshed, G., & Baumer, E. P. S. (2012). Going to college and staying connected: Communication between college freshmen and their parents. *Proceedings of the ACM SIGCHI Conference on Computer Supported Cooperative Work*, 789–798.

Smith, W. C., & Zhang, P. (2010). The impact of key factors on the transition from high school to college among first- and second-generation students. *Journal of the First-Year Experience & Students in Transition, 22*(2), 49–70.

Taylor, S. E., Sherman, D. K., Kim, H. S., Jarcho, J., Takagi, K., & Dunagan, M. S. (2004). Culture and social support: Who seeks it and why? *Journal of Personality and Social Psychology, 87*(3), 354–362.

Taylor, Z. E., Doane, L. D., & Eisenberg, N. (2013). Transitioning from high school to college: Relations of social support, ego-resiliency, and maladjustment during emerging adulthood. *Emerging Adulthood, 2*(2), 105–115.

Wills, T. A. (1985). Supportive functions of interpersonal relationships. In S. E. Cohen & S. L. Syme, *Social support and health* (pp. 61–82). Orlando, FL: Academic Press, Inc.

Wintre, M. G., & Yaffe, M. (2000). First-year students' adjustment to university life as a function of relationships with parents. *Journal of Adolescent Research, 15*(1), 9–37.

Wohn, D. Y., Ellison, N. B., Khan, M. L., Fewins-Bliss, R., & Gray, R. (2013). The role of social media in shaping first-generation high school students' college aspirations: A social capital lens. *Computers & Education, 63*, 424–436.

Section Three

Couples in a Digital Age

10

What Marriage and Family Therapists Tell Us about Improving Couple Relationships through Technology

FRED P. PIERCY
DANA RIGER
CHRISTINA VOSKANOVA
WEI-NING CHANG
EMILY HAUGEN
LEONARD STURDIVANT
Virginia Tech

AUTHOR NOTE: We would like to acknowledge support for this project from the Center for Information Technology Impacts on Children, Youth, and Families and the Department of Human Development at Virginia Tech, Blacksburg, Virginia.

Introduction

New technologies are shaping the ways we form and maintain our relationships. While technology can certainly have its shadow side, with the potential to distance partners and facilitate affairs (Cravens, Leckie, & Whiting, 2013; Kerkhof, Finkenauer, & Muusses, 2011; Toma, 2013), new technologies such as social media, Internet resources, texting, and video chatting can also help couples strengthen their relationships. For example, technology can help couples better manage conflict (Pettigrew, 2009; Scissors & Gergle, 2013). According to a Pew Research Internet Project poll (Lenhart & Duggan, 2014), digital technology such as texting helps some couples communicate better and feel closer to one another. Scissors and

Gergle (2013) found that computer-mediated communication, for example, can help angry couples slow down and cool off.

The choices a partner makes on social media can contribute to higher levels of personal and relationship satisfaction (Papp, Danielewicz, & Cayemberg, 2012). For example, the time people spend viewing and editing personal information on social media may predict relationship improvement; partner portrayal of relationships on Facebook hold importance for relationship functioning (Papp et al., 2012). Moreover, online dating sites appear to improve the efficiency with which individuals search for partners, especially individuals who have previously faced a narrow market for potential mates, such as older singles, those with disabilities, and gay men and lesbians (Rosenfeld & Thomas, 2012).

Increasingly, partners shape and sustain their relational identities through their portrayals on social media (Hesper & Whitty, 2010). In fact, some couples believe their relationship is not legitimate until its status is disclosed online and maintained through continuous displays of relationship well-being. Couples may reinforce their digital identity by communicating significant relationship details to digital communities, such as posting photos and providing status updates (Papp et al., 2012). Engaged couples may communicate jointly constructed identities by crafting narratives on their "*wed*site" (see the Daws chapter in this volume), which is a website created by many contemporary couples and designed to share details of their upcoming wedding. Wedsites also typically include the story of couple's courtship and engagement/proposal. Daws found couples often distort information on their wedsite to intentionally deceive readers about details of their relationship.

The Internet also can increase the closeness of already married or partnered couples. For example, some couples increase intimacy by viewing sexually explicit material together online (Hertlein, 2012). According to Grov et al. (2011), couples who view sexual activity together on the Internet were less likely to pass judgment on their partner's bodies, experience decreases in sexual frequency, or express boredom with their sexual repertoire.

New technology also can promote healthy boundaries (Hertlein, 2012). Internet users, for example, can choose to establish boundaries around themselves by determining who they allow within their cyber-networks and by "blocking" others. Couples also can create rules about when and where they permit technology, and when and where they prefer one-on-one contact with each other.

In this chapter, we will further examine the potential of technology to improve couple relationships by learning from the experiences of marriage and family therapists. From their perspective, we will report on the ways new technologies and computer-mediated communication are helping couples improve relationship satisfaction.

Clinical Considerations

Human–computer interaction scientists have designed many technological aids to help couples connect when they are apart from one another (Hassenzahl, Heidecker, Eckoldt, Diefenbach, & Hillmann, 2012). For example, Chang et al., (2002) created LumiTouch, which consists of two picture frames in which each partner inserts a picture of his or her partner. When one individual handles the picture frame containing the partner's picture, the remote partner's frame lights up with colors that correspond to where, how hard, and how long the frame is squeezed. Similar technologies use teddy bears, floating feathers, scented oil, and other devices to give distant partners the sense of touch (feeling a hug when the partner hugs a teddy bear), smell (scented oil), sound, and visual cues (a floating feather in a vase) that allow each partner to reciprocally connect with the other across miles (Hassenzahl et al., 2012).

Technology also can provide ways for individuals to communicate with a partner and manage daily life. For example, couples rely heavily on cell phones to connect during a day. In fact, for couples in which both partners have cellphones, 70% of people report making daily contact with a partner (Kennedy, Smith, Wells, & Wellman, 2008). Couples also use technology (online calendars, auto-reminders) to plan their days, to touch base electronically, and to plan for quality time together.

Ling (2004) defines asynchronous communication, such as emails and texts, as communication where users can edit and present information prior to sending messages; ideally this type of communication gives the opportunity to slow down, craft, and send thoughtful and clear messages to one's intimate partner. Although there also can be drawbacks to personal digital devices, according to Czechowsky (2008) couples with BlackBerrys reported that communication via their devices helped them resolve arguments over email and allowed more flexibility to schedule time with each other. Further, Czechowsky found that new media can positively affect interactions by providing entertainment couples can enjoy together, as well as opportunities to positively connect with each other.

Our Theoretical Framework

Social constructionism provides the theoretical underpinning of our study. Technology represents a new kind of social sphere, where meaning, communication, and values are evolving in new ways. Social constructionists believe that meanings are transitory and developed through interaction and social agreement (McNamee & Gergen, 1992). Couples using digital communication technologies are creating relationships through online interactions, constructing couple identities, expressing themselves as couples to others, and negotiating the meaning and value of such technologies in their lives and relationship. Rich in meaning, the cyberspace context can heighten perceptions of intimacy, even though it may, in fact, also reflect deception and fraud (as anyone spending time on dating websites learns sooner or later).

Social constructionists challenge the authority of knowledge and argue that knowledge derives from culture and agreement of group knowledge (McNamee & Gergen, 1992). By showing that human subjectivity imposes itself on objective facts and not the other way around, social constructionists have brought the idea of constructing narratives into the therapeutic realm. We see these processes at work within the digital realm as well.

Social constructionist concepts inform marital and family therapists who deconstruct and challenge their clients' problematic narratives and help them find richer, more life-giving narratives. For example, White and Epston (1990), in *Narrative Means to Therapeutic Ends* (1990), outline their social constructionist model of narrative therapy. Their chief assumption is that individuals, couples, and families jointly construct problematic realities and that, through therapy, they can develop richer narratives that underline their strengths and exceptions to the problem-saturated narratives that dominate their lives.

Computer-mediated communication is informing a new type of narrative for single and partnered individuals alike. We want to know more about computer-mediated interactions, couple's digital identities, and how both therapists and clients go about understanding, shaping, and using them. How can technology be used to re-story problematic couple relationships? How can technology be part of the solution and not just part of the problem? To answer this question, we used social constructionism as one of our touchstones.

Symbolic Interactionism

Symbolic interactionism is a sociological theory with a focus on the connection between symbols and interactions (LaRossa & Reitzes, 1993). Social interactionists seek to understand how people create symbolic worlds, and how those worlds shape behavior. Families are social groups whose members, as LaRossa and Reitzes (1993) argue, "assess and assign" (p. 136) value to family activities.

Blumer (1969) outlined basic assumptions of symbolic interactionism: First, people act toward things on the basis of meanings they ascribe; thus meaning has importance for human behavior. Second, meaning is derived from social interaction; thus meanings are managed through interpretative processes. LaRossa (1993) further explained that human action is based on meanings we ascribe through interactions and that meanings are shaped through a "sense-making" process. The key assumptions, as described by Blumer, hold that meaning is central in human behavior, that language gives humans a mode through which they can negotiate meaning through symbols, and that thought modifies interpretation of symbols (Griffin, 1997). Symbolic interactionism, then, is the engagement of language that comes to identify meaning where one's sense of identity is derived from interaction with others, and provides motivation for behavior.

We use symbolic interactionism as a framework for understanding computer-mediated communication and the effect of technology on relational well-being, which depends heavily on the creation and interpretation of symbols and language. Further, self-concepts or self-identities are increasingly being constructed through online interactions. Through digital interactions, both roles and identities are formed. The "selfie" phenomena demonstrate one way our self-concepts are being formed by perceptions of others' approval (Wortham, 2013). Online feedback we get from others shapes self-esteem, which is inherently tied to identity and social and relational role formations.

Method

Background and Sample

Our present research team included one faculty member and five doctoral students in a doctoral marriage and family therapy training program at Virginia Tech. Our participants were practicing therapists or therapists-in-training who presently conduct at least a portion of their practice with couples. We recruited through a range of national and international lists and listservs of various marriage and family therapy (MFT) training programs, practicing professionals, professional organizations, and knowledgeable contacts to generate potential respondents (e.g., National Council on Family Relations marriage and family therapy section, and technology and families section; Emotion Focused Couple Therapy Listserv; Facebook communities related to Internal Family Systems and Contextual Therapy; COAMFTE-accredited program faculty and graduate students; and a Russian society for family counselors and therapists).

Demographics

In all, 63 therapists and therapists-in-training in the United States and abroad completed our online survey. We had 18 male participants (29%), whose average age was 50, and 45 female participants (71%) whose average age was 44. The mean years of clinical experience for all participants was 15.4. These participants had an average of 36 clinical hours of therapy per month, of which 21 hours were with couples. As for their comfort with using technology, on a five-point Likert scale ranging from 1 (not at all conversant) to 5 (very conversant), they indicated a comfort level with technology of 4.2 in their personal lives and 3.4 in their clinical work. As for terminal degrees, 2% had a certificate, 6% had a bachelor's degree, 45% had a master's degree, and 47% had a doctorate. They had licensure in the following professions: marriage and family therapy (57%), psychology (17%), psychiatry (2%), professional counseling (16%), clinical social work (10%), and registered nurse (2%). Moreover, 21% were therapists-in-training. While the great majority of our participants resided in the United States (72%), we also had participants from Canada (5%), Colombia (2%), Mexico (2%), United Kingdom (6%), Belorussia (2%), Russia (11%), and the Ukraine (2%). The work settings of our participants (who could indicate more than one setting) included private practice (63%), academic (58%), clinical agency (16%), managed care (14%), and other (6%). The following is the degree to which the participants used various forms of technology in their personal life and in couple therapy: emails (100% in personal life; 64% in couple therapy); social media (87% in personal life; 18% in couple therapy); texting (96% in personal life; 51% in couple therapy); and video chatting or calling (87% in personal life; 25% in couple therapy).

Instrument Development

Over a 3-month period in the fall of 2013, we created a mostly open-ended Web-based survey related to the use of technology in couple therapy. We were interested in asking marriage and family therapists four general questions. The first author crafted the initial questions and the coauthors contributed edits and revisions. The authors also generated, discussed, and revised relevant demographic information they subsequently developed into questions. The four primary questions we asked participants in the open-ended portion of our survey were:

1. Describe one or more ways that you have successfully used technology with couples wishing to improve their relationships.
2. Describe one or more ways that couples in therapy with you have employed technology on their own to improve their relationships.
3. What challenges have you had in using technology in couple therapy? How have you dealt with these challenges?

4. Describe one or more ways that couples in therapy with you have successfully "unplugged" from technology in a manner that improved their relationships.

In addition to the primary English version of the survey, we also translated the questions into Russian, since one of the contributing authors (CV), a Russian marriage and family therapist, had a target audience of Russian couple therapists in mind as potential participants. We used systematic back translation procedures with an independent native speaker to be sure that all questions in the Russian version of the instrument conveyed the intended meaning (Matsumoto & Yoo, 2006).

We constructed our survey using Qualtrics, a proprietary online survey software. Upon initial analysis of the survey results, we identified nine different responses on which we wanted elaboration. We asked these nine participants for individual phone or Skype follow-up interviews, six of whom agreed and were interviewed. Our hope was that through these interviews participants would provide more depth and nuanced comments to their initial responses. In conducting these follow-up interviews, we adhered to a general template:

1. In your written response to the question [insert question here], you mentioned [summarize the response here].
2. Could you tell me more about your answer? For example, … [probe here; e.g., "which websites exactly do you recommend? Could you send me the links to them?"]
3. [Continue to probe for a fuller answer.]
4. Do you have any other thoughts on [depending on the participant's initial answer to a particular question] "the use of technology in couple therapy" or "couples' use of technology to improve their relationship" or "couples unplugging from technology?"

Also, in the initial survey, several participants stated that they recommended certain websites, YouTube videos, TED Talks, etc., to their client couples. We followed up by email with five of these individuals (who had given us permission to do so), asking for the specific sites they recommended. We received four responses providing this information.

Analysis

We used thematic analysis on our initial survey data to categorize participant responses into themes. Thematic analysis is a foundational, flexible method of identifying, analyzing, and reporting themes within data (Braun & Clark, 2006).

It has been compared to Grounded Theory but differs in that it is not tied to a theoretical framework. Thematic analysis serves as a tool used across epistemologies and research questions to organize complex data sets rich in qualitative detail. Thematic analysis as it pertains to this study provided us a way to uncover the nuances and general themes across and within our data, and to organize our findings in a way that would make sense to couple therapy practitioners, couple educators, as well as couples wishing to improve their relationships. We present our findings, along with illustrative examples, in a form that couples, educators, and/or marriage and family therapists might find helpful.

Results

We have organized our findings according to the therapists' answers to our four primary qualitative questions. We also provide examples from individual interviews, where appropriate.

Question One: Describe one or more ways that you have successfully used technology with couples wishing to improve their relationships.

The interventions our participants described ranged from the mundane to the inventive. (See Table 10.1 for examples of therapist interventions using technology.) As for the more mundane, our participants described practical uses of technology ranging from emails to schedule or confirm appointments, to Skype or other video-calling sessions when the clients are traveling or after the therapist has gotten to know them face to face. Several therapists reviewed videos of their couple sessions or used them in their own supervision. Many also mentioned their professional websites, the assessments their clients access there and complete before their initial session, and their use of technology to seek professional development (e.g., online webinars; research findings).

Table 10.1. Examples of Therapist Use of Technology with Couples in Marriage and Family Therapy.

Practice Issues	• To advertise practice • To receive professional supervision and development • To manage appointments • To touch base with clients

Assessment	• Online assessment instruments • Examine couple's electronic technology usage to better understand their dynamics and concerns
Psychoeducation	• Online resources such as TED Talks, guided mindfulness practices, YouTube and other videos that explain certain relationship skills and concepts important to relationship improvement • Homework assignments that include online searches
Direct Therapy Interventions	• Have couples connect through the day through texting, calling, emailing, Skype, and FaceTime • Have distant couples connect through shared experiences (e.g., picnics, hikes) via FaceTime • Slow down and better understand cycles of anger by using email, texting, and other technology • Monitor and discuss the couples' previous electronic communications • Suggest electronic communication to partners who have trouble expressing their feelings face to face • Use technology to support journaling, guided reflections, more constructive ways to communicate
Self-Help Resources	• Have the couple connect with online resources to supplement therapy
Accountability Resources	• In the wake of an affair, suggest that couples consider electronic "accountability" applications that allow them to know where their partner is, and/or what sites the partner visits on the Internet (or to engage a third party as the "accountability" person to monitor their Internet activity)

Our participants also mentioned a number of ways they use technology to enhance the face-to-face couple therapy they conduct. Many direct their clients to online psychoeducational materials, research findings, instructional videos, YouTube videos (e.g., a primer on attachment), and TED Talks. Topics from such sites that participants mentioned include guided mindfulness practices, John Gottman's online videos, Divorce Busting (Michele Weiner-Davis' site; http://www.divorcebusting.com/), Love Language resources, discernment counseling (http://www.cehd.umn.edu/fsos/projects/mcb/dcdirectory.asp), Authentic Happiness (Seligman's site at http://www.authentichappiness.sas.upenn.edu/Default.

aspx), animation therapy (www.animationtherapy.co.uk), and online newspaper articles. Our participants also mentioned a variety of assessment instruments, including such inventories as Prepare-Enrich (https://www.prepare-enrich.com/), the Myers-Briggs Personality Test (www.myersbriggs.org), and the Enneagram Personality Test (http://www.enneagraminstitute.com/intro.asp#.Ux8ptvldW-GU). Others suggested as homework that clients research topics related to their presenting issues, such as increasing trust in a postaffair relationship. Several therapists noted they get their clients started in their searches by "clicking around" the Internet for them in session. Therapists also helped couples make sense of useful information on the Internet and information that may be suspect (information that is not theory- or data-driven). One couple therapist stated, "If they come in quoting information from a Dr. Phil show or website, I tend to steer them in the direction of John Gottman instead."

Some technology-based homework assignments that participants reported involved, for example, suggesting that couples send caring or flirtatious emails or texts to their partners during the day. One therapist suggested date nights might center around technology that the couple enjoys—computer games, films, etc. Similarly, a number of therapists suggested couples use texting, email, and Skype to stay in touch and connected when one partner was out of town. One therapist suggested couples use same-time features like FaceTime to be "with" their partner when physically apart. For example, the partners could "join" one another for a picnic or hike (that they simultaneously experience in separate physical locations). Another therapist suggested that couples could actually take out their phone (or other device) "outside while they are hiking, and try to recreate that experience next to each other."

Other couple therapists were more involved in the communication process. For example, in one case where a client was upset that her boyfriend didn't tell her he loved her enough, the therapist helped her understand that she could be empowered by texting him when she missed him and ask directly for her needs to be met. The therapist explained that this was successful on several levels: The client had an "ah ha moment" when she realized that she was playing the victim instead of reaching out herself. She further realized that she was holding back in other areas of her relationship, waiting for her boyfriend to "make the first move." The therapist noted that "we even connected it to the abandonment by her father, how she needed to feel loved," and what she could now do differently.

The same therapist recounts using texting therapeutically with another couple:

> The wife called her husband at work at least 15 times a day [which became a] problem…he is constantly stopping to answer her phone call. And so I said, "if you want him to remember something, can't you just text him or send him an

> email?...that was helpful. She was in her 60s [and] did not know how to text, [so] I helped her learn how....And again, it goes far deeper than the mediums that she uses. Why [does she] need to connect so often with her partner? [So we] talked about [that].

Several therapist participants ask to see their clients' text or email exchanges. One reviews various email or text conversations in session to examine and comment on various communication issues reflected in these digital conversations. This therapist also asks couples living apart to carbon copy (cc) her on emails when they have conversations on topics important to their relationships. She comments on the conversations and even intervenes with her own comments, when appropriate. For example, she often uses Emotion Focused Couple Therapy interventions such as, "It seems to me that what you were trying to say was..."

Therapist participants reported that some socially anxious clients are better able to express themselves clearly in email or texts than they are in person. For these clients, writing down, and thus externalizing, what they are experiencing may be a good adjunct to face-to-face therapy. One therapist told us, "Emails are especially helpful for partners who have trouble expressing their emotions. They are able to organize their thoughts better (and not get) caught up in the overwhelming feelings of an argument" that may happen through texting. Another therapist recommends journaling, and sharing reflections with her (the therapist) via email, as a supplement to therapy. Here we see how the therapist uses a social constructionist framework, allowing the client to create new meaning for emails through the perception that the therapist (or someone) is reading them. She states:

> Even though they are really talking to themselves, when they email me, they direct it to somebody, and it is easier for them to write when they know that someone is going to read it. Most people...want to be heard. They want someone [to understand what they've been through]. And so writing to me gives them more of a focus and they use more words because they are trying to get me to understand them. In a [private] journal, they are going to use a lot of abbreviations.

Some couple therapists discuss the advantage of technology in slowing down the cycles of anger that couples sometimes get into. One therapist, for example, has her clients send angry emails intended for their partner to her (the therapist) first. "That way," she explained, "they are getting out what they want to say, but they are not actually doing damage to the other person or to the relationship. And then we'll go through it, or sometimes they'll say, 'I sent it to you and I do not feel the need to send it anymore,' and then they send a much calmer email, and sometimes they do not even need to send it at all. They just needed to get out their emotions."

Question Two: Describe one or more ways that couples in therapy with you have employed technology on their own to improve their relationships.

Therapists stated that some couples have used electronic media to send messages of connection and caring, and even pictures, throughout the week, and to make dates with one another electronically. One therapist reported that each partner, when in different cities, watch the same movie simultaneously and use video chat to connect about it. Another couple dines out "together" in different cities through video chat.

Also, like therapists, some couples independently use emails and texts to slow down communication and prevent arguments (with varying degrees of success). One couple, for example, sits in different rooms of the house and communicates via email or text as if they were in separate cities. Another couple sits on different sides of the same couch when they are angry and engage in an "electronic argument" to keep from yelling at one another.

Couples also use platforms like Skype and Facebook to stay connected. One couple, for example, has developed a joint Facebook page with her partner and shares pictures and experiences ("statuses") throughout the day. Similarly, many military spouses report using Skype and Facebook to stay in touch during deployments.

Couples also go online independently to seek information about relationships, self-help resources, and assessment instruments. One partner, when she hears about a good self-help book, will immediately download it on her Kindle to read later that week.

One therapist reports that "some of my couples who are dealing with infidelity have [agreed to use] one of the various location apps available so that [they can increase] trust …by…being able to track each other's whereabouts." Other couples, through the advice of their pastor, use blocking software like Covenant Eyes (http://www.covenanteyes.com/) to provide some external surveillance of the websites [they] visit. If a person visits a pornographic or dating website, the computer lets an agreed-upon third person (who could be the partner or a mutual friend) know that they are looking at a site they should not be looking at. The idea is that both partners make a firm agreement together not to visit certain websites and empower that third person to hold both partners accountable for their website visits.

Question Three: What challenges have you had in using technology in couples therapy? How have you dealt with these challenges?

Our participants were not universally positive about the effects of technology in improving couple relationships. In fact, a number of them spoke of the potential downsides of couples using technology too much. For example:

- [with texting] "There is no eye contact or ability to interpret nonverbals, which can easily lead to miscommunication."
- "People tend not to hear intonation and intentionality, especially with text messaging."
- "They got really nasty, because one person was checking the other person's Facebook, and the other person recognized that and started to use it against the other to make the other person jealous, posting on (the Facebook page) about other female Facebook friends."
- "Texting itself was seeding into their insecurities of always needing communication from each other."
- "I learned that the husband would randomly check various sites to see if her name popped up as well as have alerts on his phone that were activated if she signed up for a new site."
- "Many seem to overuse technology and needed more help to connect intimately…too many use it as their primary connection! So many fights erupt, from text messaging especially."
- "I want to video chat, but if we have a divorce, he can use this tape against me."
- "Texting and phone calls seem to trigger a negative cycle of interaction between the couple because of how easy it is to misinterpret the meaning."
- "I find texting to be hugely damaging with troubled couples and relationships because there is little that can be communicated via text that is straightforward to interpret. And texts for many of my couples have been hugely responsible for escalating fights, and/or starting fights in the first place."

Fortunately, therapists also spoke about how they address such challenges. For example, one therapist suggests couples talk about and negotiate which approach—electronic or face to face—is best for them under different circumstances. Another therapist "walks [them] through a *cost–benefit analysis* with couples regarding the pros and cons of using technology." The therapist says that they learn, "on the one hand, they have more frequent contact, but on the other hand, it is not as intimate." Several therapists expressed comments similar to this one: "It seems like texting is helpful when you need something quick, like organizing things together, but if it is about their relationship, or about how they define love, it seems to…correlate with a lot of arguments….I think people text a lot of things before they think about their outcome." Another therapist put it more bluntly: "So one thing we negotiate is not texting over important issues. No texting will be allowed when they…discuss important issues or solutions to an issue."

Other therapists suggest techniques to ensure immediate electronic messages do not spark unintended arguments. One, for example, suggests that clients not send messages immediately, or send them to themselves first and consider their potential negative impact before sending them to their partners. Another addressed the lack of nonverbal cues and intentionality in texting by suggesting the use of emoticons (cartoons that capture the emotional intent of a message). Still another favors email over texting when the issue is volatile. She states, "Email is sometimes longer, and there is not always an expectation that you'll respond right away. It's like, they process the email they receive and respond to it when they feel like it. Conversely, texting is expected to be continued, almost like a conversation."

Some therapists worry about confidentiality when sharing electronic information. One therapist explained that because his agency has a private network that covers phone and email, client confidentiality is maintained and HIPAA (Health Insurance Portability and Accountability Act) concerns are addressed. This same therapist notes phone conversation and texting in his case notes simply as "daily contact."

One challenge relates to the electronic media itself. For example, sometimes Skype or FaceTime do not work well, reception and connectivity issues may arise, recording quality may be below par, and so on. In such cases, the advantages of face-to-face communication become more apparent.

Several of our participant therapists told us they use the couples' electronic communication to better understand their communication styles, presenting problems, and issues of power, all of which inform therapy. It is their belief that the clients' use of electronic media captures and represents issues that can be addressed both in the therapy room directly and through modification of their electronic or social media practices.

Question Four: Describe one or more ways that couples in therapy with you have successfully "unplugged" from technology in a manner that improved their relationship.

For most therapists, the idea of "unplugging"—removing contact from electronic devices—goes hand in hand with honest discussions about how technology meets a couple's needs and how it might also be getting in the way of deeper intimacy.

For some therapists, the way to address the challenges mentioned above is to help couples "unplug" from technology and to learn to communicate more productively face to face. This can be done incrementally or all at once. One therapist, for example, helped a partner stop monitoring the Internet use of the other, talking directly about her fears, and consequently both are learning to trust each other more. Another therapist often gives a homework assignment to have couples turn off the television and their other electronic devices in the evening for at least an hour and just talk to each other. Yet another therapist states:

> Obviously part of the therapy was about how not to be connected to the Internet all the time—putting the phone upside down, silencing the phone so that new messages do not ring, having times during the day when the phone is out of sight and silenced during some moments such as when they are having sex.

Another therapist recommends a technology-free zone that generally involves setting 60–90 minutes aside for one another without accessing any technology. Similarly, one therapist states that some couples "have set…times…to disconnect from the computer or cell phones, creating more opportunity for eye-to-eye communication with each other."

Some therapists have asked couples to abstain completely from using technology. Here are a few examples:

> I've had a couple who abstained from texting for a few weeks and described the first week as terrible and difficult for them, the second week as a [time that they] gained insights on what makes them feel close and loved, and the third week as attaining improvement in their communications.

> In my groups, some have been asked to take a 90-day sobriety test [that involves them disconnecting] from something that is distracting their recovery. I have had some who have abstained from Facebook and/or TV.

Finally, meditation is an alternative that several therapists suggested as a way to help individuals "unplug" from technology while also becoming more present for one's partner.

Discussion

Norcross, Pfund, and Prochesca (2013) asked 70 prominent psychotherapy experts to forecast psychotherapy trends in the next decade. One prominent trend involved the use of various forms of online technology in both psychotherapy and self-help support services for clients. Clearly, technology is here to stay for couples and the therapists who treat them. Turkle (2012) emphasizes that technology has become an integral part of many individuals' lives, habits, and even identities. Our goal in conducting this study was to learn how to help couples better navigate the technology that is becoming a significant part of who they are and the identities they form—consistent with the social construction and symbolic interaction lenses guiding this investigation.

We saw a number of examples of couples developing shared identities through new technology. For example, through FaceTime, some couples, even when they were apart, learned to nurture their couple identity through activities that allowed them to experience events like hikes, picnics, breaktime chats, and other intimate experiences in real time. Others used joint Facebook accounts to support their couple identity. Still other couples created a more reflective, rational identity by becoming less reactive to one another through planful use of email and texts, and through employing technology coaches that would help them learn to use technology more constructively. Finally, another feature of identity development involved both nurturing self-agency (e.g., supporting individuals to make use of online resources like support groups and forums) and creating a more positive projected identity. For example, one therapist helped a male client to more positively present himself on Facebook and in text messages. The therapist states, "He listened and started editing his remarks, with dramatic results. He's now married and the couple's first year together looks really good." In another case, the therapist supported a transgender client's positive self-identity by connecting her to a Web-based resource that included positive information on the lives of famous transgender individuals.

We do not see technology as necessarily either good or bad but simply as a platform that allows couples to interact, sometimes well and sometimes poorly. If someone wants to have an affair or to improve a relationship, the Internet can help that person do either. Similarly, our participants mentioned both the strengths and weaknesses of texting, consistent with previous research (Coyne, Stockdale, Busby, Iverson, & Grant, 2011). Duran, Kelly, and Rotaru (2011) found that frequent cell phone calls, for some, helped partners feel connected and cared for. Others needed more autonomy, more distance. Our guess is the same is true for texting: Some like the connection it provides; some find it too smothering. On the positive side, Perry and Werner-Wilson (2011) found digital communication could de-escalate conflict and support better conflict resolution. Both partners' interactive styles and need for closeness or distance will determine whether and/or how a therapist might suggest or use texting and other digital communication in the context of therapy. Since little research has been conducted on this subject, an honest discussion with the couple about the pros and cons, and appropriate and inappropriate situations, for texting and other digital media use makes good sense.

In the present study, we focused on the positive: how couples might use technology to improve their relationships (consistent with the "positive technology" movement; see Botella, Riva, Gaggioli, Weiderhold, Alcaniz, & Banos, 2012). The ideas of our participants were rich with methods to help couples connect in positive ways and to negotiate technology in a way that supports a closer relationship. At the same time, our therapist participants were not naïve. Most saw the potential risks in these new technologies and many described ways to address these risks.

Some of our therapists' practices around digital media challenged our traditional views of the role of the marriage and family therapist. Should a therapist be reading an email from one partner to another before the partner reads it (as one of our therapist participants does)? Should a therapist encourage one partner to send his or her journal entries to the therapist to read and respond to at the next session? On the positive side, such practices support a positive bond between therapist and client, and allow the therapist information about a partner or relationship that the therapist might not otherwise have, information that the therapist can use constructively to help both partners. On the other hand, what are appropriate and inappropriate boundaries and ethical behavior around a therapist's use of social media? Is the therapist innovative and engaged or inappropriately overinvolved? Might such practices, done on a regular basis, lead to therapist burnout?

Existing ethical standards give us few guidelines. As marriage and family therapists (MFTs) adapt to the evolving digital culture, they must also be aware of and responsive to the ethical principles of confidentiality and professional behavior, and the challenges of the Health Insurance Portability and Accountability Act (HIPAA). Working with social media puts MFTs at risk of violating clients' confidentiality and crossing unclear therapist–client relationship boundaries (Lannin & Scott, 2013). The online world is characterized by pervasive incidental contact, inevitable self-disclosure, and unavoidable multiple relationships (Lannin & Scott, 2013). The American Psychological Association's Ethical Standard 5.04 advises psychologists to take reasonable precautions regarding the dissemination of public advice and comments via media that include the Internet (Lannin & Scott, 2013). But what are "reasonable precautions?"

For starters MFTs must consider the risks that their online activities might pose for clients, be upfront about acceptable and unacceptable online interactions, and seek informed consent for any behaviors out of the ordinary. MFTs should consider how private their social networking sites are as well as set appropriate boundaries with clients to avoid conflicts of interest, inappropriate alliances with one partner against another, and multiple relationships with clients online (Lannin & Scott, 2013). What should be considered encrypted communication? What are acceptable community standards for what is private and confidential for a marriage and family therapist, and to what degree do various social media meet these standards? Inadvertent disclosures of confidential information on social media may lead to HIPAA violations. Lannin and Scott suggest that practitioners take precautions to limit liability and to contact both their professional and personal liability insurance representatives to determine whether they are covered for professional practices involving social networking.

As for unplugging from technology, beyond what our participants suggested, Park, Fritz, and Jex (2011) found that those who could segment their work and nonwork lives were better able to detach from work demands and the technological communication that go with them, to unwind, and, we would presume, be more present for their partners. The issue of psychological detachment from, segmentation of, and boundaries between work and nonwork demands should be examined further, particularly in terms of what therapy interventions might facilitate this detachment.

Application

In sum, we have identified a number of promising—even exciting—ways that marriage and family therapists can support better couple relationships through new technology. Couples and couple/family educators also can improve relationships using the ideas and reports of therapists. For therapists, some ideas include the application of technology to assessment, homework assignments, and skill development. Others involve technology-related interventions that encourage connection or disrupt a couple's cycle of anger. Still others bridged distances between partners or supported their identity as a couple.

For couples themselves, our findings should provide ideas regarding how to expand their positive use of technology (e.g., flirtatious emails and texts) and support more intimate, satisfying relationships. One thing that our therapist participants emphasized is that couples should discuss how they wish to use new technology, what limits they wish to put on such technology, when they should or should not use texting, and how they might match their own unique issues and interpersonal styles (e.g., wishes for closeness and distance; verbal facility) with existing technologies. Would they benefit from technology-free times? What relationship information should they search for online, and how should they judge its validity?

For couple/family educators, our findings provide content for the development of helpful relationship education modules related to couple relationships and technology. For example, a couple/family educator could develop discussion guidelines around when and how to use technology in relationships, and invite group participants to have such a discussion with their partners (in the group or at home). Other natural aspects of couples education would involve our participants' suggestions around online relationship information, formal talks on relationship skills, the use of online assessment instruments, and conversations around how couples could use Facebook and other technology to develop more satisfying couple identities. In fact, we believe that most of the present findings could be developed into lectures, discussions, and/or learning activities that would work in a relationship education format.

Our study also raises important questions that beg empirical investigation. Researchers, for example, could investigate how and when texting may or may not be helpful. Do virtual activities (e.g., sharing a picnic or a hike via FaceTime) add to the couples' sense of intimacy? What are the best ways for couples to "unplug" periodically from technology and what are the effects of unplugging on one's relationship?

As in any new frontier, great opportunities and great challenges coexist. We believe this study can help identify ways that marriage and family therapists, couple educators, and couples themselves can benefit from the new world of technology that is touching all of our lives.

References

Blumer, H. (1969). *Symbolic interactionism: Perspective and method.* Upper Sadle River, NJ: Prentice-Hall.

Botella, C., Riva, G., Gaggioli, A., Weiderhold, B., Alcaniz, M., & Banos, R. (2012). The present and future of positive technologies. *Cyberpsychology Behavior and Social Networking, 15*(2), 78–84. doi: 10.1089/cyber.2011.0140

Braun, V. & Clark, V. (2006). Using thematic analysis in psychology. *Qualitative Research in Psychology, 3*(2). 77–101. doi: 10.1191/1478088706qp063oa

Chang, A., Resner, B., Koerner, B., Wang, X., & Ishii, H. (2001). LumiTouch: An emotional communication device. In *CHI '01 extended abstracts on human factors in computing systems* (pp. 313–314). New York: ACM Press. doi: 10.1145/634067.634252

Coyne, S., Stockdale, L., Busby, D., Iverson, B., Grant, D. (2011). "I luv u☺!" A descriptive study of the media use of individuals in romantic relationships. *Family Relations, 60,* 150–162. doi: 10:1111/j.1741–3729.2010.00639.x

Cravens, J. D., Leckie, K. R., & Whiting, J. B. (2013). Facebook infidelity: When poking becomes problematic. *Contemporary Family Therapy, 35*(1), 74–90. doi: 10.1007/s10591–012–9231–5

Czechowsky, J. D. (2008). *The impact of BlackBerry on couple relationships.* (Unpublished doctoral dissertation). Wilfrid Laurier University, California.

Duran, R., Kelly, L., & Rotaru, T. (2011). Mobile phones in romantic relationships and the dialectic of autonomy and connection. *Communication Quarterly, 59*(1), 19–36. doi: 10.1080/01463373.2011l.541336

Griffin, E. (1997). *A first look at communication theory.* New York: McGraw-Hill.

Grov, C., Gillespie, B., Royce, T., & Lever, J. (2011). Perceived consequences of casual online sexual activities on heterosexual relationships: A U.S. online survey. *Archives of Sexual Behavior, 40,* 429–439. doi: 10.1007/s10508–010–9598-z

Hassenzahl, M., Heidecker, S., Eckoldt, K., Diefenbach, S., and Hillmann, U. (2012). All you need is love: Current strategies of mediating intimate relationships through technology. *ACM Transactions on Computer–Human Interaction, 19*(4), No. 30. doi:10.1145/2395131.2395137

Hertlein, K. M. (2012). Digital dwelling: Technology in couple and family relationships. *Family Relations, 61,* 374–387. doi: 10.1111/j.1741–3729.2012.00702.x

Hesper, E. J., & Whitty, M. T. (2010). Netiquette within married couples: Agreement about acceptable online behavior and surveillance between partners. *Computers in Human Behavior, 26,* 916–926. doi: 10.1016/j.chb.2010.02.006

Kennedy, T. L. M., Smith, A., Wells, A. T., & Wellman, B. (2008). Networked families. *Pew Research Internet Project.* Retrieved from http://www.pewinternet.org/Reports/2008/Networked-Families.aspx

Kerkhof, P., Finkenauer, C., & Muusses, L. D. (2011). Relational consequences of compulsive Internet use: A longitudinal study among newlyweds. *Human Communication Research, 37*(2), 147–173. doi:10.1111/j.1468–2958.2010.01397.x

Lannin, D. G., & Scott, N. A. (2013). Social networking ethics: Developing best practices for the new small world. *Professional Psychology: Research & Practice, 44*(3), 135–141. doi:10.1037/a0031794

LaRossa, R. (1993). Stories and narratives. *Journal of Social and Personal Relationships, 12,* 553. doi: 10.1177/0265407595124009

LaRossa, R., & Reitzes, D. C. (1993). Symbolic interaction and family studies. In P. G. Boss, W. J. Doherty, R. LaRossa, W. R. Schumm, & S. K. Steinmetz (Eds.), *Sourcebook of family theories and methods: A contextual approach* (pp. 135–163). New York: Plenum Press.

Lenhart, A., & Duggan, M. (2014, February 11). Couples, the Internet, and social media. *Pew Research Internet Project.* Retrieved from http://www.pewinternet.org/2014/02/11/couples-the-internet-and-social-media/

Ling, R. (2004). *The mobile connection: The cell phone's impact on society.* San Francisco, CA: Elsevier.

Matsumoto, D., & Yoo, S. H. (2006). Toward a new generation of cross-cultural research. *Perspectives on Psychological Science, 1*(3), 234–250. doi: 10.1111/j.1745–6916.2006.00014.x

McNamee, S., & Gergen, K. J. (Eds.). (1992). *Therapy as social construction.* Thousand Oaks, CA: Sage.

Norcross, J., Pfund, R., & Prochaska, A. (2013). Psychotherapy in 2022: A Delphi poll on its future. *Professional Psychology: Research and Practice, 44*(5), 363–370.

Papp, L. M., Danielewicz, J., & Cayemberg, C. (2012). "Are we Facebook official?" Implications of dating partners' Facebook use and profiles for intimate relationship satisfaction. *Cyberpsychology, Behavior & Social Networking, 15*(2), 85–90. doi:10.1089/cyber.2011.0291

Park, Y., Fritz, C., & Jex, S. (2011). Relationships between work–home segmentation and psychological detachment from work: The role of communication technology use at home. *Journal of Occupational Health Psychology, 16*(4), 457–467. doi: 10.1037/a0023594

Perry, M., & Werner-Wilson, R. (2011). Couples and computer-mediated communication: A closer look at the affordances and use of the channel. *Family & Consumer Sciences Research Journal, 40*(2), 120–134. doi: 10:1111/j.1552–3934.2011.02099.x

Pettigrew, J. (2009). Text messaging and connectedness within close personal relationships. *Marriage and Family Review, 45*, 697–716. doi: 10.1080/01494920903224269

Rosenfeld, M. J., & Thomas, R. J. (2012). Searching for a mate: The rise of the Internet as a social intermediary. *American Sociological Review, 77*, 523–547. doi:10.1177/0003122412448050

Scissors, L. E., Gergle, D. (2013). " Back and forth, back and forth": Channel switching in romantic couple conflict. In *Proceedings of the ACM Conference on Computer Supported Cooperative Work (CSCW) 2013* (pp. 237–248). New York: ACM Press. doi:10.1145/2441776.2441804

Toma, C. L. (2013). Feeling better but doing worse: Effects of Facebook self-presentation on implicit self-esteem and cognitive task performance. *Media Psychology, 16*(2), 199–220. doi:10.1080/15213269.2012.762189

Turkle, S. (2012). *Alone together: Why we expect more from technology and less from each other*. New York: Basic Books.

White, M., & Epston, D. (1990). *Narrative means to therapeutic ends*. New York: Norton.

Wortham, J. (2013). My selfie, myself. *New York Times*. Retrieved from http://www.nytimes.com/2013/10/20/sunday-review/my-selfie-myself.html?_r=0).

11

"Technoference"

Everyday Intrusions and Interruptions of Technology in Couple and Family Relationships

Brandon T. McDaniel
Pennsylvania State University

Introduction

New technology and mobile devices, such as cell phones, smartphones, laptops, and tablets, have become common items in many families' homes in the United States. Recent surveys suggest that approximately 91% of American adults own a cell phone (with 81% of 25–34 year olds owning a smartphone), 61% have a laptop, 34% have a tablet, and 72% of online adults use social networking sites (Brenner & Smith, 2013; Lenhart, Madden, Smith, Purcell, Zickuhr, & Rainie, 2011; Pew, 2012; Rainie, 2012; Smith, 2013; Zickuhr, 2013). These numbers are likely increasing; mobile technologies and communication devices have become the fastest-growing technology in history (Castells, Fernandez-Ardevol, Qiu, & Sey, 2007). These devices have become so popular and have such attractive features that some individuals and families are beginning to use them in ways problematic for themselves and their relationships. The current chapter examines what I term "technology interference" or "technoference," which includes times when and ways that technological devices intrude, interrupt, and/or get in the way of couple or family communication and interactions in everyday life. I begin this discussion first by examining individual characteristics that predict individual use of mobile devices, as well as problematic use. I then move to an examination of characteristics of the devices themselves, those features that influence use. Then,

I turn to how even normative use of technology might produce interruptions in family life, and what the current research tells us about how technology interference might influence personal and couple well-being. Overall, preliminary work suggests that technology interference is common in couple relationships and that greater interference is related to diminished personal and relational well-being (e.g., McDaniel & Coyne, 2014a).

Mobile devices such as cell phones and smartphones are particularly important to examine because many individuals keep them on or near themselves at all times, even next to their bed as they sleep, a phenomenon known as the "always on" environment (Middleton, 2007) or being in a state of "perpetual contact" (Katz & Aakhus, 2002). To many, being perpetually "on" and available has become a way of life and to varying degrees our devices, especially cell phones, have become an extension and representation of ourselves (Campbell & Ling, 2009; Campbell & Park, 2008; Carbonell, Oberst, & Beranuy, 2013; Srivastava, 2005). We have entered a new age of personal communication technologies (Campbell & Park, 2008), where many adults now rate that they cannot live without technology (such as cell phones, the Internet, and Facebook) (Popkin, 2011; Rainie & Keeter, 2006). The Pew research group estimates that about 39% of adults have a symbiotic relationship with their mobile devices (Horrigan, 2009), and qualitative interviews reveal that many individuals experience discomfort when they have to temporarily disconnect (i.e., turn their phone off for a period of time) (Jarvenpaa & Lang, 2005). In other words, many users have "developed an intense relationship with their cell phone, much more intense than they ever did … with an ordinary (fixed-line) telephone" (Carbonell et al., 2013, p. 901).

Individual Characteristics Predicting Mobile Device Use

Not all individuals will use technology, especially mobile devices, to the same extent. For instance, Horrigan (2009) identified 10 different types of users (e.g., media movers, mobile newbies, tech indifferent, information encumbered, off the network, etc.), and Horrigan also combined users into two broad groups: (1) those whose frequency of online use is growing and who have positive attitudes about how available these devices make them (39% of users); (2) those for whom mobile technologies are not as central to their lives (61% of users). Even within these groups, individuals' views vary on whether these technologies have had a positive or negative impact on their lives. For instance, even among the group Horrigan (2009) found had the most favorable views of mobile media—the "digital collaborators"—27% did not necessarily like how *available* mobile devices have made them, and 12% felt *overloaded* by the amount of available information. Among those users in Horrigan's (2009) typologies who report less positive views of mobile media, as many as 89% did not like how *available* mobile devices have made them, 52% felt *overloaded with information*, and as many as 32% felt that technology gave them *less control* over their lives.

Younger adults (ages 20 to 39) are more likely to adopt new devices and use them more frequently (Campbell & Park, 2008; Carbonell et al., 2013), although at least one study of a large cell phone service company found that of those who use smartphones, 34% are older than 39, suggesting that as these new devices gain popularity many adults adopt and use them (Gerpott, Thomas, & Weichert, 2013). In the past, males have been more likely to own and endorse new technology; however, this gender divide has narrowed quickly in recent years (Gerpott et al., 2013), with some research finding females more likely to be heavy users of cell phones (Jenaro, Flores, Gómez-Vela, González-Gil, & Caballo, 2007). In sum, more and more individuals—male and female, young and old—are adopting and using new and mobile technology.

A variety of other factors influence the *frequency* of one's mobile technology use. Besides age and gender, personality appears to be the most studied. Results are sometimes weak and mixed. For example, one study found that personality and self-esteem variables accounted for only 3% to 7% of the variance in individuals' mobile phone use (Ehrenberg, Juckes, White, & Walsh, 2008). In general, individuals who are high on disagreeableness, extraversion, or neuroticism, or low on self-esteem tend to use their cell phones slightly more often for calling or texting (Bianchi & Philips, 2005; Butt & Philips, 2008; Ehrenberg et al., 2008). Turning to other personal indicators, Billieux, Van der Linden, and Rochat (2008) found those who reported more depressive symptoms and anxiety symptoms tended to text more, although these factors did not relate to the amount of time on the phone or number of calls per day. Those reporting feelings of loneliness are likely to spend more time on mobile phones (Takao, Takahashi, & Kitamura, 2009). These studies suggest a multitude of reasons individuals might be more likely to use their mobile devices. For example, some individuals (neurotic and depressed) might turn to mobile devices when they are feeling down or uncomfortable with real social interactions, while others (extroverts) might feel the need to be connected to others, might also have more social contacts, and would therefore give and receive more communication from others.

Attachment theory provides yet another explanation for differences in individual use of mobile phones in romantic relationships. According to attachment theory, individuals have particular *internal working models* or *states of mind* in regards to how relationships should function and the type of intimacy/closeness they desire in these relationships (e.g., Hazan & Shaver, 1987). The type of attachment state of mind that one has may guide one to using particular technologies more or less frequently. Indeed, media richness theory (Daft & Lengel, 1986) suggests that technologies differ in the type of communication they provide as well as how intimately connected one can be with one's partner while using these technologies. For example, a phone call provides a more *rich* experience with *synchronous* communication and voice tone, whereas a text or email is *less rich* as it is *asynchronous* and provides less information. Therefore, individuals who are more avoidant in their romantic attachment style likely wish to keep intimacy to a minimum, communicating less frequently via phone calls and preferring to email as opposed to call their partner (Jin & Peña, 2010; Morey, Gentzler, Creasy, Oberhauser, & Westerman, 2013). Additionally, those with more anxious tendencies in relationships tend to report using their phone more compulsively (O'Connor et al., 2013), although significant associations with actual frequency of calling and texting were not found by Morey et al. (2013). More anxious individuals are also more likely to experience a break-up via technology, such as via text message (Weisskirch & Delevi, 2013). Further, Dietmar (2005) found that those who were more securely attached used more rich and synchronous communication technologies. These individuals communicated more openly on the phone, were more likely to express feelings when texting, and less likely to avoid conflicts on the phone compared with those who were more insecure. Overall, research suggests one's attachment state of mind in romantic relationships likely influences the types of technology one uses, the frequency of use, and the types of topics one communicates via this technology.

Characteristics of Mobile Devices Influencing Use

There are many aspects of mobile phone use that can be inherently gratifying and entice individuals to use them more often. Carbonell et al. (2013) outlined a variety of factors, the most pertinent to this chapter being: (1) Mobile phones can give individuals a feeling of euphoria or feeling valued/loved as they interact with or receive messages from others; (2) phones are highly personalizable, which helps create an emotional bond and leads to one's phone becoming an extension of the self—projecting to the world clues about one's gender, social position, attitude, and personality; (3) phones have become multifunction devices serving also as one's map, calculator, alarm clock, music player, flashlight, and more; and (4) phones have become a form of entertainment during leisure or waiting times. If one has a smartphone, one can surf the Web, watch videos, and/or play games at the touch of a button or screen. Because of mobile devices' ability to fulfill a variety of needs and serve multiple purposes, they are altering our daily routines, filling leisure time, and bridging the gaps between life activities (Dimmick, Feaster, & Hoplamazian, 2011; Oulasvirta, Rattenbury, Ma, & Raita, 2012).

The characteristics of new technologies such as cell phones, smartphones, and tablets are particularly enticing and intrusive. In qualitative interviews with both younger and older adults, individuals speak of feeling pulled toward their technology and having a difficult time resisting the urge to check or respond to alerts or blinking lights on their devices (Jarvenpaa & Lang, 2005; Middleton & Cukier, 2006; Oulasvirta et al., 2012; Rainie & Keeter, 2006). The ever-present nature of mobile devices, especially phones, appears to be stressful for some individuals (Ayyagari, Grover, & Purvis, 2011); many feel they cannot escape their technology (Thomée, Dellve, Härenstam, & Hagberg, 2010). Furthermore, these enticing characteristics of new technology can lead some to develop problematic mobile phone use behaviors, such as turning to their phones when they feel down, being preoccupied with or feeling anxious about receiving a message or email, feeling lost without their phone, and spending too much time on the phone (e.g., Bianchi & Phillips, 2005). Predictors of problematic mobile phone use are almost identical to factors mentioned earlier in the prediction of the frequency of mobile phone use: being younger, female, extroverted, neurotic, anxious, depressed or lonely, having low self-esteem, or feeling anxious/insecure in relationships (Augner & Hacker, 2012; Bianchi & Phillips, 2005; Jenaro et al., 2007; O'Connor et al., 2013; Park, 2005; Takao et al., 2009; Thomée, Härenstam, & Hagberg, 2011).

Technology Interference in Couple and Family Relationships

Although there is no doubt that technology can be used in a variety of positive ways (e.g., communication, shared leisure time, life management), with so many technological devices in and around family life, it is likely that negative effects will emerge—even from normative use. Specifically, I focus here on the potential for technology interference in couple and family relationships—times when technology devices intrude, interrupt, and/or get in the way of couple and family communication and interactions. I term this "technoference."

The potential for the intrusion of technology in relationships. Simply put, the amount of technology use can interfere in relationships, causing conflicts between partners. For instance, Coyne, Busby, Bushman, Gentile, Ridge, and Stockdale (2012) found that as men's videogame playing increased, relationship conflict over media use increased, even spilling over into relational aggression (also see Ahlstrom, Lundberg, Zabriskie, Eggett, & Lindsay, 2012). Most likely, such conflict and relational aggression emerge as partners become upset with how the time spent on these media displaces time that could be spent on the relationship, as well as increases the chance that use will interrupt interactions between partners. This is especially true as the use becomes problematic (e.g., taking time away from the partner, being preoccupied with receiving messages, etc.). Fortunately, the population prevalence rates of problematic mobile phone use are relatively low, ranging from 2.8% to 10.4% (Carbonell et al., 2013).

However, even normative use and the fact that devices, such as mobile phones, are always on and ever present (Ayyagari et al., 2011; Middleton, 2007) could cause intrusions and interruptions in family life. Jarvenpaa and Lang (2005) detailed how the availability and features of new technology have led to several paradoxes, such as the present–absent paradox and the empowerment–enslavement paradox. The present–absent paradox points to how we cannot engage in a conversation and simultaneously text or call someone else, and the empowerment–enslavement paradox demonstrates how anytime/anyplace connectivity can bring great advantages but also leads individuals to feel pressured to respond immediately to their technology. In Middleton and Cukier's (2006) study, one of their participants explained this feeling: "You really don't need to check every email you receive, you really don't, but you feel like you should if it vibrates" (p. 255). Middleton and Cukier (2006) also found that users tended to suppress any dysfunctional view of mobile technology; instead, most focused on the positives even if dysfunctional behaviors were present. Even with such suppression, more than one fourth of U.S. adults report feeling like they *have to* answer their cell phones, even when it interrupts a meal or meeting (Rainie & Keeter, 2006).

Emerging evidence suggests that many individuals struggle with controlling their technology use and keeping it from intruding on family relationships. Coyne, Stockdale, Busby, Iverson, and Grant (2011) found that 38% of their sample reported sending texts or emails during a conversation with their partner. Another small study found that partners of men who own a smartphone often expressed that the phone was a constant distraction, that it negatively impacted their relationship, and that they wished their partner was more emotionally available (Czechowsky, 2008; also see Mazmanian, Orlikowski, & Yates, 2005). In qualitative interviews with couples, Middleton (2007) found that partners and spouses of employees with smartphones were upset by how often their partner monitored their email, even doing so on vacation. Miller-Ott, Kelly, and Duran (2012) also found that those who were less satisfied with the way cell phones were used in their relationship showed lower relationship satisfaction.

One intrusive aspect of the ever-present nature of new technology studied in recent years is work-to-family spillover. In a longitudinal study of couples,

Chelsey (2005) found that use of cell phones blurred boundaries between work and home and increased negative work-to-family spillover for both men and women. This spillover was also linked to increased negative mood and lower satisfaction with family life. This same relationship was not found for computers; Chelsey explains that because computers are more passive than cell phones, users have to turn them on before spillover can occur. In qualitative interviews with employees and their spouses, Mazmanian et al. (2005) found that those with mobile devices were expected to respond to email more quickly; some got caught in a self-reinforcing loop of checking email almost constantly; and spouses resented the way the devices facilitated the spillover of work into family life. The results of Middleton's (2007) and Middleton & Cukier's (2006) interviews also mirror these results. Employees suggested they had control over their always-on device, yet participants' and their spouses' answers portrayed a different reality of "fighting the urge" (Middleton & Cukier, 2006, p. 255)—an illusion of control.

A daily diary study also documented the relationship between smartphone use and work-to-family spillover (Derks & Bakker, 2012). The 69 employees in this study were compelled to use the phones by their employer, and yet many still showed signs of developing problematic use and having difficulties managing the intrusive nature of the technology. This suggests that the phenomenon of technology interference is not completely driven by individual personality characteristics leading to adoption of new technologies; as suggested earlier in the chapter, it might also be that mobile technologies, such as smartphones, have features that are inherently attractive, habit forming, and intrusive in that they are always on and ever present.

Finally, research has also begun to examine the ways use of online social networking sites (SNS), such as Facebook, are intrusive in relationships. Some research suggests use of SNS can be habit forming (Wilson, Fornasier, & White, 2009); as one study participant observed, "the temptation is great, because there's always [new] friends' updates on the screen" (Oulasvirta et al., 2012, p. 112). In a recent study, amount of time spent on Facebook was not related to relationship satisfaction until Facebook use became problematic (e.g., taking time away from others, causing arguments, interrupting tasks); then relationship satisfaction suffered (Elphinston & Noller, 2011). One explanation is that problematic use can create feelings of jealousy in one's partner (Muise, Christofides, & Desmarais, 2009).

Surveying perceptions of technology interference. All of this prior research (as well as my personal observations of how easy it is for family members or friends to pick up their devices during our conversations and interactions) led me to examine how normal, everyday use of technology might influence family relationships. Specifically, my colleague and I have begun examining relationship quality and coparenting quality (McDaniel & Coyne, 2014a, 2014b). As no prior studies have examined normative, everyday technology interruptions and intrusions in family relationships due to devices such as cell phones or tablets (instead often focusing on frequency of use or problematic use specifically), our initial work was exploratory, utilized an online questionnaire design, and sampled 143 women's perceptions (McDaniel & Coyne, 2014a). In this study, the women were married or cohabiting with a partner, were on average 30.4 years old, had a young child 9.3 months old, and 90% or more owned a cell phone/smartphone, television, and computer (McDaniel & Coyne, 2014a). We designed scales that assessed (1) the frequency of interference due to certain devices (such as cell phones/smartphones, television, computers/laptops, and iPads or other tablets) during (1a) interactions with their romantic partner and also during (1b) coparenting interactions (i.e., when the family triad—mother, father, and child—were all together); (2) the frequency with which participants experienced various real-life technology interference situations (such as a partner pulling out his/her phone when it beeps, even if they are in the middle of a conversation); and (3) the frequency of technology interference during various parenting domains (such as bedtime, playtime, mealtime). The women also reported on their personal adjustment (e.g., depressive symptoms and life satisfaction), relationship quality, and coparenting quality.

According to women's perspectives on their relationship, we found that technology interference was more common than we had expected. Sixty-two percent of the women reported that technology interfered in their couple leisure time at least once a day, and a substantial proportion reported it interfered with their conversations (35%) and at mealtime (33%) at least once a day (McDaniel & Coyne, 2014a). We also found that the frequency of these normative technology interruptions related to more frequent conflict over the use of technology, greater depressive symptoms, lower life satisfaction, and lower relationship satisfaction.

Our research is also the first to examine how technology might interfere during interactions between partners when parenting their children (McDaniel & Coyne, 2014b), a type of triadic family interaction termed coparenting (e.g., Feinberg, 2003). We gathered additional participants for this study on coparenting, leaving the final analytic sample at 203 (143 from the above study plus 60 additional mothers). The additional participants did not significantly change the demographic characteristics of the original sample. All women were married or cohabiting with a partner and were, on average, 30.6 years old, had a young child 11.7 months old, and 90% or more owned a cell phone/smartphone, television, and computer. Of this larger sample, about half of the mothers we sampled responded that cell phones or smartphones, television, and computers interfered in triadic coparenting interactions sometimes or more often, with cell phones/smartphones interfering most frequently. They also reported that technology interference occurred most frequently during playtime or free time with their child. It is important to note, though, that some mothers also reported that interference occurred sometimes or more often during educational activities (e.g., reading books) (31%), mealtimes (26%), bedtimes (26%), and even during discipline and limit setting (22%). Overall, greater technology interference in coparenting and parenting was predictive of a mother's perceptions of lower quality coparenting with her partner, even when controlling for relationship satisfaction (a strong predictor of coparenting quality). This finding suggests that when parents allow technology use to interfere in their parenting of their child, it negatively influences how they feel about the quality of coparenting with their partner. It is likely that technology interference decreases the coordination between family members during coparenting interactions, leaving mothers to feel some frustration with their partners. Our results support Jarvenpaa and Lang's (2005) present–absence paradox (e.g., individuals cannot engage in coparenting and simultaneously text or call someone else) and the empowerment–enslavement paradox (e.g., individuals likely feel pressured to respond to technology, even during important parenting moments such as discipline and limit setting).

In writing this chapter, I also wondered whether technology interference is more frequent during couple interactions versus coparenting interactions. To investigate, I ran pairwise *t*-tests to compare women's perceptions of the frequency of interference due to each device across the two domains, the couple relationship and the coparenting relationship, across the 143 women who had been given the technology interference items on *both* couple interactions and coparenting interactions. Results suggest women perceive technology interference due to any of the devices (cell phone/smartphones, computers, television, iPads or tablets) to be more common during interactions with their partner alone than during coparenting interactions when all three family members (mother, father, and child) are together; *t*-values ranged from 6.15 to 10.29, *ps* <.001. For example, for cell phones/smartphones, women rated on average 2.18 (*SD* = 1.29, 70% sometimes or more often) in couple interactions and 1.54 (*SD* = 1.01, 51%) in coparenting interactions on a 6-point scale: 0 (*Never*), 1 (*Rarely*), 2 (*Sometimes*), 3 (*Often*), 4 (*Very Often*), 5 (*All the time*). Two possible explanations include: (1) parents are better able to control their technology use when their child is present, and/or (2) the demands of whole-family interactions lessen one's ability to interact with technology devices.

Limitations and future directions. Although not definitive, our work on women's perceptions of technology interference in their family relationships is a step in the right direction for beginning to understand some of the negative implications of an always-on and always-connected environment. Like any first steps, this work is limited. As of yet, we do not understand how men's perceptions within the same family might compare; and even if men's and women's reports are comparable, we do not know whether their perceptions of technology interference would be related to personal and relational well-being in the same way as women's. It is also likely that (as is the case with most family processes) the relationships are circular in nature. As an illustration, we can imagine a distressed marriage wherein partners are more likely to "tune out" with their devices, but it is likely that even if this were the case, further technology interruptions would then continue to add to the relationship distress.

We also need to better understand how personal characteristics might influence one's perceptions of technology interference as well as one's likelihood of allowing technology interruptions in family life. For instance, we know that certain types of individuals are more prone to develop problematic use of cell phones (e.g., Bianchi & Phillips, 2005), but the scales that have been developed to measure problematic cell phone use tend not to assess the frequency of interruptions in relationships due to technology. Further, it is possible that technology interruptions might bother certain individuals to a greater extent. For example, an individual with a more insecure attachment state of mind about romantic relationships might feel more distressed during interruptions due to technology as he/she might be more likely than a more securely attached individual to feel that the interruption signals a lack of commitment to couple interactions.

Finally, technology interruptions, personal perceptions and feelings, and reactions happen on a much smaller time scale than was measured here. More intensive longitudinal designs, such as daily diaries or ecological momentary assessment, will be necessary to better understand these family processes. We would obtain a more accurate picture of the frequency of technology interruptions and how they are perceived if we have individuals record feelings after each encounter. That said, we must also be cautious not to *produce* technology interruptions through our study procedures (e.g., partners are interacting when their smartphones beep, indicating that it is time to complete their survey).

Finally, we must attempt to understand technology interruptions in context. Although not exhaustive, the following questions might guide future research on key contextual questions in the study of technology interference for couples, parents, and families: (1) Where are couples/families at the moment of the interruption and who is present? (2) What were they doing? (3) Was the interaction they were having perceived to be important by the individual or couple? (4) Was the technology interruption deemed important (i.e., was it an urgent family matter or simply a text from a friend)? (5) Who or what caused the interruption due to technology (i.e., was it the partner who decided to disengage from the couple interaction and engage with the technology? Or was it more device-driven, such as receiving a phone call or text message?).

Application

Overall, it is clear that new technology devices have become a way of life for many individuals, and although these tools are meant to connect us to others, they can easily become addictive, or at least a habit (e.g., Oulasvirta et al., 2012). Such is especially true of younger individuals growing up in a more connected world than has ever existed previously. Research on how technology might produce interruptions and intrusions in couple relationships and what these interruptions mean for relational well-being is still in its infancy. However, the literature cited in this chapter suggests that technology interference—or "technoference"—might be fairly common in interpersonal interactions, and that well-being might be compromised if technology is allowed to interfere in relationships. As technology increasingly permeates our lives and our interactions with others, couples and parents will need to regulate their own technology use when interacting with a partner or children. Some might benefit from training in technology-use etiquette, learning best practices for when devices should be put away, how to deal with phones when they beep in the middle of conversations so that one's partner continues to feel cared for, how to thoughtfully discuss rules and boundaries for technology use in the family and couple context, and so on. Setting *mutually agreed upon* rules to manage devices during family time is also likely beneficial (e.g., no phones at the table during family dinners; kids may not take phones to bed; no phone or tablet use on Sundays, etc). As technology use becomes ever more commonplace, couple communication and parenting programs will need to explicitly integrate such training into their programs in order to improve the quality of interactions between family members.

Additionally, as there are particular characteristics about ourselves, such as our personality, attachment state of mind in romantic relationships, or overall mental health, that may put us at risk of developing problematic technology use (e.g., overuse at the expense of face-to-face relationships, etc.), it is important that each of us critically evaluate ourselves and our use. Some may find it helpful to set a time each week to sit down alone (or together with a partner, although this requires careful listening and conversational skills, as topics surrounding overuse of technology may be "touchy" or "conflict-ridden" for some couples) and take a personal inventory of their daily technology use. It seems that it would be important to ask oneself at least a few important questions:

(1) At what times and *how often do I use technology* throughout the day?
(2) Is all of this use *necessary*?
(3) *What is driving me* to check or respond to my technology, such as being extroverted (i.e., having a need to be connected to many individuals), or feeling lonely or bored? You should try to identify what *need* you are trying to fulfill with your use, as your technology use may be covering up problems or other issues that would be best addressed in other ways.
(4) Is there any aspect of my use that is *affecting me negatively* (i.e., do I feel worse after getting on my phone, even though I initially thought I would feel better? Does my partner seem hurt or distant when I get on my device? Do I feel irritated, anxious, or grumpy if I do not get to use my device?). For example, it was recently found that many individuals get on Facebook believing it will make them feel better but come away feeling worse than when they began (Sagioglou & Greitemeyer, 2014).
(5) Is my technology use changing or *replacing parts of my real life* that were going well before (e.g., I used to talk with my spouse every night before going to bed and felt closer to him/her, but now we are often both on our tablets even when we climb into bed)?

This list of questions could be expanded, but these questions can act as a starting point for all of us in assessing our technology use.

You may also find it helpful to think carefully about the following sample items from the *Mobile Phone Problem Use Scale* (MPPUS, Bianchi & Phillips, 2005, p. 43). You could substitute other technology devices such as "tablet" for "mobile phone." Write down what score you would get on each item on a scale of 1 to 10, where 1 is "not at all true" and 10 is "extremely true." Then sum your total score across the 7 items.

Not at all true – 1 2 3 4 5 6 7 8 9 10 – Extremely true

____ I have used my mobile phone to make myself feel better when I was feeling down.

____ I have tried to hide from others how much time I spend on my mobile phone.

____ I lose sleep due to the time I spend on my mobile phone.

____ I find it difficult to switch off my mobile phone.
____ My friends and family complain about my use of the mobile phone.
____ My productivity has decreased as a direct result of the time I spend on the mobile phone.
____ I feel lost without my mobile phone.
____ TOTAL SCORE (out of 70)

In Bianchi and Phillips's (2005) study on 123 women and 62 men (mean age = 36.07 years) from a university/community sample, the average score adjusted by me to make it comparable to only using 7 items from the full 27-item scale was around 17. Scores on this measure were moderately related to the *MMPI-2 Addiction Potential Scale*. Although I am leery of making strict recommendations as these items are not exactly diagnostic of an addiction, you could use your total summed score on these seven items to indicate whether you might want to seek help from family, friends, or even a trained therapist or mental health specialist, especially if your score is higher than 41 (as this would be extremely high—3 standard deviations above the average—based on the statistics reported in Bianchi & Phillips, 2005). I'll add this disclaimer: These are merely my recommendations based on your score, and this cut-off score has not been tested empirically (e.g., Bianchi & Phillips did not include any cut-offs or diagnostic recommendations); it is possible for problematic use and technology interference in daily life to exist at many levels of use, and therefore some individuals' scores on this measure could be lower or higher and well-being might still be compromised. I would recommend using these items, as well as the personal inventory questions mentioned above, as a starting point to assess whether your technology use is an issue in your personal and relational life. If you have doubts, seek help from a trained professional such as a clinical psychologist or family therapist.

Moreover, technology devices such as Web-connected smartphones have begun eroding the boundaries between work and home (e.g., Chelsey, 2005). This is a difficult issue to address, as expectations have begun to change on both sides. Employers often expect employees to be more accessible and to respond more quickly to requests, and employees may find it difficult to disengage their thoughts from their work, as it often travels home with them as a blinking light or sound notification on their phone (Mazmanian et al., 2005; Middleton & Cukier, 2006). Also, it is important to note that individual characteristics likely interact with changing work pressures. Some individuals may feel especially driven to succeed in their work and may therefore more easily fall into using their technology devices for work even while at home or with family. In this regard, it again seems that *mutually agreed upon rules* at home may be the best solution for employees and their families, such as laying one's phone aside and not checking it (except for emergencies) or turning it off completely from the time one arrives home until after the kids have gone to bed and after romantic partners have had time to chat about their day. Moreover, employers could likely help by setting *clear expectations* for when work-related messages should be responded to and sent as well as *black-out times* (such as Sundays, or after 6pm) when no one is required to check messages.

Finally, a warning. Although there are times when interruptions can occur due to technology devices themselves, many personal characteristics and choices influence technology use in one's personal and family life. Technology should not receive all of the blame for personal or family problems. Even in a world where a phone can serve as our primary communication device, camera, map, agenda, and tether to our workplace, *we have the power to choose* to use our technology in good, wholesome, and responsible ways in personal and family life.

References

Ahlstrom, M., Lundberg, N., Zabriskie, R., Eggett, D., & Lindsay, G. (2012). Me, my spouse, and my avatar: The relationship between marital satisfaction and playing massively multiplayer online role-playing games (MMORPGs). *Journal of Leisure Research, 44,* 1–22.

Augner, C., & Hacker, G. W. (2012). Associations between problematic mobile phone use and psychological parameters in young adults. *International Journal of Public Health, 57*(2), 437–441.

Ayyagari, R., Grover, V., & Purvis, R. (2011). Technostress: Technological antecedents and implications. *MIS Quarterly, 35*(4), 831–858.

Bianchi, A., & Phillips J. (2005). Psychological predictors of problem mobile phone use. *CyberPsychology & Behavior, 8,* 39–51.

Billieux, J., Van der Linden, M., & Rochat, L. (2008). The role of impulsivity in actual and problematic use of the mobile phone. *Applied Cognitive Psychology, 22*(9), 1195–1210.

Brenner, J., & Smith, A. (2013). 72% of online adults are social networking site users. *Pew Internet & American Life Project.* Retrieved from http://www.pewinternet.org/Reports/2013/social-networking-sites/Findings.aspx

Butt, S., & Phillips, J. G. (2008). Personality and self-reported mobile phone use. *Computers in Human Behavior, 24,* 346–360.

Campbell, S. W., & Ling, R. (2009). Effects of mobile communication. In J. Bryant & M. B. Oliver (Eds.), *Media effects: Advances in theory and research* (3rd ed., pp. 592–606). New York: Taylor & Francis.

Campbell, S. W., & Park, Y. J. (2008). Social implications of mobile telephony: The rise of personal communication society. *Sociology Compass, 2,* 371–387.

Carbonell, X., Oberst, U., Beranuy, M. (2013). The cell phone in the twenty-first century: A risk for addiction or a necessary tool? In P. M. Miller (Ed.). *Principles of addiction: Comprehensive addictive behaviors and disorders, Vol. 1* (pp. 901–909). New York: Academic Press.

Castells, M., Fernandez-Ardevol, M., Qiu, J., & Sey, A. (2007). *Mobile communication and society: A global perspective.* Cambridge, MA: MIT Press.

Chelsey, N. (2005). Blurring boundaries: Linking technology use, spillover, individual distress, and family satisfaction. *Journal of Marriage and Family, 67*, 1237–1248.

Coyne, S. M., Busby, D., Bushman, B. J., Gentile, D. A., Ridge, R., & Stockdale, L. (2012). Gaming in the game of love: Effects of video games on conflict in couples. *Family Relations, 61*, 388–396.

Coyne, S. M., Stockdale, L., Busby, D., Iverson, B., & Grant, D. M. (2011). "I luv u:)!": A descriptive study of the media use of individuals in romantic relationships. *Family Relations, 60*, 150–162.

Czechowsky, J. D. (2008). *The impact of the BlackBerry on couple relationships.* (Unpublished doctoral dissertation, Wilfrid Laurier University). Retrieved from http://scholars.wlu.ca/cgi/viewcontent.cgi?article=2055&context=etd

Daft, R. L., & Lengel, R. H. (1986). Organizational information requirements, media richness, and structural design. *Management Science, 32*(5), 554–571.

Derks, D., & Bakker, A. B. (2012). Smartphone use, work–home interference, and burnout: A diary study on the role of recovery. *Applied Psychology*. doi: 10.1111/j.1464–0597.2012.00530.x

Dietmar, C. (2005). Mobile communication in couple relationships. In K. Nyiri (Ed.), *A sense of place: The global and the local in mobile communication.* Vienna: Passagen Verlag.

Dimmick, J., Feaster, J. C., & Hoplamazian, G. J. (2011). News in the interstices: The niches of mobile media in space and time. *New Media & Society, 13*(1), 23–39.

Ehrenberg, A., Juckes, S., White, K. M., & Walsh, S. P. (2008). Personality and self-esteem as predictors of young people's technology use. *CyberPsychology & Behavior, 11*(6), 739–741.

Elphinston, R. A., & Noller, P. (2011). Time to face it! Facebook intrusion and the implications for romantic jealousy and relationship satisfaction. *Cyberpsychology, Behavior, and Social Networking, 14*, 631–635.

Feinberg, M. E. (2003). The internal structure and ecological context of coparenting: A framework for research and intervention. *Parenting: Science and Practice, 3*(2), 95–131.

Gerpott, T. J., Thomas, S., & Weichert, M. (2013). Characteristics and mobile Internet use intensity of consumers with different types of advanced handsets: An exploratory empirical study of iPhone, Android, and other web-enabled mobile users in Germany. *Telecommunications Policy, 37*, 357–371.

Hazan, C., & Shaver, P. (1987). Romantic love conceptualized as an attachment process. *Journal of Personality and Social Psychology, 52*, 511–524.

Horrigan, J. (2009). The mobile difference: Wireless connectivity has drawn many users more deeply into digital life. *Pew Internet & American Life Project*. Retrieved from http://pewinternet.org/Reports/2009/5-The-Mobile-Difference–Typology.aspx

Jarvenpaa, S. L., & Lang, K. R. (2005). Managing the paradoxes of mobile technology. *Information Systems Management, 22*(4), 7–23.

Jenaro, C., Flores, N., Gómez-Vela, M., González-Gil, F., & Caballo, C. (2007). Problematic Internet and cell-phone use: Psychological, behavioral, and health correlates. *Addiction Research & Theory, 15*(3), 309–320.

Jin, B., & Peña, J. F. (2010). Mobile communication in romantic relationships: Mobile phone use, relational uncertainty, love, commitment, and attachment styles. *Communication Reports, 23*(1), 39–51.

Katz, J. E., & Aakhus, M. A. (Eds.) (2002). *Perpetual contact: Mobile communication, private talk, public performance.* Cambridge, UK: Cambridge University Press.

Lenhart, A., Madden, M., Smith, A., Purcell, K., Zickuhr, K., & Rainie, L. (2011). Teens, kindness, and cruelty on social network sites: How American teens navigate the new world of "digital citizenship." *Pew Internet & American Life Project.* Retrieved from http://pewinternet.org/Reports/2011/Teens-and-social-media.aspx

Mazmanian, M. A., Orlikowski, W. J., & Yates, J. (2005). Crackberries: The social implications of ubiquitous wireless e-mail devices. In C. Sørensen et al. (Eds.), *Designing ubiquitous information environments: Sociotechnical issues and challenges* (pp. 337–344). New York: Springer.

McDaniel, B. T., & Coyne, S. M. (2014a). "Technoference": The interference of technology in couple relationships and implications for women's personal and relational well-being. *Psychology of Popular Media Culture.* doi: 10.1037/ppm0000065

McDaniel, B. T., & Coyne, S. M. (2014b). *Technology interference in the parenting of young children: Implications for mothers' perceptions of coparenting.* Manuscript submitted for publication. Retrieved from http://www.brandonmcdaniel.blogspot.com

Middleton, C. A. (2007). Illusions of balance and control in an always-on environment: A case study of BlackBerry users. *Continuum: Journal of Media & Cultural Studies, 21*(2), 165–178.

Middleton, C. A., & Cukier, W. (2006). Is mobile email functional or dysfunctional? Two perspectives on mobile email usage. *European Journal of Information Systems, 15*(3), 252–260.

Miller-Ott, A. E., Kelly, L., & Duran, R. L. (2012). The effects of cell phone usage rules on satisfaction in romantic relationships. *Communication Quarterly, 60*(1), 17–34.

Morey, J. N., Gentzler, A. L., Creasy, B., Oberhauser, A. M., & Westerman, D. (2013). Young adults' use of communication technology within their romantic relationships and associations with attachment style. *Computers in Human Behavior, 29*(4), 1771–1778.

Muise, A., Christofides, E., & Desmarais, S. (2009). *CyberPsychology & Behavior, 12,* 441–444.

O'Connor, S. S., Whitehill, J. M., King, K. M., Kernic, M. A., Boyle, L. N., Bresnahan, B. W., … & Ebel, B. E. (2013). Compulsive cell phone use and history of motor vehicle crash. *Journal of Adolescent Health, 53*(4), 512–519.

Oulasvirta, A., Rattenbury, T., Ma, L., & Raita, E. (2012). Habits make smartphone use more pervasive. *Personal and Ubiquitous Computing, 16*(1), 105–114.

Park, W. K. (2005). Mobile phone addiction. In R. Ling & P. E. Pedersen (Eds.), *Mobile Communications* (pp. 253–272). London: Springer.

Pew. (2012). A closer look at gadget owernership. *Pew Internet & American Life Project.* Retrieved from http://www.pewinternet.org/Infographics/2012/A-Closer-Look-at-Gadget-Ownership.aspx

Popkin, H. A. S. (2011, September 12). British people prefer Facebook to toilets. *Msnbc.com Today.* Retrieved from http://digitallife.today.com/_news/2011/09/12/7728080-british-people-prefer-facebook-to-toilets

Rainie, L. (2012). Two-thirds of young adults and those with higher income are smartphone owners. *Pew Internet & American Life Project.* Retrieved from http://www.pewinternet.org/Reports/2012/Smartphone-Update-Sept-2012.aspx

Rainie, L., & Keeter, S. (2006). Americans and their cell phones. *Pew Internet & American Life Project.* Retrieved from http://www.pewinternet.org/Reports/2006/Americans-and-their-cell-phones.aspx

Sagioglou, C., & Greitemeyer, T. (2014). Facebook's emotional consequences: Why Facebook causes a decrease in mood and why people still use it. *Computers in Human Behavior, 35*, 359–363.

Smith, A. (2013). Smartphone ownership 2013. *Pew Internet & American Life Project.* Retrieved from http://www.pewinternet.org/Reports/2013/Smartphone-Ownership-2013/Findings.aspx

Srivastava, L. (2005). Mobile phones and the evolution of social behaviour. *Behaviour & Information Technology, 24*, 111–129.

Takao, M., Takahashi, S., & Kitamura, M. (2009). Addictive personality and problematic mobile phone use. *CyberPsychology & Behavior, 12*(5), 501–507.

Thomée, S., Dellve, L., Härenstam, A., & Hagberg, M. (2010). Perceived connections between information and communication technology use and mental symptoms among young adults: A qualitative study. *BMC Public Health, 10*(1), 66.

Thomée, S., Härenstam, A., & Hagberg, M. (2011). Mobile phone use and stress, sleep disturbances, and symptoms of depression among young adults: A prospective cohort study. *BMC Public Health, 11*(1), 66.

Weisskirch, R. S., & Delevi, R. (2013). Attachment style and conflict resolution skills predicting technology use in relationship dissolution. *Computers in Human Behavior, 29*(6), 2530–2534.

Wilson, K., Fornasier, S., White, K. (2009). Psychological predictors of young adults' use of social networking sites. *CyberPsychology & Behavior, 12*, 1–5.

Zickuhr, K. (2013). Tablet ownership 2013. *Pew Internet & American Life Project.* Retrieved from http://www.pewinternet.org/Reports/2013/Tablet-Ownership-2013/Findings.aspx

12

Love Letters Lost?

Gender and the Preservation of Digital and Paper Communication from Romantic Relationships

MICHELLE Y. JANNING
NEAL J. CHRISTOPHERSON
Whitman College

AUTHOR NOTE: The authors wish to express appreciation to Emma Snyder for her survey research assistance, and Carol Bruess for her encouragement and editorial advice. The authors also wish to thank Alissa Cordner and David Hutson for comments on earlier drafts of this chapter. Correspondence concerning this chapter should be addressed to Michelle Janning, Department of Sociology, Whitman College, Walla Walla, WA 99362. Contact: janninmy@whitman.edu

Introduction

When it comes to remembering love, does the act of unpacking and unfolding mean something different than the act of swiping and scrolling?

A recent *New Yorker* article highlights a South Korean app called "Between," a digital system for romantically involved couples to privately exchange everything from text and voice messages to photos, notes, and stickers, all of which are saved in a virtual pine-colored "memory box" meant to digitally mimic the keepsake, under-the-bed boxes and underwear drawers where special romantic messages were once preserved (Collins, 2013). More recently, an article in *The Atlantic* reveals gender differences in how young men and women save "sexts"; teenage boys tend to save and share sexts with male friends as a form of currency or status to show their friends, and girls tend to save sexts as markers of relationship stages and levels of intimacy with partners (Livingston, 2014; Rosin, 2014). Communication in contemporary romantic relationships is increasingly mediated by technology; the above examples suggest the way such communication is preserved in memory is also changing in the digital age. The latter example also demonstrates that gender can influence saving practices and the meanings of the saved messages.

Pen-and-paper letter writing has dwindled in recent years with the development of email and cell phones for texting (Brandt, 2006; Haggis & Holmes, 2011), though scholars wrestle with whether communication mediated by digital means is really that different from offline communication, both in terms of individual identity formation and in terms of how we define community (Baym, 2010; Belk, 2013; boyd, 2014; Turkle, 2011). This wrestling stretches across disciplines as diverse as literary theory, psychology, neuroscience, and consumer studies. For example, Hayles (2002), in *Writing Machines,* says the meaning of words is impacted by the form (paper versus digital) those words take. Belk (2013), in a complication and elaboration of his 1988 theory of objects as "extended selves," suggests "digital possessions are found to be almost, but not quite, the singular objects of attachment that their physical counterparts are" (p. 490).

Given that demographic categories impact the access and use of digital technology (Baym, 2010) and the behaviors within romantic relationships (Rutter & Schwartz, 2011), it is also important to understand *who* is doing the saving and storing of both paper and digital relationship messages. Gender, in particular, has been a focus of scholarly investigations about how love operates in contemporary romantic relationships (e.g., Sumter, Valkenburg, & Peter, 2013). But does gender play a role in the preservation practices associated with love letters? We combine research and theorizing about how men and women operate in contemporary romantic relationships with the scholarship on the meaning of saved objects by asking whether and how men and women save and attach meaning to digital or paper messages as mementos of romantic relationships.

While previous research reveals that gender matters in romantic relationships and that digital and physical objects may take on differential meanings in people's lives, no studies have focused on the potentially changing role of love letter saving practices in the digital age, and the potential for gender differences in those practices. Using as scaffolding current research and theorizing on digital-age human interaction and gender within couple relationships, we investigate intimate romantic relationships by studying the associated material markers of relationship memories. We ask whether saving words that express romantic love and affection on paper differs from saving them digitally, both in terms of whether and how individuals attach meaning to the letter as a symbol of the romantic relationship and in how gender might influence saving practices. The format of a saved love letter, and the manner in which it is saved—its "rituals of possession and disposition" (Belk, 2013, pp. 479–480)—might tell us something about how gender operates in romantic relationships, as well as how the meaning of the relationship, or the meaning of the possessor's self within the relationship, is represented by that letter.

Background

This project uses three important theoretical and empirical frameworks as guides for the central question, variable measures, and interpretation of findings: (1) rituals of possession and disposition of physical and digital possessions as extended selves (Belk, 2013); (2) Epp and Price's (2010) overview of the singularization and cultural biography of objects via heated and cooled storage locations as part of individuals' connections with those objects; and (3) Giordano, Longmore, and Manning's (2006) and Sumter et al.'s (2013) discussions of the conflicting research findings on gender and love in intimate romantic relationships, as well as the research on the impact of gender on the preservation of relationship mementos (Janning and Scalise, 2013) and gendered relationship communication (Baym, 2010).

Rituals of Possession and Disposition of Physical and Digital Objects as Extended Selves

Belk (1988; 1991) articulates how possessions are *extended selves* that serve as identity and memory markers. Intentionally saving objects gives them a kind of sacredness, which stems from the high level of emotional involvement imbued in the cultural biography of the object (Kopytoff, 1986) and the significance of the object to the saver's identity. Hepper and Ritchie (2011) articulate that saved objects help people remember past experiences (both one-time experiences and transitions throughout life stages), relationships, and selves, which in turn helps them define their current selves. Perhaps most salient for a project on love letters, saved objects and keepsakes can trigger nostalgic emotional responses connected to those experiences and changes, in either positive or negative ways. An object becomes a trigger when it accumulates a history from the social interactions in which it is involved. When looking at a past love letter, the accumulated history embodied in it can invoke the recalling of a version of the self as salient in the past relationship, as well as stir emotions about that relationship (Hepper & Ritchie, 2011).

When Belk first articulated his theory, he referenced solely physical objects. His updated conceptualization includes reimagining of the self via *digital* objects (2013). Belk's work underscores questions about the impact of digital versus physical objects on identity and memory creation, and asks whether "a dematerialized book, photo, or song can be integral to our extended self in the same way as its material counterpart can be. If these items are stored on a remote server, are they really ours?" (p. 479). Are digital versions of objects, because of their intangibility and easier reproducibility, therefore less singularizable (i.e., decommodified, made more emotionally attached, given personal meanings [Epp & Price, 2010]) and "less a part of the extended self" (Belk, 2013, p. 481) than would be physical objects? Can humans give their "aura" (Benjamin, 1936/1968) to a virtual object? Belk wrestles with this question when he calls to mind the importance of dematerialization: When a memory object such as a letter becomes dematerialized by virtue of it being digitized, as is the case with much contemporary email and texting correspondence, it can become largely invisible until we search for it, although it also has the capacity to elicit similar emotional responses as those attached to a physical object (Belk, 2013).

To complicate the questions about digital and physical objects as extended selves, and because social actors participate in behavioral practices that signify the preservation of objects as mementos of identities and experiences, Belk (2013) asks whether rituals of possession and disposition of virtual and material objects operate similarly. He argues that people's actions of organizing, curating, preserving, using, and perhaps dispossessing saved objects matter in determining the significance of the object as singularized and salient for identities. But he presents differing ideas about whether such rituals differ if the object is on paper or digitized, noting disagreement among scholars about whether virtual objects are as "authentic" (p. 481) as physical objects. Belk ultimately agrees with Appadurai (1986) and Denegri-Knott, Watkins, and Wood (2012), articulating the possibility for individuals to "singularize ... virtual possessions just as they can with real world possessions" in their rituals of possession and disposition (Belk, 2013, p. 480). He argues the loss of a virtual possession can have the same emotional effect on the owner. If a possession is lost, regardless of whether it is in a box or in a virtual cloud, the possessor mourns its loss. In this sense, there might not be much difference between virtual and physical objects as extended selves, and the actions people take to preserve and curate love letters as objects might not differ much either.

Belk does argue that virtual possessions lack a physical presence and carry with them an uncertainty about control and ownership, however. Storing the text of an email love letter on an online server might seem safe in the event of a house fire; on the other hand, most individuals have an emotionally more difficult time throwing away a paper greeting card than they do deleting an e-card (Siddiqui & Turley, 2006). Further, because individuals tend to define digital family mementos as less valuable than physical mementos (Petrelli & Whittaker, 2010), there might indeed be differences in how digital versus physical objects such as love letters are viewed, preserved, and visited.

Singularization and the Cultural Biography of Heated and Cooled Objects

To singularize an object means to give it personal meaning (Miller, 1987). Although directly asking someone if an object is meaningful can tell us something about its singularization, the location of the object might further reveal something about its meaning to its possessor. Putting an object in a certain place—or locating it somewhere where one is more or less likely to see or touch it—is a ritual of possession or disposition (Belk, 1988). Epp and Price (2010) call such a choice *heating* the object: to place an object in a domestic space such that it makes the object easy to see or access. Epp and Price are influenced by Kopytoff's (1986) cultural biography of things, describing as he does how an object can be heated or cooled based on its location, and on how heating and cooling tells the story of the object's significance to its possessor. For example, keeping an object in the middle of the living room where a family spends a lot of time will heat the object, making it more visible, salient, and often more readily and frequently seen or touched by family members. For an individual, an object might be heated not necessarily by being accessible in more public domestic spaces such as a living room, but by being placed in a spot that is easy to see or reach for without needing to open a door or drawer (such as on a nightstand, desk, or wall). Conversely, storing something in a cellar that is far from other living spaces or in a closet or drawer that hides its contents from the sight of household residents will cool the object (Epp & Price 2010) for both the family and individual family members. Accordingly, one could argue that the cooling of a less meaningful object occurs because it is not easy to access without opening something or removing a barrier to make it visible, and therefore that object might be less salient to an individual's self-definition. Lastovicka and Fernandez (2005), by defining spaces in a household as "hearth" and "periphery," articulate how the cooling of objects often signifies a distancing of those objects from family members' definition of selves. They find that "transition places" such as basements, porches, or unused rooms in the periphery of a home (as opposed to kitchens, living rooms, and bedrooms at the core) are often used as locations to isolate possessions in order to move them "away from the domain of 'me'" (p. 817). In this way, cooled objects are less meaningful because of their physical location within the household.

To date, scholarly work has not examined singularization via heated and cooled locations of digital versus physical objects. As Belk might argue, if an object such as a love letter is part of an extended self, it might indeed matter whether the object is paper or digital in the possessor's estimation of its singularization and whether it has salience as a heated or cooled object. If individuals are more likely to revisit and can more easily access paper letters than they can digital, perhaps paper is more heated. Perhaps computers and smartphones are more cooled in the cultural biography of love letters. Or perhaps it is the other way around: that in a digital age the ready access to mementos on a device creates opportunities for heating objects in ways not yet studied or understood prior to ubiquitous twenty-first-century communication technologies.

Gender, Love, Romantic Communication, and Saving the Stuff from Relationships

Similarities and differences in the way men and women view love and romance (Rutter & Schwartz, 2011) provide clues about how sex and gender might influence the preservations of love letters and relationship mementos. Haggis and Holmes (2011) suggest love letters represent "an exchange of emotion, thought, knowledge, feeling, and information" (p. 170), that presume a reader, a real world connection and performativity, and that have become easier to perform using new technology. The love letter, then, is a performance of emotion—and emotion and its displays are gendered within romantic relationships (Kimmel, 2012).

There are competing paradigms about gendered emotional displays and feelings of long-term romantic love within heterosexual relationships (Sumter et al., 2013; Giordano et al., 2006). On one hand, research suggests same-sex peer group socialization (along with other powerful socializing agents such as media, parental modeling, and gendered institutions) perpetuates differential emotional responses of men and women within romantic relationships (Sumter et al., 2013). In these findings, men are typically less likely to demonstrate loving commitment in their relationships than women, often due to men's adherence to traditional notions of masculinity that sanction the display or admittance of emotional attachment (Kimmel, 2012).

Alternately, researchers have found that men and women are "more similar than different in reported levels of passion, intimacy, and commitment" (Sumter et al. 2013, p. 424) in romantic relationships. Giordano et al. (2006) measure emotional engagement and find no significant gender differences in participants' "feelings of heightened emotionality in connection with the … relationship" (p. 276). Also, while lamenting the dearth of research on men and boys in romantic relationships, these authors attribute variation in gender roles within couples to meaning-making processes within the couples themselves. Using tenets of symbolic interactionism, they argue a couple's meaning-making processes might be more powerful than prescriptive gender socialization occurring outside of, or as a precursor to, the couple's relationship. For a given couple then, "the relatively private world of romantic interactions makes it likely that meanings will emerge on site, rather than simply being imported from earlier peer experiences or from the broader culture" (p. 264). These within-couple meanings may or may not adhere to traditional notions of masculinity and femininity, thus challenging the assumption that men are automatically assumed to be less emotionally attached, or less sentimental, in a romantic relationship. In terms of love letters, given these conflicting findings, it is difficult to know whether men and women will differ in their tendency to preserve and curate symbols of emotional attachment within a romantic relationship.

While the research on gender and emotional attachment in romantic relationships is conflicted, recent research has evidenced gender differences in acts surrounding the preservation of family roles and relationships via the saving of symbolic relationship mementos. Janning and Scalise (2013), for example, investigate the impact of gender on the preservation of family roles and relationships as represented in family photographs. They found women were more inclined than men to feel responsible for saving photographs as symbols of family relationships, in part a manifestation based on adherence to social expectations that connect femininity (and often motherhood, once children enter the picture) and kin-keeping. Given the research discussed earlier in this chapter (Rosin, 2014) about gender differences in motivations for saving sexual messages (young men were more likely to preserve the messages to "show off" to friends and young women more likely to preserve such items as markers of intimacy), studying the saving of romantic messages in a digital age might reveal interesting gendered practices.

Research on gendered relationship communication finds women are more often socialized to "attend more to relational dimensions of conversation while men are reared to specialize in the informative dimensions" (Baym, 2010, p. 66). Since love letters are a form of relationship communication, gender might matter in terms of the rituals of possession and disposition of them, and therefore in terms of their singularization as heated or cooled objects representing the (perhaps gendered) self. In light of the research on these topics, the following research questions guide the current investigation:

RQ1: Do men and women differ in their approach to the rituals of possession and disposition of love letters?

RQ2: Are there differences in the meaning attached to paper and digital love letters evidenced by saving practices?

Methods

After conducting a preliminary literature review and receiving IRB approval in 2012, we conducted a focus group of three college women who had been in at least one romantic relationship. We read through the transcript and found recurring themes and agreed-upon definitions of concepts, as well as concrete examples of types of relationship messages, in order to craft potential survey questions. We drafted and pretested the survey in 2013 with eight individuals of varying ages, genders, and geographic locations, since the demographics of the initial focus group participants lacked gender and age diversity. The pretest survey also included a request for respondents to tell us how long it took for them to take the survey, whether the question wording and order were clear, whether any topics seemed to be missing, and whether anything else needed improvement or clarification. After revising the questions based on the pretest responses, we implemented an online survey using Qualtrics survey software, which was open for 2 weeks in July 2013. The link was sent via a snowball method to a college student listserv and via the researchers' social networking sites (primarily Facebook, which had a maximum of 1200 initial views), thus making the sample purposive and nonrandom. People were encouraged to share or forward the survey link. After 1 week, we supplemented the initial call for survey participation by sending it to three additional student groups to yield a more geographically diverse sample, four women over 60 years old to encourage sharing with their social network, and five men between the ages of 18 and 50 outside of the student listserv in order to encourage a larger sample of men to take the survey. As is often the case with online surveys, many more people started the survey ($N = 814$) than completed it ($N = 398$), but much of the attrition was due to the fact that a bulk of the survey could only be completed by individuals who had been in at least one romantic relationship, a subsample that constitutes the sample for this analysis (specific sample sizes for each question are noted in the Findings section below).

Measures

The survey began with questions about respondents' daily technology habits to get an overall feel for the comfort level of respondents' technology use. Respondents were next asked how many relationships they had been in based on our provided definition of a romantic relationship: *"It's hard to provide a definition of 'Romantic Relationship.' For this survey, we define it to include physical intimacy, attraction, commitment, and development over time. Since we are studying communication patterns, we are interested in relationships lasting at least three months."* Respondents indicating having had at least one romantic relationship were included in this analysis. In the second set of survey questions, respondents were asked to reflect on their relationship history and select a relationship with a salient connection (however they defined salient) to giving and/or receiving love letters or romantic messages within the relationship, and then instructed to refer to and think of this relationship throughout the remainder of the survey. The subsequent questions asked what year the relationship started, what year it ended (if applicable), and whether there had been any portions of the relationship that were long distance for at least a month.

The main topic of interest for this analysis—practices of saving love letters from relationships—was operationalized by first asking context questions about general object-saving practices that funneled down into the practices of saving love letters specifically. Starting broadly, we asked whether participants considered themselves to be "savers" of meaningful objects in general, and whether they have saved any physical or digital mementos (beyond letters) from the relationship they have been thinking of. Using Belk's (1988) conceptualization of the rituals of possession and disposition, as well as Epp and Price's (2010) references to the singularization and salience of heated and cooled storage locations for preserving memories, we then specifically asked about types of saved messages from this relationship, and which types of these messages they revisit most often. For the one saved message they reported revisiting most often, respondents then answered a question about the frequency with which they revisit it, where they store this saved message, and why they revisit it. A final open-ended question asked the respondent to describe the saved message in detail. A final set of questions asked for participant demographics, including age, gender, race, education level, and income.

Data Analysis

For the quantitative data analyses, cross-tabs, means, and frequencies were calculated within either Qualtrics or, for variables that needed recoding and statistical significance tests, SPSS. In the reporting of gender comparisons below, statistical significance tests are noted when they were conducted.

The qualitative analyses of open-ended questions consisted of two rounds of pen-and-paper open coding (Berg & Lune, 2011) for thematic clusters of responses and a check for consistency between coders (the first author and a research assistant). Patterns and thematic clusters of responses to open-ended questions were recoded as categorical or nominal variables. To do this, we used the framework for qualitative data analysis developed by Miles, Huberman, and Saldaña (2013) to collapse respondent-level narrative data into aggregate findings and to note the various recurring themes emergent in the open-ended responses. Answers were compared and contrasted between coders to refine our understanding of the emerging trends and themes. After the open-ended responses were recoded as categorical variables, they were analyzed via cross-tabulations with gender, including statistical significance tests. Negative test case analysis (Creswell, 2012) was also implemented to make group comparisons when, in the first round of open coding, groups seemed quite similar. This means that a final round of coding consisted of finding instances when comments were unusual or infrequent, but raised important counterthemes or were only noted by a certain demographic of respondents (in the case of this study, if only men or only women responded with a particular answer, it was noted).

Respondent and Relationship Characteristics

In total, 97 males (20.4%) and 379 females (79.6%) answered at least one of the survey questions measuring saving practices used in this analysis; as such, 476 was the maximum sample size that could be used to conduct bivariate analyses with gender as a variable. The ages of respondents were as follows: 57% were 18–24 years old; 9% were 25–34 years old; 11% were 35–44; 11% were 45–54; 7% were 55–64; and 5% were 65–89. Of the 476 respondents, 46% reported having "some college," followed by Associate or Bachelor's Degree (26%), Master's Degree (15%), Doctorate Degree (8%), and high school degree or less (5%). Respondents' (= 428) 2012 household income range included: just over half (51%) at $100,000 or higher; 33% between $50,000 and $99,000; 10% between $25,000 and $49,999; and just under 6% less than $25,000. It was not clear if college students included parents' income as part of "family's household income"; as such, the income data might be skewed. Participants' (N = 476) self-reports of their race/ethnicity reflects numbers adding up to more than 100% because individuals could choose more than one option from the provided list. The sample is 91% White, 6% Asian American, 4% Hispanic or Latino, 1% Black or African American, 1% Native Hawaiian or Pacific Islander, and 3% "other" (among those selecting "other," the most common response was multi- or biracial).

Of the 785 respondents who answered *"Please indicate your current relationship status,"* participants were single (37%), in romantic relationships (but not married) (32%), and married (28%). Of the remaining respondents, 3% were divorced, 1% separated, 1% remarried, and 1% widowed.

In terms of involvement in romantic relationships, the highest percentage (41%) of the 747 respondents had been in one or two romantic relationships total. Thirty-one percent had between three and five, 8% between six and nine, 5% had ten or more, and 14% had none.

Respondents were asked to think of one relationship and answer the remaining questions as they pertain to that specific relationship only. This question yielded a large drop in sample size, as not everyone chose to answer questions about a relationship, and some were exempt from answering because they had not had a relationship. Of the relationships respondents reported (N = 412), 76% of respondents were female with male partners, 19.4% were male respondents with female partners, 1.2% were male respondents with male partners, and 3.2% were female respondents with female partners (1 female respondent listed "other" for her partner's sex).

Findings

Gender and Paper versus Digital Communication: Assets and Drawbacks

To gather respondents' views about the changes in communication formats in romantic relationships we asked: *"Some people debate whether digital communication has replaced handwritten communication. In your opinion, do you think letter, note, and card writing, in handwritten form, is fading in romantic relationships?"* The large majority of respondents (88%; n = 331) said "yes," and elaborated on the upsides and downsides (assets and drawbacks) of each type of communication. Key themes relating to assets and drawbacks emerged via open coding of responses, with no substantive gender differences other than those that were found using negative case analysis. Overall, men and women responded very similarly to this question; the negative case analysis found that only men mentioned "saving trees" and "being inexpensive" as assets for digital communication, and only men mentioned their "penmanship challenges" in their comments about the drawbacks of handwritten communication. Importantly, some comments were neutral, elaborating without evaluation of the practice as an asset or a drawback. These comments were not categorized as either assets or drawbacks.

The most commonly emerging assets of digital communication were ease, speed, ability to converse in real time, and justifying comments (explanations that digital communication is as meaningful as handwritten communication). The most commonly emerging drawbacks to digital communication reported were a tendency to be impersonal, promote laziness, and reinforce instant gratification.

The most common emerging assets of handwritten communication were tangibility, sacredness, rareness, and tendency to promote thoughtful and personal communication. The most commonly noted emerging drawbacks of handwritten communication were that it was cheesy, hokey, and old-fashioned, as well as justifying comments that noted it as not necessarily more meaningful than digital communication.

Gender and Saving Love Letters

In order to understand the context in which a person may save a love letter, we asked a series of questions that began with general saving practices beyond romantic relationships and ended with specific *love letter* saving practices. Specifically, first, we asked about whether individuals save meaningful objects generally; second, we asked whether they save romantic relationship objects (e.g., photos, souvenirs, articles of clothing); and third, we asked whether they save love letters specifically. Analysis of responses to these three questions reveals the following results: First, when respondents were asked to assess the extent to which the statement *"I keep objects that are meaningful to me"* reflects them and their behaviors, females scored 4.5 and males scored 4.1 on a 5-point scale where 5 = *"this definitely describes me"* and 1 = *"this definitely does NOT describe me."* T-tests reveal a statistically significant difference ($p <.05$). Women were more likely than men to see themselves as savers in general, with similar mean differences. Second, the majority of our sample (76% of 419 respondents) save physical or digital mementos (e.g., photos, souvenirs) from the relationships about which they were reporting. When asked whether they save relationship objects, 79% of women and 66% of men save objects; T-tests reveal that difference is statistically significant ($p <.05$). And third, in response to the question *"Have you saved any communication [messages] from this relationship,"* 83% of men and 90% of women said "yes." T-tests reveal a statistically significant difference on this item at the $p <.10$ level ($p =.098$). Overall, these results suggest women are disproportionately and significantly more likely to save objects generally, and objects from romantic relationships, than are men. There is a less significant difference when it comes to saving relationship messages specifically, possibly because men who are more likely to save these messages are also more likely to answer survey questions about the topic. Nonetheless, our findings suggest women seem more likely to save love letters than men.

Gender and Types of Messages Saved from the Romantic Relationship

In response to the question *"What types of communications [messages] from this relationship have you saved? (Check all that apply),"* men and women ($N = 373$) were similar to each other across both digital and paper forms. T-tests reveal no significant differences between men and women on any types of saved messages, which were transformed into singular variables (that is, each message format was turned into a separate variable) where within-gender proportional differences could be assessed for each format separately. Both women and men disproportionately save paper letters, cards, and notes (approximately 66% do so), followed by emails (approximately 50%), texting conversations (approximately 33%), Facebook message conversations (slightly less than 33%), and captured Snapchats (slightly less than 10%).

It is important to note that if a respondent indicated on the survey he or she saved a certain "type" of message, it meant the participant actually received that type of message in the relationship. It is possible that not checking a particular type meant they never received it, or it could mean they received it but did not save it. Regarding overall preference for paper or digital communication, both men and women were much more likely to save paper versus digital messages. This finding is particularly interesting given that distribution of the survey was digital and thus, one might assume, a more technologically inclined and technologically oriented sample would potentially emerge.

Gender and Type of Saved Messages Revisited Most Often

Saving an object is different from revisiting it by either physically holding it or digitally accessing it to view. If men and women are similar in the types of messages saved, we wondered whether there are differences in terms of *preferred* type of message to revisit. Out of the total number of respondents who answered this question ($N = 360$), and after transforming each type of message into a separate variable (where responses were recoded as yes or no for each type), we found that men are more likely than women to revisit letters (26.1% v. 22.5%), cards (27.5% v. 20.1%), and emails (10.1% v. 8.5%), and women are more likely than men to revisit paper notes (18.3% v. 10.1%) and texts (12.7% v. 11.6%). Since a majority of the respondents were referencing heterosexual relationships, it might be that types of messages *sent* varied by gender, since the availability of messages to revisit would logically affect whether or not they are revisited. However, T-tests reveal no significant differences between males and females along any type of messages preferred to revisit. Interestingly, in general, both men and women were more likely to prefer revisiting saved paper messages than they were digital messages.

Gender and Frequency of Looking at Saved Messages

Are men and women similar or different when it comes to how often they revisit saved relationship messages? Cross-tabulations using data from the 363 respondents who answered the question reveal a statistically significant relationship between gender and frequency of revisiting saved messages (Chi-square = 17.853, sig. .001). Specifically, 5.6% of men and 3.8% of women were in the "Daily or Almost

Daily" category of frequency of revisiting a saved message; 5.6% of men and 8% of women in the "Once or Twice a Week" category; 19.7% of men and 19.4% of women in the "Once or Twice a Month" category; 53.5% of men and 30.8% of women in the "A Few Times a Year" category; and 15.5% of men and 38.1% of women in the "Once a Year or Less" category.

This statistically significant result is likely explained by two patterns: First, among participants who revisited the saved message frequently (at least once per week or more), men were slightly more likely to do so daily or almost daily; and second, of participants who revisit infrequently (a few times a year or less), men were more likely to do so a few times a year instead of once a year or less. This explanation is complicated when the top two and bottom two categories are collapsed, resulting in three frequency categories. In this case, men and women look almost identical and the Chi-square is no longer significant (Chi-square = .016, sig. 992). When the frequency variable is treated as one that can have a calculable mean (where "Daily or Almost Daily" is coded as 1, etc.), men have a smaller mean (3.68) than women (3.91), indicating they revisit the saved message more often than women, on average. As with the cross-tabulation, the primary reason for this difference is likely that men are more likely to be in the "A Few Times a Year" (4) category and women are more likely to be in the "Once a Year or Less" (5) category. However, the T-test to compare the means shows there is not a significant difference between men and women (p =.101). This analysis reveals that, while we need to assert this finding of gender difference carefully, we know that, at least when the above original categories are included in the frequency variable, men revisit saved love letters more often than women. This is despite the fact that our earlier analysis reveals women are more likely to save love letters than men.

Gender and Reasons for Looking at Saved Messages

Why might someone revisit a saved message from a romantic relationship? Again we see more similarity than difference between men and women (N = 366). The proportions of men and women who revisit saved messages for various reasons are as follows: 47.9% of men and 51.2% of women revisit "to feel nostalgic"; 45.1% of men and 51.9% of women revisit "when I accidentally find it doing other things"; 45.1% of men and 43.4% of women revisit "when I organize objects or files where the item is located"; 43.7% of men and 43.7% of women revisit "to remind myself of the good parts of the relationship"; 39.4% of men and 34.2% of women revisit "when I am cleaning"; 9.9% of men and 10.2% of women revisit "to celebrate anniversaries or other special occasions"; and 1.4% of men and 4.4% of women revisit "to remind myself of what to avoid in a relationship."

These data suggest it seems to be as common to "stumble upon" the item as it does to intentionally revisit it, though arguably the categories included here do not all measure intentionality on the part of the possessor. Interestingly, men are slightly more likely than women to find these items while cleaning, and women are slightly more likely than men to find them while doing other things and to use the items to remind themselves of what to avoid in future relationships. Perhaps the latter finding suggests that the tone of the saved message for women might be more negative than for men. After all, encountering a saved a breakup letter or a love letter likely yields different emotional reactions, and they are saved for different reasons. However, despite these differences, T-tests show no statistically significant differences between the proportions of men and women along any of the reasons saved messages are revisited. Using these measures, then, there is not a discernable pattern to why the letters are revisited, nor is there a clear gender difference.

Gender and Location of Stored Relationship Messages

Where an item is stored can tell us something about how much an individual sees or is likely accesses the item, reminiscent of Epp and Price's (2010) notion of heated and cooled locations for memory-keeping. Survey respondents who noted they saved any messages from a past relationship were asked to then describe, in an open-ended question, where they stored them. Using the qualitative data analysis procedure described above, responses ($N = 408$) were coded into a nominal variable that included the categories "Physical Hidden," "Physical Displayed," "Digital Computer or Email," "Digital Phone," and "Files or Journals." If a respondent listed that items were in, under, or behind something, they fell into the Physical Hidden category—representing cooled locations. Letters that were positioned horizontally or vertically *on* something were in the Physical Displayed category—a heated location. Letters stored on a computer, email, or phone were divided into computer/email and phone, because of the portability differences between the devices. In the coding of digital communication patterns, as is discussed below, the open-ended responses did not contain enough details for us to code whether they were heated or cooled locations as defined by Epp and Price (2010). Finally, if respondents listed files or journals, it was not possible to discern whether they were located in physical or digital formats, so they remain a separate category.

After coding all of the responses into five storage-location categories listed above, quantitative findings were as follows: 44.6% of men and 55.9% of women stored relationship messages in the Physical Hidden Category (e.g., "in a drawer," "under my bed," "behind a picture," or "in a decorated storage box"); 16.1% of men and 5.9% of women in Physical Displayed (e.g., "on my bulletin board," "on my desk"); 25% of men and 18.1% of women in Digital Computer or Email; 8.9% of men and 13.8% of women in Digital Phone; and 5.4% of men and 6.3% of women in Files or Journals. During a negative case analysis of the responses to this question, we found that the only respondents to mention a specific type of storage container for the love letters—which included a detailed description of the storage container as "special," of a certain fabric or material, or "decorated"—were women.

Cross-tabulations with Chi-square analysis show no statistically significant relationship between gender and storage location at the $p < .05$ level. However, it is significant at the $p < .10$ level ($p = .056$). The significance might be due to impact of large differences between physical and digital storage locations more so than to gender. For both men and women, storing love letters was more likely to be in hidden places (i.e., "in," "behind," or "under" something as opposed to "on" something), and more likely to take paper than digital form.

Because of the uncertainty of the aforementioned analysis, we isolated location categories in order to examine individuals who store physical things separately from individuals who store digital things (and omitted people who listed files and journals, since their digital or physical quality is unknown). This allowed us to see if there are gender differences within those isolated categories. Analysis revealed a more nuanced picture. For the Physical Hidden and Physical Displayed groups, the Chi-square becomes significant (Chi-square = 7.28, $p = .007$), showing that men (26.5%) are significantly more likely than women (9.6%) to display the love letter rather than hide it, and women (90%) are significantly more likely than men (73.5%) to keep the letter under, in, or behind other objects. In other words, even though both men and women prefer to save physical love letters more so than digital ones, women are more likely than men to store paper love letters in cooled locations, and men are more likely than women to store paper love letters in heated locations.

For individuals who noted they stored love letters digitally, there were differences in proportions of men and women within each category, though the descriptions of the digital storage locations did not contain enough information to code them as heated or cooled locations. Nearly three-fourths (74%) of men stored the item on a computer or in email (v. 26% who store it on a phone), whereas 57% of women stored it on a computer or email (v. 43% who store it on a phone). Importantly, despite the difference in proportions, the Chi-square for this cross-tabulation is not significant (Chi-square = 1.83, sig. 176), likely because there were only 19 males in the subsample. It is difficult to tell whether computer or phone storage represents heated or cooled locations, since the data in this analysis do not include descriptions of how the letters look, or where the phone or computer is physically stored. But the data do reveal that digital love letters are much less preferred as relationship memory objects than physical ones. Because our data are limited in these ways, future researchers might discern how definitions of heated and cooled "locations" could be measured.

Discussion

Romantic Relationships in a Digital Age

Our findings reveal that, despite the overwhelming majority of respondents believing that digital communication has replaced paper communication in romantic relationships, men and women are similar in their likelihood to save and revisit saved paper messages over digital ones. In other words, where gender matters least in this analysis is in the mismatch between respondents' views about the decline in handwritten romantic communication generally, and their attachment of importance and value to it in their own relationships. Paper love letters are singularized as part of our respondents' extended selves more than are digital love letters, but nearly all respondents attest to the decline in handwritten letters as a form of romantic communication.

The finding that respondents value handwritten love letters at the same time they are unlikely to believe people will continue writing them has implications for larger questions about our understanding of intimate relationships in a digital age. Love letters are pieces of material culture that can symbolize a relationship and its contained memories, and the changing nature of the type of communication (paper versus digital) might alter the quality of the memory of the relationship itself, and perhaps even the quality of a current relationship. This latter possibility could result from a sense of disappointment when relationship realities (a love note via text) do not live up to romantic ideals (a handwritten letter that looks as if it took an hour to craft). To continue to idealize handwritten love letters in an era when digital communication is valued and in which gender roles are changing can serve to limit both men and women eager to participate in more nontraditional relationship practices.

Understanding the extended self might also change as relationship dynamics become increasingly mediated by digital communication technologies. If we use saved letters to symbolize the extended self within a relationship, then the possibility that we attach differential meaning to the importance or accessibility of digital and paper letters might mean our definitions of self within relationships may be altered.

As social relationships involve increasingly digital interactions, it will be important for scholars to investigate what happens when individuals' actions (using digital means to communicate) do not align with their idealized actions (saving paper messages as meaningful) in intimate relationships. Such cultural lag can impact innovation in digital technologies, future human–computer interaction studies, and, as mentioned above, measures of relationship satisfaction that reveal mismatch between the ideal and the real.

Gender and Love Letters

Where the gender differences in this study become most visible is in analyses of likelihood to save messages, frequency of revisiting saved messages, and heated and cooled locations of stored love letters (especially paper ones). Our findings have implications insofar as the interpretation offered here might support or refute the persistence of traditional gender roles within romantic relationships. We acknowledge that the demographics of our sample challenge generalizability of the findings to a more diverse and representative population. Nonetheless, despite this important limitation, the large response number offers relatively large subsample sizes for comparisons between men and women, which is the primary area of focus for this analysis.

Women are more likely to save love letters than men. This finding might suggest women find love letters more important than men. But, men revisit saved love letters more often than do women, even though they save fewer of them. Further, and in line with Epp and Price's (2010) definition of singularization via heated and cooled objects, men are more likely than women to display their saved paper love letters in heated locations, and women are more likely to store their paper love letters in cooled places that require looking in or under something to get to them. These findings suggest that men singularize their letters more than do women, and that for men love letters are more likely to be a part of their extended selves than they are for women. One could argue, then, that these findings reveal relatively nontraditional gender roles, consistent with past research that challenges the normative expectations for men to be less emotionally attached, or less sentimental, in a romantic relationship (Giordano et al., 2006).

On the other hand, that women are more likely than men to save love letters is consistent with past research that illustrates women's greater likelihood to participate in behaviors demonstrating attachment to kinship relations and preserving of family memories. Further, the finding that men display their love letters in heated locations more than do women might be interpreted as adhering to traditional gender norms for three reasons. First, it could align with past research on men's displays of intimate relationship symbols as trophies or status symbols. Second, it might suggest that women are more likely to make the storage of love letters a "project" that requires organizing them in designated (and perhaps decorated) storage containers—like the South Korean "Between" box in the introduction to this chapter. Or that storage of any item in, under, or behind something is part of women's traditional practice of managing household tidiness. Finally, it might be that identifying the location of a saved object as only heated or cooled by coding terms such as "on," "under," "in," or "behind," misses a more nuanced definition of a love letter's salience to its possessor, one that ought to include level of intentionality as well as the effort that goes into the designation of a storage space as special or sacred (which decorating a box can do).

Our data do not tell us the motivations behind the saving practices; future research could uncover such motivations to ascertain how much rituals of possession and disposition reinforce traditional gender norms and roles. What our data do tell us is that love letter saving practices demonstrate a mixed bag when it comes to gender roles in romantic relationships, and that competing interpretations of the same findings are possible with regard to gender roles.

Application

Our definitions of love are not fixed. They are socially constructed and can vary across time, geographic space, and even between romantic partners. For individuals who have an interest in understanding a partner's role expectations and levels of emotional investment in a romantic relationship, it is important to know that behaviors in these relationships are strongly influenced by societal norms, but also that not all individuals adhere to these norms. When figuring out what each partner brings to a romantic relationship, remember we are still living in an era when male and female roles are heavily influenced by socialization and media representations—each perpetuating heteronormative ideals of romance, chivalry, and production and consumption of hand-crafted goods to symbolize love. Each puts pressure on both men and women to behave in such a way that a partner will see him or her as loving and invested in the relationship in traditional ways.

We are also living in an era when people are disrupting traditional roles and crafting meaning within their own relationships—often in ways that counter normative societal role expectations. For this reason, anyone who is assessing whether his or her partner is invested "enough" in a relationship should know that expressions of love are influenced by factors both within and outside a relationship. Respectful and productive communication can help couples sort through which factors are influential in which contexts. Such communication might be helpful as individuals ascertain whether, and why, handwritten love letters might be a central part of their expectations of love.

Readers should also keep in mind that the rituals of possession and disposition associated with love letters only tell part of the story about how important and valued letters are to an individual. People who want to know whether love letter saving practices can tell us anything about their partner's investment in a relationship should be cautious about using *only* our measures to make such conclusions, though couples might find it fruitful to add these kinds of innovative measures to their conversations about how love is shown within a relationship. Importantly, and in addition to whether letters are saved and where, couples could discuss what the letters mean, as well as motivations for saving, revisiting, or displaying them, as a way to understand each other's "extended romantic self." Even if someone does not have a partner, it can be a worthwhile exercise to think about how the types of measures we used might be part of how we define ourselves.

In terms of understanding the meaning of objects in social relations, it is important to understand that human social behaviors always occur in relationship to our physical and digital worlds, and that examining the impact of everyday objects and spaces (even virtual ones) can shed light on how relationships function and become meaningful. Most importantly, by uncovering the meaning behind everyday domestic objects, including love letters, we bring to the forefront research questions about devalued and often hidden parts of life, aspects that can reveal much about the larger social world. Readers are urged to be mindful of the ways digital communication is altering not only how we engage in relationships, but also how we define happiness. Because we use memories to guide our everyday actions, looking at how we save "stuff," including love letters, might shed light on who we are, how we love, and what we want out of life.

Note

1 In this chapter, the term "communication" refers to the general and dynamic process of communicating within a relationship, as well as larger societal patterns of communicating that have changed over time and in different forms; the terms "message" and "love letter" are used interchangeably to refer to the objectified format of communication (i.e., paper letters, handwritten notes, paper cards, emails, texts, Facebook messages, and captured Snapchats). In the survey instrument used in the analysis in this chapter, the term "communications" is used, which refers to messages or love letters as objectified formats of communication.

References

Appadurai, A. (1986). Introduction: Commodities and the politics of value. In A. Appadurai (Ed.), *The social life of things* (pp. 3–63). Cambridge, UK: Cambridge University Press.

Baym, N. K. (2010). *Personal connections in the digital age.* Boston, MA: Polity.

Belk, R. W. (1988). Possessions and the extended self. *Journal of Consumer Research 15*, 139–168.

Belk, R. W. (1991). Possessions and sense of past. In R. W. Belk (Ed.), *Highways and buyways: Naturalistic research from the consumer behavior odyssey* (pp. 114–130). Provo, UT: Association for Consumer Research.

Belk, R. W. (2013). Extended self in a digital world. *Journal of Consumer Research 40*, 477–500.

Benjamin, W. (1936/1968). The work of art in the age of mechanical reproduction. In H. Arendt (Ed.) and H. Zohn (Trans.), *Illuminations* (pp. 219–253). San Diego, CA: Harcourt, Brace & World.

Berg, B., & Lune, H. (2011). *Qualitative research methods for the social sciences,* (8th ed.). Upper Saddle River, NJ: Pearson.

boyd, d. (2014). *It's complicated: The social lives of networked teens.* New Haven, CT: Yale University Press.

Brandt, C. (2006). Devouring time finds paper toughish: What's happened to handwritten letters in the twenty-first century? *Auto/biography studies, 21*(1), 7–19.

Collins, L. (2013, November 25). The love app: Romance in the world's most wired city. *The New Yorker*, 88–95.

Creswell, J. W. (2012). *Qualitative inquiry and research design: Choosing among five traditions* (3rd ed.). Thousand Oaks, CA: Sage Publications.

Denegri-Knott, J., Watkins, R., & Woods, J. (2012). Transforming digital virtual goods into meaningful possessions. In M. Molesworth & J. Denegri-Knott (Eds.), *Digital virtual consumption* (pp. 76–91). London: Routledge.

Epp, A. M., & Price, L. L. (2010). The storied life of singularized objects: Forces of agency and network transformation. *Journal of Consumer Research, 36*(5), 820–837.

Giordano, P. C., Longmore, M. A., & Manning, W. D. (2006). Gender and the meanings of adolescent romantic relationships: A focus on boys. *American Sociological Review, 71*(2), 260–287.

Haggis, J., & Holmes, M. (2011). Epistles to emails: Letters, relationship building, and the virtual age. *Life Writing, 8*(2), 169–185.

Hayles, N. K. (2002). *Writing machines.* Boston, MA: MIT Press.

Hepper, E. G., & Ritchie, T. D. (2011). Odyssey's end: Lay conceptions of nostalgia reflect its original Homeric meaning. *Emotion, 12*(1), 102–119.

Janning, M., & Scalise, H. (2013). Gender and generation in the home curation of family photography. *Journal of Family Issues.* Retrieved from http://jfi.sagepub.com/content/early/recent

Kimmel, M. (2012). *The gendered society* (5th ed.). Oxford, UK: Oxford University Press.

Kopytoff, I. (1986). The cultural biography of things: Commoditization as process. In A. Appadurai (Ed.) *The social life of things* (pp. 64–94). Cambridge, UK: Cambridge University Press.

Lastovicka, J. L., & Fernandez, K. V. (2005). Three paths to disposition: The movement of meaningful possessions to strangers. *Journal of Consumer Research, 31,* 813–823

Livingston, J. (2014, November 18). Sexting and gender. Retrieved from http://montclairsoci.blogspot.com/2014/11/sexting-and-gender.html.

Miles, M. B., Huberman, A. M., & Saldaña, J. (2013). *Qualitative data analysis: A methods sourcebook* (3rd ed.). Thousand Oaks, CA: Sage Publications.

Miller, D. (1987). *Material culture and mass consumption.* New York: Blackwell.

Petrelli, D., & Whittaker, S. (2010). Family memories in the home: Contrasting physical and digital mementos. *Personal Ubiquitous Computing, 14*(2), 153–169.

Rosin, H. (2014, October 14). Why kids sext. *The Atlantic*. Retrieved from http://www.theatlantic.com/magazine/archive/2014/11/why-kids-sext/380798/.

Rutter, V., & Schwartz, P. (2011). *The gender of sexuality: Exploring sexual possibilities,* 2nd ed. Lanham, MD: Rowman & Littlefield.

Siddiqui, S., & Turley, D. (2006). Extending the self in a digital world. In C. Pechmann & L. Price (Eds.), *Advances in consumer research* (Vol. 33, pp. 647–648). Duluth, MN: Association for Consumer Research.

Sumter, S. S., Valkenburg, P. M., & Peter, J. (2013). Perceptions of love across the lifespan: Differences in passion, intimacy, and commitment. *International Journal of Behavioral Development, 37*(5), 417–427.

Turkle, S. (2011). *Alone together: Why we expect more from technology and less from each other*. New York: Basic Books.

13

“Unplugging the Power Cord”

Uncovering Hidden Power Structures via Mobile Communication Technology Use within the Traditional Marital Dyad

ANDREA GUZIEC IACCHERI
Ohio University

ADAM W. TYMA
University of Nebraska at Omaha

Introduction

According to the Pew Research Internet and American Life Project (Pew Research Publications, 2014), 90% of American adults own cell phones, 81% of cell phone users use text or SMS messaging as their primary communication method, and 21% of those users participate in video chat or video calls. The ever-growing usage of mobile communication technology (MCT), specifically how text-based mobile communication is used by marriage partners, is the focus of this chapter. Although prior and current research increases our understanding of communication between spouses (e.g., Albright & Conran, 2003; Baym, Zhang, Kunkel, Ledbetter, & Lin, 2007; Garcia-Montes, Caballero-Munoz, & Perez-Alvarez, 2006; Jin & Pena, 2010; Kennedy & Wellman, 2007; Licoppe, 2004; Pettigrew, 2009; Ramirez & Broneck, 2009; Solis, 2006), developing theoretical explanations of how married couples communicate via mobile digital technologies is essential, as marital communication is becoming more commonly mediated by, and accomplished via, communication technologies (Lenhart & Duggan, 2014).

Our analysis extends current research on marital communication, computer-mediated communication, and MCT by investigating the practices of text-based mobile communication (e.g., text messages, email, Google Chat, SMS, and MMS) between spouses, or what will be referred to in this chapter as “mobiText.”

For purposes of this study, MCT is referred to as the *medium*: "a means by which something is communicated" (Mish, 2007, p. 771), while mobiText is operationalized as the *mode*: "manner, way, or method of doing or acting" (Morris, 1970, p. 843). To interpret the actions of couples' MCT use in their relationships, we employed the underlying philosophy of Fairclough's (1989) Critical Discourse Analysis (CDA)—specifically his use of *Discourse, common sense*, and *ideology*—to analyze 12 individual (six couples') interviews. Using Fairclough's assumptions as a theoretical lens helps us determine if a power structure is present within married partners because of MCT (specifically mobiText).

Fairclough's CDA as a Theoretical Lens

Critical discourse analysis provides an important lens through which scholars can theorize, analyze, and apply discourse scholarship (Van Dijlk, 2001). The major focus of Fairclough's CDA is the relationship between power and language (Fairclough, 1989). Fairclough's work focuses on how power operates in and behind discourses within a social structure, and does so by examining the language used in those structures; he argues discourse has a reproductive effect—impacting, changing, and sustaining social structures.

Fairclough places emphasis "upon 'common-sense' assumptions which are implicit in the conventions according to which people interact linguistically, and of which people are generally not consciously aware" (2001, p. 2). He identifies assumptions as "ideologies" naturally embedded in specific assumptions, while the nature of the conventions themselves are dependent on power relations. Fairclough argues "ideologies are closely linked to language, because using language is the commonest form of social behavior" (2001, p. 2). Yet, that power as a concept is rarely studied in connection to language. Fairclough focuses on power because "the exercise of power, in modern society, is increasingly achieved through ideology, and more particularly through the ideological workings of language" (2001, p. 2). One way to understand how power operates in or behind discourse is with Fairclough's theory of discourse as social practice.

Discourse as social practice operates from the understanding that discourse, "language as social practice determined by social structures," is constructed through "sets of conventions associated with social institutions" (Fairclough, 2001, p. 14). Fairclough identifies conventions "as clustering in sets or networks" which he calls "orders of discourse" (2001, p. 23). In other words, discourse can be described as language that is socially performed while embodying certain ideologies (Fairclough, 2001). For purposes of this study, we identify marriage as the social institution in which we analyze the discourse operating. For Fairclough, language is a social process that is socially conditioned. By understanding the ways discourse operates through sets of conventions shaped ideologically through power relations in specific social institutions, such as the institution of marriage, we can begin to explore the manifestation of power by examining how text-based communication operates in marriage.

Power is present in various forms. Fairclough identifies "two major aspects of the power/language relationship [:] power *in* discourse, and power *behind* discourse" *[sic]* (2001, p. 36). Power *in* discourse identifies power as a place where power relations can be exerted. Power *behind* discourse focuses on how power can operate and be shaped by relations of power in various social institutions (Fairclough, 2001). For purposes of this study, we look at power relations within the social institution of marriage, specifically focusing on how power operates in the discourse describing couples' MCT use. Fairclough's discussion on language and power is what he calls "common sense"—taken-for-granted ways "ideologies are embedded in features of discourse" (2001, p. 64). To comprehend how "common sense" plays a role in the operationalization of power, a basic understanding of Fairclough's theoretical assumptions is helpful.

Dominant and Dominated Discourse Types

Fairclough (2001) proposes a way to understand how power relations are sustained within a given social domain. He argues that, once a particular line of discourse is established or maintained as the dominant discursive framework in a given social domain (in our study, marriage), ideological assumptions are viewed and responded to as "common sense" (per Fairclough's discussion of this idea, p. 64). In the present study, such assumptions would be dominant discourse in the marital dyads. For example, suppose a couple expresses a common pattern in their marriage where one spouse regularly answers calls or responds to texts while the couple is in conversation, and the interrupted spouse voices concern about this pattern, yet the pattern does not change, that pattern is representative of dominant discourse in the dyad. Fairclough would argue the pattern sustains power relations in the marriage.

Naturalization and the Generation of Common Sense

Patterns of communication and behaviors in marriage are influenced by the dominant discourse within the dyad.

> If a discourse type so dominates an institution that dominated types are more or less entirely suppressed or contained, then it will cease to be seen as arbitrary

> (in the sense of being one among several possible ways of "seeing" things) and will come to be seen as *natural,* and legitimate because it is simply *the* way of conducting oneself. (Fairclough, 2001, p. 76)

Our study defines naturalization as the constructed ideology of situations from which the dominant discourse achieves successful recognition and becomes embodied by the couple as, to quote Fairclough "the natural way of conducting oneself." For example, if the dominant member of the couple identifies patterns or common usages for when and/or how the phone is to be used in specific instances, out of these created patterns a norm is created of daily usage patterns. Fairclough would identify this norming or routine behavior as a construction of power by the dominant member of the couple.

Ideology and Meaning

Words and symbols make up our discourse. Fairclough explains that the meaning of a word or object is not fixed; it varies in meaning in part due to the ideologies one is taught and with which one surrounds oneself, and variance occurs in the experiences attached to the object or memory through association with a particular time, object, or viewpoint. For example, the meaning given to a technological device by a couple creates specific meaning for the couple.

Interactional Routines and Their Boundaries

Fairclough describes "interactional routines" (2001, pp. 81–84) as ways we are accustomed to interacting with one other. Assumptions about normal interactional routines guide exchanges such as regularly sharing informational messages and sharing funny or tragic stories as they happen. If a "'problem'" (Fairclough, 2001, p. 82) occurs, discomfort drives attempts to repair an exchange that does not follow the "'normal course'" (p. 82) or interactional routine.

Subject Position and Situations

Subject position and situations are set by the socialization of people into a given set of normative behaviors and discursive structures (Fairclough, 2001). As Fairclough later explains: "The socialization of people involves them coming to be placed in a range of subject positions, which they are exposed to partly through learning to operate within various discourse types" (2001, p. 85). Discourse types establish sets of subject positions for individuals within varying situations (Fairclough, 2001). Socialization occurs through exposure to various discourse types and subject positions. From the myriad of discursive structures, one subject position emerges as dominant for both individuals and groups (for the present study, between married dyads). The dominant discourse, through the definitions constructed and established within the relationship, progresses to naturalization within the power structure for the couple. It is through created meanings, seen as natural, that constraint of "the contents of discourse and, in the long term, knowledge and beliefs" (Fairclough, 2001, p. 87) occurs. For example, if a couple's personal accounts of mobiText and overall MCT use are in agreement with their daily conversations about the same, a socialization has occurred. Fairclough would argue that the dominant member of the dyad constructed and established a meaning, thus creating specific knowledges and beliefs about overall MCT use. Key to the understanding of subjects and situations is how definitions are created and established for MCT and mobiText use. More specifically, we aimed in our study to identify if an individual's description of his or her own perception of MCT and mobiText use differed from their belief about MCTs and about their mobiText use. With this introductory section in mind, the next section will detail our methodology. We demonstrate how using dyadic interviews, paired with Fairclough's theoretical underpinnings, provides an understanding of how couples might employ MCT and mobiText in relationship maintenance.

Method

Personal experiences and subjective reasoning are important components for understanding the use of mobile communication within marriages. To uncover the personal experiences and subjective reasoning of married couples' use of MCT, we designed a qualitative/critical study and conducted in-depth interviews. Using Fairclough's theoretical underpinnings that inform Critical Discourse Analysis as our ideological lens, we critically interrogated the interview transcripts.

Sampling Procedures

A mixed sampling (Creswell, 2007) approach was used for this study. Both criterion and intensity sampling were used to gain rich descriptions of the phenomenon being studied. To recruit participants, we posted signs at local Midwestern colleges and universities and posted on a social networking site (Facebook) to publicize the study and announce participant requirements. All of the following criteria had to be met to participate in the study: Participants needed to (1) be a legally married heterosexual couple, (2) be between the ages of 19 and 49, and (3) be active users of MCT as a means of communication within their relationship.

Data Collection Procedures

Data were collected via semi-structured interviews; all interviews were digitally recorded. Twelve participants (six couples) participated in interviews. Prior to the start of each interview, a written consent form was reviewed and signed by each interviewee. We conducted interviews individually to ensure the accuracy of information shared and to allow for an open space of sharing regarding spousal MCT use.

Data Analysis Procedures

Once interviews were complete, and saturation was met, audio recordings were transcribed and analyzed using the theoretical frame informed by Fairclough, as described above. We narrowed our focus to specifically engage Fairclough's notions of "discourse, common sense, and ideology" (2001, pp. 64–90). Within this larger framework, the specific concepts interrogated included "Dominant and dominated discourse types; Naturalization and the generation of common sense; Ideology and meaning; Interactional routines and their boundaries; Subjects and situations" (Fairclough, 2001, pp. 69–87). Based on these five components, the following five questions were posed and guided our analysis:

1. Do the transcripts offer insight into any power imbalance within the husband/wife dyad?
2. Does a naturalization occur within the discourse of the husband/wife dyad?
3. What type or types of relationships (e.g., ideological, functional) do each of the participants have with MCT?
4. Are interactional routines via and outside of MCT present within the husband/wife dyad?
5. Does each member of a husband/wife dyad have a different expressed relationship with mobiText, or do both members have the same expressed relationship with their technology?

Providing qualitative exemplars for each component of Fairclough's theory, and specifically focusing on these components, allowed for a more focused exploration of the possible embedded ideological assumptions of power within the interpretations of how discourse is being explained and understood within the marital dyad.

Participants

Six couples (twelve total individuals) participated in the study. Couples were selected based on interest, MCT use, and meeting all criteria for the study as outlined in the sampling procedures. The average length of marriage was 3.82 years.

The average age of participants was 30.5 for women and 32 for men. Three of the six couples had children. Five couples were of white ethnicity and one couple was of Asian-Indian descent.

Analysis

In a recent study conducted by the Pew Research Center, Lenhart and Duggan (2014) identify that couples use technology to share both large and small moments. Specifically, couples negotiate usage patterns and fight about the use of technology, while also experiencing hurtful moments caused by tech use. Given such findings, it is important not only to see how power is expressed within marital dyads but to understand how power operates in and through discourse shared through and about technology. To best see how power is expressed within the dyads, analysis of the transcripts was organized around each of the concepts provided by Fairclough: "Dominant and dominated discourse types; Naturalization and the generation of common sense; Ideology and meaning; Interactional routines and their boundaries; Subject position and situations" (Fairclough, 2001, pp. 69–87).

Dominant and Dominated Discourse Types

The first question guiding our analysis asks if the transcripts provide insight into any power imbalance within the husband/wife dyad. Dominant discourse was evident throughout Becky's interview when she described communication between her and husband Steve (Couple 1). Becky's description reveals a dominating discourse over Steve. When asked, "Does your spouse ever answer your cell phone if you're unavailable or in another room?" Becky responded, "He doesn't answer mine, but I answer his. But he doesn't answer our regular phone (laughing)." She continues, "It's more of a, a he wants to be contacted when he feels like being contacted. But I do answer phone … and look at who's calling." When asked if this was a mutual understanding or something that developed over time, Steve explained:

> Ah, I don't know; it's just always been that way… Although, I will say this, she is more comfortable answering my phone than I am hers. So, it's not the same on both sides.

Steve's example reflects Becky's commanding behavior regarding answering his phone as well as her view about his mobile device use while he is at home. Steve's recognition of this unequal balance of power suggests one member of the dyad, Becky, dominates aspects of MCT use in their marriage. Fairclough notes, "where dominated discourses are oppositional, there will be pressure for them to be suppressed or eliminated" (2001, p. 76). Both illustrations show no opposition from

Steve toward Becky's dominating style, supporting both dominant and dominating discourse within the dyad.

The interview text of Stone and Sasha (Couple 5) revealed that Stone is the primary user of dominant discourse for the couple. Stone was blatant regarding her dominance when asked, "How do you feel when your spouse is on his device?"

> Most of the time I don't care 'cause I'm usually doing my own thing. But like, if I'm wanting to hang out I will just tell him, hey, quit hanging out with your phone, but Sasha is awesome and then he does. He just puts it down. He's like, oh, I'm sorry and then we hang out.

Stone's ability to "command and it is done" provides evidence of her dominating ability. Sasha acknowledges his inability to express his discontent with his wife's mobile use, as seen in this description of his preference for her to leave the room while on a call: "Some of the times I would want her to leave the room, 'cause she's so loud on her phone. But, she chooses not to so …" Sasha is seen as submissive, compared with Stone's description of the same situation: "I make Sasha leave the room because when he talks on the phone, he paces and that gives me anxiety so, every time he's on the phone, I make him leave the room." Stone illustrates not only her command over when and where she takes her calls, but over her husband's calls as well. The two examples provide evidence that one member of the dyad holds the dominant discourse: Stone.

Dominant discourse is also identified in the interviews with Couple 6, Tori and Bob. Tori refers to her husband's uncanny knack for answering calls while in conversation with her. She provides a representative anecdote:

> At night, if I'm talking to him and he picks up the phone, really annoying. Whether to text somebody back or, I mean if somebody calls, he'll always answer it whether I'm talking or not. If we're talking and somebody texts, he usually will just let it go until we're done but I haven't had to throw it anywhere, it's come through my mind though before when we're talking I'm like: put your cell phone down; I know I've said it but I haven't actually like taken it and thrown it away from him.

Fairclough argues that power relations are sustained by the dominant discourse. In the example above, Tori remarks about her ability to express annoyance to her husband regarding his usage patterns. Although she is able to express her annoyance to Bob, Tori references that her husband always answers whether she is talking or not. Bob's ability to continue his usage pattern, despite his wife's complaints, reveals Bob's dominance in the discourse.

Naturalization and the Generation of Common Sense

The second question guiding our analysis asks if naturalization occurs within the discourse of the husband/wife dyad. A natural discourse emerged in interviews with Becky and Steve (Couple 1), supporting the notion of naturalization through discourse. Naturalization occurred in their viewpoint of mobiText dinner table etiquette. When asked "Do you or your spouse ever leave the room when you take a call or a text?" both Becky and Steve had similar responses. Steve explained: "I would say from my wife's perspective it's more common courtesy than anything ... she is sensitive to the fact that you shouldn't talk on a cell phone at the table or necessarily answer your cell phone at the table." Becky clarified: "If we're in a restaurant, ah, unless I suppose we're in a fast food restaurant, that would be, eh, perhaps an exception. But if we're in a restaurant, always ... it's not appropriate to talk at the table." Steve and Becky disclose similar viewpoints regarding MCT use at the dinner table, although the similarity provides evidence that naturalization has occurred. Within Steve's statement, as quoted above, he further shares:

> But if you do answer it [the phone], you take it away from the table. Or take it outside or if you happen to be at a restaurant, or something like that. Ah, from my perspective it's a (short pause), I also like to, to not be rude while I'm sitting there on the phone so, it's kinda the same thing.

This declaration by Steve exhibits a routine for dinner table behavior regarding MCT use that is now the naturalized discourse.

Within the transcripts of Couple 4, Monica and FM, each member of the dyad alludes to a dominating pattern existing prior to FM owning his own mobile device. He remembers:

> I'd use hers [cell phone] all the time, like when I needed it, I'd be going to do something and then I gave out her number to a bunch of my friends, like (laughing) and then they would call her and wouldn't know. And then a year later, I was working with those same people ... and they'd still call her number and not mine 'cause I'd gotten a phone by then.

Monica references this same experience: "Before he had a cell phone, if he needed a mobile device, he would borrow mine. For you know whatever ... and he had 500 people calling him that day, he wouldn't have a phone, he would use mine." Monica and FM both referenced a naturalization occurring in their relationship, even prior to FM owning his own mobile device. This naturalization occurred as a product of the routine set in place by FM, who used his wife's device prior to having his own, thus dominating the usage pattern and creating the naturalization within the marriage.

FM's mobile device patterns seem to be reflected in another area of naturalization in his marriage: his family calling his wife in order to reach him. Monica recounts when she uses texting with her husband: "Sometimes he's more difficult to get a hold of, his family may call me to get a hold of him: Your mother called, call her back." FM speaks of this specific type of call and message, "My little brother or my other brother actually called her 'hey, FM's phone is full of messages. I couldn't leave him a message.' So then they left her a message about something they wanted to tell me." The calls and messages that Monica receives from his family are now a normal occurrence. Due to the lack of her husband's initial reachability, his family now opens lines of communication to his wife so he can be reached, thus showing naturalization of his dominant discourse and behavior patterns with his wife and also his immediate family.

In Tori and Bob's (Couple 6) relationship, naturalization emerges from patterns that existed during courtship. Tori speaks of Bob's constant use of his device when asked her opinion of her husband's practices: "Too much. He has always been on his phone ever since I met him. Nonstop. He loves to talk to everyone, anyone who will listen. So he's on it constantly. Texting or talking. All the time." Bob's description of his behavior is similar to his wife's description: "So, I use it all day long with work and personal use and texting and messenger all day." Although naturalization is identified by both Tori and Bob regarding his usage habits, the interview texts cannot identify when this naturalization occurred. Fairclough believes that "ideologies come to be ideological common sense to the extent that the discourse types which embody them become naturalized" (2001, p. 76). This embodiment is detected in Bob and Tori's interviews.

Ideology and Meaning

The third question guiding our analysis asks what type or types of relationships (e.g., ideological, functional) each of the participants have with MCT. Becky and Steve's (Couple 1) individual meanings of their mobile devices differ. Steve views his device as "the most awesome phone that is currently available" and uses it "primarily for work e-mail and for personal messaging." It also functions as a streaming music player and a personal planner. For Steve, the multifunctionality of his mobile device is obvious. His wife sees her device differently. "I have a smart phone because my husband has a smarter phone." She further explains, "It's a more expensive piece of equipment and there's so much on it that I have more, my phone creates more stress for me." Becky identifies her phone as a smart, stress-producing object, while Steve views his device as a multifunctional object.

Couple 2, Joyce and JB, share similar means of communicating and hold similar meaning of their devices. The couple uses mobiText as their primary mode of communication with each other as well as other family members, but each sees the purpose and features of their devices differently. Joyce defines the best feature of her phone as the Internet or the ability to always be connected. JB noted the best feature of his phone is the "feedback, the ultimate feedback, like the timely feedback from what I communicate with people, it's usually pretty quick… keeps the conversation flowing." Joyce and JB find their mobile devices offering different features, which provides different perceptions of device use.

When Joyce described the daily use of her device, she responded that texting was her primary use: "It's hooked up to my personal e-mail so I'll use it for that, but I don't have my work e-mail on here, um, day to day probably texting is the first thing, and then Facebook, and e-mail." Joyce sees her device as a way to keep connected as well as a social device. JB views the purpose of his device differently: "I think, ah, just having a kid and a wife and, and family in town, if there's an emergency or somebody that needs me, I need ta, you know, I feel like I need ta be there for them." Although both JB and Joyce identify their devices as a social connector, JB views his as consistent accessibility because of family and potential emergencies; Joyce sees hers as a means of keeping socially connected—two similar yet different meanings for the same device.

FM's (Couple 4) view of his mobile device is very detailed compared to his wife's. He describes his mobile device as "my home phone … and that's number one is phone first. Number two is a way to keep up with limited e-mail or more or less, just to read e-mails." He continues by explaining, "And then I also use it for texting, for quick messages, and to stay in communication with people … and I surf the web on it too when I drive around. Not when I drive, but when I ride around." FM's multifunctional view of his mobile device solidifies the meaning of his device as a tool for everyday communication and living. Monica perceives her device as just that, a device: "I'm not really emotionally attached to my phone." Her abrupt response—"I don't"—when asked if she has a favorite application for her phone authenticates her nonattachment to her phone. Based on answers provided by FM and Monica, MCT does vary in ideological meaning within the dyad.

The meaning given to the device by both Stone and Sasha (Couple 5) is of one accord. Stone and Sasha view their devices as a way to stay connected with family and friends. Sasha discloses:

> I would say that mostly, I mean, mostly I use it for calling my wife, for calling family and calling friends. Um, of course texting when it's not convenient to be on the phone and social media so like Facebook, things like that.

Stone shares a similar response: "I text message plans back and forth. I think I spend quite a bit of time just sending my friends messages like: Hi, how you doin'? You know or making plans." Simplistic in nature, Stone's and Sasha's interpretations of their devices are almost identical: They are media for social connection and communication.

Interactional Routines and Their Boundaries

The fourth question guiding our analysis asks if interactional routines via and outside of MCT are present within the husband/wife dyad. Interactional routines are found in Becky and Steve's (Couple 1) use of mobiText as well as their mobile devices. When asked how each interacts with his or her spouse via the device, responses were almost identical. Becky and Steve both use their device to call as well as text. Becky: "We use it a lot for texting, I'm going to be home at this time, when were you going to be home?" Steve has a similar response: "I'd say we text more than we call each other on our cell phones, if we're both out and about." Both also mentioned travel. Steve clarified, "If one of us is home, then, the one of us, we'll call the person who's at home. But if, if they're traveling, wandering around then it's, it's a more of a text thing." Becky shared a similar viewpoint: "If we're traveling separately and one of us is home with her [their daughter] and the other person is at a meeting or whatever else, take pictures with the camera and send those." Although different forms of mobiText are explained, Becky and Steve reveal the presence of interactional routines via mobiText in their marriage.

Joyce and JB (Couple 2) have a daily communication routine in place as they inform each other upon arrival to work, as well as share experiences or funny stories encountered over the course of their days. This specific routine is made possible by the vehicle in which they communicate, Google Chat. Their descriptions of their routine are almost identical. When asked to describe how he interacts with his spouse, JB shared, "I mean, it's on a day-to-day basis I guess. The way I look at it is GoogleTalk [Google Chat] is probably what we use the most to communicate." Joyce answered, "Mostly GoogleTalk [Google Chat]"; she expanded by stating, "GoogleTalk [Google Chat] you can do, it's on like our phones and also on like our computers, our desktops so, you know, if we're at our desks we can talk and then if we're not, we'll just use our phones." Her answer is also similar to JB's: "and the great thing about that [Google Chat] is I can use it on my work, on the computer but then I leave work, like the whole conversation is on my phone." These almost identical answers reveal the presence of interactional routines in Joyce and JB's daily communication.

The interactional routines revealed by Sasha and Stone (Couple 5) were almost identical to each other, supporting the presence and personal significance of their daily communication with each other. The question posed to both Sasha and Stone, "Describe how you interact with your spouse via your mobile device?" elicited an almost verbatim response from each. Sasha detailed his daily routine:

> Normally throughout my day, I would call my wife probably three times through my work shift. I would call her on my first break, my lunch, and my last break. Throughout the rest of the day we would probably, for the most part, text; it just kinda depends on the schedule. I mean, we (short pause) we call each other if we're not busy, if we're busy, we'll text each other. The texts will be short, brief, and to the point.

Stone recounts a similar pattern shared with her spouse:

> We communicate every day. He calls me on his first break and then at lunch and then we always text each other of when we're coming home or like kinda what we're doing. Or we'll send like little, I love you messages on it. The text messaging I would say is like, just little short, little blurps. Maybe like two sentence like: Love you. What are you doin'? What's up? Kinda stuff like that.

Stone provides a more detailed description of the types of messages sent but a clear interactional pattern is exhibited through both texts shared by the couple.

Bob and Tori (Couple 6) have a unique history of providing each other with location status updates. This routine was first solidified while living in New York in the early years of their marriage and reflects the major mobiText interactional routine shared by the couple. Tori described how texting is used as a routine in their daily communication: "We will text throughout the day, he'll just ask me how my day's going. Or I'll do the same. Or he'll send me the pictures." Bob had a similar recollection regarding the messages sent to his wife: "In the afternoons we'll just, we always just kinda check in to see how you're doing." Similarities exist in the couple's statements regarding their routines, exhibiting the presence of such routines as described by Fairclough.

Subject Position and Situations

The fifth question guiding our analysis asks if each member of the husband/wife dyad has a different expressed relationship with mobiText, or if both members of the husband/wife dyad have the same expressed relationship with their technology. An important aspect of CDA is the identification of mobiText perception verses the discourse of use. When asked if she thought the use of her device has hurt, helped, or done a little bit of both in her relationship, Becky (Couple 1) explained: "I would say that it has helped" and "I think maybe some of the habits that I perceived were hurtful for other people, we don't do." Her answer reflects her belief that mobiText is positive. When asked, "If you could give another couple any advice regarding it [mobiText] in their relationship, from your own experiences, what advice would you share?" Becky answered, "I think probably my rules, quite frankly. One of which is my, the very first rules that I put down, don't fight over texting." This answer is similar to her discourse throughout her interview. When asked, "Have you ever misread a message that your husband has sent you?" she answered, "I've been unclear"... "so he'll make a, a reference that's less clear assuming that I know what the reference is to." Becky clarifies, "But other than that, I don't think we have many misunderstandings ... and most misunderstandings I don't clear up through a text. I clear up through a phone call. I didn't understand it the first time around, the texting probably isn't going to help me." Becky shows consistency within her natural discourse as well as in her belief of mobiText and over MCT use in her relationship with her husband.

Steve's (Couple 1) response was similar to Becky's regarding his overall perception of mobile device use in his marriage, "I think it's only helped." He continued by stating:

> I mean there're very few times um, once, once we, we established the ground rules, of you know of none of the phone, I mean, none in the bed and you know, during dinner we don't, we don't text ... there's relatively little conflict. So it's mostly helped us keep, keep in touch.

These two explanations from Steve are similar to his answers throughout his interview—that mobiText is used as a primary means to coordinate "the where we are, when we're coming home and ah, what our schedules are." When asked to share advice to couples regarding mobile technology use in their relationship, Steve's response was different from the thoughts described above:

> Well, use it as a tool to stay in touch. Um, as, as people get busier and as our lives get more complex it's easier ta move away and be more of roommates than a couple. Or a married couple ... using the functions to bring you together and not to throw yourself into a little asylum are the ones that I would, I would throw out there.

Although Steve's interview does not reflect solitary use of his device, when asked, "How often do you use your phone, all of the bells and whistles?" he responded, "I probably use it about, I'd say when I'm at home, I use it every 15 minutes." Steve shows discord within his answers. Overuse can be seen as "the little asylum," the very thing Steve advised against in a relationship. This example shows discrepancy between how Steve uses MCT and mobiText technology and his beliefs regarding this form of communication in marriages, including his own.

Joyce and JB (Couple 2) both recognized how mobiText is helpful in their marriage, which corresponds to their interview dialogue. Joyce identified the helpful nature of mobiText:

> I think it's one of the better parts of my day that I can talk to him all day, you know? Not all day, you know? Throughout the day … that we can kinda maintain the communication all day so, I, I think it's good and we still communicate face to face well.

JB mirrors his wife's response by sharing, "I think it's [mobiText] made it better, honestly I do." He continues:

> It's been great because it just allows us to just show more about ourselves and our day that we wouldn't bring up in conversation like (small pause), stuff at work that happens; like I wouldn't remember to bring that up to her later on. You know, we get a good laugh out of something or you know [it] allows us to share just more of ourselves with each other.

The above detailed responses regarding the helpful nature of mobiText use in their relationship supports the couple's belief in the positive influence of mobiText in their relationship. JB and Joyce's opinion regarding this mode of communication matches the examples supporting the other four tenets as discussed for this couple.

Monica's (Couple 4) interview suggests she does not use her device in such a manner that creates dependency on the device. She said that the use of MCT, specifically mobiText has been helpful in her relationship with her husband, which corresponds to her natural discourse as revealed during her interview. Her advice to other couples: "From my perspective, don't discuss difficult and delicate subjects by text message because I think it's too easy to, potentially too easy to misread it or shorten it or make it too, make issues out of it that aren't there." This advice corresponds with her view of mobiText as seen throughout her interview.

FM (Couple 4) summarizes his perspective of overall MCT use, specifically mobiText in his relationship:

> It's been a tool for communication but yet as it's a tool, if it's not always used when the other person thinks you should use it, then it can be somewhat, I don't know, a detriment or whatever. Not really a detriment, but like something that isn't as good.

Both FM and Monica's personal accounts of mobiText and overall MCT use are in agreement with the discourse throughout their individual interviews.

The discourse presented in Stone's (Couple 5) interview shows a consistent view and belief of mobiText in her marriage. She summarizes:

> I think that it's [MCT and mobiText] very good for our relationship. I think that we, um, we're able to communicate, keep in touch, make each other feel like, you know, we are about each other and we're thinking about each other.

Stone's personal reflection exhibits consistency as seen within the examples to support the previous four tenets of CDA for the couple.

Sasha's (Couple 5) interview shows discord with his overall view of MCT and mobiText in his relationship. He believes that the use of the mobile device has "definitely done a little bit of both." He expands on his reasoning:

> Because there's definitely certain things that need to be discussed in person and just so you can understand that person's emotion and what they really mean. And if you're doing it over the phone or texting and, and you're trying to be emotional or not trying to be emotional, things can be misunderstood.

If no conflict had occurred via MCT or mobiText, as Sasha claimed in his interview, emotion and misunderstanding would not be an issue for him. His assertion that no conflict has occurred—"I would say no, I usually know what she means"—was contradicted when he confirmed he had misread a message from his spouse due to "her lack of effort to spell check her messages." This provides evidence that his belief of mobiText in his relationship does not match his discourse.

Tori and Bob (Couple 6) provide a unique perspective on MCT and mobiText communication. Unlike the other couples that participated in the study, Bob and Tori showed no discrepancy within their own interview discourse or when referencing their spouse's usage or behavioral patterns of MCT and/or mobiText use. Tori's viewpoint on MCT use in her marriage reflects her interview discourse in that she stresses, "I think it's so easy to communicate but sometimes it's probably not the best way." Her advice to other couples:

> Listen to and be attentive to the other person. So, if you are in the same room or you are having a conversation or doing other things, don't pick up your phone (laughing). Don't pick it up, leave your texts, it can wait like two minutes until you're done.

Tori's honest advice is a direct reflection of her interview discourse as presented earlier in this chapter.

Bob highlighted the importance of daily communication, "Just use it as, you know, an easy way to communicate. I wouldn't use it as a crutch by any means, but, you know, it's the small things that count. So that's kinda how we use it." Bob's viewpoint matches how he personally described his usage of his device throughout his interview. He provided this insight of MCT/mobiText use:

> But yeah, I mean as far as helping, think about it. You know, the only times you could, what was it, probably not even 20 years ago, where there was not this type of communication. So, I think it can only help, you know, who knows; down the road, the next 20 years, what it may bring.

Findings and Discussion

We originally queried: Can a power structure within an intimate dyad be identified via MCT discourse? We discovered the answer is "sometimes." Power structures are present via two of the five tenets in Fairclough's CDA: dominant and dominated discourse types, and naturalization and the generation of common sense. When power operates in discourse, we see the powerful participant "controlling and constraining the contributions of non-powerful participant" (Fairclough, 2001, pp. 38–39). More specifically, we see constraints on "contents (what is said or done), relations (the social relations people enter into in discourse), and subjects (the 'subject positions' people can occupy" (Fairclough, 2001, p. 39). Five of the six couples had one member of the dyad express a dominant power discourse through the use of commanding and suggestive communication behavior. The presence of a power structure reflects Fariclough's belief that power relations exist between men and women, between old and young, and "between social groupings in institutions" (2001, p. 28) and with constraints on contents and subjects, as described earlier.

Fairclough argues that dominant discourse sustains power within relationships. Participants expressed one member of the dyad using a form of dominant discourse via MCT and regarding MCT usage patterns revealing the presence of a power structure, thus answering our guiding question. The findings revealed that commanding behavior, acceptable verses unacceptable behavior of MCT and mobiText use, and appropriate communication via mobiText were the preferred ways to influence partner views of MCT and mobiText, thus creating the presence of a power relationship within the dyad.

Our analyses suggest mobiText and the device used for mobiText is a symbol of power in the marital relationship. The participants conveyed a reliance on mobiText, turning it into the mode, or way and manner, in which something is experienced and expressed. MobiText takes the place of verbal sharing, as it is viewed as a personal assistant (logistics coordinator), acts as a means to express conflict, and helps locate an individual. MobiText is also perceived as a way to command behavior, dictate what is viewed as acceptable or unacceptable behavior, and as a way to control what is appropriate communication within the dyad.

We suggest that the dominant members of the dyad use these various forms of MCT and mobiText as the mode in which they hold power over the nondominant member. The meaning we attach to a symbol ultimately defines the individual and the reality they experience (Mead, 1934). Participants alluded to meanings they have of their devices as discussed in the third tenet of CDA: ideology and meaning (Fairclough, 2001). Although at times meanings within the dyads varied, an overall, mutually conditioned understanding of the device was evident in how each person described and accepted device use by her or his spouse. The use of MCT within the marital dyad suggests that a mutual conditioning of this form of communication is present, thus allowing the potential of one member of the dyad to exhibit a dominant discourse over the other.

Finally, we argue that the use of mobiText creates a third spouse in the marital relationship. This third "person," the device, creates a secondary avenue for the dominant discourse to emerge, thus favoring the dominant individual and dominant discourse of the dyad. MobiText communication involves a dyad, separated in place and time; often, the power relation performed is not understood or clear to the reader of the message. Unsaid or under-communicated messages are being sent via text message, without context and lacking voice inflection. Undercommunicated messages are defined as messages lacking depth and/or detail. The text, the choice of words by the sender, is the only message the receiver sees and is able to process. Within this study, reference was only made to text messages; no other forms of messages were discussed. This medium of communication gives precedence to the dominant discourse as the lack of face-to-face interaction works to the advantage of the dominant discourse. Power is now controlled via two means: face-to-face encounters and mobile-to-mobile encounters.

MCT, specifically mobiText, has arguably changed the way individuals communicate with each other. McLuhan's (1964) notion that "the medium is the message" effectively addresses the implications of this study. The findings presented herein argue that mobiText is a new medium. MobiText alters not only the pattern and the pace of our communication (McLuhan, 1964) but changes how couples communicate throughout their day, at home, and with other individuals, even that the absence of landlines is now the norm. Communication patterns and styles of communication used by married couples continue to occur with the technological advancement of mobile communication devices. McLuhan (1964) asserts:

> The content or uses of such media [in this study, mobiText] are as diverse as they are ineffectual in shaping the form of human association. Indeed, it is only too typical that the "content" of any medium blinds us to the character of that medium. (p. 9)

He asserts, "the 'content' of any medium is always another medium" (p. 8). The "content" of mobiText is the actual message being sent: text or picture. The ease of sending any message via mobiText blinds the user to the fact that he or she is using a device to communicate personal information and messages; couples are so entrapped by the quickness of getting the "content" or their "message" out, they are almost oblivious to the fact of being reliant on that medium, mobiText, to send their message.

Our analysis also found that power is ultimately given to the device itself, suggesting that the medium has truly become "the message" (McLuhan, 1964, p. 7). The message—communication via MCT, specifically mobiText—is a preferred method of maintaining aspects of the marital relationship. It is within this relationship that talk has now become textualized. Relationship talk, once face to face, is now device to device, or mobi to mobi.

Application

With the rise and continued use of MCT by individuals, families, family professionals, and scholars must be informed and educated in the ways that power is present and is used as a tool of control in marital relationships. Practical applications of our research are provided for professionals working to improve the family relationship, family members themselves, as well as scholars and communication theorists.

Implications for Family Professionals

The findings presented here will be useful for family professionals looking for information about the impact MCT use has on the marital dyad. Family professionals can use the interpretation of Fairclough's CDA as a framework to engage in discussions with couples, married and nonmarried, seeking to better their relational communication patterns. Using the tenets provided herein can equip family professionals with a framework to assist couples in seeing how power operates within the dyad via MCT use. Having real-life examples of conversations to aid in the discussion of the possible consequences of MCT use in marriage can assist family professionals and family members in opening up a space for improving overall communication about MCT use and communication via MCT.

Implications for Couples and Family Members

As we move toward the use of digital communication as a primary means of interacting, couples and family members can gain valuable information from our study. First, our analysis suggests couples and family members should be more aware of how a dominant member of the marital dyad might use technology as a means of holding the dominant position in the marriage. Second, couples and family members might use examples provided throughout the chapter as conversation starters to facilitate dialogue about possible destructive and productive communication patterns in one's couple or family system. Finally, for couples or individual members of family or couple systems, the real-life narratives shared in our study might ring true, suggesting that struggles for power through digital communication are indeed real—not only in one's mind or misperceived. Once such patterns can be recognized and labeled, conversation about their potentially destructive nature, and eventual change and resolution, is more probable.

Implications for Scholars

Our ability to communicate through mobile devices has provided us the opportunity to select what messages we want to send, when we want to send them, and most importantly, how we want our messages to be received. The ability to use mobiText at any given time makes it a new vehicle for everyday talk in marital dyads. This idea of continuous communication is found within our study with the use of mobiText to share information throughout the day, to engage in a quick message to check schedules, and to engage in behavior to gain power and control within the marital dyad. Scholars must begin to investigate how the increase in MCT use is changing our communicative behaviors by looking at the intricacies of everyday communication via mobiText. Focusing on communication patterns, message types, usage habits, and message construction will provide insight into how MCT use impacts our interpersonal relationships, specifically in the marital dyad.

Implications for Theory

Addressing how constant connectivity impacts our marital relationship is imperative for extending our theoretical understanding of MCT and mobiText use. Two theories worth exploring in this context are Licoppe's (2004) theory of connected presence and Duck's (1994) theory of relationship talk. Licoppe (2004) describes connected presence as a continual connection. Licoppe believes that, in relationships where individuals are separated, members increase their mediated communication to create a co-presence or "connected presence." Duck's (1994) relationship talk theory explains the importance of everyday talk in relationships. Everyday talk assists relationships "because it continues to embody partners' understanding or shared meaning, and it continues to represent their relationship to one another in ways that each accepts and is comfortable with" (Duck, 1994,

p. 54). Examining these two theories within the specific context of mobiText use for marital communication can further our understanding of how MCT use is changing marital communication interactions and patterns.

References

Albright, J. M., & Conran, T. (2003). Desire, love, and betrayal: Constructing and deconstructing intimacy online. *Journal of Systemic Therapies, 22,* 42–53.

Baym, N. K., Zang, Y. B., Kunkel, A., Ledbetter, A., & Lin, M. C. (2007). Relational quality and media use in interpersonal relationships. *New Media and Society, 9,* 735–752. doi: 10.1177/1461444807080339

Creswell, J. W. (2007). *Qualitative inquiry and research design: Choosing among five approaches* (2nd ed.). Thousand Oaks, CA: Sage Publications Inc.

Duck, S. (1994). Steady as (s)he goes: Relational maintenance as a shared meaning system. In D. J. Canary & L. Stafford (Eds.), *Communication and relational maintenance* (pp. 45–60). San Diego, CA: Academic Press, Inc.

Fairclough, N. (1989). *Language and Power.* London: Longman.

Fairclough, N. (2001). *Language and Power* (2nd ed.). London: Pearson.

Garcia-Montes, J. M., Caballero-Munoz, D., & Perez-Alvarez, M. (2006). Changes in the self resulting from the use of mobile phones. *Media, Culture, & Society, 28,* 67–82. doi: 10.1177/0163443706059287

Jin, B., & Pena, J. F. (2010). Mobile communication in romantic relationships: Mobile phone use, relational uncertainty, love, commitment, and attachment styles. *Communication Reports, 23*(1), 39–51. doi:10.1080/08934211003598742

Kennedy, T. L. M., & Wellman, B. (2007). The networked household. *Information, Communication, & Society, 10,* 645–670. doi:10.1080/13691180701658012

Lenhart, A., & Duggan, M. (2014, February 11). Couples, the Internet, and social media: How American couples use digital technology to manage life, logistics, and emotional intimacy within their relationships. Retrieved from http://www.pewinternet.org/2014/02/11/couples-the-internet-and-social-media/

Licoppe, C. (2004). "Connected" presence: The emergence of a new repertoire for managing social relationships in a changing communication technoscape. *Environment and Planning D: Society and Space, 22,* 135–156. doi:10.1068/d323t

McLuhan, M. (1964). *Understanding media: The extensions of man.* New York: McGraw-Hill.

Mead, G. H. (1934). *Mind, self, and society: From the standpoint of a social behaviorist.* Chicago: The University of Chicago Press.

Mish, F. C. (Ed.). (2007). *Merriam-Webster's collegiate dictionary* (11th Ed.). Springfield, MA: Merriam-Webster, Inc.

Morris, W. (Ed.). (1970). *The American heritage dictionary of the English language.* New York: American Heritage Publications.

Pettigrew, J. (2009). Text messaging and connectedness within close interpersonal relationships. *Marriage and Family Review, 45,* 697–716. doi:10.1080/01494920903224269

Pew Research Center Publications. (2014). Mobile Technology Fact Sheet. Retrieved from http://www.pewinternet.org/fact-sheets/mobile-technology-fact-sheet/

Ramirez, Jr., A., & Broneck, K. (2009). "IM me": Instant messaging as relational maintenance and everyday communication. *Journal of Social and Personal Relationships, 26*, 291–314. doi:10.1177/0265407509106719

Solis, R. J. C. (2006). Mobile romance: An exploration of the development of romantic relationships through texting. *Proceedings of the Asia Culture Forum.* Retrieved from: http://cct.pa.go.kr/data/acf2006/mobile/mobile_0205_Randy%20Jay%20C.%20Solis.pdf

Van Dijk, T. A. (2001). Critical discourse analysis. In D. Tannen, D. Schiffrin, & D. Hamilton (Eds.), *Handbook of discourse analysis* (pp. 352–371). Malden, MA: Blackwell Publishing, Ltd.

14

Couples' Communication of Rules and Boundaries for Social Networking Site Use

JACLYN D. CRAVENS
JASON B. WHITING
Texas Tech University

Introduction

Technology and Internet use in our daily lives has rapidly grown over the past 15 years. As of 2014, in the United States 90% of adults have cell phones, 58% own smartphones, and 42% have a tablet computer (Pew Internet and American Life Project, 2014). The increase in Internet and social networking site (SNS) use has become a major factor in U.S. couples' relationships. Researchers found that couples use technology in their relationships to facilitate communication and support, to resolve arguments and for sexting (Lenhart & Duggan, 2014). Further, couples reported that the Internet has had a major impact—both good and bad—on their relationships, particularly for the 18–29-year-old cohort.

Technology has many positive impacts on relationships, such as helping maintain relationships (Sidelinger, Ayash, Gordorhazy, & Tibbles, 2008) and increasing connection (Pettigrew, 2009). One fifth of participants in a recent study on couple relationships reported use of technology has helped them feel closer to their partner (Lenhart & Duggan, 2014). Researchers have also explored how computer-mediated communication (CMC) compares to face-to-face communication (Ross & Kauth, 2002). CMC facilitates feelings of anonymity, allowing Internet users to communicate with other users with less inhibition, which can lead to more honest, open, and personal conversations (Spears & Lea, 1994).

Use of technology and the Internet have not come without relational and personal consequences. Internet users face temptations related to the ease with which they can access sexually explicit materials and engage in infidelity behaviors online. A recent survey found that 40% of U.S. adults report they use their email to engage in flirtatious behavior with people they are attracted to (Pew Internet and American Life Project, 2006). Additionally, compulsive Internet users and their problematic use has been found to negatively impact their offline relationship: diminished time spent together, issues with conflict resolution, lack of emotional support, and low levels of intimacy (Cooper, Månsson, Daneback, Tikkanen, & Ross, 2003). SNS also have been found to create negative consequences for relationships. Researchers have found that certain Facebook behaviors such as interacting with ex-partners, sending private messages, and commenting on users' pictures may create problems for relationships (Clayton, Nagurney, & Smith, 2013) including relationship satisfaction, trust, and create feelings of jealousy (Elphinston & Noller, 2011). Further, Facebook infidelity has been found to be just as painful as offline infidelity, to cause similar emotional experiences for the nonparticipating partner (e.g., hurt, anger, loss of trust), and to result in the dissolution of the relationship (Cravens, Leckie, & Whiting, 2013).

The vulnerabilities that relationships face due to new communication technologies demand couples and families, and those that serve them, to carefully consider the complexities of relationship dynamics in the digital age. Hertelin (2012) (also see Hertlein & Blumer and Blumer & Hertlein chapters in this volume) created the first ever mutlitheoretical model, the Couple and Family Technology Framework (CFT), conceptualizing the way the Internet and technology influence couples and families. Reflective of the current study, the CFT Framework provides one way to conceptualize the process couples in committed relationships must go through to adapt to the integration of technology in their daily lives: "technology influences the way couples and families establish rules, roles, and boundaries" (Hertlein, 2012, p. 375), which in turn can impact relationship initiation, maintenance, and dissolution (Hertlein & Blumer, 2013). The multitheoretical model stresses the need for couples to revisit their relational rules and consider how the boundaries between online and offline relationships may become blurred with the multiple forms of communication technology offers (Hertlein, 2012). The idea that relational rules should be revised to consider technology and the Internet is further stressed by Daneback, Cooper, and Månsson (2005), who suggest couples who avoid such a discussion may perceive their partner to be operating online in ways that violate their relationship. It is clear that researchers have identified a need for couples to communicate about rules and boundaries for the Internet and technology; however, it is currently unknown to what extent couples engage in such conversations. The purpose of this chapter is to review literature related to online rules and boundaries and report a study examining how couples establish rules and boundaries for SNS use in their relationship, and how such rules and boundaries are communicated and maintained.

Appropriate and Inappropriate Offline and Online Behaviors

Researchers have investigated the process of married couples developing rules about acceptable or unacceptable behaviors, the majority focusing specifically on infidelity behaviors (Murray, Holmes, Bellavia, Griffin, & Dolderman, 2002; Wilson, Roloff, & Clark, 1998; Wilson, Mattingly, Clark, Wiedler, & Bequette, 2011). Often such rules are unspoken, and assumptions are made that one's partner shares her or his beliefs about what is appropriate (Murray et al., 2002). Unfortunately, assumptions don't always mirror what a partner perceives as inappropriate behavior. Researchers have consistently evidenced gender differences in reactions to sexual and emotional infidelity (Roscoe, Cavanaugh, & Kennedy, 1988; Yarab, Allgeier, & Sensibaugh, 1999). In those studies, men and women were in agreement about which sexual behaviors were inappropriate; however, wide inconsistencies were found of individuals' perceptions of the (in)appropriateness of nonsexual behaviors. For example, female participants were more likely than male participants to perceive keeping secrets (Roscoe et al., 1988), romantic attachments, flirting, and sexual fantasies (Yarab et al., 1999) as cheating.

Researchers have predominately focused on participants' perceptions of offline behaviors; however, several studies suggest individuals perceive certain online behaviors to be forms of cheating (Cravens & Whiting, in press; Mileham, 2007; Parker & Wampler, 2003; Whitty, 2003). Parker and Wampler (2003) explored individuals' perceptions of online infidelity, finding that participants ranked online sexual behavior (e.g., visiting adult websites, cybersex) as less of an affair than physical, offline sexual behaviors. Despite this, participants still reported online sexual behaviors to be an affair and the behavior to distract from the primary offline relationship. Further, Whitty (2003) found that participants ranked online sexual acts, such as hot chatting, cybersex, and pornography, as being ranked most strongly as infidelity, but that pornography was viewed as least threatening. Other studies found online infidelity behaviors to be just as damaging to relationships as offline infidelity and that online infidelity behaviors have negative consequences for the offline relationship (loss of trust, breaking up) (Cravens & Whiting, in press; Whitty, 2005).

Overall, research to date highlights that, within and across relationships, individuals and couples may have vastly different ideas of what counts as cheating behavior. Couples likely have similar differences about other behaviors (noncheating) deemed inappropriate within the context of their committed relationship, suggesting the need for more research on the extent to which couples set rules or boundaries in their relationship, in particular those related to online choices.

Setting Online Boundaries

Researchers have revealed the intrapersonal and interpersonal consequences of individuals' inappropriate online behaviors (Cooper et al., 2003; Schneider, 2003), suggesting couples are wise to engage in prevention, including rule development. Rules establish boundaries and help couples explicitly define expectations. Relational rules specify what behavior individuals "think or believe should or should not be performed" (Argyle & Henderson, 1985, p. 63). Further, boundary setting is one of the primary ways partners inhibit disruptive, exploitative, and unsupportive actions within relationships (Wilson et al., 1998). When partners lack clear or compatible rules, research has found that tension may develop (Petronio, 2002). Both researchers and clinicians alike can benefit from a more robust understanding of how couples define and negotiate online boundaries, yet a paucity of research exists about online boundary setting, with only two known studies on the topic (Helsper & Whitty, 2010; Norton, 2011).

Helsper and Whitty (2010) investigated the shared netiquette, "the unspoken and spoken rules about acceptable and unacceptable online activities" (p. 919) of married couples, including online monitoring and surveillance of partner behaviors. Results suggest the largest number of agreed-upon, unacceptable online behavior were activities considered "infidelity" (e.g., falling in love with someone else online and engaging in cybersex). The largest area of disagreement was about whether it was acceptable or not to look at sexual material online. Gambling and shopping online were also areas of significant disagreement between couples.

Norton (2011) examined the nature of SNS boundaries and rules as protective factors in marital relationships, exploring the relationship among trust, relationship satisfaction, and online rules and boundaries. Results suggest couples in long-term marital relationships do have rules for SNS (although the study did not assess if such were explicit or implicit), and that couples, boundaries and rules for SNS reflect two main types: (1) boundaries about "openness," such as sharing passwords, allowing partners to access each other's SNS accounts, and knowing the people they were friends with on the SNS accounts; and (2) boundaries related to "fidelity," including the way emotional fidelity should extend to online behaviors (e.g., no flirting, no "friending" previous romantic partners). Trust and boundary setting were positively related, indicating that as relational trust increased in marital relationships, the use of openness and the setting of fidelity boundaries for Internet use also increased.

Purpose of Study

Given how little is currently known about how couples communicate about boundaries and rules for Internet use, research exploring the topic of couple boundary-setting for online behavior is warranted. As such, the purpose of the current study was to explore how couples establish rules and boundaries for SNS use in their relationship, and how such rules and boundaries are communicated and maintained. The following three research questions guided the study: (1) What rules and boundaries about social networking site use do couples have? (2) How are these rules and boundaries communicated in the relationship? (3) How are these rules and boundaries monitored?

Methods

To answer the research questions, couples were interviewed and the data were analyzed using a constructivist grounded theory methodology (Charmaz, 2006). This methodology aims to build a theory that is data driven, not constructed from preexisting conceptualizations. The researchers adopted a subjective or "not-knowing" stance, and operated from a constructivist paradigm (Charmaz, 2006). The resulting theoretical model was influenced by the interaction between researcher and participants, and the final model should be understood as representing one conceptualization among many of the phenomenon (Daly, 2007).

Data Collection

After receiving Institutional Review Board approval, participants were recruited from an on-campus family therapy clinic that serves individuals in the university community as well as from the general public, which allowed the researchers to interview couples that were currently in therapy and those from the general public. Participants had an opportunity to be entered into a drawing for one of two $50.00 Visa gift cards conducted at the conclusion of data collection. Inclusion criteria for the study were that participants must be at least 18 years old, English speaking, and currently in a committed relationship. For the purposes of this study, committed relationship was defined as a current relationship between two partners who both define the relationship as committed.

Sample Characteristics

A sample of 10 couples (20 individuals) was recruited from the community (n = 6) and a family therapy clinic (n = 4). Of the participants, 11 were female and nine were male. The majority of the couples reported being in a heterosexual relationship, with one couple reporting a same-sex relationship. Participants' relationship status included: dating (n = 4, 20%), cohabiting (n = 10, 50%), and married (n = 6, 30%). The length of current relationship ranged from less than a year to 10 years. Participants identified their ethnicities as Caucasian (n = 17, 85%), multiracial (n = 2, 10%) and African American/Black (n = 1, 5%). Participants' highest level of education ranged from middle school to college degree or higher, with the majority of participants having a high school degree (n = 7, 35%) to a college degree or higher (n = 7, 35%).

Measures

Demographic information regarding age, gender, current relationship status, length of relationship, education, and SNS use was gathered from a simple questionnaire. Semi-structured interviews were then conducted with each participant couple; both partners were required to be present for the interview. Interview questions explored areas related to SNS use and their offline relationship. Questions asked participants about time spent online, how SNS enhances or detracts from their offline relationship, what behaviors are perceived as inappropriate, and what rules and boundaries for online behaviors—if any—they had established. Couples who had established rules were asked why they established rules and how they negotiated differences. For couples who had not established SNS rules in their relationship, the interviewer focused on asking each partner to discuss specific problematic SNS behaviors and how specific behaviors might impact their relationship.

Data Analysis

The semi-structured interviews were recorded using a handheld recorder and were subsequently transcribed. Memo writing is the practice of recording reflexive notes about the researcher's conceptualization of the data, which helps track analytic decisions, code development, and researcher's reflections. Memos add to the credibility and trustworthiness of qualitative research and were used extensively in this study.

Four stages of qualitative data coding, as recommended by Charmaz (2006), were used: initial, focused, axial, and theoretical coding. During the initial coding stage, each line of the transcript was read, making analytic interpretations that moved beyond the participants' concrete statements to identify codes. For example, the following codes were named during the initial coding stage: *no written rule, following norms,* and *no established rules.* These codes remained close to the data and revealed actions related to the development of rules. The next stage, focused coding, involved a process of refining initial codes by comparing data to data, seeking to find events, interactions, or perspectives. Focused coding allowed for the synthesis of *no written rules, following norms,* and *no established rules* into the code *implicit rules.*

Axial coding is a process of relating categories to subcategories, and specifying dimensions of categories (Charmaz, 2006). The process of sorting, synthesizing, and organizing categories revealed that *implicit rules, explicit rules*, and *rule consensus* were actions related to how couples made a determination about whether specific online behaviors were relationship violations. It was then determined that these codes were specific properties of the final process-models stage *appraising the online issue*, leading to the development of each of these codes as subcategories of appraising the online issue. The final stage of coding is theoretical coding—a process of articulating relationships between the coded categories with the aim of telling a coherent analytic story about the participants' experiences. In this final stage of coding the researcher organized each category as a stage of the final process model, representing the stages couples go through after a problematic online behavior occurs. Prior to finalizing the model, the researcher's memos and the original data were revisited to ensure the process model reflected the couples' narratives.

Results

Grounded theory analysis resulted in the development of the Process Model of Online Issues in Intimate Partner relationships (Figure 14.1). The circular model represent the process couples experience after an inappropriate online behavior has occurred in their relationship. It includes five stages: identify online issue; appraise online issue; discuss online issue; resolution; and consequence. The process starts with identification of the online issue and is punctuated by three possible outcomes: (1) resolution of the issue, (2) relational consequences, and/or (3) additional online issues occur—bringing the couple back to the start of the process model. The model also indicates that several preventative barriers exist—honesty, trust, and respect—which protect the couple from experiencing issues with SNS in their relationship. Preventative barriers are depicted as encompassing the five stages of the model and reflect participants' beliefs that, when present, couples are less likely to experience online issues and thus less likely to enter the cycle. In the remainder of this section, each stage of the process is presented, including descriptions of each category and subcategory model (see Figure 14.1).

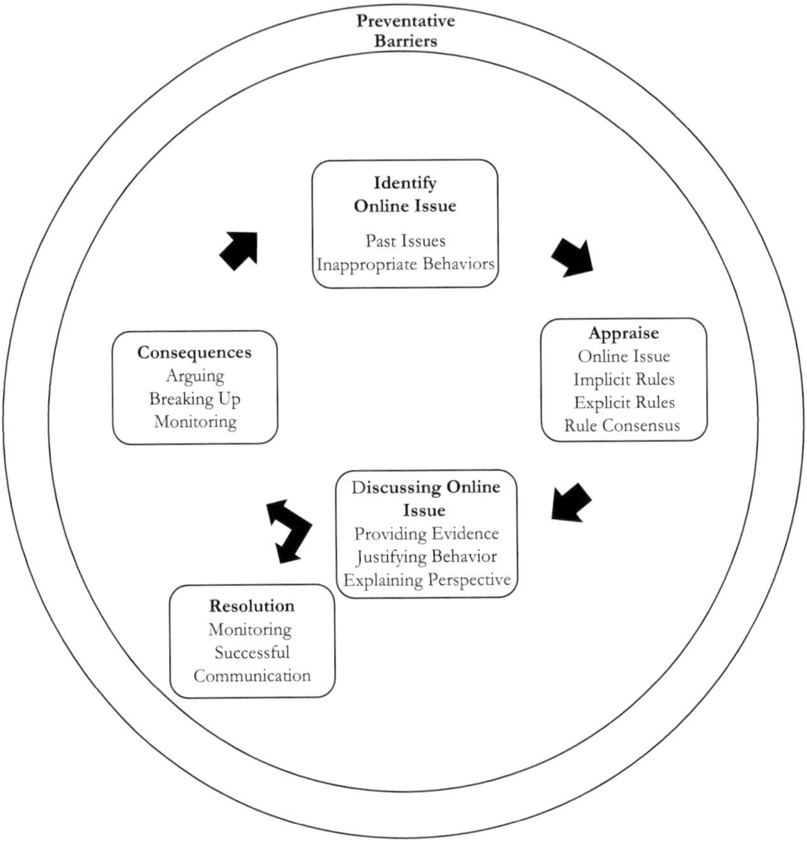

Figure 14.1. Process Model of Online Issues in Intimate Partner Relationships.

Identify online issue. Couples were asked whether there were specific online behaviors they would consider appropriate or inappropriate within the context of their relationship. Two subcategories were revealed: *Past Issues* and *Inappropriate Behaviors*.

Past issues. Past issues are defined as an online behavior that at least one partner viewed as being an issue and that had occurred previously in either the current relationship or in one or more past relationships. When asked to identify inappropriate online behaviors, partners not only shared specific behaviors, many also related the behavior back to issues encountered in the past, as illustrated in the following:

> Partner 6B: I have either been contacted or been in contact with pretty much everyone from every dark corner or dark part of my past....One was a friend, the first girlfriend that I ever had [*partner interrupts*].
>
> Partner 6A: That he talked about so much it drove me nuts.

Similarly, couple 4AB had concerns about how the partner would respond to other Facebook users' private messages and whether the conversation was appropriate:

> Partner 4B: Messaging, she was starting to get uneasy because there was a couple people saying, cutie or something like that, and she didn't know all the facts yet. But it got to the point where previous conversations supposedly got deleted and she would get on my case about things.

In addition to discussing SNS issues within their current relationship, couples also shared issues from previous relationships. For example, one partner (8B) stated "Not our relationship, well we haven't had any issues with it [SNS], the only issue was when I was with my ex-wife." His partner (8A) shared: "I did have a joint account with my ex-husband for the sole purpose that I knew he was doing inappropriate things on Facebook."

Inappropriate behaviors. Inappropriate behaviors were defined as any online behavior considered inappropriate according to one or both partners and the behavior had occurred in their relationship. Participants' narratives indicated each partner identified specific behaviors as inappropriate within the context of their current relationship. Two couples specifically talked about what should be posted online. One partner (3A) shared that you shouldn't post "stupid pictures," while partner 7A discussed her boyfriend's strict privacy rules: "Well if I ever put up a picture of him, I feel like that would be crossing a line, because he doesn't want any of that." Other couples identified specific inappropriate behaviors ranging from mirroring inappropriate offline behaviors (e.g., emotional affairs, flirting) to looking for another partner online.

Appraise online issue. Individual partners went through a process where the online issue was appraised based on each person's rules for appropriate online behavior. A common theme emerging from this category was whether couples had implicit or explicit rules for online behaviors. The two types of rules (implicit, explicit) and whether there was consensus between the partners influenced how the behavior was appraised. Three subcategories were identified: *implicit rules*, *explicit rules,* and *rule consensus.*

Implicit rules. The subcategory of implicit rules is a set of one partner's implied or identified but not expressed rules for what constitutes inappropriate online behavior. When one partner engaged in an inappropriate online behavior, the other partner indicated that she or he should have known the behavior was inappropriate, despite the fact that no rule had been expressed. For example, one partner (7B) shared: "No we really don't have any rules…they just mirror our offline rules." Other partners conveyed they did not have established rules, but there were behaviors that would cross an implicit boundary. Partner 2B: "I haven't really figured it out yet. I don't have rules, I just have guidelines. And there is stuff I am comfortable with and there is stuff that I am not." Although the partner had not established a rule, he was communicating to his partner there are behaviors he would be uncomfortable with his partner engaging in. One couple shared that they were aware of "unwritten rules" but that they had not discussed them:

Partner 6B: No, we just have unwritten rules that we just both probably agreed would be distasteful.

Partner 6A: Maybe there is a list of rules that we should be going over with each other.

Another couple indicated that each partner knew what inappropriate behaviors were and that they had even tried to tell each other what they liked. Partner 9B: "I know I communicate a lot of what I like and don't like…so maybe that is why there haven't been rules laid down." While this couple revealed coming close to having an actual discussion about rules, both members stated they had not actually established concrete rules.

Explicit rules. Although implicit rules were the predominant way rules were constructed, a few couples stated they had formally established rules for their online behaviors by explicitly identifying and setting a boundary. For example, one couple talked about how a past issue resulted in establishment of a new and explicit rule:

Partner 1B: There was a specific event that occurred and that is when it happened.

Partner 1A: Ah, there was a specific event that occurred. …I didn't tell him what I did; he saw it [online]. But then I took it off. I don't really think you said I had to.

Partner 1B: Well yeah, so if like she thinks a picture might be too risqué, then she has to send it to me first.…And then I get to make a decision.

Another couple shared that, due to previous issues in their relationship with SNS, they decided they needed to discuss rules and create clear boundaries.

Partner 10A: We are really careful with our account. We set out expectations before we joined our accounts together. Different people that we'd had a relationship (with) before we got together—we don't friend those people.

Partner 10B: Yeah, we had some guidelines beforehand.

Rule consensus. The final subcategory, rule consensus, is defined as the degree to which each partner in the relationship agreed with the designation of the specific online behaviors as inappropriate and the severity of the behavior's effect on the relationship. Regardless of whether rules were implicit or explicit, there was great variation in rule consensus that often led to arguments. One couple disagreed about whether or not it was okay to talk about sexual issues to opposite-sex individuals, while another couple disagreed about who was an acceptable Facebook friend. Each disagreement reflected a lack of rule consensus, as exemplified by this couple's comments:

Partner 2A: I don't like him doing a lot of talking to other females.

Partner 2B: At all, at all!

Partner 2A: [*laughs*] I don't like other girls talking to him like... [*Partner interrupts*].

Partner 2B: Not even about sex, just at all. Of course I don't follow that rule at all.

Another couple argued about adding friends on Facebook, a disagreement revealed in their ongoing argument about what is and isn't appropriate:

Partner 5B: Oh, I have gotten mad about her not adding my friends. I ask her to add my friends, and she doesn't want to.

Partner 5A: But then he thinks I should, but... [*partner interrupts*].

Partner 5B: 'Cause I think that since we are a couple she, 'cause if I am friends with someone, then she and they are good friends in real life, well... that it is rude for her to ignore them wanting to be her friend.

Partner 5A: ...I don't know why it matters, but I mean if his friends ask now, I will do it. I just don't need a million people on my Facebook....

Partner 5B: I don't know, I just think it is rude. It is like a slap in the face.

Discussing online issue. After couples identified and appraised the problematic online issue, they moved to the *Discussing Online Issue* stage. Discussions focused on factors related to the online behavior, and such conversations did not always immediately follow the appraisal stage. For example, partner 9B: "The one time one of the examples that I gave happened, eventually we were able to talk about it." Further, discussions were not always easy. For example, some participants who were accused of engaging in problematic online behavior denied that they had actually done so or used justifications or minimizations to reduce the perceived severity of the behavior. According to interviewees, discussing the online issue was most successful when each partner had the opportunity to communicate his or her perspective. Three main subcategories emerged identifying dimensions of discussing the online issue: *providing evidence, justifying behavior,* and *explaining perspective.*

Providing evidence. When discussing the online issue, many couples reported that when one partner was accused of engaging in the problematic behavior, she or he would deny the accusation—forcing the accusing partner to provide evidence to support the claim. For instance, partner 2B said there was no reason not to trust him, while his partner responds: "Well, that is not necessarily true, because the whole incident with his ex-wife and the incident with [*name*]." In another example, evidence from the accusing partner was provided to the researcher after her partner had declared, "There was no inappropriate interaction."

> Partner 6A: [*partner interrupts*] …the girl that you told was sexy, then the other one was the chick who always had her tits hanging out in her profile picture, because I have a big problem with that. Because you know most of the women he is friends with, he actually sought friendships with them on Facebook. Most of them didn't seek him out. It was going through other people's profiles and looking for women, and next thing I know there are just hundreds of good-looking women and… [*partner interrupts*]
>
> Partner 6B: That was not actually true.
>
> Partner 6A: I watched him do it.

Justifying behavior. Individuals defend or justify their online behavior. For some partners, justification was a way to reduce the perceived impact of the behavior on the relationship. For example, partner 6A was upset with her partner for commenting about how sexy a woman's photo was and that she thought the woman's profile pictures were inappropriate. Partner 6B responds with a justification: "I had no control over that." Another partner justified by arguing her partner wanted her to engage in the online behavior:

> Partner 2A: Well, yeah, you have contacted people without my permission before and just randomly came up with some picture of some girls… [*partner interrupts*].
>
> Partner 2B: You've said that you were interested in that.

Others engaged in justifications by attempting to convince a partner the identified inappropriate online behavior was not an issue. When one partner identified she had issues with her partner interacting with women online, her partner (6B) stated "Why? They have kids, they have artwork, they do stuff, and they like to look at my stuff. You know? My motorcycle and my kids, tattoos, and stuff like that I like to see." The partner continues by explaining to the interviewer his wife would like the women if she got to know them.

Several partners justified behavior by minimizing it. One participant (9A) shared she had been curious about an interaction her partner had with someone, so she checked her partner's account to read her private messages: "And that was really the only time that I ever did that." Another participant tried to justify his behavior by minimizing the impact of the behavior because of its infrequency:

Partner 6A: A couple of years ago it was a lot more childish, because every time we'd get into a fight he would get online and call me names.
Partner 6B: That was only a couple of times, and I didn't get that extreme.
Partner 6A: Seven times is a lot okay? And I don't forget these things....

Explaining perspective. When the couples communicated about the problematic online issue, one partner was often expected to explain why the behavior was problematic—most often when there was not consensus between partners on what constitutes inappropriate online behavior. Partner 6A identified interacting with attractive women as problematic. She explained how she kept thinking about him writing inappropriate comments to other women: "But then going through their pictures and commenting on them, that bothers me because then I have a bad taste in my mouth about them."

Another partner (9A) identified that spending too much time on Facebook was an issue in their relationship: "She can be on there [Facebook] for hours. I think if she had the chance, she would sit on there all day long. Like she just will stalk people." Partner 9A went on to explain her perspective, pointing out that her partner's time on Facebook takes quality time away from their relationship.

Consequences. Although problematic online issues always resulted in a dialogue, the dialogues did not always result in positive resolutions. In the appraisal and discussing online issue stages, several factors contributed to couples experiencing negative relational consequences. For example during the appraisal stage, couples did not always reach consensus about the (in)appropriateness of certain behaviors. In the discussing online issue stage, some partners denied they had engaged in the behavior or used cognitive distortions such as minimization and justifications to reduce the perceived severity of their behaviors. When interaction during these two stages was not accompanied by open communication, including explaining one's perspective, couples were much more likely to experience negative relational consequences. Three subcategories emerged from the analysis: *arguing, breaking up*, and *monitoring.*

Arguing. While discussing online issues, many couples struggled to stay de-escalated, to reduce the severity of the conflict or remain calm. Several couples identified Facebook as the source of many arguments in their relationship. Couple 6AB stated: "Yeah we had other reasons for arguments, but Facebook has been a big catalyst in our relationship." Another couple (9AB) observed that Facebook behaviors caused many "bickers" in their relationship.

Couples' discussions often resulted in arguments, particularly when they disagreed about whether an online behavior was inappropriate. One partner admitted she did not want her partner talking about their relationship to other women online. Their discussion became more intense when the male partner stated that the rule is not one he is going to follow, to which his partner responded:

> Partner 2A: I don't find it very appropriate to talk to another female about sex, about something in our relationship. I get a little irritated at that. I wouldn't do that.

Breaking up. Although arguing was the most common consequence, several couples revealed that disagreements about SNS issues resulted in a break-up or separation. Partner 2A explained what happened when her partner broke up with her because of her online behavior: "Deep down inside it was the thrill of getting caught and being punished for it, and it backfired on me because it made him leave me." The couple agreed that they experienced a process of trial and error with online behaviors, a process that resulted in breaking up and getting back together several times:

> Partner 2A: We have haphazardly fallen through on these things.
> Partner 2B: And, it tested the water on some things.
> Partner 2A: Experimented on some things.
> Partner 2B: And seeing what happens with some things. It has broken us up a few times because of the private sex messages with people and then him spying on me.

For another couple, Facebook was a contributing factor to previous marriages ending. One partner (8A) reported that her partner was doing inappropriate things on Facebook, so she made him get rid of his account, "He just ended up getting another account under a name that I wouldn't find." Another couple explained how previous romantic partners sending private Facebook messages led the couple to briefly separate. One partner (10A) shared: "I guess we had a little hiatus where we were separated for a month because of Facebook."

Monitoring. Couples explained that monitoring (e.g., checking a partner's Internet browser history, logging into their partner's SNS accounts either secretly or with permission) was both a consequence of, and a resolution to, inappropriate online behavior. One couple explained that, because trust was lacking in their relationship, each monitored the other's Facebook account by using the other's password. However, they came to recognize that such monitoring had negative consequences for their relationship. When asked about having access to each other's SNS accounts, partner 6B explained he does not log into her account. His partner responded:

> Partner 6A: No, he has used it before when he knew my password. It wasn't a secret or anything.
>
> Partner 6B: No, I have, but we both decided that it is in bad taste, so we don't anymore.
>
> Partner 6A: I think we both grew up about that sort of thing. What is the word, *evolved*, because it caused a lot of problems. It would cause arguments, and I would find out information.

Monitoring also emerged when partners became suspicious of online behaviors. For instance, one male participant observed that his partner monitored his account because she herself was guilty of inappropriate online choices, specifically receiving nude pictures ("pics") from other men on Facebook:

> Partner 2B: I had never looked through her phone or on other people's accounts before we met each other. But she went through my phone once. So I asked her, "Why are you doing this?" At which point I saw why she was doing this, there were four or five di- pics on her account. I am like, okay, the reason you are obviously looking through my phone is that you have a guilty conscience.

Another couple (9AB) shared that they each get on the other's accounts despite having no established agreement that they could. One of the partners (9A) discussed how she would get on her partner's phone to check her Facebook without asking her permission. She admitted: "Which I don't know if that is a good or bad thing, I am nosy, so I just do it." She explains further: "Most of the time it is just out of curiosity or boredom." Her partner (9B) described how she was suspicious when a friend from her past had come into town to visit. She stated, "I wanted to see how they communicated…I was just like, why are y'all reconnecting and talking? So I went on Facebook to see it because it wasn't on her phone."

Resolution. The process model depicts three possible outcomes following an inappropriate online behavior: (1) The couple experiences consequences related to the behavior; (2) the couple continues to experience issues with the Internet and remains in the cycle; or (3) the couple reaches a resolution to the problem. Following the stage of discussing the online issue, several couples discussed two primary ways they were able to resolve the issue: *Monitoring* and *Successful Communication.*

Monitoring. While monitoring was identified as a negative consequence, it was also identified as a positive behavior for helping couples resolve issues. Participants described the positive aspects of monitoring in two ways: (a) being responsible for monitoring one's own online behavior, and (b) creating a shared account. One partner (2A) explained it was her responsibility to monitor her own online behavior: "I know personally what needs to be done, so I just do what feels right." Another participant explained that when a woman tries to add him as a friend on Facebook, he responds in a way that prevents future problems:

> Partner 6B: I monitor my own behavior. If I get a request—I have gotten I guess 6 in the past couple of months from women that I don't recognize— I have sent them a message back: "How do I know you? And if I don't, then I don't think it is appropriate that I friend you." And then I have messages saved.

The second form of monitoring identified by couples as positive was the creation of a shared account. One couple explained how Facebook had created previous issues in their relationship, and to resolve them they created a shared Facebook account:

> Partner 10A: Us having separate accounts and it not going well, it motivated us to have a joint account. We were trying to make things better.
>
> Partner 10B: Yeah. It has helped us a lot. I think we had to build up some trust.

Successful communication. By successfully communicating about the SNS issue, couples reported they were able to prevent the problematic behavior from being repeated. One couple resolved their concern about who shouldn't be friended on Facebook (e.g., previous dating partners, coworkers, high school friends) by simply discussing the issue. Through successful communication the couple was able to come to an agreement concerning friending on Facebook. Another partner (6B), who identified private messaging other women on Facebook as inappropriate behavior, shared that through openly discussing her concerns with her husband, they were able to resolve the issue: "And we actually resolved that. You know I told him how I felt, and I told him why I felt that way, and then we talked about it, and we didn't get into a fight."

Another couple with separate Facebook accounts actually separated because of multiple issues resulting from having individual accounts. When they started rebuilding their relationship, they explained needing to discuss Facebook rules and boundaries, and become clear about motivations for creating a joint account:

> Partner 10A: I think you have to be really careful setting guidelines, because obviously having a joint account takes away each person's privacy. I think it takes two people to not really mind that it is a shared account; that way it is not intruding on each other's personal space. We were both really open with having this and being careful, knowing what the purpose of having our account is. Not just using it for social networking but to stay in contact with our friends and family and that is pretty much it.

Preventative barriers. Many couples identified aspects of their relationship that served as preventative barriers to common online issues, each aspect related in some way to trust and honesty. For example, one couple indicated not having issues with SNS, largely because of the trust they had established in their relationship: "No, I mean we pretty much trust each other, we know that we trust each other and that's about it" (1B). Another couple compared their current relationship to previous relationships; both were situations in which the exes engaged in inappropriate Facebook behaviors:

> Partner 8A: Yeah, so I think it just made both of us realize when the trust is there, you don't have to worry. 'Cause we were both not trusted by our exes, but really they were the ones doing things that were not trustworthy. And we were not the guilty party, but we were both made to feel guilty. I think once you've gotten into a healthy relationship, you don't question things.

Another participant explained she had moved past previous Facebook issues in her current relationship by not only working on trust but also by learning to communicate better: "As far as assumptions go, I think we are past that." She credited counseling and talking about expectations for the change.

Finally, couples identified respect and "considering the other person" as effective preventative techniques for avoiding inappropriate online choices. Participant 8B explained mutual respect is important in the relationship: "So I am not going to do it to you, so you should not do it to me." Her partner (8A) further explains: "If I wouldn't do it with you sitting right next to me, then I am not going to do it all." Participant 7B highlighted how respect makes him confident they won't have Facebook issues: "I think for the most part things that would end any relationship would be rules, but in terms of our character…I just don't see that happening." One couple exemplified the importance of respect as a preventative barrier:

Partner 1A: I think social media can really ruin a relationship, but I have actually noticed that it is pretty okay in our relationship. So it doesn't really affect ours too much.

Partner 1B: It is just being respectful.

Partner 1A: [*jumps in*] Being respectful of each other and he always told me put yourself in my shoes and I started to think of that and what he would and wouldn't like and he is the same way towards me.…we care, so we try.

Discussion

Results suggest that couples in committed relationships experience issues related to SNS in their relationships. When an issue occurs, couples go through a process of identifying the specific problematic online behavior, followed by an *Appraisal* process during which each partner considers the behavior within the context of their implicit or explicit rules—attempting to arrive at consensus about the perceived severity of the problem. After the *Appraisal* stage, couples move to the *Discussing Online Issue* and concerns about the behavior—including explanations and perspective sharing, or justifications. The process results in *Resolution*, relational *Consequences*, or the online issues continuing to occur.

As the process model reveals, most couples do not explicitly communicate rules or boundaries for SNS use as a preventative measure in their relationship. Our results reveal most couples are confronted with communicating about the online issue *after* issues arise. Among the most important findings of the current study is that partners were more likely to have created implicit rules for SNS behaviors. Even though couples discussed the inappropriate online behavior, discussions did not result in the creation of rules or boundaries. Our findings mirror the results of Murray et al. (2002), who found partners rarely develop spoken rules for acceptable behavior and that individual partners assumed their partner shared their views. In the current study, it is possible that couples did not develop rules because they couldn't come to consensus about which online behaviors were inappropriate. As Wilson et al. (2011) found, men and women tend to disagree about what are un/acceptable behaviors, especially related to infidelity.

Couples in our study revealed that a couple's communication strategy when addressing online issues—e.g., "justifications" and "providing further evidence"— impacted their ability to successfully resolve the problem, often leading to arguments. In the stage *Discussing Online Issues*, justifying behavior was a type of cognitive distortion, in which the accused partner aims to justify the behavior as nonproblematic. Ours were resonant of Mileham's (2007) findings in her ethnographic study of chat room affairs, where she found individuals often engaged in a behavioral rationalization, attempting to justify their behavior as morally acceptable. Similar to participants in our study, individuals often justified their behavior as a way to reduce its negative impact, and positioned the behavior in a way that it would have the least severe implications for the relationship.

Finally, in our study *Monitoring* was identified as both a consequence of and resolution to problematic Facebook behaviors, with many participants reporting having engaged in some form of monitoring behavior during their relationship. Similarly, Helsper and Whitty (2010) found that one in three participants reported having monitored their partner's online account. In another study of the impact of Facebook infidelity on offline relationships, Cravens and Whiting (in press) found that, even when a partner was engaging in an online affair, the non-participating partner was perceived as crossing a boundary by going on a partner's Facebook account. Taken together, these studies highlight the complexity of online monitoring in committed relationships.

One limitation of the current study was that the researchers were unable to utilize member checking, a process by which the researcher shares final results of the data analysis with participants to ensure the theoretical model reflects the participants' experiences (Charmaz, 2006). At the conclusion of each interview, participants were asked if the researcher could contact them for further information related to finalizing the results. Of the ten couples, only two agreed. Unfortunately, neither of the agreeing couples responded to the researcher's contact attempts, and thus we could not receive participant feedback on the validity of the developing model. A second limitation is generalizability. Our study participants were predominately white and in their 20s and early 30s. Although constructivist grounded theory methodology does not assume that results of the study are representative of everyone's experience, a more diverse sample of couples would likely have yielded more robust and illuminating results on how couples across life stages manage rules and boundaries in digital age relationships.

Application

The results of this study are applicable in both clinical and nonclinical settings. In the following, we will discuss: (1) how clinicians working with couples might use the results of this study to help couples address issues related to problematic SNS behaviors, and (2) how couples can benefit by creating rules about online behaviors.

Clinical Applications for Couples Therapy

The grounded theory model can be used to assist clinicians in understanding the communication process of couples when addressing problematic SNS behaviors. An important finding from the current study was how rarely couples reported establishing rules or boundaries, despite the fact that many had experienced an issue related to SNS use. Although all couples in the current study discussed having conversations about the online issue after it occurred, conversations did not result in establishing rules. Clinicians might encourage couples to have a conversation about what each partner would consider inappropriate online behavior and help them establish shared rules. Clinicians can facilitate the discussion in-session by asking questions similar to those asked in the semi-structured interviews of our study. Initially, clinicians might assess whether SNS have created relationship problems: "Have you had any issues related to SNS in your relationship? What impact have these issues had on your relationship?" And, "How were these issues resolved?" After an initial assessment, clinicians might then explore what each partner would consider an inappropriate online behavior, asking each partner: "What online behaviors would you find problematic if your partner were to engage in that specific behavior?" By exploring with each partner their responses, the couple and clinician can explore implicit rules individuals might have but have not yet shared with a partner.

Several of the couples reported not reaching consensus about which online behaviors crossed a boundary, often the catalyst for an argument. Clinicians can be prepared to help couples understand each other's perspectives about how and why specific behaviors might be perceived as problematic. Clinicians could ask each partner questions to get at beliefs about identified online behavior, such as: "I hear that this specific behavior is a concern for you. Can you please tell your partner what this behavior signifies to you? What are your concerns about this behavior; specifically what impact do you perceive it will have on you or your relationship if your partner should engage in it? What do you think has motivated you to create this rule?"

After assessing for previous issues with SNS behaviors and helping partners create explicit rules, the clinician can also focus on helping couples with basic communication skills. Several of the clinical-population couples reported they have had fewer issues with Facebook and their relationship since they started couples therapy. When asked how therapy had influenced the observed changes, couples discussed they were better able to talk about difficult issues because they had been given tools to bring up problems in a face-to-face context, instead of using Facebook to address such issues. Finally, couples in the current study that had experienced issues with Facebook mentioned that trust was still an issue.

Reestablishing trust will be a necessary step in counseling to help couples move forward after experiencing issues with SNS.

Creating Internet Rules within Intimate Partner Relationships

Couples therapy is one option for couples that have experienced online issues in their relationship; however, this option is typically employed only *after* a problem has occurred. Couples should consider using the findings of this study—and even the questions posed above for clinicians to use—to openly discuss rules and boundaries for online behaviors with their partner.

Couples can begin the discussion by having each partner share which online behaviors would be considered inappropriate within the context of their relationship. Partners should be as specific as possible when identifying problematic behaviors. Following this identification process, couples should explain why these behaviors are problematic and what consequences the partner perceives such behaviors might have on their relationship. Specifically, because the Internet offers users a myriad of opportunities to interact with people both known and unknown, couples are wise to focus their discussion on with whom partners can interact, in what ways, and what types of information can be shared. Couples should also be aware that research on SNS and relationships has identified that most often couples have issues related to partners interacting with ex-partners, sharing private information, and commenting on attractive users' photos (Clayton et al., 2013).

If couples struggle to identify specific problematic behaviors, they could begin a broad discussion about behaviors in general that might constitute a boundary violation in their relationship. They could then discuss whether these general rules can be applied to the Internet or if there are specific online behaviors that now must be considered. Researchers have found that, when considering offline violations relating to infidelity, only two categories are frequently cited: emotional and sexual. However, when considering Internet infidelity, a third category of pornography was identified (Whitty, 2005). Couples could specifically ask questions such as:

1. Are there any websites that you believe would be inappropriate for me to visit?
2. When using SNS, are there any groups of users or specific people with whom you would be uncomfortable with me interacting?
3. Is there any information you feel should or should not be posted online about me, you, or our relationship?
4. Do you consider pornography to be a violation of our relationship?

In addition to developing clear rules and boundaries for the Internet, the Process Model of Online Issues in Intimate Partner Relationships revealed that monitoring behaviors can result in both positive and negative relationship consequences. If couples decide to develop specific rules and boundaries for Internet use, they should discuss how these rules will be reinforced or monitored. Partners should be clear about whether or not each partner can have access to the other's Internet accounts, can check the other's browser history, or if they should have joint accounts. Research is mixed about monitoring behaviors: research reveals monitoring can increase trust in a relationship (Norton, 2011), and other research has found that monitoring behaviors lead to feelings of privacy violation, creating negative consequences for the relationship (Cravens & Whiting, in press). Thus, each couple must decide how or when monitoring behaviors would be used, if at all, in their relationship.

Finally couples in our study revealed that preventative barriers are specific factors (i.e., honesty, trust, and respect) that can reduce the negative impact of the digital age on their relationship. While such are commonly recognized positive attributes of healthy relationships, they can be specifically conceptualized in terms of SNS behaviors. The privacy that comes with SNS accounts may require that partners be honest with each other about the behaviors they are engaging in and that each partner respects the boundaries developed around Internet use. Couples must work to trust that a partner is abiding by the rules.

References

Argyle, M., & Henderson, M. (1985). *The Anatomy of relationships: Rules and skills needed to manage them successfully.* London: Pelican Books.

Charmaz, K. (2006). *Constructing grounded theory: A practical guide through qualitative analysis.* Thousand Oaks, CA: Sage.

Clayton, R. B., Nagurney, A., & Smith, J. R. (2013). Cheating, breakup, and divorce: Is Facebook to blame? *CyberPsychology, Behavior, and Social Networking, 16*(10), 717–720. doi:10.1089/cyber.2012.0424

Cooper, A., Månsoon, S., Daneback, K., Tikkanen, R., & Ross, M. W. (2003). Predicting the future of Internet sex: Online sexual activities in Sweden. *Sexual and Relationship Therapy, 18,* 277–291.

Cravens, J. D., Leckie, K. R., & Whiting, J. B. (2013). Facebook & infidelity: When poking becomes problematic. *Contemporary Family Therapy, 35,* 74–90.

Cravens, J. D., & Whiting, J. B. (in press). Fooling around on Facebook: The perceptions of infidelity behaviors on social networking sites. *Journal of Couple and Relationship Therapy.*

Creswell, J. W. (2007). *Qualitative inquiry and research design: Choosing among five approaches* (2nd ed.). Thousand Oaks, CA: Sage.

Daly, K. J. (2007). *Qualitative methods for family studies and human development.* Thousand Oaks, CA: Sage.

Daneback, K., Cooper, A., & Månsson, S. (2005). An Internet study of cybersex participants. *Archives of Sexual Behaviors, 34,* 321–328.

Elphinston, R. A., & Noller, P. (2011). Time to face it! Facebook intrusion and the implications for romantic jealousy and relationship satisfaction. *CyberPsychology, Behavior, & Social Networking, 14,* 631–635.

Helsper, E. J., & Whitty, M. T. (2010). Netiquette within married couples: Agreement about acceptable online behavior and surveillance between partners. *Computers in Human Behavior, 26,* 916–926.

Hertlein, K. M. (2012). Digital dwelling: Technology in couple and family relationships. *Family Relations, 61,* 374–387.

Hertlein, K. M., & Blumer, M. L. C. (2013). *The couple and family technology framework: Intimate relationships in a digital age.* New York: Routledge.

King, S. (1999). The impact of compulsive sexual behaviors on clergy marriages: Perspectives and concerns of the pastor's wife. *Sexual Addiction & Compulsivity, 10,* 193–199.

Lenhart, A., & Duggan, M. (2014). Couples, the Internet, and social media: How American couples use digital technology to manage life, logistics, and emotional intimacy in their relationships. *Pew Research Internet Project.* Retrieved from http://www.pewinternet.org/2014/02/11/couples-the-internet-and-social-media/

Mileham, B. (2007). Online infidelity in Internet chat rooms: An ethnographic exploration. *Computers in Human Behavior, 23,* 11–31.

Murray, S. L., Holmes, J. G., Bellavia, G., Griffin, D. W., & Dolderman, D. (2002). Kindred spirits? The benefits of egocentrism in close relationships. *Journal of Personality and School Psychology, 82,* 563–581.

Norton, A. M. (2011). Internet boundaries for social networking: Impact of trust and satisfaction. (Master's thesis, Kansas State University, Manhattan, KS).

Parker, T. S., & Wampler, K. S. (2003). How bad is it? Perceptions of relationship impact of different types of Internet sex activities. *Contemporary Family Therapy, 25,* 415–429.

Petronio, S. (2002). Boundaries of privacy: Dialectics of disclosure. Albany: State University of New York Press.

Pettigrew, J. (2009). Text messaging and connectedness within close interpersonal relationships. *Marriage & Family Review, 45,* 697–716.

Pew Internet and American Life Project. (2006). *Online dating.* Retrieved from http//:www.pewinternet.org/pdfs/PIP_Online_Dating.pdf

Pew Internet and American Life Project. (2014). Mobile technology fact sheet. Retrieved from http://www.pewinternet.org/fact-sheets/mobile-technology-fact-sheet/

Roscoe, B., Cavanaugh, L. E., & Kennedy, D. R. (1988). Dating infidelity: Behaviors, reasons and consequences. *Adolescence, 23,* 34–43.

Ross, M. W., & Kauth, M. R. (2002). Men who have sex with men, and the Internet: Emerging clinical issues and their management. In A. Cooper (Ed.), *Sex and the Internet: A guidebook for clinicians* (pp. 47–69). New York: Brunner-Routledge.

Schneider, J. P. (2003). The impact of compulsive cybersex on the family. *Sexual Relationship Therapy, 18*, 329–354.

Sidelinger, R. J., Ayash, G., Godorhazy, A., & Tibbles, D. (2008). Couples go online: Relational maintenance behaviors and relational characteristics use in dating relationships. *Human Communication, 11,* 341–355.

Spears, R., & Lea, M. (1994). Panacea or panopticon? The hidden power in computer-mediated communication. *Communication Research, 21,* 427–459.

Whitty, M. T. (2003). Pushing the wrong buttons: Men's and women's attitudes toward online and offline infidelity. *CyberPsychology and Behavior, 6,* 569–579.

Whitty, M. T. (2005). The realness of cybercheating: Men's and women's representations of unfaithful Internet relationships. *Social Science Computer Review, 23,* 57–67.

Wilson, K., Mattingly, B. A., Clark, E. M., Weidler, D. J., & Bequette, A. W. (2011). The gray area: Exploring attitudes toward infidelity and the development of the Perceptions of Dating Infidelity Scale. *The Journal of Social Psychology, 151*(1), 63–86.

Wilson, L. L., Roloff, M. E., & Carey, C. M. (1998). Boundary rules: Factors that inhibit expressing concerns about another's romantic relationship. *Communication Research, 25*, 618–640.

Yarab, P. E., Allgeier, E. R., & Sensibaugh, C. C. (1999). Looking deeper: Extradyadic behaviors, jealousy, and perceived unfaithfulness in hypothetical dating relationships. *Personal Relationships, 6,* 305–316.

15

Creating Couples' Identities

Telling and Distorting via "Wedsite" Relationship Narratives

LAURA BETH DAWS

Southern Polytechnic State University

Introduction

Lindsey and Chris met in college, and after a few years of dating exclusively they decided to get married. Upon getting engaged, Lindsey immediately created a website to share the details of the upcoming wedding with their friends and family. Such a website is also known as a "wedsite" (Daws, 2009). Lindsey and Chris's wedsite was informative for wedding guests: It contained information about where and when the ceremony and reception would be located, where the couple was registered for gifts, who was in their bridal party, and suggested hotels for out-of-town wedding guests. But there was other information on the site indicating they didn't create the site *only* to share the details of their upcoming wedding. For example, visitors had the option to take a quiz about the couple with questions such as "What's Lindsey's favorite food? What's Chris's hometown? What's Lindsey's and Chris's height difference?" The "about us quiz" was designed to test friends' and family members' knowledge of the couple they'd soon be supporting at a wedding. In this case, the wedsite went beyond the pragmatic function of a cost-effective, efficient way to keep guests informed of the details of their wedding.

Another engaged couple, Casey and Tommy, also chose to create a wedsite. Like Lindsey and Chris's, their wedsite communicated important information about their upcoming wedding and contained many of the same informative features such as dates, times, and locations. Their wedsite also revealed performative elements of the upcoming wedding ceremony. Casey and Tommy referred to their "Bridesmaids and Groomsmen" as the "Cast and Crew." Much like a stage performance, the important players were given roles and brief descriptions of their qualifications for performing in their wedding. The wedding was framed as a performance, fitting because Casey and Tommy frequently performed at regional Renaissance Faires. In fact, the couple became engaged during one such faire performance. Casey recalls that day: "(Tommy) was (on stage and) dressed as a pirate. And he was talking about how he'd been searching his whole life for 'the greatest treasure in all the world!' and (he) finally found it. And, (he pointed at her and said) 'here, she's over here!' He pulled me up on stage and it was very sweet." He then presented her with an engagement ring and proposed.

These two examples demonstrate how wedsites are often used by couples getting married to convey practical information or to preview for wedding guests the style and level of formality of the upcoming wedding and/or the personal tastes of the soon-to-be bride, but wedsites are also used to deceive. Alexis used her wedsite to maintain a lie she originally told her parents about her relationship. Alexis' parents were not aware she was living with her boyfriend of 3 years at the time he proposed. In fact, Alexis explained, had they found out about her living arrangements they would not have paid for the wedding. As such, when Alexis wrote the narrative for her wedsite, she was extremely careful not to reveal that her fiancé proposed at their shared home. Alexis carefully constructed and edited the wedsite narrative to sound as if they lived apart. She told the online lie to preserve the relationship with her parents, even though all of her friends reading the story knew she'd written a lie.

These three examples highlight an important issue facing family communication today: Using the Internet to disclose personal identifying information can strengthen or threaten familial relationships. Romantic partnerships are generally formed in social contexts outside the direct supervision of immediate family members, and as this chapter will show, there are times adult children feel compelled to maintain or create a lie for parents, extended family, or others in their social networks about aspects of their engaged/romantic relationships. This chapter will explain how wedsites simultaneously communicate factual, truthful information as well as distorted stories designed to help couples fit societal or familial norms. In carefully crafting narrative content for their wedsites, individuals engage in the online performance of identity during a time in which their individual identities are shifting from "single" to "married."

What Is a Wedsite?

As mentioned, wedsites are Web pages created in conjunction with an upcoming wedding. Currently, the wedding industry has no statistics available indicating the popularity of wedsites. However, a simple Internet search in summer 2014, using the keywords "wedding websites," produced 353 million results and revealed at least eight online companies currently offering to host or help create wedsites, some for free, some for a fee, and many with predesigned templates. They are commonly hosted on sites like weddingwire.com and theknot.com, and wedsite hosts primarily target brides instead of grooms or couples.

Wedsites serve many pragmatic functions. They are an efficient, cost-effective way to share information about an upcoming wedding. Dates, times, and locations of ceremonial and reception-related events are usually shared on wedsites, along with information for out-of-town guests about hotels, attractions, and weather forecasts. Often, wedsites offer descriptive information about the bridesmaids and groomsmen. More complex wedsites also have interactive features such as guest books, informational polls, song request forms, and the ability to RSVP for the wedding and related events. Consistent with what would be expected on a well-designed website, wedsites contain both narrative and visual information—the latter in the form of pictures, graphics, and color schemes matching the style and level of formality a guest could expect at the wedding.

However, wedsites serve more than just a pragmatic function for couples and their invited guests. A close examination of interview data with brides and corresponding narratives on their wedsites, specifically those about the couple, reveal much about online identity presentations. In such narratives, couples solidify the details of their relationship for friends and family. In heterosexual relationships, the responsibility for creating the wedsite generally falls to the bride, consistent with the cultural gender role expectation that women do most of the physical and emotional labor associated with a relationship (Ferree, 1990; Haas, 1999; Hochschild & Machung, 2003) and planning the wedding (Humble, Zvonkovic, & Walker 2008; Sniezek, 2005). Not surprisingly, most wedsites are created by women. An examination of wedsites in this chapter will reveal how women appear to be seizing the opportunity to create narratives that justify how they (the bride- and groom-to-be)—as well as their wedding itself—fit normative expectations, and further how their gender role performances are in sync with cultural expectations of heterosexual relationships.

Wedsites are a venue for sharing a couple's story to important others and, in doing so, permits the couple or the partner who creates the site to maintain or transform (Carey, 1989) each partner's individual identity and/or their identity as a couple. The tension between maintaining an existing identity while simultaneously transforming that identity to fit social norms, family expectations, and the changes that come with getting married serves as an interesting context for studying online deception. What happens when part of a person's relationship has been kept secret from an important other and suddenly he or she must decide whether to disclose the secret online? Could online narratives be used to both reinforce the "truth" of a relationship and simultaneously deceive others in an effort to preserve family expectations or adhere to social norms? A growing body of literature on the presentation of the self, performativity, and the online world offers a starting point from which to study these and similar questions.

Identity Presentation Online: A Literature Review

Performativity and Online Communication

Performativity (Butler, 1999) suggests that mundane or routine actions, thoughts, conversations, and habits help create and maintain social reality. Even the most taken-for-granted action carries meaning, is value-laden, and is a result of socialization. Thus, every social interaction has social significance. This theoretical framework has been applied to communication in both face-to-face interactions (Little, 2002; Maltz, 1998) and online communication (Charles, 2007; Maltz, 1998; Payne, 2007). Performativity in the online communicative context is important to examine; like all aspects of our identities, computer-meditated interactions are a process of creating and negotiating who we are, what we value, and where we fit in the world (Bagozzi, Dholakia, & Klein Pearo, 2007; Coon Sells, 2013; Davidovici-Nora, 2009; Hine, 2001; Matic, 2011; Phillips, 2002; Rolland, 2013).

Butler (1999) suggested that gendered identities are performed: Gender isn't a characteristic people possess; rather gender reflects the repeated actions of people. Like all identities, gender is learned and coconstructed through interactions with others and reinforced in everyday actions. Butler argues that cultural discourses and routine behaviors normalize and maintain a dichotomous (masculine/feminine) gender scheme. Research suggests that gendered identities are presented and performed online, not just in face-to-face settings (Gomez, 2010). Gender identity is crucial to explore when studying weddings; in American culture, women are generally encouraged—starting at a very young age—to think about, look forward to, and begin planning their wedding. Media heavily influence and shape the heteronormative wedding ideal (White, 2011), thus reinforcing traditional notions of femininity, romance, chivalry, and gender performance.

Weddings, Online Identity Performance, and Deception

Identity performance on the Internet is complex. Online communication facilitates multiple opportunities for the presentation of self. Even under the guise of "anonymous" interactions, people who communicate online are creating an identity. Whether that identity is consistent with the identity presented in nonmediated interactions—as one might see on a professional social networking profile—or reflects a completely different "self"—as one might see in an online game avatar—it is largely up to the social actor to decide how and what to communicate online. Users rely on the Internet for multiple self-presentational goals: self-presentation of one's "true" self (Bargh, McKenna, & Fitzsimmons, 2002; Baym, 2000; DeHaan, Kuper, Magee, Bigelow, & Mustanski, 2013; Kennedy, 2006; McKenna, Green, & Gleason, 2002; Miller & Arnold, 2001; Ollier-Malaterre, Rothbard, & Berg, 2013; Ross, 2011); creating different identities or "selves" (Bullingham & Vasconcelos, 2013; Phillips, 2002); and lying about self (Whitty, 2008).

Online lying and deception, particularly about one's identity, has generated a substantial amount of research across multiple contexts: deception in online business relationships (Baker, 2002; Logsdon & Patterson, 2009); manipulating an identity on dating websites (Ellison, Heino, & Gibbs, 2006; Hall, Park, Song, & Cody, 2010; Yurchisin, Watchravesringkan, & McCabe, 2005); motivations for lying online (Huang & Yang, 2013; Utz, 2005); and the ways media might influence the probability of lying online (Utz, 2005; Whitty, Buchanan, Joinson, & Meredith, 2011). Researchers have also investigated motivations for children lying to parents (Jensen, Arnett, Feldman, & Cauffman, 2004), parents lying to children (Bustle, 2008), and computer-mediated communication within families (Goby, 2011), but little research currently exists in the area of online deception in family relationships or the couple-identity creation contexts. This chapter attempts to contribute to that literature, investigating a rather new context in which relational deception occurs online.

Online communication about weddings provides a ready context for examining the complex set of questions about identity performance, lying, and deception. Much research has explored mediated communication and weddings, with particular emphasis on the ways media messages influence the cultural expectations and norms surrounding weddings (Engstrom & Semic, 2003; Engstrom, 2008; Engstrom, 2012; Ingraham, 1999; Lewin, 2004; Mead, 2007; Otnes & Pleck, 2003; Patterson, 2005; Yep & Camacho, 2004). There is a substantial body of literature indicating weddings are cultural rituals that reinforce and transform personal identities (Dean, 2011; Dunak, 2009; Leeds-Hurwitz, 2002; Morrill, 2012; Sharaby, 2006). However, little attention has been given to the ways individuals getting married use mass media—specifically the Internet—for the construction of relationship narratives, which in turn also influence the construction of identities. Wedsites offer an avenue from which to study that phenomenon.

Wedsites are worthy of study for several reasons. First, wedsites offer a way to examine a central aspect of a person's identity: the views an individual has of perhaps his or her most important personal relationship during a crucial time of identity articulation. Weddings offer those participating in the cultural ritual of the wedding an opportunity to reinforce and express personal and cultural identities (Dean, 2011; Dunak, 2009; Leeds-Hurwitz, 2002; Morrill, 2012; Sharaby, 2006). Second, talking with those who create wedsites can shed light on how narratives help construct an identity online. Third, wedsites offer an interesting site from which to study mediated deception, specifically as the creator(s) desire to communicate only those aspects of identity consistent with normative social expectations—assuring the rest of the world the couple is happy, in love, and "normal." As such, the questions guiding this research are:

RQ1: How do relationship narratives on wedsites facilitate the production, maintenance, and/or transformation of a couple's identity?

RQ2: What are the motives for lying about elements of a couple's identity on wedsites?

This research will demonstrate that there are two major factors guiding decisions women make in the construction of narratives on wedsites: the desire to appear "normal" to others, and the desire to maintain lies previously told to families members about the details of a relationship. This work will also demonstrate how, in making decisions under those guidelines, wedsites reinforce dominant ideological beliefs regarding gender performance and gender expectations, as well as those regarding traditional, conservative, heteronormative relationships.

Methodology

To answer the research questions, I conducted in-depth photo-elicitation interviews (Lindlof & Taylor, 2009; Harper, 2002) with women who were actively planning a wedding and who had created a wedsite. Full understanding of a social phenomenon requires a researcher's commitment to seeking in-depth knowledge from the perspective of the social actors involved. Qualitative research methods, which emphasize understanding meaning of everyday interactions, are well suited for this approach (Lindlof & Taylor, 2009). Previous research has demonstrated the ability to gain an understanding of the meaning of online communication by interviewing those who create Web content (Hine, 2001; Papacharissi, 2002).

Photo-elicitation involves the use of a visual prompt in an interview to obtain more in-depth information from respondents than allowed in a traditional face-to-face interview without a prompt. In the current study, the technique involved the researcher beginning the interview in the traditional analytic style (Lindlof & Taylor, 2009), and after establishing rapport with the respondent, the interview moved to the photo-elicitation tradition. As pictures "portray the intimate dimensions of the social family or other intimate social group" (Harper, 2002, p. 13), photo-elicitation studies often result in clear, detailed responses and are useful when investigating identity (Gauntlett & Holzwarth, 2007; Harper, 2002) and when the researcher hopes to generate detail about individual experiences (Frith & Harcourt, 2007; Thomson & Gunter, 2007). In the photo-elicitation part of the interview, the researcher used an Internet-connected laptop computer to view the respondent's wedsite via a Web browser. Interview questions then focused on eliciting the respondent's decisions made when creating the wedsite.

In total, I interviewed 28 women in heterosexual relationships who were actively planning a wedding and who had created a wedsite. Opting to interview only women in heterosexual relationships was a purposeful choice. Given that women are traditionally responsible for the emotional and physical labor associated with wedding planning (Humble, Zvonkovic, & Walker 2008; Sniezek, 2005), it made sense that more women than men were ultimately responsible for the creation of the couple's wedsite. Only women in heterosexual couples were included, to increase understanding of gendered cultural expectations of traditional femininity in relationship to masculinity, as those identities were performed in the context of weddings.

Participants were recruited in a number of ways. First, with permission from forum moderators, a call was posted for study participants on two popular online wedding forums: theknot.com and offbeatbride.com. Those two sites were chosen because of the significant number of women who participate in their daily forums to discuss wedding planning. Further, women who consider themselves "traditional" brides, planning weddings consistent with cultural norms surrounding weddings, tend to gravitate to forum discussions on theknot.com, while women planning weddings they feel are nontraditional in some way tend to gravitate to offbeatbride.com. Including women from both forums offered data more representative of the diverse approaches to wedding planning. The postings resulted in 10 of the 28 participants: six from theknot.com and four from offbeatbride.com.

Four participants were recruited from a large Southern U.S. university. Personal referrals and snowball sampling procedures were used to recruit additional participants. Colleagues referred qualified individuals, which resulted in 12 additional respondents. At the close of each interview, I used a snowball sampling technique and asked the interviewee if she knew any other women who might be interested in participating. In those cases, I made initial contact with the potential respondent. These procedures resulted in two additional respondents.

Participants ranged in age from 21 to 29, were all white, in heterosexual relationships, and living in cities across the Southeast United States. Budgets for their weddings ranged from $800 to $35,000. Fifteen of the participants were undergraduate or graduate students (12 of whom were also working part or full time), and thirteen were working professionals in the areas of law, medicine, and service industries. Participants were not financially compensated for their participation. IRB approval was obtained before the study began, and each participant signed an informed consent form before beginning the interview.

Each interview was recorded with a digital voice recorder and later transcribed verbatim by the researcher. Interviews averaged one hour, 25 minutes, 14 seconds, with a total of 42 hours, 36 minutes and 57 seconds of interview data. Once the transcripts had been typed and printed, the resulting data was 866 single-spaced pages. Narratives on the 28 unique wedding-related websites were used to verify information learned in the interviews.

Data analysis took place in several phases. First, in-process analytical notes (Lindlof & Taylor, 2009) were taken during the transcription process to help form emergent themes later. Once all interviews were completed, I read through the 866 single-spaced pages of interview transcripts following Lindlof and Taylor's (2009) recommendations for open coding. As they note, beginning with open coding in initial analysis accommodates creativity and flexibility. Later, I refined the data and developed a formal codebook. During the initial coding process, I searched for commonalities in the data, then created a final codebook based on emergent themes arising from the data. The interpretive process required careful attention not only to what interview respondents explicitly stated but also to what was implied within the context of the conversation.

After the initial round of coding, data were read one more time to further refine the codebook. Thus, open coding led to a refinement of categories of data, which then provided answers to the research questions. Ultimately, data were categorized into eight main themes with three subthemes for each category. Two of those main themes and six subthemes will be presented in the results section. These two themes provide data that best answer my research questions.

Results

The current study sought to answer questions about how relationship narratives on wedsites facilitate the production, maintenance, and/or transformation of a couple's identity, with particular focus on motives for instances of lying on wedsites. Data analysis of interviews revealed that wedsites facilitated the construction of a couple's shared identity through narratives about how they met and how they got engaged. Among the emergent themes that arose from data analysis, two broad themes answered the primary research questions guiding this study: (1) the desire to communicate a shared identity to a public audience for the purposes of generating social support; and (2) the desire to appear to adhere to traditional, heteronormative relationship expectations.

Constructing a Shared Identity on Wedsites for Social Support

A description of the couple on a wedsite marked the first time the couple was publicly introduced to the world. Constructing a wedsite meant the simultaneous construction of the identity for the couple as a soon-to-be-married unit. Women told the story of who they were as a couple not just through narratives but even more through pictures that were carefully selected to communicate the most positive aspects of the couple's relationship.

Selection of pictures. Another subcategory in the theme of identity construction came from the bride's choice of pictures for the wedsite. Sarah shared that at the time of the interview, she had not yet met her fiancé's mother. However, she knew his mom would eventually look at the site. When she chose pictures to go on the site, she chose "pictures that, where he looked happy, and we look happy, and [his mother] can look at them and go, 'I haven't met her, but she looks like a nice person. He makes her happy and she makes him happy.' So that's the only reason for certain photos." Similarly, Alyssa shared pictures in which she and her fiancé looked happy, because she felt the purpose of wedsites was partially to find out "why [couples] are right for each other." Alyssa also discussed making sure her narrative content focused on the similarities in their personalities, evidence to further reinforce to others that they belonged together.

Jayme posted pictures she felt best represented her relationship with her fiancé, with particular emphasis on pictures in which she and her fiancé looked happy. She said her wedsite was "an outlet to show people about us, and how much we love each other, and how much fun we have, and how we're right for each other." Similarly, Carrie had a gallery of photographs on her wedsite ranging from casual snapshots taken during her and her fiancé's time in college together to professionally done engagement photographs. She included them to "show who we are; the different stuff we're doing." Megan agreed that the pictures and content she wrote would make people who knew them very well agree, "that's very 'them.' And people who don't know us will get an idea of [who we are]."

All participants reported purposefully selecting photographs they felt best represented the couple as happy, which was the most important shared identity characteristic to portray on their wedsites. Despite the differences in personalities, style, or approaches to wedding planning, every bride in this study discussed the importance of communicating a shared identity as a couple that had common interests and enjoyed spending time together. The amount of time spent selecting and sharing pictures of the couple suggests brides felt it important for site visitors to believe the couples were right for each other, and they did so in an effort to generate social support from important others.

Social support for shared identity. Participants' comments consistently revealed how wedsites operate as a vehicle for generating social support even before the wedding ceremony—where social support is typically and overwhelmingly displayed. Brides reported expecting to hear positive feedback about their wedsites, either verbally or publicly via the site itself. For instance, Meredith admitted her wedsite was "an outlet…[for] people that support us; with the guest book people can say, 'oh we're excited for you!' It kind of lets everyone know that everyone's behind us." Online guest books were used as publicly viewable areas for visitors to the wedsite to leave comments about the site, the wedding, or the couple. At 21, Megan was the youngest bride-to-be in the sample and admitted often feeling judged by others—when they questioned her in person—for marrying so young. However, her wedsite guest book contained only positive comments, a form of support for her decision to marry her boyfriend of 5 years.

Guest books were not the only venue for wedsite visitors to offer positive feedback. Visible counters were common, displaying how many unique visits had been made to the site. Deborah was one of the few respondents who did not publicly display a tally of how many views her site generated, but she did use analytics to determine how many views the site gathered—something brides interpreted as social support or lack thereof (if the number of visits wasn't perceived as high). Brides were concerned about how many people viewed their sites, admitting they wanted everyone with whom they shared the site to interact with it some way. Women's level of feeling validated—feeling supported—was perceived as related to the number of views the site had, the number of guest book comments, and the number of people who interacted with the site via other features.

Data analysis further revealed that, on their wedsites, brides purposefully highlighted the most positive aspects of their relationship with their fiancé in an effort to generate social support and, as is addressed further in the discussion section, to attempt to meet normative expectations about relationships. Brides admitted carefully selecting information about themselves and their relationships to be shared via their narratives and pictures, most of which was consistent with an identity that close family members and friends knew. However, 11 out of 28 brides admitted they were not completely truthful about one or more aspects of their identities as a couple or about the circumstances surrounding their wedding. The next section reveals the second emergent theme, the types of lies told on wedsites, and is followed by a discussion of motivations for brides' wedsite deceptions.

Types of Lies on Wedsites

Data analysis revealed three categories of lies told by brides on their wedsites: (1) lies about the couple's lifestyle choices; (2) lies about the couple's living arrangements; and (3) lies about the bride's feelings about her fiancé's proposal.

Lifestyle choices. Despite a large amount of self-disclosure on wedsites, five brides chose to edit their narratives to hide specific lifestyle choices—most commonly behavior related to alcohol consumption. Lying about drinking habits was to preserve parents' perceptions of the couple as "sober" or because brides did not want to disclose to parents they had engaged in underage drinking or drinking during college. Brides revealed alcohol was a taboo topic in some families, to the point that women were expected to create wedsite narratives reflecting the couple's sobriety even if recreational and safe alcohol consumption was a routine part of the couple's life.

Lindsey recalled writing the part of their wedsite about her fiancé Chris's hobbies, one being that he is a bourbon aficionado. In Lexington, Kentucky, where this couple resided, bourbon drinking was a popular activity among their friend group; Lindsey and Chris were also both of legal drinking age at the time of their engagement. When she showed Chris the wedsite for the first time, he asked her to omit any evidence that he drank alcohol. She explained:

> His dad's family doesn't really believe in drinking, and I guess they had a major problem with him drinking. *They* drink all the time; they just don't make it public. It's a religious [thing]; they're not Catholic, but their religion doesn't believe in drinking, so they act like it's a mortal sin, but they have whiskey in the closet. And I had put that he liked bourbon and wine tastings, and you know, he was like, "I'm going to sound like an alcoholic to my family."

When I asked her if the family would have an issue with alcohol at her wedding, she replied, "it's gonna be interesting. But we're just letting it go. It's who we are." Her explanations revealed the couple was experiencing tension between demonstrating who they really are as a couple—recreational consumers of alcohol—while attempting to honor his family's expectations that they would publicly appear sober for religious reasons.

Anne had a similar issue related to alcohol consumption, influencing her decision to maintain a previous lie she'd told her family about how the couple met. She explained:

> The "our story" [section on their wedsite was] hard to put together because I had to edit a lot. Because when we first met, it was at a party, and um, my parents didn't know how much I partied when I was in college. And, it was hard to edit because I think there's a lot of parts of our story that would stress my parents out.

Her family knew the couple met in college through mutual friends. However, the true story was that they had first met at a fraternity/sorority party on Saint Patrick's Day—a night she "got really drunk." Although they had not met before, Wes invited her to stay in his room since she was too drunk to make it home. Anne passed out in his bed, fully clothed, and when she woke up she realized what had happened. She felt relieved when she realized Wes "didn't take advantage of [me]; instead, he had just left his number and a note for me to call him, on a napkin." All of these details were intentionally not included on the wedsite.

Living arrangements. Generally, women who had been cohabiting with a partner before getting engaged were concerned about disclosing that fact on wedsites. Alyssa's mom requested she edit her proposal narrative to leave out the fact that her boyfriend—now fiancé—had spent the night at the parents' home before the proposal. Alyssa explained: "He has a 'cot,' you know, or an air mattress [at my parents' house]. Which my mom's like, 'don't tell people that he did it in the morning in your room!' And I'm like, 'oh my God, Mom, people don't care. No one would even worry about that besides you.'"

Alexis ran into similar issues regarding more permanent living arrangements with her fiancé. After living with her fiancé for 3 years, Alexis admitted that her "mom still doesn't know he lives with me. So it's, like, a big lie. They know he 'comes and visits' me on the weekends, and he apparently stays with a friend Monday through Friday, which is obviously not true.…I know it's not really the right thing to do, but I'm so thankful for the experience we've had living together." Alexis's parents "actually threatened to not give us a wedding." She took great care to edit her proposal story to make it seem like she and her fiancé did not live together, just to keep her parents in the dark. "On the bottom down here I have that he came to visit me—then 'he came for a surprise visit' (and he'd) 'put me to bed'" before sending her Chihuahua upstairs with a proposal note and a ring tied to her collar. Alexis admitted that "all my friends know that I'm bullshitting" on the wedsite, but she edited the story to preserve the relationship she had with her parents. Further, Alexis expressed concern that her parents would not help her pay for her $10,000 wedding if they found out they lived together. To Alexis, it was a very important reason to keep secret that aspect of their relationship.

Anne's situation was slightly different. Her parents knew she was living with her fiancé, and they disapproved of the living arrangements. Thus, she opted not to include any information about their living arrangements on the wedsite, even though they had shared a house and a life together for several years. "When I moved in with Wes, my parents didn't talk to me for a month. And the rest of the family decided not to talk to me either. And then they all got over it." After they got engaged, she explained that her parents "felt about a million times better. And it turns out, [Wes had] actually snuck away at Thanksgiving to talk to my dad first about it, which just made it even better. So, everything worked out. Almost, pretty much perfectly, I can't imagine it being much better. Because it'd been really hard for him…my family was not happy about the whole living-together situation. I come from a very, very conservative, religious family."

Proposal narratives. Women revealed experiencing social pressure to make their own proposal story match cultural expectations of proposal stories: Specifically, proposals needed to demonstrate the future husband attempted to surprise the future bride; the proposal story needed to demonstrate elements of uniqueness of method or approach; and the story needed to contain elements of chivalry, masculinity, and romance. Some respondents' proposal narratives fit normative expectations—that a marriage proposal was an elaborate, romantic, chivalrous, and surprise event with fairytale elements—and those women whose fiancés proposed in such a way had no problem disclosing the exact details of the story on their wedsite. Meredith's face lit up as she recalled the story of the "most romantic night of her life"—a proposal on a boat, at night, with a bottle of wine and a steak dinner. Denise admitted she relished writing every detail about the elaborate, complicated beach proposal that took her fiancé two days to effectively complete. Sarah's fiancé proposed without warning in their newly purchased house, with promises to build a life together there. These stories contained elements of the stereotypical, chivalrous, fairytale proposal and revealed little about their outside life other than that they were happy, in love, and that their fiancés played their culturally expected role. These proposal narratives also fit the normative expectation that men are supposed to plan a proposal that women are proud to share.

However, some respondents were not pleased with how their partners proposed. Common reasons for disappointment included someone ruining the surprise ahead of time or displeasure with the setting in which the proposal took place. Even brides who were unhappy with the proposal reported feeling it was still important to edit the proposal part of their narrative to make it sound as if they were happy. In some cases, this meant lying about their feelings or even lying about how the proposal happened.

For example, Renee explained with sadness in her voice that the way in which her fiancé proposed was

> not [an] exciting story. He doesn't know this, but I knew that he'd gotten the ring. It was a Tuesday, and I honestly had this sick feeling. I felt like I was gonna pass out. And I get home, and I'm like, in tears, I feel so bad. And we live on the lake. And he was gonna take me down there to do it, but he, when he saw that I was in tears, he didn't know what else to do. So basically I was like, "I need some Tylenol." And he just came up (with the ring) and said 'what about this?' And I was like, what is that?! I wish it was more of a story, like we went down to the lake. I wish it would've been something so magical, you know?

Renee did not reveal her disappointment on the wedsite; instead, she gave a shortened version—edited to make her sound excited about the proposal her fiancé planned. She communicated excitement by the frequent use of exclamation marks in the story and by reminding readers she was excited about having an engagement ring. According to her, her fiancé still did not know she was upset about the way he proposed.

Rose felt that her story was "really stupid.... [Steve's] mother gave him an heirloom ring" to use in the proposal, but it was a ring she didn't like. Steve's sister told Rose that Steve had a ring and was about to propose; Rose then "got kinda drunk" and confronted Steve about when he was going to propose. His response: "I was waiting for the right time...so, ok, here you go." Rose felt she "kinda proposed to (her)self," which she admitted in the interview was also disappointing, in addition to being upset about the ring she did not want to wear. This was a story she didn't feel comfortable sharing on the wedsite for a number of reasons. She would have risked offending her future mother-in-law with her disdain for the ring. Also, Steve still didn't know that his sister "ruined" the surprise element he'd hoped for initially—information Rose thought could have been damaging to an otherwise positive brother–sister relationship.

In summary, many women freely communicated accurate, completely truthful details about their relationships, lives, and upcoming weddings online, especially when the details of their lives adhered to what brides perceived were normative expectations about relationships. Women tended to lie on their wedsites when they felt information could threaten family or other relationships, or when they felt some part of their story did not fit normative expectations regarding dominant cultural ideas about weddings or romance. As this research shows, even when women lied on their wedsites and other friends knew about the lies, they had very little fear that their lies would be uncovered or that their friends would tell those they were trying to protect by editing parts of their stories. Women in this sample overwhelmingly trusted their friends to keep secrets from family members who would have had a problem with their lifestyles or living arrangements. About proposal narratives, women felt it smart to keep their true feelings of displeasure to themselves, in most cases to avoid upsetting their future husbands.

Discussion

This study sought to answer the following research questions: How do relationship narratives on wedsites facilitate the production, maintenance, and/or transformation of a couple's identity? And what are the motives for lying about relationships on wedding wedsites? Analysis of interview data revealed that women constructed an identity for themselves and their fiancés online through the use of verbal and visual cues, primarily in the form of narratives and photographs. These elements allowed the women to perform an identity consistent with heteronormative expectations, familial expectations, and previous lies told to family members about the relationship. Such identities were maintained and validated by site visitors who left positive comments in guest books and used the interactive features available on the wedsites. Not only were women who created wedsites constructing an identity for the soon-to-be-married couple, so, too, were family members and friends who visited the site participating in the performance and cocreation of the newly constructed couple identity through publicly validating the wedsite content.

Using the theoretical framework of performativity to understand interview data, it becomes apparent that women carefully selected parts of their relationships with their fiancés to publicly display on their wedsites. They performed identities consistent with normative behavior, including the demonstration that the couple was "right" for each other, that the couple was happy, that the groom's proposal contained elements of surprise and romance (even when it didn't), and that the couple would be living together only after marriage. The ultimate factor in decisions about content—and identity construction—on wedsites was whether the information adhered to traditional notions of masculinity and femininity associated with relationships. Women chose to lie about their identity as a couple unit for similar reasons; in some cases, performing their true identities as a couple would have proven problematic for one or more family relationships, or would have appeared to violate traditional expectations for dating couples. Performance of an identity consistent with cultural norms resulted in positive, public feedback.

Interestingly, despite all of the disclosure on wedsites related to the couple's identity, no discussion of one crucial element to the identity transformation for women migrating from single to married appeared on any site: No bride discussed the issue of taking her new husband's last name upon marriage. In fact, when I asked respondents about this element of identity change upon marriage, many said they'd never given it any thought and had just assumed they would change their names upon marriage. Karen's response summed it up best. When asked about whether she would change her name, she, like the majority of respondents, admitted: "I don't know; I haven't given much thought to it. I guess I'll do whatever's normal. So, yeah, I guess I'll change it." Only two brides in the sample of 28 said they intended to keep their family-of-origin's name upon getting married. One was for professional reasons; the other was because "I'm getting married; I'm not becoming a new person." Although it would have been beyond the scope of the wedsite to disclose every element of a couple's new identity as newly married, it was of interest that even the two brides who intended to keep their maiden names made no mention of this violation of cultural norms on their wedsites.

Future Directions

Future research in this topic should explore same-sex couples' weddings and wedsites. Of particular interest would be research on the ways same-sex couples create narratives consistent with dominant ideological notions of love and romance, and on what are the differences in the way same-sex versus opposite sex couples communicate about their relationships. It would be interesting to have both members' perspectives on wedsite development and content. In heterosexual relationships—like those studied here—do brides and grooms have differing perceptions and thoughts on wedsites? Further, since many women today perform much of the emotional labor of wedding planning using the social media site Pinterest—a free site that allows users to collect ideas and images about their future weddings in the form of online message boards—researchers would be wise to explore the use of Pinterest and other social networking sites in the context of wedding planning, identity performance, and relationship negotiations. Much is yet to be understood about the way public discourse in the digital age influences couples' rituals and ceremonies, as well as their current and future relationship choices.

Conclusion

Wedsites give women the ability to communicate honestly—and distort—the truth about their relationships with their life partners. They cocreate shared meanings about their relationships using a number of symbolic strategies: the inclusion or exclusion of specific details of their life with their partners; the emphasis on the happiness the couple experienced together; and the extent to which they adhered to normative expectations relating to gender performance and the cultural performance of weddings and relationships. Although women recognize wedsites' power to communicate practical details of an upcoming wedding, it is through the telling of their relationship stories that they are able to also communicate that the couple is happy, in love, worthy of reinforcement from others for their decision, and ultimately acting in ways consistent with culturally sanctioned relationship expectations. When part of their story does not mesh with expectations, the bride takes creative liberty with the story and changes it, using the Internet as one tool with which to intentionally construct and express identity.

Application

This chapter explored the phenomenon of the wedsite, particularly how it goes beyond a pragmatic function in communicating the details of a wedding to offer the opportunity for engaged couples (primarily brides) to generate social support in ways consistent with normative expectations surrounding romance and relationships. The information presented here is especially useful for future brides, as well as families and friends of those couples.

Brides who are creating a wedsite should think critically about how their presentation of selves and their relationships online may impact family relationships. Any bride or fiancé creating a wedsite should talk to his or her partner to learn which relationship details both are comfortable sharing with family, important friends, and the public. Another level of conversation for couples is that of boundaries, specifically how relationship boundaries and communication patterns between the couple and any number of combinations of family members and friends might change after the wedding. If brides (or grooms) choose to disclose previously held secrets that might damage existing relationships, it is important both partners consider the ramifications of that level of sharing before the wedsite goes live.

Further, by the time a woman (in particular, given gendered cultural expectations) gets married, she has likely been the recipient of a multitude of messages encouraging her to dream of a "perfect" wedding that includes a romantic, chivalrous proposal story. Thus, there are likely a host of cultural and normative expectations she may feel she needs to meet, such as making sure the wedding day and all surrounding details are seemingly perfect. Since information about ideal weddings is so prevalent online, and a woman is likely to have seen other wedsites before creating her own, there is a good chance she may feel social pressure to edit her own narratives to fit what she feels is consistent with this prevailing notion of perfection, particularly because, as this research shows, other brides are also editing their narratives to make their stories sound ideal, even when they are not. As such, it is best for brides to resist the urge to engage in too much social comparison with others' wedsites.

Families and friends of couples getting married can also benefit from this research. It is important that those involved in the lives of the couple during their engagement understand the role of a wedsite as going beyond just communicating about the wedding. All brides in this study felt their wedsites were an important part of their weddings, and they desired public validation for not just the site but also the relationship itself. Supporters of the couple should remember to also take the wedsite seriously and use it as an opportunity to offer social support and encouragement to the couple embarking on a major life change.

References

Bagozzi, R. P., Dholakia, U. M., & Klein Pearo, L. R. (2007). Antecedents and consequences of online social interactions. *Media Psychology, 9,* 77–114.

Baker, C. R. (2002). Crime, fraud, and deceit on the Internet: Is there hyperreality in cyberspace? *Critical Perspectives on Accounting, 13,* 1–15.

Bargh, J. A., McKenna, K. Y. A., & Fitzsimmons, G. M. (2002). Can you see the real me? Activation and expression of the "true self" on the Internet. *Journal of Social Issues, 58,* 33–48. doi:10.1111/1540–4560.00247

Baym, N. (2000). *Tune in, log on: Soaps, fandom, and online community.* Thousand Oaks, CA: Sage.

Bullingham, L., & Vasconcelos, A. C. (2013). 'The presentation of self in the online world': Goffman and the study of online identities. *Journal of Information Science, 39*(1), 101–112. doi:10.1177/0165551512470051

Bustle, J. (2008, November). Honey, the dog ran away: Key aspects, situational exigencies, and motivating factors of parental deception. Paper presented at the meeting of the National Communication Association, San Diego, CA.

Butler, J. (1999). *Gender trouble: Feminism and the subversion of identity.* New York: Routledge.

Carey, J. (1989). *Communication as culture.* Boston, MA: Unwin-Hyman.

Charles, C. (2007). Digital media and 'girling' at an elite girls' school. *Learning, Media & Technology, 32,* 135–147.

Coon Sells, T. G. (2013). The construction of sexual identities in an online gay, lesbian, and bisexual bulletin board system. *Journal of Human Behavior in the Social Environment, 23*(8), 893–907.

Davidovici-Nora, M. (2009). The dynamics of co-creation in the video game industry: The case of World of Warcraft. *Communications & Strategies,* 73, 43–66.

Daws, L. B. (2009). Performance of gender identity on wedsites. Paper presented at the Association for Education in Journalism and Mass Communication annual conference, Chicago, IL.

Dean, J. J. (2011). The cultural construction of heterosexual identities. *Sociology Compass, 5*(8), 679–687.

DeHaan, S., Kuper, L. E., Magee, J. C., Bigelow, L., & Mustanski, B. S. (2013). The interplay between online and offline exploration of identities: A mixed-methods study with LGBT youth. *Journal of Sex Research, 50*(5), 421–434. doi:10.1080/00224499.2012.661489

Dunak, K. M. (2009). Ceremony and citizenship: African American weddings, 1945–60. *Gender & History, 21*(2), 402–424.

Ellison, N., Heino, R., & Gibbs, J. (2006). Managing impressions online: Self-presentation processes in the online dating environment. *Journal of Computer-Mediated Communication,* 415–441. doi:10.1111/j.1083-6101.2006.00020.x

Engstrom, E. (2008). Unraveling the knot: Political economy and cultural hegemony in wedding media. *Journal of Communication Inquiry, 32,* 60–82. doi:10.1177/0196859907306833

Engstrom, E. (2012). *The bride factory: Mass media portrayals of women and weddings.* New York: Peter Lang.

Engstrom, E., & Semic, B. (2003). Portrayal of religion in reality TV programming: Hegemony and the contemporary American wedding. *Journal of Media & Religion, 2,* 145–163. doi:10.1207/S15328415JMR0203_02

Ferree, M. M. (1990). Beyond separate spheres: Feminism and family research. *Journal of Marriage and Family, 52,* 866–884.

Frith, H., & Harcourt, D. (2007). Using photographs to capture women's experiences of chemotherapy: Reflecting on the method. *Qualitative Health Research, 17,* 1340–1350. doi:10.1177/1049732307308949

Gauntlett, D., & Holzwarth, P. (2006). Creative and visual methods for exploring identities. *Visual Studies, 21,* 82–91. doi:10.1080/14725860600613261

Goby, V. P. (2011). Psychological underpinnings of intrafamilial computer-mediated communication: A preliminary exploration of CMC uptake with parents and siblings. *CyberPsychology, Behavior, and Social Networking, 14*(6), 365–370. doi:10.1089/cyber/2010.0289

Gomez, A. G. (2010). Competing narratives, gender, and threaded identity in cyberspace. *Journal of Gender Studies, 19*(1), 27–42.

Haas, L. (1999). Families and work. In M. B. Sussman, S. K. Steinmetz, & G. W. Peterson (Eds.), *Handbook of marriage and the family* (2nd ed., pp. 571–612). New York: Plenum Press.

Hall, J. A., Park, N., Song, H., & Cody, M. J. (2010). Strategic misrepresentation in online dating: The effects of gender, self-monitoring, and personality traits. *Journal of Social & Personal Relationships, 27*(1), 117–135. doi10.1177/0265407509349633

Hancock, J. T. (2007). Digital deception: Why, when, and how people lie online. In A. N. Joinson, K. Y. A. McKenna, T. Postmes, & U. D. Reips (Eds.), *The Oxford Handbook of Internet Psychology* (pp. 289–301). Oxford, UK: Oxford University Press.

Harper, D. (2002). Talking about pictures: A case for photo elicitation. *Visual Studies, 17,* 13–26. doi:10.1080/14725860220137345

Hine, C. (2001). Web pages, authors, and audiences: The meaning of a mouse click. *Information, Communication & Society, 4,* 182–198.

Hochschild, A., & Machung, A. (2003). *The second shift.* New York: Penguin Books.

Huang, C. L., & Yang, S. C. (2013). A study of online misrepresentation, self-disclosure, cyber-relationship motives, and loneliness among teenagers in Taiwan. *Journal of Educational Computing Research, 48*(1), 1–18.

Humble, A. M., Zvonkovic, A. M., & Walker, A. J. (2008). "The royal we": Gender ideology, display, and assessment in wedding work. *Journal of Family Issues, 29,* 3–25. doi:10.1177/0192513X07305900

Ingraham, C. (1999). *White weddings: Romancing heterosexuality in popular culture.* London: Routledge.

Jensen, L. A., Arnett, J. J., Feldman, S., & Caufmann, E. (2004). The right to do wrong: Lying to parents among adolescents and emerging adults. *Journal of Youth and Adolescence, 33*(2), 101–112.

Kennedy, H. (2006). Beyond anonymity, or future directions for Internet identity research. *New Media & Society, 8,* 859–876. doi:10.1177/1461444806069641

Leeds-Hurwitz, W. (2002) *Wedding as text: Communicating cultural identities through ritual.* Mahwah, NJ: Erlbaum.

Lewin, E. (2004). Does marriage have a future? *Journal of Marriage and Family, 66,* 1000–1006. doi:10.1111/j.0022–2445.2004.00071.x

Lindlof, T. R., & Taylor, B. C. (2009). *Qualitative communication research methods* (3rd. ed.). Thousand Oaks, CA: Sage.

Little, J. (2002). Rural geography: Rural gender identity and the performance of masculinity and femininity in the countryside. *Progress in Human Geography, 26,* 665–670.

Logsdon, J. M., & Patterson, K. D. W. (2009). Deception in business networks: Is it easier to lie online? *Journal of Business Ethics, 90,* 537–549. doi:10.1007/s10551–010–0605-z

Lu, H. (2008). Sensation-seeking, Internet dependence, and online interpersonal deception. *CyberPsychology & Behavior, 11*(2), 227–231. doi:10.1089/cpb.2007.0053

Maltz, R. (1998). Real butch: The performance/performativity of male impersonation, drag kings, passing as male, and stone butch realness. *Journal of Gender Studies, 7,* 273–286.

Matic, I. (2011). The social construction of mediated experience and self-identity in social networking. *International Journal of Interdisciplinary Social Sciences, 5*(11), 13–21.

McKenna, K. Y. A., Green, A. S., & Gleason, M. E. J. (2002). Relationship formation on the Internet: What's the big attraction? *Journal of Social Issues, 58,* 9–31. doi:10.1111/1540–4560.00246

Mead, R. (2007). *One perfect day: The selling of the American wedding.* New York: Penguin Publishing.

Miller, H., & Arnold, J. (2001). Breaking away from grounded identity? Women academics on the Web. *CyberPsychology and Behavior, 4,* 95–108. doi:10.1089/10949310151088451

Morrill, B. T. (2012). Performing the rite of marriage: Agency, identity, and ideology. *Proceedings of the North American Academy for Liturgy,* 93–105.

Ollier-Malaterre, A., Rothbard, N. P., & Berg, J. M. (2013). When worlds collide in cyberspace: How boundary work in online social networks impacts professional relationships. *Academy of Management Review, 38*(4), 645–669. doi:10.5465/amr.2011.0235

Otnes, C. C., & Pleck, E. H. (2003). *Cinderella dreams: The allure of the lavish wedding.* Los Angeles: University of California Press.

Papacharissi, Z. (2002). The self online: The utility of personal home pages. *Journal of Broadcasting & Electronic Media, 46*, 346–368.

Patterson, L. (2005). Why are all the fat brides smiling? *Feminist Media Studies, 5*, 243–246.

Payne, R. (2007). Str8acting. *Social Semiotics, 17*, 525–538.

Phillips, D. J. (2002). Negotiating the digital closet: Online pseudonymity and the politics of sexual identity. *Information, Communication & Society, 5*, 406–424. doi:10.1080/13691180210159337

Rolland, S. E. (2013). The benefit of social media: Bulletin board focus groups as a tool for co-creation. *International Journal of Market Research, 55*(6), 809–827.

Ross, J. (2011). Traces of self: Online reflective practices and performances in higher education. *Teaching in Higher Education, 16*(1), 113–126. doi:10.1080/13565217.2011.530753

Sharaby, R. (2006). The bride's henna ritual: Symbols, meanings, and changes. *Nashim: A Journal of Jewish Women's Studies and Gender Issues, 11*, 11–42. doi:10.2979/NAS. 206.-.11.11

Sniezek, T. (2005). Is it our day or the bride's day? The division of wedding labor and its meaning for couples. *Qualitative Sociology, 28*, 215–234. doi:10.1007/s11133–005–63687

Thomson, P., & Gunter, H. (2007). The methodology of students-as-researchers: Valuing and using experience and expertise to develop methods. *Discourse: Studies in the Cultural Politics of Education, 28*, 327–342. doi:http://dx.doi.org/10.1080/01596300701458863

Utz, S. (2005). Types of deception and underlying motivation: What people think. *Social Science Computer Review, 23*, 49–56.

White, M. (2011). Engaged with eBay. *Feminist Media Studies, 11*(3), 303–319.

Whitty, M. T. (2008). Revealing the 'real' me, searching for the 'actual' you: Presentations of self on an Internet dating site. *Computers in Human Behavior, 24*, 1707–1723. doi:10.1016/j.chb.2007.07.002

Whitty, M. T., Buchanan, T., Joinson, A. N., & Meredith, A. (2011). Not all lies are spontaneous: An examination of deception across different modes of communication. *Journal of the American Society for Information Science and Technology, 63*(1), 208–216.

Yep, G., & Camacho, A. O. (2004). The normalization of heterogendered relations in *The Bachelor*. *Feminist Media Studies, 4*, 338–341.

Yurchisin, J., Watchravesringkan, K., McCabe, D. B. (2005). An exploration of identity re-creation in the context of Internet dating. *Social Behavior and Personality, 33*(8), 735–750.

Section Four

Parenting in a Digital Age

16

Social Context Influences on Parenting

A Theoretical Model of the Role of Social Media

Susan K. Walker
University of Minnesota

Introduction

Parents' use of the Internet and social media is now central to their daily problem solving, relationship maintenance, and parenting activities (Dworkin, Connell, & Doty, 2013; Plantin & Daneback, 2009; Takeuchi, 2011; Walker & Rudi, 2014; Wartella, Rideout, Lauricella, & Connell, 2013). While the direct impacts of parents' use of information and communication technologies (ICT) on their intimate relationships with children or on children's developmental outcomes are unclear (Hertlein, 2012), research strongly points to the role ICT play as a resource of support and influence to parents by connecting individuals and enabling parents access to information. Professionals now employ and design new social and informational technologies to promote parent learning, family engagement, and to build parents' connections (Hughes, Bowers, Mitchell, Curtiss, & Ebata, 2012).

As we advance ICT research in service to families, our explorations need to be grounded within theoretical frameworks that guide our understanding of new media's influence. Systems models related to ICT impacts on family life functioning in general (Lanigan, 2009) and family relationships specifically (Hertlein, 2012) have been offered, each articulating family structures and processes influenced by unique characteristics of new technologies and highlighting individual differences in use. To date, however, a model specific to technology use by parents and impacts on childrearing is absent. Given that parenting is greatly influenced by interactions within the social context (Luster & Ogakaki, 2007) and that the "social affordances" of the Internet (Bradner, Kellogg, & Erickson, 1999, p. 153) facilitate interpersonal connectivity, it is particularly fitting that a framework of parenting impacts be constructed that embraces new media's social potential.

Therefore, the aim of this chapter is to offer a theoretical model of parenting that suggests the role played by ICT in promoting social context interactions. First, ecological theory on parenting, which embraces the role of the social context, is reviewed. Then, research situating parents' ICT use in the ecological framework is summarized, providing evidence of new media's role in mobilizing social context resources influencing parenting. Factors that differentiate ICT use among parents and reflect characteristics of technology that mediate relational interactions are also summarized, offering important considerations for further development of the theoretical model. Finally, with assistance from Cochran's (1990) social network perspective of parenting in particular, a model of social context influences on parenting facilitated by ICT is proposed. The model unpacks parents' social contexts by articulating the structures and processes of their social relationships as influences on parenting quality, and highlights the real and potential roles played by social media in facilitating parents' social interactions. The chapter ends with suggestions for research and applications for the design of technology-rich platforms to promote effective parenting.

Ecological Perspectives on Human Development and Parenting

A foundation for considering social context influences on human development and parenting is Bronfenbrenner's (1995) bioecological perspective. Through a bioecological lens, individual behavior and growth is recognized as influenced by interacting systems, sensitive to change and to time, in which the individual is variably affected. Influence on development largely relates to qualities unique to the individual and to processes or "enduring forms of interaction in the immediate environment" (p. 620). Nested systems that contain interactions with others and in settings with proximal or distal relationship to the developing individual can have both direct and indirect impacts. The individual's *microsystem*, for example, includes connections with those most intimate, immediate, and consistent. The home and relationships with the child, coparent, and/or other family members are those most often cited within a parent's microsystem. *Mesosystem* influences occur with interactions of two or more settings of the microsystem (e.g., home and neighborhood) and can reinforce, validate, and conflict, contributing to growth. Barron (2006) suggests that development occurs as individuals take agency in identifying opportunities to extend learning from setting to setting across personal learning ecologies.

Distal influences—such as those of the parent's culture or presented through media—have indirect yet often potent effects through the flow of information across ties that interconnect individuals' systems of influence. For example, fathering practices may be shaped over time by public discussion of media messages and by the promotion of work–family policies that more strongly support women's nurturing roles in childrearing.

Determinants of Parenting

Belsky (1984) applied the ecological perspective to childrearing by analyzing the research literature and conceptualizing the determinants of parenting across three primary interacting spheres: the individual parent, his or her social context, and the child. Accordingly, parenting is influenced by individual characteristics of the parent including developmental history (e.g., how she or he was parented), personal traits that are fixed (e.g., gender, age), and malleable (e.g., emotional well-being, maturational level of development, knowledge). The child influences parenting and requires "fit" to the child's needs through factors unique to the child (e.g., developmental stage, health, temperament, gender). Reciprocal interactions with the child stimulate parent maturation and growth in understanding of self relative to others (the needs of the child) (Barnard & Solchany, 2002). When successful, parenting not only results in positive child outcomes and in healthy relationships between parent and child, but also in fostering the caregiver's own maturation and development. Relationships with others who share in caregiving (e.g., the co-parent) and consideration for the needs of other family members contribute to the parent's emotional and cognitive resources and to parenting behavior.

Interaction with the social context influences the parent through offers of support and resources that can shape, reinforce, and possibly thwart parenting. Information, advice, practical forms of assistance, and other types of contextual supports can help parents acquire a greater repertoire of relational skills, manage life stress, deepen and gain a more complex understanding of childrearing, and reinforce identification in the role (Azar, 2003). Messages from the social context about parenting that are reinforced across parents' settings shape parents' perceptions, knowledge, and responses to childrearing situations. The context can also help scaffold parents' movement to a higher level of functioning, provided such functioning is within their developmental reach based on existing capacities (Marineau & Segal, 2006; Vygotsky, 1978). Characteristics of the parent and of the child can shape parents' interactions with the social context. For example, events that cause a change in parents' personal identity and group association (e.g., divorce, the transition to parenthood) can affect changes in social context memberships (Bost, Cox, & Payne, 2002). Figure 16.1 depicts Belsky's multidimensional perspective of social context, parent, and child interactions that influence parenting behavior and the parent–child relationship.

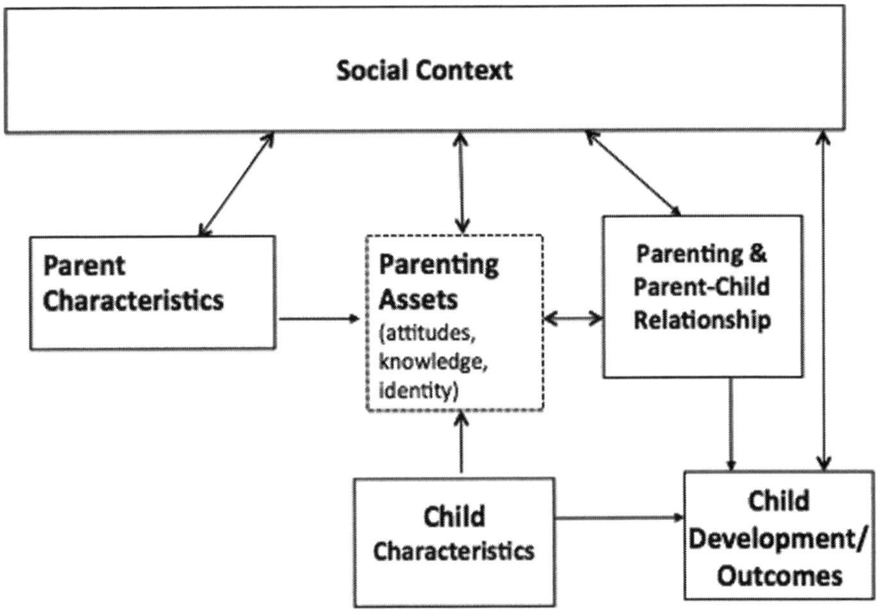

Figure 16.1. General model of parent–child context influences on parenting (adapted from Belsky, 1984).

Parenting Influences and Outcomes Suggested from Research on Parents' Use of ICT

Research to date on parents' ICT use suggests that a multideterminant, ecological framework of parenting is a suitable lens through which to understand parent motivations for the selection of ICT and the role ICT plays as an influence on parenting (Dworkin et al., 2013; Plantin & Danebeck, 2009). Recent research by this chapter's author (Walker and Rudi, 2014) analyzed parents' self-identified reasons for using a variety of new media coded into categories represented in Belsky's model. Data from a national online survey of parents (n = 1,804; see research citation and Connell, 2012 for details of the research project) were used for the study.

Use for Parenting, Family, and Social Context Connections

ICTs are used as a platform for maintaining the relationship between parent and child, and for the parent to fulfill parenting duties such as monitoring. Texting, email, and social media were most commonly cited for maintaining parent–child connections in the Walker and Rudi (2014) research. Parents used these media to communicate, offer emotional and cognitive nurturance, and stay connected to their children. Other research indicates that parents vary in their use of ICT for communication with the child, based on the child's age (Rudi, Dworkin, Walker, & Doty, 2014). Parents are more likely to use texting and social networking with adolescents, for example, than with young children. Parents may be more motivated to go online based on their child's age (e.g., mothers of preteens use technology as a way to monitor activity) (Wartella et al., 2013). Yet technological skill may play a part in parent use. Lack of comfort with and knowledge of social technologies can hamper parents' confidence in their ability to keep up with their adolescent children's online and offline lives (Palfrey, Gasser, & boyd, 2010; Yardi & Bruckman, 2011).

Family and coparenting relations are supported through parents' communication activities. In the Walker and Rudi (2014) study, 78% reported using email, 64% used voice over IP (e.g., Skype), 81% used Facebook, and 91% reported sharing photos as a means of communication with family members. As others have noted (Devitt & Roker, 2009; Wellman, Smith, Wells, & Kennedy, 2008), cell phones and shared Internet platforms are used to increase and enhance family connectedness. Social media is also used to connect with extended family (Rudi et al., 2014; see also Bruess, Li, & Polingo chapter in this volume). Yet, Tee, Brush, and Inkpen (2009) noted that although most parents expressed a desire for more communication and sharing with their extended family via ICT, many felt that an increase would be realistically difficult to achieve due to challenges such as busy schedules or extended family members' lack of technology use.

Regarding connections with the social context, a variety of media were used to connect with friends, as reported by parents in Walker and Rudi's (2014) study; more than two thirds reported using text, email, and social networking for this purpose. Parents reported reading blogs and newsletters to connect with professionals. And social networking and discussion boards were reported by more than half as ways to build the parents' social network. Other studies similarly identify social networking sites (SNS) like Facebook as frequently identified by parents for making contact with family, friends, and wider social connections (Bartholomew, Schoppe-Sullivan, Glassman, Kamp Dush, & Sullivan, 2012; McDaniel, Coyne, & Holmes, 2012; see also the Sharabi, Roache, & Pusateri chapter in this volume).

Use in Support of Parents' Learning, Well-being, and Development

Research suggests looking deeper than the explicit functions of devices used (e.g., cell phones for communication) to observe the relational resources being mobilized by these devices that may contribute to outcomes beneficial to parenting. For example, Hall and Irvine's (2008) analysis of mothers' exchanges in online forums revealed benefits of the Internet as a place for social interactions. Mothers could develop relational community connections, request and provide emotional support, facilitate their learning, and normalize their parenting experience. Discussed below, Walker and Rudi's (2014) analysis of parents' reasons for using IC revealed three direct benefits to their cognitive and emotional resources for parenting, with each of the three influenced by social interactions.

Acquisition of parenting knowledge. A predominant use of the Internet for parenting is in the search for information, especially about a child's health, to assist with problem solving and decision making (Dworkin et al., 2013). Walker and Rudi (2014) reported that 82% of parents reported gathering information on childrearing by searching the Internet, and 59% by reading newsletters. And such searches for information are tailored to the timing and developmental interests of parents. New parenthood, for instance, is an active time for online activity. Plantin and Daneback (2009) report that the majority (86%) of parents-to-be go online to find information about pregnancy and delivery. Yet, the online search for information about parenting is also a social enterprise. Parents vet the information with familiar and trusted sources of information such as their own parents and friends (Bernhardt & Felter, 2004; Radey & Randolph, 2009). Further, in the Walker & Rudi (2014) research, parents use discussion boards (85%), and read and comment on blogs (65%) as means for gathering information and advice. Parents reported that these applications help identify problems their child might be experiencing, and provide normative information on the child's behavior. One of the conclusions of the study was that parents might use a variety of ICT devices and applications to accomplish a particular parenting goal, in this case gathering information.

Parent well-being. Walker and Rudi's (2014) study revealed parent use of discussion boards and social networking as means of feeling validated in their parenting choices and beliefs, and to gain confidence. Though limited, other studies (e.g., Scharer, 2005; Blackburn & Read, 2005; O'Connor & Madge, 2004) indicate that parents' online exchange of information and emotional social support is largely positive and contributes to their emotional well-being and confidence in parenting.

Maturation and identity with the parenting role. Walker & Rudi (2014) also observed that parents express their views and gain diverse perspectives about parenting through discussion boards, social networking, and email. Qualitative and ethnographic research (Gibson and Hanson, 2013; Madge & O'Connor, 2006) of mothers' interactions in online discussion groups identifies the Internet as a safe space for women to try out their identities as new mothers and form judgments about appropriate parenting practices. McDaniel and colleagues (2012) report that mothers host blogs as a way to share experiences and insights about motherhood to both familiar and anonymous readers.

Overall, the literature suggests ICT acts as a vehicle for parenting within the ecology of childrearing, with ICT use influenced by family and social context dimensions that contribute to child development. And ICT facilitates support and resources to the parent in ways that appear to influence learning, feelings of well-being, and an identity and confidence with parenting.

Technological Considerations

Important to the construction of any model of human impacts by technology are considerations that characterize the unique qualities and capacities of new media (Hertlein, 2012). Three considerations appear important: individual differences in use, device differences and affordances, and use in spaces that are virtual and coordinated with offline ecologies.

Individual differences in use. Many factors influence the selection and behavior of individuals and families related to ICT (Dworkin et al., 2013; Lanigan, 2009; Plantin & Danebeck, 2009). Specific to parents, Walker, Dworkin, and Connell (2011) determined 10 different user groups based on parents' reports of technology use according to device access and ownership, preference for use, and attitudes. Group types ranged from parents who were hyperconnected through frequent use of many types of technologies and who possessed highly positive attitudes about technology, to others with more moderate attitudes or who preferred to use technology on an as-needed basis (e.g., primarily as a communication device); still others revealed minimal use, with possibly negative attitudes toward technology.

Access to devices may be limited by economics, location, or language, although socioeconomic status seems less of a digital dividing point for parents than comfort with use and attitude (Doty, Dworkin, & Connell, 2012). Lack of digital experience, computer skills, and usage opportunities are dimensions of the division. As such these technological limitations can affect attitudes and use in general, use for specific purposes (e.g., as previously noted in parents' use of social networking with their teens, Palfrey et al., 2010), or use of information found online (Ham & Walker, 2012).

Device differences and affordances. The Internet allows connections with more and different people, more quickly, and the ability to share information across large numbers of people in different networks. The text-based nature of communication means that less visual information about socioeconomic status and the physical self is conveyed. Communication scholars have documented that online information sharing and communication may be *hyperpersonal,* in other words, even more social and intimate than face-to-face communication (Walther & Parks, 2002). Because human interactions are expressed through online ecologies, expressions of support are more cognitive (e.g., information and advice) and emotion-based than face-to-face support that includes offers of practical aid.

Therefore, considerations of relational impacts in research and design must account for the characteristics inherent in these new technologies. Hertlein (2012, p. 376) reminds family researchers to consider what she labels the "vulnerabilities" of new media as they are used to initiate or maintain relationships. These include representational differences of anonymity, approximation (of the reality of the person), access to individuals that is more frequent (and enables the expectation of frequent access) and sometimes intrusive, and ambiguity. Hertlein warns of boundaries in relationships that can be blurred with the use of new media, as can roles such as a parent and child who possess unequal levels of technological aptitude.

Use in spaces that are virtual and coordinated with offline ecologies. The Internet offers a space for parents' personal interaction, information acquisition, and sharing that is separate from an offline world. In a study of teen parents for example, Valaitis and Sword (2005) noted that online communication was preferred over face-to-face group discussions. Study participants reported that being anonymous in online discussion groups encouraged open and honest feedback. This online world may offer parents supplementary resources missing in their offline worlds (Scharer, 2005). Social and digital media are also used complementary to offline activities and interactions. Wartella et al. (2013) report the majority of parents of young children first consult family, friends, and the pediatrician as trusted sources of parenting information before seeking online assistance. Parents may also go online to find support for their own beliefs because of a conflict perceived in information received from a doctor (Bernhardt & Felter, 2004). Or they may consult friends and the coparent to discuss or validate information found online (Radey & Randolph, 2009).

With this foundation of technology-use considerations in parenting, the next step toward building an ICT-integrated model of parenting influence is to identify elements within the social context that contribute to parent knowledge, well-being, and development as influences on parenting. The sections that follow explore the theory and research on social context structure or process influences on parenting, and ICT roles in facilitating these influences. As depicted in Figure 16.2, parents' social networks explicate the role of structural dimensions of relationship connections (e.g., number of members, similarity or differences in the members). Relational associations of network memberships provide identity and personal meaning (e.g., parental role, neighborhood community). Within those network connections and relational associations are the social processes that convey the flow of influence across the connections to the parent that have direct impact on parent development, well-being, and parenting. These processes include social learning, social support, and social capital.

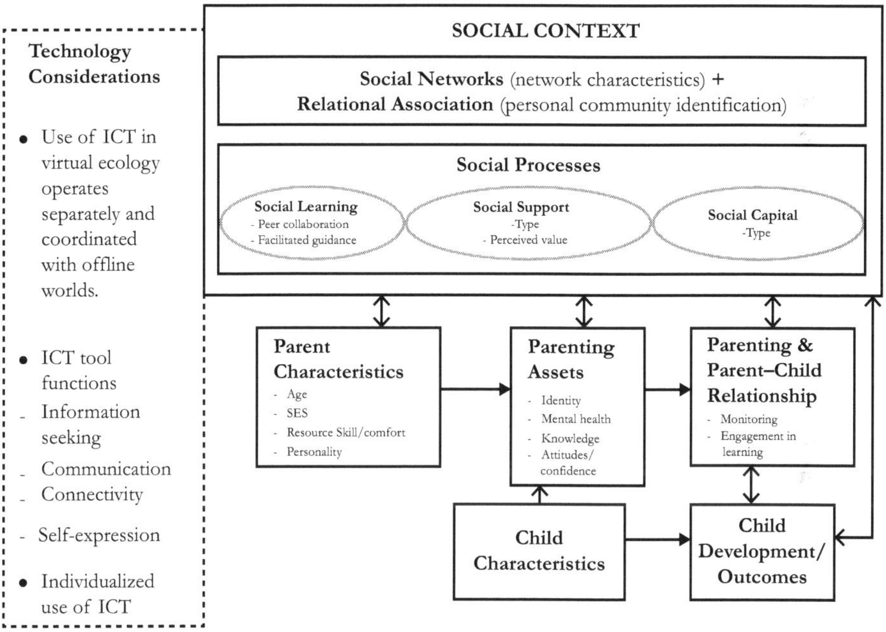

Figure 16.2. Social context influences on parenting facilitated by information and communications technology (ICT).

Social Context Structures: Networks and Relational Associations

Theoretical Foundations

Cochran's conceptualization of parents' personal social networks (Cochran & Brassard, 1979; Cochran, 1990) suggests how the larger ecological, structural, and relational dynamics of parents' lives might impact child well-being, either through the parent or operating directly on the child. Cochran (1990) observed that relationships with members of the network transcended a specific setting, conveying significance and meaning to the individual anchoring the network. Through the structure of connections and relational associations (personal communities that have meaning to the individual), networks transmit information through models of behavior, norms, and influence from the larger society.

A key characteristic of social networks is *connections between individuals*. Social network structures vary by the *number* of connections, the *density* of interconnections (which network members know each other), and individuals' *positions* within the network. Network connections can be *proximal* or *distant*, depending on their relative closeness to the individual. Network connections, as they function in aggregate, embrace the *whole network* (Garton, Wellman, & Haythornthwaite, 1997), whereas connections anchored to a single individual are viewed as *personal social networks*.

A network's value lies in the resources shared and influence conveyed, yet the quality and kind of resources depend on the nature of the dyadic ties and networks (Wellman, 2007). *Strong ties* link to those who are most meaningful, and *weak ties* to those who offer more singular roles and purposes. Granovetter (1973) revealed that members weakly linked to the individual could provide valuable information not known to those in closer relationships. *Latent* ties are those with little meaning until they are activated when the individual has a need (Haythornthwaite, 2002).

According to Wellman, Boase, and Chen (2002), as our society became more industrialized and families more mobile, communities became more dispersed, diverse, and transitory, and relationship structures took on new characteristics. Structures developed are "*personal* communities that supply the essentials of community separately to each individual: support, sociability, information, social identities, and a sense of belonging" (Wellman et al., 2002, p. 160).

Networks have *interconnectedness* and have *spatial* and *temporal* dimensions. Single networks have a size, shape, and structure, but they are also connected to network members' networks, providing ever-expanding links of influence, outreach, and connections. Kadushin (2002) labels those whose distant connections might connect other networks as "brokers," enabling the flow of novel information from one network to another (e.g., influence of minority culture to a dominant culture network).

Research has revealed that parents' relationships with more proximal members (usually the coparent, family, and friends) are denser and more tightly knit and trend toward bonds with those safe and familiar (for a review, see Cochran & Walker, 2005). Yet parents in smaller, more cohesive, homogeneous networks are less satisfied with their network relations and demonstrate more intrusive, less emotionally warm styles of parenting. This is believed to be due, in part, to the lack of innovation in support and fewer resources provided by network members. Parents create personal communities to complement other social resources in their lives. Those belonging to networks including more weak ties with more heterogeneous members through which novel information is transmitted across ties demonstrate more competent parenting.

Cochran (1990; Cochran & Walker, 2005) proposed two forces that influence parents' social networks. Parents' social network membership is built from a pool of potential members that is constrained by social forces, such as social-structural position (including race, gender, family structure, income, and education). These directly influence network density and degree of contact, network composition, and social exchanges of assistance. What Cochran labels as "personal initiative" aspects (e.g., personality, a life event, developmental phase) are other forces that operate independently on network engagement or might interact with other aspects. Cochran and Walker (2005) note that during divorce, for example, parents' networks might shift in membership or engagement, and stronger ties with children and new network memberships may result.

Social Networks Observed through Study of Parents Online

Wellman and colleagues' (2002) observation of personal communities extended to the social affordances of the Internet, noting that they have facilitated a kind of "networked individualism" that enables us to connect with our multiple networks or communities unique to the individual (p. 158). The advent of applications like Facebook encourages networks to be interconnected and enables individuals to bridge multiple networks.

boyd & Ellison (2007) suggest that "friending" behaviors through social network sites can result in more and different types of connections between individuals that would not otherwise be made. SNSs can serve a range of purposes, including helping users learn new skills and behaviors (Greenhow & Robelia, 2009), along with personal expression and relationship initiation and maintenance. Such relationship building can be accomplished through a range of features that accommodate personal information sharing in a variety of formats and through content created by the user.

Parent reports on reasons for use of SNS suggest that the purposes and artifacts shared through these sites may help parents strengthen network ties and build networks in size and membership. Bartholomew and colleagues (2012) observe that during the transition to parenthood, when new mothers' SNS associations are largely composed of family and friends, personal adjustment as measured through parent satisfaction and parenting stress improved. Walker and Rudi (2014) note that parent reports of using SNS, email, and text messages with family and friends suggest that ties are being strengthened. They report that 91% of parents post photos of their own family and 97% stay in touch with friends rarely seen. Parents also add members to their social networks by making connections to parents through discussion boards and forums, which provide access to a parent-related community (Gibson & Hanson, 2013). Although these ties may be weak, discussion board contacts may offer diverse perspectives on parenting, thus offering novel information. Walker and Rudi's research also indicated that parents use email and SNS to connect with professionals, thereby extending and possibly strengthening weak ties beyond their family and friend personal networks.

Applying the construct of an online ecology to Cochran's (1990; Cochran & Walker, 2005) observation about situational constraints and personal initiatives as influences on parents' social networks, recent research suggests that access to technology, comfort, skills, and preference for technology will influence SNS use, and thus opportunities for strengthening or adding networked connections (McDaniel et al., 2012; Palfrey et al., 2010; Yardi & Bruckman, 2011). Research has also revealed how during life transitions, such as becoming parents, individuals might expand the size and membership of new parents' networks as they find parents like themselves online through Facebook (Bartholomew et al., 2012).

Social Processes: Social Capital, Social Support, and Social Learning

Social networks' influence is primarily considered to be the reinforcement of norms and behaviors an individual believes to be significant (Christakis & Fowler, 2009). For the most part, social support and social capital have been offered as the processes through which the network influences parenting (Cochran, 1990). In this section, those processes and their influence on parent development and parenting facilitated by ICT will be discussed. A third social process as observed from parenting research and relevant to a discussion of online relational influence on parents is social learning. Although these processes are described individually, their actions as conduits of influence on parent learning, well-being, and development are interactive and combined.

Social Capital

Social capital refers to resources or benefits available to people through their social interactions (Lin, 1999) and is valuable to feelings of trust, reciprocity, and social cohesion (Putnam, 2000). Investment in social networks might benefit individuals through greater access to and use of information, influence, social credentials, and reinforcement of identity and recognition (Lin, 1999). Terrion (2006) reports that individuals with a high level of social capital generally have a higher sense of life satisfaction, reduced depression, and perceive access to social resources they need to support their parenting. Social capital varies with the type, strength, and interconnection of linkages conferring feelings of trust and belongingness, and exposure to diverse perspectives. Research in education and human development has typically focused on two broad types of social capital: *bridging capital* derived from weak ties that affords diverse perspectives and new information and *bonding capital* derived from strong ties that comes from close friends and family (Putnam, 2000).

Social capital observed through parents' online interactions. Mothers have been the focus of much of the research on ICT-facilitated social capital, primarily qualitative analyses of discussion groups or online support groups for specific parents (e.g., Fletcher & St. George, 2011; Drentea & Moren-Cross, 2005; Valaitis & Sword, 2005). A predominant insight from these studies was that participation yielded a sense of connectedness. In an examination of lesbian mothers' use of a specific website, Lev and colleagues (2005) observed that mothers found community online and experienced decreased isolation.

Translation of possible social capital benefits to parents through social network use might be found in social media research on other populations. Valenzuela, Park, and Kee (2009) speculated that SNSs like Facebook promote the accumulation of social capital through (1) multiple channels for interpersonal feedback and peer acceptance, which help with personal identity construction; (2) status update features, which reinforce existing ties and communities by fulfilling users' need to know about their contacts; and (3) prominently featured personal profiling, which helps increase individuals' knowledge of other members, fostering norms of reciprocity and trust. Lampe and Ellison (2012) examined social capital acquisition in college undergraduates using Facebook. They found that intensive use of Facebook was associated mainly with higher levels of *bridging* capital by virtue of the ease and efficiency of maintaining and accessing contacts. According to the authors, Facebook increased bridging capital by "reducing the cost of finding and maintaining large, distributed groups of social ties" (p. 91).

Social Support

Social support has long been identified as an ecological construct that influences individual parent well-being (Schwarzer & Knoll, 2007), often operating as a buffer to stress, as moderator of stress's effects, or as direct psychological, cognitive, or practical aid. Reciprocity of social support conveys social capital and social cohesion when people reciprocate with support similar to the kind they receive (Plickert, Côté, & Wellman, 2007). Traditional assessments of social support in families examine type, amount, source, and perceived value of support from others relative to the perception of the stressor (Cleary, 1988).

In general, parents who report greater levels of social support display more competent parenting (Crnic & Low, 2002). Parents seek supports differently depending on their network member relationships and composition, for instance turning to family and friends for emotional, informational, and practice support and to the Internet or professionals for specific, informational assistance (Walker, Hoodecheck, & Landers, 2013).

Parent online behavior and social support. Research revealing parents' perceived social support through their online exchanges is prevalent (e.g., Brady & Guerin, 2010; Drentea & Moren-Cross, 2005; Fletcher & St. George, 2010; McDaniel et al., 2012). Parents' social support has been identified from participation in Internet community discussion forums, chat rooms, email listservs, and in groups targeted to specific parents (e.g., young single mothers, teen mothers, nursing mothers, fathers). Through asynchronous discussion of topics and live chats, parents have the ability to share thoughts, ideas, and experiences about parenting and hear the perspectives of others. Not only do these discussions help normalize parents' experience and validate their beliefs, serving as an emotional aid, they offer an opportunity to display a certain expertise. Social exchanges online can offer parents information that might exceed, clarify, or reinforce information received from family and friends.

As a result of participating in online activities facilitating support, a number of benefits to parents' mental health and well-being have been reported. McDaniel and colleagues (2012) revealed blogging-related perceived social support contributed to decreased stress, decreased marital conflict, and increased marital satisfaction, and indirectly reduced depression. Other research observed that parents report feeling encouraged to take more responsibility in their role as a parent, more confidence, and validated for their beliefs (Hall & Irvine, 2008; O'Connor & Madge, 2004). Brady and Guerin's (2010) analysis of mothers' posts in an online discussion forum suggested the likelihood of reciprocal support, expressed as feelings about other posters.

Method of social media use may have differential effects, however. Although McDaniel and colleagues (2012) determined that mothers' blogging had positive impact on perceived increased support, mothers' social networking behavior did not show these relationships. In an examination of social support and Facebook use by college students, Liu and Yu (2013) suggest that using SNS does not directly impact well-being but can help individuals obtain online social support that in turn can help individuals access offline, generalized supportive resources.

Social Learning

Social learning is a third social process that is conferred through network linkages. It is active change that occurs in understanding and meaning-making through observation of and interaction with others—others who reinforce and validate understanding and cultural norms, and provide mentoring and modeling (Bandura, 1977). Sociocultural perspectives on learning recognize how domain knowledge (such as parenting) is a social construction (Rogoff, 2003), and that social settings and systems reinforce concepts and practices that maintain conventions. Analyses of brain research and learning suggest that community-centered environments promote learning through collaborative interactions aimed at shared goals and identities as learners (Bransford, Brown, & Cocking, 2000). Wenger's (1998) promotion of social learning systems, or "Communities of Practice," elucidates the role of relational association and identity with a certain competence and area of skill acquisition. Affiliation with other practitioners can deepen understanding through focus on shared learning products and intentions.

These social concepts of learning processes have value to parenting, an enterprise for many adults that is new and requires role identification and a base of knowledge as experience develops. Parent learning benefits from a supportive, trusting, relational context that offers safe and critical self-reflection of understanding, challenging assumptions, and validating personally constructed knowledge (Marineau & Segal, 2006). Peer interactions can provide critical reflection on one's life experience to reach new constructions of knowledge and revised interpretations to guide future action. Berg, Meegan, and Deviney (1998) suggest that when it occurs in the company of others, problem resolution and discovery of new knowledge can build a relational appraisal and group identity that leads to involvement in more collaborative problem-solving approaches, perceptions of community connectedness, and interest in participation in more community-bounded relationships. Hypothetically, parents' association with others who share the parenting role may provide them with a sense of membership in a practice-like "Community of Parenting," conferring benefit as a collective, social context for learning and development. Thus, when learning occurs by virtue of engaged and trusted social relationships, there is potential receipt of social capital (a sense of belongingness with community) and social support (reciprocal offers of emotional and informational assistance), contributing to parent well-being, identity, and knowledge and parenting skill.

Parent social learning online. Much of the research explicitly on parent learning online comes from reports of content website use (Zaidman-Zait & Jamieson, 2007) or fully online programs aimed as education efforts to individuals (e.g., Steimle & Duncan, 2004). These generally measure site participation and satisfaction, and assess changes in knowledge from exposure to novel content. Although only a small portion of parents use Internet-offered classes related to childrearing (about 10% according to Walker & Rudi, 2014), further research on participation in dedicated online platforms might indicate ways that social interaction can be structured and facilitated to benefit parent learning.

The more predominant use of ICTs by parents is learning that is informal and self-directed. As previously noted, parents seek information through websites and take information back to their informal social networks for validation and decision making, or may seek out online information resources to resolve decision-making needs as a complement to offline sources. Discussion boards enable parents to learn informally through participation with others who gather around topics of common interest, exchange information, ask questions, and share passions (Henri & Pudelko, 2003). Although expectations for sharing in these venues are low, Drentea and Moren-Cross (2005) suggest that parents might form a bond in these groups, so even a minimum of involvement with other "practitioners" may provide a sense of participation in a community of practice.

The sharing and exchange of information appears to influence parents' perceptions about parenting and deepen identity in the role. Work by researchers like O'Connor and Madge (2004) suggests that when mothers participate in online discussions about parenting, they provide narratives on their parenting lives and decisions, validate their identities of motherhood, and can critically reflect on their parenting. True to constructivist perspectives of social learning, Huws, Jones, and Ingeldew's (2001) analysis of mothers' exchanges in email listservs related to autism suggests that groups may do more than offer parents a sense of support and community; they might also contribute to the development of parental representations of autism.

In summary, theories of human development and of parenting point to the key role of the social context in interaction with characteristics of the parent that influence parent well-being and parenting behavior. Within the social context, structural dimensions of personal connections through social networks can affect the content and flow of information through the strength and interconnectedness of social ties that link the parent to his or her wider relational world. Bounded relational associations or personal networks provide specialized communities for identification and interest pursuits. And social processes within these structures convey influence in ways that affect parent development, attitudes, knowledge, and behavior. Social capital provides the sense of connectedness between relationship ties, and social support is a product that can act as a buffer, can moderate stress, and can provide parents with direct informational or emotional aid. Social learning deepens understanding, provides critical perspectives for reflection, and can promote identification and articulation of the parenting role. The Internet in general and social media in particular offer platforms for these social structures and processes to play out. The model presented here, adapted and expanding on Belsky's (1984) determinants of parenting and on Cochran's (1990) perspective of social network influences, offers promise for further research on parents' use of social technology and resultant outcomes on parenting.

Application

Research Considerations

Although there is evidence to support this model as one that frames parents' social relationships amid new technological landscapes, research is needed to explicate each element as it relates to parent technology use and how use relates to parenting assets and relationship dimensions that affect child outcomes. In short, as others have observed with regard to family impacts of technology (Aponte, 2009; Lanigan, 2009), we are at the very early stages of understanding the facilitative role of ICT in helping parents mobilize social resources in ways that affect their parenting, positively or negatively. Research has yet to document or map parents' online relationships, their structural features or social processes, and how online and offline network dynamics affect parenting.

As the review in this chapter indicates, the social context and social context relationships play out and can be measured in vastly different ways. Research on social dynamics of ICT use by parents needs to tease out differences in use of social technologies (e.g., descriptive reports of SNS use), use of technologies for social purposes (e.g., reasons for using technology to engage with others online), and use of technologies that facilitate social processes (e.g., what emotional support perceived from online interactions achieves). This research needs to maintain the focus on use by parents for parenting purposes (rather than sample adults who are parents and attribute use of ICT to fulfill parenting roles; Walker & Rudi, 2014 determined this is not the same). And this might mean that traditional measures of social processes be redesigned to fit with perceptions of Internet relationships (Williams, 2006).

Relatedly, how technology complements parents' multiple learning ecologies (Barron, 2006) should also be explored. Building and then testing platforms that encourage cross-ecology parent learning and development is one way to determine this (Wenger, White, & Smith, 2009). For example, analysis of focus group and survey data from parents of young children who attend an early childhood family education program revealed that parents report learning about parenting through association with multiple relational communities, including family and friends, their child's class, the early childhood program, and the local neighborhood in which the program is based (Walker et al., 2013). Does social media that enables easy access to members of these communities aid learning across these communities and encourage interconnectedness, thus involving the parent in a larger, more diverse network? Would participation with such a socially mediated technology platform that encourages interconnectedness also then contribute to heightened perceptions of social support and social capital?

Finally, research must regard differences represented by mechanisms and platforms used for interaction. The online experience can affect participant motivation, behavior, and attitudes that affect communication and social exchange (Bradner et al., 1999). As online representation may be anonymous or an identity may be disguised, parent commitment and feelings of belongingness to groups, the motivation to return, or to provide information may vary. Discussions that are public, private, monitored, or facilitated may convey different meaning to individuals and may affect their behavior and presentation of self.

Considerations for Design

The model outlined in this chapter, in the aggregate, proposes that online interventions built on social context theories of human development and social networking principles that encourage social interactions have the potential to contribute to parent well-being. To work toward these goals, platforms aimed at strengthening and supporting parents should consider the following elements:

(1) Provide activities that nudge parents' networks to be larger and more heterogeneous. Parents are drawn to Web platforms that offer information or resources for their children, supports for themselves, and outlets for self-expression (Hughes et al., 2012). Platforms for parents can embrace their desire to interact with communities of comfort, safety, and familiarity, yet encourage development and learning through larger, networked connections borne from involvement in interest and identity communities. Discussion groups and social networking applications are ways to build and see contacts that connect parents with other parents.

(2) Include social features within sites that permit identity formation of groups (e.g., a place for stepparents to separately discuss common interests on a more general site for parents), sharing of content, peer-to-peer expertise, and

validation of beliefs (Henri & Pudelko, 2003). As Walker & Rudi (2014) determined, a feature like a discussion group can yield a variety of benefits. Participation on a discussion board might help the mother of a child with autism to gain confidence in her parenting, acquire information from other parents on the child's social development, and learn about community resources for the child. Yet consider components of structured online platforms aimed at learning and support outcomes (Hughes et al., 2012). Use of an expert or moderator can facilitate learning (e.g., problem posing for deeper learning) or manage and monitor activity to keep the communication constructive and inviting.

(3) Encourage and enable sharing of content in ways that bridge personal networks. For example, a feature that enables parents to share among email, a website, and Facebook encourages sharing within informal networks that offer familiar, trusted, and enduring relationships (email exchanges between family members; bonding social capital) and respect the linkages that parents rely on. Yet it enables links to wider networks and can make the parent the broker of interconnected networks and at the center of the information flow (Kadushin, 2002).

(4) Consider online *projects* that encourage community building, identity validation in parenting, and give parents an outlet for creativity and expression. An example of this is a social production community that produces a knowledge artifact that has value to the community (Gilbert & Karahalios, 2009) (e.g., a wiki of recommended places to take children on outings). Collaborative activity in an online practice-focused project can serve as a social context vehicle for parent learning and development (Wenger, 1998; Marineau & Segal, 2006).

And finally, true to any application for individual learning through support and engagement: (5) Regard individual differences in ways that respect parents' range of access to comfort using and skill level with technology. Design for and expect use by a wide range of users, and support greater use through features that are easy to use and conveniently accessed. Conscientious technological consideration of the parent as developing individual and learner will encourage the creation of online environments that promote positive parenting and the greatest likelihood of supporting parenting outcomes.

References

Azar, S. T. (2003). Adult development and parenthood: A social-cognitive perspective. In J. Demick & C. Andreoletti (Eds.), *Handbook of adult development* (pp. 391–415). New York: Springer.

Aponte, R. (2009). The communications revolution and its impact on the family: Significant, growing, but skewed and limited in scope. *Marriage & Family Review, 45*(6–8), 576–586. doi:10.1080/01494920903396778

Bandura, A. (1977). *Social learning theory.* Oxford, UK: Prentice-Hall.

Barnard, K. E., & Solchany, J. E. (2002). Mothering. In M. H. Bornstein (Ed.), *Handbook of parenting, vol. 3: Being and becoming a parent* (2nd ed., pp. 3–25). Mahwah, NJ: Erlbaum.

Barron, B. (2006). Interest and self-sustained learning as catalysts of development: A learning ecology perspective. *Human Development, 49,* 193–224.

Bartholomew, M., Schoppe-Sullivan, S., Glassman, M., Kamp Dush, C., & Sullivan, J. (2012). New parents' Facebook use at the transition to parenthood. *Family Relations, 61*, 455–469.

Belsky, J. (1984.) The determinants of parenting. *Child Development, 55*(1), 83–96.

Berg, C., Meegan, S., & Deviney, F. (1998). A social-contextual model of coping with everyday problems across the lifespan. *International Society for the Study of Behavioral Development, 22*(2), 239–261.

Bernhardt, J. M., & Felter, E. M. (2004). Online pediatric seeking among mothers of young children: Results from a qualitative study using focus groups. *Journal of Medical Internet Research, 6,* 1, e7.

Blackburn, C. and Read, J. (2005). Using the Internet? The experiences of parents of disabled children. *Child: Care, Health and Development, 31,* 507–515.

Bost, K., Cox, M., & Payne, C. (2002). Structural and supportive changes in couples' family and friendship networks across the transition to parenthood. *Journal of Marriage and the Family, 64*, 517–531.

boyd, d. m., & Ellison, N. B. (2007). Social network sites: Definition, history, and scholarship. *Journal of Computer-Mediated Communication, 13*(1), article 11.

Bradner, E., Kellogg, W., & Erickson, T. (1999). The adoption and use of "Babble": A field study of chat in the workplace. In *Proceedings of the 6th European Conference on Computer Supported Cooperative Work* (pp. 139–158). New York: ACM Publishing.

Brady, E., & Guerin, S. (2010). Not the romantic, all happy, coochy coo experience: A qualitative analysis of interactions on an Irish parenting web site. *Family Relations, 59*(1), 14–27.

Bransford, J. D., Brown, A. L., & Cocking, R. R. (2000). *How people learn: Brain, mind, experience, and school.* Washington, DC: Committee on Developments in the Science of Learning.

Bronfenbrenner, U. (1995). Developmental ecology through space and time: A future perspective. In P. Moen, G. Elder Jr., and K. Luscher (Eds.), *Examining lives in context: Perspectives on the ecology of human development* (pp. 619–647). Washington, DC: American Psychological Association.

Christakis, N. & Fowler, J. (2009). Connected: the surprising power of our social networks and how they shape our lives. New York: Little, Brown & Co.

Cleary, P. (1988). Social support: Conceptualization and measurement. In H. Wess and F. Jacobs. *Evaluating family programs* (pp. 195–216). New York: Aldine de Gruyter.

Cochran, M. (1990). The network as an environment for human development. In M. Cochran, M. Larner, D. Riley, L. Gunnarsson, & C. Henderson Jr., *Extending families: The social networks of parents and their children* (ch. 14). London: Cambridge University Press.

Cochran, M., & Brassard, J. (1979). Child development and personal social networks. *Child development, 50,* 609–615.

Cochran, M., & Walker, S. (2005). Parenting and personal social networks. In T. Luster & L. Ogakaki (Eds.) *Parenting: An ecological approach* (pp. 235–274). Mahwah, NJ: Earlbaum.

Connell, J. (2012, March). *Parenting 2.0 summary report: Parents' use of technology and the Internet.* Retrieved from http://www.cehd.umn.edu/fsos/projects/parent20/pdf/p20summaryreport-july2012.pdf

Crnic, K., & Low, C. (2002). Everyday stresses and parenting. In M. Bornstein (Ed.), *Handbook of parenting, Vol 5: Practical issues in parenting* (2nd ed., pp. 243–267). Mahwah, NJ: Lawrence Erlbaum Associates.

Devitt, K., & Roker, B. (2009). The role of mobile phones in family communication. *Children & Society, 23*(3), 189–202. doi:10.1111/j.1099–0860.2008.00166.x

Drentea, P., & Moren-Cross, J. (2005). Social capital and social support on the web: The case of an Internet mother site. *Sociology of Health and Illness, 27*, 920–943.

Dworkin, J., Connell, J., & Doty, J. (2013). A literature review of parents' online behavior. *Cyberpsychology: Journal of Psychosocial Research on Cyberspace, 7*(2). Retrieved from http://cyberpsychology.eu/view.php?cisloclanku=2013052301&article=2

Fletcher, R. J., & St. George, J. M. (2010). Practitioners' understanding of father engagement in the context of family dispute resolution. *Journal of Family Studies, 16*(2), 101–115.

Garton, L., Wellman, B. & Haythornthwaite, C. (1997). Studying online social networks. *Journal of Computer-Mediated Communication, 3*(1). Retrieved from jcmc.indiana.edu/vol3/issue1/garton.html

Gibson, L., & Hanson, V. L. (2013). "Digital motherhood": How does technology support new mothers? In *CHI 2013* (pp. 313–322). Paris.

Gilbert, E., & Karahalios, K. (2009). Using social visualization to motivate social production. *IEEE Transactions on Multimedia, 11*(3), 413–421.

Granovetter, M. (1973). The strength of weak ties. *American Journal of Sociology, 78*, 1360–1380.

Greenhow, C., & Robelia, E. (2009). Old communication, new literacies: Social network sites as social learning resources. *Journal of Computer-Mediated Communication, 14*, 1130–1161.

Hall, W., & Irvine, V. (2008). E-communication among mothers of infants and toddlers in a community-based cohort: A content analysis. *Journal of Advanced Nursing, 65*(1), 175–183.

Ham, Y. H., and Walker, S. (2012, November 2). Determinants of parents' challenges in searching for and using parenting information online. Paper presented at the National Council on Family Relations annual conference, Phoenix, AZ.

Haythornthwaite, C. (2002). Strong, weak, and latent ties and the impact of new media. *The Information Society, 18*, 385–401.

Henri, F., and Pudelko, B. (2003). Understanding and analyzing activity and learning in virtual communities. *Journal of Computer Assisted Learning, 19*, 474–487.

Hertlein, K. M. (2012). Digital dwelling: Technology in couple and family relationships. *Family Relations, 61*(3), 374–387. doi:10.1111/j.1741–3729.2012.00702.x

Hughes, R., Bowers, J., Mitchell, E., Curtiss, S., & Ebata, A. (2012). Developing online family life prevention and education programs. *Family Relations, 61*, 711–727.

Huws, J., Jones, R., & Ingeldew, D. (2001). Parents of children with autism using an email group: A grounded theory study, *Journal of Health Psychology 6*, 569–584.

Kadushin, C. (2002). The motivational foundation of social networks. *Social Networks, 24*, 77–91.

Lampe, C., & Ellison, N. (2012). Understanding Facebook: Social Computing Isn't "Just" Social. *Computer, September*, 98–100. Retrieved from http://computingnow.computer.org

Lanigan, J. D. (2009). A sociotechnological model for family research and intervention: How information and communication technologies affect family life. *Marriage & Family Review, 45*(6–8), 587–609. doi:10.1080/01494920903224194

Lev, A. I., Dean, G., DeFilippis, L., Evernham, K., McLaughlin, L., & Phillips, C. (2005). Dykes and tykes: A virtual lesbian parenting community. *Journal of Lesbian Studies, 9*, 81–94.

Lin, N. (1999). Building a network theory of social capital. *Connections, 22*(1), 28–51.

Liu, C.-Y., & Yu, C.-P. (2013). Can Facebook use induce well-being? *Cyberpsychology, Behavior, and Social Networking, 16*(9), 674–678. doi:10.1089/cyber.2012.0301

Luster, T., & Ogakaki, L. (Eds.). (2005). *Parenting: An ecological perspective* (2nd ed.). Mahwah, NJ: Erlbaum.

Madge, C., & O'Connor, H. (2006). Parenting gone wired: Empowerment of new mothers on the Internet? *Social and Cultural Geography, 7*(2), 199–220.

Marienau, C., and Segal, J. (2006). Parents as developing adult learners. *Child welfare, 85*(5), 768–784.

McDaniel, B. T., Coyne, S. M., & Holmes, E. K. (2012). New mothers and media use: associations between blogging, social networking, and maternal well-being. *Maternal and Child Health Journal, 16*(7), 1509–1517. doi:10.1007/s10995–011–0918–2

O'Connor, H., and Madge, C. (2004). "My mum's thirty years out of date": The role of the Internet in the transition to motherhood. *Community, work, and family, 7*(3), 351–369.

Palfrey J., Gasser, U., & boyd, d. (2010). Response to FCC Notice of Inquiry 09–94: Empowering parents and protecting children in an evolving media landscape. Cambridge, MA: Berkman Center for Internet and Society at Harvard University. Retrieved from http://papers.ssrn.com/sol3/papers.cfm?bstract_id=1559208

Plantin, L. & Daneback, K. (2009). Parenthood, information, and support on the Internet: A literature review of parents and professionals online. *BMC Family Practice, 10*, 34–52.

Plickert, G., Côté, R. R., & Wellman, B. (2007). It's not who you know, it's how you know them: Who exchanges what with whom? *Social Networks, 29*(3), 405–429. doi:10.1016/j.socnet.2007.01.007

Putnam, R. (2000). *Bowling alone: The collapse and revival of American community.* New York: Simon & Schuster.

Radey, M., & Randolph, K. A. (2009). Parenting sources: How do parents differ in their efforts to learn about parenting? *Family Relations, 58*, 536–548.

Rogoff, B. (2003). *The cultural nature of human development.* New York: Oxford University Press.

Rudi, J., Dworkin, J., Walker, S., and Doty, J. (2014). Parents' use of information and communications technologies for family communication: differences by age of children. *Information, Communication and Society,* DOI: 10.1080/1369118X.2014.934390

Scharer, K. (2005). Internet social support for parents: The state of science. *Journal of Child and Adolescent Psychiatric Nursing, 18*(1), 26–35.

Schwarzer, R., & Knoll, N. (2007). Functional roles of social support within the stress and coping process: A theoretical and empirical overview. *International Journal of Psychology, 42*(4), 243–252.

Steimle, B., & Duncan, S. (2004). Formative evaluation of a family life education web site. *Family Relations, 53*, 367–376.

Takeuchi, L. M. (2011). *Families matter: Designing media for a digital age.* New York: The Joan Ganz Cooney Center at Sesame Workshop.

Tee, K., Brush, A. J. B., & Inkpen, K. M. (2009). Exploring communication and sharing between extended families. *International Journal of Human–Computer Studies, 67 (2)*, 128–138.

Terrion, J. (2006). Social capital in vulnerable families: Success of a school-based intervention program. *Youth and Society, 38*, 155–175.

Valaitis, R., & Sword, W. (2005). Online discussions with pregnant and parenting adolescents: Perspectives and possibilities. *Health Promotion Practice, 4,* 464–471.

Valenzuela, S., Park, N., & Kee, K. F. (2009). Is there social capital in a social network site? Facebook use and college students' life satisfaction, trust, and participation. *Journal of Computer-Mediated Communication, 14*, 875–901.

Vygotsky, L. S. (1978). *Mind in society: The development of higher psychological processes.* Cambridge, MA: Harvard University Press.

Walker, S., Dworkin, J., & Connell, J. (2011). Variation in parent use of information and communications technology: Does quantity matter? *Family and Consumer Sciences Research Journal, 40*(2), 106–119.

Walker, S., Hoodecheck, E., & Landers, A. (2013, November 10). Participatory design research to extend place-based parent learning and support through technology: Phase 1. Paper presented at the National Council on Family Relations annual conference, San Antonio, TX.

Walker, S., & Rudi, J. (2014). Parenting across the social ecology facilitated by information and communications technology: Implications for research and educational design. *Journal of Human Sciences and Extension, 2*(2), 2–19.

Walther, J. B., & Parks, M. R. (2002). Cues filtered out, cues filtered in: Computer mediated communication and relationships. In M. L. Knapp, J. A. Daly, & G. R. Miller (Eds.), *The handbook of interpersonal communication* (3rd ed., pp. 529–563). Thousand Oaks, CA: Sage.

Wartella, E., Rideout, V., Lauricella, A., & Connell, S. (2013). *Parenting in the age of digital technology: A national survey.* Evanston, IL: Northwestern University, Center on Media and Human Development. Retrieved from http://web5.soc.northwestern.edu/cmhd/wp-content/uploads/2014/03/ParentingAgeDigitalTechnology.REVISED.FINAL_.2014.pdf

Wellman, B. (2007). The network is personal. *Social Networks 29,* 349–356.

Wellman, B., Boase, J., & Chen, W. (2002). The networked nature of community on and off the Internet. *IT and Society, 1*(1), 151–165.

Wellman, B., Smith, A., Wells, A. & Kennedy, T. (2008). *Networked families.* Pew Internet and American Life Project. Washington, DC. Retrieved from http://www.pewinternet.org/2008/10/19/networked-families/

Wenger, E. (1998). *Communities of practice learning, meaning, and identity.* Cambridge, UK: Cambridge University Press.

Wenger, E., White, N., & Smith, J. D. (2009). *Digital habitats: Stewarding technology for communities.* Portland, OR: CPSquare.

Williams, D. (2006). On and off the 'net: Scales for social capital in an online era. *Journal of Computer-Mediated Communication, 11*, 593–628.

Yardi, S., and Bruckman, A. (2011). Social and technical challenges in parenting teens' social media use. In *CHI 2011* (pp. 1–10). Vancouver: Canada.

Zaidman-Zait, A., & Jamieson, J. (2007). Providing web-based support for families of infants and young children with established disabilities. *Infants & Young Children, 20*(1), 11–25. Retrieved from http://journals.lww.com/iycjournal/Abstract/2007/01000/Providing_Web_based_Support_for_Families_of.3.aspx

17

Gr8 Textpectations

Parents' Experiences of Anxiety in Response to Adolescent Mobile Phone Delays

STEPHANIE TIKKANEN
Ohio University

WALID AFIFI
University of Iowa

ANNE MERRILL
Pennsylvania State University

Introduction

Innovations of the past few decades such as mobile phones and text messaging have created new ways of staying in touch with family, friends, and colleagues. In fact, the International Telecommunication Union reports that over 96% of the world's population now uses mobile phone technology (ITU Statistics, 2013), which has an enormous impact on the landscape of modern communication. At minimum, many people are no longer tethered to a particular location from which to contact others, but—importantly—they are also reachable nearly anywhere. Consequently, scholars suggest that cell phones have created the perception that individuals are always accessible and are expected to immediately respond to contact efforts (Baron, 2008). Indeed, Carey and Elton (2010) report interviewees claimed that one of the biggest downsides to having a cellular phone was the expectation that they could be reached anytime and should either pick up immediately or call back as soon as possible. One context in which expectations of constant availability may have important implications is in the interactions between parents and their teenage children.

Increasingly, teenagers are given a mobile phone in order to keep parents informed about matters of safety and security (Schiano, et al., 2002) but also as a tool for parental monitoring (Blair & Fletcher, 2011). Alongside a mobile phone's function as a key to adolescent autonomy comes the expectation that children will respond quickly to parental contact efforts. As adolescents begin to assert their individuality apart from their parents, they might resist parental efforts at surveillance and violate parents' expectations for an immediate or prompt response. Little is known, however, about the implications related to the violation of these expectations for parents' experiences, such as uncertainty and anxiety, or what can be done to address the effects they may have on families. Other areas of literature, however, offer insight on this front. Broadly, literature in the areas of expectancy violations and uncertainty suggest that the violation of expectancies often results in uncertainty (Kellerman & Reynolds, 1990). In turn, considerable evidence suggests uncertainty is associated with anxiety (Miceli & Castelfranchi, 2005). These relationships should be especially strong when the expectancy being violated concerns matters of health and well-being, and the associated uncertainty is threat related. As such, one would expect that children's failure to rapidly respond to parents' contact efforts should produce psychological distress. Yet, a recent approach to individuals' responses to uncertainty suggests that the association between uncertainty and anxiety may not be simple. Kruglanski and colleagues' work on the need for closure (NFC) (Dechesne & Kruglanski, 2009; Kruglanski & Webster, 1996) argues that personality differences in the processing of uncertainty affect individuals' responses to uncertainty-producing events. Essentially, those with a low need for closure tolerate higher levels of uncertainty than those with a characteristic high need for closure. As mobile technology that offers parents a tool for monitoring the activities of their children becomes increasingly important in family communication, research must also recognize its potential to create threat-related uncertainty and anxiety. This investigation uses the theoretical framework surrounding NFC as central to understanding the implications of adolescents' delayed response time to parental contact efforts on parents' psychological distress.

Rules and Norms Surrounding Mobile Phone Use

Adolescent mobile phone use has increased dramatically. According to a recent survey conducted by the Pew Internet and American Life Project, over 78% of teens aged 12–17 owned mobile phones in 2013, up from 45% in 2004 (Lenhart, 2010; Madden, Lenhart, Duggan, Cortesi, & Gasser, 2013). Additionally, 12–17 year old sends a median of 60 texts on a typical day (Lenhart, 2012). With increasing usage, mobile phones have become integral to many teenagers' lives. Indeed, several scholarly efforts to understand the functions of cell phones for adolescents have emerged. Their overall conclusion is that cell phones generally serve three primary purposes for a teenage population: (a) for maintenance of social relationships (Licoppe & Smoreda, 2005; Ling & Yttri, 2002); (b) as a status symbol (Blair & Fletcher, 2010); and (c) for a sense of security (Aoki & Downes, 2003, Schiano et al., 2002). For example, Schiano et al. (2002) report cell phones are generally purchased to provide security and emergency protections when teens start dating or driving. Similarly, Aoki and Downes (2003) argue that cell phones give teenage respondents "psychological security when out on the street at night" (p. 354). The underlying features that make these three general functions primary to cell phone usage are ready access and convenience (Leung & Wei, 2000). Of course, with these features also comes the potential for expectations of availability: Just as users can make calls or send text messages from anywhere, they can also be reached anywhere.

The notion that cell phones create an expectation of rapid and constant accessibility implies that individuals evaluate others based on the speed with which they respond to contact efforts. Although not studied using cell phone messages, a few investigations testing other technologies confirm that individuals find response delays to hold meaning. In one of the earliest such efforts, Walther and Tidwell (1995) had participants evaluate (fictional) task- and socially oriented emails sent between an employer and an employee. The times sent and received were manipulated in order to assess perceptions of the sender and receiver in terms of perceived intimacy and dominance. Results indicated that slower replies to task-oriented messages resulted in the lowest ratings of intimacy, but slow replies to social content were perceived as the most intimate of all. More recently, Sheldon, Thomas-Hunt, and Proell (2006) reported two studies in which response latency during online interactions was held constant, but the length of the response delay and the responder's status were manipulated. They found that slow responses from higher-status responders were perceived less negatively than similarly delayed responses from low-status responders. Relatedly, Döring and Pöschl (2008) conducted a similar experiment, instead manipulating the time and content of text messages sent and received. All three investigations noted that the lag time before a response influenced judgments of status; those who took less time to answer a message were perceived as relationally subordinate to the sender. Finally, Kalman and Rafaeli (2011) found that the response latency of hypothetical job applicants to email correspondence was significantly associated with negative evaluations and a lack of credibility, among other negative perceptions. These findings are consistent with evidence that response time in interactions is tied to power relations (cf., Burgoon, Buller, & Woodall, 1996) but play an especially important role for our purposes because they are the only studies of which we are aware that examine consequences, of any sort, tied to response-time lags in technology-based interactions.

If individuals hold expectations for response times and lags are imbued with meaning, then the violation of such expectations undoubtedly has consequences (e.g., Afifi & Metts, 1998; Burgoon & Walther, 1990). Afifi and colleagues' work on the Aversive Uncertainty within Valence (AUV) model (Afifi & Burgoon, 2000; Afifi & Metts, 1998) suggests that one of these consequences is uncertainty. These scholars have shown, both in experimental, lab-based designs and in longitudinal, self-report methods, that negative violations from liked others generally increase uncertainty about the violator. When applied to the context of interest in this investigation, we predict that:

> H1: Parents who experience longer-than-expected delays in their child's cell phone response time will experience more uncertainty about their child's activities than those who do not experience such a delay.

The Link between Uncertainty and Anxiety

If response delays create uncertainty, what are the implications for parents? Scholars have long argued that uncertainty causes anxiety (for review, see Afifi, 2009; for exceptions, see Brashers, 2001; Ford, Babrow, & Stohl, 1996). Indeed, scholars often *define* anxiety as emerging from uncertainty or related constructs. For example, in clarifying his appraisal approach to emotions, Lazarus (1998) conceptualized anxiety as emerging from a specific threat that is "uncertain [and] existential" (p. 40). Consistent with Lazarus's conceptualization of anxiety, Miceli and Castelfranchi (2005) advance an Uncertainty Theory of Anxiety, in which they argue that that anxiety stems from "uncertainty about some event or state which implies a possible danger" (p. 295). Relatedly, Power and Dalgleish (1997) propose that individuals' anxiety stems from their inability to control an event, itself a form of outcome uncertainty. These conceptual links between uncertainty and anxiety are also supported by volumes of empirical data, across multiple methods, which show the anxiety-producing qualities of uncertainty (for review, see Afifi, 2009). Importantly, though, and consistent with the above conceptualizations, uncertainty's effects on anxiety are typically constrained to contexts in which the uncertainty is appraised as a possible threat (e.g., see Babrow & Matthias, 2009).

So, we would expect adolescents' delays in response to parents' contact efforts to produce threat-related uncertainty and lead to anxiety. Of course, the critical feature of that process is the threat appraisal: How do parents interpret the threat?

We propose two factors likely to impact the likelihood of threat appraisal associated with uncertainty: (a) trait-level parental differences on need for closure (NFC) and (b) state-level differences on perceived risk.

Need for Closure

Kruglanski and colleagues (Dechesne & Kruglanski, 2009; Kruglanski & Webster, 1996) propose multiple ways for individuals to cognitively manage ambiguity. These methods vary along a continuum of a person's ability to tolerate uncertainty, called *need for [cognitive] closure*, or NFC. Closure is defined as "*an* answer on a given topic, *any* answer, [...] compared to confusion and ambiguity" (Kruglanski, 1990, p. 337). Typically, NFC is conceptualized dichotomously as being either high or low; individuals with a low NFC are tolerant of uncertainty in ambiguous situations, or may even cherish it, whereas individuals with a high NFC are uncomfortable with uncertainty. More specifically, Webster and Kruglanski (1994) conceptualize people with a high need for closure as (a) preferring structure and order in their surroundings; (b) experiencing emotional discomfort (e.g., anxiety) by uncertainty; (c) earnestly desiring closure; (d) wanting steady knowledge that permits confident forecasting of events; and (e) being relatively unwilling to allow their knowledge to be challenged by inconsistent evidence. In contrast, those with a low need for closure are comfortable with ambiguity, have little interest in reducing uncertainty, and seek out inconsistent evidence before ultimately reaching a conclusion. The impact of these individual differences has been validated across several contexts (for review, see Dechesne & Kruglanski, 2009).

Consistent with the conceptualization of NFC, Kruglanski and colleagues have found a difference among those high and low on NFC in how they use information (see Kruglanski & Webster, 1996). While those with a low NFC have a higher tolerance for uncertainty and generally leave several possibilities open to consideration until a thorough information search is complete (Dechesne & Kruglanski, 2009), persons with a high NFC generally accept the first account that allows the reduction of uncertainty and associated cognitive closure, regardless of the account's objective validity—a tendency called "seizing and freezing." In other words, people with a high NFC respond to uncertainty by "seizing" upon the first possible account that eliminates the uncomfortable state of ambiguity, then "freezing" on that same information (Kruglanski & Webster, 1996). "Freezing" is characterized by the discontinuation of information gathering, heightened confidence in one's conclusion, and difficulty in countering the conclusion. Support for this pattern is strong (for review, see Dechesne & Kruglanski, 2009; Vermeir, Van Kenhove, & Hendrickx, 2002). Importantly, researchers (see De Grada, Kruglanski, Mannetti, & Pierro,

1999) have shown that the impact of NFC motivations varies situationally. One particular context in which the motivational forces of high NFC and related "seize and freeze" tendencies are heightened is in cases involving perceived risk or threat.

Perceiving Threat

The literature on the use of heuristics, or mental shortcuts, in the context of uncertainty is vast (for review, see Kahneman, Slovic, & Tversky, 2001). It is particularly useful for our purposes because our interests involve an event with uncertainty-producing potential (i.e., delay in response to contact efforts) and that might elicit threat- or risk-based attributions. Indeed, Kahneman and Tversky's seminal work (1973) in the domain of cognitive processing and heuristics (also Tversky & Kahneman, 1973) pays special attention to the role of risk perceptions, where the availability heuristic plays an especially dominant role (cf., Gärling, 1989). The availability heuristic reflects a cognitive mechanism that relies on the ease with which one recalls event-relevant information to make assessments about the probability of that event (e.g., Schwarz et al., 1991). In the context of this investigation, we might envision a child's previous history of risky behaviors or brushes with danger to serve as particularly relevant information as the parent works to make sense of the response delay. For example, if a child has had a tendency to get into trouble or risky situations in the past, the parents might perceive higher threat related to cell phone response delays because the likelihood of risk is more "available" in their minds. Other possible heuristic indicators of threat in this context include the time of the day or day of the week (e.g., weekend nights are perceived to be the time when adolescents are more likely to engage in risky behavior), and trust in the child, among others.

As such, how does this reliance on heuristics in the face of uncertainty resulting from response delay apply to differential information processing tendencies associated with need for closure? If we apply Kruglanski and colleagues' theorizing, we would expect parents with a low NFC to closely examine the context surrounding the uncertainty and generate several possible explanations for why the delay occurred (Dechesne & Kruglanski, 2009). They are likely to search for a host of possible causes for such delays and rely less exclusively on heuristically gathered judgments, compared to high-NFC parents. Specifically, the assessment of risk to the child is only one of several pieces of information they would use in their uncertainty-reduction efforts.

In contrast, parents with a high NFC are likely to process uncertainty very differently, thereby heightening the likelihood of a threat appraisal. In accordance with the high-NFC tendency to "seize and freeze," these parents' need for closure will encourage them to put the bulk of weight in accounting for the uncertainty upon a single minimally relevant piece of information, with the threat heuristic reliably serving that role (seizing). Their confidence in the veracity of this judgment is thus heightened (freezing). This process is likely to produce one of two polarized threat appraisals: (a) certainty that the child is under no risk, with accompanying low levels of anxiety, or (b) certainty that she or he is at risk, with resultant high levels of anxiety.

In other words, the assessment of risk to the child should play an uneven role in affecting distress for low-NFC parents but a consistent and systematic role for those with high NFC. Together, these logics lead to the prediction that NFC and risk perception both moderate the impact of uncertainty on parental anxiety in the context of response delays. Specifically, we predict that:

> H2: High risk assessment heightens the association between uncertainty and parental anxiety among high-NFC parents but will not have a significant effect among low-NFC parents.

Method

Participants

Parents were recruited through students in introductory communication courses at a university in the western United States. Students (N = 251) received extra course credit in return for their completion of a survey unrelated to this investigation and their recruitment of a parent or family friend willing to participate in this study. In order to qualify, the parent/family friend had to serve as the primary caregiver for a child aged 13–19 who was currently living with them. Caregivers who agreed to participate were entered into a drawing to win a $25 gift card. The analyses for this investigation were limited to the 132 (53%) of the 251 parent participants who completed the entry survey and reported at least two contact efforts (an attempt to reach the child via phone call or text message), in total, across four nightly surveys.

Seventy-eight percent of that subsample was female (n = 104). Participants ranged in age from 27 to 62 years old (M = 49 years, SD = 5.5), and their adolescent children ranged in age from 13 to 19 (M = 18 years, SD = 2.3). Most of the parents were Caucasian (n = 92, 69.2%), with Asian/Asian-American characterizing the second largest ethnic group (n = 18, 13.5%). The household income ranged from less than $40,000 to over $140,000 annually, with a median income category of $121,000–$140,000.

Procedures and Measures

Participants were asked to complete a total of five online questionnaires: one entry questionnaire and another per night for four nights, between Thursday and Sunday, inclusive. The entry survey was completed the same day as the first nightly survey. The length of the study and the focus on a weekend was chosen for two reasons. The number of days came from results of a pilot study (N = 11) in which nightly data were collected across seven consecutive days, and which revealed fatigue among participants. The selection of particular days (focused on the weekend), rose from a conjecture that the likelihood of a threat-related account for response delays is heightened on weekends, when fatal accidents involving risky behaviors are elevated (National Highway Traffic Safety Administration, 2006). Finally, data were collected across multiple nights, as opposed to just one, in order produce a more representative sample of contact efforts and related response delays.

At the end of each of the four nights, parents were asked to record detailed information about the first three contact efforts (text messages or phone calls) that they initiated to their child's mobile phone after 5:00 p.m., when the chances for threat-related appraisals are elevated (Williams & Wells, 1995). The entries were also explicitly restricted to those texts or calls for which the parent expected a response. Like the limit to the number of days, the limit of the first three contact efforts was done in order reduce participants' fatigue. Keeping in mind that the sample was restricted for analysis to those who reported at least two contact efforts across at least two nights, the number of reported contacted efforts across the four nights in the restricted sample spanned the theoretical range (*min* = 2, *max* = 12; M = 5.44).

Entry survey. The entry questionnaire included several measures. To begin, parents were asked to think of one child aged 13–19 who was currently living with them. To ensure focus on one child, participants were asked to identify that child by initials, age, and gender. Participants then completed several measures, including mental health and need for closure.

Mental health. Mental health was included as a possible covariate. Participants responded to an abbreviated version of the "Mental Health Inventory" called the MHI-5, a well-tested instrument that includes five items (e.g., "How much of the time during the last month have you felt calm and peaceful?"), assessed on a six-point scale ranging from (1) "None of the time" to (6) "All of the time," and intended to capture individuals' mental health (McDowell, 2006). Two items were recoded so that lower scores represented higher mental health, creating a summed theoretical range of 5–30 (α = 0.83, M = 11.71, SD = 3.86).

Need for closure. The original Need for Closure Scale (NFCS) was developed by Kruglanski, Webster, and Klem (1993). We used a shortened version of the Need for Closure Scale (NFCS) (Pierro, Schultz, & Kruglanski, 2008), which included 13 items assessing cognitive desire for closure across various contexts, rated on a six-point scale, ranging from (1) "None of the time" to (6) "All of the time" (e.g., "In cases of uncertainty, I prefer to make an immediate decision, whatever it may be"). Higher scores indicated greater need for closure (α = 0.86, *M* = 3.09, *SD* = 0.78).

Nightly surveys. Participants completed a nightly survey before bed each night. Each survey asked for assessments of the first three contact efforts, regardless of whether they were text-based efforts or involved a phone call. The caveat was that they were required to be contact efforts for which the parent expected a response. For each of the first three contact efforts, participants recorded the time that the contact effort was made, the content of the message, and the time when the child first responded.

There were two follow-up sections associated with each contact effort: (a) the first assessed the participants' cognitive and emotional states *at the time that the contact effort was made*, and the second (b) focused on cognitive and emotional states during the *delay period between the contact effort and response*. Given that data from the second section were intended to reflect a period of delay between the contact effort and the response, it was preceded by a question that asked participants if they had "experienced a gap (i.e., more than 1–2 minutes) between the time that [they] tried to contact their son/daughter and the time [they] received a response." Those who responded negatively skipped that section. In addition, since our interest for this investigation was in the impact of delays that exceeded normative expectations, the first question in the second section asked participants if their child's response to that contact effort occurred within the expected amount of time ("1" = "Yes, it was within the time period I was expecting"; "2" = "No, it took a little longer than I expected for him/her to respond"; 3 = "No, it took a lot longer than I expected for him/her to respond"). Data from this item were dichotomized (0 = the response fell within the expected time frame; 1= the response time was longer than expected) and served as the operationalization of expectancy violations, hereafter labeled "violation."

Beyond the assessment of a response-time violation, other measures of interest for this investigation (all part of the "delay period" section), included: (a) a one-item measure of perceived risk or danger to the child that was assessed on a five-point scale, ranging from (1) "No risk" to (5) "Great risk" ("S/he was engaging in behavior or was in a situation that reflected ____ to his/her health/well-being,") (*M* = 1.38, *SD* = 0.55); (b) a one-item measure of parental uncertainty regarding the child's whereabouts and safety, also assessed on a five-point scale, in this case ranging from

(1) "No uncertainty" to (5) "High uncertainty" ("How uncertain were you about his/her whereabouts and/or behavior?") (M = 4.37, SD = 3.95); and (c) a six-item measure of anxiety state, adapted from O'Neil and Richardson (1977), with items tapping the degree of calmness, tension, ease, jitteriness, anxiety, and relaxation on a four-point scale from (1) "Not at all" to (4) "Very much so" (α = 0.91, M = 2.00, SD =.055). The risk and uncertainty measures were limited to one item in an attempt to alleviate participant fatigue in a relatively lengthy survey.

Results

In order to capture overall parental experiences across data from four nights while allowing for a range of missingness in "delay period" data across both days and contact effort, daily indices that collapsed data across both contact efforts and days were used.

H1: Negative Expectancies and Uncertainty

The first hypothesis proposed that parents' experiences of delays in expected response times are associated with uncertainty. Because the outcome involves uncertainty experienced during the response delay, only participants who reported experiencing a delay (i.e., those who completed the second section) at any time during the four nights were included in this analysis (n = 105). Of those, 55% (n = 58) experienced a delay that negatively violated their time expectations.

A preliminary analysis was conducted to account for the influence of three variables that the literature suggested might influence parents' experience of delays (Peters, Burraston, & Mertz, 2004; Slovic, 1999): parent sex, child sex, and parent mental health at the entry survey. Specifically, a univariate analysis of covariance (ANCOVA) was conducted with uncertainty as the dependent variable and the experience of a negative violation as the independent variable.

Because none of the covariates was a significant predictor of uncertainty [parent sex, $F(1,104)$ =.254, p >.05; child sex, $F(104, 1)$ =.737, p >.05; parent mental health, $F(1,104)$ = 1.780, p >.05], an independent-samples t-test was conducted to test the hypothesis. Results revealed that the two groups differed in their levels of uncertainty about the child's safety, $t(104)$ = 2.06, p <.05. Inspection of the means revealed that parents who experienced a violation reported higher uncertainty (M = 2.28, SD =.125) than those who did not (M = 1.90, SD =.14). As such, the prediction was supported—parents whose children took longer than expected to respond to a contact effort experienced more uncertainty than those whose children responded within the expected time frame.

H2: The Impact of NFC on Anxiety

The second hypothesis proposed that trait-level differences on NFC and state-level differences on risk perceptions jointly moderate the impact of uncertainty on anxiety. Specifically, for high-NFC participants, risk perception during the delay period was expected to impact the relationship between uncertainty and anxiety during that same period such that perceptions of high risk would be associated with higher levels of anxiety, and perceptions of little to no risk would be associated with lower levels of anxiety. In contrast, for low-NFC individuals, risk perception during the delay period was not expected to play a role in the size of the uncertainty–anxiety association during that same period.

Growth curve analysis was used initially to determine whether there was significant variability in anxiety within and between participants over time. An unconditional model or baseline model was estimated to test for these changes in anxiety. However, the results revealed no significant variability in the random intercept within the participants (i.e., no systematic difference across days; γ =.02, $t(48)$ =.02, p >.05) or between participants (*Wald Z* =.31, p >.05). Some of this lack of significance could be due to the fact that only 48 of the parents reported response delays on more than one occasion during the four nights (i.e., were able to be used in the assessment of within-person variance). Given that there was no significant change in the parents' anxiety over time, the variables of interest (i.e., uncertainty, risk, anxiety) were analyzed as fixed and were averaged across the nightly surveys.

Given that the prediction argued for a difference between high- and low-NFC groups (on the moderating role of risk perception), the analyses were conducted separately within high- and low-NFC groups. To do so, NFC scores were divided at the median (*Median* = 3) resulting in 66 participants in the high-NFC group and 62 participants in the low. Like H1, preliminary analyses showed the three covariates did not significantly impact the outcome of interest. As such, they were excluded from the hypothesis test. To test H2, a hierarchical regression was conducted within each of the two levels of NFC, with parental anxiety as the outcome, the main effects for uncertainty and perceived risk entered in the first step, and their interaction entered in the second step. Typically, significant interaction terms signal the presence of a moderating relationship and are followed up with analysis of the slope of the simple regression line (reflecting the association between the predictor and outcome) at three levels of the moderator: one standard deviation below the mean, at the mean, and one standard deviation above the mean (see Aiken & West, 1991; Frazier, Tix, & Barron, 2004). However, the interaction term is notoriously sensitive to low power. In fact, Aguinis (2004) argues that the power of that test to detect true differences in slopes is often as low as 50% and recommends sample sizes of at least 200 to feel confident the accuracy of the interaction term is a reflection of the presence of a moderating relationship (see also McClelland & Judd, 1993). Because of our small sample size, and because we had theoretical justification to go beyond the omnibus results, we relied on the simple-effect test of the slopes at low, moderate, and high levels of the moderator for evidence of a moderating relationship, as opposed to the interaction term. An SPSS macro (MODPROBE), developed by Hayes and Matthes (2009) to examine moderators in regression analyses, was used to perform those simple-effect tests. All variables were mean centered.

Individuals with low NFC. Consistent with H2, the association between uncertainty and anxiety was similar (nonsignificant) across all three levels of perceived risk. Specifically, results showed that the association between uncertainty and anxiety was nonsignificant at low, $b = .07$, $SE = .12$, $t(47) = 0.57$, $p > .05$; moderate, $b = .11$, $SE = .09$, $t(47) = 1.16$, $p > .05$; and high levels of risk, $b = .14$, $SE = .12$, $t(47) = 1.16$, $p > .05$. In other words, perceived risk did not moderate uncertainty's impact on anxiety.

Individuals with high NFC. Also consistent with H2, the analyses of the slopes showed differential impacts of uncertainty on anxiety for high-NFC parents across low, moderate, and high levels of perceived risk. Specifically, the analyses revealed a significant association between uncertainty and anxiety at moderate, $b = .22$, $SE = .08$, $t(49) = 2.77$, $p < .01$; and high, $b = .30$, $SE = .12$, $t(49) = 2.51$, $p < .05$, levels of perceived risk, but not at low levels, $b = .14$, $SE = .10$, $t(49) = 1.35$, $p > .05$. In other words, consistent with the prediction, uncertainty negatively impacted anxiety for the high-NFC individuals but only at elevated levels of perceived risk.

Discussion

The principal purpose of this investigation was to examine the impact on parents' anxiety of delays in their children's response to cell phone contact efforts, using the theoretical framework of need for closure, together with literature on cognitive heuristics. Results generally suggested that (a) such delays did produce uncertainty for parents and (b) the negative impact of uncertainty differed according to parents' propensity toward high or low need for closure. These findings have implications at both theoretical and applied levels.

Response Delays and Parental Uncertainty

The first hypothesis predicted that parents would experience uncertainty about their adolescent child's well-being to the extent that the child's response to their contact efforts was slower than expected. Results were consistent with that prediction, indicating that the violation of expected response time was indeed associated with the experience of uncertainty among parents. It is also worth noting that 23% of parents (58 out of 251 participants) reported at least one occasion during the four-night period of the study in which they experienced a longer-than-expected delay in their child's response to the contact effort. Given that these data reflect experiences from only one of approximately 48 weekends each year, and that cell phone use among teenagers continues to rise, the relevance of this type of uncertainty to parent–child relationships is not inconsequential.

Importantly, while previous studies have noted negative perceptions associated with significant time gaps between contact efforts and received response using mobile technology (e.g., Kalman & Rafaeli, 2011; Walther & Tidwell, 1995), these findings are the first to establish the negative uncertainty-related consequences of mobile phone use. Three clear implications emerge from these data. First, they support the utility of threat-related uncertainty as a construct for examining the consequence of new technologies, particularly within the context of close relationships such as the parent–child relationship. While scholars have long examined individuals' uncertainty about the benefits and costs of a technology as predictors of its adoption (see Marra, Pannell, & Ghadim, 2003), they have ignored the possibility that these technologies might add threat-related uncertainty to our lives as a result of features they possess and expectations they may create. Second, the data suggest that scholars should play closer attention to how mobile technology affects the parent–child relationship. A growing body of research has established that uncertainty experienced in relational contexts plays an important role for a wide range of relationship outcomes, from closeness to trust (for review, see Knobloch & Satterlee, 2009). The current finding that the violation of response-time expectations is relatively common among teenagers communicating with their parents, which in turn often begets parental uncertainty, underscores the need to more closely examine the relational implications for parent–child relationships. Finally, extrapolating these data (e.g., the commonality of delays) to the range of adolescent years implies that some parents experience chronic bouts of uncertainty regarding their children's well-being as a result of these response delays. An increasing number of studies are showing that such experiences may have deleterious consequences for well-being (for review, see Afifi, Felix, & Afifi, 2012). Indeed, with that possibility in mind, we examined the impact of parental uncertainty on their levels of anxiety.

Response Delays and Parental Anxiety

The second hypothesis examined the doubly moderating roles of trait-level differences in need for closure and state-level perceptions of risk on the association between parental uncertainty about their child's safety and parental anxiety. Specifically, we argued that uncertainty's effect on anxiety is greater when risk assessment is high than when it is low, but that moderating effect of risk on the uncertainty–anxiety association only applies to high-, not low-, NFC parents. Indeed, that is what we found. For low-NFC parents, a main effect for risk on anxiety emerged such that higher perceptions of risk to the child were associated with higher anxiety but, interestingly, uncertainty about the child's whereabouts was not associated with anxiety. As predicted, risk did not moderate the relationship between uncertainty and anxiety. This pattern is relatively consistent with prior studies related to cognitive processing among low-NFC individuals (e.g., Webster & Kruglanski, 1994). It is likely that low-NFC parents who experienced a longer-than-expected response delay considered multiple explanations for their child's delay rather than dwelling solely upon their assessment of risk. The result was that (a) perceived risk was a good indicator of threat (as it should be), (b) uncertainty—as an experience that could be appraised in many ways (Brashers, 2001)—was not related to anxiety in any systematic way, and (c) perceived risk was not privileged in the appraisal of uncertainty more than other appraisal contributors.

In contrast, the appraisal of—and subsequent reaction to—uncertainty was more predictable/less complex for high-NFC parents: If they perceived that the child was at risk, their uncertainty was appraised as threat and it produced high levels of anxiety; if they did not, their uncertainty was appraised as nonthreatening, resulting in low levels of anxiety. Consistent with the notion of "seizing and freezing" (Kruglanski & Webster, 1996) and previous work finding that heuristically processed information that an individual judges to be credible leads to stronger confidence in its veracity (Trumbo, 2002), high NFC individuals, once committed to an explanation for their child's delay, appeared to disregard all other possible explanations. Thus, those high-NFC parents who perceived little risk to their child did not report high anxiety because they felt highly confident in their conclusion that their child was safe. Those who reached the conclusion that their child was in some danger, however, also felt confident in their conclusion; as such, they experienced heightened anxiety in response to the uncertainty created by their child's expectancy violation.

These results highlight the importance of personality traits in the assessment of and subsequent emotional reaction to risk. Extant literature suggests universally negative emotional outcomes resulting from threat-related uncertainty (for review, see Afifi, 2009), but the present findings suggest that this relationship may be more complex. As a result of their tendency to heuristically process risk, some individuals may actually experience reduced anxiety in response to uncertainty, contradicting the conventionally accepted uncertainty–anxiety link. This phenomenon is especially important in the context of parent–child relationships. We found that parents who demonstrate a high need for closure and are prone to judgments of elevated risk are especially susceptible to elevated levels of anxiety, a tendency that is likely to have negative consequences for overall well-being. These findings have implications for not only the way parents can evaluate and monitor their own responses to uncertainty but also for how parents can manage their communication with adolescents in an effort to reduce violations and subsequent anxiety.

Limitations

Though the findings of this study offer valuable contributions to the existing literature as well as our understanding of the role of mobile technology in parent–adolescent relationships, they must be interpreted within the nature of the sample and research design. Participation in the study required parents who were willing to assist their children by completing a series of questionnaires over a four-day period. As a result, the sample of parents is likely especially involved in the lives of their children, which may in turn affect their perception of threats to their child, producing elevations in reports of anxiety. This effect is potentially heightened by the fact that a majority of the respondents (78%) were mothers, who have been shown to worry more about their children than fathers (Walzer, 1996). The design of the research might have also impacted the results; although the survey captured longitudinal data, the abbreviated requirement of days and the restriction to only the first three contact efforts each evening placed an artificial ceiling on their reported experiences. The result may have been the loss of experiences that came near the end of the night, beyond the third contact effort. Importantly, though, the vast majority of participants (74–82%) reported fewer than three contact efforts on any one night during the period of the study, making it unlikely that the artificial ceiling affected our findings in any substantial way. In fact, the bigger limitations came from a small sample of contact efforts with response delays, thereby reducing power. The emergence of the predicted patterns in H2 despite the low power speaks to its strength as a pattern of behavior. Finally, this investigation did not include measures of information seeking. Given the wide range of possible strategies for gathering information (see Hogan & Brashers, 2009), future studies would benefit from a more thorough examination of the actions parents took to manage their uncertainty following response delays. Regardless of these limitations, however, the study still suggests several practical applications for parents.

Applications

The results of this study carry important implications for how family communication is influenced by new technology and pave the way for fruitful directions for this area of research. One of the clearest implications is the area of misunderstanding between parents' and children's expectations for the role of cell phones and how communication plays a central role in managing these misunderstandings. Parents often give adolescents a cell phone so that they can know where they are and get a hold of them more easily. As previous scholars note, parents tend to view cell phones as a tool of security or as a digital leash to allow their children to go out on their own while ensuring parents and children can always contact each other (Campbell, 2006; Ling & Yttri, 2002; Nafus & Tracey, 2002). Paradoxically, it seems that parents' implicit and explicit expectations that their teens will respond to contact efforts are regularly lost in translation between parents and their adolescent children. In other words, this tool designed to give parents increased peace of mind as to their children's safety might actually serve to increase parents' uncertainty and anxiety when their expectations for their children's responsiveness are violated. This is not of course to imply that cell phones are doing more harm than good for parent–child relationships; instead, it illustrates the importance of children's understanding of parents' expectations as well as parents' awareness of their own potential cognitive biases (i.e., high NFC leading to jumping to conclusions or "seizing and freezing").

Based on these findings, future research should explore to what extent parents establish explicit expectations or rules for cell phone use and what those conversations look like. Families in which cell phone use expectations are explicitly established (and followed) might experience fewer expectation violations and presumably less uncertainty and anxiety. However, when these expectations go assumed or unspoken between parents and their children, there is increased possibility for greater uncertainty and anxiety as a result of response delays, as well as potential for greater likelihood of subsequent parent–child conflict. Past research on parent rules for teen driving (a context very similar to teen cell phone use) has shown that, while teens and parents report being aware of similar rules, both parents and teens report that some of these rules are not explicit, but instead "unspoken" (Hartos, Shattuck, Simons-Morton, & Beck, 2004). Similarly, the current findings show a disconnect in parent–child response expectations given the frequency of response violations. Although it is common to assume other family members share an understanding of unspoken rules, this assumption should not preclude parents having explicit conversations with their children about cell phone rules and expectations.

While most of this study focused on the parents' experiences, the present results also hold implications for adolescents' experiences of cell phones and family communication. From these data, it seems that adolescents' view of an appropriate response time can differ from their parents' expectations. While many external factors (e.g., not having the phone nearby, being busy with another task, and running out of battery charge) can influence how quickly one can respond to another's contact attempts, another possibility for these delays might be strategic avoidance on an adolescent's part. In a qualitative study of interviews with teenage girls, Campbell (2006) found that, in response to their mothers' calls, girls reported pretending that their phone was off, giving misleading information about their whereabouts or activities, as well as assigning parents special ringtones so they immediately know who is calling and can choose not to answer. In this way, while cell phones might come with at least an implicit obligation to respond to parents' contact efforts, they also provide adolescents the *choice* of when to respond and what information to give, resulting in information manipulation and strategic avoidance. As they are enjoying increases in independence, adolescents likely use their cell phones as a tool to manage their privacy with their parents. Examining the individual, contextual, as well as relational or family factors that might play a role in adolescents' strategic mediated responses to their parents would be a worthwhile direction for future research. Furthermore, existing theoretical frameworks, such as family communication schemata (i.e., conformity orientation and conversation orientation; see Fitzpatrick & Ritchie, 1994) and the circumplex model (see Olson, 2000), would be useful approaches to study parent–child communication via new technology given their focus on family-level variables such as openness and conformity.

In addition to the important theoretical implications for the experience of uncertainty and anxiety in a new technology context, this research can offer important practical takeaways for researchers, students, therapists, family professionals, as well as, of course, parents and their children. Given how often parents perceived a time delay and the possible link to their increased uncertainty and anxiety, it is imperative that parents and children talk about what constitutes a time delay and their expectations for responses. If parents' expectations differ from those of their children (e.g., parents expect a call to be answered, whereas teens prefer to answer a text, or find hitting the "ignore" button to be an acceptable response), then that must be made clear in advance of these delays so that high-NFC parents do not experience elevated anxiety as a result of jumping to conclusions. Parents and teens could set up rules for how to deal with response delays: How long is too long of a delay? When is it acceptable for the parent to call the teen's friend to get a hold of him or her without embarrassing the teen? Is a text message a possible alternative? Having conversations *before* giving a child a cell phone could help parents who want to keep clear expectations and an open dialogue with their children.

Further, parents should be conscious of the issues that this research brings to light when making decisions about when to give their children their own cell phones. Given the importance of heuristics in risk assessment—and their subsequent effect on parents' experiences of anxiety—the child's past actions are important in determining parents' present reactions. As such, ensuring that their child is at the right age and maturity level, consistently demonstrates responsibility, and is willing to follow rules for cell phone use may lower parents' assessment of risk as well as the frequency of response-expectancy violations; parents will know the teen is both responsible and responsive. Furthermore, although clear communication of rules has been emphasized thus far, consistent enforcement of family rules about adolescent cell phone use should also be considered as a crucial method for minimizing parent–child miscommunication and misunderstandings. In the context of teen driving rules, Hartos et al. (2004) argue that flexibility and inconsistent enforcement of rules can lead to teens finding "exceptions" to the rules and increased parent–child disagreement over a given rule. As cell phone responses are related to adolescents' safety like driving rules are, the need for parents to consistently enforce their cell phone rules is likely integral to increasing the likelihood that adolescents will follow those rules and understand their parents' expectations.

Establishing more predictable communication patterns with their children is one step that parents might take toward knowing whether a delayed response might merit concern. However, parents must also engage in self-reflection; becoming more aware of the why one might be feeling uncomfortable could help manage uncertainty before feeling too anxious. If high-NFC parents can become more conscious of their tendency to jump to conclusions, they can also try stopping themselves from prematurely seizing and freezing on potentially false information that might confirm their worst fears about their child's welfare. Instead, by establishing more predictable patterns of communication with their child, they might not be caught off guard as often by latencies in their child's replies. This strategy does require cooperation on the child's part, such as sharing their daily schedules with their parents (e.g., "I'm going to the mall, and then to my friend's house. I'll be back in time for dinner") or letting parents know in advance about potential barriers to responding promptly ("I'll be in a movie until 8 p.m., so I won't be able to call or text until afterwards"). Finally, the role of trust and disclosure is vital not only for improving parent–child communication in this context but pervades most contexts of family communication. If children feel like they can open up to their parents (even about things that might be undesirable), building trust in the relationship is much easier. Overall, having explicit conversations about response expectations, determining the appropriate time to give a teen a cell phone, consistently enforcing rules, reflecting on how one's personality may affect interpretations, and generally promoting a culture of trust and disclosure can help keep expectations uniform between parents and their children, minimize parent–child conflict, and promote open parent–child communication.

Taken as a whole, the present findings offer insight into parents' cognitive processes during periods of expectation violation, an important context in today's technologically mobile society. These results provide important evidence that personality traits such as NFC impact the relationship between uncertainty and anxiety, offering a more complex view of the cognitive processes occurring in parents experiencing a delay in response times. They are likely reflective of processes that occur in contexts outside of the present study of parents and children; individuals who possess high NFC may experience greater levels of anxiety as a result of uncertainty in various relationships. To the extent to which the processes occur in various relationships, this knowledge may help high-NFC individuals manage their own uncertainty and subsequent anxiety. Finally, these results lend insight into a number of practical applications to improve parent–adolescent relationships and reduce parental experiences of uncertainty and anxiety.

References

Afifi, W. A. (2009). Uncertainty and information management in interpersonal contexts. In S. Smith & S. R. Wilson (Eds.), *New directions in interpersonal communication* (pp. 94–114). Thousand Oaks, CA: Sage.

Afifi, W. A., & Burgoon, J. K. (2000). The impact of violations on uncertainty and the consequences for attractiveness. *Human Communication Research, 26,* 203–233. doi:10.1111/j.1468–2958.2000.tb00756.x

Afifi, W. A., & Metts, S. (1998). Characteristics and consequences of expectation violations in close relationships. *Journal of Social and Personal Relationships, 15,* 365–392. doi:10.1177/0265407598153004

Afifi, W. A., Felix, E. D., & Afifi, T. D. (2012). The impact of uncertainty and communal coping on mental health following natural disasters. *Anxiety, Stress & Coping, 25,* 329–347. doi:10.1080/10615806.2011.603048

Aguinis, H. (2004). *Moderated regression*. New York: Guilford.

Aiken, L. S., & West, S. G. (1991). *Multiple regression: Testing and interpreting interactions.* Newbury Park, CA: Sage.

Aoki, K., & Downes, E. J. (2003). An analysis of young people's use of and attitudes towards cell phones. *Telematics and Informatics, 20,* 349–364. doi:10.1016/S0736–5853(03)00018–2

Babrow, A. S., & Matthias, M. S. (2009). Generally unseen challenges in uncertainty management: An application of Problematic Integration Theory. In T. D. Afifi & W. A. Afifi (Eds.), *Uncertainty, information management, and disclosure decisions: Theories and applications* (pp. 9–25). New York: Routledge.

Baron, N. S. (2008). *Always on: Language in an online and mobile world.* Oxford, UK: Oxford University Press.

Blair, B. L., & Fletcher, A. C. (2011). "The only 13-year-old on planet earth without a cell phone": Meanings of cell phones in early adolescents' everyday lives. *Journal of Adolescent Research, 26*, 155–177.

Brashers, D. E. (2001). Communication and uncertainty management. *Journal of Communication, 51*, 477–497. doi:10.1111/j.1460–2466.2001.tb02892.x

Burgoon, J. K., Buller, D., & Woodall, W. G. (1996). *Nonverbal communication: The unspoken dialogue.* New York: McGraw-Hill.

Burgoon, J. K., & Walther, J. B. (1990). Nonverbal expectancies and the consequences of violations. *Human Communication Research, 17*, 232–265. doi:10.1111/j.1468–2958.1990.tb00232.x

Campbell, R. (2006). Teenage girls and cellular phones: Discourse of independence, safety, and "rebellion." *Journal of Youth Studies, 9*, 195–212. doi:10.1080/13676260600635649

Carey, J., & Elton, M. C. J. (2010). *When media are new: Understanding the dynamics of new media adoption and use.* Ann Arbor: The University of Michigan Press.

De Grada, E., Kruglanski, A. W., Mannetti, L., & Pierro, A. (1999). Motivated cognition and group interaction: Need for closure affects the contents and processes of collective negotiations. *Journal of Experimental Social Psychology, 35*, 346–365. doi:10.1006/jesp. 1999.1376

Dechesne, M., & Kruglanski, A. W. (2009). Motivated cognition in its interpersonal context: Need for closure and its implications for information regulation and social interaction. In T. D. Afifi and W. A. Afifi (Eds.), *Uncertainty, information management, and disclosure decisions: Theories and applications.* New York: Routledge.

Döring, N., & Pöschl, S. (2008). Nonverbal cues in mobile phone text messages: The effects of chronemics and proxemics. In R. S. Ling and S. W. Campbell (Eds.), *The reconstruction of space and time* (pp. 109–136). New Brunswick, NJ: Transaction Publishers.

Fitzpatrick, M. A., & Ritchie, L. D. (1994). Communication schemata within the family: Multiple perspectives on family interaction. *Human Communication Research, 20*, 275–301.

Ford, L. A., Babrow, A. S., & Stohl, C. (1996). Social support messages and the management of uncertainty in the experience of breast cancer: An application of problematic integration theory. *Communication Monographs, 63*, 189–207. doi:10.1080/03637759609376389

Frazier, P. A., Tix, A. P., & Barron, K. E. (2004). Testing moderator and mediator effects in counseling psychology research. *Journal of Counseling Psychology, 51*, 115–134. doi:10.1037/0022–0167.51.1.115

Gärling, A. (1989). Parents' heuristics for judging children's accident risk. *Scandinavian Journal of Psychology, 30*, 134–145. doi:10.1111/j.1467–9450.1989.tb01075.x

Hartos, J. L., Shattuck, T., Simons-Morton, B. G., & Beck, K. H. (2004). An in-depth look at parent-imposed driving rules: Their strengths and weaknesses. *Journal of Safety Research, 35*, 547–555. doi:10.1016/j.jsr.2004.09.001

Hayes, A. F., & Matthes, J. (2009). Computational procedures for probing interactions in OLS and logistic regression: SPSS and SAS implementations. *Behavior Research Methods, 41*, 924–936. doi:10.3758/BRM.41.3.924

Hogan, T. P. & Brashers, D. E. (2009). The theory of communication and uncertainty management: Implications from the wider realm of information behavior. In T. D. Afifi & W. A. Afifi (Eds.), *Uncertainty, information management, and disclosure decisions: Theories and applications* (pp. 45–66). New York: Routledge.

ITU Statistics. (2013). Aggregate data. Retrieved from http://www.itu.int/en/ITU-D/Statistics/Pages/stat/default.aspx

Kahneman, D., Slovic, P., & Tverksy, A. (2001). *Judgment under uncertainty: Heuristics and biases.* New York: Cambridge University Press.

Kahneman, D. & Tversky, A. (1973). On the psychology of prediction. *Psychological Review, 80,* 237–251. doi:10.1037/h0034747

Kalman, Y. M. & Rafaeli, S. (2008, May). Chronemic nonverbal expectancy violations in written computer-mediated communication. Paper presented at the annual meeting of the International Communication Association, Montreal, Canada.

Kellerman, K., & Reynolds, R. (1990). When ignorance is bliss: The role of motivation to reduce uncertainty in uncertainty reduction theory. *Human Communication Research, 17*, 5–75. doi:10.1111/j.1468–2958.1990.tb00226.x

Knobloch, L. K., & Satterlee, K. L. (2009). Relational uncertainty: Theory and application. In T. D. Afifi & W. A. Afifi (Eds.), *Uncertainty, information management, and disclosure decisions: Theories and applications* (pp. 106–127). New York: Routledge.

Kruglanski, A. W. (1990). Motivations for judging and knowing: Implications for causal attribution. In E. T. Higgins & R. M. Sorrentino (Eds.), *The handbook of motivation and cognition: Foundation of social behavior* (Vol. 2, pp. 333–368). New York: Guilford Press.

Kruglanski, A. W., & Webster, D. M. (1996). Motivated closing of the mind: "Seizing" and "freezing." *Psychological Review, 103,* 263–283. doi:10.1037/0033–295X.103.2.263

Kruglanski, A. W., Webster, D. M., & Klem, A. (1993). Motivated resistance and openness to persuasion in the presence or absence of prior information. *Journal of Personality and Social Psychology, 65,* 861–876. doi:10.1037/0022–3514.65.5.861

Lazarus, R. S. (1998). Emotions and adaptation. In J. M. Jenkins, K. Oatley, and N. L. Stein (Eds.), *Human emotions: A reader* (pp. 38–44). Malden, MA: Blackwell.

Lenhart, A. (2010). Teens, cell phones, and texting: Text messaging becomes centerpiece communication. Pew Internet and American Life Project. Retrieved from http://pewresearch.org/pubs/1572/teens-cell-phones-text-messages

Lenhart, A. (2012). Teens, smartphones & texting. Pew Internet and American Life Project. Retrieved from http://www.pewinternet.org/files/old-media/Files/Reports/2012/PIP_Teens_Smartphones_and_Texting.pdf

Leung, L., & Wei, R. (2000). More than just talk on the move: Uses and gratifications of the cellular phone. *Journalism and Mass Communication Quarterly, 77*, 308–320.

Licoppe, C., & Smoreda, Z. (2005). Are social networks technologically embedded? How networks are changing today with changes in communication technology. *Social Networks, 27,* 317–335. doi:10.1016/j.socnet.2004.11.001

Ling, R., & Yttri, B. (2002). Hyper-coordination via mobile phones in Norway. In J. E. Katz & M. Aakhus (Eds.), *Perpetual contact: Mobile communication, private talk, public performance* (pp. 139–169). Cambridge, UK: Cambridge University Press.

Madden, M., Lenhart, A., Duggan, M., Cortesi, S., & Gasser, R. (2013). Teens and technology 2103. Pew Research Internet Project. Retrieved from http://www.pewinternet.org/2013/03/13/teens-and-technology-2013/

Marra, M., Pannell, D. J., & Ghadim, A. A. (2003). The economics of risk, uncertainty, and learning in the adoption of new agricultural technologies: Where are we on the learning curve? *Agricultural Systems, 75,* 215–234. doi:10.1016/S0308–521X(02)00066–5

McClelland, G. H., & Judd, C. M. (1993). Statistical difficulties of detecting interactions and moderator effects. *Psychological Bulletin, 114,* 376–390. doi:10.1037/0033–2909.114.2.376

McDowell, I. (2006). *Measuring health: A guide to rating scales and questionnaires.* New York: Oxford University Press.

Miceli, M., & Castelfranchi, C. (2005). Anxiety as an "epistemic" emotion: An uncertainty theory of anxiety. *Anxiety, Stress, and Coping, 18,* 291–319. doi:10.1080/10615800500209324

Nafus, D., & Tracey, K. (2002). Mobile phone consumption and concepts of personhood. In J. E. Katz & M. Aakhus (Eds.), *Perpetual contact: Mobile communication, private talk, public performance* (pp. 206–221). Cambridge, UK: Cambridge University Press.

National Highway Safety Administration. (2006). Traffic safety annual assessment. Retrieved from http://www.nhtsa.dot.gov/

Olson, D. H. (2000). Circumplex model of marital and family systems. *Journal of Family Therapy, 22,* 144–167.

O'Neil, H. F., & Richardson, F. C. (1977). Anxiety and learning in computer-based learning environments: An overview. In J. E. Sieber, H. F. O'Neil, & S. Tobias (Eds.), *Anxiety, learning, and instruction* (pp. 133–146). New York: Lawrence Erlbaum Associates.

Peters, E. M., Burraston, B., & Mertz, C. K. (2004). An emotion-based model of risk perception and stigma susceptibility: Cognitive appraisals of emotion, affective reactivity, worldviews, and risk perceptions in the generation of technological stigma. *Risk Analysis, 25,* 1349–1367. doi:10.1111/j.0272–4332.2004.00531.x

Pierro, A., Schultz, J., & Kruglanski, A. (2008). Revised need-for-closure scale: Short-form. Unpublished data.

Power, M. J., & Dalgleish, T. (1997). *Cognition and emotion: From order to disorder.* Hove, UK: Psychology Press.

Schiano, D. J., Chen, C. P., Ginsberg, J., Gretarsdottir, U., Huddleston, M., & Isaacs, E. (2002). Teen use of messaging media. *Proceedings of ACM Conference on Human Factors in Computing Systems CHI '02* (Minneapolis, MN, 2002), New York: ACM Press.

Schwarz, N., Bless, H., Strack, F., Klumpp, G., Rittenauer-Schatka, H., & Simons, A. (1991). Ease of retrieval as information: Another look at the availability heuristic. *Journal of Personality and Social Psychology, 61,* 195–202. doi:10.1037/0022–3514.61.2.195

Sheldon, O. J., Thomas-Hunt, M. C., & Proell, C. A. (2006). When timeliness matters: The effect of status on reactions to perceived time delay within distributed collaboration. *Journal of Applied Psychology, 91,* 1385–1395. doi:10.1037/0021–9010.91.6.1385

Slovic, P. (1999). Trust, emotion, sex, politics, and science: Surveying the risk-assessment battlefield. *Risk Analysis, 19,* 689–701. doi:10.1023/A:1007041821623

Trumbo, C. W. (2002). Information processing and risk perception: An adaptation of the Heuristic-Systematic Model. *Journal of Communication, 52,* 367–382. doi:10.1111/j.1460–2466.2002.tb02550.x

Tversky, A., & Kahneman, D. (1973). Availability: A heuristic for judging the frequency and probability. *Cognitive Psychology, 5,* 201–232. doi:10.1016/0010–0285(73)90033–9

Vermeir, I., Van Kenhove, P., & Hendrickx, H. (2002). The influence of need for closure on consumers' choice behaviour. *Journal of Economic Psychology, 23,* 703–727. doi:10.1016/S0167–4870(02)00135–6

Walther, J. B., & Tidwell, L. C. (1995). Nonverbal cues in computer-mediated communication, and the effect of chronemics on relational communication. *Journal of Organizational Computing, 5,* 355–378. doi:10.1080/10919399509540258

Walzer, S. (1996). Thinking about the baby: Gender and divisions of infant care. *Social Problems, 43,* 219–234.

Webster, D. M., & Kruglanski, A. W. (1994). Individual differences in need for cognitive closure. *Journal of Personality and Social Psychology, 67,* 1049–1062.

Williams, A. F., & Wells, J. K. (1995). Deaths of teenagers as motor-vehicle passengers. *Journal of Safety Research, 26,* 161–167. doi:10.1016/0022–4375(95)00012-F

18

Parental Uncertainty and Information Seeking on Facebook

LIESEL L. SHARABI
DAVID J. ROACHÉ
KIMBERLY B. PUSATERI
University of Illinois at Urbana-Champaign

Introduction

The impact of mediated communication on interpersonal relationships has been well documented (for review, see Walther, 2011). However, the pervasive role of mediated communication—social network sites (SNSs) in particular—in family communication has received scant attention. In fact, only recently have scholars begun to unpack the ways families communicate and relate through SNSs. Of those with Internet access, more than two thirds of middle-aged adults (ages 30–49) and young adults (ages 18–29) use SNSs (Duggan & Smith, 2013). This suggests that a large number of parents and their college-aged children are on Facebook and are "friends" with each other (e.g., Child & Westermann, 2013; Kanter, Afifi, & Robbins, 2012).

This chapter explores, through the lens of uncertainty reduction theory (URT; Berger & Calabrese, 1975), how, if at all, parents use Facebook to obtain information about their child's life at college. Originally applied to initial interactions, URT has since been applied to SNSs (e.g., Antheunis, Valkenburg, & Peter, 2010) and long-distance relationships (LDRs; Maguire, 2007). SNSs are effective information-seeking channels (Westerman, Van Der Heide, Klein, & Walther, 2008), and Facebook has even become a socially acceptable way to monitor romantic partners (Utz & Beukeboom, 2011). However, it is not yet known if parents take advantage of Facebook's affordances to reduce their uncertainty about their long-distance kin. Tokunaga's (2011) study revealed that romantic dyads engage in interpersonal electronic surveillance, yet it is unclear whether parents perform similar actions to monitor their college-aged children. On average, young adult children who are away at college spend 9 months apart from their parents during the academic year. By nature, it is a relationship with the high potentiality for uncertainty, and therefore ideal for a digital age extension of URT.

Uncertainty in Long-Distance Relationships

A child's graduation from high school marks the beginning of a new phase in the parent–child relationship (Levitt, Silver, & Santos, 2007). During this time many young adults move away from home to attend college, sometimes in different cities, states, or even countries, thereby transforming their relationships with their parents from proximal to long-distance. Maguire and Connaughton (2011) define a LDR as one in which "the unit members perceive they are unable to interact [facetoface] FtF for prolonged periods of time on a regular and/or frequent basis to accomplish their goals" (p. 246). Much of the research about LDRs centers on young adults' dating relationships (Stafford, 2004). Yet the experience of living apart from a loved one is clearly not confined to a particular relationship type. During the transition to college, parents and their young adult children also must acclimate to not seeing each other FtF on a daily basis, which requires, among other things, that they adapt their communication approaches and patterns.

Parent–child relationships often undergo a number of changes when children decide to leave home for the first time (Jablonski & Martino, 2013; Kloep & Hendry, 2010). At this point in children's development, they are expected to pursue individuation and increased separation from their parents, and to establish their own identities as young adults (Aquilino, 1997; Philip, 1988). For young adult children, this typically involves learning how to be self-sufficient and moving away from the friends and family that supported them throughout childhood (Philip, 1988). Parents, on the other hand, typically want to continue as a source of support, while respecting their children's autonomy (Padilla-Walker, Nelson, & Knapp, 2014). As a result, parents are likely to find that they have less authority over their children, that their children rely on them less, and that they do not spend as much time with their children as they used to (Aquilino, 1997). Yet that is not to say that the transition to college has a negative effect on the parent–child bond. Quite the contrary, in fact. Arnett (1997) revealed college-aged adults felt less like dependents and more like equal partners in their relationships with their parents.

Likewise, Jablonski and Martino (2013) found that parents and children alike reported that the transition to adulthood positively impacted their communication and turned their relationship into something more closely resembling a friendship.

Although understudied, the ways parents navigate their LDR with a young adult child during the child's transition to college can have important implications for the future of their relationship. In the context of romantic relationships, some studies suggest physical distance presents challenges for dyads (Sahlstein, 2006). Partners in long-distance dating relationships (LDDRs), for example, are more likely than those in proximal relationships to break up within a 1-year period (Cameron & Ross, 2007). Of course, the parent–child relationship is distinct from the relationship between romantic partners in many ways: It is involuntary, defined by familial ties, and platonic. Other research on romantic relationships suggests individuals in LDDRs have higher quality relationships than do those who are proximal to their partner (Kelmer, Rhoades, Stanley, & Markman, 2013). These discrepant findings might stem from differences in how partners respond to changes in their relationship once they are no longer living proximally or, in the case of parents and children, under the same roof. For instance, Le, Korn, Crockett, and Loving (2010) found the more committed participants were to their romantic relationship, the more they missed a partner when they were temporarily separated, and as such were more motivated to put extra effort into maintaining the relationship (e.g., through positivity, openness, and assurances). In this case, the distance between partners led them to choose communication strategies associated with more positive relational outcomes.

One change parents might experience is nascent uncertainty about what their young adult child is doing, now that he or she is living away from home. Physical separation, coupled with an increased amount of time spent apart from one's partner, can give rise to a climate of ambiguity in LDRs (Sahlstein, 2004, 2006). Maguire and Kinney (2010) confirmed the prominence of uncertainty in LDRs, finding uncertainty to be one of the chief sources of anxiety for female college students in distressed LDDRs. Likewise, Maguire (2007) observed students were less satisfied with their LDDR when they were unsure if they would ever be proximal to their partner again. Despite the fact uncertainty has been primarily explored from the perspective of young adults, it is likely a cognitive state parents experience as well. In fact, Cole et al. (2013) found 70% of parents in their study used Facebook to monitor a child who was still living at home, indicative of uncertainty in the relationship even when it is proximal. In parent–child relationships, parents question and wonder about a range of issues, from a child's homesickness and ability to make new friends (Vianden & Ruder, 2012) to whether their children will ask them for help when in trouble (Kenyon & Koerner, 2009).

Parents might also find as a result of their LDR they spend less time with their child FtF and more time communicating through mediated channels (see Smith chapter in this volume). For all relationship types, a key difference between proximal and long-distance relationships is that the latter largely depend on technology for communication (Maguire & Connaughton, 2011). Facebook is one such digital-age tool, designed specifically to enable convenient contact between partners during periods of physical separation (Baym, 2010), and is used frequently to maintain relationships (Tosun, 2012). Facebook is unique among communication technologies (e.g., text messaging and phone calls) in that it allows college students to integrate their old relationships with family and high school friends and their new relationships with college peers (Stephenson-Abetz & Holman, 2012). Consequently, it makes sense that Facebook would be crucial to the maintenance of the new LDRs between parents and their children transitioning to college.

Uncertainty Reduction and Information Seeking on Facebook

Facebook is now a ubiquitous SNS, one that is changing communication in close relationships (Wilson, Gosling, & Graham, 2012), including that of family members (see Bruess, Li, and Polingo chapter in this volume). Similar to other SNSs, Facebook offers users the ability to create a profile, display their list of friends, and engage with the content shared by those in their network (Ellison & boyd, 2013). As of September 2013, Facebook had 1.19 billion active users each month and 727 million active users each day (Facebook.com, 2013). According to Duggan and Smith (2013), in the United States alone, 71% of adult Internet users are on Facebook. Of these users, 63% log in daily and 40% log in more than once per day (Duggan & Smith, 2013).

Facebook originated on college campuses and was once only available to college students with an .edu email address (boyd & Ellison, 2008). In 2006, Facebook was opened to the general public. One of the top reasons college students report still using Facebook is to maintain long-distance relationships (Tosun, 2012). Facebook makes it easy to communicate across distance by offering a combination of synchronous (e.g., chat) and asynchronous (e.g., wall posts, private messaging) features (Bryant, Marmo, & Ramirez, 2011). Not surprisingly, many college students post on Facebook to reveal information about themselves to their social networks (Waters & Ackerman, 2011). In many ways, Facebook acts as a virtual diary for disclosing both mundane and extraordinary events of daily life to friends and family (Choi & Toma, 2014; Nosko, Wood, & Molema, 2010). For many families, Facebook has become a ritual of connection and functions to support relationship maintenance between extended and immediate family members over time, space, and generations (see Bruess et al. in this volume).

Facebook profiles provide vast amounts of information about others; as such people use the site to learn more about one another (Bryant et al., 2011; Lampe, Ellison, & Steinfield, 2006). In college samples, Facebook has proven to be a valuable uncertainty reduction tool (Stefanone, Hurley, & Yang, 2013). "Creeping" is widely used vernacular referring to how people gather information on Facebook without their target's knowledge. As a strategy for uncertainty reduction, it is appealing to young adults because it is unobtrusive (Stefanone et al., 2013; Trottier, 2012). For instance, users can learn more about their Facebook friends by perusing anything publicly posted on their pages. Research suggests it has become commonplace for college students to reduce uncertainty by creeping on the Facebook pages of individuals in whom they have a keen interest, such as romantic partners both potential (e.g., Fox, Warber, & Makstaller, 2013) and former (e.g., Tong, 2013). It's logical to assume parents might use similar strategies to gather information without their child's knowledge. Bruess et al. (this volume) found family members report actually feeling closer to other family members by monitoring those members' posts and photos on Facebook. The monitoring ritual, one of six identified by Bruess et al., serves a relational maintenance function for members separated by geographical distance. Participants reported that monitoring others' Facebook activity increased perceptions of closeness by allowing information about other family members without the obligation of reciprocity.

Parents can turn to Facebook for a timeline of their young adult child's activities and whereabouts, assuming they are friends with their child on the site. Interestingly, most young adults who receive a Facebook friend request from one of their parents do not perceive it as an invasion of their privacy (Kanter et al., 2012), and most accept the request outright (Child & Westermann, 2013). What is more, Coyne, Padilla-Walker, Day, Harper, and Stockdale (2014) found that children who were friends with their parents on Facebook reported a stronger sense of parent–child connectivity, more prosocial behaviors, and fewer instances of aggression, delinquency, and internalizing problems, perhaps because they knew their parents were monitoring the information they posted. Indeed, one of Facebook's main functions is to help users browse and search for social information, and parents and children are no exception (Wise, Alhabash, & Park, 2010). Even among college students, information seeking is one of the primary internal motivators of Facebook use (Kwon, D'Angelo, & McLeod, 2013). Consequently, parents also might be relying on Facebook for information about their children, including young adult children away at college. To investigate the topic, specifically what kinds of information parents seek and attend to on their child's Facebook page, the following research questions are posed:

RQ1: Do parents seek information on their young adult child's Facebook page?
RQ2: What kinds of information do parents seek on their young adult child's Facebook page?
RQ3: What kinds of information do parents pay the most attention to on their young adult child's Facebook page?

Uncertainty Reduction Theory and Parent Information Seeking

Uncertainty Reduction Theory (URT; Berger & Calabrese, 1975) provides a useful heuristic for examining the association between parental uncertainty and information seeking about their children on Facebook. At the theory's core is the assumption that, as human beings, we have a low tolerance for ambiguity resulting in our desire to explain and predict others' behavior. The theory is premised on seven axioms and 21 theorems linking uncertainty with a number of communication behaviors, including information seeking. According to URT, high levels of uncertainty lead to greater amounts of information seeking, which, in turn, produce lower levels of uncertainty. Although originally intended to explain FtF interactions, scholars have recently begun to apply URT to the online context (e.g., Antheunis et al., 2010; Tidwell & Walther, 2002).

Berger (1979) proposed that people reduce uncertainty through a variety of information-seeking strategies. Specifically, Ramirez, Walther, Burgoon, and Sunnafrank (2002) identified four strategies used in computer-mediated communication (CMC): passive, active, extractive, and interactive. The first three strategies occur in the absence of interaction with the target of one's interest. *Passive strategies* involve observation of a target, such as viewing the information on his or her Facebook page. *Active strategies* are characterized by requests for information from a third party, for example privately messaging a mutual friend on Facebook with questions about a target. *Extractive strategies* consist of searching online databases for information, such as using Facebook to find out where a target attends school and then searching for his or her university on Google for additional information. In contrast to the first three, the last strategy requires direct contact with the other person. *Interactive strategies* are marked by the exchange—including direct questions—of reciprocal self-disclosure, such as asking a target questions via Facebook chat.

URT suggests parents will attempt to resolve uncertainty about their child through information seeking. Even though URT is a theory about relationship development between previously unacquainted individuals, recent research demonstrates even people in close relationships experience relational uncertainty, for instance when one has doubts about the nature of their partnership (Knobloch & Solomon, 1999). In the family context, uncertainty has proven to be a salient experience for couples in the adjustment to an empty nest (Nagy & Theiss, 2013), for parents-in-law during the transition to an extended family (Mikucki-Enyart, 2011), and for adolescents throughout a parent's military deployment (Huebner, Mancini, Wilcox, Grass, & Grass, 2007). Importantly, the content of the uncertainty can differ depending on relationship type (Knobloch, 2008). Bevan, Stetzenbach, Batson, and Bullo (2006), for example, found that in sibling dyads, young adults were more uncertain about their sibling's attitudes and behaviors than they were about the state of the relationship. Thus, although relational uncertainty focuses on ambiguity about the stability or status of the relationship itself, we believe that in the context of long-distance relationships parents will naturally be uncertain about aspects of their college-aged child's choices, both personally and academically. Although parents who choose Facebook to seek information about their child will have access to the full range of information-seeking strategies, given how common passive strategies are on SNSs (Antheunis et al., 2010; Doodson, Gavin, & Joiner, 2013), we believe passive information seeking will have special appeal to parents wanting to reduce uncertainty, leading us to the following hypothesis:

H1: Parental uncertainty will be positively associated with passive information seeking on Facebook.

What is more, internal and external forces likely shape whether parents who are uncertain will rely on Facebook for clarity and the reduction of their uncertainty. Afifi and Schrodt (2003) found that children and adolescents were more likely to discuss their uncertainty about the state of their family when they had a high-quality relationship with their parents, suggesting a close parent–child relationship could lessen the need to engage in passive information seeking on Facebook. Instead, parents who are close to their young adult children and have questions about their lives at college might be more likely to choose direct communication with those children, either through Facebook or other mediated channels. Geographic distance is yet another factor that might mitigate needs for parents' information seeking about their college-aged child, as physical distance often dictates how much time parents and children can spend together in person (Maguire & Connaughton, 2011; Maguire & Kinney, 2010). The farther away their children live, the more parents might depend on Facebook for information to reduce uncertainty. As such, we propose the following moderating effects on the association between uncertainty and information seeking:

H2: Relational closeness will moderate the positive association between parental uncertainty and passive information seeking on Facebook.
H3: Geographic distance will moderate the positive association between parental uncertainty and passive information seeking on Facebook.

Method

Participants

Students enrolled in undergraduate communication courses at a large Midwestern university recruited their parents (N = 205) to participate in this study. Students received a small amount of extra credit when a parent agreed to participate. To be eligible for participation, parents needed to (a) have an active Facebook account and (b) be friends with their child on Facebook.

The resulting sample included more mothers (76.1%; n = 156) than fathers (23.9%; n = 49). Parents ranged in age from 37 to 77 years (M = 49.84; SD = 5.61) and reported their children's ages as between 17 and 31 (M = 20.05; SD = 1.65). The majority of participants were Caucasian (71.7%; n = 147), followed by Asian (10.7%; n = 22), Latino/Latina (5.9%; n = 12), African American or Black (6.3%; n = 13), and other (5.4%; n = 11). Most parents reported on a child who lived more than 60 miles from home (M = 829.44; SD = 2187.28), with distances ranging from 0 to 10,300 miles.

Instruments

Parental uncertainty. A measure of uncertainty was developed via an adaptation of Clatterbuck's (1979) Attributional Confidence Scale. The six-item measure was used to assess how unsure participants were about their child who is away at college and was found to be reliable (α =.88). Participants reported below the midpoint (M = 2.09; SD =.73) on the six-point Likert-type measure, ranging from one (Completely or Almost Completely Certain) to six (Completely or Almost Completely Uncertain), indicating parents demonstrated a moderately low level of uncertainty about their child. Sample items included "How sure are you that your child is doing well (healthy) while away at college?" and "How confident are you that your child is acting responsibly at college?"

Relational closeness. The level of relational closeness participants experienced in the parent–child relationship was measured using the Psychological

Closeness dimension of Vangelisti and Caughlin's (1997) Relational Closeness Questionnaire (*M* = 6.49; *SD* =.55), with the mean level demonstrating parents in our sample felt very close to their child. The five-item Psychological Closeness subscale has been previously validated and also achieved acceptable reliability in the present sample (α =.76). Sample items included "How close are you to your child?" and "How much do you enjoy spending time with your child?" All items were calculated on a one (Not at All) to seven (A Great Deal) Likert-type scale.

Table 18.1. Measure of Passive Information Seeking on Facebook.

Survey Item	Mean (Standard Deviation)
I scan my child's pictures on Facebook to see with whom he/she is spending time.	4.47 (2.02)
I never go to my child's Facebook friends' profiles to seek information.	4.08 (1.90)
I like having the ability to see what my child is doing by looking on his/her Facebook profile.	5.16 (1.58)
I browse my child's pictures on Facebook for information.	4.44 (1.94)
I do not look at comments made on my child's Status Updates for information about him/her.	4.32 (1.77)
Looking at my child's Facebook profile is the best way to check up on my child without directly questioning him/her.	3.44 (1.73)
I read the picture comments left by my child's Facebook friends for information.	3.86 (1.82)

Passive information seeking. An original measure was devised to assess passive information seeking on Facebook (*M* = 4.25; *SD* = 1.38). The seven-item measure achieved acceptable reliability (α =.87) and included items such as "I browse my child's pictures on Facebook for information" and "I like having the ability to see what my child is doing by looking on his/her Facebook profile." All items were calculated on a one (Strongly Disagree) to seven (Strongly Agree) Likert-type scale. See Table 18.1 for the complete Measure of Passive Information Seeking on Facebook.

Open-ended items. Participants were also invited to answer two open-ended questions about how they used Facebook to seek information about their child. More specifically, participants were asked to share what kinds of information they sought on their child's Facebook page and what kinds of information they paid the most attention to. Participants were not limited in the length of their responses.

Coding

Analytic induction (Bulmer, 1979; Znaniecki, 1934) was used to code for the *kinds of information* parents seek and the information parents *pay the most attention to* on their child's Facebook page. Following the guidelines of Bulmer (1979), we began by reading through the entire data set and developing tentative category descriptions. Then, two of the authors inspected a subset of the data using the tentative coding scheme. Identification of deviant cases led to subsequent revisions of the coding scheme (Bulmer, 1979; Znaniecki, 1934). This iterative process continued until all responses were accounted for and our classification system appeared to capture every case represented in the sample.

Once categories were complete, two authors began coding the data. First, we discussed the coding scheme to ensure full understanding of each proposed category. Then we unitized and coded 20% of the data with the goal of reaching 80% agreement (Bauer, 2000). We calculated Krippendorff's alpha values for the *kinds of information* parents seek on their child's Facebook profile and the information parents *pay most attention to* on their child's Facebook profile (.92 and .81, respectively; Krippendorff, 1980). Krippendorff's alpha values demonstrated acceptable levels of intercoder reliability.

When the two raters did not initially agree on coding decisions, each rater stated his or her reasons for the code he or she assigned based on the codebook. In some cases, one of the raters agreed that the other rater was correct based on the criteria, and the data were coded accordingly. When the two raters felt it was not clear how to code a unit of the data, the codebook was modified by redefining the category or adding additional detail to category descriptions. After discrepancies were addressed, the remaining data were divided evenly between the two raters and coded.

Results

Information Parents Seek and Attend to on Their Child's Facebook Page

Our first research question sought to understand whether parents seek information on their child's Facebook page. Mentions of information seeking were frequent (82.5%; $n = 311$), with the majority of parents affirming they use Facebook to search for information about their child (see Table 18.2). A minority of parents reported they *do not* seek information on their child's Facebook page (17.5%; $n = 66$) (see Table 18.3). Some parents noted that they do not use Facebook to seek information out of *respect for child's privacy* (7.4%; $n = 28$) or because *a close relationship makes seeking information on Facebook unnecessary* (4.2%; *n* = 16). Others said they only look at their child's page out of *curiosity or for fun* (5.8%; *n* = 22), not using Facebook as an information-seeking tool.

Table 18.2. Categories and Frequencies of What Kinds of Information Parents Seek on Their Child's Facebook Page.

Category	Example	Count	Percent
Who the child's friends are: Want to know who their child is spending time with.	"I like to see who she is going out with."	56	14.9%
What the child is doing: Want to see what the child is doing/activities he/she engages in.	"To see what he may have done over the weekend."	53	14.1%
Pictures: Look at pictures the child is posting/pictures posted of their child.	"Pictures of the friends/ events she told me about."	49	13.0%
Information to stay informed: Want to know what is going on in the child's life.	"It keeps me connected to their life away from home."	41	10.9%
General well-being: Use in order to check on child's emotional or physical health.	"To make sure everything is alright and she is safe."	38	10.1%
Risky behaviors: Want to make sure the child is making good decisions/not getting into trouble.	"I want to make sure he is making smart decisions."	27	7.1%
Other: Did not provide a direct response to the question; mention was infrequent.	"I don't like to look at it."	21	5.6%
New information: Can discover information that the child does not share.	"This is the info she is least likely to tell me on her own."	17	4.5%
Child's romantic interests: Use in order to see who their child's romantic interests are.	"Who she is dating at the time."	9	2.4%

N* = *311

The second research question asked for the kinds of information parents seek on their child's Facebook page. Respondents most frequently reported seeking information about *who the child's friends are* (14.9%; *n* = 56). Others sought information about *what the child is doing* while away at school (14.1%; *n* = 53), *pictures* their child posted or was tagged in (13.0%; *n* = 49), *information to stay informed* (10.9%; *n* = 41), information about their child's *general well-being* (10.1%; *n* = 38), information about the child's *risky behaviors* (7.1%; *n* = 27), *new information* about their child (4.5%; *n* = 17), and the *child's romantic interests* (2.4%; *n* = 9). Descriptions of these categories, examples, and frequencies are presented in Table 18.2. Importantly, some respondents reported seeking more than one kind of information on their child's Facebook page.

Table 18.3. Categories and Frequencies of Reasons Why Parents Do Not Seek Information on Their Child's Facebook Page.

Category	Example	Count	Percent
Respect for child's privacy: Feel that they do not use Facebook to seek information.	"I only look at her profile when I'm on Facebook. I don't go on with the intent of checking up on her."	28	7.4%
Only look at profile out of curiosity or for fun: Check the child's profile for fun or recreation.	"I am curious about his likes/dislikes and opinions."	22	5.8%
A close relationship makes seeking information on Facebook unnecessary: Relationship is close enough that they do not need Facebook to seek information.	"I have a fantastic relationship with my child and did not get a Facebook account in order to spy."	16	4.2%

***N* = 66**

Table 18.4. Categories and Frequencies of Kinds of Information Parents Pay the Most Attention to on Their Child's Facebook Page.

Category	Example	Count	Percent
Pictures: Most interested in pictures the child is posting/pictures posted of their child.	"Her pictures to make sure they are appropriate for posting."	102	36.6%
Content posted by the child: Attend to status updates and posts the child generates.	"Her posts that directly show her opinions and thoughts."	55	19.7%
Relationships: Most interested in the child's relationships with friends or romantic interests.	"New friends since I am not with him every day."	28	10.0%

Other: Did not provide a direct response to the question; mention was infrequent.	"Like to look at the outfits."	27	9.7%
Content posted by child's friends: Attend to comments or posts made by the child's friends.	"Comments made by friends that are close to him."	27	9.7%
General information: Most interested in general information about the child or daily activities.	"I try to get a general picture of how and what my son is doing."	17	6.1%
Do not seek information out of respect for child's privacy: Feel that they do not use Facebook to seek information.	"I rarely look at my son's profile, I feel I know my son fairly well, I trust him, and I also respect his privacy."	16	5.7%
What the child is doing: Most interested in what the child is doing/activities he/she engages in.	"Destinations, just out of curiosity and concern."	9	3.2%
New information: Information that the child does not directly share with parents.	"I think I know my daughter well enough, but sometimes I learn new information about her."	4	1.4%
School: Attend to information posted about the child's classes or assignments.	"I like to read poems that she may have written for class."	3	1.1%

***N* = 279**

Our third research question asked what kinds of information parents pay the most attention to on their child's Facebook page. Results indicated parents most often pay closest attention to *pictures* (36.6%; *n* = 102), followed by *content posted by the child* (19.7%; *n* = 55), *relationships* (10.0%; *n* = 28), *content posted by child's friends* (9.6%; *n* = 27), *general information* (6.1%; *n* = 17), *what the child is doing* (3.2%; *n* = 9), *new information* about the child (1.4%; n = 4), and information about *school* (1.1%; *n* = 3). Similar to results of the first research question, some parents said they do not seek information on their child's Facebook page out of *respect for child's privacy* (5.7%; *n* = 16). Again, there were also respondents who attended to multiple kinds of information about their child on Facebook. Descriptions of these categories, examples, and frequencies are presented in Table 18.4.

Parental Uncertainty and Information Seeking on Facebook

To test the hypotheses, we conducted hierarchical multiple regression in IBM SPSS Statistics 21. Considering our interest in long-distance parent–child relationships, and in accordance with Stefanone et al.'s (2013) LDR definition, we only included participants who reported being in a long-distance parent–child relationship where distance reported was greater than or equal to 60 miles (n = 196). We held constant parent age and sex in the first step of each model. In all of the models, age was grand mean centered, and geographic distance was centered at 60 miles.

The first hypothesis posited that parental uncertainty would be positively associated with passive information seeking on Facebook. Standardized betas are reported, unless specified otherwise; full results of the regression analyses are presented in Table 18.5. Results of the regression analyses revealed the model significantly predicted information seeking on Facebook, $F(3, 177) = 2.92, p <.05$. Uncertainty significantly predicted information seeking on Facebook, β =.16, $t(177) = 2.18, p <.05$, accounting for an additional 3% of the variance. Thus, these results garnered support for H1: As parents' uncertainty increased, they sought more information about their child on Facebook.

Table 18.5. Summary of Hierarchical Regression Analysis for Parents' Uncertainty Predicting Information Seeking (N = 180).

	Model 1			Model 2		
Variable	*B*	*SE B*	*β*	*B*	*SE B*	*β*
Sex	-0.07	0.25	-0.02	-0.05	0.24	-0.01
Age	-0.04	0.02	**-0.15***	-0.03	0.02	**-.15***
Uncertainty				0.31	0.14	**.16***
ΔR^2		.02			.03	
F for change in R^2		1.96			**4.74***	

Note. Overall model is significant, $F(3, 177) = 2.92, p <.05$.
*$p <.05$.

The second hypothesis posited that relational closeness would moderate the positive association between parental uncertainty and passive information seeking on Facebook. Standardized betas are reported, unless specified otherwise; full results of the regression analyses are presented in Table 18.6. Using hierarchical multiple regression, results revealed the model significantly predicted information seeking on Facebook, $F(5, 169) = 2.58, p <.05$. Results revealed a significant interaction for closeness and uncertainty, β = -1.30, $t(169) = -2.07, p <.05$. There was also a significant effect for uncertainty, β = 1.57, $t(169) = 2.27, p <.05$; however, closeness failed to reach significance, β = 0.40, $t(169) = 1.83$, $p = .07$. Given the statistical significance of the interaction term, we retained the interaction in the model. The model including the interaction term accounted for an additional 2% of the variance. In sum, results of the analyses provided support for H2, such that parents' perceived closeness to their child served to dampen the effect of uncertainty on information seeking (see Figure 18.1).

Table 18.6. Summary of Hierarchical Regression Analysis for Parents' Uncertainty and Closeness Predicting Information Seeking (N = 174).

	Model 1			Model 2			Model 3		
Variable	*B*	*SE B*	*β*	*B*	*SE B*	*β*	*B*	*SE B*	*β*
Sex	-.07	.25	-.02	-.04	.25	-.01	-0.02	.25	-.01
Age	-.04	.02	-.15	-.04	.02	-.15	-.04	.02	**-.18***
Uncertainty				.30	.16	.15	3.06	1.35	**1.57***
Closeness				-.05	.21	-.02	1.04	.57	.40
UNC x CLS							-.44	.21	**-1.30***
ΔR^2		.02			.03			.02	
F for change in R^2		1.89			2.30			**4.27***	

Note: UNC x CLS is interaction term for uncertainty and relational closeness.
Overall model is significant, $F(5, 169) = 2.58$, $p < .05$.
*$p < .05$.

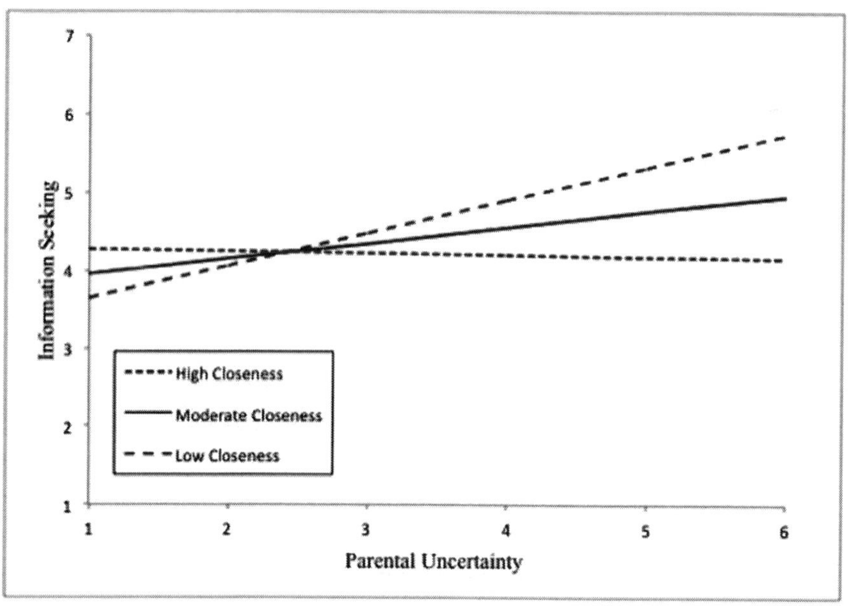

Figure 18.1. Moderating effect of closeness on the association between parental uncertainty and information seeking.

Finally, the third hypothesis proposed that geographic distance would moderate the positive association between parental uncertainty and passive information seeking on Facebook. Standardized betas are reported, unless specified otherwise; full results of the regression analyses are presented in Table 18.7. Results revealed a nonsignificant model when the interaction of distance from child and uncertainty were included. Therefore, we retained the model including uncertainty and distance as predictors only, $F(4, 176) = 2.60, p < .05$. Only uncertainty significantly predicted information seeking on Facebook, $\beta = 0.15, t(176) = 1.97, p = .05$. Geographic distance failed to reach statistical significance, $\beta = 0.10, t(176) = 1.27, p = .21$. Thus, our results did not support H3.

Table 18.7. Summary of Hierarchical Regression Analysis for Parents' Uncertainty and Distance from Child Predicting Information Seeking (N = 180).

	Model 1			Model 2			Model 3		
Variable	*B*	*SE B*	*β*	*B*	*SE B*	*β*	*B*	*SE B*	*β*
Sex	-.07	.25	-.02	-.00	.25	.00	.02	.25	.01
Age	-.04	.02	**-.15***	-.03	.02	-.14	-.03	.02	-.14
Uncertainty				.29	.15	**.15***	.33	.16	**.17***
Distance				.00	.00	.10	.00	.00	0.24
UNC x Distance							-.00	.00	-.16
ΔR^2		.02			.03			.00	
F for change in R^2		1.96			**3.19***			.42	

Note: UNC x Distance is interaction term for uncertainty and distance (in miles) from child. Model 3 failed to reach significance and was therefore not retained. Model 2 is significant $F(4, 176) = 2.60, p < .05$.
$^*p < .05$.

Discussion

The transition from high school to college is the start of a new chapter in the parent–child relationship that may bring with it heightened perceptions of uncertainty (e.g., Sahlstein, 2004, 2006) and an increased dependence on mediated communication (e.g., Maguire & Connaughton, 2011). Consequently, we set out to uncover the kinds of information that parents sought and attended to on Facebook, a SNS that is popular among young and middle-aged adults alike (Rainie, Lenhart, & Smith 2012). At the same time, we were also interested in determining whether parents who were uncertain about their young adult child used Facebook as a source of information. Results showed that parents did indeed seek information on Facebook (RQ1), and they looked for everything from who their child's friends were and what their child was doing at college to whether he or she was engaging in risky behaviors (RQ2). In doing so, they paid the most attention to visual information (e.g., pictures) and content posted by the child him- or herself (e.g., status updates) (RQ3). Furthermore, we found a positive association between parental uncertainty and information seeking (H1) that was moderated by closeness (H2) but not geographic distance (H3). These findings document important changes to how parents manage their uncertainty and acquire information in a digitally saturated age, an age when their young adult children share often multiple aspects of themselves and their lives on Facebook.

Given that college students use Facebook to share information with their friends (Waters & Ackerman, 2011), we reasoned that parents would turn to the site for updates on their young adult child's life. Our qualitative results confirmed this suspicion and showed that parents were most interested in general information about their child's activities and social circles, including *who the child's friends are* and *what the child is doing* while away at school. Some participants also sought information that allowed them to parent from a distance by checking on their child's *general well-being*, such as his or her emotional and physical health, and making sure their child was not engaging in *risky behaviors*. College-aged adults are tasked with learning how to exist separately and independently from their parents (Padilla-Walker et al., 2014; Philip, 1988), and our findings imply that parents might indeed be using Facebook as a means of checking up on their child during this transformative period without threatening his or her independence. Furthermore, a small number of comments came from parents who reported that they did not look for information on Facebook, largely because they thought doing so meant they did not trust their child or that their child was not telling them something. One reason parents articulated for not engaging in creeping behavior was because they only look at their child's profile *out of curiosity or for fun*. At first this appears to be a contradiction—after all, these parents were still searching for information, albeit for a different reason than the explicitly information seeking participants. However, attributing their own actions to "curiosity" might allow these parents to justify their need for information while simultaneously honoring their child's right to privacy, which perhaps they thought they were violating by looking at the child's page at all.

Parents also reported attending to myriad sources of information on their child's Facebook page, with *pictures* and *content posted by the child* being the most often sought information. The literature on college students' Facebook creeping suggests young adults tend to gravitate toward information that is difficult for their friends to manipulate, such as pictures (Fox et al., 2013) and comments that other people post on their friends' walls (Walther, Van Der Heide, Kim, Westerman, & Tong, 2008). Our data show parents might be interested in pictures for similar reasons, perhaps because they are not as easy for their child to control and thus provide a more accurate depiction of his or her life at school. Moreover, although children can be more strategic about presentations of selves through content they generate (e.g., status updates and wall posts) than they can with pictures, their disclosures may still provide useful information. Whereas *pictures* and friend-generated content (e.g., *content posted by child's friends*) are indicative of what the child is doing and with whom, *content posted by the child* gives parents insight into the child's general well-being. For example, parents said they looked at content their child posted to find out "how he is doing" or "just to make sure that everything is ok." Hence, as one of several strategies available to parents for resolving their uncertainty via Facebook (Berger, 1979; Ramirez et al., 2002), passive strategies might be particularly well suited for uncertainty reduction about certain types of issues, like a child's social network and general state of well-being.

Consistent with URT, which posits higher levels of uncertainty lead to greater amounts of information seeking (Berger & Calabrese, 1975), our quantitative results demonstrate that the more uncertain parents are about their child, the more likely they are to passively seek information on Facebook. Parents, like their college-aged children, seem attuned to the wealth of information that can be extracted from Facebook (cf. Stefanone et al., 2013). However, prior research suggests that even though passive information seeking on SNSs is common, it is not always an effective strategy for reducing uncertainty (Antheunis et al., 2010; Doodson et al., 2013). For instance, parents interested in how their child is performing in school might benefit more from a direct strategy, such as a phone call, than they would from trying to infer information from a status update. Consequently, future research should explore whether parents are learning things about their child on Facebook that mitigate and/or exacerbate parental uncertainty.

We also found that relationship closeness weakened the positive association between parental uncertainty and passive information seeking. It is possible that parents who are close to their child believe they have less need to gather information unobtrusively. Just as children and adolescents are more likely to talk to their parents about the state of their family when they are satisfied with the relationship (Afifi & Schrodt, 2003), so too might parents be more inclined to discuss issues that could decrease uncertainty in their LDR with their child when they have a close bond. For these parents, a conversation with their child might provide more useful information than can Facebook. Conversely, parents who are less close to their child may turn to Facebook for reducing uncertainty, either because they do not want to pry or because the information on an SNS provides information their child does not. It stands to reason Facebook is a more valuable source of information for some parents than it is for others. Future researchers are wise to explore the many variables at work in such a relationship.

Contrary to our expectations, the association between uncertainty and passive information seeking was not conditional on the geographic distance between parent and child. Unlike parents who live hundreds of miles away from their child, those who are within driving distance from their child's school have the option of reducing their uncertainty FtF. This leads us to believe that parents are probably using Facebook as a supplement to traditional modes of information seeking (e.g., FtF contact), perhaps because it offers something that other channels cannot easily provide: the ability to gather firsthand information about their child without having to ask for it. Of course, an alternative explanation is that even though geographic distance might increase uncertainty by limiting the amount of time parents spend with their child FtF (Maguire & Connaughton, 2011; Maguire & Kinney, 2010), the actual number of miles between them does not matter once the distance becomes great enough. Because we were interested in LDRs, we only included parents in our quantitative analyses if they lived 60 miles or more from their child, and our results might have been different had we not excluded parents who lived proximally to their child.

There were several limitations to our study. We noticed a floor effect in our data, with most parents reporting that they were at least slightly certain about what their child was doing at college. Additionally, to qualify for our study, parents had to be friends with their child on Facebook. Parents who have unbridled access to their child's Facebook page might be closer to him or her than the average parent (see Child & Westermann, 2013), and future research should determine whether this has any bearing on the strategies they use for managing uncertainty.

In the future, family scholars also may want to explore what parents do with the information they gather on their child's Facebook page. For instance, if and how they talk to their child about what they find may have an effect on their subsequent uncertainty and their decision about whether to keep using Facebook as a source of information. Additionally, the moderating effect of closeness suggests Facebook use does not occur in isolation to the whole of the parent–child relationship. This is consistent with emerging research that calls for the study of transitions (e.g., Ramirez & Wang, 2008; Ramirez & Zhang, 2007) and interconnections (e.g., Caughlin & Sharabi, 2013) between mediated and FtF communication. Moving forward, it would be worth knowing if what parents and children do when they are together is connected to the ways parents use Facebook when they are apart. We might also predict that family appearances on public Facebook walls would indicate more seamless communication between Facebook and other modes of contact.

Application

Our results have a number of practical implications for parents who might want to use Facebook in their LDR with their child. For parents who are uncertain about the well-being, activities, and/or choices of their young adult child away at college, our data suggest that SNS information seeking can indeed be a useful strategy for staying privy to some of your child's new life experiences while not offending his or her privacy or autonomy. For instance, according to the parents in our study, the majority (82.5%) disclosed some attempt at information seeking, and the data reveal how the rather non-obtrusive method of browsing Facebook pictures and others' comments can be useful to parents. Perhaps the digital age is providing a new method of assuaging parents' age-old concerns about young adults' choices, especially when the parent–child relationship is not close enough to warrant conversation about parental concerns, curiosities, and worries.

Our data also point to ways that parents can use Facebook more effectively to stay informed about their child's new life at college. In some cases, Facebook may provide parents with information about their child that could not be easily gleaned from asking him or her directly. For example, on Facebook you can observe your child's interactions with friends and learn about the mundane details of his or her life, thus providing information that might not come up in routine conversation. As such, Facebook can be a useful addition to the communication parents have with their children through other channels. Of course, some caution is warranted, as any information passively acquired on Facebook has the potential to be taken out of context or misperceived. What is more, children can be selective in what they present on their Facebook pages. As such, if parents have legitimate concerns about their child's health or safety, they should seek out multiple sources of information rather than rely on Facebook as their sole means of uncertainty reduction.

Counselors, therapists, child life educators, student affairs professionals, and others who assist parents in launching children to college may also find our study results useful. For example, when a child leaves for college, parents who do not already have a Facebook account might benefit from creating one so they can stay up-to-date on the activities and events in their child's life. Additionally, a select number of parents in our sample reported that they did not seek information about their child on Facebook, often because their relationship was already close or because they did not want to intrude. By assuring parents that checking on their child via social media does not reflect poorly on their relationship, professionals might better support parents and instruct them on how to appropriately use Facebook as an uncertainty-reduction tool. As our study indicates, Facebook has become a popular way for parents to maintain their relationship with their young adult children, and doing so is not always a bad thing.

References

Afifi, T. D., & Schrodt, P. (2003). Uncertainty and the avoidance of the state of one's family in stepfamilies, postdivorce single-parent families, and first-marriage families. *Human Communication Research, 29,* 516–532. doi:10.1093/hcr/29.4.516

Antheunis, M. J., Valkenburg, P. M., & Peter, J. (2010). Getting acquainted through social network sites: Testing a model of online uncertainty reduction and social attraction. *Computers in Human Behavior, 26,* 100–109. doi:10.1016/j.chb.2009.07.005

Aquilino, W. S. (1997). From adolescent to young adult: A prospective study of parent–child relations during the transition to adulthood. *Journal of Marriage and the Family, 59,* 670–686. doi:10.2307/353953

Arnett, J. J. (1997). Young people's conceptions of the transition to adulthood. *Youth & Society, 29,* 3–23. doi:10.1177/0044118X97029001001

Bauer, M. (2000). Classical content analysis: A review. In M. Bauer & G. Gaskell (Eds.), *Qualitative research with text, image, and sound* (pp. 131–151). London: Sage.

Baym, N. K. (2010). *Personal connections in the digital age.* Malden, MA: Polity.

Berger, C. R. (1979). Beyond initial interaction: Uncertainty, understanding, and the development of interpersonal relationships. In H. Giles & R. N. St. Clair (Eds.), *Language and social psychology* (pp. 122–144). Oxford, UK: Blackwell.

Berger, C. R., & Calabrese, R. J. (1975). Some explorations in initial interaction and beyond: Toward a developmental theory of interpersonal communication. *Human Communication Research, 1,* 99–112. doi:10.1111/j.1468–2958.1975.tb00258.x

Bevan, J. L., Stetzenbach, K. A., Batson, E., & Bullo, K. (2006). Factors associated with general partner and relational uncertainty within early adulthood sibling relationships. *Communication Quarterly, 54,* 367–381. doi:10.1080/01463370600878479

boyd, d. m., & Ellison, N. B. (2008). Social network sites: Definition, history, and scholarship. *Journal of Computer-Mediated Communication, 13,* 210–230. doi:10.1111/j.1083–6101.2007.00393.x

Bryant, E. M., Marmo, J., & Ramirez, Jr., A. (2011). A functional approach to social networking sites. In K. B. Wright & L. M. Webb (Eds.), *Computer-mediated communication in personal relationships* (pp. 3–20). New York: Peter Lang.

Bulmer, M. (1979). Concepts in the analysis of qualitative data. *Sociological Review, 27,* 651–677. doi:10.1111/j.1467–954X.1979.tb00354.x

Cameron, J. J., & Ross, M. (2007). In times of uncertainty: Predicting the survival of long-distance relationships. *The Journal of Social Psychology, 147,* 581–606. doi:10.3200/SOCP. 147.6.581–606

Caughlin, J. P., & Sharabi, L. L. (2013). A communicative interdependence perspective of close relationships: The connections between mediated and unmediated interactions matter. *Journal of Communication, 63,* 873–893. doi:10.1111/jcom.12046

Child, J. T., & Westermann, D. A. (2013). Let's be Facebook friends: Exploring parental Facebook friend requests from a communication privacy management (CPM) perspective. *Journal of Family Communication, 13,* 46–59. doi:10.1080/15267431.2012.742089

Choi, M., & Toma, C. L. (2014). Social sharing through interpersonal media: Patterns and effects on emotional well-being. *Computers in Human Behavior, 36,* 530–541. doi:10.1016/j.chb.2014.04.026

Clatterbuck, G. W. (1979). Attributional confidence and uncertainty in initial interaction. *Human Communication Research, 5,* 147–157. doi:10.1111/j.1468–2958.1979.tb00630.x

Cole, J. I., Suman, M., Schramm, P., Zhou, L., & Salvador, A. (2013). The 2013 digital future report: Surveying the digital future. Los Angeles: USC Annenberg School Center for the Digital Future.

Coyne, S. M., Padilla-Walker, L. M., Day, R. D., Harper, J., & Stockdale, L. (2014). A friend request from dear old dad: Associations between parent–child social networking and adolescent outcomes. *CyberPsychology, Behavior, and Social Networking, 17,* 8–13. doi:10.1089/cyber.2012.0623

Doodson, J., Gavin, J., & Joiner, R. (2013, June). *Getting acquainted with groups and individuals: Information seeking, social uncertainty, and social network sites.* Paper presented at the Seventh International AAAI Conference on Weblogs and Social Media, Boston, MA.

Duggan, M., & Smith, A. (2013, December 30). Social media update 2013. Washington, DC: Pew Internet and American Life Project.

Ellison, N. B., & boyd, d. m. (2013). Sociality through social network sites. In W. H. Dutton (Ed.), *The Oxford handbook of Internet studies* (pp. 151–172). Oxford, UK: Oxford University Press.

Facebook.com. (2013, September 30). Key facts. Retrieved from http://newsroom.fb.com/Key-Facts

Fox, J., Warber, K. M., & Makstaller, D. C. (2013). The role of Facebook in romantic relationship development: An exploration of Knapp's relational stage model. *Journal of Social and Personal Relationships, 30,* 771–794. doi:10.1177/0265407512468370

Huebner, A. J., Mancini, J. A., Wilcox, R. M., Grass, S. R., & Grass, G. A. (2007). Parental deployment and youth in military families: Exploring uncertainty and ambiguous loss. *Family Relations, 56,* 112–122. doi:10.1111/j.1471–3729.2007.00445.x

Jablonski, J. F., & Martino, S. (2013). A qualitative exploration of emerging adults' and parents' perspectives on communicating adulthood status. *The Qualitative Report, 18,* 1–12.

Kanter, M., Afifi, T., & Robbins, S. (2012). The impact of parents "friending" their young adult child on Facebook on perceptions of parental privacy invasion and parent–child relationship quality. *Journal of Communication, 62,* 900–917. doi:10.1111/j.1460–2466.2012.01669.x

Kelmer, G., Rhoades, G. K., Stanley, S., & Markman, H. J. (2013). Relationship quality, commitment, and stability in long-distance relationships. *Family Process, 52,* 257–270. doi:10.1111/j.1545–5300.2012.01418.x

Kenyon, D. B., & Koerner, S. S. (2009). Examining emerging adults' and parents' expectations about autonomy during the transition to college. *Journal of Adolescent Research, 24,* 293–320. doi:10.1177/0743558409333021

Kloep, M., & Hendry, L. B. (2010). Letting go or holding on? Parents' perceptions of their relationships with their children during emerging adulthood. *British Journal of Developmental Psychology, 28,* 817–834. doi:10.1348/026151009X480581

Knobloch, L. K. (2008). The content of relational uncertainty within marriage. *Journal of Social and Personal Relationships, 25,* 467–495. doi:10.1177/0265407508090869

Knobloch, L. K., & Solomon, D. H. (1999). Measuring the sources and content of relational uncertainty. *Communication Studies, 50,* 261–278. doi:10.1080/10510979909388499

Krippendorff, K. (1980). *Content analysis: An introduction to its methodology.* Thousand Oaks, CA: Sage.

Kwon, M. W., D'Angelo, J., & McLeod, D. M. (2013). Facebook use and social capital: To bond, to bridge, or to escape. *Bulletin of Science Technology & Society, 33,* 35–43. doi:10.1177/0270467613496767

Lampe, C., Ellison, N., & Steinfield, C. (2006). A Face(book) in the crowd: Social searching vs. social browsing. *Proceedings of CSCW-2006* (pp. 167–170). New York: ACM Press.

Le, B., Korn, M. S., Crockett, E. E., & Loving, T. J. (2010). Missing you maintains us: Missing a romantic partner, commitment, relationship maintenance, and physical infidelity. *Journal of Social and Personal Relationships, 28,* 653–667. doi:10.1177/0265407510384898

Levitt, M. J., Silver, M. E., & Santos, J. D. (2007). Adolescents in transition to adulthood: Parental support, relationship satisfaction, and post-transition adjustment. *Journal of Adult Development, 14,* 53–63. doi:10.1007/s10804–007–9032–5

Maguire, K. C. (2007). "Will it ever end?" A (re)examination of uncertainty in college student long-distance dating relationships. *Communication Quarterly, 55,* 415–432. doi:10.1080/01463370701658002

Maguire, K. C., & Connaughton, S. L. (2011). A cross-cultural examination of technologically-mediated communication and social presence in long-distance relationships. In K. B. Wright & L. M. Webb (Eds.), *Computer-mediated communication in personal relationships* (pp. 244–265). New York: Peter Lang.

Maguire, K. C., & Kinney, T. A. (2010). When distance is problematic: Communication, coping, and relational satisfaction in female college students' long-distance dating relationships. *Journal of Applied Communication Research, 38,* 27–46. doi:10.1080/00909880903483573

Mikucki-Enyart, S. L. (2011). Parent-in-law privacy management: An examination of the links among relational uncertainty, topic avoidance, in-group status, and in-law satisfaction. *Journal of Family Communication, 11,* 237–263. doi:10.1080/15267431.2010.544633

Nagy, M. E., & Theiss, J. A. (2013). Applying the relational turbulence model to the empty-nest transition: Sources of relationship change, relational uncertainty, and interference from partners. *Journal of Family Communication, 13,* 280–300. doi:10.1080/15267431.2013.823430

Nosko, A., Wood, E., & Molema, S. (2010). All about me: Disclosure in online social networking profiles: The case of FACEBOOK. *Computers in Human Behavior, 26,* 406–418. doi:10.1016/j.chb.2009.11.012

Padilla-Walker, L. M., Nelson, L. J., & Knapp, D. J. (2014). "Because I'm still the parent, that's why!" Parental legitimate authority during emerging adulthood. *Journal of Social and Personal Relationships, 31,* 293–313. doi:10.1177/0265407513494949

Philip, A. F. (1988). Parents, sons, and daughters: Growth and transition during the college years. *Journal of College Student Psychotherapy, 2,* 17–32. doi:10.1300/J035v02n01_03

Rainie, L., Lenhart, A., & Smith, A. (2012, February). The tone of life on social networking sites. Washington, DC: Pew Internet and America Life Project.

Ramirez, Jr., A., & Wang, Z. (2008). When online meets offline: An expectancy violations theory perspective on modality switching. *Journal of Communication, 58,* 20–39. doi:10.1111/j.1460–2466.2007.00372.x

Ramirez, Jr., A., & Zhang, S. (2007). When online meets offline: The effect of modality switching on relational communication. *Communication Monographs, 74,* 287–310. doi:10.1080/03637750701543493

Ramirez, Jr., A., Walther, J. B., Burgoon, J. K., & Sunnafrank, M. (2002). Information-seeking strategies, uncertainty, and computer-mediated communication: Toward a conceptual model. *Human Communication Research, 28,* 213–228. doi:10.1093/hcr/28.2.213

Sahlstein, E. M. (2004). Relating at a distance: Negotiating being together and being apart in long-distance relationships. *Journal of Social and Personal Relationships, 21,* 689–710. doi:10.1177/0265407504046115

Sahlstein, E. M. (2006). Making plans: Praxis strategies for negotiating uncertainty–certainty in long-distance relationships. *Western Journal of Communication, 70,* 147–165. doi:10.1080/10570310600710042

Stafford, L. (2004). Romantic and parent–child relationships at a distance. In P. Kalbfleisch (Ed.), *Communication yearbook* (pp. 37–85). Mahwah, NJ: Lawrence Erlbaum.

Stefanone, M. A., Hurley, C. M., & Yang, J. (2013). Antecedents of online information seeking. *Information, Communication & Society, 16,* 61–81. doi:10.1080/1369118X.2012.656137

Stephenson-Abetz, J., & Holman, A. (2012). Home is where the heart is: Facebook and the negotiation of "old" and "new" during the transition to college. *Western Journal of Communication, 76,* 175–193. doi:10.1080/10570314.2011.654309

Tidwell, L. C., & Walther, J. B. (2002). Computer-mediated communication effects on disclosure, impressions, and interpersonal evaluations: Getting to know one another one bit at a time. *Human Communication Research, 28,* 317–348. doi:10.1093/hcr/28.3.317

Tokunaga, R. S. (2011). Social networking site or social surveillance site? Understanding the use of interpersonal electronic surveillance in romantic relationships. *Computers in Human Behavior, 27,* 705–713. doi:10.1016/j.chb.2010.08.014

Tong, S. T. (2013). Facebook use during relationship termination: Uncertainty reduction and surveillance. *CyberPsychology, Behavior, and Social Networking, 16,* 788–793. doi:10.1089/cyber.2012.0549

Tosun, L. P. (2012). Motives for Facebook use and expressing "true self" on the Internet. *Computers in Human Behavior, 28,* 1510–1517. doi:10.1016/j.chb.2012.03.018

Trottier, D. (2012). Interpersonal surveillance on social media. *Canadian Journal of Communication, 37,* 319–332.

Utz, S., & Beukeboom, C. J. (2011). The role of social network sites in romantic relationships: Effects on jealousy and relationship happiness. *Journal of Computer-Mediated Communication, 16,* 511–527. doi:10.1111/j.1083–6101.2011.01552.x

Vangelisti, A. L., & Caughlin, J. P. (1997). Revealing family secrets: The influence of topic, function, and relationships. *Journal of Social and Personal Relationships, 14,* 679–705. doi:10.1177/0265407597145006

Vianden, J., & Ruder, J. T. (2012). "Our best friend is moving away": Exploring parent transition and involvement during their student's first year in college. *The Journal of College and University Student Housing, 38,* 62–77.

Walther, J. B. (2011). Theories of computer-mediated communication and interpersonal relations. In M. L. Knapp & J. A. Daly (Eds.), *The SAGE handbook of interpersonal communication* (pp. 443–479). Washington, DC: Sage.

Walther, J. B., Van Der Heide, B., Kim, S. Y., Westerman, D., & Tong, S. T. (2008). The role of friends' appearance and behavior on evaluations of individuals on Facebook: Are we known by the company we keep? *Human Communication Research, 34,* 28–49. doi:10.1111/j.1468–2958.2007.00312.x

Waters, S., & Ackerman, J. (2011). Exploring privacy management on Facebook: Motivations and perceived consequences of voluntary disclosure. *Journal of Computer-Mediated Communication, 17,* 101–115. doi:10.1111/j.1083–6101.2011.01559.x

Westerman, D., Van Der Heide, B., Klein, K. A., & Walther, J. B. (2008). How do people really seek information about others? Information seeking across Internet and traditional communication channels. *Journal of Computer-Mediated Communication, 13,* 751–767. doi:10.1111/j.1083–6101.2008.00418.x

Wilson, R. E., Gosling, S. D., & Graham, L. T. (2012). A review of Facebook research in the social sciences. *Perspectives on Psychological Science, 7,* 20–220. doi:10.1177/1745691612442904

Wise, K., Alhabash, S., & Park, H. (2010). Emotional responses during social information seeking on Facebook. *CyberPsychology, Behavior, and Social Networking, 13,* 555–562. doi:10.1089/cyber.2009.0365

Znaniecki, F. (1934). *The method of sociology.* New York: Farrar & Rinehart.

19

Parents' Use of New Media for Communication about Parenting

A Consideration of Demographic Differences

JODI DWORKIN
SUSAN WALKER
JESSICA RUDI
JENNIFER DOTY
University of Minnesota

Introduction

Over the past 15 years, use of the Internet and social media has multiplied at a rapid rate. The Pew Internet and American Life Project (2014) reported that, as of September 2013, 86% of American adults were using the Internet. Additionally, in September 2013, 73% of adults reported using online social media, and 42% of adults used multiple social networking websites (SNS) (Duggan & Smith, 2013). Similar to the broad population, parents are increasingly using new media technologies (Allen & Rainie, 2002; Plantin & Daneback, 2009), and their use is diverse (Rothbaum, Martland, & Jannsen, 2008; Walker, Dworkin, & Connell, 2011).

However, parents have different needs for communication using new media than do adults who are not parents. Healthy and effective parenting involves household management and maintenance of interpersonal relationships, and evidence increasingly suggests that new media aids in these efforts. As parenting models inclusive of the social context suggest (e.g., Belsky, 1984), these parenting activities are accomplished through bidirectional relationships with children and other family members and with others who influence the well-being of the children (e.g., teachers). Smith, Cudaback, Goddard, and Myers-Walls (1994) classified parenting roles as involving activities such as caring for oneself, managing resources (e.g., money, housing, and food), guiding and motivating children, and connecting effectively to social systems such as child care and schools, to ensure that children get the resources they need. Evidence suggests that Internet-capable devices help parents accomplish some of these activities. For example, online, parents provide and receive emotional support related to parenting, share strategies and advice, seek information about programs in their communities, and connect with others to normalize parenting experiences (Dworkin, Connell, & Doty, 2013; Hall & Irvine, 2009). Parents use social networking sites to communicate with children, those in their children's network, as well as to monitor children's activities (Doty & Dworkin, 2013); parents and grandparents actively use social, mobile technologies to exchange information, photos, and calendars (Tee, Brush, & Inkpen, 2009). Certain populations of parents (e.g., new parents, deployed military fathers) use new media to assist with life transitions and maintaining family relationships (e.g., Schachman, 2010). Walker et al. (2011) observed that parents are using multiple devices for a variety of purposes. These new media support parenting and provide tools that can complement parents' offline worlds. Online communication with family and friends through Skype, email, and Facebook (Kennedy, Smith, Wells, & Wellman, 2008; see also the Bruess, Li, & Polingo chapter in this volume) for instance, may serve to reinforce and strengthen communication in daily life. In fact, some families report feeling more connected overall because of their ability to maintain connections online throughout the day (Hertlein, 2012).

However, evidence suggests that demographic variables influence use of new media. Some argue that income has the most impact on technology use because it directly affects families' ability to acquire technology devices and services (Martin & Robinson, 2007); however, findings are mixed. For example, one study found that 66% of mothers on a support site were below average in income, while a second study found 40% of parents on a website were low income (Plantin & Daneback, 2009; Sarkadi & Bremberg, 2004). While some studies have found disparities in technology access by race, others have found differences disappear at higher income levels (Plantin & Daneback, 2009). Doty, Dworkin, and Connell (2012) found that comfort with technology was a more salient predictor of online behavior than socio-economic status or parent age.

Although much has been learned about which parents are using new media and to some extent how, why, and which new media, we need a more complete picture of how new technologies are used for communication in daily life to fulfill parents' responsibilities (e.g., Dworkin et al., 2013). For example, although most parents generally use email, is email a form of communication used to interact with other caregivers about children? And is this use specific to certain groups of parents (e.g., rural parents who may have less access to face-to-face communication with other parents)? To best understand parents' technology behavior, research needs to draw from large samples of parents who are online (Richiardi, Pizzi, & Pearce, 2013). Unfortunately, other than a study by Allen and Rainie (2002) more than a decade ago, most recent studies rely on small samples drawn from users of particular websites or specialized groups of parents seeking services (Dworkin et al., 2013; Plantin & Daneback, 2009). With the constant development and adoption of multiple new communication technologies, it is imperative that researchers and family practitioners stay up to date on parents' use of technology and new media. Learning more specifically how parents are using a variety of new media for communication is crucial to our understanding of the role of technology in family life; specifically, it informs our understanding of the role of new media in supporting family relationships and thus allows practitioners to more effectively use new media in their work with parents.

Current Study

To address the need for more research on parents' use of new technologies, an online survey was used to investigate parents' online behavior. There were two specific objectives: (1) to understand demographic differences in how parents use new media for communication; and (2) to explore which new media activities parents use to communicate with family and other members in their social networks.

Method

Procedures

A comprehensive literature review was conducted on parents' general technology and Internet use (Dworkin et al., 2013). The findings were used to create an online survey that elicited information from parents who were online about technological devices used, attitudes and comfort using the Internet and new media in general, frequency of doing various online activities in general and specifically for parenting, and the purposes served by online activities for parenting. Since the majority of adults have access to the Internet through computers and portable media such as smartphones, and the intention of this survey was to study use of new media, data were collected online, the most appropriate method for the population and goals of the study (Dillman, Smyth, & Christian, 2009).

Parents were recruited to participate in this study through a variety of email listservs that reach a nationwide and demographically diverse sample. These listservs targeted parents and professionals who work with parents, and included National Institute of Food and Agriculture (NIFA) divisions and initiatives such as Cooperative Extension including eXtension, and CYFAR projects (Children, Youth and Families at Risk projects funded by the United States Department of Agriculture), early education efforts through state Departments of Education, as well as other statewide and national networks that reach families and professionals with parenting resources. Recruiting efforts also included links on Facebook pages and parenting websites, face-to-face efforts, and the distribution of postcards at public events with study information and the survey URL. Potential participants were directed to a website to learn more about the project and complete the online survey. Participants could choose to be entered into a drawing for one of several $100.00 Amazon.com gift cards after completing the survey.

Participants

One thousand six hundred and fifty-three parents (M_{age} = 43.6 years) participated in this study between May and November 2010. Most parents (91.8%) were biological parents. Parents were primarily White (89.9%) mothers (87.4%) who were married (88.0%). Fifty-four parents (3.3%) were expecting a child. The majority (73.8%) had at least two children, ranging in age from newborns to adults (M_{age} = 11.4 years). Although the sample is somewhat skewed by race, gender, and marital status, respondents are representative of parents who are online, and similar to samples found in other studies examining parent use of new media (Plantin & Daneback, 2009).

Measures

In addition to demographic information, parents were asked how often they engaged in 17 online activities and the purpose of those online activities.

Online activities in general and specifically for parenting. Parents were asked how often they engaged in 17 online activities in general (see Table 19.1). Participants who reported engaging in an activity received a follow-up question that asked how often they engaged in the activity specifically for parenting. Parenting was defined for parents as "all things you do to take care of your children and support their growth and development." Participants reported the frequency they performed each activity online for parenting using a seven-point Likert-scale (1 = *Never*, 7 = *Several times a day*).

Table 19.1. Frequency of Parents' Online Activities for Parenting (N = 1653).

Activity[a]	*M*	*SD*
Send or read email	3.76	1.33
Look for general information (health and wellness, ideas for activities, research a topic)	2.78	1.15
Send or receive text messages (SMS)	2.51	2.12
Read emailed newsletters (e.g., newsletters from school or youth organizations)	2.47	1.38
Use social networking services (Facebook, MySpace, Cafemom, etc.)	2.17	1.94
Send or receive photos	2.16	1.25
Post on or read discussion boards or chat rooms	1.06	1.54
Use instant messaging (AIM, MSN messenger, Yahoo! Chat, etc.)	1.02	1.64
Read or comment on blogs	1.02	1.47
Watch, create, or share video files online (movies, TV, home videos)	0.89	1.23
Audio conference or make phone calls using the Internet (e.g. Skype)	0.71	1.17
Listen to, create, or share audio files online	0.70	1.18
Use webcam or video conference	0.52	1.05
Participate in online classes, workshops, or webinars	0.51	1.02
Create, maintain, or write blogs	0.41	1.07
Create, maintain, or follow microblogs (Twitter)	0.30	0.94
Create or maintain a website	0.28	0.87

[a] 0 = never; 1 = less than once a month; 2 = monthly; 3 = weekly; 4 = once a day; 5 = several times a day

Purposes of online activities for parenting. The online activity items were followed with a question asking parents how each activity "helps you as a parent." Parents were presented with a list of up to 15 possible reasons (e.g., "communicate with my child," "communicate with my child's other parent") and were asked to select all of the ways the online activity helped them fulfill their role as a parent. Parents were asked to respond "yes" or "no" to each item. Parents were only asked about the purpose of an online activity if they indicated that this activity was frequently performed. The "frequent use" threshold was different for each activity as some activities are naturally more frequent than others (i.e., it is common that individuals use email at least weekly but unlikely they participate in online classes weekly or more often). For example, a parent who responded "weekly or more" to the question about using SNS received the follow-up list of reasons, while those who responded "monthly or less" did not. We focus here on the new-media activities parents used to communicate with their child(ren), nonresident family members, their child(ren)'s other parent, parents of their child(ren)'s friends, and others who care for their child(ren).

Data Analysis

To explore parent use of new media technologies for communication, descriptive statistics were computed. To explore demographic variations in how parents used these technologies, independent samples *t*-tests were conducted to identify differences in new media technology activities by parent gender (mother or father) and race (White or Non-White). A series of ANOVA analyses, with Tukey post-hoc tests, were conducted to identify differences in activities by income, parent education, and geographic area (see Table 19.2). For all post-hoc analyses, the significance level was adjusted to .002 using the Bonferroni adjustment. Pearson's correlations were computed to identify differences in activity participation by parent age. Because of the large sample size, only correlations of .10 or greater were considered.

Table 19.2. Demographic Differences in Parents' Online Activities.

Activity[a]	Race[b] t (df)	Area[c] F (df)	Income[d] F (df)	Parent Education[e] F (df)	Parent Age Pearson's r
Look for information	2.04 (1459)	0.31 (2, 1613)	3.88 (2, 1429)*	0.72 (2, 1621)	-.16***
Make phone calls/ Skype	3.53 (756)**	1.61 (2, 829)	1.62 (2, 734)	0.38 (2, 831)	.03
Use webcam	4.37 (680)**	1.18 (2, 749)	4.67 (2, 671)*	2.38 (2, 750)	-.09
Use IM	2.17 (898)	1.52 (2, 991)	1.70 (2, 888)	4.85 (2, 995)**	.17***
Text message	-0.28 (1143)	5.31 (2, 1252)**	7.02 (2, 1112)**	6.16 (2, 1258)**	.26***
Discussion boards/ chat rooms	2.02 (933)	5.82 (2, 1037)**	5.83 (2, 933)**	3.19 (2, 1042)*	-.26***
Email	-0.47 (1437)	1.36 (2, 1591)	9.59 (2, 1409)**	7.87 (2, 1598)***	.15***

Read emailed newsletters	4.09 (1343)**	0.33 (2, 1486)	0.54 (2, 1321)	1.62 (2, 1493)	-.06
Send/receive photos	2.50 (1340)	0.72 (2, 1482)	1.13 (2, 1319)	0.16 (2, 1488)	-.16***
Share audio files	4.81 (889)**	0.31 (2, 985)	4.10 (2, 888)*	3.09 (2, 988)*	-.07
Share video files	3.82 (974)**	1.24 (2, 1076)	7.27 (2, 970)**	0.47 (2, 1082)	-.14***
Read/comment on blogs	2.24 (1022)	4.33 (2, 1135)*	4.86 (2, 1027)*	2.84 (2, 1139)	-.26***
Create/write blogs	1.31 (434)	4.59 (2, 476)*	6.78 (2, 433)**	0.69 (2, 476)	-.17***
Microblog (Twitter)	0.99 (336)	1.26 (2, 378)	1.58 (2, 342)	1.46 (2, 379)	-.05
Create/maintain website	3.43 (460)**	2.86 (2, 509)	5.01 (2, 463)*	8.28 (2, 512)***	-.10**
Use SNS	-0.87 (1181)	1.06 (2, 1302)	1.80 (2, 1171)	3.93 (2, 1310)*	.04
Take online classes	4.02 (906)**	5.69 (2, 1015)**	20.18 (2, 913)**	6.11 (2, 1017)**	-.09

[a] 0 = never; 1 = less than once a month; 2 = monthly; 3 = weekly; 4 = once a day; 5 = several times a day. [b] 2 = White, 1 = Non-White. [c] 1 = rural, 2 = suburban, 3 = urban. [d] 1 = low income (less than \$50,000), 2 = middle income (\$50,000–less than \$100,000), 3 = high income (\$100,000 or more). [e] 1 = less than college, 2 = college degree, 3 = postgraduate training.

* $p < .05$ ** $p < .01$ *** $p < .001$

To identify which new media technology activities parents used to communicate with child(ren), nonresident family members, child(ren)'s other parent, parents of child(ren)'s friends, and others who care for child(ren), a series of Cochran's Q tests with post-hoc analyses were conducted within activity (independent variable was online activity frequency: *never* to *several times a day*) across function (dependent variable was function of online activity: *yes* or *no*). The Cochran's Q statistic is appropriate for dichotomous data and is used to test whether the proportions of the independent variable (activity) are the same across the multiple dependent variables (function). Similar to other nonparametric tests, when using the Cochran's Q statistic, the assumption of a normal distribution is not required (Cochran, 1950; Siegel, 1957). Because of the large number of post hoc analyses conducted, the significance level was adjusted to .002 using the Bonferroni adjustment.

Results

Demographic Variations in How Parents Use New Media for Communication

Table 19.1 provides a summary of parents' average frequency of use of various new media for parenting; Table 19.2 reveals demographic variations in parents' use. Mothers were more frequent users than fathers of three online activities: visiting discussion boards/chat rooms, $M = 1.70$, $SD = 1.68$ versus $M = 1.20$, $SD = 1.44$; $t(1, 1038) = -3.47$, $p < .001$; reading/commenting on blogs, $M = 1.51$, $SD = 1.58$ versus $M = 1.02$, $SD = 1.42$; $t(1, 1135) = -3.67$, $p < .001$; and reading emailed newsletters, $M = 2.66$, $SD = 1.26$ versus $M = 2.20$, $SD = 1.44$; $t(1, 1487) = -4.61$, $p < .001$. No other significant differences emerged.

Compared to White parents, Non-White parents reported more frequently making phone calls/using Skype, $M = 1.87$, $SD = 1.68$ versus $M = 1.31$, $SD = 1.25$; using a webcam, $M = 1.78$, $SD = 1.60$ versus $M = 1.05$, $SD = 1.25$; sharing audio files, $M = 1.80$, $SD = 1.55$ versus $M = 1.08$, $SD = 1.29$; sharing video files, $M = 1.81$, $SD = 1.56$ versus $M = 1.28$, $SD = 1.26$; creating/maintaining a website, $M = 1.49$, $SD = 1.76$ versus $M = 0.79$, $SD = 1.30$; taking online classes, $M = 1.30$, $SD = 1.57$ versus $M = 0.77$, $SD = 1.14$; and reading emailed newsletters, $M = 3.05$, $SD = 1.38$ versus $M = 2.55$, $SD = 1.27$, $p < .001$ (see Table 19.2).

When exploring geographic area, differences for five activities emerged (see Table 19.2). Urban parents used discussion boards/chat rooms more frequently than rural parents, $M = 1.95$, $SD = 1.71$ versus $M = 1.43$, $SD = 1.53$, $p = .002$. Rural parents participated in online classes more frequently than suburban parents, $M = 0.98$, $SD = 1.27$ versus M = 0.69, $SD = 1.11$, $p = .002$, though overall both reported low use. For text messaging, reading/commenting on blogs, and creating/maintaining blogs, the ANOVA was significant; however, post hoc analyses were not.

Patterns by income also emerged (see Table 19.2). For discussion boards/chat rooms, sharing video files, and creating/maintaining blogs, low-income parents, $M = 1.97$, $SD = 1.79$; $M = 1.67$, $SD = 1.46$; $M = 1.89$, $SD = 1.74$, respectively, reported significantly ($p < .002$) more frequent use than high-income parents, $M = 1.46$, $SD = 1.59$; $M = 1.22$, $SD = 1.25$; $M = 1.12$, $SD = 1.41$, respectively. For emailing, high-income parents, $M = 3.94$, $SD = 1.22$, reported significantly ($p < .002$) more frequent use than low-income parents, $M = 3.60$, $SD = 1.45$, and middle-income parents, $M = 3.64$, $SD = 1.36$; and for text messaging, high-income parents reported significantly more frequent use than middle-income parents, $M = 3.43$, $SD = 1.78$ versus $M = 3.00$, $SD = 1.87$, $p < .001$. For taking classes online, lower-income parents reported significantly more frequent use than high-income parents, $M = 1.29$, $SD = 1.45$ versus $M = 0.60$, $SD = 1.05$, $p < .001$.

Differences in use by education emerged for eight activities (see Table 19.2). Parents with a college degree reported significantly more frequent text messaging than those with a postgraduate degree or training, $M = 3.45$, $SD = 1.77$ versus $M = 3.03$, $SD = 1.89$, $p < .001$. Parents with less than a college degree reported creating/maintaining a website significantly more frequently than parents with a postgraduate degree or training, $M = 1.29$, $SD = 1.53$ versus $M = 0.64$, $SD = 1.18$, $p < .001$. The opposite pattern emerged for emailing. Parents with a college degree reported emailing significantly more frequently than those with less than a college degree, $M = 3.94$, $SD = 1.22$ versus $M = 3.61$, $SD = 1.53$, $p < .001$. Post hoc analyses for IM, discussion board/chat room, and share audio files were not significant.

Younger parents reported looking for information, using discussion boards/chat rooms, sending/receiving photos, sharing video files, reading/commenting on blogs, creating/writing blogs, and creating/maintaining a website significantly more frequently than older parents. Older parents reported using IM, text messaging, and emailing significantly more frequently than younger parents (see Table 19.2).

Use of New Media Activities for Communication with Parents' Social Networks

Next, we examined the variety of ways that parents used new media for communicating with their child(ren), nonresident family members, their child(ren)'s other parent, parents' of their child(ren)'s friends, and others who care for their child(ren) using Cochran's Q. Significant differences emerged for all activities, except microblogging (e.g., using Twitter) and creating/maintaining a website (see Table 19.3). Post hoc analyses revealed that parents were significantly more likely ($p < .001$) to use email, SNS, blogs, video, webcams, and photos to communicate with nonresident family members than to communicate with others, and significantly more likely ($p < .001$) to use text messaging to communicate with their children than with others. Parents were significantly more likely ($p < .001$) to use IM, Skype, and share audio files for communicating with children and nonresident family members than for communicating with others.

Table 19.3. Differences in Who Parents Communicate with by Activity (% (*n*)).

	My child(ren)	Family members who do not live with me	My child(ren)'s other parent	Parents of my child(ren)'s friends	Others who care for my child	Cochran's *Q* (*df*)
Weekly or More						
Email (n = 1388)	54.0 (749)	75.8 (1052)	43.7 (607)	44.2 (613)	24.0 (333)	819.17(4)**
Text message (n = 901)	70.4 (634)	57.3 (516)	52.8 (476)	40.2 (362)	22.2 (200)	495.49(4)**
Use SNS (n = 769)	46.6 (358)	76.3 (587)	21.2 (163)	48.4 (372)	17.4 (134)	769.39(4)**
Use IM (n = 356)	60.1 (214)	60.4 (215)	33.7 (120)	–	16.3 (58)	201.02(3)**
Microblog (n = 93)	23.7 (22)	18.3 (17)	18.3 (17)	18.3 (17)	–	5.30(3)
Monthly or More						
Read, comment, create, or write blogs (n = 467)	15.3 (52)	37.1 (126)	9.1 (31)	14.1 (48)	–	131.94(3)**
Share video files (n = 426)	40.6 (173)	62.4 (266)	22.8 (97)	24.2 (103)	12.9 (55)	344.66(4)**
Make phone calls/Skype (n = 345)	56.8 (196)	58.6 (202)	12.2 (42)	5.8 (20)	2.9 (10)	488.91(4)**
Use webcam (n = 244)	38.9 (95)	65.6 (160)	13.1 (32)	4.5 (11)	4.1 (10)	328.74(4)**
Share audio files (n = 313)	46.0 (144)	42.8 (134)	19.5 (61)	19.2 (60)	12.5 (39)	179.01(4)**
Create/maintain website (n = 116)	17.2 (20)	–	13.8 (16)	–	–	0.80(1)
Ever (Less than once a month)						
Send/receive photos (n = 1377)	47.1 (649)	84.0 (1156)	28.1 (387)	–	13.9 (192)	1448.26(3)**

Note: – not a response option for the activity. For all activities 0 = never; 1 = less than once a month; 2 = monthly; 3 = weekly; 4 = once a day; 5 = several times a day. For all reasons 0 = no, 1 = yes.

** p <.001

Discussion

To understand how new media are being incorporated into the lives of parents, in this study we took the next essential step to understand the specific purposes technologies serve for parents' communication with various members of their intimate and extended personal networks. A strength of the current study is our large sample size that allowed us to explore demographic differences between groups less represented in other research (e.g., fathers and rural parents).

The findings that low-income parents were more likely to frequently use discussion boards/chat rooms, share video files, create blogs, and participate in online classes corroborates earlier findings that low-income parents may gravitate toward social media (Doty et al., 2012). Similarly, Sarkadi and Bremberg (2004) found that parents on discussion boards tended to have lower than average income. In contrast, the current study found that those with a higher level of education and with a higher income were more likely to use email.

Parents with lower incomes and non-White parents reported more frequently engaging in online classes and sending videos. They were less frequently using email and sending text messages, reporting between daily and weekly use of those media. Data suggest that lower income parents and non-White parents may seek out a greater range of devices and engage in different activities than White or higher income parents. For example, non-White parents reported more frequent use than White parents of a variety of communication activities. This is consistent with other studies (Smith, 2010; Zickuhr & Smith, 2012) that found African Americans and Latinos were somewhat less likely than Whites to access the Internet but more likely to have mobile devices that provided the potential to access a range of activities. Younger and non-White parents might enjoy experimenting with multiple applications, platforms, and devices. Those with limited resources might select devices such as smartphones that fulfill multiple purposes, as opposed to paying for multiple, less mobile devices that are used for a single purpose.

Texting and email, activities easily done with handheld devices such as smartphones and tablets but also with less mobile devices such as computers, appear more frequent by parents who are older, with higher income and more education. Online classes (though infrequent for most parents) were more popular among rural and low income parents. For parents who are geographically isolated with perhaps less access to transportation, online resources are an imperative alternative to face-to-face classes or sessions. Social activities like discussion boards and chat rooms are popular among mothers, lower income parents, and parents living in urban areas.

Perhaps certain subgroups of parents value connection to others for parenting needs and experiences more than other subgroups of parents. For instance, new mothers have been found to use blogs to connect with others and gain social support (McDaniel, Coyne, & Holmes, 2011; Sarkadi & Bremberg, 2004). Also, parents whose children have special needs or who face illness may find mutual support in online groups (e.g., Han & Belcher, 2001; Scharer, 2005; Scharer, Colon, Moneyham, Tavakoli, Hussey, & Shugart, 2009).

Although we had a limited subsample of fathers in this sample, it is clear there is a need for more attention on fathers. For instance, in this study, we found that fathers were significantly less likely than mothers to visit discussion boards/chat rooms, read/comment on blogs, and read emailed newsletters. These findings suggest that mothers and fathers have different needs for parenting information and find different types of parenting information appealing, but they reveal little in the way of what does work for fathers. The few studies that have considered fathers provide evidence that online parenting spaces are often unwelcoming for fathers and that fathers are more likely to find support in an online environment where mothers are not dominating the conversation (Brady & Guerin, 2010; Ericksson & Salzmann-Erickson, 2013; Fletcher & St. George, 2010).

Results support the idea that parents are using multiple technology activities to communicate with others important to their parenting, also known as "media multiplexity" (Haythornthwaite, 2005). Analyses revealed that parents are using text messaging, email, IM, and applications such as Skype to connect with children. This is not surprising, given that 52.69% of parents had children who were 13–22 years old; older children are more likely to own their own technology devices and have more freedom in using these devices than younger children (Lenhart, Madden, Smith, Purcell, Zickuhr, & Rainie, 2011; Subrahmanyam & Greenfield, 2008).

Parents are also using technology, particularly new media with visual interfaces, to maintain connection with extended family members who do not live with them. Skype and video phone calls (58.6%), along with webcams (65.6%), sharing photos (84.0%), and sharing video files (62.4%) can be used so extended family members can stay in touch with growing children. Visual and audio methods allow for engagement with extended family who are not with the parents and enable them to see and hear the children. These connections with extended family might help reinforce values and norms within the larger family system, providing support for parenting, such as information about childrearing and emotional support.

Compared to communication with children and other family members, communicating with the child's other parent is not frequently done through the new media included in this study. Just over half of parents reported using text messaging to communicate with a coparent, and 43.7% reported using email for this purpose. These interactions are likely still happening face to face and via phone, and technology has not replaced these more traditional forms of communication between parents. For instance, in a study of divorced coparents, Ganong, Coleman, Feistman, Jamison, and Stafford Markham (2012) found that in families where the coparenting relationship was contentious, parents used new media to reduce conflicts. However, the ability to avoid face-to-face communication also supported parents in less positive ways, like enabling them to withhold information. Similarly, few parents reported communicating with others who care for children via technology; across the entire sample, 24% used email and 22.2% used text message. Communication with parents of children's friends was primarily through written messages via email, text message, and SNS, likely around coordinating plans and simply checking in.

The present study contributes a more complete picture of how parents are using technology for parenting. Still, the sample was weighted toward parents with higher incomes and education, who were mostly White, female, and married. While this reflects parent samples in other research on technology use (Plantin & Daneback, 2009; Radey & Randolph, 2009), it suggests the need for more rigorous methods of recruitment that result in more diverse samples of parents. In addition, these data were collected in 2010, and since then there have been sudden and frequent shifts in technology, such as trends toward heavier use of mobile multifunction media like smartphones and tablets, and applications that permit text, video, audio, and image sharing for communication. For example, in May 2010, only 3% of adults owned a tablet, but this number increased to 35% by September 2013 (Rainie & Smith, 2013). Similarly, in May 2011, 35% of adults owned a smartphone, and this number increased to 56% in May 2013 (Smith, 2013). Among parents of 0–8 year olds in 2013, 42% owned a tablet and 71% owned a smartphone (Wartella, Rideout, Lauriella, & Connell, 2013). Researchers must work to understand these rapid changes in technology use and their impact on family life.

Application

There is an ever-emerging and more complex understanding of the role new media plays in parenting and family life. This study contributes to that body of knowledge by exploring use of new media for communication among a national sample of parents who are online. The Internet and new media simply expand where and how relationships may be engaged, and increases opportunities for communication across larger and more diverse personal networks.

Analyses from the present investigation suggest that the design of programs that use new media must respect differences in parent use, preferences, and context, while recognizing the different functions served by different devices to meet parents' needs (Hughes, Bowers, Mitchell, Curtiss, & Ebata, 2012). Regardless of education, socioeconomic status (SES), or other demographics, parents seek information online to support them in their parenting role. For example, they use websites to find information that help with solving problems. Parents also do this by connecting and communicating with other parents, professionals, and family members to acquire and exchange information. Sometimes these sources are used to validate information found through websites or simply to reinforce parents' beliefs and understanding. Professionals can help parents navigate the wealth of information available and effectively use new media to best meet parents' needs.

In addition to capitalizing on the unique strengths of technology that are valued by parents such as convenience, access at any time of day, anonymity, and the ability to connect with diverse individuals around the globe (Brady & Guerin, 2010; Drentea & Moren-Cross, 2005; Madge & O'Connor, 2006), educational programs and resources for parents can capitalize on the social expression and connectivity of SNS, blogs, and websites (e.g., online support groups and websites with child development information). Incorporating new media within educational programs and resources for parents allows connections between parents at any time without the logistical barriers of traditional face-to-face programs or resources. For those concerned with stigma around receiving parenting services, new media also allow for anonymous communication and connectivity, overcoming an important barrier to accessing parenting services. Family professionals might stay actively engaged with discussion boards and chat rooms popular with parents to facilitate parental learning by clarifying information about parenting or sharing new knowledge about topics important to parents.

These data are clear that parents are using multiple devices and multiple online activities to connect with children, and it is likely that technology use to communicate with children varies depending on the children's ages. Research shows that children's technology use increases with age (Lenhart et al., 2011; Subrahmanyam & Greenfield, 2008), and with age, youth become more independent users of technology. The majority of adolescents and emerging adults own their own mobile phone, and many own a personal laptop or tablet (Madden, Lenhart, Duggan, Cortesi, & Gasser, 2013). As such, older children have more control over how and with whom they communicate, compared to younger children. It is important for parents to adapt to these changes in order to maintain a positive parent–child connection. Parents can use technology to check in with their child, such as sending a text message to ask when they will be home or who they are with. Parents report mobile phones as being particularly helpful in making family plans and monitoring their children (Devitt & Roker, 2009).

These data suggest important ways to capitalize on parents' interest in maintaining connections to family members with whom they do not live. More specifically, designers of new technologies and online tools for parents can build on opportunities for within-site parent-to-parent connectivity, and facilitate the ease of sharing content with others (e.g., forwarding a parenting article through Facebook, offering tools for video chat). Designers also need to work to capitalize on parents' use of mobile technologies through the development of mobile compatible websites and information, as well as building apps and other online tools. For example, geo-location applications like the Find My Kids—Footprints app allow parents to monitor their child's location or the Good Food Near You app informs parents about healthy eating options nearby. Utility apps like Babymate help parents track health and growth information during the early years, share the information easily with others, and be reminded of important health and wellness dates. Safety Web could be a useful app to protect children from cyber-bullying. Family-life educators can provide information and resources to help parents learn to feel comfortable using these new communication-rich technologies. Parents might also be expected to explain how to use devices and technology applications to extended family members.

Practitioners working with parents might also conduct needs assessments to identify which new media are used by which parents to capitalize on those most preferred for engagement and learning. By collecting local data about parents' current use and preferences for resource delivery, practitioners can tailor resources and services to meet parents' wants and needs, possibly increasing the impact that services and resources can have on parents' behaviors, confidence, and self-efficacy. For instance, data could reveal to practitioners which parents like to communicate via email or text message, and which parents might be more interested in and receptive to interacting via SNS.

Finally, these findings set the stage for continued research that more fully investigates the processes through which complex "personal communities" or networks support parents (Wellman, 2007) and to consider what these communities mean for parenting and ultimately child outcomes (Cochran, 1990). In an age when digital and social media are saturating the majority of families' lives, much research is needed to understand the increasingly complex set of choices, consequences, and opportunities provided by such technologies.

References

Allen, K., & Rainie, L. (2002). Parents online. Pew Internet and American Life Project. Retrieved from: http://www.pewinternet.org/~/media/Files/Reports/2002/PIP_Parents_Report.pdf.pdf

Belsky, J. (1984). The determinants of parenting: A process model. *Child Development, 55*(1), 83–96.

Brady, E., & Guerin, S. (2010). Not the romantic, all happy, coochy coo experience: A qualitative analysis of interactions on an Irish parenting web site. *Family Relations, 59*(1), 14–27.

Cochran, M. (1990). The network as an environment for human development. In M. Cochran, M. Larner, D. Riley, L. Gunnarsson, & C. Henderson, Jr. (Eds.), *Extending families: The social networks of parents and their children* (pp. 265–276). Cambridge, UK: Cambridge University Press.

Cochran, W. G. (1950). The comparison of percentages in matched samples. *Biometrika, 37*(3/4), 256–266.

Devitt, K., & Roker, B. (2009). The role of mobile phones in family communication. *Children & Society, 23(3), 189–202.*

Dillman, D. A., Smyth, J. D., & Christian, L. M. (2009). *Internet, mail, and mixed-mode surveys: The tailored design method* (3rd ed.). Hoboken, NJ: John Wiley & Sons.

Doty, J., & Dworkin, J. (2013). Parents' of adolescents use of social networking sites. *Computers in Human Behavior.* Advance online publication. doi:http://dx.doi.org/10.1016/j.chb.2013.07.012

Doty, J., Dworkin, J., & Connell, J. (2012). Examining digital differences: Parents' online activities. *Family Science Review, 17*(2), 18–39.

Drentea, P., & Moren-Cross, J. (2005). Social capital and social support on the Web: The case of an Internet mother site. *Sociology of Health and Illness, 27*, 920–943.

Duggan, M., & Smith, A. (2013). *Social media update 2013. Pew Research Internet Project.* Retrieved from http://www.pewinternet.org/2013/12/30/social-media-update-2013/

Dworkin, J., Connell, J., & Doty, J. (2013). A literature review of parents' online behavior. *Cyberpsychology: Journal of Psychosocial Research on Cyberspace, 7*(2). Retrieved from http://cyberpsychology.eu/view.php?cisloclanku=2013052301&article=2

Ericksson, H., & Salzmann-Erikson, M. (2013). Supporting a caring fatherhood in cyberspace: An analysis of communication about caring within an online forum for fathers. *Scandinavian Journal of Caring Sciences, 27*(1), 63–69.

Fletcher, R. J., & St. George, J. M. (2010). Practitioners' understanding of father engagement in the context of family dispute resolution. *Journal of Family Studies, 16*(2), 101–115.

Ganong, L. H., Coleman, M., Feistman, R., Jamison, T., & Stafford Markham, M. (2012). Communication technology and postdivorce coparenting. *Family Relations, 61,* 397–409.

Hall, W., & Irvine, V. (2008). E-communication among mothers of infants and toddlers in a community-based cohort: A content analysis. *Journal of Advanced Nursing, 65*, 175–183.

Han, H. R., & Belcher, A. E. (2001). Computer-mediated support group use among parents of children with cancer: An exploratory study. *Computer, 19*(1), 27–33.

Haythornthwaite, C. (2005). Social networks and Internet connectivity effects. *Information, Communication and Society, 8*(2), 125–147.

Hertlein, K. M. (2012). Digital dwelling: Technology in couple and family relationships. *Family Relations, 61*(3), 374–387.

Hughes, R., Bowers, J. R., Mitchell, E. T., Curtiss, S., & Ebata, A. T. (2012). Developing online family life prevention and education programs. *Family Relations, 61*(5), 711–727.

Kennedy, T. L. M., Smith, A., Wells, A. M., & Wellman, B. (2008). Networked families. Pew Internet and American Life Project. Retrieved from http://www.pewinternet.org/~/media//Files/Reports/2008/PIP_Networked_Family.pdf.pdf

Lenhart, A., Madden, M., Smith, A., Purcell, K., Zickuhr, K., & Rainie, L. (2011). Teens, kindness and cruelty on social network sites. Retrieved from http://pewinternet.org/~/media//Files/Reports/2011/PIP_Teens_Kindness_Cruelty_SNS_Report_Nov_2011_FINAL_110711.pdf

Madden, M., Lenhart, A., Duggan, M., Cortesi, S., & Gasser, U. (2013). Teens and technology 2013. Retrieved from http://www.pewinternet.org/2013/03/13/teens-and-technology-2013/

Madge, C., & O'Connor, H. (2006). Parenting gone wired: Empowerment of new mothers on the Internet? *Social and Cultural Geography, 7*, 199–220.

Martin, S. P., & Robinson, J. P. (2007). The income digital divide: Trends and predictions for levels of Internet use. *Social Problems, 54*, 1–22.

McDaniel, B. T., Coyne, S. M., & Holmes, E. K. (2011). New mothers and media use: Associations between blogging, social networking, and maternal well-being. *Maternal and Child Health Journal, 16*(7), 1–9.

Pew Research Internet Project. (2014). *Internet use over time.* Retrieved from http://www.pewinternet.org/data-trend/internet-use/internet-use-over-time/

Plantin, L., & Daneback, K. (2009). Parenthood, information, and support on the Internet: A literature review of research on parents and professionals online. *BMC Family Practice, 10*, 34.

Radey, M., & Randolph, K. A. (2009). Parenting sources: How do parents differ in their efforts to learn about parenting? *Family Relations, 58*, 536–548.

Rainie, L., & Smith, A. (2013). Tablet and e-reader ownership update. Pew Internet and American Life Project. Retrieved from http://www.pewinternet.org/2013/10/18/tablet-and-e-reader-ownership-update/

Richiardi, L., Pizzi, C., & Pearce, N. (2013). Commentary: Representativeness is usually not necessary and often should be avoided. *International Journal of Epidemiology, 42*(4), 1018–1022.

Rothbaum, F., Martland, N., & Jannsen, J. (2008). Parents' reliance on the Web to find information about children and families: Socio-economic differences in use, skills and satisfaction. *Journal of Applied Developmental Psychology, 29*, 118–128.

Sarkadi, A., & Bremberg, S. (2004). Socially unbiased parenting support on the Internet: A cross-sectional study of users of a large Swedish parenting website. *Child: Care, Health, and Development, 31*(1), 43–52.

Schachman, K. A. (2010). Online fathering: The experience of first-time fatherhood in combat-deployed troops. *Nursing Research, 59*(1), 11–17.

Scharer, K. (2005). An Internet discussion board for parents of mentally ill young children. *Journal of Child and Adolescent Psychiatric Nursing, 18*(1), 17–25.

Scharer, K., Colon, E., Moneyham, L., Tavakoli, A., Hussey, J., & Shugart, M. (2009). Comparison of two types of social support for mothers of mentally ill children. *Journal of Child and Adolescent Psychiatric Nursing, 22*(2), 86–98.

Siegel, S. (1957). Nonparametric statistics. *The American Statistician, 11*(3), 13–19.

Smith, A. (2010). Americans and their gadgets. Pew Internet and American Life Project. Retrieved from http://www.pewinternet.org/Reports/2010/Gadgets/Overview.aspx

Smith, A. (2013). Smartphone ownership 2013. Pew Internet and American Life Project. Retrieved from http://www.pewinternet.org/2013/06/05/smartphone-ownership-2013/.

Smith, C. A., Cudaback, D., Goddard, H. W., & Myers-Walls, J. A. (1994). *National extension parent education model.* Manhattan, KS: Kansas Cooperative Extension Service. Retrieved from http://www.k-state.edu/wwparent/nepem/nepem.pdf

Subrahmanyam, K., & Greenfield, P. (2008). Online communication and adolescent relationships. *The Future of Children, 18*(1), 119–146.

Tee, K., Brush, A. J. B., & Inkpen, K. M. (2009). Exploring communication and sharing between extended families. *International Journal of Human–Computer Studies, 67,* 128–138.

Walker, S. K., Dworkin, J., & Connell, J. H. (2011). Variation in parent use of information and communications technology: Does quantity matter? *Family & Consumer Sciences Research Journal, 40,* 106–119.

Wartella, E., Rideout, V., Lauriella, A., & Connell, S. (2013). *Parenting in the age of digital technology: A national survey.* Northwestern University, Center on Media and Human Development. Retrieved from http://web5.soc.northwestern.edu/cmhd/wp-content/uploads/2013/05/Parenting-Report_FINAL.pdf

Wellman, B. (2007). The network is personal. *Social Networks, 29,* 349–356.

Zickuhr, K., & Smith, A. (2012). Digital Differences: Pew Internet and American Life. Retrieved from http://pewinternet.org/Reports/2012/Digital-differences.aspx

20

Digital Generation Differences in Parent–Adolescent Relationships

J. Mitchell Vaterlaus
Montana State University

Sarah Tulane
Utah State University

Introduction

Generation gaps are presumed differences between adolescents and their parents in terms of values and attitudes. Generation gaps between parents and adolescents received copious research attention during the 1960s and 1970s (Smith, 2000). The 1950s were marked by general adolescent conformity, whereas the 1960s and 1970s saw movement away from rigid societal roles (Falk & Falk, 2005; Vaterlaus, 2012). Generation gap research emerged during a period of social change (e.g., legalization of the contraceptive pill, more liberal political views, ongoing war and military draft, illicit drug use; Falk & Falk, 2005; Maga, 2003). With the onset of these dramatic social changes, many believed dramatic differences in parent and adolescent attitudes and values also emerged during this period. However, generation gap research indicated the presence of only small or insignificant gaps when investigating *actual* gaps (i.e., comparing adolescent beliefs with parent's beliefs; Jacobsen, Berry, & Olsen, 1975). When researchers then examined *perceived* gaps (i.e., what adolescents think their parents believe compared to what adolescents believe) noted differences emerged (Acock & Bengtson, 1980).

As communication technologies have changed, research has attempted to document societal changes in how people interact, spend time, and find entertainment (Jones, 2009; Vaterlaus, 2012). Technology is no longer limited to noninteractive media (e.g., television or movies); rather, opportunities to interact with and through technology are popular and readily available (e.g., Internet, cell phones; Jones, 2009). As use of interactive technologies has spread over multiple generations—from children and adolescents to those in later adulthood—(Duggan & Rainie, 2012; Lenhart, 2010; Zickuhr, 2011), research attention on generational differences in technology use has simultaneously increased (Clark, 2009; Livingstone, 2003; Vaterlaus, 2012; Vaterlaus, Jones, & Tulane, 2014a). The current chapter explores recent developments in generational gap research on interactive technologies (i.e., email, social networking, cell phone technology/apps, and video chat), specifically addressing implications of these digital generational differences on parent–adolescent relationships. As this chapter will demonstrate, current research suggests there are generational differences between parents and adolescents in terms of digital technology use, knowledge, and acquisition.

Adolescence

The study of human development includes, but is not limited to, how humans systematically change biologically, cognitively, emotionally, and socially over time (Lerner, 2013). Stages of human development (e.g., infancy, childhood, adolescence) have emerged based on the developmental tasks accomplished during specific time periods. There has long been debate about when the developmental time period of adolescence ends and adulthood begins (Bynner, 2007). Early developmental scholars proposed that the time period of adolescence extended into the mid-twenties (Hall, 1904). A more contemporary approach has been to use the chronological age of 18 to define the ending point of adolescence and beginning of adulthood (Feixa, 2011). However, contemporary approaches to defining adolescence have recently been challenged; many of the developmental tasks of adolescence are, according to some observers, continuing into the early twenties (Shwartz, Côté, & Arnett, 2005).

Although disagreements exist about when adolescence ends (Bynner, 2007), there is general consensus about the psychosocial developmental markers during adolescence, which include the formation of individual identity (Erikson, 1950) and negotiation of autonomy in the parent–adolescent relationship (Zimmer-Gembeck & Collins, 2003). Zimmer-Gembeck and Collins (2003) defined autonomy as the process of adolescents developing independence and becoming self-regulating, while maintaining connection with parents. Adolescents develop autonomy along three dimensions: (a) behavioral—independent self-regulation of behavior; (b) cognitive—thinking independently and developing confidence in their own abilities; and (c) emotional—adolescent relinquishment of dependence on parents. Research indicates many 18–25 year olds today, compared to previous generations, are delaying some adult developmental tasks such as procurement of their own residence, marriage, and parenthood (Arnett, 2000). These 18–25 year olds also frequently rely on their parents for emotional support, financial support, and housing (Aquilino, 2006). Bynner (2007) argued that 18–25 year olds are still adolescents because they have not yet accomplished the primary developmental tasks (autonomy and identity) of this stage of human development. Consistent with Bynner's perspective, we define adolescence as typically existing between the onset of puberty and the time an individual reaches his or her mid-twenties.

Theoretical Grounding

Adolescent development is best understood in the context of adolescents' environments (e.g., family, culture, society, etc.). Bronfenbrenner (1979) proposed that humans develop in a set of concentric ecosystems (i.e., micro-, meso-, exo-, macro-, and chronosystems). The microsystem level is the smallest level of examination and includes the developing human and his or her most frequent and enduring interactions. This system level includes parent and adolescent interactions. As concentric systems evolve and change, the developing human learns to adapt. Adaption is evidence of development, as well as an antecedent to development.

McHale, Dotterer, and Kim (2009) extended Bronfenbrenner's (1979) theory by proposing an ecological perspective on youth media use. The microsystem includes the adolescent and his or her day-to-day activities. These activities change as an adolescent ages and are conceptualized as a "cause and a consequence of development" (McHale et al., 2009, p. 1187). The adolescents' most enduring relationships such as with parents, siblings, and peers are part of the microsystem. Further, the microsystem includes technology owned by the adolescents, technology made available by parents, technology accessible at school, technology reachable through peers, parental regulation (e.g., rules) of technology use, and technological education facilitated by schools. Technology, according to Vaterlaus, Beckert, Tulane, and Bird (in press), is part of the proximal processes of the microsystem. For example, technology can facilitate relational interactions between parents and adolescents (e.g., texting), but also influences the quality of parent–adolescent interaction (e.g., conflict over technology use). As adolescents begin to develop autonomy from parents, peers become increasingly important. As McHale et al. (2009) indicated, "like family members, peers provide models for, companions in, and reinforcement of youth's involvement in media-oriented activities" (p. 1194). As technology has infiltrated their microsystems, developing humans and their families have had to adapt.

Integrating Uses and Gratifications Theory (U&G) with the ecological prospective provides a useful lens for understanding how parents and adolescents adapt to technology at a microsystem level. The use of U&G in media and communication research dates back to the 1950s and 1960s (Ruggiero, 2000). With the advent of the Internet and other interactive technologies, attention has returned to the U&G framework. U&G postulates that media consumers are active and goal focused (Katz, Blumler, & Gurevitch, 1973), and that media users select media sources that meet the media user's needs. U&G also states that media sources compete with other media sources for need fulfillment (e.g., to most users, text messaging is more convenient and instantaneous than email for interaction).

Additionally, parents' and adolescents' developmental needs differ: Adolescents' developmental needs are primarily social and parents' needs are primarily instrumental (Erikson, 1950). Considering a U&G perspective and Erikson's (1950) theoretical evidence, parents and adolescents likely use technology differently to meet their primary developmental needs. For example, parents may view cell phone use as a way to monitor their adolescent's behavior when they are apart (instrumental need), whereas adolescents might see cell phones as a tool to build and maintain social networks (social needs). These generational differences in the goals associated with technology will likely influence the interaction between parents and adolescents at a microsystem level.

Digital Generation Differences

Dialogue about consequences of digital inequalities has largely focused on social exclusion at the global or macrosystem level (Norris, 2003). Research on technological gaps provides a historical explanation for how interest in digital generation differences between parents and adolescents emerged. For example, the term *digital divide* is used to describe disparities in accessibility to technology (Compaine, 2001; Norris, 2003). The term describes the accessibility of technology based on individuals' geographic location (e.g., technology accessibility comparisons between people in North America and Africa) and accessibility for individuals in various contexts within a geographic region (e.g., technology accessibility of children in different schools in the same state in the United States). Hargittai (2002) extends the digital-divide research by proposing a *second-level digital divide*, which focuses on the divide in level of technology-use ability. Recognizing differences in ability to use technologies expands the limited access-to-technology dichotomy (e.g., those who have access versus those who don't), something van Dijk (2005) calls a *usage divide*, and is essential to examine and consider.

Currently, the digital divide between parent and adolescent access to technology appears to be small. For example, 95% of adolescents in the United States (12–17 years old) reported being online (Madden, Lenhart, & Duggan, 2013) and 85% of adults reported having online access (Pew Research Center, 2013). Prensky (2001) describes usage differences by the terms (a) *digital natives*—children, adolescents, and young adults who were born into the digital age and adapt easily to technology; and (b) *digital immigrants*—the adult population who have immigrated into the digital age and generally have more difficulty adapting to new technology. Although widely used and accepted, at least some researchers are currently challenging the terms, suggesting ability to use technology does not equate to technological proficiency (Koutropolulos, 2011). Building on the seminal generational work of Mannheim (1952), Bolin and Westlund (2009) proposed the term *media generations* to suggest people are not separated in their media experience by age but rather by individual media experience.

This brief history of generational differences provides evidence for increasing interest in how technology influences parents and adolescents. It further tells us it is not prudent to collapse all digital generational differences into one simple set of conclusions; rather, researchers suggest technological generational differences between parents and adolescents are more accurately approached in three primary categories: (1) purposes and use of technology; (2) acquisition of technology knowledge; and (3) technological knowledge. Each is discussed in the following sections.

Generational Differences in the Purpose and Use of Technology

Recent research captures the digital generation differences in the perceived purposes and uses of interactive technology. Adults (34–45 years old) are more likely to use noninteractive online media compared to the younger generation (18–33 year olds; Zickuhr, 2010) and do not typically use cell phones for nonvoice functions (e.g., texting, picture messages; Zickuhr, 2011). In contrast, adolescents are often at the forefront of new technology use. For example, adolescents were the early adopters of social networking, smartphone technology, instant messaging, and peer-to-peer file sharing (Brown & Bobkowski, 2011; Xenos & Foot, 2008). Adolescents adapt easily to new technologies by using skills they developed with previous technologies (Facer, Sutherland, Furlong, & Furlong, 2001).

Differences in purposes and use. According to U&G, individuals select technology sources based on needs (Katz et al., 1973). Such needs are often different between adolescents and parents (Doty & Dworkin, 2013; Oksman & Turtiainen, 2004; Swift & Taylor, 2003). When parents and children (6–16 years old) were asked to rank the most significant online activities for children, parents ranked homework number one and children ranked homework eighth (Swift & Taylor, 2003). Parents typically view interactive technology as a way to accomplish instrumental tasks, while adolescents more often see interactive technology's primary purposes as social (Morrill, Jones, & Vaterlaus, 2013) and entertainment (Lenhart, 2010). While both parents and adolescents use technology for social interaction and building meaningful relationships (Thurlow & McKay, 2003), parents more often use technology to maintain relationships with children and extended family (Doty & Dworkin, 2013), while adolescents use interactive technology to meet their social relational needs (Oksman & Turtiainen, 2004). With technology convergence (e.g., Internet accessibility on cell phones), adolescents often carry their entire social community wherever they go, day and night (Brown & Bobkowski, 2011).

Parents' perceptions of purpose and use of interactive technology influence their decisions about granting their adolescents access to such technologies (Oksman & Turtiainen, 2004). Adolescents view the acquisition of a cell phone as a rite of passage (Blair & Fletcher, 2011), while parents consistently report allowing adolescent cell phone ownership for safety, as well as opportunities for parental monitoring of adolescents' behavior (Oksman & Turtiainen, 2004). Williams and Williams (2005), studying parental monitoring and cell phones, suggest, "this authority-at-a-distance is in some senses illusionary" (p. 326). Adolescents report they use the argument of safety and increased contact with their parents to acquire a cell phone, but believe the primary purpose of a cell phone is to stay connected and close with friends (Oksman & Turtiainen, 2004). According to Blair and Fletcher (2011), cell phone ownership facilitates adolescent autonomy from parents by providing a conduit to activities outside the direct supervision of parents. Adolescents become frustrated when the phone becomes an "electronic tether" rather than an opportunity for freedom from parents (Lenhart, 2010, p. 5). Adolescents view interactive technology as a private experience and a tool to define personal space (Oksman & Turtiainen, 2004; Tutt, 2005).

Youth culture. Oksman and Turtiainen (2004) believe "the youth culture that has developed around new communication technology encompasses many features that are invisible to adults" (p. 322). For instance, Tulane (2012) concludes in her social analysis of adolescent cell phone use:

> Adolescents appeared to understand their culture surrounding text messaging and pointed out that adults could not see this. One participant encouraged her mother to quit calling her during class, because it is not an appropriate cell phone behavior. Another participant noted teens are building a valuable social network, and adults did not understand the value of texting to build connections. (p. 79)

This emerging youth culture surrounding new technologies appears to create generational differences in perceptions of the purposes of technology.

Further, the adolescent microsystem has created a set of cultural values, mores, and rules about technology that make technology's purpose and use for most adolescents a normal aspect of daily living. For example, adolescents report that cell phone technology is not remarkable—it's just a regular part of everyday life (Cupples & Thompson, 2010). Many adults view the consequences of interactive technology to be largely negative (Thurlow & Bell, 2009) and some even argue it is a waste of time (Cupples & Thompson, 2010). On the contrary, while adolescents acknowledge some negative aspects to interactive technology use, they believe adults often generalize from the minority problematic user to all adolescent technology users (Tulane, 2012). Some researchers suggest that when an individual's behaviors and values mature beyond adolescence and youth culture, he or she uses technology differently (Tulane & Beckert, 2013). Other researchers argue generational differences are apparent in youths' and adults' perceptions of what personal information should be private—what should and should not be shared on social networking sites (Levin, Foster, West, Nicholson, Hernandez, & Cukier, 2008). For members of youth culture, very little personal information needs to be kept private on social networking sites, further suggesting emergence of a technological youth culture about which many parents are unaware, and with which they are unfamiliar and often uncomfortable.

Generational Differences in Technology Knowledge Acquisition

Adolescents have been the early adopters of new technology (Xenos & Foot, 2008), and adults report that adapting to new technology can be difficult (Kelty, 2000). As new technologies emerge, research is turning to examining how adolescents and parents learn about technology. Parents and adolescents appear to be consulting different sources to acquire knowledge and experience with technology. Sánchez-Navarro and Aranda (2013) found that adolescents learned about using the Internet primarily on their own, followed by learning from a relative (e.g., siblings or parents), and then in a school setting. Finnish adolescents report they serve as the source of their parents' and grandparents' learning about cell phone technology (Oksman & Turtiainen, 2004).

Vaterlaus, Jones, and Tulane (2014b) used a multiple-response format (allowing participants to report more than one learning source) and asked parents and adolescents in the United States where they learned about email, cell phone, social networking, and video chat technologies. The majority of adolescents reported they had taught themselves about email and cell phones, but peers were the most mentioned educational source for social networking and video chat technology. Parents, too, taught themselves about email and cell phone technologies. However, the majority of parents indicated consulting their children to learn about social networking and video chat. Additionally, parents and adolescents indicated what source they would consult to learn about a new technology. For adolescents, peers were the most common source for learning about new technology. Parents reported children as the most frequently selected source for learning about new technology. Overall, current research suggests most technology knowledge acquisition occurs through informal sources.

Generational Differences in Technology Knowledge

As evidenced by the wide social acceptance of the terms *digital native* and *digital immigrant,* society assumes adolescents have more technological knowledge or digital literacy than their parents. Digital literacy refers to people's ability to use a technology "medium effectively, and efficiently" (Hargittai & Hsieh, 2012, p. 95). Digital literacy work has primarily focused on the Internet, with little research on literacy across the variety of new technologies (e.g., cell phones, video chat, Instagram, Snapchat). Research suggests demographic factors influence young adults' level of Web skills (Hargittai, 2010). For instance, Hargittai (2010) found adolescents and young adults (18–29 years old) who are Caucasian and with highly educated parents and high socioeconomic status are more likely to demonstrate more advanced Internet skills. These results indicate digital differences in Internet ability *within* the adolescent age group. Additional research has validated within-group differences of adolescents' ability to look for and evaluate Web content (Hargittai, Fullerton, Menchen-Trevino, & Thomas, 2010). Such within-group differences in ability to use technology discredit the idea of digital natives as one homogeneous group (Koutropolulos, 2011). The identification of within-group differences is consistent with the concept of media generations (Bolin & Westlund, 2009), which implies there exist varying technology-use abilities *within* generations, not just between.

The term *digital generation gap* describes the differences between parents and adolescents in knowledge of how to use technology (Livingstone, 2003; Vaterlaus, 2012; Vaterlaus et al., 2014a). In an interview study with parents and adolescents, Clark (2009) identified a perceived digital generation gap between parents and adolescents as indicated by a perception that adolescents possess more technological knowledge than parents. Vaterlaus and colleagues (2014a) sought to quantitatively measure this perceived digital generation gap. Adolescents rated their own knowledge and their parents' knowledge of how to use a variety of features of email, cell phone, social networking, and video chat technologies; parents then reported their own knowledge of the use of the aforementioned technologies. The comparison of adolescents' knowledge and their perceptions of their parents' knowledge revealed that indeed adolescents perceived they knew more than their parents on all technology sources, evidence of a perceived digital generation gap. Such perceived digital generation differences were further supported when comparing differences between adolescent self-reported knowledge and parent self-reported knowledge about technologies. Documentation of *actual* digital generation gaps—using standardized testing of actual technological knowledge, not self-reports—has yet to be published.

Digital Generational Differences and Parent–Adolescent Relationships

Access to interactive technology (e.g., Internet and cell phones) creates the opportunity for greater access to information and communication. And without equitable access to technology, a divide between the "info-haves and have-nots" can result in other negative outcomes, such as social exclusion (Norris, 2003, p. 11). Hargittai (2002) argues that the limited binary of the "haves and have-nots" fails to address the importance not only of having access to technology but also of knowing how to use it. Consequences of a second-level digital divide include decreased access to information (or accurate information), frustration with the medium of technology, and possibly decreased use of technology. With these consequences in mind, and by focusing on the parent–adolescent microsystem, we have a richer lens for understanding and exploring the *influence* of digital generation differences on parent–adolescent relationships; specifically, parent–adolescent quality time, parent–adolescent conflict, and parental knowledge of adolescents' behaviors.

Parent–Adolescent Quality Time

The adolescent–parent microsystem includes enduring interactions that, naturally, change over time. Research documents that, as adolescents age and pursue increased autonomy, they spend less time with parents and more time with peers (Fulkerson, Neumark-Sztainer, & Story, 2006). Even though adolescents spend less *time* with their families overall, they continue to stay connected with their families through face-to-face communication and technological communication (Vaterlaus, Jones, & Beckert, 2014). While *quantity* of time spent with family decreases throughout adolescence, it is unclear whether there is any change in the *quality* of parent–adolescent time. Parent–adolescent quality time is defined as parents' and adolescents' joint time when they feel close and together (Fallon & Bowles, 1997). To date, the majority of research on technology and parent–child quality time has focused only on noninteractive technology (Vaterlaus, 2012) and generally suggests a relationship between noninteractive technology use and decreases in adolescent quality time with parents. For example, a five-year study tracking parent–adolescent time spent together identified an increase of 25 minutes in parent–adolescent time spent watching television together but a decrease of 14 minutes of parents and adolescents going somewhere together (Dubas & Gerris, 2002). Additionally, in a four-year observational study of working-parent reunions with their children, approximately half of the time children ignored a working parent when he or she arrived home. Instead of attending to their parents, the children focused on electronic gadgets (Ochs, Graesch, Mittman, Bradbury, & Repetti, 2006).

Interactive technologies certainly create opportunities for family members to both connect and disconnect, with digital generational differences potentially playing a key role. Recent research suggests that when parents had the ability to communicate with their adolescents over the phone, adolescents reported close, satisfying, and supportive parent–child relationships (Gentzler, Oberhauser, Westerman, & Nadorff, 2011). However, in this same study, when parents communicated with adolescents using social networking, adolescents reported conflict, anxious attachments, and high levels of loneliness. Considering U&G theory, adolescents likely perceive different uses and purposes for phone and social networking technologies than do their parents. Adolescents might perceive social networking as neither a quality time activity nor an effective parent–child method of communication. Vaterlaus and colleagues (2014) indicate that adolescents and young adults perceive more closeness in parent–child communication through modalities that replicate face-to-face communication (i.e., video chat) or allow for immediate feedback (i.e., telephone, video chat, and text messaging).

In Vaterlaus's (2012) investigation of the relationship between quality time and perceived interactive technology knowledge differences and similarities between adolescents and parents, adolescent males reported more maternal quality time when they perceived that their mothers had less knowledge about social networking than they themselves did. Adolescent males also reported 46.4% more maternal quality time when adolescents perceived that their mother's knowledge about basic email skills was similar to their own compared to adolescents who perceived they knew more than their mothers about basic email skills. It appears male adolescents perceive more quality time when their mothers have at least basic interactive technology skills, but less quality time when mothers have similar skill levels with more advanced interactive technologies. When a digital generation gap is absent or mothers have similar knowledge about advanced interactive technologies, they too may become distracted by technology resulting in lower quality time with their children.

Parent–Adolescent Conflict

Although parent–child conflict can have negative consequences (see Petersen, 1988), some conflict in the parent–adolescent microsystem is a natural part of adolescents' negotiation of autonomy (Schwartz & Buboltz, 2004). Parents and adolescents most often experience conflict over day-to-day activities (e.g., chores, friends, or when they go out) rather than large macrosystem topics (e.g., war or social movements) or deviant behaviors (e.g., drugs; Galambos & Almeida, 1992; Montemayor, 1983; Renk et al., 2006). As McHale and colleagues (2009) have indicated, technology and communication about new technologies have become a part of the day-to-day reality for the parent–child microsystem.

Research is beginning to shed light on parent–adolescent conflict and generational differences in the perceptions of the purposes or use of interactive technologies (Cooper, 2009; Weisskrich, 2009, 2011). In these studies, parent–adolescent conflict often arose when parents used cell phones to monitor adolescent behaviors, to track homework, and when parents initiated cell phone calls to adolescents when parents were upset. Mesch (2006b) reports adolescents perceived parent–adolescent conflict when the adolescent used the Internet for social purposes (e.g., communication with friends, online games). No association between parent–adolescent conflict existed when adolescents used the Internet for school-related purposes. These findings provide evidence for the following claim: Parent–adolescent conflict is more likely when there are generational differences in the perceived purposes of interactive technology. From a U&G perspective, adolescents are finding their social need fulfillment through interactive technology while parents are more likely to view interactive technology as important to fulfilling instrumental needs.

Parent–adolescent conflict also appears with generational differences in technology *knowledge*. Vaterlaus (2012) reported that, in general, parent–adolescent conflict increased with more disparity in perceived generational gaps in technology knowledge surrounding newer technology (e.g., Twitter, video chat, and social networking). Furthermore, male adolescents reported higher levels of conflict when they perceived their mothers had a similar level of knowledge about social networking—or a smaller perceived digital generation gap. In general, research finds increased parent–adolescent conflict when adolescents are perceived to have more knowledge of technology than their parents (Mesch, 2006a; Vaterlaus, 2012). For example, Mesch (2006a) investigated perceived intergenerational technology knowledge differences and parent–adolescent conflict. Forty percent of parents indicated parent–adolescent conflict about adolescent Internet use, and rates of parent–adolescent conflict increased with the perception of adolescents as technology experts in the home (Mesch, 2006a).

Subrahmanyam and Greenfield (2008) argue too little research is available concerning interactive technology and parent–child conflict; the same is true about parent–child conflict and digital generation differences. To date no studies have investigated how generational differences in acquisition of technology knowledge relate to parent–adolescent conflict. Vaterlaus and colleagues (2014b) report parents rely on adolescent children to learn about technology. They hypothesize that this child-teaching-parent dynamic could be related to parent–adolescent conflict and urge researchers to investigate further.

Parental Knowledge of Adolescents' Behavior

Parental knowledge refers to a parent's awareness of his or her child's behavior when they are not together (Kerr, Stattin, & Burk, 2010). Parental knowledge most often comes to parents through their children's self-disclosure. Research on this topic has focused on parental monitoring (surveillance of children's behavior), but parental monitoring alone rarely leads to parental knowledge (Kerr et al., 2010). In the digital age, parental knowledge of adolescents' behavior has become important; parents perceive increased risks associated with their kids' use of interactive technologies. Small and portable devices have indeed created opportunities for private access to and use of interactive technologies. Adolescents have access to pornography, engage in sexting (sending or receiving sexual images), and face the realities of cyber-bullying. With perceptions of increased risk come parental attempts to monitor adolescents' interactive technology use (Vaterlaus et al., in press), a behavior called *parental mediation* (Livingstone & Helsper, 2008). Parents mediate their adolescents' interactive technology use through checking data and usage (e.g., checking the phone bill or Internet browser history), active mediation (openly talking about technology use), restriction (e.g., preventing device ownership, using Internet filters), and rule setting (e.g., rules about time with technology; Vaterlaus et al., in press).

Parental mediation can be more challenging when parents do not have knowledge about the technology sources their adolescents are using. In one study, parents report they would like additional transparency about their adolescents' interactive technology use (Yardi & Bruckman, 2011). However, parents reported that parental mediation was difficult because they were unfamiliar with the technology their adolescents were using. Yardi and Bruckman (2011) suggest digital generational differences in technological knowledge can decrease the ability of parents to mediate technology within the parent–adolescent microsystem.

Fewer studies have looked at parental knowledge and digital generation differences. As mentioned previously, parental monitoring alone rarely leads to parental knowledge (Kerr et al., 2010). Swift and Taylor (2003) found 83% of parents in their sample implemented some parental mediation techniques for adolescents' Internet use, but these same parents reported very low knowledge about what their adolescent children were actually doing online. Vaterlaus (2012) explored the relationship between parental knowledge (i.e. about adolescent behaviors at night, after school, with money, during free time, with friends, and deviant behaviors) and a perceived digital generation gap. When adolescents perceived their mothers had similar knowledge about email technology, they also reported their mothers had more parental knowledge of their behaviors. Male adolescents reported their fathers had more parental knowledge when they perceived similar father–adolescent knowledge about more advanced technologies (i.e., Twitter or video chat). This pattern was also true for female adolescents and their mothers with similar social networking knowledge. It appears that when perceived digital generation gaps are absent (parents and adolescents have similar technological knowledge) parents have more knowledge of their adolescents' behaviors. Overall, digital generation differences in knowledge appear to impede parental mediation of adolescent interactive technology use.

Conclusion

There is growing empirical evidence of generational differences in the defined purposes and uses of interactive technology (Oksman & Turtiainen, 2004; Swift & Taylor, 2003), the acquisition of interactive technology knowledge (Vaterlaus et al., 2014b), and in the amount of perceived interactive technology knowledge (Clark, 2009; Vaterlaus et al., 2014a) between parents and adolescents. These digital generation differences are associated with potential challenges within the parent–adolescent microsystem (Vaterlaus, 2012). As an emerging area of research, there are several directions for future research to further define these digital generational differences and clarify their influence on the parent–adolescent relationship, as well as to investigate the importance of family communication as a mediator of healthy digital-age choices. As Davis (2013) eloquently summarizes, "Digital natives may appear on the surface quite different from their pre-digital forebears, but they still require supportive, face-to-face relationships in order to thrive" (p. 2289). In light of what the contemporary generational research tells us, we conclude with preliminary ideas for how educators, parents, and practitioners who work with adolescents and parents can successfully navigate the digital age.

Application

Is Education the Answer?

Teaching parents. Education is a valid solution to bridging generational differences in technology. Hargittai (2002) argues it is not enough to provide people with access to technology; individuals need support and training to minimize technological differences. Adolescents and parents report they rarely seek formal sources to learn about interactive technology and are more likely to learn from informal sources (Vaterlaus et al., 2014b). This poses a challenge for Family Life Educators (FLE) because programming designed to educate is more formal in nature. FLE could consider using less formalized or lower levels of education (see Hawkins, Carroll, Doherty, & Willoughby, 2004) to overcome this potential barrier. In practice this might involve partnering with local schools and posting technology tip videos for parents on the school website, distributing brief pamphlets at community agencies or schools indicating simple "how to" instructions for newer media such as Snapchat, or providing media contests with desirable incentives for parents on newer technology platforms to stimulate interest in newer technologies (e.g., Instagram photo contests). These or similar endeavors could increase awareness about technology education and stimulate interest in more comprehensive educational offerings. FLE could consider collaborating with technology specialists in the community to develop courses for parents using a variety of interactive technologies.

Teaching adolescents. Parents report they have consulted and would consult with their children to learn about existing and new interactive technologies. This children-teaching-parents dynamic is relatively new and its impact on the parent–child relationship largely unknown at this point. Further, as discussed in this chapter, there is variance in the digital literacy among adolescents themselves (Hargittai, 2010), which might not make all adolescents the best technology instructors. Adolescents likely receive some education about technology in school (McHale et al., 2009), but it may not be expansive enough to account for cell phones and various social media applications made available on the Internet. FLE could consider developing courses for adolescents that assess and build on adolescent knowledge of interactive technology *and* facilitate opportunities for adolescents to learn best practices in how to teach people to use technology. These courses may also include components addressing the potential benefits of teaching parents how to use technology (e.g., if your parents learn how to Skype, you can video chat while away at college). Educators should evaluate these programs and in turn contribute to the research related to technology acquisition. An evaluation might involve (a) a pre-test assessing adolescent and parent interactive technology knowledge, (b) formal education for adolescents about interactive technology and how to effectively teach someone to use technology, and (c) a follow-up evaluation of the parents' digital literacy (assuming parents would consult their children about technology).

A developmental approach. A more isomorphic method might be to take a broader educational approach by teaching parents and adolescents about the major psychosocial tasks of adolescent development—identity and autonomy development. The educational objectives could include tips and skills for developing identity and negotiating autonomy as well as discussing how technology plays (or could play) a role in this adaptive process within the parent–adolescent microsystem. Using U&G as a framework, education for parents and adolescents could include information about how interactive technologies meet adolescents' developmental needs. This approach could shed some light on the different purposes and uses of interactive technology between parents and adolescents.

Talk about It Offline

Clinicians and educators alike should consider the role technology plays in parent–adolescent relational distress. Technological knowledge is not the only area where digital generation differences exist. Increasing communication about the *purpose* of technology for adolescents might help bridge some digital generation differences. Oksman and Turtiainen (2004) indicate that many adults are unaware of the culture that has developed around new interactive technologies. Clinicians and educators should create opportunities and questions that elucidate the values, rules, and mores that underlie the youth culture. Such communication has the potential to increase adolescents' own understanding of their youth culture and allow parents the opportunity (at least in part) to acculturate into this youth culture. This suggestion could be implemented concurrently with therapy plans related to social skill development and communication training.

Parental Mediation

Involving the digital native. Kerr and colleagues (2010) indicate that parental knowledge of adolescents' behaviors occurs when adolescents self-disclose to parents. Parents might not have to be technological experts in order to provide structure and safety within adolescent interactive technology use. Creating and maintaining an open dialogue about multiple topics in the parent–adolescent microsystem can lead to more adolescent self-disclosure. Vaterlaus and colleagues (in press, pp. 23–27) propose principles for the implementation of parental mediation of adolescent technology use:

1. Parents should assume the responsibility of regulating adolescent interactive technology use.
2. Parents could consider including adolescents in the conversation when deciding what parental mediation techniques should be implemented (e.g., rules, restrictions) to mediate adolescent technology use.
3. Parents need to select mediation technique(s) that are within their level of technological competence and with which they can be consistent.
4. After implementing techniques, parents should evaluate the influences of parental mediation technique on their adolescent's behavior and the parent–adolescent relationship. In addition, parents should evaluate how consistent they are applying the selected approach.

The parent–adolescent communication resulting from application of these principles could be an adaptive process in the parent–adolescent microsystem: Parents are granting some autonomy while maintaining some authority and connection to their adolescent.

When adolescents turn 18, is parental mediation complete? For adolescents in the digital age, the parent–adolescent microsystem involves achievement of some levels of autonomy (e.g., leaving home for college). However, most adolescents rely on their parents for a variety of resources (e.g., financial and emotional support; Aquilino, 2006). What is a parent's role in mediating technology when their children turn 18, or leave the nest? Coyne, Padilla-Walker, and Howard (2013) point out how little is known about parental mediation during this part of adolescence (18–25 years old) and encourage future research. Conceptualizing how to mediate technology after the age of 18 is difficult because the parent–adolescent microsystem changes significantly during this part of adolescence. Furthermore, the differences in the perceived uses and gratifications of technology between parents and adolescents make it hard to suggest mediation techniques that might be ideal and successful. We propose that active mediation techniques (e.g., being "friends" with the adolescent on social networking sites, discussing adolescent technology use) with adolescents 18 years or older could increase parents' awareness of any technological behaviors that might be harmful to their adolescent and/or people within the adolescents' digital social circle. However, if digital generational differences prevent parental mediation in earlier adolescence, mediation is likely to be more challenging in later adolescence. As such, parents should engage early and often in the mediation of their children's technology and media use.

References

Acock, A. C., & Bengtson, V. L. (1980). Socialization and attribution processes: Actual versus perceived similarity among parents and youth. *Journal of Marriage and Family, 42*, 501–515.

Aquilino, W. S. (2006). Family relationships and support systems in emerging adulthood. In J. J. Arnett & J. L. Tanner (Eds.), *Emerging adults in America* (pp. 193–218). Washington, DC: American Psychological Association.

Arnett, J. J. (2000). Emerging adulthood: A theory of development from the late teens through the twenties. *American Psychologist, 55*, 469–480. doi:10.1037/0003–066X.55.5.469

Blair, B. L., & Fletcher, A. C. (2011). "The only 13-year-old on planet Earth without a cell phone": Meanings of cell phones in early adolescents' everyday lives. *Journal of Adolescent Research, 26*, 155–177. doi:10.1177/0743558410371127.

Bolin, G., & Westlund, O. (2009). Mobile generations: The role of mobile technology in the shaping of Swedish media generations. *International Journal of Communication, 3*, 108–124.

Bronfenbrenner, U. (1979) *The ecology of human development.* Cambridge, MA: Harvard University Press.

Brown, J. D., & Bobkowski, P. S. (2011). Older and newer media: Patterns of use and effects on adolescents' health and well-being. *Journal of Research on Adolescence, 21*, 95–113. doi:10.111/j.1532–7795.2010.00717.x

Bynner, J. (2007). Rethinking the youth phase of the life-course: The case for emerging adulthood? *Journal of Youth Studies, 8*, 367–384. doi:10.1080/13676260500431628

Clark, L. S. (2009). Digital media and the generation gap: Qualitative research on US teens and their parents. *Information, Communication, & Society, 12*, 388–407. doi:10.1080/13691180902823845

Compaine, B. M. (2001) *The digital divide: Facing a crisis or creating a myth?* Cambridge, MA: MIT Press.

Cooper, C. (2009). The blurring of interpersonal and mass communication: Generation net and the cell phone. *American Communication Journal, 11*. Retrieved from http://ac-journal.org/journal/2009/Spring/GenerationNetandCell phones.pdf

Coyne, S. M., Padilla-Walker, L. M., & Howard, E. (2013). Emerging in a digital world: A decade review of media use, effects, and gratifications in emerging adulthood. *Emerging Adulthood, 1*(2), 125–137. doi:10.1177/2167696813479782

Cupples, J., & Thompson, L. (2010). Heterotextuality and digital foreplay. *Feminist Media Studies, 10*, 1–17. doi:10.1080/14680770903457063.

Davis, K. (2013). Young people's digital lives: The impact of interpersonal relationships and digital media use on adolescents' sense of identity. *Computers in Human Behavior, 29*, 2281–2293. doi:10.1016/j.chb.2013.05.022

Doty, J., & Dworkin, J. (2013). Parents' of adolescents use of social networking sites. *Computers in Human Behavior.* Retrieved from http://www.sciencedirect.com/science/article/pii/S0747563213002501

Dubas, J. S., & Gerris, J. R. M. (2002). Longitudinal changes in the time parents spend in activities with their adolescent children as a function of child age, pubertal status, and gender. *Journal of Family Psychology, 16*, 415–427. doi:10.1037/0893–3200.16.4.415

Duggan, M., & Rainie, L. (2012). Cell phone activities 2012. Pew Internet and American Life Project. Retrieved from http://www.pewinternet.org/Reports/2012/Cell-Activities/Additional-Demographic-Analysis/Demographics.aspx

Erikson, E. H. (1950). *Childhood and Society*. New York: Norton.

Facer, K., Sutherland, R., Furlong, R., & Furlong, J. (2001). What's the point of using computers? The development of young people's computer expertise in the home. *New Media Society, 3*, 199–219. doi:10.1177/1461444801003002004

Falk, G., & Falk, U. A. (2005). *Youth culture and the generation gap*. New York: Algora.

Fallon, B. J., & Bowles, T. V. (1997). The effect of family structure and family functioning on adolescents' perceptions of intimate time spent with parents, siblings, and peers. *Journal of Youth and Adolescence, 26*, 25–43. doi:10.1023/A:1024536128038

Feixa, C. (2011). Past and present of adolescent society: The "teen brain." *Neuroscience and Biobehavioral Reviews, 35*, 1634–1643. doi:10.1016/j.neubiorev.2011.02.013

Fulkerson, J. A., Neumark-Sztainer, D., & Story, M. (2006). Adolescent and parent views of family meals. *The Journal of the American Dietetic Association, 106*, 526–532. doi:10.1016/j.jada.2006.01.006

Galambos, N. L., & Almeida, D. M. (1992). Does parent–adolescent conflict increase in early adolescence? *Journal of Marriage and Family, 54*, 737–747.

Gentzler, A. L., Oberhauser, A. M., Westerman, D., & Nadorff, D. K. (2011). College students' use of electronic communication with parents: Links to loneliness, attachment, and relationship quality. *Cyberpsychology, Behavior, and Social Networking, 14*, 71–74. doi:10.1089/cyber.2009.0409

Hall, G. S. (1904). *Adolescence: Its psychology and its relation to physiology, anthropology, sociology, sex, crime, religion, and education*. Englewood Cliffs, NJ: Irvington.

Hargittai, E. (2002). Second-level digital divide: Differences in people's online skills. *First Monday, 7*(4). Retrieved from http://firstmonday.org/ojs/index.php/fm/article/viewArticle/942

Hargittai, E. (2010). Digital na(t)ives? Variation in Internet skills and uses among members of the "Net Generation." *Sociological Inquiry, 80*, 92–113. doi:10.1111/j.1475-682X.2009.00317.x

Hargittai, E., Fullerton, L., Menchen-Trevino, E., & Thomas, K. Y. (2010). Trust online: Young adults' evaluation of Web content. *International Journal of Communication, 4*, 468–494.

Hargittai, E., & Hsieh, Y. P. (2012). Succinct survey measures of Web-use skills. *Social Science Computer Review, 30*, 95–107. doi:10.1177/0894439310397146

Hawkins, A. J., Carroll, J. S., Doherty, W. J., & Willoughby, B. (2004). A comprehensive framework for marriage education* *Family Relations, 53*(5), 547–558.

Jacobsen, R. B., Berry, K. J., & Olson, K. F. (1975). An empirical test of the generation gap: A comparative intrafamily study. *Journal of Marriage and Family, 37*, 841–852.

Jones, S. (2009). Generations online in 2009. Retrieved from Pew Research Internet Project website: http://pewresearch.org/pubs/1093/generations-online

Katz, E., Blumler, J. G., & Gurevitch, M. (1973). Uses and gratifications research. *The Public Opinion Quarterly, 37*, 509–523.

Kelty, N. (2000). Computer proficiency: The digital generation gap. Retrieved from http://eric.ed.gov/PDFS/ED471132.pdf

Kerr, M., Stattin, H., & Burk, W. J. (2010). A reinterpretation of parental monitoring in longitudinal perspective. *Journal of Research on Adolescence, 20*, 39–64. doi:10.1111/j.1532–7795.2009.00623.x

Koutropolulos, A. (2011). Digital natives: Ten years after. *Journal of online learning and Teaching, 7*. Retrieved from http://jolt.merlot.org/vol7no4/koutropoulos_1211.htm

Lenhart, A. (2010). *Teens, cell phones, and texting*. Retrieved from Pew Research Internet Project website: http://pewresearch.org/pubs/1572/teens-cell-phones-text-messages

Lerner, R. M. (2013). *Concepts and theories of human development*. New York: Psychology Press.

Levin, A., Foster, M., West, B., Nicholson, M. J., Hernandez, T., & Cukier, W. (2008). *The next digital divide: Online social networking privacy*. Ryerson University, Toronto, ON: Privacy and Cyber Crime Institute.

Livingstone, S. (2003). Children's use of the Internet: Reflections on the emerging research agenda. *New Media and Society, 5*, 147–166.

Livingstone, S., & Helsper, E. (2008) Parental mediation of children's Internet use. *Journal of Broadcasting & Electronic Media, 52*, 581–599. doi:10.1080/08838150802437396

Madden, M., Lenhart, A., & Duggan, M. (2013). Teens and Technology 2013. Retrieved from Pew Research Internet Project website: http://www.pewinternet.org/Reports/2013/Teens-and-Tech.aspx

Maga, T. (2003). *The 1960s*. New York: Infobase.

Mannheim, K. (1952). The problem of generations. In P. Kecskemeti (Ed.), *Essays on the Sociology of Knowledge* (pp. 276–322). London: Routledge.

McHale, S. M., Dotterer, A., & Kim, J. (2009). An ecological perspective on the media and youth development. *American Behavioral Scientist 52*, 1186–1203. doi:10.1177/0002764209331541

Mesch, G. S. (2006a). Family characteristics and intergenerational conflicts over the Internet. *Information, Communication, and Society, 9*, 473–495. doi:10.1080/13691180600858705

Mesch, G. S. (2006b). Family relations and the Internet: Exploring a family boundaries approach. *The Journal of Family Communication, 6*, 119–138. doi:10.1207/s15327698jfc0602_2

Montemayor, R. (1983). Parents and adolescents in conflict: All families some of the time and some families most of the time. *Journal of Early Adolescence, 3*, 83–103.

Morrill, T. B., Jones, R. M., & Vaterlaus, J. M. (2013). Motivations for text messaging: Gender and age differences among young adults. *North American Journal of Psychology, 15*, 1–16.

Norris, P. (2003). *Digital divide: Civic engagement, information poverty, and the Internet Worldwide*. Cambridge, UK: Cambridge University Press.

Ochs, E., Graesch, A. P., Mittman, A., Bradbury, T., & Repetti, R. (2006). Video ethnography and ethnoarchaeological tracking. In M. Pitt-Castouphes, E. E. Kossek, & S. Sweet (Eds.), *The work and family handbook: Multi-disciplinary perspectives and approaches* (pp. 387–409). Mahwah, NJ: Erlbaum.

Oksman, V., & Turtiainen, J. (2004). Mobile communication as a social stage: Meanings of mobile communication in everyday life among teenagers in Finland. *New Media and Society, 6*, 319–339. doi:10.1177/1461444804042518

Petersen, A. C. (1988). Adolescent development. *Annual Reviews of Psychology, 39*, 583–607. doi:10.1146/annurev.ps. 39.020188.003055

Pew Research Center (2013). Trend data (adults). Retrieved from Pew Research Internet Project website: http://www.pewinternet.org/Static-Pages/Trend-Data-(Adults)/Whos-Online.aspx

Prensky, M. (2001). Digital natives, digital immigrants, part II: Do they really think differently? *On the Horizon, 9*, 1–6. Retrieved from http://www.marcprensky.com/writing/Prensky%20%20Digital%20Natives,%20Digital%20Immigrants%20-%20Part2.pdf

Renk, K., Roddenberry, A., Oliveros, A., Roberts, R., Meehan, C., & Liljequist, L. (2006). An examination of conflict in emerging adulthood between college students and their parents. *Journal of Intergenerational Relationships, 4*, 41–59. doi:10.1300/J194v04n04_04

Ruggiero, T. E. (2000). Uses and gratifications theory in the 21st century. *Mass Communication & Society, 3*(1), 3–37. doi:10.1207/S15327825MCS0301_02

Sánchez-Navarro, J., & Aranda, D. (2013). Messenger and social network sites as tools for sociability, leisure, and informal learning for Spanish young people. *European Journal of Communication, 28*(1), 67–75. doi:10.1177/0267323111432411

Schwartz, J. P., & Buboltz, W. C. (2004). The relationship between attachment to parents and psychological separation in college students. *Journal of College Student Development, 45*, 566–577. doi:10.1353/csd.2004.0062

Schwartz, S. J., Côté, J. E., & Arnett, J. J. (2005). Identity and agency in emerging adulthood: Two developmental routes in the individualization process. *Youth and Society, 37*, 201–229. doi:10.1177/0044118X05275965

Smith, T. W. (2000). *Changes in the generation gap, 1972–1998*. GSS Social Change Report No. 43. Arlington, VA: National Science Foundation.

Subrahmanyam, K., & Greenfield, P. (2008). Online communication and adolescent relationships. *The Future of Children, 18*, 119–146. doi:10.1353/foc.0.0006

Swift, C., & Taylor, A. (2003). The digital divide—a new generation gap: Parental knowledge of their children's Internet use. *Pediatrics and Child Health, 8*, 275–278.

Thurlow, C., & Bell, K. (2009). Against technologization: Young people's new media discourse as creative cultural practice. *Journal of Computer-Mediated Communication, 14*, 1038–1049. doi:10.1111/j.1083–6101.2009.01480.x.

Thurlow, C., & McKay, S. (2003). Profiling "new" communication technologies in adolescence. *Journal of Language and Social Psychology, 22*, 94–103.

Tulane, S. (2012). *Social implications of adolescent text messaging* (Unpublished doctoral dissertation). Utah State University, Logan.

Tulane, S., & Beckert, T. E. (2013). Perceptions of texting: A comparison of female high school and college students. *North American Journal of Psychology, 15*, 395.

Tutt, D. (2005). Mobile performances of a teenager: A study of situated mobile phone activity in the living room. *Convergence: The International Journal of Research into New Media Technologies, 11*, 58–75.

van Dijk, J. A. (2005). *The deepening divide: Inequality in the information society*. Thousand Oaks, CA: Sage.

Vaterlaus, J. M. (2012). *Late adolescents' perceptions of a digital generation gap and perceived parent–child relations* (Unpublished doctoral dissertation). Utah State University, Logan.

Vaterlaus, J. M., Beckert, T. E., Tulane, S., & Bird, C. V. (in press). "They always ask what I'm doing and who I'm talking to": Parental mediation of adolescent interactive technology use. *Marriage and Family Review.*

Vaterlaus, J. M., Jones, R. M., & Beckert, T. E. (2014). *Parent–child time together and interactive technology in adolescence and young adulthood.* Manuscript submitted for publication.

Vaterlaus, J. M., Jones, R. M., & Tulane, S. (2014a). *Digital generation gaps: An investigation of perceived gaps in technological knowledge between late adolescents and their parents.* Manuscript submitted for publication.

Vaterlaus, J. M., Jones, R. M., & Tulane, S. (2014b). *Generational differences in learning about technology.* Manuscript submitted for publication.

Weisskirch, R. S. (2009). Parenting by cell phone: Parental monitoring of adolescents and family relations. *Journal of Youth and Adolescence, 38,* 1123–1138. doi:10.1007/s10964–008–9374–8

Weisskirch, R. S. (2011). No crossed wires: Cell phone communication in parent–adolescent relationships. *Cyberpsychology, Behavior, and Social Networking, 14*(7–8): 447–451. doi:10.1089/cyber.2009.0455.

Williams, S., & Williams, L. (2005). Space invaders: The negotiation of teenage boundaries through the mobile phone. *The Sociological Review, 53,* 314–331. doi:10.1111/j.1467–954X.2005.00516.x.

Xenos, M., & Foot, K. (2008). Not your father's Internet: The generation gap in online politics. In W. L. Bennett (Ed.). *Civic life online: Learning how digital media can engage youth,* (pp. 51–70). Cambridge, MA: MIT Press.

Yardi, S., & Bruckman, A. (2011). *Social and technical challenges in parenting teens' social media use.* Retrieved from http://www.cc.gatech.edu/~yardi/pubs/Yardi_ParentsTechnology11.pdf

Zickuhr, K. (2010). *Generations.* Retrieved from Pew Research Internet Project website: http://pewinternet.org/Reports/2010/Generations-2010.aspx

Zickuhr, K. (2011). *Generations and their gadgets.* Retrieved from Pew Research Internet Project website: http://pewinternet.org/~/media//Files/Reports/2011/PIP _Generations _and_Gadgets.pdf

Zimmer-Gembeck, M. J., & Collins, W. A. (2003). Autonomy development during adolescence. In G. R. Adams & M. Berzonsky (Eds.), *Blackwell handbook of adolescence* (pp. 175–204). Oxford, UK: Blackwell Publishers.

21

Nonresidential Parenting and New Media Technologies

A Double-Edged Sword

FALON KARTCH
California State University, Fresno

LINDSAY M. TIMMERMAN
University of Wisconsin–Milwaukee

Introduction

Nonresidential parents (NRPs) are defined as parents who do not live with one or more of their biological children all or most of the time (Braithwaite & Baxter, 2006; Herrerias, 1995). Individuals can become NRPs in a number of ways: after a divorce, after a cohabiting relationship ends, or if children are born outside of a marital/committed relationship. Even in joint custody situations, it is common for one parent to have primary physical placement, making the other parent nonresidential by default (Ganong & Coleman, 2004). The focus of this chapter will be post-divorce NRPs, parents who often must redefine and modify parenting practices to adapt to their new family system. Because NRPs are geographically separated from their children on a regular basis, they often use various technologies to maintain familial connections with their children (Rollie Rodriguez, 2014). As such, post-divorce, nonresidential parenting is an important context in which to examine digital-age family communication.

Nonresidential Parenting

Previous research on nonresidential parenting has focused on patterns of contact and visitation (Cooksey & Craig, 1998; Stewart, 1999), child support (Natalier & Hewitt, 2010), child adjustment (Falci, 2006; Gunnoe & Hetherington, 2004), father involvement (Carlson & McLanahan, 2010; Fagan & Barnett, 2003; Tach, Mincy, & Edin, 2010), levels of coparenting (Carlson, McLanahan, & Brooks-Gunn, 2008), incarceration and absenteeism (Geller, Cooper, Garfinkel, Schwartz-Soicher, & Mincy; 2012), paternal engagement (Zhang & Fuller, 2012), and nonresidential parent adjustment (Anderson, Kohler, & Letiecq, 2005; Arditti & Madden-Derdich, 1993; Kartch & Tenzek, 2012; Kielty, 2008). Most of the research to date has taken a quantity approach to understanding nonresidential parenthood, with a focus on the number of times the nonresidential parent has been in contact with a child within the last 12 months, or how often the nonresidential parent was late with child support payments. While such research provides important information about the relationship between the NRP and their child(ren), frequency of NRP–child contact does not provide insight into the quality of the contact itself. Research suggests it is the *quality* of the interaction that promotes relational closeness and increased personal well-being for both the parent and the child (Nielsen, 2011).

Some recent research has begun to explore the nature of talk in the NRP–child relationship (Rollie, 2006; Rollie Rodriguez, 2014; Yarosh, Chiech, Chew, & Abowd, 2009). For instance, Rollie Rodriguez (2014) explored how absence as a result of the visitation schedule impacts NRP–child communication. Results indicated that NRPs struggled with gaining access to information about their children's lives, and that they used telephone calls to catch up on what was happening in their children's lives. Results also indicated NRPs often had to extract information from their children, from the residential parent, and from others about the lives of their children, and that the information their children did provide were more like "highlights"—the big events that transpired in the child's life (Rollie Rodriguez, p. 12). While research suggests those topics are important for NRPs and children to discuss, communication research also points to the importance of mundane, day-to-day talk for creating and maintaining relationships (Duck, 1995; Rollie Rodriguez, 2014). Due to periods of forced physical separation between NRPs and their children, it is increasingly difficult to maintain these familial relationships through mundane talk (Rollie Rodriguez).

Family Communication and Technology

Research has also explored familial use of new media technology to facilitate relational closeness (Coyne, Padilla-Walker, Fraser, Fellows, & Day, 2014; Padilla-Walker, Coyne, & Fraser, 2012). Coyne et al. explored the use of new media technology as a "tool" to build and maintain closeness within families. Results indicated participants used these tools to increase their parental involvement within their children's lives.

Research has established the importance of technology in maintaining interpersonal relationships at a distance (Johnson, Haigh, Becker, Craig, & Wigley, 2008). Johnson et al. explored how college students enacted relational maintenance through email with long-distance family, friends, and romantic partners. Results indicated participants reported the use of openness, social networks, and positivity as the most common maintenance strategies used within their email communication with family members (Johnson et al.). Similarly, research has indicated that new media technologies, such as email and social networking websites, are commonly used to maintain parent/child connections (Walker, this volume).

Nonresidential parenting and technology. Yarosh et al. (2009) explored the use of technology in post-divorce families, providing further insight into the challenges of the NRP–child relationship and the role of technology in maintaining parent–child contact. Results suggest that NRPs used phone calls as the primary medium to stay connected with their children; however, NRPs and children both found audio-only communication to be difficult because they are unable to see one another and therefore are unable to communicate nonverbally beyond the use of vocalics (Yarosh et al.). In addition, other reasons NRPs reported feeling dissatisfied with audio-only communication included: being unable to hug or touch their children; the possibility of their conversations being overheard by others; and their desire not to interrupt the daily activities of their children, which they felt limited their ability to maintain parent–child connections. Participants also reported difficulties encouraging deeper conversation over the telephone. The current investigation extends the work of Rollie Rodriguez (2014) and Yarosh et al. by explicitly exploring NRPs' use of, and challenges with, new media technologies for communicating and maintaining relationships with their children.

In addition, new media tools provide opportunities for parenting from a distance. In a study of post-divorce nonresidential parenting, Bailey (2003) explored how NRPs who resided more than 50 miles from their children maintain familial bonds with those children through a qualitative analysis of NRPs' descriptions of the challenges and strengths of nonresidential parenting. Results indicated these NRPs used telephone calls, email, and snail mail to keep in contact with their children during times of separation. The present chapter extends this line of inquiry by exploring a wider range of new media technologies and how NRPs use them to parent their children when they are not physically together. Also, rather than exploring the strengths and weaknesses of nonresidential parenting in general, the current research specifically explores the strengths and limitations of the use of new media technologies within the context of the NRP–child relationship.

Family Systems Theory

The current research employs a family systems theory framework for exploring the intersection between nonresidential parenting and new media technologies. According to family systems theory, families develop patterns that make life predictable and stable (Galvin, Dickson, & Marrow, 2006), establishing regularity and order for the family (Gottman, 1991). Rules help maintain patterns in the system, a process of calibration whereby feedback regulates behavior according to family rules. Communication rules often require recalibration during the transition from residential parent to NRP. Such a change in the system naturally represents a shift in family life, characterized by changes in family roles, patterns, and relationships.

The common conceptualization of parenting in U.S. American culture occurs within the context of daily physical presence and cohabitation. Children are raised in the parental household, as "parents and young children are supposed to share a residence" (Stafford, 2005, p. 1). In this model, parents and children interact with one another face to face on a daily basis. Parents often engage in a variety of mundane parenting activities. Rollie (2006) described these activities as "opportunities" (p. 186). Residential parents are afforded many more parental opportunities, which affect the relationships they develop with their children (Rollie). NRPs must figure out how to parent with more limited opportunities. According to Rollie, "because they live in a different household, NRPs often have limited opportunities to enact the full range of behaviors and expressions that normally make up the parent identity" (p. 188). Because NRPs' parenting roles are limited (Yarosh et al., 2009), they have reported experiencing feelings of loss (Hagestad & Smyer, 1982; Rollie; Shapiro & Lambert, 1999; Wilbur & Wilbur, 1988), due to a "loss of emotional attachments," an "inability to preform valued roles," and the "loss of routines" (Rollie, p. 189–190). These challenges are a result of their transition to nonresidential parenting and illustrate NRPs' need to recalibrate within the context of their new parental status.

In order for the family to create new patterns in their family system, parents must reconceptualize what it means to be a "parent," as well as how they parent (Rollie, 2006; Seltzer, 1991; Stueve & Pleck, 2001; Yarosh et al., 2009). Research illustrates the role of parent comprises a variety of accompanying roles including breadwinner, teacher, caretaker, protector, and moral developer, among others (Lupton & Barclay, 1997; Minton & Pasley, 1996; Seltzer, 1991). According to Rollie, "NRPs are unable to enact some aspects of the parent role in the traditional, culturally prescribed and immediate manner" (p. 190). Because of these limitations, it is important to NRPs to recalibrate their parental role and develop new means of parenting within the context of their now nonresidential status.

Research indicates NRPs do, in fact, refine their roles and develop new ways of spending time with their children when they are together (Hawkins, Amato, & King, 2006). One means of recalibration for NRPs is the use of new media technologies to facilitate parent–child communication when the parent and child are physically separated. In order to explore the relationship between new media technologies and nonresidential parenting, the following research questions were posed:

RQ1: For what purposes do NRPs use new media technologies to communicate with their children?

RQ2: What challenges do NRPs experience in the use of new media technologies for communicating with their children?

Method

Participants were recruited using criterion sampling (Patton, 2002). To be eligible for participation in this study, an individual had be a nonresidential parent, defined for purposes of this study as a divorced parent who did at one time, but currently does not, live with one or more of his or her biological children. All participants were offered a $5 Target gift card for their participation. Participation was voluntary. All participants have been given pseudonyms to protect their confidentiality.

After receiving approval from the institutional review board, 40 nonresidential parents were interviewed (20 fathers, 20 mothers). Participants ranged in age from 23 to 66, with an average age of 40.35 years. Thirty-three participants self-identified as White or Caucasian, two participants as Mexican, and two participants as Asian. The remaining three participants each self-identified as American Indian, African American, and Celtic respectively. Participants were living in a wide range of regions within the United States (23 from the Midwest; six from the South; four from the Southwest; three from the West; three from the East) and one participant was currently living abroad in Mexico. Respondents varied in length of time they had been a NRP at the time of the study, ranging from 4 months to 19 years, with an average length of 4.93 years.

Because of the nature of the study only respondents with minor children and/or young adult children (not older than 22 years old) were actively recruited to participate in the study. Children of the participants ranged in age from two to 27, with an average age of 13.19 years. In the case of the parent with the 27 year old, the parent's youngest child was 20; therefore, the interview questions focused on the 20 year old.

While the large majority of participants had one or two nonresidential children (one, *n* = 17; two, *n* = 17), some of the participants had three (*n* = 5) or four (*n* = 1). Twelve participants also had residential, biological children (one, *n* = 8; two, *n* = 1; three, *n* = 2; four, *n* = 1). Eight respondents reported having stepchildren (one, *n* = 4; two, *n* = 2, three, *n* = 1; five, *n* = 1). In some cases stepchildren were residential, and in other cases they were living predominantly with their other biological parent.

Data were collected through in-depth, qualitative interviews (either face to face or via telephone) with nonresidential parents. The interview protocol was divided into four main sections. The first section was composed of basic demographic items as well as questions that explore the basic context of each NRP's unique circumstance. This section included questions regarding how many children the participant had, including sex and age for each child, and a description of how they each became a nonresidential parent. The second section solicited participant perspectives on parental roles, including questions about the responsibilities of both residential and nonresidential parents. Participants were also asked to reflect on their own parental role. The third section focused on frequency of contact between NRPs and their children, as well as the communication channels used within these relationships (e.g., text messaging, Skype, Facebook, etc.). The final section explored NRP–child interactions through a series of questions designed to facilitate discussion regarding the NRP's perceived parental control, perceived level of involvement, and communication behaviors. Participants were asked to provide detailed descriptions of the conversations they have with their children using various communication technologies, as well as the types of messages they send to their children through these mediums. Participants were also asked to list and describe any topics that are difficult to discuss with their children, why they believe these topics are difficult, how they attempt to cope with these difficult topics, and how they attempt to communicate intimacy within their relationships with their children. Participants were then asked to reflect on how these relational variables have evolved since becoming a nonresidential parent. Participants who are nonresidential parents to more than one child were asked to report on their interactions and experiences with each child.

All interviews were audio-recorded and transcribed for further analysis. Interview length ranged from just under 20 minutes (19:02) to nearly 90 minutes (1:27:22); the average length was 48:18 minutes. Transcribing resulted in 473 single-spaced pages of data for analysis.

Interview data were analyzed inductively (Patton, 2002), using systems theory as a general framework for understanding NRPs' use of new media technologies to communicate with their children as a means of recalibration after divorce. A four-step coding process, as outlined by Emerson, Fretz, and Shaw (1995) was used to facilitate data analysis. First, all interview transcripts were open coded (Emerson et al.). During this stage, all transcripts were read closely with an eye toward identifying data that reflected the two RQs and creating general codes within each RQ.

The second step of data analysis involved writing initial memos (Emerson et al., 1995), constructed by identifying and electronically sorting all open-coded data excerpts by research question and general codes. The third step of data analysis was focused coding (Emerson et al.). During focused coding, all initial memos were read and the data were coded again. The fourth and final stage of data analysis involved writing integrated memos (Emerson et al.). Focused codes were electronically grouped together to explore variations (sub-themes) within the broader themes.

Results

Every participant (N = 40) mentioned technology when discussing communication with their nonresidential child(ren). NRPs described a variety of technologies they sporadically and/or regularly employ to communicate with their children, including landline phones, cell phones, Skype, Facebook (posts and chat), Twitter, email, text messaging, and video messaging.

Research Question One

RQ1 asked, for what purposes do NRPs use new media technologies to communicate with their children. Participants described their use of new media technologies to communicate with their nonresidential children a total of 89 times within the data. Inductive analysis of these excerpts resulted in the identification of four major uses of new media technologies: *daily presence*, *show affection*, *show support*, and *involvement in the NRP's household*. Throughout the results section, *n*s in parentheses refer to number of messages in that category (i.e., for RQ1, out of 89); percentages refer to how many parents are represented in that category (out of 40).

Daily presence. When participants described their use of new media technologies to communicate with their children, they most frequently described using technology for *daily presence* (n = 38; 65%). According to interview data, parents are frequently physically separated from their children and use technology to stay connected with them. Parents report using telephone calls (both landlines and cell phones), emails, Facebook messages, Tweets, text messages, and video messages to maintain a daily presence within the lives of their children and as a way to keep as up-to-date as possible with what is happening in their children's lives. Quinn described her use of daily phone calls as a way of checking in with her nonresidential son and daughter:

> I try to have daily contact with the children. Then I can check in and see how they are doing with their school and their friends, and just have a day-to-day connection with them. Just to see where they are in their heads and physically what is going on.

Text messaging was another important medium for NRPs to stay connected with their children. Arielle described the use of text messaging in daily communication with her nonresidential sons and daughter:

> Text is instantaneous … [we text] daily, multiple times a day. Even if it is a text saying "hey this song came on the radio and I love you," or something that my daughter and I have gotten into. She'll watch *Glee* and I'll watch *Glee* and we'll talk about it, or we do different games we play together. That drawing game, Pictionary or we do like Song Pop, we instant message when we're doing those games.

Show affection. The second most frequently reported way NRPs use new media technologies when communicating with their children is to *show affection* (n = 19; 40%). Data revealed that due to geographical separation, NRPs' means of showing affection to their children was limited before new communication technologies became widely available for doing so through multiple media. Participants reported showing affection through new media technologies in a variety of ways and with various types of technology. The use of the telephone was important for participants (e.g., always saying "I love you" before hanging up), as was the use of Facebook messaging, text messaging, Twitter, Skype, and using the mail to send postcards and pictures. Phoebe described using Facebook to show affection to her son: "On Facebook I tell him I love him and I will see him on whatever day that I am supposed to get him or I do like, on Facebook they have the smiley face or the smooch face." NRPs like Quinn take advantage of both Skype and telephone calls in order to mimic physical forms of showing affection. Quinn said, "With Skype we always do a pretend hug and a kiss. We do that on the phone too; kind of make a hugging sound and a kiss sound." Interviews revealed new media technologies are providing new and various outlets for NRPs to show affection to their children.

Show support. The third most frequently reported purpose for using new media technologies when communicating with their nonresidential children was to *show support* (n = 17; 30%). Parents reported using technology as a means of making themselves available for emotional support to their children, something they deemed essential because they are not always able to do this face to face. Caroline described using Twitter as a means of providing emotional support to her daughter: "When she Tweets something like that she is upset, I will start a conversation with her and I'll be like 'hey, what's going on?' We send text messages … I think technology helps a lot." Caroline went on to explain that she reaches out to her nonresidential daughter with Tweets, cell phone calls and text messages to initiate and engage in such conversations.

When discussing his responsibilities as a NRP, Dean described telephone calls as a means of providing social support to his son: "He knows he can call me anytime if he needs anything. [My job is to] just be as supportive as I can." Dean reveals that he has a cell phone that he has with him all of the time so his son is able to get in touch with him whenever he needs to.

Involvement in the NRP's household. The final theme reflects NRPs using new media technologies when communicating with their children to facilitate *involvement in the NRP's household* (n = 15; 18%). The *daily presence* category described above captures these parents' attempts to stay connected to the lives of their children when they are physically separated. *Involvement in the NRP's household* is composed of instances when participants reported using new media technologies to facilitate a continued connection between their children and the NRP's life and household. Here, NRPs shared information with their children about what has been happening in their own lives, with their pets, with their home, and/or with the child's siblings. Research indicates mundane talk about daily life and events are an important way for individuals to maintain their connections with others (Duck, 1995). In the case of *involvement in the NRP's household*, these parents are attempting to use technology to keep their children not only informed but also connected to their own daily lives. Alan sends pictures and videos of his home and the weather he is experiencing to his five-year-old daughter:

> Sometimes I will make funny videos walking around the house and I'm in her old bedroom. I still have her old bedroom here, and I still have all of her stuff in it because they did not take anything, so it still is like a little girl's room, and so sometimes I will [make videos] so she does not forget about some things that she has here. I will take little videos and walk around the house, stuff like that.

He explains making the videos to maintain a bond with his young daughter and because he doesn't want her to forget about his home; he wants it to continue to feel like her home and her space as well.

Caroline described sending text messages to her nonresidential daughter to keep her informed about what was happening in the lives of her residential children:

> I make sure when the kids, when the little ones [her residential children and her nonresidential daughter's half-siblings], they run track … so when they make it to nationals and all these things I make sure that I text her [nonresidential daughter] right away and include her in that right away, like "hey, Zoey just took third." She was here this summer and spent a lot of time with us at track meets twice a week, every week, so she is kind of in the loop with all that stuff. I keep her in the loop.

Research Question Two

RQ2 asked what challenges NRPs experience when using new media technologies to communicate with their children. Participants described challenges of using new media technologies a total of 83 times within the data (*ns* in this section will refer to the number of references out of 83). Inductive analysis of the 83 excerpts resulted in emergence of five major themes: *residential parent interference*, the *mediated nature of the communication*, *access*, *child unresponsiveness*, and *child's age*.

Residential parent interference. The most commonly reported challenge of using new media technologies to communicate with children was *residential parent interference* ($n = 29$; 40%). Residential parents became barriers to NRP–child communication through technology in two ways: *gatekeeping* ($n = 18$; 30%) and *monitoring* ($n = 11$; 15%). While these challenges are not inherent to the technologies themselves, the mediated nature of the parent–child interactions provided multiple opportunities for the residential parent to become a barrier in the NRP–child interactions.

Gatekeeping. *Gatekeeping* was the most common method residential parents employed to create communication barriers between NRPs and their children. Family scholars studying RPs and NRPs have identified gatekeeping as actions of the residential parent to control and limit the interactions between the nonresidential parent and the child (Rollie, 2006; Seltzer & Brandreth, 1994). In our study, participants described the multiple ways residential parents control the NRP's access to their children through new media technologies. Candice described how gatekeeping became a source of frustration when her ex-husband and his new wife actively blocked her—the nonresidential mother's—communication attempts with the kids:

> The judge said I can call every 48 hours and that if the kids needed to talk to me anytime, they should be allowed to call me. So I call every 48 hours. Sometimes I get a call back and sometimes I don't. So I bought my daughter a cell phone. They [residential father and stepmother] would not allow it [would not allow the daughter to use the cell phone], and they bought my son a cell phone that a lot of the times I cannot text it because they have me blocked. So sometimes I cannot call him because they have it restricted.

Technology for this NRP has become a new source of stress and tension in her parenting role.

Dean also described the way gatekeeping limits the usefulness of new media technologies for communicating with his son: "She [residential mother] plays it to however she feels. There are times that I have gotten my son and he has told me that he was not able to call me." Dean discovered the gatekeeping behaviors when the residential parent would not allow the child to use the telephone, and the child reported back to him.

Monitoring. The second method residential parents employed to create challenges in NRP–child mediated communication was *monitoring*. *Monitoring* refers to instances when the residential parent listened in on communication that takes place via new media technologies between the nonresidential parent and the child, and which impedes either party from communicating openly. For instance, knowing (or perceiving) that the residential parent is eavesdropping on conversations creates a challenge for NRPs communicating openly with their children. Meg discussed how monitoring has made it difficult for her to have authentic conversations with her daughter over Skype:

> She told me everything when we lived together. She told me everything, like we talked every night before she went to bed, but then now she does not tell me anything even when we Skype. She answers a couple quick questions like when I asked, "oh how are you doing? How is your school?" She says "okay," it seems like she hesitates to tell me through Skype, because sometimes she knows that her dad is around, so she does not tell her honest feelings and it is totally different from before.

Another participant, Kate, described having similar issues with both Skype and the telephone:

> A lot of times I feel that our conversations are monitored and I can't talk freely when I call … I can't tell with Skype anymore. It used to be that I could tell that he was walking past the door, through the room. Sometimes when I call it seems like it is in their kitchen and they [residential father and stepmother] are listening to the conversation and they are talking to the children when they are talking to me.

Kate cites evidence of the monitoring behaviors; she actually would see the residential father walking nearby during their conversations and hear him communicating with the children while she is on the phone with them. Due to the nature of these data—based on perceptions of the NRPs—it cannot be known whether gatekeeping and/or monitoring are actually taking place in each instance. However, the challenge is a perceived reality for these NRPs and thus creates a barrier for NRP–child communication.

Mediated nature of the communication. The second most frequently reported challenge of new media technologies for communicating with nonresidential children was actually the *mediated nature of the communication* (n = 18; 35%). While parents acknowledged new technologies are often a vital tool, they are also inherently limited and can't fully replace face-to-face communication with their children. Kate used to frequently read her son books when she was a residential mother, something she is no longer able to do, although she's tried via Skype: "I've actually tried to [read him books] while I'm over the phone or Skype. I've tried to do the book reading thing, especially with my son and he just won't have any part of it. That part is hard."

Damon similarly described the inherent limitations of mediated communication with his son:

> I do not get to have that three to four hours after school, after work, up until bedtime and things like that … having organic conversation with him [son]. If it is a phone call it's only ten to 20 minutes and you really cannot get the whole day out of the child in ten to 20 minutes.

Access. The third most frequently reported challenge NRPs experience using new media technologies to communicate with their children is *access* (n = 16; 28%), emerging as two distinct subcategories: *general access* (n = 10; 20%) and *child being disciplined* (n = 6; 13%).

General access. *General access* refers to instances when lack of access to technologies was a limitation for the NRPs. When neither the NRP nor the child has access to the Internet or a cell phone, communication decreases and frustration increases. Kate, who is currently living abroad in Mexico while her son lives in the United States with his father, reported: "I do not have access to the Internet at all, so I was having trouble keeping in contact." She lamented that telephone communication is rare because of the expense of international calls; she also does not have Internet access and thus communication with her son is severely limited.

Xander is a naval officer, and when he is at sea his access to telephone calls is limited: "When my ship was underway I cannot call them so I will normally send an email to my ex-wife, who I believe communicates to them [daughters], and in most cases I get a response like [daughter] says this or [other daughter] says that." Because Xander's daughters are seven and five, the email communication is an alternative to phone calls, but must be mediated through the residential mother.

Child being disciplined. The second subcategory of *access* is *child being disciplined.* In each of these instances, participants reported the residential parent "grounded" the child from using communication technologies such as Facebook or cell phones, which then created a barrier for NRP–child communication. Lanie explains, "I would say they [text messages to daughter] are infrequent, because my ex-husband [the residential father] likes to take away her phone frequently to ground her." She further explains the frustration of wanting to text with her daughter more often but being unable to because her daughter's access to that technology is sporadic—her father often removes access to her phone as a disciplinary measure. Ryan reported a similar issue:

> If they got in trouble, she [residential mother] will ground them from the cell phone and she will never let me know that they are grounded from the cell phone. So I'll be sitting here trying to text them, call them, whatnot and I can't get ahold of them and wondering what's going on, and little do I know, she's grounded them from the cell phone.

For some parents such as Ryan, not receiving a response from his children and not knowing why is a source of anxiety.

Child unresponsiveness. The fourth most frequently reported challenge of NRPs using new media technologies to communicate with their children was *child unresponsiveness* (n = 12; 18%). Two subcategories emerged within the data: *no response* (n = 7; 13%) and *delayed response* (n = 5; 10%).

No response. *No response* represented cases when participants expressed frustration or concern due to children not responding to Facebook messages, text messages, or cell phone calls. Parents discussed the challenge of not being guaranteed a response from their child and not being able to do much about it beyond continuing to post, text, or call to solicit a response. When talking about her 16-year-old son, Gina explains, "If I would call him, he would not answer his phone. If I would text him, he would not text back." In Caroline's case, she was deeply saddened to have missed her daughter's eighth grade graduation, which was due to the daughter's lack of responsiveness:

> I was like, dude, I texted you three times last week. I texted trying to figure out the date and the time and she was like "oh, my number changed" and I was like "well, okay so I'm texting this number that does not exist." I'm like "you probably should've called and told me that." But she, a spacey teenager, does not really get that part of it. She is not always as quick to figure things out like that.

Delayed response. The second subcategory of *child unresponsiveness* is *delayed response*, referring to instances when children's responses to communication attempts using technology from the NRPs are significantly delayed. Parents discussed how interaction still occurred but the long wait for a response was perceived as a significant barrier for communication with nonresidential children.

Damon described frustrating delays in receiving emails from his son: "He does email me once in a while, but he does not check it frequently … he might check it once a month." Stana said, "he [nonresidential son] is not an email person … then I have to call him to tell him to go check his Facebook." Stana is still able to communicate with him via telephone but admits it can be frustrating to have to call him to remind him to check his other devices.

Child's age. The final reported challenge of using new media technologies was *child's age* (n = 8; 20%). Technologies can be limiting because nonresidential children need to be old enough to use the technology. When they are not, communication occurring via the technology is often unsatisfactory for the NRP. Alan, for instance, has a difficult time connecting with his five-year-old daughter over the telephone or through Skype:

> I have Skyped with her before, but she just gets infatuated with the screen and she does not really pay any attention to me. So it's cool to see her, but again it is kind of like the phone call. It is not exactly what I want to get out of it. I'm not sure that it's really that great for either of us.

Discussion

The present study provided a qualitative, descriptive look at the purposes that ground NRPs use of new media technologies to communicate with their children, as well as the challenges of using technologies for communication with their children. Results indicate NRPs' use of new media technologies can be a double-edged sword. Technologies function for parents to maintain a *daily presence*, *show affection*, *show support*, and facilitate their nonresidential children's *involvement in the NRP's household*, which are all important means of parent–child communication and function to assist NRPs in recalibrating their parenting post-divorce. However, these technologies also pose new challenges for many NRPs, including: *residential parent interference*, *access*, the *mediated nature of the communication*, *child unresponsiveness*, and the *child's age*. In the context of NRP–child communication through technology, our participants confirm that with the good comes the bad. According to the NRPs in this study, without technologies NRPs would have far fewer options for staying connected with their children. Simultaneously, new technologies have added to the list of the many parenting challenges and frustrations for NRPs.

Previous research on NRPs' use of technology to communicate with their children focused predominantly on the use of the telephone (Rollie Rodriguez, 2014; Yarosh et al., 2009). Rollie Rodriguez called for future research on how NRPs and their children use a variety of other technologies to communicate with one another.

Rollie Rodriguez explored how absence influenced how NRPs communicate with their children. Results indicated NRPs emphasized "catching up" conversations as an important yet restrictive focus of communication during visitations. Here, communication centered around NRPs' attempts to seek information about what has been going on in the lives of their children during periods of separation; however, NRPs reported feeling frustrated by this because a lack of knowledge of their children's daily lives can make initial communication during visits difficult, as the NRP is not sure what to talk about with their child. This process was also frustrating for NRPs because they reported feeling like they had to "extract" information from their children.

The current study extended this line of inquiry by exploring how new media technology was used by NRPs to communicate with their children during times of separation. These results indicate NRPs can employ a variety of technologies in order to maintain more of a daily presence in their children's lives. It is hoped this daily presence will allow NRPs to feel more connected to the daily lives of their children and help them stay more up-to-date with information regarding their children's lives, so that during visitation they do not feel as much pressure to find out about everything that has gone on during the past week (or more) of their children's lives.

Bailey (2003) found NRPs used the telephone, snail mail, and email as means of contact with their children when they were not physically together. While the current study also examined NRPs' use of the telephone, snail mail, and email, a range of other technologies were explored including Skype, Facebook, Twitter, and text messaging. While the telephone continues to be a popular means of NRP–child communication, other new media technologies are commonly being used by both NRPs and their children. These findings are consistent with research on family communication in the mediated environment (Bruess, Li, & Polingo, this volume; Coyne et al., 2014; Padilla-Walker et al., 2012). Coyne et al. (2014) found family members used a variety of new media technologies to communicate with their family members. Participants in their study reported using telephone calls, text messaging, picture sharing, email, Skype, and Facebook to communicate with family members. Participants also describe sharing YouTube videos and music electronically as a means of staying connected and facilitating closeness. While Coyne et al. were not specifically interested in long-distance family relationships, one of their participants did mention the importance of mediated communication for staying connected with distant family members. The current results extend Coyne et al.'s line of inquiry by illustrating that many of these same technologies are, in fact, used to maintain a specific type of family relationship that is characterized by a lack of daily, physical presence.

In addition, our results both support and extend the work of Yarosh et al. (2009), who explored the limitations of NRPs' use of audio-only technologies when communicating with their children. Participants in the current study also reported the limitations of mediated communication and identified difficulties of not being able to see their children during phone conversations. Yet participants also noted a variety of additional challenges using other technologies. For example, Skype provides a valuable means for NRPs to both hear and see their children; however, when residential parents monitor the interactions, the NRPs reported feeling dissatisfied with the technology. While text messaging does not allow NRPs to see their children, it does offer a quick means of connection with them, and NRPs in this study found it a great way to communicate throughout the day, even while engaged in other activities (e.g., watching television, playing games, etc.).

Historically, cyberspace communication has been viewed as separate from and inferior to communication that occurs in "real space" (Haythornthwaite & Wellman, 2002). These views of the relationship among technology, communication, and relationships are inherently problematic as many individuals communicate within a given relationship through both mediated and unmediated channels. According to Baym, Zhang, & Lin (2004), relationships are maintained through a mixture of media. Individuals use a mixture of face-to-face communication, text messaging, email, Skype, Facebook, and a wide variety of other media to maintain their relationships. Scholars have referred to these relationships as "mixed-media relationships" (Walther & Parks, 2002). This is evident in the NRP–child relationship. Because these relationships are characterized by periods of physical absence, it makes sense that these parents and children would use technology to maintain their familial connection during their times apart. The use of new media technology has the power to enrich these parent–child relationships and facilitate closeness. We argue the NRP–child relationship is an important context for which scholarship should consider how new media technology can enhance parent–child connections by providing a means of connection during periods of separation.

The nonresidential parenting role continues to suffer from a lack of institutionalization (Arditti, 1995). A dearth of norms associated with role enactment creates role ambiguity and leaves NRPs with little guidance or preparation for how best to function in this capacity (Rollie, 2006). NRP role ambiguity is further complicated by the fact that traditional parenting rules and roles are based on co-residency of parent and child. In the case of NRPs, "they must redefine or modify the traditional parent role to better fit within the structural and social constraints of their nonresidential status" (Rollie, p. 190). The process of redefining or modifying the parental role will have a direct impact on how the NRP interacts with their child and how involved they are in their child's life (Rollie). This process is also crucial as NRPs work to recalibrate the family system after divorce.

Since these parents are more often than not geographically separated from their children, using technology to parent becomes a primary means for redefining the parent role. The technologies often become the building blocks of continued parent–child connections.

Family systems theory is a lens that can be used to understand how change and transition can impact families (Ahrons, 1980). Divorce represents a significant family transition (Ahrons), as family boundaries change (Madden-Dedich, Leonard, & Christopher, 1999). Family roles must be reconceptualized (Elder, 1991) as parents begin simultaneously renegotiating their parental roles while also attempting to understand and accept many other changes they are experiencing as a result of the divorce. Results of this study illustrate that the road to recalibration of the family system after divorce can be complicated. Post-divorce NRPs are moving from a parenting situation based on a significant amount of co-presence to a parenting context that demands new approaches and ways of interacting with their children, as well as with ex-partners—and most are doing so in the context of many new communication technologies. Our results indicate there are a variety of challenges and limitations to the use of new media technologies within the NRP–child relationship, yet the technologies are also invaluable to the NRPs as they recalibrate, offering new options for communication outside the residential parenting model.

The current study is limited and thus the results must be considered in light of such limitations. First, data were only collected from NRPs. As such, our data are not able to confirm the complexities of recalibration or interdependence in the systems. Specifically, while our data suggest that residential parents are *gatekeeping* and/or *monitoring* NRP–child communication, the reports are based on perceptions and experiences of only the NRPs. Future researchers would be wise to collect data with multiple members of the family system for triangulation of voices and experiences on communication challenges in a new parenting context. At the same time, while a limitation of the current investigation, it is also important to note that in the interpretive tradition, researchers are interested in describing meanings—and representing the experiences—of participants, more so than discovering one reality. As such, the insights and perceptions of the NRPs as represented in this study are significant and helpful as we attempt to understand the family system in transition.

Another limitation of the current study is the lack of depth we were able to achieve on the wide variety of new media technologies being used by NRPs to communicate with their children. The most commonly reported technological device used was the telephone (whether the landline or cell phone), although many parents mentioned using, at least to some degree, other communication technologies, including email, texting, Facebook, and Twitter. Given the design of our study, we were not able to explore in as much depth as would be ideal how text- and video-based technologies are specifically serving the communication and relationship needs of NRPs and their children. Future researchers should focus specifically on these new media technologies in particular.

Application

For Nonresidential Parents

Our findings illustrate several different ways for you to adjust to your new parental role, and your parenting style, to reflect the "new normal" within your family system. Our results indicate you should experiment with a variety of technologies to facilitate continued interaction and engagement with your children. By exploring your options, you will discover the technologies that fit best within the context of your relationship with your child.

Based on the parents in our study, we suggest NRPs intentionally work to stay current with communication technologies. Learn what's out there, and try using several different options to interact with your child so you can see what feels right for you and what they like the best. Some families thrive using FaceTime or Skype; others prefer Facebook or Snapchat. By the time this book goes to print, new technologies will probably be available! Kids are often the early adopters and knowledge-heads of new technologies, so check in with them and let them teach you about a new option every once in awhile.

Our results also highlight the continued importance of your relationship with the residential parent. Parents in post-divorce families must consider how to adjust and maintain a functional relationship with one another. This is an important step for you because it will directly impact your relationship with your child. Although your marital relationship is over, you still coexist within the larger family unit as a co-parent to your child(ren). Our findings suggest that the relationship between the parents does indeed have an effect on the NRP–child relationship, so make your best effort to promote and engage in constructive communication with your ex.

You can also use new media technologies to communicate with the residential parent about your child(ren). One of our participants described plans to use Google Calendar as a way for him and his ex-wife to keep up-to-date with their son's schedule:

> We [he and his ex-wife] were discussing making a Google Calendar, putting stuff on that. We both can access and change things … that way if anything comes up that I want to take him to, I can put it up on the calendar. That way we both can see it without having to really talk to each other … you've got to love technology.

Consider the many ways that new media technologies can be used to maintain a positive and effective co-parenting relationship. You should consider which media best fit your relationship with your ex. We recommend discussing options for technology use with your ex, if possible, and selecting the media most comfortable for both of you.

Elena, one of the NRPs who participated in this study, described the role of the NRP as follows: "work on the relationship with the kids to let them know that there is love from both sides [residential parent and NRP], and … let them know that even though they are separate, they are still important." Through the use of new media technologies, you can communicate to your child(ren) that, even though you are not together as much as you used to be—or as much as you would perhaps like to be—they are still important, they are still your child, and you value your relationship with them.

For Residential Parents

Our findings illustrate several different ways for you to facilitate the relationship between your child and their NRP. The most common challenge NRPs reported in this study was the residential parent, through gatekeeping and monitoring. It is important for you to support your child's interactions with their NRP by avoiding these destructive behaviors. This will also assist you in maintaining a positive co-parenting relationship with the NRP, which is beneficial for everyone involved. Another way that you, as an important influence in your child's life, can facilitate the relationship between your child and the NRP is by being mindful that your child is communicating with their NRP. Our participants described child unresponsiveness as another challenge when using technology to communicate with their kids. As the residential parent, you are in the position to support your child(ren)'s relationship with their NRP, simply by checking in with them about it. You can do your part to make sure they are responding to their NRP's text messages, and when the NRP calls your home you can be sure that your child takes the phone call.

Another important way that you can facilitate communication between your child and the NRP is by keeping up-to-date with current technologies yourself. By doing this, you can suggest technologies that your child and their NRP could use, and you can feel confident and secure in those suggestions. You can also do what you can to give your child access to technologies they can use to feel connected to their NRP. For example, you might decide to allow your child to have a cell phone, even if they are only allowed to use it to communicate with you and their NRP. These technologies will also be helpful to your relationship with your child, because when they are with their NRP they will be able to communicate with you using these technologies.

References

Ahrons, C. R. (1980). Divorce: A crisis of family transition and change. *Family Relations, 29,* 533–540.

Anderson, E. A., Kohler, J. K., & Letiecq, B. L. (2005). Predictors of depression among low-income, nonresidential fathers. *Journal of Family Issues, 26,* 547–567. doi: 10.1177/0192513042727 53

Arditti, J. A. (1995). Noncustodial parents: Emergent issues of diversity and process. *Marriage & Family Review, 20,* 283–304.

Arditti, J. A., & Madden-Derdich, D. A. (1993). Noncustodial mothers: Developing strategies of support. *Family Relations, 42,* 305–314.

Bailey, S. J. (2003). Challenges and strengths in nonresidential parenting following divorce. *Marriage & Family Review, 35,* 29–44. doi:10.1300/J002v35n01

Baym, N. K., Zhang, Y. B., & Lin, M. (2004). Social interactions across media: Interpersonal communication on the Internet, face-to-face, and the telephone. *New Media & Society, 63,* 299–318. doi:10.1177/1461444804041438

Braithwaite, D. O., & Baxter, L. A. (2006). "You're my parent but you're not": Dialectical tensions in stepchildren's perceptions about communicating with the nonresidential parent. *Journal of Applied Communication, 34,* 30–48. doi:10.1080/00909880500420200

Carlson, M. J., & McLanahan, S. S. (2010). Fathers in fragile families. In M. E. Lamb (Ed.), *The role of the father in child development* (pp. 241–269). Hoboken, NJ: John Wiley & Sons, Inc.

Carlson, M. J., McLanahan, S. S., & Brooks-Gunn, J. (2008). Coparenting and nonresident fathers' involvement with young children after a nonmarital birth. *Demography, 45,* 461–488. doi:10.1353/dem.0.0007

Cooksey, E. C., & Craig, P. H. (1998). Parenting from a distance: The effects of paternal characteristics on contact between nonresidential fathers and their children. *Demography, 35,* 187–200. doi:10.2307/3004051

Coyne, S. M., Padilla-Walker, L. M., Fraser, A. M., Fellows, K., & Day, R. D. (2014). "Media time–family time": Positive media use in families with adolescents. *Journal of Adolescent Research, 29,* 663–688. doi:10.1177/0743558414538316

Duck, S. (1995). Talking relationships into being. *Journal of Social and Personal Relationships, 12,* 535–540. doi:10.1177/0265407595124006

Elder, G. H. (1991). Family transitions, cycles, and social change. In P. A. Cowan & M. Hetherington (Eds.), *Family Transitions, Vol. 2* (pp. 31–57). Hillsdale, NJ: Erlbaum.

Emerson, R. M., Fretz, R. L., & Shaw, L. L. (1995). *Writing ethnographic fieldnotes.* Chicago: The University of Chicago Press.

Fagan, J., & Barnett, M. (2003). The relationship between maternal gatekeeping, paternal competence, mothers' attitudes about the father role, and father involvement. *Journal of Family Issues, 24,* 1020–1043. doi:10.1177/0192513X03256397

Falci, C. (2006). Family structure, closeness to residential and nonresidential parents, and psychological distress in early and middle adolescence. *The Sociological Quarterly, 47,* 123–146. doi:10.1111/j.1533-8525.2006.00040.x

Galvin, K. M., Dickson, F. C., & Marrow, S. R. (2006). Systems theory: Patterns and (w)holes in family communication. In D. O. Braithwaite & L. A. Baxter (Eds.), *Engaging theories in family communication: Multiple perspectives* (pp. 309–324). Thousand Oaks, CA: Sage Publications.

Ganong, L. H., & Coleman, M. (2004). *Stepfamily relationships: Development, dynamics, and interventions.* New York: Kluwer Academic, Plenum.

Geller, A., Cooper, C. E., Garfinkel, I., Schwartz-Soicher, O., Mincy, R. B. (2012). Beyond absenteeism: Father incarceration and child development. *Demography, 49,* 49–76. doi:10.1007/s13524–011–0081–9

Gottman, J. M. (1991). Chaos and regulated change in families: A metaphor for the study of transitions. In P. A. Cowen & E. M. Hetherington (Eds.), *Family Transitions* (pp. 247–272). Hillsdale, NJ: Lawrence Erlbaum.

Gunnoe, M. L., & Hetherington, E. M. (2004). Stepchildren's perceptions of noncustodial mothers and noncustodial fathers: Differences in socioemotional involvement and association with adolescent adjustment problems. *Journal of Family Psychology, 18,* 555–563. doi:10.1037/0893–3200.18.4.555

Hagestad, G. O., & Smyer, M. A. (1982). *Out of touch.* New York: Oxford University Press.

Hawkins, D. N., Amato, P. R., & King, V. (2006). Parent–adolescent involvement: The relative influence of parent gender and residence. *Journal of Social and Personal Relationships, 12,* 313–320. doi:10.1111/j.1741–3737.2006.00238.x

Haythornthwaite, C., & Wellman, B. (2002). The Internet in everyday life: An introduction. In B. Wellman & C. Haythornthwaite (Eds.), *The Internet in Everyday Life* (pp. 3–42). Malden, MA: Blackwell.

Herrerias, C. (1995). Noncustodial mothers following divorce. *Marriage and Family Review, 10,* 233–255.

Johnson, A. J., Haigh, M. M., Becker, J. A. H., Craig, E. A., & Wigley, S. (2008). College students' use of relational management strategies in email in long-distance and geographically close relationships. *Journal of Computer-Mediated Communication, 13,* 381–404. doi:10.1111/j.1083–6101.2008.00401.x

Kartch, F., & Tenzek, K. E. (2012, November). *"I wish someone knew the pain that I feel": The voices of nonresidential mothers.* Paper presented at the National Communication Association Convention, Orlando, FL.

Kielty, S. (2008). Non-resident motherhood: Managing a threatened identity. *Child and Family Social Work, 13,* 32–40. doi:10.1111/j.1365–2206.2007.00512.x

Lupton, D., & Barclay, L. (1997). *Constructing fatherhood: Discourses and experiences.* London: Sage.

Madden-Derdich, D. A., Leonard, S. A., & Christopher, F. S. (1999). Boundary ambiguity and coparental conflict after divorce: An empirical test of a family systems model of the divorce process. *Journal of Marriage and Family, 61,* 588–598.

Minton, C., & Pasley, K. (1996). Fathers' parenting role identity and father involvement: A comparison of nondivorced and divorced, nonresident fathers. *Journal of Family Issues, 17,* 26–45. doi:10.1177/019251396017001003

Natalier, K., & Hewitt, B. (2010). "It's not just about money": Non-resident fathers' perspectives on paying child support. *Sociology, 44,* 489–505. doi:10.1177/00383510362470

Nielsen, L. (2011). Shared parenting after divorce: A review of shared residential parenting research. *Journal of Divorce and Remarriage, 52,* 586–609. doi:10.1080/10502556.2011.619913

Padilla-Walker, L. M., Coyne, S. M., & Fraser, A. M. (2012). Getting a high speed family connection: Associations between family media use and family connection. *Family Relations, 61,* 426–440. doi:10.1111/j.1741–3729.2012.00710.x

Patton, M. Q. (2002). *Qualitative research & evaluation methods* (3rd ed.). Thousand Oaks, CA: Sage Publications.

Rollie, S. S. (2006). Nonresidential parent–child relationships: Overcoming the challenges of absence. In D. C. Kirkpatrick, S. Duck, & M. K. Foley (Eds.), *Relating difficulty: The processes of constructing and managing difficult interactions* (pp. 181–201). Mahwah, NJ: Erlbaum Associates, Inc.

Rollie Rodriguez, S. (2014, February). "We'll only see parts of each other's lives:" The role of mundane talk in maintaining nonresidential parent–child relationships. *Journal of Social and Personal Relationships*. doi:10.1177/0265407514522898

Seltzer, J. A. (1991). Relationships between fathers and children who live apart: The father's role after separation. *Journal of Marriage and the Family, 53,* 79–101.

Seltzer, J. A., & Brandreth, Y. (1994). What fathers say about involvement with children after separation. *Journal of Family Issues, 15,* 49–77.

Shapiro, A., & Lambert, J. D. (1999). Longitudinal effects of divorce on the quality of the father–child relationship and on fathers' psychological well-being. *Journal of Marriage and the Family, 50,* 663–677.

Stafford, L. (2005). *Maintaining long-distance relationships and cross-residential relationships*. Mahwah, NJ: Erlbaum.

Stewart, S. D. (1999). Disneyland dads, Disneyland moms? How nonresidential parents spend time with absent children. *Journal of Family Issues, 20,* 539–556. doi:10.1177/019251399020004006

Stueve, J. L., & Pleck, J. H. (2001). "Parenting voices": Solo parent identity and co-parent identities in married parents' narratives of meaningful parenting experiences. *Journal of Social and Personal Relationships, 18,* 691–708. doi:10.1177/0265407501185007

Tach, L., Mincy, R., & Edin, K. (2010). Parenting as a "package deal": Relationships, fertility, and nonresident father involvement among unmarried parents. *Demography, 47,* 181–204. doi:10.1353/dem.0.0096

Walther, J. B., & Parks, M. R. (2002). Cues filtered out, cues filtered in: Computer-mediated communication and relationships. In M. L. Knapp & J. A. Daly (Eds.), *Handbook of interpersonal communication* (3rd ed.), (pp. 529–563). Thousand Oaks, CA: Sage.

Wilbur, J. R., & Wilbur, M. (1988). The noncustodial parent: Dilemmas and interventions. *Journal of Counseling and Development, 66,* 434–437.

Yarosh, S., Chieh, Y., Chew, D., & Abowd, G. D. (2009). Supporting parent–child communication in divorced families. *International Journal of Human–Computer Studies, 67,* 192–203. doi:10.1016/j.ijhcs. 2008.09.005

Zhang, S., & Fuller, T. (2012). Neighborhood disorder and paternal involvement of nonresident and resident fathers. *Family Relations, 61,* 501–513. doi:10.1111/j.1741–3729.2012.00705.x

Section Five

A Practical Tool for Understanding and Helping Families in a Digital Age

22

The Technology-Focused Genogram

A Tool for Exploring Intergenerational Family Communication Patterns around Technology Use

Markie L. C. Blumer
University of Wisconsin–Stout

Katherine M. Hertlein
University of Nevada, Las Vegas

AUTHORS NOTE: A note of thanks to Megan VandenBosch, Graduate Assistant, University of Wisconsin–Stout Human Development and Family Studies Department, Marriage and Family Therapy Program, for her assistance with references and editing of earlier drafts.

Introduction

According to the Internet World Statistics (2012), as of June 2012 approximately 2.5 billion of the more than 7 billion people in the world are Internet users. Indeed, communication via various technologies for many is an everyday occurrence, particularly in the global regional areas known as Asia, Europe, and North America (Internet World Statistics, 2012). Technology's immersion is not just pervasive, it is also prominent in daily life—some days more so than others. For instance, recently I (M. L. C. B.) met with a colleague for dinner—for the first time—an occurrence that started and ended on a smartphone. Although we were in the same restaurant, we used our smartphones to "find" each other because neither had met the other before or knew what the other looked like, and each was waiting in separate areas of the building thinking the other was probably late. After texting and finding each other across the room, we started our dinner.

Each of us shared a little of our professional and personal life stories, including our digital life stories. My colleague shared her recent increased use of social networking and how it has made her feel more connected to her brother than she could remember in the last 40 years. I shared with her how social networking has made it easier for my family and friends to stay connected with me while I currently enjoy a more nomadic lifestyle—moving about every 3 to 5 years. Certainly, staying connected would be much more difficult across these transitions and great distances if not for modern technology. I would likely miss my family of origin more, and my child would not have as much opportunity to have his grandparents in his life, nor they him, if not for video conferencing, texting, emailing, social networking, and similar communication technologies. As we shared more of our digital stories we recognized that they were neither all positive nor all negative. We recognized, rather, the meaningful way technology plays a part in all of our lives, and across generations. We parted and followed up with "thank you" text messages on our smartphones and later again with emails.

This story reads as what at one time would be a work of science fiction but is now commonplace: Technology connects people—digitally and otherwise, across time, space, and generations—in ways that once were barely imaginable, and yet now the absence of that connection is almost unimaginable. Both my dinner partner's and my digital stories reveal technology-based communication, the primary focus of this chapter. Specifically, in this chapter we provide an overview of the current research on intergenerational technological communication, then present a mechanism for assessing such intergenerational communication using the Technology-Focused Genogram. Finally, we provide an example of this assessment and discuss ways it can be applied in varied contexts.

Intergenerational Technological Communication

Prevalence of Intergenerational Technology Use

According to a Pew Internet and American Life Project study (Kennedy, Smith, Wells, & Wellman, 2008) focused on networking in families, data from that nationally representative sample of 2,252 adults found that, of the various household configurations in the United States, those most likely to be Internet users are those identifying as married with children (data of this nature are not available at this time for cohabiting parental households, same-gender cohabiting or marital parenting households, or multipartnered households). They further found it most likely that everyone in those homes are Internet users (Kennedy et al., 2008). Specifically, in married-with-children households, 93% have at least one parent who uses the Internet, 76% have two parents who go online, and 84% have children between the ages of 7 and 17 who are Internet users (Kennedy et al., 2008). More recent research identifies teen use of the Internet by those between the ages of 12 to 17 as higher, with 93% getting online and roughly 60% having their own desktop or laptop computer (Rainie, 2009).

Further, most of the members of the families in the Pew study (Kennedy et al., 2008) own and use cell phones. Often in these families, both parents own a cell phone (78%), with children less likely to own a cell phone (57%; Kennedy et al., 2008). An even more recent analysis reveals about 3% of children under the age of 10 have their own cell phones, compared to 6% of ten year olds and 11% of eleven year olds (Lenhart, 2010). In the United States, the majority of adolescents acquire their first cell phones when they are between 12 and 13 years old (Lenhart, 2010). Texting is the digital activity in which teens engage most frequently: 63% of teens report texting every day, and older girls text more on a daily basis than boy teens and younger girl teens of other ages (Lenhart, 2012).

Use of Technology to Communicate Intergenerationally

How are family members using technology to communicate across generations? Many Internet-using adults spend considerable time with various technologies, often with other family members jointly exploring things online in real time. Such activity is considered to promote closeness (Hertlein & Blumer, 2014). In married-with-children families, 13% go online with members of their families on a daily basis, 9% do so almost every day, and 30% go online with family members more than once per week (Kennedy et al., 2008). Nearly nine in 10 (87%) of the survey respondents reported they are online with another member of their household at least occasionally: 54% reported doing so a few times per week or more, and 47% of parents reported going online with their children often (Kennedy et al., 2008). There appear to be gender differences in family use of communication technologies; women are more likely to go online with just their children, and men are more likely to go online with their spouse and their children (Kennedy et al., 2008).

Often new media have been a part of a child's life well before they enter the lives of their care providers (Hertlein & Blumer, 2014). For instance, expectant parents access multiple websites to help select names for their children and use social networking sites (SNSs) for sharing information about a child before arrival. I (M. L. C. B.) have personally observed many pregnant friends and family members post multitudes of pictures of their bodies changing during pregnancy, share ultrasound photos, administer "guess the sex" online surveys, and blog about their pregnancy experiences. Thus, many families begin a digital webprint documenting a child's life before arrival, a record that often remains readily available after birth and is typically expanded as the child grows, producing documentation of the child's development and interests.

Many technology-using families are going online in real time together, many doing so to communicate with each other when not in a shared physical space. In comparison to nonparenting families, parenting families communicate more frequently via technologies throughout the day (Kennedy et al., 2008). In Kennedy et al.'s study (2008), a majority of parents (74%) contact a spouse one or more times per day to just say "Hi" and chat (compared to 58% of nonparenting spouses), 70% contact a spouse to coordinate schedules, (51% of nonparenting spouses do so), and 42% contact each other to discuss important matters (compared to 34% of nonparenting spouses). The only instances in which parenting spouses and nonparenting spouses are equally likely to use technology to interact over the course of a day is to plan events with family and friends (20% and 17%, respectively; Kennedy et al., 2008). Further, cell phones in parenting families are the primary mechanism through which parents keep in touch with their children over the course of a day (Kennedy et al., 2008). A little less than half (42%) of parents call their children (aged 7–17) from a cell phone one or more times per day (Kennedy et al., 2008). In contrast, only 7% text their children daily, and less than 1% engage in instant messaging on SNSs with their children (Kennedy et al., 2008).

Technology-based interactions can play a part in family communication in postparenting stages, specifically as adult children launch into the workforce or participate in postsecondary education (Hertlein & Blumer, 2014; Mesch, 2006; Watt & White, 1999). For instance, in a study by Gentzler, Oberhauser, Westerman, and Nadorff (2011), two thirds of college students away from home use email, phone calls, and text messaging to stay in touch with their families of origin. The researchers also found 25% of college students consistently use SNSs to communicate with their parents.

In a more recent study, we examined the texting, sexting, use of applications, and new media practices of 431 college students in a large, metropolitan-based university setting using survey questions derived from the Ecological Elements Questionnaire (Hertlein & Blumer, 2014). In this study, the majority of participants reported living with their biological parents (n = 163, 37.82%). Generally speaking, although it appears college students engage in conversations about some technology-related interactions with their parents, the bulk do not discuss topics like sex-related activities that occur via new media. For instance, 83.29% (n = 359) report "never" talking with their parents about smartphone sex-related activities, and 96.98% (n = 418) report "never" doing so with their grandparents. This lack of dialogue between adult children and their parents and grandparents regarding sex-related practices engaged in via new media mirrors the lack of conversation regarding sex-related practices in general (Fitzharris & Werner-Wilson, 2004; Johnson & Thompson, 2009). Interestingly, some researchers have concluded that college students would like more communication with their parental figures regarding sex (Johnson & Thompson, 2009), and the same may also be true for communication around sex-related activities taking place via technology.

Technology-based interactions also occur between parents of parents, and grandparents with grandchildren (Hertlein & Blumer, 2014; Mesch, 2006). For example, both authors' children maintain a high degree of connectivity and closeness with our respective parents, despite living in other states, in part thanks to our use of digital communication technologies. Often, when my (M. L. C. B.) child is going somewhere new or wants to talk about something exciting from school, I find him using the Facetime app on my phone with my parents.

Our family experiences are certainly not unique. Video conferencing software allows family members across three or more generations to interact with one another in meaningful ways despite geographical separation (Harley & Fitzpatrick, 2009). Not only are family members able to interact via video-mediated communication technologies, they are able to do so in ways that mediate closeness in their relationships. In a qualitative study of 17 people communicating with various family members across 12 households using video-mediated communication technologies, participants were able to mediate their desire for face-to-face closeness using video-based communications occurring in real time (Kirk, Sellen, & Cao, 2010). Grandparents and their grandchildren also engage in meaningful and educational activities through the Internet and video-conferencing software. For instance, a software system called "Family Story Play" is being used by grandparents and grandchildren to read books together in real time via Internet-based video conferencing (Raffle et al., 2010).

Effects of Technology in Intergenerational Communication

Given the extent of technology-assisted intergenerational communication, the influence of technology on family dynamics, and electronic development across the family lifespan—also known as "e-development" (Blumer & Hertlein, 2013)—it is essential to consider the impact of technology on family relationships. Generally speaking, families who use Facebook among themselves report feeling closer (see Bruess, Li, & Polingo chapter this volume) and closer *because* of these technologies than are families with lower reported use of technologies (Hertlein & Blumer, 2014). Kennedy et al. (2008), found that 23% of participants reported their connections with family members greatly improved by using technological communication, and 25% reported that the Internet and cell phones have had the effect of bringing their family closer than their family of origin was growing up (Kennedy et al., 2008). However, the majority of participants (60%) reported that such technologies have not made much difference in the degree of closeness experienced in their families, and 11% report that their family today is not as close as their family of origin *because* of new technologies (Kennedy et al., 2008).

Depending on one's degree of digital competency as it relates to generational cohort membership, there do appear to be differences in the effects of technology usage and perceived closeness within families (Prensky, 2001). For instance, younger Americans, often referred to as "digital natives" or those who have grown up in a digitally saturated environment (Prensky, 2001), tend to see little difference in the closeness of their current and childhood families (Kennedy et al., 2008). Specifically, about two thirds (67%) of young adults between the ages of 18 and 29 report that communication technologies have not made much difference in how close their present family is in comparison to their family of origin (Kennedy et al., 2008).

"Digital settlers"—people who grew up in an analog world but who in young adulthood entered a digital world and hence are relatively capable of being bilingual in the language of both the digital and analog languages (Prensky, 2001)—tend to see little difference in closeness between their current and childhood families. Indeed, 62% of 30–49 year olds report that technologies have not made much difference in their perceived closeness of present family versus family of origin (Kennedy et al., 2008). Both "digital natives" and "digital settlers" view the closeness in their families of origin and their current families as relatively the same regardless of the role of technology—most likely because for most of their lives they have had exposure to and encounters with technology. This differs from a third group, "digital immigrants"—those who were not born into the digital age and have had to adopt a completely new digital language, at times with difficulty (Prensky, 2001)—who see a difference in terms of closeness between their current and childhood families. Specifically, 45% of adults age 65 and older report that technologies have made a significant difference in perceived closeness in their present family when compared to their families of origin (Kennedy et al., 2008). As most of this latter group's lives have occurred prior to the current digital age, it is not surprising they report feeling greater closeness between their families of procreation than origin, as they have experienced a clear demarcation in their lives before technology was embedded into it and after.

Differences in perceptions of technological usage, abilities, competencies, and literacy among members of these varying digital generations—digital natives, settlers, and immigrants—can influence intergenerational communication. For example, differences in digital competency between Millennials, who are often digital natives (Taylor, Doherty, Parker, & Krishnamurthy, 2014), and their Generation X or Boomer parents or grandparents, who are frequently digital settlers or immigrants, can influence their intergenerational digital experiences (Hertlein & Blumer, 2014). Millennials tend to take more digital pictures of themselves via smartphones ("selfies") and share them via texting or social networking than do their Generation X or Boomer counterparts (Taylor, 2014). Differences in selfie taking and sharing can be a source of misunderstanding between generations. For instance, I (M. L. C. B.) have worked clinically with parents of Millennials who perceive their children's selfies as frivolous, annoying, and connoting "self-importance." Their children make the case that the selfie is meant to be fun, a form of expression, and a way of distinguishing themselves from others. Intergenerational digital differences, as in this example of the selfie, are often about smaller misunderstandings.

Yet, with increasing and expanded use of technologies across multiple generations, misunderstandings and miscommunication are becoming more serious. For instance, although Millennials are the most avid users of new technologies like SNSs, 9 in 10 believe people share too much information about themselves online, a view opposite of that held by older generations (Taylor et al., 2014). This intergenerational difference in sharing information online can lead to misunderstandings over what is meant to be kept private versus shared publicly (see the Child & Petronio chapter in this volume). Such misunderstandings commonly occur when parents "check in" or "post" pictures that include their Millennial children on Facebook, often without the children's consent, knowledge, or permission. In such instances what parents see as a common and inclusive practice, their children view as indiscreet and a potential violation of their privacy, particularly if unwanted people unexpectedly arrive in their now disclosed location.

Assessment of Intergenerational Technological Communication

Given the increasing use of technology to communicate intergenerationally, it is essential to assess intergenerational patterns of technological interactions among individuals, couples, and families. However, to date there has been little focus on assessment by family therapy professionals (Blumer, Hertlein, Smith, & Allen, 2014; Cravens, Hertlein, & Blumer, 2013; Hertlein & Blumer, 2014; see also the Hertlein & Blumer chapter in this volume and the Piercy et al. chapter in this volume). For instance, in a 2011 Alaska Association for Marriage and Family Therapy grant–funded national survey study of 227 family therapy professionals, the majority reported "rarely" or "never" assessing clients for technology-related problems among intergenerational configurations like couples and families with children (Hertlein, Blumer, & Smith, 2012). More specifically, of the participants who work with couples, more than one third "often" or "always" assess for technology use (*n* = 89, 39.2%) while just over half (*n* = 116, 51.1%) indicate they "rarely" or "never" assess for couples' technology issues (Hertlein et al., 2012). Among those working with families, 37.9% (*n* = 86) indicate "often" or "always" inquiring about technology; just over half (*n* = 118, 52%) indicate they "rarely" or "never" ask about these issues (Hertlein et al., 2012). Of the participants who indicate they work with children and adolescents, nearly half report "often" or "always" asking about technology issues (*n* = 103, 45.5%); the other approximately half indicate they ask about technology issues "rarely" or "never" (*n* = 98, 43.2%) (Hertlein et al., 2012).

Although there are existing assessments for some technology-use concerns, such as the Online Cognition Scale (Davis, Flett, & Besser, 2002), the Problematic Internet Usage Questionnaire (Demetrovics, Szeredi, & Rozsa, 2008), the Ecological Elements Questionnaire (Hertlein & Blumer, 2014), and the Internet Addiction Test (Young, 1998), few family therapy professionals are inquiring about such issues (Cravens et al., 2013; Hertlein et al., 2012). In the same study of family therapy professionals, Hertlein, Blumer, and Smith (2012) also inquired about the extent to which professionals assess for technology-related issues that are more common in intergenerational family configurations, including Internet infidelity, Internet addiction, online gaming addiction, online family networking, online social networking, online dating, and safety measures to protect from online sexual predators. Participants provided their responses along a continuum of 1 to 6, with 1 indicating no assessment of the topic and 6 indicating assessment of the topic to the highest degree.

The two areas assessed by family therapy professionals to the highest degree (as indicated by a 6) were safety regarding online sexual predators (*n* = 22, 9.7%) and online social networking practices (*n* = 21, 9.3%) (Hertlein et al., 2012). Even though these were the two areas assessed to the highest degree, in general, the majority of all of the technology-related issues are not being assessed for at all when working with clients. The areas that family therapy professionals reported assessing for least frequently (as indicated by a 1) included online gaming addiction (*n* = 63, 27.8%), online family networking practices (*n* = 61, 26.9%), and safety regarding online sexual predators (*n* = 64, 28.2%) (Hertlein et al., 2012). These findings indicate that family therapy professionals seem polarized on their assessments of safety and networking in particular, as these are the two areas assessed for to the greatest and least degrees.

Technology-Focused Genogram

Family professionals might not be conducting assessments about technology-related concerns because finding appropriate assessment tools is difficult, specifically tools that are broad and inclusive enough to work with multiple units of analysis (i.e., individuals, couples, families, children, etc.) and robust enough to assess multiple technological topics simultaneously. One option is the technology-focused genogram. Not only can this assessment tool be used to assess varied units of analysis and with virtually any technology-related concern, it can be conducted by family professionals of all kinds (e.g., certified family life educators, social workers, family therapists, child life specialists), as well as by people outside of these professional contexts (e.g., students, clients, parents, couples, individuals).

Constructing basic and focused genograms. The use of genograms to assess family patterns, trace intergenerational communication, treat common presenting problems, and generate greater understanding of familial relationships and life events has been taking place in the field of family therapy for close to 50 years (Bowen, 1966; McGoldrick & Gerson, 1985). However, the process of conducting genograms has received little attention outside of this discipline. Focused genograms, which emerged in the family therapy field in the late 1990s, are particularly useful for exploring generational patterns on specific topics in a concentrated manner (DeMaria, Weeks, & Hof, 1999).

The basics of constructing of a genogram have been extensively outlined, documented, and explained (see Bowen, 1966; McGoldrick, Gerson, & Shellenberger, 1999). Essentially, a genogram includes family information for all individuals in the assessment and looks much like a symbolic, detailed family tree. The genogram includes information from the individual and his or her family of procreation, family of origin (including parents and grandparents), and/or the person's family of choice (i.e., a socially constructed family that might include friends or those not traditionally recognized as "family" by law or other common definitions). The gender of each member identified in the genogram is denoted using a defined symbol (i.e., male-identifying with a square; female-identifying with a circle; gender queer, bigender, androgynous with a circle that has a square inside it or a square that has a circle inside it; two-spirit with a circle that has a square inside it or a square that has a circle inside it with a superscript "2" in the upper corner; trans-identifying with ⚧). For a comprehensive list of various gender-identifying symbols, see Belous, Timm, Chee, and Whitehead (2012).

Also included in basic genograms is information related to marriages, partnerships, cohabiting relationships, deaths, divorces, separations, and dissolutions. Deaths are typically denoted with an X over the person who has died. Divorce is indicated with two diagonal lines // and dissolution is indicated with one diagonal line /. The degree of closeness, distance, or conflict in the various relationships is denoted in the following ways: For a very close relationship three parallel, horizontal lines ≡ are drawn; for a close relationship two parallel, horizontal lines = are depicted; for a distant relationship a broken line - - - is used; and for a conflictual or hostile relationship an up and down line or zigzag is used. After constructing the symbolic representation of the basic genogram, typical assessment questions are asked to explore information related to family relationships, dynamics, and life-cycle transitions. Such questions are designed to help develop a narrative of the family's intergenerational pattern and story.

Focused genograms are pictorially and symbolically constructed in the same way as a basic genogram, and many of the same basic assessment questions are used. The difference with focused genograms is the addition of multiple, detailed questions into one particular area of interest (DeMaria et al., 1999). Focused genograms have been used historically to assess targeted areas such as money and finances (Mumford & Weeks, 2003), ecological sustainability (Blumer, Hertlein, & Fife, 2012), work and family (Kakiuchi & Weeks, 2009), intimacy (Sherman, 1993), or military service (Blumer, Papaj, & Robinson, 2012; Brelsford & Friedberg, 2011; Papaj, Blumer, & Robinson, 2011; Weiss, Coll, Gerbauer, Smiley, & Carillo, 2010)—to name just a few. To elaborate upon what can be gained by constructing a focused genogram, an exploration of some of the benefits of conducting a military-focused genogram follows.

In conducting a military-focused genogram, one can gain greater insight into some of the more common problems and strengths associated with individuals, couples, and families in military culture(s). This assessment asks specific questions and identifies unique patterns within military families such as those around relocation and travel, deployments and reunions, shifting attachment bonds and styles, wartime experiences, and military-related traumas and posttraumatic stress (Papaj et al., 2011). If service members within the family happen to be racial, gender, and/or sexual orientation minorities, inquires focused on identifying patterns of discrimination; roles and expectations around gender; equality in job title, rank, and type; as well as policies and practices that are affirming of minority service members can also be helpful to explore (Blumer et al., 2012).

Constructing a Technology-Focused Genogram

The use of a technology-focused genogram, also known as "technological genogram" or "technogram" (Hertlein & Blumer, 2014), has only recently become an option, as not until the past two decades have at least three generations in a family had the opportunity to engage in consistent digital technology use. To create a technology-focused genogram, one decides first who to include in the basic genogram; then, one completes the basic genogram symbolic construction; finally, one employs a symbol for technology usage to identify the various technologies not merely as tools or patterns of communication but as members of the system itself (Hertlein & Blumer, 2014).

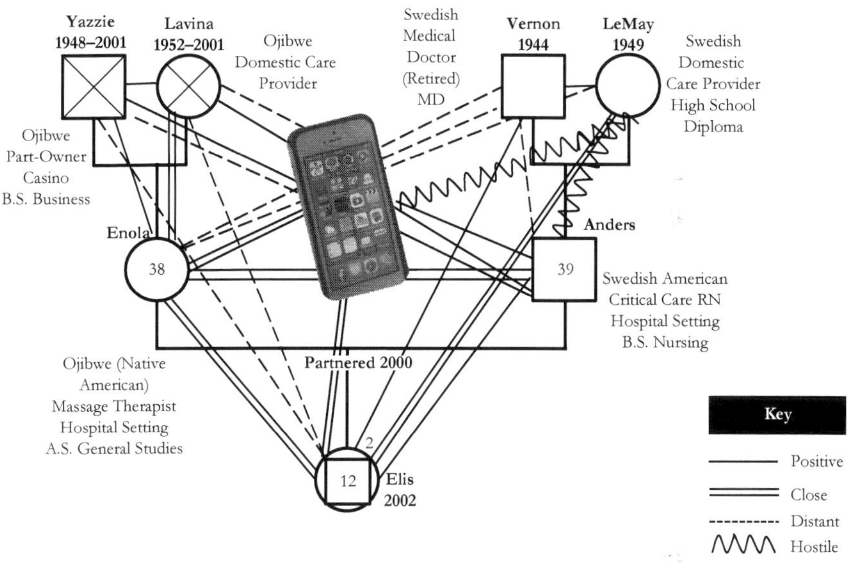

Figure 22.1. Example of a technology-focused genogram. Credit: Katherine M. Hertlein.

Conducting a technology-focused genogram also includes general exploration of the dynamics and patterns previously described in basic genograms but adds an assessment and exploration of each member's relationship with their technologies. As an example, see Figure 22.1, which depicts a technology-focused genogram, and then read the next section for a vignette of the fictional family depicted.

To assist in the development of a technology-focused genogram, several sets of questions are available (see appendices in Hertlein & Blumer, 2014, for the following: General Technological Focused Genogram Questions; Couple and Family Technology Focused Genogram Questions; and Questions for Consideration across an Electronic Developmental Lifespan). In part inspired by the work of Hertlein and Blumer (2013), the following questions are useful for developing a technology-focused genogram and assessing intergenerational technology use, communication, and potential areas of technology-related concern:

- What is each family member's relationship with technology (e.g., close, positive, distant, hostile)?
- How does each family member's relationship with technology influence their relationships with one another?
- How does each family member's relationship with each other influence their relationship with technology?
- What were the relationships between family members like prior to the development of any technology-based relationships?
- What is the percent of communication between family members that occurs face to face versus online?
- What kind of technology-mediated communication (e.g., SNS, texting, emailing, i-chatting, etc.) do family members engage in with each other? What kind of technology-mediated communication do family members engage in with others outside the family?
- What are some of the positive ways that technology is used to communicate with each other in the family? With others outside the family?
- What are some of the negative ways that technology is used to communicate with each other? With others outside the family?
- How much dialogue have various family members had with each other regarding possible areas of technology-related concerns, such as sex-related activities, Internet infidelity, Internet addiction, online gaming addiction, online family networking, online social networking, online dating, online safety?
- If the family has experienced technology-related issues or concerns, how have they successfully (or unsuccessfully) managed them?
- What are the already-existing rules, roles, and boundaries about technology use with family members? With others?

Technology-focused genogram vignette: The Magnusson family. The Magnusson family consists of a heterosexual, cisgender (a gender identifier referring to a person whose own gender matches their medically assigned or designated gender or sex—commonly thought of as a nontransgender or nontranssexual person [Edelman, 2009]), partnered couple, Anders and Enola (both late 30s in age), and their preadolescent child, Elis, who is 12. Anders, who is of Swedish descent, is a critical care nurse in a large hospital's emergency department. Enola is of Ojibwe descent and is a massage therapist. Elis identifies with a two-spirit gender (a social and spiritual identifier referring to a person of Indigenous descent and cultures in which an individual is recognized as possessing both a male and a female spirit) Tayfoya, 1997) and is in middle school. The family resides in an urban area of the midwestern United States.

All members of the immediate Magnusson family share positive connections with technology, and Enola and Elis have particularly close relationships with technology. Enola uses technology quite a bit to communicate with her patients —scheduling appointments, sending health tips, engaging in social networking via Twitter, Facebook, and LinkedIn, suggesting helpful apps, and the like. Elis has a close relationship to technology—regularly using it to complete school activities; connect with friends and family; engage in social networking via Facebook, Snapchat, Vine, Twitter, and Instagram; take part in online groups with other two-spirited people; play online games, and so on. Anders makes use of technology by emailing coworkers, friends, and family members; surfing the Internet; and other activities. All three members of the immediate Magnusson family regularly connect with each other via technology by emailing, chatting, texting, and calling each other. All three also share positive offline relationships with each other; Enola and Anders are close and Enola and Elis are close as well.

When exploring the relationships with technology and family members one generation back on either side, different patterns begin to emerge. Enola's parents, Yazzie and Lavina, died in an automobile accident in 2001—before the past decade's boom of smartphone usage and social networking; they had no opportunity to develop a deep degree of relational connectivity to technology. Yazzie and Lavina shared positive relationships with both Enola and Anders but never met Elis.

Anders's parents, Vernon and LeMay, have a much more complex relationship with technology and with the younger generation of Magnussons. Until a year and a half ago, LeMay shared a close connection to technology and used it to communicate with the younger Magnussons via email, social networking sites, phone calling, and texting. A shift happened a year ago, when Elis began identifying as two-spirited and began participating in online groups of like-gendered folks. Elis found support in his gender identity in these online groups. However, he shared with his grandmother, LeMay, that he also started encountering some gender-spectrum phobia (Blumer & Barbachano, 2008), cisgenderism (Ansara, 2010; Blumer, Ansara, & Watson, 2013), and bullying from "trolls" (persons who participate in online groups, SNSs, chats, blogs, or discussion threads with the intention of arguing with, provoking, or upsetting people, and/or positing inflammatory, extraneous, or off topic content). LeMay, who is very close to Elis, thought that Elis's parents should ban Elis's participation in these groups to protect him from online predators.

In response to LeMay's concerns, Anders and Enola sat down with Elis and discussed the pros and cons related to safety when participating in the online groups. Elis reported that it was better to have the support online than not, and thus worth a little risk and encountering a few trolls here or there. Anders shared with LeMay their decision to allow Elis to continue in the online groups, and LeMay became furious. Since then she has withdrawn from having as much technological communication as before with Anders and Enola, and has grown angry at technology and the harm it can bring. She is also somewhat angry at her son, Anders, for not doing more to protect her only grandchild, and has been distant to Enola. LeMay has shared her concerns repeatedly with Vernon, and he supports her—in part because he has never been close to or really understood technology, and also because, in his and LeMay's relationship, they have typically supported each other above all others. Further, Vernon's relationship with his son, Anders, has been more distant, and his relationship with Enola, which used to be quite positive, has grown more distant as well. LeMay does, however, maintain a close relationship with Elis, and they have continued to communicate via technology. Vernon also has maintained a positive relationship with Elis, but they do not communicate via technology (nor does Vernon with anyone else, for that matter).

Recently, Elis expressed concern to Anders and Enola regarding how little time the three of them spend with the extended family. Elis reports wanting the "whole family to be close again." Enola and Anders would like the same thing but are unsure how to go about repairing the relationships, and have even begun to wonder whether they made the best decision about Elis's technology use, particularly as the involvement in the online groups, as of late, seems to occupy more and more of Elis's time. They report that it is as if Elis wants to spend more time with online support family members than offline immediate family members.

Discussion of the Magnusson family. Intergenerational technological communication patterns, the influence of technology on Magnusson family dynamics, and the e-development across the Magnusson family lifespan becomes clear through both the visual depiction of the technology-focused genogram and the narrative based upon responses to the technology-focused genogram questions. In many ways the technological story of the Magnusson family echoes the work of scholars cited throughout this chapter. For instance, all members of the immediate Magnusson family use technology as individuals and to communicate with each other, as is the case with the majority of married-with-children families in the United States (Kennedy et al., 2008). Moreover, the mother in the immediate family, Enola, has more technological communication with the child, Elis, than with the father, Anders, which is also consistent with the research (Kennedy et al., 2008). Finally, older members of the Magnusson family, who are of the Boomer generation, appear to have a technological competency level of digital immigrants (Prensky, 2001). Thus, it is not surprising that in this vignette these older family members see technological communications as potentially problematic, because, on average, members of this cohort are better able than members of younger generational cohorts to recognize differences in communication in relation to technological use (Kennedy et al., 2008).

The technological practices of the adolescent, Elis, also mirror many practices of age and gender-mate peers. For example, Elis's involvement and experiences of being supported through participation in online support groups of like-gendered people mirrors experiences reported by transgender- and nonbinary-gender-identifying persons in the literature (Gauthier & Chaudoir, 2004). In addition, Elis's attention to gender identity in cyber-settings confirms recent research that identifies the practice of managing of one's sexual- and/or gender-orientation minority identity in online environments as electronic visibility (e-visibility) management (Blumer, Bergdall, & Ullman, 2014). For Elis in this vignette practicing e-visibility management, in part, aligns with the need to be mindful of and manage one's identity in electronic environments to help protect oneself from cyber-bullies, trolls, and other online predators (Blumenfeld & Cooper, 2010; Blumer et al., 2014).

Application

Assessment using genograms goes beyond family studies and family therapy contexts. Historically speaking, in addition to these settings, genograms have been applied to personal (Connolly, 2005), medical (Daly et al., 1999; McIlvain, Crabtree, Medder, Stange, & Miller, 1998; Schilson, Braun, & Hudson, 1993), educational (Daughhetee, 2001), and occupational (Gibson, 2005; Malott & Magnuson, 2004) settings. For instance, in medical settings genograms have been used to assess family practice configurations (McIlvain et al., 1998), cancer risk in families (Daly et al., 1999), and patient–doctor collaborative interactions (Schilson et al., 1993). In educational settings, ranging from elementary to university levels, the genogram has been a common tool teachers have applied to help students gain insight into their prospective college (Daughhetee, 2001) and careers (Gibson, 2005; Malott & Magnuson, 2004).

Just as genograms have been used across these varied settings, the technology-focused genogram can be applied in any setting where the exploration of technological patterns is considered beneficial. For instance, in my (M. L. C. B.) undergraduate family studies basic counseling skills training course (in both online and in-person delivery formats) I have students complete a technology-focused genogram. This activity is helpful for many reasons: Students learn how to conduct genogram assessments in their future family studies–based careers. Students also gain insight into their own families, as well as into their technological practices, which will help them offer the most informed and focused services as family studies professionals.

Returning to the findings from the survey study of 227 family therapy (a subdiscipline within the family studies field) professionals, the majority reported not learning about cyber-based technologies in any context (n = 76, 24.2%); however, when they did, it was primarily through coursework (n = 51, 16.24%) (Blumer, Hertlein, Tran, & Koble, 2014). Therefore, by completing a technology-focused genogram, a possible gap in much of the college curriculum is at least in part addressed. Recognizing this gap is essential because most current traditional-age college students are of the "net generation" (Carlson, 2005, Blumer & Hertlein, 2011) or are digital natives (Prensky, 2001) and thus need more opportunity to discuss within the college classroom the part technology plays in their professional and personal lives. Upon completing a technology-focused genogram, students report that it helps them become more mindful of their technology use and patterns; establish clearer expectations of roles, rules, and boundaries around technological engagement; and develop a better understanding of professional netiquette.

References

Ansara, Y. G. (2010). Beyond cisgenderism: Counselling people with non-assigned gender identities. In L. Moon (Ed.), *Counselling ideologies: Queer challenges to heteronormativity* (pp. 167–200). Aldershot, UK: Ashgate.

Belous, C. K., Timm, T. M., Chee, G., & Whitehead, M. R. (2012). Revisiting the sexual genogram. *The American Journal of Family Therapy*, *40*, 281–296. doi:10.1080/01926187.2011.627317

Blumenfeld, W. J., & Cooper, R. M. (2010). LGBT and allied youth responses to cyberbullying: Policy implications. *The International Journal of Critical Pedagogy, 3*, 114–133. Retrieved from http://libjournal.uncg.edu

Blumer, M. L. C., Ansara, Y. G., & Watson, C. M. (2013). Cisgenderism in family therapy: How everyday practices can delegitimize people's gender self-designations. *Journal of Family Psychotherapy, 24*, 267–285. doi:10.1080/08975353.2013.849551

Blumer, M. L. C., & Barbachano, J. M. (2008). Valuing the gender-variant therapist: Therapeutic experiences, tools, and implications of a female-to-male transvariant clinician. *Journal of Feminist Family Therapy: An International Forum, 20*, 46–65. doi:10.1080/0895280801907135

Blumer, M. L. C., Bergdall, M., & Ullman, K. (2014, November). *E-visibility management of LGB identities*. Poster, Scientific Society for Sexuality Studies Annual Conference. Omaha, NE.

Blumer, M. L. C., & Hertlein, K. M. (2011). "Twitter, and texting, and youtube, oh my!" MFT networking via new media. *Family Therapy Magazine*, 24–25. Retrieved from http://www.aamft.org/imis15/Content/Resources/FTM_Articles.aspx

Blumer, M. L. C., & Hertlein, K. M. (2013, February). *Exploring the e-developmental family lifespan*. Lecture, XXI World International Family Therapy Association Congress, Lake Buena Vista, FL.

Blumer, M. L. C., Hertlein, K. M., & Fife, S. T. (2012). It's not easy becoming green: The role of family therapists in an eco-sustainability age. *Contemporary Family Therapy: An International Journal, 34*, 1–17. doi:10.1007/s10591–012–9175–9

Blumer, M. L. C., Hertlein, K. M., Smith, J. M., & Allen, H. (2014). How many bytes does it take? A content analysis of cyber issues in couple and family therapy journals. *Journal of Marital and Family Therapy, 40*, 34–48. doi:10.1111/j.1752–0606.2012.00332.x

Blumer, M. L. C., Hertlein, K. M., Tran, L., & Koble, J. (2014, October). *MFTs' education of online practices and online professional networking.* Poster, American Association for Marriage and Family Therapy Annual Conference, Milwaukee, WI.

Blumer, M. L. C., Papaj, A. K., & Robinson, L. D. (2012, September). *Therapeutic framework to deploy for serving the servicewoman.* Workshop, American Association for Marriage and Family Therapy Annual Conference, Charlotte, NC.

Bowen, M. (1966). *Family therapy in clinical practice.* Northvalle, NJ: Jason Aronson.

Brelsford, G. M., & Friedberg, R. D. (2011). Religious and spiritual issues: Family therapy approaches with military families coping with deployment. *Journal of Contemporary Psychotherapy, 41*, 255–262. doi:10.1007/s10879–011–9174–4

Carlson, S. (2005, October 5). The net generation goes to college: Tech-savvy "Millennials" have lots of gadgets, like to multitask, and expect to control what, when, and how they learn. Should colleges cater to them? *The Chronicle of Higher Education: Information Technology, 52*, A34. Retrieved from http://chronicle.com/weekly/v52/i07/07a03401.htm

Connolly, C. M. (2005). Discovering "family" creatively: The self-created genogram. *Journal of Creativity in Mental Health, 1*, 81–105. Retrieved from http://eric.ed.gov/?id=EJ844338

Cravens, J. D., Hertlein, K. M., & Blumer, M. L. C. (2013). Online mediums: Assessing and treating Internet issues in relationships. *Family Therapy Magazine*, 18–23. Retrieved from https://www.aamft.org/imis15/Documents/MAFTMSinglePages.pdf

Daly, M., Farmer, J., Harrop-Stein, C., Montgomery, S., Itzen, M., Costalas, J. W., … Gillespie, D. (1999). Exploring family relationships in cancer risk counseling using the genogram. *Cancer, Epidemiology, Biomarkers & Prevention, 8*, 393–398. Retrieved from http://cebp.aacrjournals.org/content/8/4/393.full.pdf+html

Daughhetee, C. (2001). Using genograms as a tool for insight in college counseling. *Journal of College Counseling, 4*, 73–76. doi:10.1002/j.2161–1882.2001.tb00184.x

Davis, R. A., Flett, G. L., & Besser, A. (2002). Validation of new scale for measuring problematic Internet use: Implications for pre-employment screening. *Cyberpsychology Behavior: The Impact of the Internet, Multimedia and Virtual Reality on Behavior and Society, 5*, 331–345. doi:10.1089/109493102760275581

DeMaria, R., Weeks, G., & Hof, L. (1999). *Focused genograms: Intergenerational assessment of individuals, couples, and families.* New York: Brunner/Mazel.

Demetrovics, Z., Szeredi, B., & Rozsa, S. (2008). The three-factor model of Internet addiction: The development of the problematic Internet use questionnaire. *Behavior Research Methods, 40*, 563–574. doi:10.3758/BRM.40.2.563

Edelman, E. A. (2009). (In)visible sites of male-to-female transsexual resistance. In E. Lewin & W. L. Leap (Eds.), *Out in public: Reinventing lesbian/gay anthropology in a globalizing world* (pp. 164–179). West Sussex, UK: Wiley/Blackwell.

Fitzharris, J. L., & Werner-Wilson, R. J. (2004). Multiple perspectives of parent adolescent sexual communication: Phenomenological description of a Rashoman effect. *American Journal of Family Therapy, 34*, 273–288. doi:10.1080/01926180490437367

Gauthier, D. K., & Chaudoir, N. K. (2004). Tranny boyz: Cyber community support in negotiating sex and gender mobility among female to male transsexuals. *Deviant Behavior, 25*, 375–398. doi:10.1080/01639620490441272

Gentzler, A. L., Oberhauser, A. M., Westerman, D., and Nadorff, D. K. (2011). College students' use of electronic communication with parents: Links to loneliness, attachment, and relationship quality. *CyberPsychology, Behavior & Social Networking, 14*, 71–74. doi:10.1089/cyber.2009.0409

Gibson, D. M. (2005). The use of genograms in career counseling with elementary, middle, and high school students. *The Career Development Quarterly, 53*, 353–362. doi:10.1002/j.2161–0045.2005.tb00666.x

Harley, D., & Fitzpatrick, G. (2009). YouTube and intergenerational communication: The case of Geriatric1927. *Universal Access in the Information Society, 8*, 5–20. doi:10.1007/s10209–008–0127-y

Hertlein, K. M., & Blumer, M. L. C. (2014). *The couple and family technology framework: Intimate relationships in a digital age*. New York: Routledge.

Hertlein, K. M., Blumer, M. L. C., & Smith, J. M. (2012, November). *Family therapists' considerations of Web-based technologies in clinical practice*. Paper, National Council on Family Relations Annual Conference, Phoenix, AZ.

Internet World Stats. (2012). *Internet users in the world distribution by world regions*. Internet World Stats Usage and Population Statistics. Retrieved from http://www.internetworldstats.com/stats.htm

Johnson, D., & Thompson, T. (2009). Parent communication and college students' sexual attitudes. *University of Wisconsin–Stout Journal of Student Research, 9*, 97–120. Retrieved from http://www2.uwstout.edu/content/rs/2009/2009contents.shtml

Kakiuchi, K. K. S., & Weeks, G. R. (2009). The occupational transmission genogram: Exploring family scripts affecting roles of work and career in couple and family dynamics. *Journal of Family Psychotherapy, 20*, 1–12. doi:10.1080/08975350802716467

Kennedy, T. L. M., Smith, A., Wells, A. T., & Wellman, B. (2008). Networked families: Parents and spouses are using the Internet and cell phones to create a "new connectedness" that builds on remote connections and shared Internet experiences. Pew Internet and American Life Project. Retrieved from http://www.pewinternet.org/files/old-media/Files/Reports/2008/PIP_Networked_Family.pdf.pdf

Kirk, D., Sellen, A., & Cao, X. (2010). Home video communication: Mediating "closeness." *Computer Supported Cooperative Work '10*, 135–144. doi:10.1145/1718918.1718945

Lenhart, A. (2010). Is the age at which kids get cell phones getting younger? Pew Internet and American Life Project. Retrieved from http://pewinternet.org/Commentary/2010/December/Is-the-age-at-which-kids-get-cell-phones-getting-younger.aspx

Lenhart, A. (2012). Teens, smartphones & texting. Pew Internet and American Life Project. Retrieved from http://www.pewinternet.org/files/old-media/Files/Reports/2012/PIP_Teens_Smartphones_and_Texting.pdf

Malott, K. M., & Magnuson, S. (2004). Using genograms to facilitate undergraduate students' career development: A group model. *The Career Development Quarterly, 53*, 178–186. doi:10.1002/j.2161–0045.2004.tb00988.x

McGoldrick, M., & Gerson, R. (1985). *Genograms in family assessment*. New York: Norton.

McGoldrick, M., Gerson, R., & Shellenberger, S. (1999). *Genograms: Assessment and intervention* (2nd ed.). New York: Norton.

McIlvain, H., Crabtree, B., Medder, J., Stange, K. C., & Miller, W. L. (1998). Using practice genograms to understand and describe practice configurations. *Family Medicine, 30*, 490–496. Retrieved from http://www.ncbi.nlm.nih.gov/pubmed/9669161

Mesch, G. S. (2006). Family relations and the Internet: Exploring a family boundaries approach. *The Journal of Family Communication, 6*, 119–138. doi:10.1207/s15327698jfc0602_2

Mumford, D. J., & Weeks, G. R. (2003). The money genogram. *Journal of Family Psychotherapy, 14*, 33–44. doi:10.1300/J085v14n03_03

Papaj, A. K., Blumer, M. L. C., & Robinson, L. D. (2011). The clinical deployment of therapeutic frameworks and genogram questions to serve the servicewoman. *Journal of Feminist Family Therapy: An International Forum, 23*, 263–284. doi:10.1080/08952833.2011.604533

Prensky, M. (2001). Digital natives, digital immigrants, part 2: Do they really think differently? *On the horizon, 9*(6), 1–6. doi:10.1108/10748120110424843

Raffle, H., Ballagas, R., Revelle, G., Horii, H., Follmer, S., Go, J., … Spasojevic, M. (2010). Family story play: Reading with children (and Elmo) over a distance. *Human Factors in Computing Systems '10*, 1583–1592.

Rainie, L. (2009). Teens in the digital age. Pew Internet and American Life Project. Retrieved from http://www.nationaltechcenter.org/documents/conf09/back_to_the_future_rainie.pdf

Schilson, E., Braun, K., & Hudson, A. (1993). Use of genograms in family medicine: A family physician/family therapy collaboration. *Family Systems Medicine, 11*, 201–208. doi:10.1037/h0089389

Sherman, R. (1993). The intimacy genogram. *The Family Journal, 1*, 91–93. doi:10.1177/106648079300100117

Tayfoya, T. (1997). Native gay and lesbian issues: The two-spirited. In B. Greene (Ed.), *Ethnic and cultural diversity among lesbians and gay men: Psychological perspectives on lesbian and gay issues* (Vol. 3) (pp. 1–10). Thousand Oaks, CA: Sage.

Taylor, P. (2014). More than half of Millennials have shared a "selfie." *Factank News in the Numbers*. Pew Research Center. Retrieved from http://www.pewresearch.org/fact-tank/2014/03/04/more-than-half-of-millennials-have-shared-a-selfie/

Taylor, P., Doherty, C., Parker, C., & Krishnamurthy, V. (2014). Millennials in adulthood: Detached from institutions, networked with friends. *Pew Research Social and Demographic Trends*. Retrieved from http://www.pewsocialtrends.org/2014/03/07/millennials-in-adulthood/

Watt, D., & White, J. M. (1999). Computers and family life: A family development perspective. *Journal of Comparative Family Studies, 30*, 1–15. Retrieved from http://www.jstor.org/stable/41603606

Weiss, E. L., Coll, J. E., Gerbauer, J., Smiley, K., & Carillo, E. (2010). The military genogram: A solution-focused approach for resiliency building in service members and their families. *The Family Journal, 18*, 395–406. doi:10.1177/1066480710378479

Young, K. S. (1998). *Caught in the Net: How to recognize the signs of Internet addiction and a winning strategy for recovery.* New York: John Wiley & Sons.

Contributors

Walid A. Afifi (BA, 1990, University of Iowa & PhD, 1996, University of Arizona) is Professor and Chair of the Department of Communication Studies at the University of Iowa. He is an author of over 60 articles, chapters, and books, and has served as chair of the Interpersonal Division for both the National Communication Association and the International Communication Association. His program of research revolves around uncertainty and information-management decisions and has led to the development and refinement of the Theory of Motivated Information Management. He is committed to respecting and involving the communities from which we all learn. His program of life revolves around, and the (usually) calming influence on his personal experiences of uncertainty are, his wife, their two children, and three dogs (Charles Jackson, Mashi & Maddi). He can be reached at Walid-afifi@uiowa.edu

Bethany L. Blair, PhD, is Assistant Professor in Family and Child Sciences at Florida State University. She received her doctoral degree in Human Development and Family Studies from The University of North Carolina at Greensboro, where she was granted a Fulbright award to study Finnish adolescents' use of social technology with friends and family. Her program of research examines social and emotional precursors to the development of healthy peer relationships, the ways in which children's social technology use reflects their social and emotional development, and parental influences on children's peer relationships and social technology use. She can be reached at blblair@fsu.edu.

Markie Louise Christianson (L. C.) Blumer, PhD, is Associate Professor in the Human Development and Family Studies Department and Marriage and Family Therapy Program and the Certificate in Sex Therapy Program Coordinator at the University of Wisconsin–Stout. Markie is an Affiliate of the Wisconsin HOPE (Harvesting Opportunities for Postsecondary Education) Lab at the University of Wisconsin–Madison, and a Licensed Marriage and Family Therapist (IA, NV) and Mental Health Counselor (IA), AAMFT Clinical Fellow and Approved Supervisor, and an AASECT-Certified Sexuality Educator. Dr. Blumer is coauthor (with Katherine M. Hertlein) of the book *The Couple and Family Technology Framework: Intimate Relationships in a Digital Age* and has published 45 articles, 8 book chapters, and presented over 100 times in various venues. Markie serves as an editorial board member for the *Journal of Feminist Family Therapy: An International Forum* and the *Journal of Couple and Relationship Therapy*. Contact email: blumerm@uwstout.edu.

Carol J. Bruess (last name rhymes with "peace"), PhD, is Professor in the Communication and Journalism Department and Director of Family Studies at the University of St. Thomas, Minnesota. For over 25 years she has been passionate about the study of communication in healthy family, couples, and interpersonal relationships. She is coauthor (with Mark P. Orbe) of *Contemporary Issues in Interpersonal Communication* and three self-help books: *What Happy Couples Do* (2008); *What Happy Parents Do* (2009); and *What Happy Women Do* (2010) (with coauthor Anna Kudak). She is a trained Gottman Seven Principles Educator and has been frequently quoted in national and regional media outlets including PBS, NBC, CBS, *The Chronicle of Higher Education, Men's Health, American Health* and *Cosmopolitan* magazine. She has also been heard on over 4 dozen radio programs, including Oprah Radio, and admits to using many emoji in every text message and Facebook post. She can be reached at cjbruess@stthomas.edu.

Wei-Ning Chang, MEd, is a doctoral student in marriage and family therapy in the Department of Human Development at Virginia Tech. Her email address is weiningc@vt.edu

Jeffrey T. Child is Associate Professor of Communication Studies at Kent State University. Jeff earned his PhD in communication from North Dakota State University in 2007. Jeff received his BA in 2002 from Wayne State College in northeastern Nebraska. Jeff's primary research explores how people manage their privacy in relation to social media interactions and the impact of a variety of factors on the subsequent communication practices. His primary scholarship bridges the interpersonal and mediated contexts of interaction with a special focus on issues related to effective privacy management, disclosure, and privacy repair strategies. Jeff has over 30 publications in a range of journals and a basic course textbook called *Experience Communication* (with coauthors Judy C. Pearson and Paul Nelson, 2015). Jeff has presented over 40 research paper presentations at regional, national, and international conventions related to the advancement of communication scholarship. He can be reached at jchild@kent.edu.

Neal Christopherson is Director of Institutional Research at Whitman College, where he occasionally teaches in the Sociology Department and is also the Assistant Cross Country Coach. He has an MA and PhD in sociology from the University of Notre Dame, and a BA in philosophy from Wheaton College, Illinois. A fan of both qualitative and quantitative research methods, he has published in the areas of sociology of religion and sociology of sports. His current focus is on applied higher education research. He can be reached at christnj@whitman.edu.

Emily M. Cramer, PhD, is Assistant Professor of Communication in the Department of Communication at North Central College, an independent liberal arts college in the southwest suburbs of Chicago. Her PhD is in communication from the University of Wisconsin–Milwaukee; she also has an MA in communication from DePaul University and a BA in communication studies from Marquette University. She currently teaches foundational and advanced-level courses in new media, public relations, persuasion theory, and interpersonal communication. Her current program of research focuses on new media and health disparities in access to information and technology. She can be reached at: emcramer@noctrl.edu.

Jaclyn D. Cravens, PhD, is Assistant Professor in the Community, Family, and Addiction Sciences Department at Texas Tech University in Lubbock, Texas. Her PhD and MS degrees are in marriage and family therapy and she is a licensed marriage and family therapist (Washington) and approved supervisor candidate. She teaches both undergraduate and graduate courses on marriage and family therapy theories, addiction and recovery, and practicum supervision. Her research examines the role of technology, specifically social networking sites, on intimate partner relationships. She can be reached by email at: jaclyn.cravens@ttu.edu.

Laura Beth Daws, PhD, is Assistant Professor of Communication in the Department of Communication at Kennesaw State University in Kennesaw, Georgia. Her PhD is in communication from the University of Kentucky; she also has an MA in mass communication from Auburn University and a BA in communication arts: public communication from the University of North Alabama. She currently teaches courses at the undergraduate and graduate level in communication skills, research methods, small group communication, health communication, and media studies. Her current program of research focuses on media history, digital/new media, and gender representations in media. She can be reached at ldaws@kennesaw.edu.

Jennifer Doty, PhD, has an interdisciplinary postdoctoral fellowship at the University of Minnesota focused on healthy youth development. Jennifer's research interests are built around the idea that parent–child relationships are a key leverage point for improving adolescent health and well-being. She views the online environment as a potential outlet for the dissemination of parent-based prevention programming. She has authored six publications, four as first author, with a focus on parents in an online environment. In her dissertation research, she focused on the relationship between parents and adolescents prospectively over three generations in the Youth Development Study. She was awarded a Kappa Omicron Nu Research Award for this work. Jennifer's research interests include the well-being of parents and adolescents, translational research using online tools, and parent-based prevention. Her long-term goal is to build bridges between basic research and applied prevention settings. She can be reached at dotyX093@umn.edu.

Jodi Dworkin, PhD, is Associate Professor and Extension Specialist in the Department of Family Social Science at the University of Minnesota. Her research and outreach focuses on risk-taking among adolescents and college students, promoting positive family development, parenting adolescents and college students, and the role of technology in these relationships. A critical piece of her work is developing research-based outreach services to promote positive family development. One of her current research projects is Parenting2.0 (http://www.cehd.umn.edu/fsos/parent20/), a collaborative project designed to gain a better understanding of the ways in which, and the reasons that, parents use technology; and to better understand the outcomes from parents' use of technology. She can be reached at jdworkin@umn.edu.

Megan Kenny Feister has a PhD in organizational communication from Purdue University. Her research focuses on issues of identity, identification, team and ethical decision-making, and engineering education.

Anne C. Fletcher, PhD, is Associate Professor in the Department of Human Development and Family Studies at the University of North Carolina at Greensboro. She obtained her doctorate in developmental psychology from Temple University and her BA in psychology from Haverford College. Dr. Fletcher studies parenting and parent–child relationships across ages ranging from middle childhood through adolescence. Her specific areas of interest include parenting styles and stylistic dimensions of parenting, ways in which parents use relationships with other parents to inform their parenting, and parental management of adolescents' use of social technologies. Dr. Fletcher teaches classes at the graduate and undergraduate levels focusing in adolescent development, research methods, and lifespan development. She can be reached at acfletch@uncg.edu.

Elizabeth Dorrance Hall, PhD, is Assistant Professor of Communication in the Department of Languages, Philosophy, and Communication Studies at Utah State University. Elizabeth's PhD is in interpersonal and family communication from Purdue University. Her program of research integrates the study of how family relationships evolve over time with health, close relationship, and organizational communication theory. Elizabeth views families as organizing forms which engage in processes that impact all members of the family. Elizabeth's recent work investigates the processes of marginalization and resilience in families and the role of family support in adjustment to college across cultures. Elizabeth can be reached at elizabeth.dorrance@gmail.com.

Emily Haugen, MS, LAMFT, is a doctoral candidate in marriage and family therapy in the Department of Human Development at Virginia Tech. Her email address is hauge307@vt.edu.

Katherine M. Hertlein, PhD, is Professor and Program Director of the Marriage and Family Therapy Program at the University of Nevada, Las Vegas. She received her master's in marriage and family therapy from Purdue University Calumet and her doctorate in human development with a specialization in marriage and family therapy from Virginia Tech and is an AAMFT approved supervisor. Across her academic career, she has published over 50 articles, 6 books, and over 25 book chapters. She has coedited a book on interventions in couples treatment, interventions for clients with health concerns, and a book on infidelity treatment. Dr. Hertlein has also produced the first multitheoretical model detailing the role of technology in couple and family life, published in her latest book, *The Couple and Family Technology Framework*. She presents nationally and internationally on sex, technology, and couples. Email contact: katherine.hertlein@unlv.edu.

Andrea Iaccheri, MA, is a PhD candidate at Ohio University. Her research interests focus on health and well-being as situated within and shaped by sociocultural, sociopolitical, and historical contexts. Grounding her work in Foucault and post-structuralist commitments, her research utilizes critical and rhetorical means to interrogate the cultural, historical, and personal narratives surrounding past and current health issues. Email contact: andrea.guziec.iaccheri@gmail.com.

Michelle Janning, PhD, is Professor of Sociology at Whitman College in Walla Walla, Washington, and Co-Chair of the Board of Directors of the Council on Contemporary Families, a national organization dedicated to connecting journalists with family scholars and practitioners. Her research and teaching focuses on culture, families, childhood, education, design and aesthetics, and community-based research. She has published research and presented speeches on post-divorce home spaces and parent-child relations, motherhood and family photos, gender and home decorating, symbolic work-family boundaries for married co-workers, early learning and kindergarten readiness, Scandinavian childhoods, and the symbolic importance of saved love letters (contained in this collection). Michelle has served as a visiting professor at the University of York's (UK) Centre for Women's Studies, and as a Fulbright scholar and frequent visiting professor at the Danish Institute for Study Abroad in Copenhagen, Denmark. She has been quoted in the *Chicago Tribune*, *Real Simple, Women's Health*, and many other national print and radio outlets, and writes a blog about the sociology of everyday life at www.michellejanning.com. She can be reached at janninmy@whitman.edu.

Meg Wilkes Karraker, PhD, studies that which makes a good society for families in a changing world (her interests rooted in a childhood living abroad in a military family). She is the author, coauthor, or editor of four books: *Global Families; The Other People: Interdisciplinary Perspectives on Migration; Families with Futures: Family Studies into the Twenty-first Century;* and *Diversity and the Common Good: Civil Society, Religion, and Catholic Sisters in a Small City.* Karraker is Professor of Sociology, Family Business Center Fellow, and University Scholar at the University of St. Thomas in St. Paul, Minnesota; President emerita of Alpha Kappa Delta (the international sociology honor society); and recipient of her university's John Ireland Presidential Award for Outstanding Achievement as a Teacher/Scholar; Aquinas Scholars Honors Program Teacher of the Year Award; and the Midwest Sociological Society's Jane Addams Award for Service to Women and Girls. She can be reached at mwkarraker@stthomas.edu.

Falon Kartch, PhD, is Assistant Professor of Communication at California State University, Fresno. Her program of research examines how various populations define what it means to be "family" as well as the intersection between family communication and the dark side of close relationships. This work centers on the experiences of nontraditional family types including stepfamilies, LGBT families, and nonresidential parenting. She is also interested in the process of coming out, as it occurs within families, and the negotiation of ownership over information related to sexual orientation. She teaches undergraduate and graduate classes in interpersonal communication, communication theory, and research methods. fkartch@csufresno.edu.

Xiaohui Sophie Li, PhD, is Assistant Professor of Family and Child Studies in the School of Family, Consumer, and Nutrition Sciences at Northern Illinois University. Her PhD is in family social science from the University of Minnesota at Twin Cities; she also has an MA in health and clinical psychology from Beijing Normal University (Beijing, China) and a Bachelor of Economics from China Agricultural University (Beijing, China). She currently teaches courses at the undergraduate and graduate level in family financial planning and family resources management. Her program of research focuses on understanding diverse couple and family systems, investigating systemic and ecological influence on child development, and promoting learned resilience and resourcefulness. She can be reached at xli@niu.edu.

Edward A. Mabry, PhD, is Emeritus Associate Professor of Communication, Department of Communication, University of Wisconsin–Milwaukee. During his 42 years in the department, his face-to-face and online classroom teaching focused on group, interpersonal, and organizational communication topics and quantitative research methods. His research addressed a range of issues including communication in face-to-face and mediated groups, effects of communication technology on groups and personal relationships, communication and instructional technology, and psycho-social factors predicting drug use. Most recently, he has collaborated on research about cyber-bullying and gender style and familial differences in mediated communication.

Brandon T. McDaniel is a PhD student in the Department of Human Development and Family Studies at The Pennsylvania State University. He received his Master's degree from this same program and received his Bachelor's degree in psychology from Brigham Young University. His current research is primarily focused on couple and coparenting relationships. Contexts in which he often studies these relationships include the transition to parenthood and early infancy/childhood, as well as very specific contexts such as bedtime or technology use. Brandon also has experience with intensive data designs (such as daily diaries) and can be found using these methods to examine family processes. His work has been featured in various national and international media outlets including NPR, *The Today Show, US News & World Report, Men's Health*, and *The New York Times*. Brandon can be reached at btmcdaniel.phd@gmail.com.

Anne Merrill, PhD, is a post-doctoral fellow in the Department of Communication Arts and Sciences at Pennsylvania State University. Anne received her PhD (2014) and MA (2011) from the Department of Communication at the University of California Santa Barbara. Her research focuses on processes such as information regulation (i.e., topic avoidance, disclosure, secrecy, and privacy), conflict, uncertainty, stress, and coping within close relationships, such as romantic relationships and families. Her email address is annefmerrill@gmail.com.

Sandra Petronio, PhD, is Professor in the Indiana University Department of Communication Studies, Indiana University School of Medicine on the campus of Indiana University–Purdue University, Indianapolis, and was recently appointed Director of the newly formed Communication Privacy Management Center. Petronio has expertise in interpersonal, health, social media, and family communication. She developed the evidenced-based Communication Privacy Management (CPM) theory over the last 35 years. Her 2002 book on CPM, *Boundaries of Privacy: Dialectics of Disclosure,* won the Gerald R. Miller Award from the National Communication Association and a book award from the International Association of Relationship Research. CPM theory is used across many cultures and contexts. Petronio has published five other books, numerous articles and chapters, and served as journal editor for several journals. She received the National Communication Association's Bernard J. Brommel Lifetime Award for Excellence in Family Communication, the National Communication Association's Mark Knapp Award in Interpersonal Communication, and the WSCA Distinguished Scholar Award. Contact information: petronio@iupui.edu.

Fred Piercy, PhD, is Professor of Marriage and Family Therapy in the Department of Human Development at Virginia Tech. He is also the current editor of the *Journal of Marital and Family Therapy*. His email address is piercy@vt.edu.

Tamara J. Polingo, BA, is a 2013 graduate of the University of St. Thomas in Minnesota, where she studied psychology and family studies. She is currently in her second year of the Master of Social Work program at the University of Chicago in the School of Social Service Administration, with a goal of earning her license to practice social work in the school setting. Tamara is passionate about working with adolescents and promoting positive environments where every young person has the opportunity to succeed. She can be reached at tammipolingo@gmail.com.

Kimberly Pusateri (MA, University of Illinois at Urbana-Champaign) is a doctoral candidate in the Department of Communication at the University of Illinois, Urbana-Champaign. She studies interpersonal communication with a focus on the intersection of health and family communication. Kimberly recently published pieces concerning communication satisfaction and caregiving intentions in grandparent-grandchild relationships and health-related confrontations between emerging adult children and their parents. Kimberly's current program of research focuses on parent–adult child communication in the context of cancer. She can be reached at kpusate2@illinois.edu.

Dana Riger, MA, is a doctoral candidate in marriage and family therapy in the Department of Human Development at Virginia Tech. She previously coauthored a chapter in *The Effects of the Internet on Social Relationships: Therapeutic Considerations* (2011). Her email address is driger@vt.edu.

David J. Roaché (MA, University of Illinois, 2013) is a doctoral student in the Department of Communication at the University of Illinois at Urbana-Champaign. His research resides at the intersection of computer-mediated communication and interpersonal communication, with an emphasis on how dating partners navigate relational conflict using mediated and face-to-face communication. His work has been recognized by the National Communication Association with a Top Student Paper Award in the Interpersonal Communication Division (2012) and a Top Paper Award in the Family Communication Division (2014). He can be reached at roache2@illinois.edu.

Jessie Rudi, PhD, is a research associate in the Department of Family Social Science at the University of Minnesota. Her program of research focuses on promoting strong and supportive parenting and parent-child relationships during adolescence and the transition to adulthood. Much of her work has examined technology use in the family context, specifically the use of communication technology in parenting and parent-child communication and its role in family relationships and youth development. Her recent work has explored how parents and teens use communication technology as part of the parental monitoring process. Her ultimate goal is to provide professionals with practical, beneficial research that responds to families' needs specifically related to supporting parenting, strengthening families, and promoting positive youth development. Jessie can be reached at conne262@umn.edu.

Liesel L. Sharabi (MA, University of New Mexico, 2010) is a doctoral candidate in the Department of Communication at the University of Illinois at Urbana-Champaign. Her research program primarily explores the use of communication technologies in close relationships. Within this area, much of her work focuses specifically on dating and courtship. She is especially interested in how communication technologies—from cell phones to social media and everything in between—are being used to initiate and develop romantic relationships. For her dissertation, she is conducting a longitudinal study of relationship development in online dating, with the goal of identifying various factors responsible for more or less successful first dates. Her research on communication in romantic relationships has appeared in edited volumes and peer-reviewed journals such as *Communication Monographs, Journal of Communication,* and *Journal of Social and Personal Relationships.* She can be contacted at sharabi2@illinois.edu.

Madeline E. Smith is a PhD candidate in technology and social behavior at Northwestern University, a joint doctoral program in computer science and communication studies. Her research is in the field of human-computer and focuses on the use of communication technology for maintaining social and family relationships. She is currently writing her dissertation centered on college students' use of communication technology with family during the stressful transition from high school to college. Her research is supported by a National Science Foundation Graduate Research Fellowship, as well as research grants from the Northwestern University Graduate School, School of Communication, and Department of Communication Studies. She has an MS in information science from Cornell University and a BS in computer science from Ithaca College. She can be reached at madsesmith@u.northwestern.edu.

Leonard Sturdivant, MS, is a third-year doctoral student in marriage and family therapy in the Department of Human Development at Virginia Tech. His dissertation research focuses on marital reconciliation for couples who have separated and filed for divorce. As a child advocate, the aim of his research is to help couples discover how their intergenerational pathology affects the marriage and how to prevent the pattern from being passed on to the children. Since some studies show that the trajectory of children's lives are better when parents avoid divorce and stay together, children become the benefactors of a model of resilience as their parents successfully navigate the vicissitudes of marriage. Len's publications include *Increasing Positive Behavior in Couples* (National Council on Family Relations) and a book review of *30 Lessons for Living: Tried and True Advice from the Wisest Americans* by K. Pillemer in the *Journal of Intergenerational Relationships.* Len can be reached at lenstar@vt.edu.

Stephanie A. Tikkanen, PhD, is Assistant Professor in the School of Communication Studies at Ohio University (Go Bobcats!), where she teaches undergraduate and graduate courses in social media, interpersonal communication, and empirical methods. She received her MA and PhD in communication from the University of California Santa Barbara, and her research program currently focuses on the intersection of interpersonal communication and new media, particularly on the choices surrounding disclosure decisions and implications of new media on health and romantic relationships. Her work has been published in journals such as *Journal of Communication* and *Communication Research Reports*. She can be reached at tikkanen@ohio.edu.

Lindsay Timmerman, PhD, is Associate Professor in the Department of Communication at the University of Wisconsin–Milwaukee. Her primary research interests center around close relationships, including romantic relationships, family dynamics, and friendships. She is particularly interested in under-studied close relationships. Her research has focused on jealousy expression, long-distance relationships, family secrets, and disclosure of HIV status in families. Currently, she is working on projects related to stigmatized or difficult disclosures, and using social media (e.g., Facebook or Twitter) as relationship maintenance. Lindsay can be reached at lindsayt@uwm.edu.

Sarah Tulane, PhD, is Clinical Assistant Professor in the Department of Family, Consumer, and Human Development at Utah State University. She received her PhD from Utah State University in family and human development with an emphasis in adolescence. Her research interests include adolescent psychosocial development, technology and relationships, and family life education. Email: sarah.tulane@usu.edu.

Adam W. Tyma, PhD, is Associate Professor of Communication (critical media studies) in the School of Communication at the University of Nebraska at Omaha (UNO). In addition, he is the Graduate Program Chair for the school's Masters Program and co-founder of the UNO Social Media Lab for Research and Engagement. Tyma's research areas include online life, popular culture, film, the history of theory, media literacy, and identity construction in online spaces. His work has been published in *Journal of Communication Inquiry*, *Communication Teacher*, and the *International Journal of Communication*, among others, presented at multiple conferences, and he has been interviewed by local and regional media outlets. He is also a coauthor and coeditor for *Beyond New Media: Discourse and Critique in a Polymediated Age* (Lexington Press). Tyma can be reached at ATyma@UNOmaha.edu or followed on Twitter @AdamWTyma.

J. Mitchell Vaterlaus, PhD, LMFT is Assistant Professor in the Department of Health and Human Development at Montana State University. He studies the role of new media and technology in human development and family relationships. His published research has focused on motivations for adolescent and young adult technology use in different contexts, technology and health, parental mediation, youth culture, and generational differences in technology knowledge. Email: j.vaterlaus@montana.edu.

Christina Voskanova, MPsy, MMFT, is a doctoral student in marriage and family therapy in the Department of Human Development, Virginia Tech. Her email address is vcris13@vt.edu.

Susan Walker is Associate Professor and Director of Parent and Family Education in the Department of Family Social Science, University of Minnesota. With over 30 years of translating research to the design, delivery, and evaluation of educational programs to enrich family life, Susan now oversees a masters and state teacher license (in parenting) preparation program for professional development. She teaches courses on parent learning theory, parent–child relations, curriculum design, and program evaluation. Her research investigates social context factors that influence parenting and the role of professionals in facilitating parent learning and well-being. She has long been fascinated by the intersection of personal, community, and professional influences on human development and finding ways to build relationships and interconnections to encourage wider bases of support for those fulfilling society's most important role: parents. Given their power and potential, information technology and the Internet are natural avenues for research and theory building.

Lynne M. Webb, PhD, is Professor in Communication Arts at Florida International University in Miami, Florida. She held previous tenured appointments at the Universities of Florida, Memphis, and most recently Arkansas, where she was named a J. William Fulbright Master Researcher. Her research examines romantic communication, family communication, and social media. She has coedited multiple scholarly readers including *Computer-Mediated Communication in Personal Relationships* (Peter Lang, 2011) and *Communication for Families in Crisis* (Peter Lang, 2012). Her 80+ published essays include theories, research reports, methodological pieces, and pedagogical essays. Her work appears in the *Journal of Applied Communication Research*, *Journal of Family Communication,* and *Health Communication* as well as important collections including the *Sage Handbook of Family Communication, Motherhood Online,* and *Social Media: Usage and Impact*. Dr. Webb is a past president of the Southern States Communication Association and has received a Presidential Citation for her service to the National Communication Association.

Jason B. Whiting, PhD, is Professor in the Community, Family, and Addiction Sciences Department at Texas Tech University. He studies deception and rationalization in intimate relationships, especially as it contributes to violence and conflict. His research has also focused on relationship education and he has led several federally-funded projects examining the effectiveness of short term enrichment for couples, including those who have been aggressive or abusive. He also has an interest in mindfulness, as well as the role of emotional regulation and the brain in aggression and addiction. Dr. Whiting presents regularly at national conferences and won an Outstanding Researcher award from Texas Tech University for his work aimed at helping couples have happier and more trusting relationships.

Subject Index

A

B

C

D

E

F

G

H

I

J

K

L

M

N

O

P

R

S

T

U

V

W

Y

LIFESPAN COMMUNICATION

Children, Families, and Aging

Thomas J. Socha, *General Editor*

From first words to final conversations, communication plays an integral and significant role in all aspects of human development and everyday living. The Lifespan Communication: Children, Families, and Aging series seeks to publish authored and edited scholarly volumes that focus on relational and group communication as they develop over the lifespan (infancy through later life). The series will include volumes on the communication development of children and adolescents, family communication, peer-group communication (among age cohorts), intergenerational communication, and later-life communication, as well as longitudinal studies of lifespan communication development, communication during lifespan transitions, and lifespan communication research methods. The series includes college textbooks as well as books for use in upper-level undergraduate and graduate courses.

Thomas J. Socha, Series Editor | *tsocha@odu.edu*
Mary Savigar, Acquisitions Editor | *mary.savigar@plang.com*

To order other books in this series, please contact our Customer Service Department at:

(800) 770-LANG (within the U.S.)
(212) 647-7706 (outside the U.S.)
(212) 647-7707 FAX

Or browse online by series at www.peterlang.com